国外大学优秀教材——工业工程系列（影印版）

生产与运作分析
（第7版）

Production and Operations Analysis
(Seventh Edition)

［美］史蒂文·纳米亚斯（Steven Nahmias） 编著

成晔 改编

清华大学出版社

北京

Production and Operations Analysis，7th Edition，Steven Nahmias
Copyright © 2015 by Steven Nahmias and Tava Lennon Olsen

The English language edition of this book is published by Waveland Press, Inc. 4180 IL Route 83, Suite 101, Long Grove, Illinois 60047 United States of America.

ENGLISH language adaptation edition published by **TSINGHUA UNIVERSITY PRESS** Copyright © 2018.
本书影印改编版由清华大学出版社出版发行。未经许可，不得以任何方式复制或抄袭本书的任何部分。

ENGLISH language adaptation edition is manufactured in the People's Republic of China, and is authorized for sale only in the People's Republic of China.

北京市版权局著作权合同登记号　图字：01-2018-6264

版权所有，侵权必究。举报：010-62782989，beiqinquan@tup.tsinghua.edu.cn。

图书在版编目(CIP)数据

　　生产与运作分析：第 7 版 = Production and Operations Analysis, 7th Ed.：英文 /(美) 史蒂文·纳米亚斯 (Steven Nahmias) 编著；成晔改编. —影印本. —北京：清华大学出版社，2018(2022.12重印)
　　(国外大学优秀教材. 工业工程系列)
　　ISBN 978-7-302-51665-1

　　Ⅰ.①生… Ⅱ.①史… ②成… Ⅲ.①企业管理－生产管理－高等学校－教材－英文 Ⅳ.①F273

中国版本图书馆 CIP 数据核字（2018）第 257495 号

责任编辑：冯　昕
封面设计：常雪影
责任印制：丛怀宇

出版发行：清华大学出版社
　　　　　网　　　址：http://www.tup.com.cn, http://www.wqbook.com
　　　　　地　　　址：北京清华大学学研大厦 A 座　　　邮　　编：100084
　　　　　社　总　机：010-83470000　　　　　　　　　　邮　　购：010-62786544
　　　　　投稿与读者服务：010-62776969, c-service@tup.tsinghua.edu.cn
　　　　　质　量　反　馈：010-62772015, zhiliang@tup.tsinghua.edu.cn
印 装 者：北京建宏印刷有限公司
经　　销：全国新华书店
开　　本：185mm×230mm　　　印张：35
版　　次：2018 年 11 月第 1 版　　　　　印　　次：2022 年 12 月第 5 次印刷
定　　价：89.00 元

产品编号：079868-02

出版说明

为了满足国内广大读者了解、学习和借鉴国外先进技术和管理经验的需要，清华大学出版社与国外几家著名的出版公司合作，影印出版了一系列工业工程英文版教材。鉴于大部分外版教材篇幅过长，且其中的部分内容与我国的教学需要不符，我们请专家结合国内教学的实际需要，对所选图书进行了必要的删节。经过删节处理后的图书，页眉保留原版书的页码，页脚是连续的新书页码。文中提到的页码均为原版书页码。有的内容或页码也有可能已被删除从而无法找到，由此会给读者带来诸多不便，在此深表歉意！

欢迎广大读者给我们提出宝贵的意见和建议！

清华大学出版社
2018.8

Foreword

This textbook series is published at a very opportunity time when the discipline of industrial engineering is experiencing a phenomenal growth in China academia and with its increased interests in the utilization of the concepts, methods and tools of industrial engineering in the workplace. Effective utilization of these industrial engineering approaches in the workplace should result in increased productivity, quality of work, satisfaction and profitability to the cooperation.

The books in this series should be most suitable to junior and senior undergraduate students and first year graduate students, and to those in industry who need to solve problems on the design, operation and management of industrial systems.

Gavriel Salvendy

Department of Industrial Engineering, Tsinghua University
School of Industrial Engineering, Purdue University
April, 2002

序 言

本教材系列的出版正值中国学术界工业工程学科经历巨大发展，实际工作中对工业工程的概念、方法和工具的使用兴趣日渐浓厚之时。在实际工作中有效地应用工业工程的手段将无疑会提高生产率、工作质量、合作的满意度和效果。

该系列中的书籍对工业工程专业的本科生、研究生和工业界中需要解决工程系统设计、运作和管理诸方面问题的人士最为适用。

加弗瑞尔·沙尔文迪
清华大学工业工程系
普渡大学工业工程学院（美国）
2002 年 4 月

Brief Contents

About the Author xv
Preface xvi
Introduction xvii

1. Strategy and Competition 1
2. Forecasting 52
3. Sales and Operations Planning 128

Supplement 1 Linear Programming 169

4. Inventory Control Subject to Known Demand 198
5. Inventory Control Subject to Uncertain Demand 249
6. Supply Chain Management 315
7. Service Operations Management 367

Supplement 2 Queueing Techniques 417

8. Push and Pull Production Control Systems: MRP and JIT 437
9. Operations Scheduling 490
10. Project Scheduling 543
11. Facilities Layout and Location 593
12. Quality and Assurance 666
13. Reliability and Maintainability 742

APPENDIX: TABLES 796
INDEX 814

Contents

About the Author xv
Preface xvi
Introduction xvii

Chapter 1
Strategy and Competition 1

Chapter Overview 1
    Snapshot Application: Apple Adopts a New Business Strategy and Shifts Its Core Competency from Computers to Portable Electronics 3
1.1 Manufacturing Matters 5
    Manufacturing Jobs Outlook 7
1.2 A Framework for Operations Strategy 8
    Strategic Dimensions 9
1.3 Competing in the Global Marketplace 10
    Snapshot Application: Global Manufacturing Strategies in the Automobile Industry 13
    Problems for Sections 1.1–1.3 13
1.4 Strategic Initiatives: Reengineering the Business Process 14
1.5 Strategic Initiatives: Just-in-Time 17
1.6 Strategic Initiatives: Time-Based Competition 19
1.7 Strategic Initiatives: Competing on Quality 20
    Problems for Sections 1.4–1.7 22
1.8 Strategic Initiatives: Servicization 23
    Servicization: Moving Downstream 23
    The IBM Story 24
    Performance Based Contracts 25
    Leasing Versus Buying 25
    Green Leasing 26
    Problems for Section 1.8 27
1.9 Matching Process and Product Life Cycles 27
    The Product Life Cycle 27
    The Process Life Cycle 28
    The Product–Process Matrix 29
    Problems for Section 1.9 31
1.10 Learning and Experience Curves 31
    Learning Curves 32
    Experience Curves 34
    Learning and Experience Curves and Manufacturing Strategy 36
    Problems for Section 1.10 36
1.11 Capacity Growth Planning: A Long-Term Strategic Problem 38
    Economies of Scale and Economies of Scope 38
    Make or Buy: A Prototype Capacity Expansion Problem 39
    Dynamic Capacity Expansion Policy 40
    Issues in Plant Location 44
    Problems for Section 1.11 46
1.12 Summary 47
    Additional Problems for Chapter 1 48
Appendix 1–A Present Worth Calculations 50
Bibliography 51

Chapter 2
Forecasting 52

Chapter Overview 52
2.1 The Time Horizon in Forecasting 55
2.2 Characteristics of Forecasts 56
2.3 Subjective Forecasting Methods 57
2.4 Objective Forecasting Methods 58
    Causal Models 58
    Time Series Methods 59
    Snapshot Application: Advanced Forecasting, Inc., Serves The Semiconductor Industry 60
    Problems for Sections 2.1–2.4 60
2.5 Notation Conventions 62
2.6 Evaluating Forecasts 62
    Problems for Section 2.6 64
    Snapshot Application: Pfizer Bets Big on Forecasts of Drug Sales 65
2.7 Methods for Forecasting Stationary Series 66
    Moving Averages 66
    Problems on Moving Averages 69
    Exponential Smoothing 69
    Multiple-Step-Ahead Forecasts 73
    Comparison of Exponential Smoothing and Moving Averages 74
    Problems for Section 2.7 75
    Snapshot Application: Sport obermeyer slashes costs with improved forecasting 76
2.8 Trend-Based Methods 77
    Regression Analysis 77
    Problems for Section 2.8 78
    Double Exponential Smoothing Using Holt's Method 79
    More Problems for Section 2.8 80

2.9 Methods for Seasonal Series 81
    Seasonal Factors for Stationary Series 81
    Determining the Deseasonalized Series 83
    Problems for Section 2.9 84
    Snapshot Application: Nate Silver Perfectly Forecasts 2012 Presidential Election 85
    Winters's Method for Seasonal Problems 85
    More Problems for Section 2.9 90
2.10 Box-Jenkins Models 90
    Estimating the Autocorrelation Function 91
    The Autoregressive Process 94
    The Moving-Average Process 95
    Mixtures: ARMA Models 97
    ARIMA Models 97
    Using ARIMA Models for Forecasting 99
    Summary of the Steps Required for Building ARIMA Models 100
    Case Study. Using Box-Jenkins Methodology to Predict Monthly International Airline Passenger Totals 101
    Snapshot Application: A Simple Arima Model Predicts The Performance of The U.S. Economy 105
    Box-Jenkins Modeling—A Critique 105
    Problems for Section 2.10 105
2.11 Practical Considerations 106
    Model Identification and Monitoring 106
    Simple versus Complex Time Series Methods 107
2.12 Overview of Advanced Topics in Forecasting 108
    Simulation as a Forecasting Tool 108
    Forecasting Demand in the Presence of Lost Sales 107
2.13 Linking Forecasting and Inventory Management 111
    Case Study. Predicting the Growth of Facebook 112
2.14 Historical Notes and Additional Topics 116
2.15 Summary 117
    Additional Problems on Forecasting 117
Appendix 2–A Forecast Errors for Moving Averages and Exponential Smoothing 122
Appendix 2–B Derivation of the Equations for the Slope and Intercept for Regression Analysis 124
Appendix 2–C Glossary of Notation for Chapter 2 126
Bibliography 126

Chapter 3
Sales and Operations Planning 128

Chapter Overview 128
3.1 The S&OP Process 130
    Snapshot Application 133
    Problems for Section 3.1 134
3.2 Key Performance Indicators 135
    Problems for Section 3.2 136
3.3 The Role of Uncertainty 137
    Problems for Section 3.3 138
3.4 Aggregate Planning of Capacity 138
    Costs in Aggregate Capacity Planning 139
    A Prototype Problem 141
    Chase, Level, and Mixed Strategies 143
    Problems for Sections 3.4 143
    Snapshot Application: HP Enterprise Services Uses Optimization for Workforce Planning 144
3.5 Solving Aggregate Planning Problems 145
    Cost Parameters and Given Information 145
    Problem Variables 146
    Problem Constraints 146
    Rounding the Variables 147
    Extensions 148
    Problems for Section 3.5 154
3.6 Disaggregating Plans 157
    Aggregate 157
    Snapshot Application: Welch's Uses Aggregate Planning for Production Scheduling 159
    Problems for Section 3.6 160
3.7 Sales and operation Planning on a Global Scale 160
3.8 Historical Notes 161
3.9 Summary 162
    Additional Problems on Aggregate Planning 163
Appendix 3–A Glossary of Notation for Chapter 3 167
Bibliography 167

Supplement 1   Linear Programming 169

S1.1 Introduction 169
S1.2 A Prototype Linear Programming Problem 169
S1.3 Statement of the General Problem 171
    Definitions of Commonly Used Terms 172
    Features of Linear Programs 173
S1.4 Solving Linear Programming Problems Graphically 174
    Graphing Linear Inequalities 174
    Graphing the Feasible Region 176
    Finding the Optimal Solution 177

Identifying the Optimal Solution Directly by Graphical Means 179
S1.5 The Simplex Method: An Overview 180
S1.6 Solving Linear Programming Problems with Excel 181
 Entering Large Problems Efficiently 185
S1.7 Interpreting the Sensitivity Report 187
 Shadow Prices 187
 Objective Function Coefficients and Right-Hand Sides 188
 Adding a New Variable 188
 Using Sensitivity Analysis 189
S1.8 Recognizing Special Problems 191
 Unbounded Solutions 191
 Empty Feasible Region 192
 Degeneracy 194
 Multiple Optimal Solutions 194
 Redundant Constraints 194
S1.9 The Application of Linear Programming to Production and Operations Analysis 195
Bibliography 197

Chapter 4
Inventory Control Subject to Known Demand 198

Chapter Overview 198
4.1 Types of Inventories 201
4.2 Motivation for Holding Inventories 202
4.3 Characteristics of Inventory Systems 203
4.4 Relevant Costs 204
 Holding Cost 204
 Order Cost 206
 Penalty Cost 207
 Problems for Sections 4.1–4.4 208
4.5 The EOQ Model 210
 The Basic Model 210
 Inclusion of Order Lead Time 213
 Sensitivity 214
 EOQ and JIT 215
 Problems for Section 4.5 216
4.6 Extension to a Finite Production Rate 218
 Problems for Section 4.6 219
4.7 Quantity Discount Models 220
 Optimal Policy for All-Units Discount Schedule 221
 Summary of the Solution Technique for All-Units Discounts 223
 Incremental Quantity Discounts 223
 Summary of the Solution Technique for Incremental Discounts 225
 Other Discount Schedules 225
 Problems for Section 4.7 226
 Snapshot Application: SmartOps Assists in Designing Caterpillar's Inventory Control System 227
*4.8 Resource-Constrained Multiple Product Systems 227
 Problems for Section 4.8 231
4.9 EOQ Models for Production Planning 231
 Problems for Section 4.9 235
4.10 Power-of-Two Policies 236
 Case Study. Betty Buys a Business 238
4.11 Historical Notes and Additional Topics 240
4.12 Summary 241
 Additional Problems on Deterministic Inventory Models 242
Appendix 4–A Mathematical Derivations for Multiproduct Constrained EOQ Systems 246
Appendix 4–B Glossary of Notation for Chapter 4 248
Bibliography 248

Chapter 5
Inventory Control Subject to Uncertain Demand 249

Chapter Overview 249
 Overview of Models Treated in this Chapter 253
5.1 The Nature of Randomness 254
5.2 Optimization Criterion 256
 Problems for Sections 5.1 and 5.2 257
5.3 The Newsvendor Model 258
 Notation 258
 Development of the Cost Function 259
 Determining the Optimal Policy 260
 Optimal Policy for Discrete Demand 262
 Extension to Include Starting Inventory 262
 Snapshot Application: Using Inventory Models to Manage the Seed-Corn Supply Chain at Syngenta 263
 Extension to Multiple Planning Periods 264
 Problems for Section 5.3 265
5.4 Lot Size–Reorder Point Systems 267
 Describing Demand 268
 Decision Variables 268
 Derivation of the Expected Cost Function 268
 The Cost Function 270
 Inventory Level versus Inventory Position 272
 Snapshot Application: Inventory Management Software for the Small Business 273
5.5 Service Levels In (Q, R) Systems 274
 Type 1 Service 274
 Type 2 Service 274

x Contents

        Optimal (Q, R) Policies Subject to Type 2 Constraint 275
        Imputed Shortage Cost 277
        Scaling of Lead Time Demand 277
        Estimating Sigma When Inventory Control and Forecasting Are Linked 278
        *Lead Time Variability 279
        Calculations in Excel 279
        Negative Safety Stock 280
        Problems for Sections 5.4 and 5.5 280

5.6 Additional Discussion of Periodic-Review Systems 282
        (s, S) Policies 282
        *Service Levels in Periodic-Review Systems 283
        Fixed Order Size Model 284
        Problems for Section 5.6 284
        Snapshot Application: Tropicana Uses Sophisticated Modeling for Inventory Management 285

5.7 Multiproduct Systems 286
        ABC Analysis 286
        Exchange Curves 288
        Problems for Section 5.7 290

*5.8 Overview of Advanced Topics 291
        Multi-echelon Systems 291
        Perishable Inventory Problems 293
        Snapshot Application: Intel Uses Multiechelon Inventory Modelling to Manage the Supply Chain for Boxed CPUs 294

5.9 Historical Notes and Additional Readings 295

5.10 Summary 296
        Additional Problems on Stochastic Inventory Models 297

Appendix 5–A Notational Conventions and Probability Review 303

Appendix 5–B Additional Results and Extensions for the Newsvendor Model 304

Appendix 5–C Derivation of the Optimal (Q, R) Policy 308

Appendix 5–D Probability Distributions for Inventory Management 308

Appendix 5–E Glossary of Notation for Chapter 5 312

Bibliography 313

Chapter 6
Supply Chain Management 315

Chapter Overview 315
        The Supply Chain as a Strategic Weapon 318

6.1 Supply Chain Strategy 319
        Snapshot Application: Wal-Mart Wins with Solid Supply Chain Management 320

6.2 The Role of Information in the Supply Chain 321
        Snapshot Application: Anheuser-Busch Re-engineers their Supply Chain 322
        The Bullwhip Effect 322
        Electronic Commerce 326
        RFID Technology 327
        Problems for Sections 6.1 and 6.2 329

6.3 The Transportation Problem 329

6.4 Generalizations of the Transportation Problem 333
        Infeasible Routes 334
        Unbalanced Problems 334

6.5 More General Network Formulations 335
        Snapshot Application: IBM Streamlines Its Semi-conductor Supply Chain Using Sophisticated Mathematical 338
        Problems for Sections 6.3–6.5 338

6.6 Determining Delivery Routes in Supply Chains 341
        Practical Issues in Vehicle Scheduling 345
        Snapshot Application: J.B. Hunt Saves Big with Routing and Scheduling Algorithm 346
        Problems for Section 6.6 346

6.7 Risk Pooling 347
        Inventory/Location Pooling 348
        Product Pooling and Postponement 351
        Capacity Pooling 352

6.8 Designing Products for Supply Chain Efficiency 353
        Additional Issues in Supply Chain Design 354
        Snapshot Application: Dell Computer Designs the Ultimate Supply Chain 356

6.9 Multilevel Distribution Systems 356
        Problems for Sections 6.7–6.9 358

6.10 Incentives in the Supply Chain 359
        Problems for Section 6.10 362

6.11 Global Supply Chain management 362
        Problems for Section 6.11 363

6.12 Summary 364

Bibliography 365

Chapter 7
Service Operations Management 367

Chapter Overview 367

7.1 Service Operations Strate Gy 370
        The Service Economy 370
        Service Quality 371
        Measuring Quality 372
        Controlling Quality 372
        Paying for Quality 372

Key Decisions for Service Businesses 373
Snapshot Application: Southwest Airlines
 Competes with Service 374
Managing Variability 374
Service Competition 375
Problems for Section 7.1 376
7.2 Flow Systems 377
Process Flow Diagrams 377
Capacity 378
Flow Rates and Utilization 378
Problems for Section 7.2 379
7.3 Modeling Unscheduled Arrivals 380
Poisson Process 380
Exponential Interarrival Times 382
General Arrival Processes 383
Pooling in Services 384
Probability of Delay 384
Problems for Section 7.3 385
7.4 Queueing Systems 386
Structural Aspects of Queueing Models 387
Notation 387
Little's law 388
The M/M/1 Queue 389
Problems for Section 7.4 391
7.5 General Queueing Models 392
Expected Time in System for a Single Server
 System 393
Multiple Parallel Servers 395
Systems with Abandonment 396
Priorities 397
Other Queueing Extensions 399
Simulation 399
Improving a Service Process 400
Problems for Section 7.5 401
7.6 The Human Element in Service
 Systems 401
Snapshot Application: Using Queueing to
 make Staffing Decisions Saves Lives 402
The Psychology of Queueing 402
Introducing Technology into Services 403
Guidelines for Service Guarantees and
 Refunds 404
Snapshot application: Disney uses both the
 Science and the Psychology of Queueing 405
7.7 Call and Contact Centers 405
Call Center Basics 405
Metrics 406
Call Routing 407
7.8 Revenue Management 407
Airline Revenue Management Overview 407
Revenue Management Basics 408

Lead Time Pricing 409
Nontraditional Applications for Revenue
 Management 410
Problems for Sections 7.6–7.8 410
7.9 Historical Notes and Additional
 Readings 411
7.10 Summary 411
Additional Problems for Chapter 7 412
Appendix 7–A Simulation Implementation 414
Random Number Generation 414
Entity Driven Logic 414
Bibliography 415

Supplement 2 Queueing Techniques 417

S2.1 Details of the Poisson Process and Exponential
 Distribution 417
S2.2 Analysis of the M/M/1 Queue 418
Waiting Time Distribution 421
S2.3 Further Results for M/M Queues 422
The M/M/s Queue 424
The M/M/1 Queue with a Finite Capacity 427
S2.4 Infinite Server Results 430
The M/g/∞ queue 430
Infinite Server Limits 431
S2.5 Queueing Networks 432
S2.6 Optimization of Queueing Systems 433
Typical Service System Design Problems 433
Modeling Framework 434
Bibliography 436

Chapter 8
**Push and Pull Production Control Systems:
MRP and JIT 437**

Chapter Overview 437
MRP Basics 440
JIT Basics 442
8.1 The Explosion Calculus 443
Problems for Section 8.1 447
8.2 Alternative Lot-Sizing Schemes 449
EOQ Lot Sizing 449
The Silver–Meal Heuristic 450
Least Unit Cost 451
Part Period Balancing 452
Problems for Section 8.2 453
8.3 Incorporating Lot-Sizing Algorithms into the
 Explosion Calculus 455
Problems for Section 8.3 456
8.4 Lot Sizing with Capacity Constraints 457
Problems for Section 8.4 460

8.5 Shortcomings of MRP 461
    Uncertainty 461
    Capacity Planning 462
    Rolling Horizons and System Nervousness 463
    Additional Considerations 465
    Snapshot Application: Raymond Corporation Builds World-Class Manufacturing with MRP II 466
    Problems for Section 8.5 467
8.6 JIT Fundamentals 468
    The Mechanics of Kanban 468
    Single Minute Exchange of Dies 470
    Advantages and Disadvantages of the Just-in-Time Philosophy 471
    Implementation of JIT in the United States 474
    Problems for Section 8.6 475
8.7 A Comparison of MRP and JIT 476
8.8 JIT or Lean Production? 477
8.9 Historical Notes 478
8.10 Summary 479
    Additional Problems for Chapter 8 480
Appendix 8–A Optimal Lot Sizing for Time-Varying Demand 484
Appendix 8–B Glossary of Notation for Chapter 8 488
Bibliography 489

Chapter 9
Operations Scheduling 490

Chapter Overview 490
9.1 Production Scheduling and the Hierarchy of Production Decisions 493
9.2 Important Characteristics of Job Shop Scheduling Problems 495
    Objectives of Job Shop Management 495
9.3 Job Shop Scheduling Terminology 496
9.4 A Comparison of Specific Sequencing Rules 498
    First-Come, First-Served 498
    Shortest Processing Time 499
    Earliest Due Date 499
    Critical Ratio Scheduling 500
9.5 Objectives in Job Shop Management: An Example 501
    Problems for Sections 9.1–9.5 502
9.6 An Introduction to Sequencing Theory for a Single Machine 503
    Shortest-Processing-Time Scheduling 504
    Earliest-Due-Date Scheduling 505
    Minimizing the Number of Tardy Jobs 505
    Precedence Constraints: Lawler's Algorithm 506

    Snapshot Application: Millions Saved with Scheduling System for Fractional Aircraft Operators 508
    Problems for Section 9.6 508
9.7 Sequencing Algorithms For Multiple Machines 510
    Scheduling n Jobs on Two Machines 511
    Extension to Three Machines 512
    The Two-Job Flow Shop Problem 514
    Problems for Section 9.7 517
9.8 Stochastic Scheduling: Static Analysis 518
    Single Machine 518
    Multiple Machines 519
    The Two-Machine Flow Shop Case 520
    Problems for Section 9.8 521
9.9 Stochastic Scheduling: Dynamic Analysis 522
    Selection Disciplines Independent of Job Processing Times 524
    Selection Disciplines Dependent on Job Processing Times 525
    The $c\mu$ Rule 527
    Problems for Section 9.9 527
9.10 Assembly Line Balancing 528
    Problems for Section 9.10 532
    Snapshot Application: Manufacturing Divisions Realize Savings with Scheduling Software 534
9.11 Historical Notes 535
9.12 Summary 535
    Additional Problems on Scheduling 536
Bibliography 542

Chapter 10
Project Scheduling 543

Chapter Overview 543
10.1 Representing a Project as a Network 546
10.2 Critical Path Analysis 548
    Finding the Critical Path 551
    Problems for Sections 10.1 and 10.2 554
10.3 Time Costing Methods 556
    Problems for Section 10.3 560
10.4 Solving Critical Path Problems with Linear Programming 561
    Linear Programming Formulation of the Cost–Time Problem 564
    Problems for Section 10.4 566
10.5 Pert: Project Evaluation and Review Technique 566
    Path Independence 571

Problems for Section 10.5   574
Snapshot Application: Warner Robins Streamlines Aircraft Maintenance with CCPM Project Management   576
10.6 Resource Considerations   576
Resource Constraints for Single-Project Scheduling   576
Resource Constraints for Multiproject Scheduling   578
Resource Loading Profiles   579
Problems for Section 10.6   581
10.7 Organizational Issues in Project Management   583
10.8 Historical Notes   584
10.9 Project Management Software for the PC   585
Snapshot Applications: Project Management Helps United Stay on Schedule   586
Thomas Brothers Plans Staffing with Project Management Software   586
Florida Power and Light Takes Project Management Seriously   586
10.10 Summary   587
Additional Problems on Project Scheduling   588
Appendix 10–A   Glossary of Notation for Chapter 10   591
Bibliography   592

Chapter 11
Facilities Layout and Location   593

Chapter Overview   593
11.1 The Facilities Layout Problem   596
11.2 Patterns of Flow   597
Activity Relationship Chart   598
From-To Chart   600
11.3 Types of Layouts   602
Fixed Position Layouts   602
Product Layouts   602
Process Layouts   603
Layouts Based on Group Technology   603
Problems for Sections 11.1–11.3   605
11.4 A Prototype Layout Problem and the Assignment Model   607
The Assignment Algorithm   608
Problems for Section 11.4   610
*11.5 More Advanced Mathematical Programming Formulations   611
Problem for Section 11.5   612
11.6 Computerized Layout Techniques   612
CRAFT   613
COFAD   617
ALDEP   618
CORELAP   619
PLANET   620
Computerized Methods versus Human Planners   620
Dynamic Plant Layouts   621
Other Computer Methods   621
Problems for Section 11.6   622
11.7 Flexible Manufacturing Systems   625
Advantages of Flexible Manufacturing Systems   627
Disadvantages of Flexible Manufacturing Sysems   627
Decision Making and Modeling of the FMS   628
The Future of FMS   631
Problems for Section 11.7   632
11.8 Locating New Facilities   632
Snapshot Application: Kraft Foods Uses Optimization and Simulation to Determine Best Layout   633
Measures of Distance   634
Problems for Section 11.8   635
11.9 The Single-Facility Rectilinear Distance Location Problem   635
Contour Lines   638
Minimax Problems   639
Problems for Section 11.9   642
11.10 Euclidean Distance Problems   643
The Gravity Problem   643
The Straight-Line Distance Problem   644
Problems for Section 11.10   645
11.11 Other Location Models   646
Locating Multiple Facilities   647
Further Extensions   648
Problems for Section 11.11   650
11.12 Historical Notes   651
11.13 Summary   652
Additional Problems on Layout and Location   653
Spreadsheet Problems for Chapter 11   658
Appendix 11–A   Finding Centroids   659
Appendix 11–B   Computing Contour Lines   661
Bibliography   644

Chapter 12
Quality and Assurance   666

Chapter Overview   666
Overview of this Chapter   670
12.1 Statistical Basis of Control Charts   671
Problems for Section 12.1   673

xiv Contents

12.2 Control Charts for Variables: The $\bar{X}$ and R Charts 675
  $\bar{X}$ Charts 678
  Relationship to Classical Statistics 678
  R Charts 680
  Problems for Section 12.2 681
12.3 Control Charts for Attributes: The p Chart 683
  p Charts for Varying Subgroup Sizes 685
  Problems for Section 12.3 686
12.4 The c Chart 688
  Problems for Section 12.4 690
12.5 Classical Statistical Methods and Control Charts 691
  Problem for Section 12.5 691
*12.6 Economic Design of $\bar{X}$ Charts 692
  Problems for Section 12.6 698
12.7 Overview of Acceptance Sampling 699
  Snapshot Application: Navistar Scores with Six-Sigma Quality Program 701
12.8 Notation 702
12.9 Single Sampling for Attributes 702
  Derivation of the OC Curve 704
  Problems for Section 12.9 706
*12.10 Double Sampling Plans for Attributes 707
  Problems for Section 12.10 708
12.11 Sequential Sampling Plans 709
  Problems for Section 12.11 713
12.12 Average Outgoing Quality 714
  Snapshot Application: Motorola Leads the way with Six-Sigma Quality Programs 716
  Problems for Section 12.12 716
12.13 Total Quality Management 717
  Definitions 717
  Listening to the Customer 717
  Competition Based on Quality 719
  Organizing for Quality 720
  Benchmarking Quality 721
  The Deming Prize and the Baldrige Award 722
  ISO 9000 724
  Quality: The Bottom Line 725
12.14 Designing Quality into the Product 726
  Design, Manufacturing, and Quality 728
12.15 Historical Notes 730
12.16 Summary 731
  Additional Problems on Quality and Assurance 733
Appendix 12–A Approximating Distributions 737
Appendix 12–B Glossary of Notation for Chapter 12 on Quality and Assurance 739
Bibliography 740

Chapter 13
Reliability and Maintainability 742

Chapter Overview 742
13.1 Reliability of a Single Component 746
  Introduction to Reliability Concepts 746
  Preliminary Notation and Definitions 747
  The Exponential Failure Law 749
  Problems for Section 13.1 752
13.2 Increasing and Decreasing Failure Rates 754
  Problems for Section 13.2 756
13.3 The Poisson Process in Reliability Modeling 757
  Series Systems Subject to Purely Random Failures 760
  Problems for Section 13.3 761
13.4 Failures of Complex Equipment 762
  Components in Series 762
  Components in Parallel 763
  Expected Value Calculations 763
  K out of N Systems 764
  Problems for Section 13.4 766
13.5 Introduction to Maintenance Models 766
13.6 Deterministic Age Replacement Strategies 768
  The Optimal Policy in the Basic Case 768
  A General Age Replacement Model 770
  Problems for Section 13.6 774
13.7 Planned Replacement under Uncertainty 774
  Planned Replacement for a Single Item 774
  Block Replacement for a Group of Items 778
  Problems for Section 13.7 780
*13.8 Analysis of Warranty Policies 782
  The Free Replacement Warranty 782
  The Pro Rata Warranty 784
  Extensions and Criticisms 786
  Problems for Section 13.8 786
13.9 Software Reliability 787
  Snapshot Application: Reliability-Centered Maintenance Improves Operations at Three Mile Island Nuclear Plant 788
13.10 Historical Notes 789
13.11 Summary 790
  Additional Problems on Reliability and Maintainability 791
Appendix 13–A Glossary of Notation on Reliability and Maintainability 793
Bibliography 795

Appendix: Tables 796

Index 814

About the Authors

Steven Nahmias is Professor of Operations Management and Information Systems in the Leavey School of Business Administration at Santa Clara University. He holds a B.A. in Mathematics and Sciences from Queens College, and B.S. in Operations Research from Columbia University, and the M.S. and Ph.D. degrees in Operations Research from Northwestern. He previously served on the faculties of the University of Pittsburgh, Georgia Tech, and Stanford University.

He is widely known for his research on stochastic inventory models with an emphasis on perishables. He has authored or co-authored more than 50 scientific articles which have appeared in a variety of national and international journals. He has served as Area Editor in Supply Chain Logistics for *Operations Research*, senior editor for *M&SOM*, associate editor for *Management Science*, and associate editor for *Naval Research Logistics*. He earned first prize in the Nicholson Student Paper competition (1971) and second prize in the TIMS student paper competition (1972) and the University Award for Sustained Excellence in Scholarship from Santa Clara University (1998). In 2011 he was named Distinguished Fellow of the Manufacturing and Service Operations Management Society and in 2014 Distinguished Fellow of *INFORMS*.

In addition to his academic activities he has served as a consultant to a variety of companies and agencies. In his spare time he enjoys biking and golf. He is also a semi-professional jazz trumpet player and performs regularly with several bands in the Bay Area.

Tava Olsen holds the Ports of Auckland chair in Logistics and Supply Chain Management at the University of Auckland Business School. Prior to joining Auckland, she was Professor of Operations and Manufacturing Management in the Olin Business School at Washington University in St. Louis, which she joined after serving as an Assistant Professor in the Department of Industrial and Operations Engineering at the University of Michigan, Ann Arbor. Dr. Olsen received her B.Sc. (honours) in Mathematics from the University of Auckland. She earned both her M.S. in Statistics and her Ph.D. in Operations Research from Stanford University.

Dr. Olsen's research interests include supply chain management; pricing and inventory control; and stochastic modeling of manufacturing, service, and healthcare systems. Among other journals, her publications have appeared in *Management Science*, *Operations Research*, *Manufacturing and Service Operations Management (M&SOM)*, and the *Journal of Applied Probability*. In 2012, she received Auckland Business School's Sustained Research Excellence Award.

Dr. Olsen is the Academic Director of the Centre for Supply Chain Management. She is currently an Associate Editor for *Management Science, M&SOM* and *Operations Research*, is a senior editor of *Production and Operations Management*. She is a past president of the Manufacturing and Service Operations (MSOM) society for which she received the society's distinguished service award. She enjoys hiking, biking, and spending time with her husband and two daughters.

Preface to the Seventh Edition

This edition is the most substantial to date. All of the changes have been to the first half of the book, which appears to comprise the most popular chapters. Chapter 1 is basically intact with the addition of a major section on servicization. In Chapter 2, the tables that appeared in the first six editions have been replaced with screen shots of spreadsheets with cell formula definitions. The section on seasonal decomposition has been streamlined, and several new snapshot applications were added. Chapter 3 has been retitled and repositioned. The chapter is now titled "Sales and Operations Planning." It incorporates the aggregate planning material from prior editions, but includes new material on the planning process and discusses how production plans grow out of demand forecasts. Chapter 4 on deterministic demand includes a new Snapshot Application and a brief case study at the end of the chapter. In Chapter 5, there is a new appendix that derives a closed form expression for the expected cost function in a newsvendor model with normal demand. Chapter 6 on supply chains has been substantially revised and repositioned. Chapter 7 is new. It presents a comprehensive treatment of the analytical models for service systems and incorporates material on queueing and the Poisson process from the prior editions. The remaining chapters (8 through 13) are largely the same as the sixth edition.

Finally, I am very happy to welcome Tava Lennon Olsen as a co-author. She has brought a fresh perspective to the book and broadened the coverage substantially.

Steven Nahmias

Chapter One

Strategy and Competition

"However beautiful the strategy, you should occasionally look at the results."
—Winston Churchill

Chapter Overview

Purpose

The purpose of this chapter is to introduce the student to a variety of strategic issues that arise in the manufacturing function of the firm.

Key Points

1. *Manufacturing matters.* This writer contends that the loss of the manufacturing base in the U.S. economy is not healthy and will eventually lead to an overall loss in the standard of living and quality of life in this country. It counters the argument that our evolution into a service economy is a natural and healthy thing.
2. *Strategic dimensions.* Along with cost and/or product differentiation, other dimensions along which firms distinguish themselves include (a) quality, (b) delivery speed, (c) delivery reliability, and (d) flexibility.
3. *Global competition.* How do we measure our success and economic health on a global scale? One way is to examine classical measures of relative economic strength, which include (a) balance of trade, (b) share of world exports, (c) creation of jobs, and (d) cost of labor. However, such macro measures do not adequately explain why certain countries dominate certain industries. National competitive advantage is a consequence of several factors (factor conditions, demand conditions, related and supporting industries, firm strategy structure, and rivalry), although productivity also plays an important role.
4. *Strategic initiatives.* We discuss several strategic initiatives that have allowed many companies to shine in their respective arenas. These include (a) business process reengineering, (b) just-in-time manufacturing and purchasing systems, (c) time-based competition, and (d) competing on quality.
5. *Product and process life cycles.* Most of us understand that products have natural life cycles: start-up, rapid growth, maturation, stabilization, or decline. However, it is rarely recognized that processes too have life cycles. Initially, new manufacturing processes have the characteristics of a job shop. As the process matures, automation is introduced. In the mature phases of a manufacturing process, most major operations are automated. A firm needs to match the phases of product and process life cycles to be the most successful in its arena.

6. *Learning and experience curves.* These are helpful in forecasting the decline in unit cost of a manufacturing process as one gains experience with the process. Learning curves are more appropriate when modeling the learning of an individual worker, and experience curves are more appropriate when considering an entire industry.
7. *Capacity growth planning.* Another important strategic issue in operations is determining the timing and sizing of new capacity additions. Simple models (make or buy problem) and more complex exponential growth models are explored in Section 1.11. In addition, some of the factors that determine appropriate location of new facilities is explored.

Strategy is a long-term plan of action designed to achieve a particular goal, most often winning. Its root is from the Greek *stratēgos*, which referred to a "military commander" during the age of Athenian Democracy. Strategy was originally conceived in the military context. Two famous books dealing with military strategy are *The Prince* by Machiavelli and *The Art of War* by Sun Tzu.

Hence, we can see that business strategy relates closely to military strategy. Companies fight on an economic battlefield, and long-term strategies determine winners and losers. Business strategy is the highest level of corporate activity that bundles together the disparate functional area strategies. Business strategy sets the terms and goals for a company to follow.

Perhaps the reason that chief executive officers (CEOs) are compensated so highly in the United States is the realization that the strategic vision of the CEO is often the difference between the success and failure of a company. The strategic visions of industry giants such as Henry Ford, Jack Welch, and Bill Gates were central to the success of their companies that have, at one time or another, dominated their competition.

Perhaps the most dramatic example is Apple Corporation. With the introduction of the iPod in 2002 and the iPhone is 2007, Apple transformed itself from a failing computer company to a major force in portable computing and telecommunications. The fascinating transformation of the firm is described in the Snapshot Application on the next page.

Success requires a vision, and visions must be articulated so all of the firm's employees can share in that vision. The formal articulation of the vision is known as the company mission statement. A good mission statement should provide a clear description of the goals of the firm and is the first step toward formulating a coherent business strategy. Poor mission statements tend to be wordy and full of generalities. Good mission statements are direct, clear, and concise. In their book, Jones and Kahaner (1995) list the 50 corporate mission statements that they perceive as the best. One example is the Gillette Corporation. Their mission statement is: "Our Mission is to achieve or enhance clear leadership, worldwide, in the existing or new core consumer product categories in which we choose to compete." They then go on to list exactly which areas they perceive as their core competencies. Intel defines their mission as: "Do a great job for our customers, employees, and stockholders by being the preeminent building block supplier to the computing industry." The statement then provides details on "Values and Objectives." In many cases, their objectives are quite specific (e.g., "Lead in LAN products and Smart Network Services"). Certainly, the award for conciseness has to go to the General Electric Corporation, whose mission statement is three words: "Boundaryless . . . Speed . . . Stretch." The commentary following the statement provides an explanation of exactly what these words mean in the context of the corporation.

Snapshot Application

APPLE ADOPTS A NEW BUSINESS STRATEGY AND SHIFTS ITS CORE COMPETENCY FROM COMPUTERS TO PORTABLE ELECTRONICS

Apple Computer was the kind of success story one sees in the movies. Two youngsters, Steve Wozniak and Steve Jobs, grew up with an interest in hobbyist computers. Working from a garage, they founded Apple Computer in April 1976, and soon after, introduced a build your own hobbyist computer called the Apple I. The firm was incorporated a year later with the help of Mike Markula, and the Apple II was introduced in April 1977, ushering in the world of personal computing. Perhaps it was the fact that it was selected as the platform for Visicalc, the first spreadsheet program, that led to its success, as much as the superior capabilities of the hardware.

While personal computers have become a common part of our everyday lives, we forget that they are a relatively new invention. The nature of the personal computer marketplace was dramatically altered by the introduction of the first PC by IBM in 1981. IBM's open architecture allowed for inexpensive clones to enter the market, and crowd out Apple's significantly more expensive products. By the turn of the century, Apple's future looked to be in doubt.

Apple's subsequent transformation and rebirth is a fascinating bit of business history. Around 2001, an independent consultant, Tony Fadell, was shopping around his concept of an MP3 music player linked to a music sales service. At that time, MP3 players were not new; one could "rip" music from one's CD collection, and load the songs on the player. While no one else was interested in Fadell's idea, he was hired by Apple and assigned to a team of 30 people, including designers, programmers, and hardware engineers.

When Apple decided to go ahead with the MP3 player concept, they also decided that they needed a new design to separate themselves from the rest of the marketplace. Apple subcontracted much of the development and design work to PortalPlayer, who devoted all of their resources to the project. Steve Jobs himself was intimately involved with the design and function of the new player. The iPod was a huge success and has been redesigned over several models and generations. The most current reports record worldwide sales of over 350 million units.

While the iPod was a huge success, Apple did not rest on its laurels. In 2007, Apple launched the first iPhone. Again, the concept of a smartphone was not new. Several companies, notably Motorola, Samsung, Palm, and Nokia, had smartphones on the market for several years prior. But as with the iPod, Apple again produced an innovative product with unique features. Apple continues to improve upon the iPhone and introduces a new generation of the product virtually every year. As of this writing, sales have reached over 500 million worldwide.

Apple's most recent product, the iPad, was also an instant success and essentially defined a new market category. This tablet computer, introduced in March 2010, is convenient for web surfing and reading e-books, and again, has become the product the competition measures itself against. Apple registered more than 1 million sales of the iPad in the first three months alone. As a testament to Apple's phenomenal success in portable computing, the market capitalization of Apple surpassed that of the software behemoth Microsoft in 2010.

Source: Various websites and L. Kahney "Inside Look at the Birth of the iPod" July 2004 (http://www.wired.com).

Once having articulated a vision, the next step is to plan a strategy for achieving that vision. This is the firm's business strategy. The overall business strategy includes defining

1. The market in which the enterprise competes.
2. The level of investment.
3. The means of allocating resources to and the integrating of separate business units.
4. Functional area strategies, including
   - The marketing strategy
   - The financial strategy
   - The operations strategy

Broadly defined, the operations strategy is the means by which the firm deploys its resources to achieve its competitive goals. For manufacturing firms, it is the sum total of all decisions concerning the production, storage, and distribution of goods. Important operations strategy decisions include where to locate new manufacturing facilities, how large these facilities should be, what processes to use for manufacturing and moving goods through the system, and what workers to employ. Service firms also require an operations strategy. The United States continues to be a leader in financial services, which must be supported by effective and reliable operations departments in order to remain competitive. The Disney theme park's continuing record of success is due in part to its careful attention to detail in every phase of its operations.

Does the American culture place too much emphasis on marketing (selling the product) and finance (leveraged buyouts, mergers, stock prices) and too little on operations (making and delivering the product)? Years ago, this was certainly the case. However, we are quick learners. The enormous success of the Japanese auto industry, for example, provided strong motivation for the American big three to close their inefficient plants and change the way things were done. The dramatic differences that were brought to light by Womack, Jones, and Roos (1990) have largely been eliminated. Today, the best American auto plants rival their Japanese counterparts for quality and efficiency.

Still, a coherent operations strategy is essential. When the Apple Macintosh was introduced, the product was extremely successful. However, the company was plagued with backorders and failed to keep up with consumer demand. According to Debbi Coleman, Apple's former director of worldwide manufacturing:

> Manufacturing lacked an overall strategy which created problems that took nine months to solve . . . we had extremely poor forecasting. Incoming materials weren't inspected for defects and we didn't have a mechanism for telling suppliers what was wrong, except angry phone calls. Forty percent of Mac materials were coming from overseas and no one from Apple was inspecting them before they were shipped. . . . One of the biggest tasks that high-tech manufacturers face is designing a manufacturing strategy that allows a company to be flexible so it can ride with the highs and lows of consumer and business buying cycles. (Fallon, 1985)

Although it is easy to be critical of American management style, we must be aware of the factors motivating American managers and those motivating managers from other cultures. For example, the Japanese have not achieved their dramatic successes without cost. Sixteen-hour work days and a high rate of nervous breakdowns among management are common in Japan.

Measuring a firm's success by the performance of its share price can result in short-sighted management practices. Boards of directors are more concerned with the next quarterly report than with funding major long-term projects. In fact, Hayes and Wheelwright (1984) make a compelling argument that such factors led to a myopic management style in the United States, characterized by the following:

1. Managers' performance is measured on the basis of **return on investment** (ROI), which is simply the ratio of the profit realized by a particular operation or project over the investment made in that operation or project.
2. Performance is measured over short time horizons. There is little motivation for a manager to invest in a project that is not likely to bear fruit until after he or she has moved on to another position.

In order to improve ROI, a manager must either increase the numerator (profits) or decrease the denominator (investment). In the short term, decreasing the denominator by cutting back on the investment in new technologies or new facilities is easier than trying to increase profits by improving efficiency, the quality of the product, or the productivity of the operating unit. The long-term effects of decreasing investment are devastating. At some point, the capital costs required to modernize old factories become more than the firm can bear, and the firm loses its competitive position in the marketplace.

It would be encouraging if the problems of U.S. industries arising from overemphasis on short-term financial performance were decreasing, but sadly, they appear to be worsening. Because of gross mismanagement and questionable auditing practices, two giants of American industry were brought down in 2001: Enron and Arthur Andersen. "Enron went from the No. 7 company on the Fortune 500 to a penny stock in a stunning three weeks because it apparently lied on its financial statements," said Representative John D. Dingell, one-time member of the House Energy Committee. While other parts of the world have experienced spectacular problems as well (such as the Asian financial crisis that hit in the late 1990s), few Americans can understand how a company that had recently expanded and profited from the energy crisis, and an American icon such as Arthur Andersen, could both be brought down so quickly and completely. It is our continual focus on short-term performance and the incentive system we have built up around this objective that led to these crises.

Measuring individual performance over the short term is a philosophy that seems to pervade American life. Politicians are elected for two-, four-, or six-year terms. There is a strong incentive for them to show results in time for the next election. Even university professors are evaluated yearly on their professional performance in many institutions, even though most serious academic projects extend over many years.

1.1 MANUFACTURING MATTERS

A question that is being debated and has been debated by economists for several decades is the importance of a strong manufacturing base. The decline of manufacturing domestically has led to a shift in jobs from the manufacturing sector to the service sector. Because there are major disparities in labor costs in different parts of the world, there are strong incentives for American firms to locate volume manufacturing facilities overseas to reduce labor costs. Is a strong manufacturing base important for the health of the economy?

There is little debate that manufacturing jobs have been steadily declining in the United States. The growth of manufacturing overseas, and in China in particular, is well documented. If we compare the proportion of nonagriculture jobs in the United States in service versus manufacturing in 1950 versus 2002, the change is quite dramatic. In 1950, manufacturing jobs accounted for 34 percent of nonagriculture labor and service jobs accounted for 59 percent. In 2002, however, manufacturing jobs only accounted for 13 percent of nonagriculture jobs, while service jobs soared to 82 percent of the total (Hagenbaugh, 2002).

One mitigating factor in the loss of manufacturing was the dramatic rise in manufacturing productivity during this same period. Average annual manufacturing productivity growth was 2.57 percent annually during the 1980s and 3.51 percent annually during the 1990s (Faux, 2003). This dramatic rise in manufacturing productivity has had the effect of offsetting the loss of high-paying manufacturing jobs at home, thus partially accounting for the success of the U.S. economy in the latter part of the first decade of the century.

An argument put forth by several scholars (e.g., Daniel Bell, 1976) is that we are simply evolving from an industrial to a service economy. In this view, the three stages of economic evolution are (1) agrarian, (2) industrial, and (3) service. In the early years of our country, we were primarily an agrarian economy. With the industrial revolution, a large portion of the labor force shifted from agriculture to manufacturing. In recent years it seems that there is less interest in manufacturing. These scholars would argue that we are merely entering the third stage of the evolutionary process: moving from an industrial economy to a service economy.

It is comforting to think that the American economy is healthy and simply evolving from an industrial to a service economy. One might even argue that manufacturing is not important for economic well-being. According to economist Gary S. Becker (1986), "Strong modern economies do not seem to require a dominant manufacturing sector."

It is far from clear, however, that we evolved from an agrarian economy to an industrial economy. Although fewer American workers are employed in the agricultural sector of the economy, agricultural production has not declined. Based on U.S. Department of Commerce data, Cohen and Zysman (1987) state that "agriculture has sustained, over the long term, the highest rate of productivity increase of any sector." By utilizing new technologies, agriculture has been able to sustain growth while consuming fewer labor hours. Hence, the figures simply do not bear out the argument that our economy has shifted from an agricultural one to an industrial one.

The argument that the economy is undergoing natural stages of evolution is simply not borne out by the facts. I believe that all sectors of the economy—agricultural, manufacturing, and service—are important and that domestic economic well-being depends upon properly linking the activities of these sectors.

The return on innovations will be lost if new products are abandoned after development. The payoff for research and development (R&D) can come only when the product is produced and sold. If manufacturing is taken offshore, then the "rent on innovation" cannot be recaptured. Furthermore, manufacturing naturally leads to innovation. It will be difficult for the United States to retain its position as a leader in innovation if it loses its position as a leader in manufacturing.

That manufacturing naturally leads to innovation is perhaps best illustrated by the Japanese experience in the video market. After Japan had captured the lion's share of the world market for televisions, the next major innovation in consumer video technology, the videocassette recorder (VCR), (at least, the inexpensive consumer version) was developed in Japan, not the United States. Virtually all VCRs sold were manufactured in Asia.

A more recent book by Pisano and Shih (2012) underscores many of the same themes that appeared in Cohen and Zysman (1987). They point to other products that were invented in the United States but whose base of manufacturing is now overseas. An example is the PV (photovoltaic) cell (more commonly known as the solar cell). PV cells were invented in Bell Labs, but only a very small percentage of the world demand is filled by American companies.

One of the more disturbing trends discussed by Pisano and Shih (2012) is the widening trade deficit in manufactured goods. The foreign trade deficit has continued to increase, resulting in the United States going from the largest creditor nation in the 1970s to the largest debtor nation today. The overwhelming source of this deficit is the continued negative trade balance in manufactured goods (the trade balance in services is actually increasing).

Where to locate manufacturing as well as R and D facilities is one of the key management decisions a firm must make. During the 1990s we saw an exodus of domestic manufacturing to China. The offshoring movement was rampant, not only in the United States but in most developed countries. The primary driver of this exodus is wage rates, but other factors were relevant as well. Favorable tax treatments, proximity to natural resources, and proximity to markets are also reasons companies locate facilities offshore.

In recent years, the advantage of offshoring is decreasing. For example, as the standard of living in China has improved, manufacturing wage rates have risen. When the disadvantages of offshoring are taken into account, the best course of action is no longer obvious. These disadvantages include longer lead times, infrastructure deficiencies, local politics, and quality problems.

An example cited in Reshoring Manufacturing (2013) is the start-up company ET Water Systems. In 2005 the firm moved manufacturing operations to China in search of lower labor costs. However, the disadvantages of locating offshore became apparent as the company starting suffering losses due to several factors, including the cost of funds tied up in goods in transit, the disconnect between manufacturing and design, and recurring quality problems. When the firm's chief executive, Mark Coopersmith, carefully looked at the total cost difference between manufacturing in China versus California he was amazed to discover that California was only 10% more expensive than China. He concluded that this cost difference was more than offset by the advantages of locating manufacturing domestically. ET Water Systems closed their plant in China and reshored the manufacturing function to General Electronics Assembly in San Jose.

Unfortunately, ET's experience is rare. More companies are continuing to choose the offshoring option. However, that reshoring is occurring at all is a positive step. Perhaps more companies will come to the same conclusion that ET Water Systems did when taking into account the full spectrum of the costs of offshoring.

In order to get some idea of the extent of reshoring compared to offshoring, Porter and Rivkin (2012) conducted an extensive survey of Harvard Business School alumni who made location decisions for their companies in 2011. They found that only 9% of the respondents were considering moving offshore activities back to the United States, 34% were planning on keeping their facilities where they were, and 57% were considering moving existing facilities out of the United States. Their results suggest that offshoring still dominates both staying put and reshoring. The respondents' main reasons for offshoring were lower wages, proximity to customers, better access to skilled labor, higher labor productivity, lower taxes, proximity of suppliers, and proximity to other company operations. The respondents' main reasons for staying put or reshoring were proximity to the U.S. market, less corruption, greater safety, better intellectual property protection, similar language and culture, better infrastructure, and proximity to other company operations.

Has offshoring been a help or a hindrance to the U.S. economy? The answer is not simple. On one hand, offshoring has resulted in loss of jobs domestically, lower average domestic wages which in turn have yielded a lower tax base and a smaller domestic market. On the other hand, offshoring has improved the bottom line for many domestic firms, and have resulted in lower costs of manufactured goods for the American consumer.

Manufacturing Jobs Outlook

The U.S. Bureau of Labor Statistics (a subsidiary of the Department of Labor) provides up-to-date information on the prospects for jobs in the manufacturing sector by industry. According to the *Occupational Outlook Handbook* (OOH), 2010–2011 Edition (http://www.bls.gov/oco/), even though manufacturing jobs are expected to decline overall, there are some areas of growth and opportunity. Consider the individual sectors:

1. *Aerospace products and parts*. This sector is projected to grow, but more slowly than the economy in general. Earnings are higher here than in most other manufacturing industries, as workers must be highly skilled. Opportunities will result from a large number of anticipated retirements.
2. *Chemical (except pharmaceuticals and medicines)*. The chemical industry continues to be a major employer of professionals, producing over 500,000 jobs.

However, employment is projected to decline and competition for better jobs to increase over the coming years.

3. *Computer and Electronic Products.* Employment is projected to decrease nearly 20 percent in the decade 2008–2018 due to productivity improvements and movement of jobs to lower wage countries.
4. *Food Manufacturing.* The jobs picture in this industry is stable, but production workers continue to have the highest incidences of injury and illness among all industry, with seafood product preparation and packaging being the worst sector in this regard.
5. *Machinery.* Productivity improvements will lead to fewer jobs overall, but opportunities will arise as a result of anticipated retirements. Machinery manufacturing has some of the most highly skilled, and highly paid, production jobs in manufacturing.
6. *Motor Vehicles and Parts.* Almost half the jobs are located in Michigan, Indiana, and Ohio, but jobs continue to shift away from this area to the South. Average earnings continue to be high in this sector, but employment is expected to decline in coming years.
7. *Pharmaceuticals and Medicine.* This continues to be a growth area, with earnings higher than in other manufacturing industries. Job prospects are particularly favorable for candidates with advanced degrees.
8. *Printing.* Most printing establishments are very small, with 70 percent employing under 10 people. Traditional printing is a declining industry due to increased computerization, but digital press operators will continue to be in demand.
9. *Steel.* Steel continues to be a declining industry domestically, with fewer jobs projected as a result of consolidation and automation. Opportunities will be best for engineers and skilled production and maintenance workers.
10. *Textiles, Textile Products, and Apparel.* About half the jobs are located in three states: California, North Carolina, and Georgia. Employment is expected to decline rapidly because of technological advances and imports of apparel and textiles from lower wage countries.

1.2 A FRAMEWORK FOR OPERATIONS STRATEGY

Classical literature on competitiveness claims that firms position themselves strategically in the marketplace along one of two dimensions: lower cost or product differentiation (Porter, 1990).

Often new entrants to a market position themselves as the low-cost providers. Firms that have adopted this approach include the Korean automakers (Hyundai, Daewoo, Kia), discount outlets such as Costco, and retailers such as Wal-Mart. While being the low-cost provider can be successful over the near term, it is a risky strategy. Consumers ultimately will abandon products that they perceive as poor quality regardless of cost. For example, many manufacturers of low-cost PC clones popular in the 1980s are long gone.

Most firms that have a long record of success in the marketplace have differentiated themselves from their competitors. By providing uniqueness to buyers, they are able to sustain high profit margins over time. One example is BMW, one of the most profitable auto firms in the world. BMW continues to produce high-performance, well-made cars that are often substantially more expensive than those of competitors in their class. Product differentiation within a firm has also been a successful strategy. Consider the success of General Motors in the early years compared to Ford. GM was able to successfully capture different market segments at the same time by forming five distinct divisions, while Henry Ford's insistence on providing only a single model almost led the company to bankruptcy (Womack et al., 1990).

Strategic Dimensions

However, cost and product differentiation are not the only two dimensions along which firms distinguish themselves. The following additional factors relate directly to the operations function:

- Quality
- Delivery speed
- Delivery reliability
- Flexibility

What does *quality* mean? It is a word often bandied about, but one that means different things in different contexts. Consider the following hypothetical remarks.

1. "That hairdryer was a real disappointment. It really didn't dry my hair as well as I expected."
2. "I was thrilled with my last car. I sold it with 150,000 miles and hardly had any repairs."
3. "I love buying from that catalogue. I always get what I order within two days."
4. "The refrigerator works fine, but I think the shelves could have been laid out better."
5. "That park had great rides, but the lines were a mess."
6. "Our quality is great. We've got less than six defectives per one million parts produced."

In each case, the speaker is referring to a different aspect of quality. In the first case, the product simply didn't perform the task it was designed to do. That is, its function was substandard. The repair record of an automobile is really an issue of reliability rather than quality, per se. In the third case, it is delivery speed that translates to quality service for that customer. The fourth case refers to a product that does what it is supposed to do, but the consumer is disappointed with the product design. The product quality (the rides) at the amusement park were fine, but the logistics of the park management were a disappointment. The final case refers to the statistical aspects of quality control.

Hence the word *quality* means different things in different contexts. A Honda Civic is a quality product and so is a Ferrari Testarosa. Consumers buying these products are both looking for quality cars but have fundamentally different objectives. The fact is that everyone competes on quality. For this reason, Terry Hill (1993) would classify quality as an order qualifier rather than an order winner. An option is immediately eliminated from consideration if it does not meet minimum quality standards. It is the particular aspect of quality on which one chooses to focus that determines the nature of the competitive strategy and the positioning of the firm.

Delivery speed can be an important competitive weapon in some contexts. Some firms base their primary competitive position on delivery speed, such as UPS and Federal Express. Mail-order and Web-based retailers also must be able to deliver products reliably and quickly to remain competitive. Building contractors that complete projects on time will have an edge.

Delivery reliability means being able to deliver products or services when promised. Online brokerages that execute trades reliably and quickly will retain customers. Contract manufacturers are measured on several dimensions, one being whether they can deliver on time. As third-party sourcing of manufacturing continues to grow, the successful contract manufacturers will be the ones that put customers first and maintain a record of delivering high-quality products in a reliable fashion.

Flexibility means offering a wide range of products and being able to adjust to unexpected changes in the demand of the product mix offered. Successful manufacturers in the 21st century will be those that can respond the fastest to unpredictable changes in customer tastes. This writer was fortunate enough to tour Toyota's Motomachi Plant located in Toyoda City, Japan. What was particularly impressive was the ability to produce several different models in the same plant. In fact, each successive car on the assembly line was a different model. A right-hand drive Crown sedan, for the domestic market, was followed by a left-hand drive Lexus coupe, designated for shipment to the United States. Each car carried unique sets of instructions that could be read by both robot welders and human assemblers. This flexibility allowed Toyota to adjust the product mix on a real-time basis and to embark on a system in which customers could order custom-configured cars directly from terminals located in dealer showrooms (Port, 1999).

Hence, one way to think of operations strategy is the strategic positioning the firm chooses along one of the dimensions of cost, quality, delivery speed, delivery reliability, and flexibility. Operations management is concerned with implementing the strategy to achieve leadership along one of these dimensions.

1.3 COMPETING IN THE GLOBAL MARKETPLACE

International competitiveness has become a national obsession. Americans are concerned that their standard of living is eroding while it seems to improve elsewhere. Evidence exists that there is some truth to this perception. Our balance of trade with Japan has been in the red for decades, with no evidence of a reversal. American firms once held a dominant position worldwide in industries that have nearly disappeared domestically. Consumer electronics, steel, and machine tools are some examples. All the news is not bad, however. The American economy is strong and continues to grow. American firms still have the lion's share of the world market in many industries.

In his excellent study of international competitiveness, Porter (1990) poses the following question: Why does one country become the home base for successful international competitors in an industry? That certain industries flourish in certain countries cannot be disputed. Some examples are

1. Germany: printing presses, luxury cars, chemicals.
2. Switzerland: pharmaceuticals, chocolate.
3. Sweden: heavy trucks, mining equipment.
4. United States: personal computers, software, films.
5. Japan: automobiles, consumer electronics, robotics.

What accounts for this phenomenon? One can offer several compelling explanations, but most have counterexamples. Here are a few:

1. *Historical*. Some industries are historically strong in some countries and are not easily displaced. *Counterexample*: The demise of the steel industry in the United States is one of many counterexamples.
2. *Tax structure*. Some countries, such as Germany, have no capital gains tax, thus providing a more fertile environment for industry. *Counterexample*: However, there is no reason that favorable tax treatment should favor certain industries over others.
3. *National character*. Many believe that workers from other countries, particularly from Pacific Rim countries, are better trained and more dedicated than American workers. *Counterexample*: If this is true, why then do American firms dominate in some industry

segments? How does one explain the enormous success Japanese-based corporations have had running plants in the United States with an American workforce?

4. *Natural resources*. There is no question that some industries are highly resource dependent and these industries have a distinct advantage in some countries. One example is the forest products industry in the United States and Canada. *Counterexample*: Many industry sectors are essentially resource independent but still seem to flourish in certain countries.

5. *Government policies*. Some governments provide direct assistance to fledgling industries, such as MITI in Japan. The role of the U.S. government is primarily regulatory. For example, environmental standards in the United States are probably more stringent than almost anywhere else. *Counterexample*: This does not explain why some industries dominate in countries with strict environmental and regulatory standards.

6. *Advantageous macroeconomic factors*. Exchange rates, interest rates, and government debt are some of the macroeconomic factors that provide nations with competitive advantage. For example, in the 1980s when interest rates were much higher in the United States than they were in Japan, it was much easier for Japanese firms to borrow for new projects. *Counterexample*: These factors do not explain why many nations have a rising standard of living despite rising deficits (Japan, Italy, and Korea are some examples).

7. *Cheap, abundant labor*. Although cheap labor can attract new industry, most countries with cheap labor are very poor. On the other hand, many countries (Germany, Switzerland, and Sweden are examples) have a high standard of living, high wage rates, and shortages of qualified labor.

8. *Management practices*. There is evidence that Japanese management practices are more effective in general than Western-style practices. Counterexample: If American management practices are so ineffective, why do we continue to dominate certain industries, such as personal computers, software development, and pharmaceuticals?

Talking about competitiveness is easier than measuring it. What are the appropriate ways to measure one country's success over another? Some possibilities are

- Balance of trade.
- Share of world exports.
- Creation of jobs.
- Low labor costs.

Arguments can be made against every one of these as a measure of international competitiveness. Switzerland and Italy have trade deficits, and at the same time have experienced rising standards of living. Similar arguments can be made for countries that import more than they export. The number of jobs created by an economy is a poor gauge of the health of that economy. More important is the quality of the jobs created. Finally, low labor costs correlate with a low standard of living. These counterexamples show that it is no easy task to develop an effective measure of international competitiveness.

Porter (1990) argues that the appropriate measure to compare national performance is the rate of productivity growth. Productivity is the value of output per unit of input of labor or capital. Porter argues that productivity growth in some industries appears to be stronger in certain countries, and that there are reasons for this. In some cases we can find the reasons in domestic factor advantages. The factor theory says all countries have access to the same technology (an assumption that is not strictly true) and that national advantages accrue from endowments of production factors such as land, labor, natural resources, and capital.

There are some excellent examples of factor theory. Korea has relatively low labor costs, so it exports labor-intensive goods such as apparel and electronic assemblies. Sweden's iron ore is low in impurities, which contributes to a strong Swedish steel industry. As compelling as it is, there are counterexamples to the factor endowment theory as well. For example, after the Korean War, South Korea developed and excelled in several highly capital-intensive industries such as steel and shipbuilding even though the country was cash poor. Also, many countries have similar factor endowments, but some seem to excel in certain industries, nonetheless. These examples suggest that factor endowments do not explain all cases of nations with dominant industry segments.

Porter (1990) suggests the following four determinants of national advantage:

1. Factor conditions (previously discussed).
2. Demand conditions. If domestic consumers are sophisticated and demanding, they apply pressure on local industry to innovate faster, which gives firms an edge internationally. Consumers of electronics in Japan are very demanding, thus positioning this industry competitively in the international marketplace.
3. Related and supporting industries. Having world-class suppliers nearby is a strong advantage. For example, the Italian footwear industry is supported by a strong leather industry and a strong design industry.
4. Firm strategy, structure, and rivalry. The manner in which firms are organized and managed contributes to their international competitiveness. Japanese management style is distinctly different from American. In Germany, many senior executives possess a technical background, producing a strong inclination to product and process improvement. In Italy, there are many small family-owned companies, which encourages individualism.

Even though Porter makes a very convincing argument for national competitive advantage in some industries, there is a debate among economists as to whether the notion of international competitiveness makes any sense at all. Companies compete, not countries. This is the point of view taken by Paul Krugman (1994). According to Krugman, the United States and Japan are simply not competitors in the same way that Ford and Toyota are. The standard of living in a country depends on its own domestic economic performance and not on how it performs relative to other countries.

Krugman argues that too much emphasis on international competitiveness can lead to misguided strategies. Trade wars are much more likely in this case. This was the case in mid-1995 when the Clinton administration was planning to impose high tariffs on makers of Japanese luxury cars. Most economists agree that trade wars and their consequences, such as tariffs, benefit no one in the long run. Another problem that arises from national competitive pride is it can lead to poorly conceived government expenditures. France has spent billions propping up its failing computer industry. (Certainly, not all government investments in domestic industry can be considered a mistake. The Japanese government, for example, played a major role in nurturing the flat-panel display industry. Japanese-based firms now dominate this multibillion dollar industry.)

Another point supporting Krugman's position is that the lion's share of U.S. gross domestic product (GDP) is consumed in the United States, thus making a firm's success in our domestic market more important than its success in the world market. Krugman agrees that productivity growth is a valid concern. He argues, however, that we should be more productive in order to produce more, not to better our international competitors.

The debate over competitive advantage will continue. Policy makers need to be aware of all points of view and weigh each carefully in formulating policy. Although Krugman makes several telling points, there is no question that globalization is a trend

Snapshot Application

GLOBAL MANUFACTURING STRATEGIES IN THE AUTOMOBILE INDUSTRY

Consider the following four foreign automobile manufacturers: Honda, Toyota, BMW, and Mercedes Benz. As everyone knows, Honda and Toyota are Japanese companies and BMW and Mercedes are German companies. The four account for the lion's share of foreign nameplates sold in the U.S. auto market. However, many assume that these cars are manufactured in their home countries. In fact, depending on the model, it could be more likely that a consumer buying a Honda, Toyota, BMW, or Mercedes is buying a car manufactured in the United States.

Honda was the first of the foreign automakers to commit to a significant investment in U.S.-based manufacturing facilities. Honda's first U.S. facility was its Marysville Motorcycle plant, which started production in 1979. Honda must have been pleased with the Ohio-based facility, since an automobile plant followed shortly. Automobile production in Marysville began in 1982. Today, Honda operates four plants in west-central Ohio, producing the Accord sedan and coupe, the Acura TL sedan, the Honda Civic line, and the Honda Element, with the capacity to produce a whopping 440,000 vehicles annually.

Next to make a significant commitment in U.S. production facilities was Toyota. Toyota's plant in Georgetown, Kentucky, has been producing automobiles since 1986 and accounts for all of the Camrys sold in the domestic market. It is interesting to note that the Honda Accord and the Toyota Camry are two of the biggest-selling models in the United States, and are also produced here. They also top almost all reliability surveys.

The two German automakers were slower to commit to U.S.-based manufacturing facilities. BMW launched its Spartanburg, South Carolina, plant in March of 1995. BMW produces both the Z series sports cars and its SUV line in this plant. It is interesting to note that BMW's big sellers, its 3, 5, and 7 series sedans, are still manufactured in Germany.

Mercedes was the last of these four to make a significant commitment to production facilities here. The facility in Tuscaloosa, Alabama, is dedicated to producing the line of Mercedes SUVs. As with BMW, the more popular C, E, and S class sedans are still manufactured in Germany.

(One might ask why Volkswagen is not on this list. In fact, Volkswagen has 45 separate manufacturing facilities located in 18 countries around the world, but no significant manufacturing presence in the mainland United States.)

Sources: Honda's Web site (http://www.ohio.honda.com/), Toyota's Web site (http://www.toyota.com), Autointell's Web site (http://www.autointell-news.com/european_companies/BMW/bmw3.htm), Mercedes Benz's Web site (http://www.mbusi.com/).

---

that shows no sign of reversing. We cannot stick our heads in the sand and say that foreign markets are not important to us. Economic borders are coming down all across the globe.

Problems for Sections 1.1–1.3

1. Why is it undesirable for the United States to evolve into a service economy?
2. What disadvantages do you see if the chief executive officer (CEO) is primarily concerned with short-term ROI?
3. Can you think of companies that have gone out of business because they focused only on cost and were not able to achieve a minimum quality standard?
4. What are the different quality standards referred to in the example comparing the Honda Civic and the Ferrari?
5. Discuss the pros and cons of trade barriers from the industry point of view and from the consumer point of view.
6. What are the advantages and disadvantages of producing new products in existing facilities?
7. What are the four determinants of national advantage suggested by Porter? Give examples of companies that have thrived as a result of each of these factors.
8. What factor advantage favors the aluminum industry in the United States over Japan and makes aluminum much cheaper to produce here? (Hint: Aluminum

production is very energy intensive. In what part of the country is an inexpensive energy source available?)
9. Paul Krugman argues that because most of our domestic product is consumed domestically, we should not dwell on international competition. What industries in the United States have been hardest hit by foreign competition? What are the potential threats to the United States if these industries fail altogether?
10. Krugman points out some misguided government programs that have resulted from too much emphasis on international competitiveness. What risks are there from too little emphasis on international competitiveness?
11. Consider the Snapshot Application in this section concerning foreign automakers locating manufacturing facilities in the United States. Discuss the advantages and disadvantages of the strategy of locating manufacturing facilities where the product is consumed rather than where the company is located.
12. The North American Free Trade Agreement (NAFTA) was established in 1994 under the Clinton administration.
    a) What was the purpose of NAFTA?
    b) At the time, political opponents characterized "the big sucking sound" as jobs would be lost as a result. Is there any evidence that this was, in fact, the case?

1.4 STRATEGIC INITIATIVES: REENGINEERING THE BUSINESS PROCESS

Seemingly on schedule, every few years a hot new production control method or management technique comes along, almost always described by a three-letter acronym. While it is easy to be skeptical, by and large, the methods are sound and can have substantial value to corporations when implemented intelligently. *Business process reengineering* (BPR) caught on after the publication of the book by Hammer and Champy (1993). BPR is not a specific technique, such as materials requirements planning or a production-planning concept like just-in-time. Rather, it is the idea that entrenched business processes can be changed and can be improved. The process is one of questioning why things are done a certain way, and not accepting the answer, "because that's the way we do it."

Hammer and Champy, who define BPR as "starting over," provide several examples of successful reengineering efforts. The first is the IBM Credit Corporation, a wholly owned subsidiary of IBM, that, if independent, would rank among the *Fortune* 100 service companies. This arm of IBM is responsible for advancing credit to new customers purchasing IBM equipment. The traditional credit approval process followed five steps:

1. An IBM salesperson would call in with a request for financing and the request would be logged on a piece of paper.
2. Someone carried the paper upstairs to the credit department, where someone else would enter the information into a computer system and check the potential borrower's credit rating. The specialist wrote the results of the credit check on a piece of paper, which was sent off to the business practices department.
3. A third person, in the business practices department, modified the standard loan document in response to the customer request. These modifications, which were done on yet another computer system, were then attached to the original request form and the credit department specialist's report.

4. Next the request went to a pricer, who keyed the information into a spreadsheet to determine the appropriate interest rate to charge the customer. The pricer's recommendation was written on a piece of paper and delivered (with the other papers) to the clerical group.
5. The information was turned into a quote letter that would be delivered to the field salesperson by Federal Express.

This process required an average of six days and sometimes as long as two weeks. Sales reps logged endless complaints about this delay: during this time, the customer could find other financing or another vendor. In an effort to see if this process could be streamlined, two senior managers decided to walk a new request through all five steps, asking personnel to put aside what they were doing and process it as they normally would. They found that the entire five-step process required an average of only 90 minutes of work! The rest of the time, requests were either in transit from one department to another or queueing up on somebody's desk waiting to be processed. Clearly the problem did not lie with the efficiency of the personnel but with the design of the credit approval process itself.

The solution was simple: the four specialists handling each loan request were replaced by a single loan generalist who handled each request from beginning to end. Up-to-date software was designed to support the generalist, who had no trouble dealing with most requests. The credit approval process was designed assuming that each request was sufficiently complex to require someone with special knowledge in each area. In truth, most requests were routine, and specialists generally did little more than a simple table lookup to determine the appropriate figure.

What was the result of this change? The six-day turnaround for loan requests was slashed to only four hours! And this was accomplished with fewer personnel and with a hundredfold increase in the number of deals handled.

While each reengineering effort requires careful thought and no two solutions will be exactly alike, Hammer and Champy (1993) suggest that reengineering efforts utilize the following general principles:

1. *Several jobs are combined into one.* Few examples of BPR are as dramatic as that of IBM Credit, but there are other success stories in the literature as well. Many of the successful cases have a common thread: the reduction of a complex process requiring many steps to a simpler one requiring fewer steps. In the case of IBM Credit, a five-step process was reduced to only a single step. This suggests a general principle. The IBM Credit process was a natural evolution of the concept of division of labor. The economist Adam Smith espoused this principle as far back as the 18th century (see the quote from *The Wealth of Nations* at the beginning of Section 1.10 of this chapter). However, a good thing can be carried too far. If one divides a process into too many steps, one eventually reaches the point of diminishing returns. BPR's most dramatic successes have come from complex processes that were simplified by reducing the number of steps required.

2. *Workers make decisions.* One goal is to reduce the number of levels of reporting by allowing workers to make decisions that were previously reserved for management. In the case of IBM Credit, most decisions once reserved for specialists are now done by a single generalist. Giving workers greater decision-making power may pose a threat to management, who might see such a step as encroaching on their prerogatives.

3. *The steps in the process are performed in a natural order.* Process steps should not be performed necessarily in rigid linear sequence, but in an order that makes sense in the context of the problem being solved. In particular, in many cases, some tasks can be

done simultaneously rather than in sequence. (These ideas, of course, are well known and form the basis for the concepts of project management in Chapter 10.)

4. *Processes should have multiple versions.* One should allow for contingencies, not by designing multiple independent processes, but by designing one flexible process that can react to different circumstances. In the case of IBM Credit, for example, the final credit issuance process had three versions: one for straightforward cases (handled by computer), one for cases of medium difficulty (handled by the deal structurer), and one for difficult cases (performed by the deal structurer with help from specialist advisers).

5. *Work is performed where it makes the most sense.* One of the basic principles of reengineering is not to carry the idea of division of labor too far. Another is not to carry the idea of centralization too far. For example, in most companies, purchasing is done centrally. This means that every purchase request is subject to the same minimum overhead in time and paperwork. A consequence might be that the cost of processing a request exceeds the cost of the item being purchased! A great deal can be saved in this case by allowing individual departments to handle their own purchasing for low-cost items. (Hammer and Champy discuss such a case.)

The authors list several other basic principles, involving minimizing checks and reconciliations, having a single point of contact, and being able to employ hybrid centralized/decentralized operations.

It is easier to list the steps one might consider in a reengineering effort than to actually implement one. In the real world, political realities cannot be ignored. For many of the success stories in the literature, not only are the processes simplified, but the headcount of personnel is reduced as well. It is certainly understandable for employees to see BPR as a thinly veiled excuse for downsizing (euphemistically called "right-sizing"). This was exactly the case in one financial services company. When word got out that management was planning a reengineering effort, most assumed that there would be major layoffs. Some even thought the company was on the verge of bankruptcy. In another instance, union leadership saw reengineering as a means for management to throw away the job categories and work rules they had won in hard-fought negotiations over the years, and persuaded the members to strike. In a third case, a senior manager was unhappy with the potential loss of authority that might accompany a reengineering effort. He resigned to start his own company. (These examples are related in a follow-up book by Hammer and Stanton, 1995.)

These stories show that starting a reengineering effort is not without risks. Rarely is the process as simple as IBM's. Reengineering has been described by Ronald Compton, the CEO of Aetna Life and Casualty, as "agonizingly, heartbreakingly, tough." There needs to be some cost–benefit analysis done up front to be sure the potential gains compensate for the risks.

Process optimization is not new. In its early years, the field of industrial engineering dealt with optimal design of processes, setting standards using time and motion studies, and flowcharting for understanding the sequence of events and flow of material in a factory. Why is BPR different? For one, BPR is concerned with business process flows rather than manufacturing process flows. Second, the concept is not one of optimizing an existing process, but one of rethinking how things should be done from scratch. As such, it is more revolutionary than evolutionary. It is likely to be more disruptive but could have larger payoffs. To make BPR work, employees at every level have to buy into the approach, and top management must champion it. Otherwise, the reengineering effort could be a costly failure.

1.5 STRATEGIC INITIATIVES: JUST-IN-TIME

Just-in-time (JIT) is a manufacturing process on one hand and a broad-based operations strategy on the other. The process elements of JIT will be discussed in detail in Chapter 8 as part of a complete analysis of push and pull inventory systems. However, JIT (or lean production, as it is also known) is a philosophy that includes treatment of inventory in the plant, relationships with suppliers, and distribution strategies. The core of the philosophy is to eliminate waste. This is accomplished by efficient scheduling of incoming orders, work-in-process inventories, and finished goods inventories.

JIT is an outgrowth of the **kanban system** introduced by Toyota. Kanban is a Japanese word meaning card or ticket. Originally, kanban cards were the only means of implementing JIT. The kanban system was introduced by Toyota to reduce excess work-in-process (WIP) inventories. Today, JIT is more ambitious. Both quality control systems and relationships with suppliers are part of an integrated JIT system. JIT systems can be implemented in ways other than using kanban cards. Integrating JIT philosophies with sophisticated information systems makes information transfer faster. The speed with which information can be transferred from one part of the firm to another is an important factor in the success of the JIT system.

JIT is a philosophy of operating a company that includes establishing understandings and working relationships with suppliers, providing for careful monitoring of quality and work flow, and ensuring that products are produced only as they are needed. Although JIT can be used simply as it was originally designed by Toyota, namely as a means of moving work-in-process (WIP) from one work center to another, proponents of the method recommend much more. They would have a firm integrate the JIT philosophy into its overall business strategy.

Inventory and material flow systems are classified as either **push** or **pull systems.** A push system is one in which decisions concerning how material will flow through the system are made centrally. Based on these decisions, material is produced and "pushed" to the next level of the system. A typical push system is materials requirements planning (MRP), which is discussed in detail in Chapter 8. In MRP, appropriate production amounts for all levels of the production hierarchy are computed all at once based on forecasts of end-product demand and the relationship between components and end items. In JIT, production is initiated at one level as a result of a request from a higher level. Units are then "pulled" through the system.

JIT has many advantages over conventional systems. Eliminating WIP inventories results in reduced holding costs. Less inventory means less money tied up in inventory. JIT also allows quick detection of quality problems. Since units are produced only as they are needed, the situation in which large amounts of defective WIP inventory are produced before a quality problem is detected should never occur in a properly running JIT system. JIT also means that relationships with suppliers must be tightened up. Suppliers must be willing to absorb some uncertainty and adjust delivery quantities and the timing of deliveries to match the rates of product flows.

Part of what made the kanban system so effective for Toyota was its success in reducing setup times for critical operations. The most dramatic example of setup time reduction is the so-called SMED, or single-minute exchange of dies. Each time a major change in body style is initiated, it is necessary to change the dies used in the process.

The die-changing operation typically took from four to six hours. During the die-changing operation the production line was closed down. Toyota management heard that Mercedes Benz was able to reduce its die-changing operation to less than one hour. Realizing that even more dramatic reductions were possible, Toyota set about focusing on the reduction of the time required for die changing. In a series of dramatic improvements, Toyota eventually reduced this critical operation to only several minutes. The essential idea behind SMED is to make as many changes as possible off-line, while the production process continues.

An important part of JIT is forming relationships with suppliers. What separates JIT purchasing from conventional purchasing practices? Freeland (1991) gives a list of characteristics contrasting the conventional and JIT purchasing behavior. Some of these include

Conventional Purchasing	JIT Purchasing
1. Large, infrequent deliveries.	1. Small, frequent deliveries.
2. Multiple suppliers for each part.	2. Few suppliers; single sourcing.
3. Short-term purchasing agreements.	3. Long-term agreements.
4. Minimal exchange of information.	4. Frequent information exchange.
5. Prices established by suppliers.	5. Prices negotiated.
6. Geographical proximity unimportant.	6. Geographical proximity important.

In his study, Freeland notes that the industries that seemed to benefit most from JIT purchasing were those that typically had large inventories. Companies without JIT purchasing tended to be more job-shop oriented or make-to-order oriented. Vendors that entered into JIT purchasing agreements tended to carry more safety stock, suggesting manufacturers are reducing inventories at the expense of the vendors. The JIT deliveries were somewhat more frequent, but the differences were not as large as one might expect. Geographical separation of vendors and purchasers was a serious impediment to successful implementation of JIT purchasing. The automotive industry was one that reported substantial benefit from JIT purchasing arrangements. In other industries, such as computers, the responses were mixed; some companies reported substantial benefits and some reported few benefits.

Although reducing excess work-in-process inventory can have many benefits, JIT is not necessarily the answer for all manufacturing situations. According to Stasey and McNair (1990),

> Inventory in a typical plant is like insurance, insurance that a problem in one area of a plant won't affect work performed in another. When problems creating the need for insurance are solved, then inventories disappear from the plant floor.

The implication is that we merely eliminate all sources of uncertainty in the plant and the need for inventories disappears. The problem is that there are some sources of variation that can never be eliminated. One is variation in consumer demand. JIT is effective only if final demand is regular. Another may be sources of variation inherent in the production process or in the equipment. Can one simply legislate away all sources of uncertainty in the manufacturing environment? Of course not. Hence, although the underlying principles of JIT are sound, it is not a cure-all and will not necessarily be the right method for every production situation.

1.6 STRATEGIC INITIATIVES: TIME-BASED COMPETITION

Professor Terry Hill of the London School of Business has proposed an interesting way to look at competitive factors. He classifies them into two types: "qualifiers" and "order winners." A product not possessing a qualifying factor is eliminated from consideration. The order winner is the factor that determines who gets the sale among the field of qualifiers.

Two factors about which we hear a great deal are quality and **time to market.** In the past decade, the Japanese and Germans gained a loyal following among U.S. consumers by producing quality products. American firms are catching up on the quality dimension. From the discussion in Section 1.6, we see that successful U.S.–based companies have been able to produce products that match the defect rates of foreign competitors. If this trend continues, product quality will be assumed by the consumer. Quality may become an order qualifier rather than an order winner.

If that is the case, what factors will determine order winners in years to come? Japanese automobile companies provided and continue to provide high-quality automobiles. In recent years, however, the major automobile producers in Japan have begun to focus on aesthetics and consumer tastes. They have branched out from the stolid small cars of the 1970s and 1980s to new markets with cars such as the Toyota-made Lexus luxury line and Mazda's innovative and successful Miata.

The timely introduction of new features and innovative design will determine the order winners in the automobile industry. In the computer industry, Compaq built its reputation partly on its ability to be the first to market with new technology. Time-based competition is a term that we will hear more and more frequently in coming years.

What is **time-based competition**? It is not the time and motion studies popular in the 1930s that formed the basis of the industrial engineering discipline. Rather, according to Blackburn (1991),

> Time-based competitors focus on the bigger picture, on the entire value-delivery system. They attempt to transform an entire organization into one focused on the total time required to deliver a product or service. Their goal is not to devise the best way to perform a task, but to either eliminate the task altogether or perform it in parallel with other tasks so that over-all system response time is reduced. Becoming a time-based competitor requires making revolutionary changes in the ways that processes are organized.

Successful retailers understand time-based competition. The success of the fashion chains The Gap and The Limited is due largely to their ability to deliver the latest fashions to the customer in a timely manner. Part of the success of the enormously successful Wal-Mart chain is its time-management strategy. Each stock item in a Wal-Mart store is replenished twice a week, while the industry average is once every two weeks. This allows Wal-Mart to achieve better inventory turnover rates than its competition and respond more quickly to changes in customer demand. Wal-Mart's strategies have enabled it to become the industry leader, with a growth rate three times the industry average and profits two times the industry average (Blackburn, 1991, Chapter 3).

Time-based management is a more complex issue for manufacturers, and in some industries it is clearly the key factor leading to success or failure. The industry leaders in the dynamic random access memory (DRAM) industry changed four times between 1978 and 1987. In each case, the firm that was first to market with the next-generation

DRAM dominated that market. The DRAM experience is summarized in the following table (Davis, 1989):

Product	Firm	Year Introduced	First Year of Volume Production	Market Leaders in First Year of Volume Production
16 K	Mostek	1976	1978	Mostek (25%) NEC (20%)
64 K	Hitachi	1979	1982	Hitachi (19%) NEC (15%)
256 K	NEC	1982	1984	NEC (27%) Hitachi (24%)
1 MB	Toshiba	1985	1987	Toshiba (47%) Mitsubishi (16%)

I am aware of no other example that shows so clearly and so predictably the value of getting to the market first.

1.7 STRATEGIC INITIATIVES: COMPETING ON QUALITY

What competitive factors do American managers believe will be important in the next decade? Based on a survey of 217 industry participants, the following factors were deemed as the most important for gaining a competitive edge in the coming years; they are listed in the order of importance.

1. Conformance quality
2. On-time delivery performance
3. Quality
4. Product flexibility
5. After-sale service
6. Price
7. Broad line (features)
8. Distribution
9. Volume flexibility
10. Promotion

In this list we see some important themes. **Quality** and **time management** emerge as leading factors. Quality control was brought to public attention with the establishment of the prestigious Malcolm Baldrige Award (modeled after the Japanese Deming Prize, which has been around a lot longer). Quality means different things in different contexts, so it is important to understand how it is used in the context of manufactured goods. A high-quality product is one that performs as it was designed to perform. Products will perform as they are designed to perform if there is little variation in the manufacturing process. With this definition of quality, it is possible for a product with a poor design to be of high quality, just as it is possible for a well-designed product to be of poor quality. Even granting this somewhat narrow definition of quality, what is the best measure? Defect rates are a typical barometer. However, a more appropriate measure might be reliability of the product after manufacture. This measure is typically used to monitor quality of products such as automobiles and consumer electronics.

There has been an enormous groundswell of interest in the quality issue in the United States in recent years. With the onslaught of Japanese competition, many American industries are fighting for their lives. The business of selling quality is at an all-time high. Consulting companies that specialize in providing quality programs to industry, such as the Juran Institute and Philip Crosby Associates, are doing a booming business. The question is whether American firms are merely paying lip service to quality or are seriously trying to change the way they do business. There is evidence that, in some cases at least, the latter is true.

For example, in a comparison of American and Japanese auto companies, quality as measured by defects reported in the first three months of ownership declined significantly from 1987 to 1990 for U.S. companies, narrowing the gap with Japan significantly. The Buick Division of General Motors, a winner of the Baldrige Award, has made dramatic improvements along these lines. Between 1987 and 1990 Buick decreased this defect rate by about 70 percent, equaling the rate for Hondas in 1990 (*Business Week*, October 22, 1990).

There are many success stories in U.S. manufacturing. Ford Motors achieved dramatic success with the Taurus. Ford improved both quality and innovation, providing buyers with reliable and technologically advanced cars. In 1980, James Harbour reported that Japanese automakers could produce a car for $1,500 less than their American counterparts. That gap has been narrowed by Ford to within a few hundred dollars. Part of Ford's success lies in former CEO Donald Petersen's decision not to invest billions in new plants incorporating the latest technology as GM did in the mid-1980s. This is only part of the story, however. According to Faye Wills (1990),

If you are looking for surprise answers to Ford's ascendancy, for hidden secrets, forget it. Good solid everyday management has turned the trick—textbook planning and execution, common-sense plant layouts and procedures, intelligent designs that not only sell cars, but also cut costs and bolster profit margins. It's that simple.

We can learn from our successes. The machine tool industry was one in which the Japanese made dramatic inroads in the 1980s. Many American firms fell to the onslaught of Asian competition, but not the Stanley Works of New Britain, Connecticut. In 1982, the firm's president was considering whether Stanley should remain in the hardware business as Asian firms flooded the U.S. market with low-priced hammers, screwdrivers, and other tools. Stanley decided to fight back. It modernized its plants and introduced new quality control systems. Between 1982 and 1988 scrap rates dropped from 15 percent to only 3 percent at New Britain. Stanley not only met the competition head-on here at home, but also competed successfully in Asia. Stanley now runs a profitable operation selling its distinctive yellow tape measures in Asia.

Where are most PC clones made? Taiwan, China? Korea? Guess again. The answer may surprise you: Texas. Two Texas firms have been extremely successful in this marketplace. One is Compaq Computer (now part of HP), which entered the market in the early 1980s with the first portable PC. It continued to build well-designed and high-quality products, and rose to command 20 percent of the world's PC market. Compaq established itself as a market leader. The other successful PC maker, Dell Computer, is also from Texas. The sudden rise of Dell is an interesting story. Michael Dell, a former University of Texas student, started reselling IBM PCs in the early 1980s. He later formed PC's Limited, which marketed one of the first mail-order PC clones. Dell is now a market leader in the PC marketplace, offering a combination of state-of-the-art designs, high-quality products, and excellent service.

Another American firm that has made a serious commitment to quality is Motorola. Motorola, winner of the Baldrige Award in 1987, has been steadily driving down the rate of defects in its manufactured products. Defects were reported to be near 40 parts per million at the end of 1991, down from 6,000 parts per million in 1986. Motorola has announced that its goal is to reach six-sigma (meaning six standard deviations away from the mean of a normal distribution), which translates to 3.4 parts per million. Motorola feels that the process of applying for the Baldrige Award was so valuable that it now requires all its suppliers to apply for the award as well.

Success stories like these show that the United States can compete successfully with Japan and other overseas rivals on the quality dimension. However, total quality management must become ingrained into our culture if we are going to be truly world class. The fundamentals must be there. The systems must be in place to monitor the traditional quality measures: conformance to specifications and defect-free products. However, quality management must expand beyond statistical measures. Quality must pervade the way we do business, from quality in design, quality in manufacture, and quality in building working systems with vendors, to quality in customer service and satisfaction.

Problems for Sections 1.4–1.7

13. What is an operational definition of quality? Is it possible for a 13-inch TV selling for $100 to be of superior quality to a 35-inch console selling for $1,800?

14. Studies have shown that the defect rates for many Japanese products are much lower than for their American-made counterparts. Speculate on the reasons for these differences.

15. What does "time-based competition" mean? Give an example of a product that you purchased that was introduced to the marketplace ahead of its competitors.

16. Consider the old maxim, "Build a better mousetrap and the world will beat a path to your door." Discuss the meaning of this phrase in the context of time-based competition. In particular, is getting to the market first the only factor in a product's eventual success?

17. What general features would you look for in a business process that would make that process a candidate for reengineering? Discuss a situation from your own experience in which it was clear that the business process could have been improved.

18. In what ways might the following techniques be useful as part of a reengineering effort?
    - Computer-based simulation
    - Flowcharting
    - Project management techniques
    - Mathematical modeling
    - Cross-functional teams

19. What problems can you foresee arising in the following situations?

    a. Top management is interested in reengineering to cut costs, but the employees are skeptical.

    b. Line workers would like to see a reengineering effort undertaken to give them more say-so in what goes on, but management is uninterested.

20. Just-in-time has been characterized as a system whose primary goal is to eliminate waste. Discuss how waste can be introduced in (a) relationships with vendors,

(b) receipt of material into the plant, and (c) movement of material through the plant. How do JIT methods cut down on these forms of waste?

21. In what ways can JIT systems improve product quality?

1.8 STRATEGIC INITIATIVES: SERVICIZATION

Hyundai is a huge multinational company based in South Korea, known as a chaebol, meaning a collection of diverse companies under a single umbrella. Prior to spinning off several of its businesses as separate companies following the Asian financial crisis in 1997, Hyundai was the largest chaebol in South Korea. The Hyundai Motor Company was established in 1967 and first began selling cars in the United States in 1986. At that time, Japanese, American, and European carmakers were firmly entrenched in the lucrative U.S. market. One way in which Hyundai sought to differentiate itself from its competitors was by offering an exceptional warranty. Today Hyundai offers a comprehensive warranty package, including a seven year/100,000 mile powertrain warranty. Sales of Hyundai models have risen steadily since 1986, with the company now offers high-end luxury vehicles, along with its low-cost entry models.

While there is no question that competitive pricing and improving reliability and performance of its products account for much of the company's success, one cannot deny that their exceptional warranties played a role as well. We will use the term "servicization" to describe the trend of manufacturing companies to bundle additional services with their products. Adding services is a means for firms to gain an edge over their competitors, and to provide an alternative to inexpensive Asian labor. (Note that the Europeans have coined the term "servitization". The term appears to have been first used by Vandermerwe and Rada (1988).

Cost-only considerations have driven much of the worldwide manufacturing to China. The Chinese economy has benefitted enormously from the investments from foreign economies, led by the United States and Japan. However, there is more to being an effective manufacturer than low labor rates. The quality of service in many overseas factories can be disappointing. Quality problems are common and turnaround times can be crippling. Such factors have lead many firms to rethink their decision to subcontract their manufacturing to Chinese factories.

Consider the case of Sleek Audio, a producer of high-end earphones. Following the trend of his competitors, the CEO, Mark Krywko, decided to have his product manufactured in a factory in Dongguan, China. Unfortunately, Krywko and his son Jason found it necessary to travel to Dongguan every few months because of persistent quality problems. For example, an entire shipment of 10,000 earphones had to be scrapped because of improper welding. Delivery delays resulted in emergency air freighting to meet promised deadlines. Furthermore, design changes took months to be implemented. As problems continued to mount, the Krywko's finally decided they'd had enough. Once the decision to come back to the states was made, Sleek Audio had no problem finding a suitable domestic partner. The earphones are now manufactured by Dynamic Innovations, whose facility is located only 15 minutes away from the company's headquarters in Palmetto, Florida. And how has the decision panned out? After more than a year producing in the United States, Sleek Audio is projecting 2011 to be the most profitable year in the company's history (Koerner, 2011).

Servicization: Moving Downstream

Wise and Baumgartner (1999) have noted that many manufacturing companies have moved their energies downstream to remain competitive. As the installed base of products increase, and the demand for new products decrease, firms are changing their business model in order to remain competitive. The focus is no longer on the manufacturing function alone, but on those services required to operate and maintain products. During the 40-year period of 1960–2000, the service sector share of the U.S. economy grew 16 percentage points while manufacturing's share declined by 10 percentage points. What are some of the downstream activities that manufacturers are becoming more involved with? The answer is financing, after sales parts and services, and possibly training. The profit margins on service typically exceed those of manufacturing, thus providing an incentive for firms to move in this direction. Of course, the model of vertical integration is far from new. Part of Henry Ford's success was the complete vertical integration of the firm. Ford not only produced the cars, but owned the dealerships where the cars were sold and even owned the stands of rubber trees used to make tires.

As firms became more specialized, they moved away from vertical integration. However, changing patterns of demands and profits are leading many companies back in this direction. As an example, the Boeing Company, the world's foremost manufacturer of commercial aircraft, has significantly broadened its view of the value chain. The company now offers financing, local parts supply, ground maintenance, logistics management, and even pilot training. Servicization can be the key to maintaining competitiveness.

The IBM Story

IBM has become almost synonymous with computing, but few realize that IBM had its roots in mechanical tabulating machines dating to the late 1800s. The company's start came in 1890 when the German immigrant, Herman Hollerith, developed a new process to track the U.S. census. Hollerith's concept involved the use of punched cards, which persisted into the 1960s. The original firm established by Hollerith was the Tabulating Machine Company. In 1924, 10 years after T.J. Watson joined the firm, the name was changed to International Business Machines, or IBM. IBM continued to innovate mechanical computing machines, but was actually a relative late comer into the electronic computer business. In fact, the first commercial computer was produced by Engineering Research Associates of Minneapolis in 1950 and sold to the U.S. Navy. Remington Rand produced the Univac one year later, which was the first commercially viable machine. They sold 46 machines that year at a cost of over $1 million each. IBM entered the fray in 1953 when it shipped its first computer, the 701. During three years of production, IBM only sold 19 machines. In 1955, AT&T Bell Laboratories announced the first fully transistorized computer, the TRADIC, and a year later the Burroughs Corporation threw its hat into the ring and later became a major player in the computer business. Eventually, Burroughs merged with Sperry Rand to form Unisys.

In 1959, IBM produced its first transistorized-based mainframe computer, the 7000 series. However, it was not until 1964 that the firm became a leader in computer sales. That was the year that IBM announced the system 360. This was a family of six mutually compatible computers and 40 peripherals that worked seamlessly together. There is little question that the system 360 computers were state of the art at the time. Within two years IBM was shipping 1000 systems per month. IBM has been dominant in the mainframe business ever since. While all of us are familiar with personal computers of various types and configurations, the mainframe business has not gone away. Even today, IBM continues to be a presence in the mainframe business with their newest system z architecture.

While the quality of their hardware was an important factor in IBM's success, it was not the only factor. What really sealed IBM's domination of the business market was the total customer solution. IBM's industry-specific software and the 360 operating system were a large part of attracting customers away from its competitors. IBM not only had one of the most successful sales forces in the business, but also was a master of after-sales service. Each client would have an SE (systems engineer) assigned to make sure that their needs were met. As much as anything else, it was IBM's commitment to after-sales service that locked in their position as market leader in mainframe computing. Clearly, the idea of edging out competitors by bundling services with products is not new, however, today the servicization concept is becoming an increasingly important means of gaining competitive advantage. (Information was gathered from www.computerhistory.org and the IBM company website for this section).

Performance Based Contracts

The impetus behind performance based contracting (PBC) was to reduce excessive costs in government contracting. Costs were being driven up by unnecessary provisions that specified exactly how each contract was to be carried out. According to Jon Desenberg of the Washington-based Performance Institute, a think tank dedicated to improving government performance, the idea "is to let the contracted group come up with the best possible solution and only pay them based on solving the problem . . . not on the individual steps and minutia that we have for so many years required."

Government contracts are a "why," "how," and "what" proposition. The "why" is established by the funding agency. Under PBC the "how" is shifted from the government to the contractor to determine the best way to achieve the "what". This is not always a win-win for the contractor. The task of pricing a contract now becomes much more onerous. It can be difficult to estimate all costs in advance, and who pays for contract changes can be problematic.

PBC's are typical for consumers seeking professional services. A plumber may quote a fixed price in advance for a simple job, but if there's uncertainty about the time required, might want to be compensated on a time plus materials basis. Anyone who has had a major remodeling of their homes is likely to have entered into a PBC with their contractor. However, it is rare that the final cost matches the quoted number for a variety of reasons: weather delays, poor estimation of material costs, difficulty in finding subcontractors, and more often than not, changes made in the original project by the homeowner.

While PBC's sound like a good solution for government contracting, it can lead to the wrong kind of behavior. As an example, Shen (2003) examines the result of PBC's in the Maine Addiction Treatment System. Because the system was being measured on the success of curing addicts, the center had a strong incentive to only treat the less severe cases. This, of course, runs counter to the purpose of a treatment center; it is the most severe cases of abuse that need attention. We can conclude that a PBC is not appropriate in all circumstances. For any contract it is important that incentives be properly aligned with desired outcomes.

Leasing Versus Buying

Leases may be viewed as a service provided to the consumer by the seller. In most cases, leasing is simply another way for the consumer to finance a purchase. It can also be viewed as a means for the consumer to reduce risk. The trend towards leasing of goods and services has increased substantially in recent years for several reasons.

Car leasing has long been an option for consumers. Leases are more popular when financing is difficult or expensive to obtain. The prospect of a low monthly payment attracts consumers, who may ultimately pay more in the long run. Consider the buyer that likes to drive a relatively new car and trades in their automobile every three years. This buyer faces the risk of not being able to accurately predict the trade-in value of the car three years down the road. In a lease situation, this residual risk is assumed by the seller. The terms of the lease are predicated on an assumption about the residual value of the car at the end of the lease. If the manufacturer overestimates the residual value of the car, the consumer benefits by simply turning the car in at the end of the lease period. If the manufacturer underestimates the residual value, the leaser wins by purchasing the car at the end of the lease and selling it for a higher market price. Hence, the manufacturer absorbs the risk of estimating the depreciation, which provides an incentive to the consumer to lease rather than buy. Of course, since automobiles tend to depreciate most in the first several years, buying and holding a car will be a less expensive alternative in the long run for most vehicles—especially those that are more durable and more reliable. Since auto leases are typically two to four years, the buyer that keeps cars for a long time will not choose to lease.

Leasing (that is, renting) versus buying is also an important choice for the consumer when it comes to choosing how and where to live. While owning a home has been touted as the "American Dream," there are clearly many who should not be homeowners. In the United States, most homeowners have a mortgage on their primary property. A mortgage is simply a loan provided to homeowner, with the home itself as the collateral. In periods when housing prices are rising faster than inflation, homeowners have done very well. However, as we've seen in recent years, rising housing prices is not a certainty. There have been several periods in which housing prices have dropped precipitously, including the Great Depression of the 1930s. In fact, as of this writing, the housing industry has been in a slump since 2008.

The mortgage crisis of 2008 led to a total collapse of many major financial institutions, and nearly caused a worldwide depression. What precipitated this crisis? In a nutshell, it was awarding mortgages to individuals that did not qualify for them. Why did this happen? There were a variety of factors including government deregulation, unscrupulous mortgage brokers, and naive consumers. The stringent standards that banks traditionally applied before awarding mortgages were thrown out the window. When real estate prices were on an apparent never-ending upward spiral, homeowners borrowed well beyond their means to finance other houses, or large capital expenditures such as boats or cars. People who had never owned a home in their lives were cajoled by unscrupulous mortgage brokers into taking loans they had no chance of paying off. Housing prices climbed far beyond reasonable levels, and when the bubble burst, millions of homeowners found themselves underwater (meaning their houses were worth less than the balance of their mortgage loans). Since many loans were granted with little or no down payment, many just walked away from their homes leaving entire neighborhoods vacant. Homes were looted for valuable materials, such as copper piping, thus assuring that these homes would never be sellable.

Renting is a sensible choice for many. While there appears to be a stigma associated with being a renter, it became clear from the subprime loan debacle that, in fact, many folks have no business owning a home. Landlords must absorb the risks of repairs and price fluctuations. It is no longer obvious that real estate is necessarily a safe investment. Perhaps the mortgage crises can be viewed as a case of servicization gone out of control.

Green Leasing

A recent trend has been towards green leasing. According to the U.S. Green Building Council, buildings account for more than one-third of all energy use, carbon dioxide emissions, waste output, and use of raw materials in the United States. While green leasing is a relatively new concept to American companies, it has been a practice in other parts of the world for years. Several foreign governments have promulgated environmental-based rules for their properties. In America, however, the movement is far less centralized.

Most green leasing initiatives in the United States have been proposed by state and local governments. Government agencies and academic institutions have been the front runners in green building technology, representing approximately 26 percent of all LEED certified buildings. LEED, developed by the Green Building Counsel, is an internationally recognized certification system that measures building performance in categories such as: energy savings, water efficiency, carbon dioxide emissions, indoor environmental quality, and resource management. LEED also provides a framework for stages throughout a building's lifecycle, from design and construction to operation and management. LEED provides several levels of certification. Most green building initiatives provide either incentives or penalties based upon a building's LEED certification level.

Problems for Section 1.8

22. Define "servicization" and provide an example from your own experience of a case where services were the deciding factor in a purchase.
23. What are some of the services that IBM provided for its mainframe customers during its meteoric rise in sales in the 1960s?
24. Why can car leasing be viewed as a service? What are the advantages and disadvantages of car leasing from the buyer's point of view? Why do manufacturers offer leases?

1.9 MATCHING PROCESS AND PRODUCT LIFE CYCLES

The Product Life Cycle

The demand for new products typically undergoes cycles that can be identified and mapped over time. Understanding the nature of this evolution helps to identify appropriate strategies for production and operations at the various stages of the product cycle. A typical product life cycle is pictured in Figure 1–3. The product life cycle consists of four major segments:

1. Start-up
2. Rapid growth
3. Maturation
4. Stabilization or decline

During the start-up phase, the market for the product is developing, production and distribution costs are high, and competition is generally not a problem. During this phase the primary strategy concern is to apply the experiences of the marketplace and of manufacturing to improve the production and marketing functions. At this time, serious design flaws should be revealed and corrected.

FIGURE 1–3
The product life-cycle curve

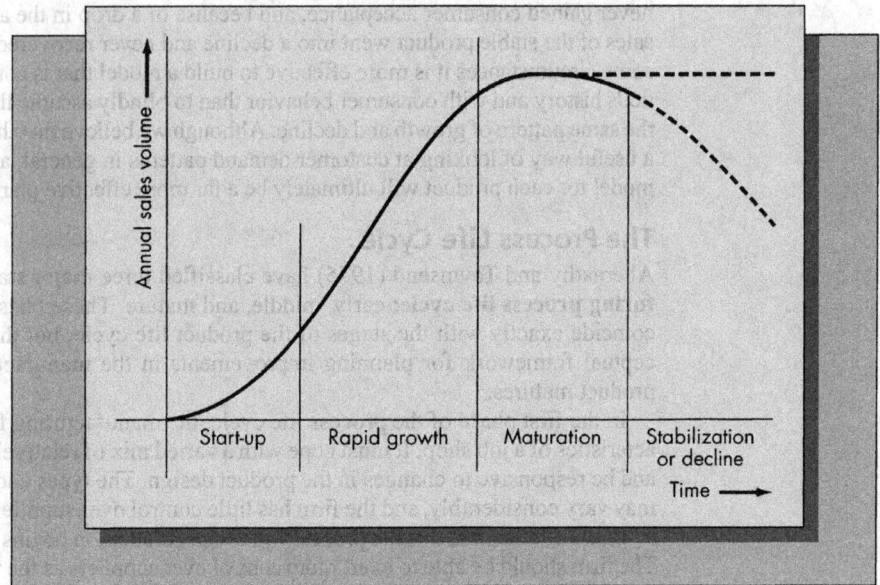

The period of rapid growth sees the beginning of competition. The primary strategic goal during this period is to establish the product as firmly as possible in the marketplace. To do this, management should consider alternative pricing patterns that suit the various customer classes and should reinforce brand preference among suppliers and customers. The manufacturing process should be undergoing improvements and standardization as product volume increases. Flexibility and modularization of the manufacturing function are highly desirable at this stage.

During the maturation phase of the product life cycle, the objective should be to maintain and improve the brand loyalty that the firm cultivated in the growth phase. Management should seek to increase market share through competitive pricing. Cost savings should be realized through improved production control and product distribution. During this phase the firm must listen to the messages of the marketplace. Most problems with product design and quality should have been corrected during the start-up and growth phases, but additional improvements should also be considered during this phase.

The appropriate shape of the life-cycle curve in the final stage depends on the nature of the product. Many products will continue to sell, with the potential for annual growth continuing almost indefinitely. Examples of such products are commodities such as household goods, processed food, and automobiles. For such products the company's primary goals in this phase would be essentially the same as those described previously for the maturation phase. Other products will experience a natural decline in sales volume as the market for the product becomes saturated or as the product becomes obsolete. If this is the case, the company should adopt a strategy of squeezing out the most from the product or product line while minimizing investment in new manufacturing technology and media advertising.

Although a useful concept, the product life-cycle curve is not accurate in all circumstances. Marketing departments that base their strategies on the life-cycle curve may make poor decisions. Dhalla and Yuspeh (1976) report an example of a firm that shifted advertising dollars from a successful stable product to a new product. The assumption was that the new product was entering the growth phase of its life cycle and the stable product was entering the declining phase of its life cycle. However, the new product never gained consumer acceptance, and because of a drop in the advertising budget, the sales of the stable product went into a decline and never recovered. They suggest that in some circumstances it is more effective to build a model that is consistent with the product's history and with consumer behavior than to blindly assume that all products follow the same pattern of growth and decline. Although we believe that the life-cycle concept is a useful way of looking at customer demand patterns in general, a carefully constructed model for each product will ultimately be a far more effective planning tool.

The Process Life Cycle

Abernathy and Townsend (1975) have classified three major stages of the **manufacturing process life cycle:** early, middle, and mature. These phases do not necessarily coincide exactly with the stages of the product life cycle, but they do provide a conceptual framework for planning improvements in the manufacturing process as the product matures.

In the first phase of the process life cycle, the manufacturing function has the characteristics of a job shop. It must cope with a varied mix of relatively low-volume orders and be responsive to changes in the product design. The types and quality of the inputs may vary considerably, and the firm has little control over suppliers.

In the middle phase of the process life cycle, automation begins to play a greater role. The firm should be able to exert more control over suppliers as the volume of production

FIGURE 1–4
The process life cycle and the experience curve

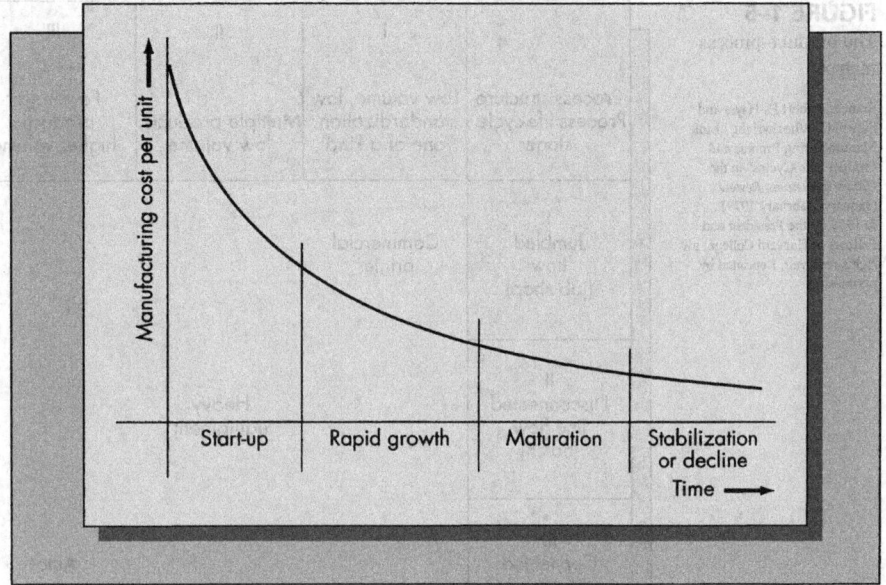

increases. Unit production costs decline as a result of learning effects. The production process may involve batch processing and some transfer lines (assembly lines).

In the last phase of the process life cycle, most of the major operations are automated, the production process is standardized, and few manufacturing innovations are introduced. The production process may assume the characteristics of a continuous flow operation.

This particular evolutionary scenario is not appropriate for all new manufacturing ventures. Companies that thrive on small one-of-a-kind orders will maintain the characteristics of a job shop, for example. The process life-cycle concept applies to new products that eventually mature into high-volume items. The issue of matching the characteristics of the product with the characteristics of the process is discussed subsequently.

Experience curves show that unit production costs decline as the cumulative number of units produced increases. One may think of the experience curve in terms of the process life cycle shown in Figure 1–4. An accurate understanding of the relationship between the experience curve and the process life cycle can be very valuable. By matching the decline in unit cost with the various stages of the process life cycle, management can gain insight into the consequences of moving from one phase of the process life cycle into another. This insight will assist management in determining the proper timing of improvements in the manufacturing process.

The Product–Process Matrix

Hayes and Wheelwright (1979) consider linking the product and process life cycles using the **product–process matrix** pictured in Figure 1–5. The matrix is based on four phases in the evolution of the manufacturing process: (1) jumbled flow, (2) disconnected line flow, (3) connected line flow, and (4) continuous flow. This matrix may be viewed in two ways. One is to match the appropriate industry in its mature phase with

FIGURE 1-5

The product–process matrix

Source: Robert H. Hayes and Steven C. Wheelwright, "Link Manufacturing Process and Product Life Cycles" in the *Harvard Business Review* (January–February 1979). © 1979 by the President and Fellows of Harvard College; all rights reserved. Reprinted by permission.

Process structure Process life-cycle stage	I Low volume, low standardization, one of a kind	II Multiple products, low volume	III Few major products, higher volume	IV High volume, high standardization, commodity products
I Jumbled flow (job shop)	Commercial printer			Void
II Disconnected line flow (batch)		Heavy equipment		
III Connected line flow (assembly line)			Auto assembly	
IV Continuous flow	Void			Sugar refinery

the appropriate process. This point of view recognizes that not all industries necessarily follow the process evolution described in the previous section on the process life cycle. Certain companies or certain products could remain in an early phase of the process life cycle indefinitely. However, even firms that do not evolve to a position in the lower right-hand corner of the matrix should, in most cases, be located somewhere on the diagonal of the matrix.

Located in the upper left-hand corner of this matrix are companies that specialize in "one of a kind" jobs in which the manufacturing function has the characteristics of a jumbled flow shop. A commercial printer is an example of a jumbled flow shop. Production is in relatively small lots, and the shop is organized for maximum flexibility.

Farther down the diagonal are firms that still require a great deal of flexibility but produce a limited line of standardized items. Manufacturers of heavy equipment would fall into this category because they would produce in somewhat higher volumes. A disconnected line would provide enough flexibility to meet custom orders while still retaining economies of limited standardization.

The third category down the diagonal includes firms that produce a line of standard products for a large-volume market. Typical examples are producers of home appliances or electronic equipment, and automobile manufacturers. The assembly line or transfer line would be an appropriate process technology in this case.

Finally, the lower right-hand portion of the matrix would be appropriate for products involving continuous flow. Chemical processing, gasoline and oil refining, and sugar refining are examples. Such processes are characterized by low unit costs, standardization of the product, high sales volume, and extreme inflexibility of the production process.

What is the point of this particular classification scheme? It provides a means of assessing whether a firm is operating in the proper portion of the matrix; that is, if the process is properly matched with the product structure. Firms choosing to operate off the diagonal should have a clear understanding of the reasons for doing so. One example of a successful firm that operates off the diagonal is Rolls-Royce. Another is a company producing handmade furniture. The manufacturing process in these cases would have the characteristics of a jumbled flow shop, but competitors might typically be located in the second or third position on the diagonal.

There is another way to look at the product–process matrix. It can be used to identify the proper match of the production process with the phases of the product life cycle. In the start-up phase of product development, the firm would typically be positioned in the upper left-hand corner of the matrix. As the market for the product matures, the firm would move down the diagonal to achieve economies of scale. Finally, the firm would settle at the position on the matrix that would be appropriate based on the characteristics of the product.

Problems for Section 1.9

25. *a.* What are the four phases of the manufacturing process that appear in the product–process matrix?

    b. Discuss the disadvantages of operating off the diagonal of the matrix.

26. Give an example of a product that has undergone the four phases of the product life cycle and has achieved stability.

27. Discuss the following: "All firms should evolve along the diagonal of the product–process matrix."

28. Locate the following operations in the appropriate position on the product–process matrix.

    a. A small shop that repairs musical instruments.

    b. An oil refinery.

    c. A manufacturer of office furniture.

    d. A manufacturer of major household appliances such as washers, dryers, and refrigerators.

    e. A manufacturing firm in the start-up phase.

1.10 LEARNING AND EXPERIENCE CURVES

As experience is gained with the production of a particular product, either by a single worker or by an industry as a whole, the production process becomes more efficient. As noted by the economist Adam Smith as far back as the 18th century in his landmark work, *The Wealth of Nations:*

> The division of labor, by reducing every man's business to some one simple operation, and by making this operation the sole employment of his life, necessarily increases very much the dexterity of the worker.

By quantifying the relationship that describes the gain in efficiency as the cumulative number of units produced increases, management can accurately predict the eventual capacity of existing facilities and the unit costs of production. Today we recognize that many other factors besides the improving skill of the individual worker contribute to this effect. Some of these factors include the following:

- Improvements in production methods.
- Improvements in the reliability and efficiency of the tools and machines used.
- Better product design.
- Improved production scheduling and inventory control.
- Better organization of the workplace.

Studies of the aircraft industry undertaken during the 1920s showed that the direct-labor hours required to produce a unit of output declined as the cumulative number of units produced increased. The term **learning curve** was adopted to explain this phenomenon. Similarly, it has been observed in many industries that marginal production costs also decline as the cumulative number of units produced increases. The term **experience curve** has been used to describe this second phenomenon.

Learning Curves

As workers gain more experience with the requirements of a particular process, or as the process is improved over time, the number of hours required to produce an additional unit declines. The learning curve, which models this relationship, is also a means of describing dynamic economies of scale. Experience has shown that these curves are accurately represented by an exponential relationship. Let $Y(u)$ be the number of labor hours required to produce the uth unit. Then the learning curve is of the form

$$Y(u) = au^{-b},$$

where a is the number of hours required to produce the first unit and b measures the rate at which the marginal production hours decline as the cumulative number of units produced increases. Traditionally, learning curves are described by the percentage decline of the labor hours required to produce item $2n$ compared to the labor hours required to produce item n, and it is assumed that this percentage is independent of n. That is, an 80 percent learning curve means that the time required to produce unit $2n$ is 80 percent of the time required to produce unit n for any value of n. For an 80 percent learning curve

$$\frac{Y(2u)}{Y(u)} = \frac{a(2u)^{-b}}{au^{-b}} = 2^{-b} = .80.$$

It follows that

$$-b \ln(2) = \ln(.8)$$

or $b = -\ln(.8)/\ln(2) = .3219$. (ln is the natural logarithm.)

More generally, if the learning curve is a $100L$ percent learning curve, then

$$b = -\ln(L)/\ln(2).$$

Figure 1–6 shows an 80 percent learning curve. When graphed on double-log paper, the learning curve should be a straight line if the exponential relationship we have assumed is accurate. If logarithms of both sides of the expression for $Y(u)$ are taken, a linear relationship results, since

$$\ln(Y(u)) = \ln(a) - b \ln(u).$$

FIGURE 1–6
An 80 percent learning curve

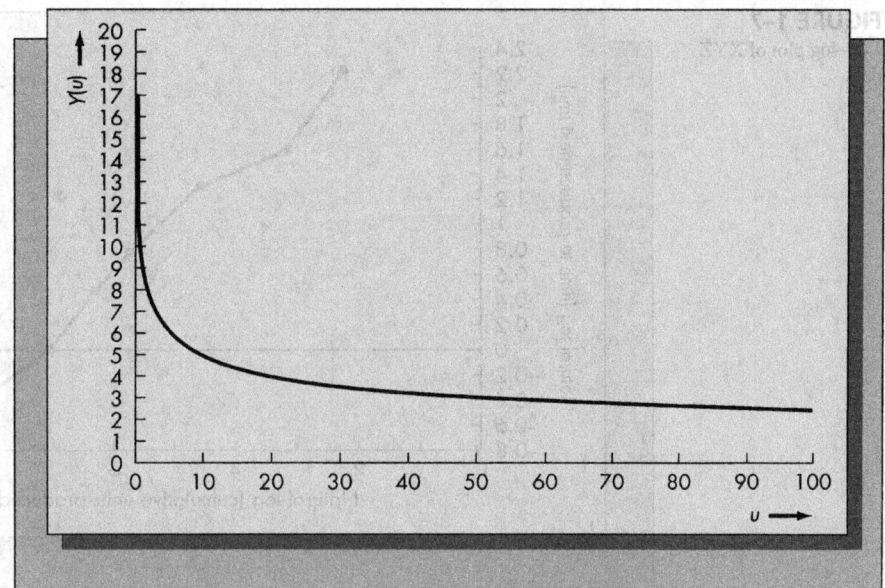

Linear regression is used to fit the values of a and b to actual data after the logarithm transformation has been made. (General equations for finding least squares estimators in linear regression appear in Appendix 2–B.)

Example 1.1 XYZ has kept careful records of the average number of labor hours required to produce one of its new products, a pressure transducer used in automobile fuel systems. These records are represented in the following table.

Cumulative Number of Units Produced (A)	Ln (Column A)	Hours Required for Next Unit (B)	Ln (Column B)
10.00	2.30	9.22	2.22
25.00	3.22	4.85	1.58
100.00	4.61	3.80	1.34
250.00	5.52	2.44	0.89
500.00	6.21	1.70	0.53
1,000.00	6.91	1.03	0.53
5,000.00	8.52	0.60	−0.51
10,000.00	9.21	0.50	−0.69

According to the theory, there should be a straight-line relationship between the logarithm of the cumulative number of units produced and the logarithm of the hours required for the last unit of production. The graph of the logarithms of these quantities for the data above appears in Figure 1–7. The figure suggests that the exponential learning curve is fairly accurate in this case. Using the methods outlined in Appendix 2–B, we have obtained estimators for the slope and the intercept of the least squares fit of the data in Figure 1–7. The values of the least squares estimators are

Intercept = 3.1301,
Slope = −.42276.

Since the intercept is ln(a), the value of a is exp(3.1301) = 22.88. Hence, it should have taken about 23 hours to produce the first unit. The slope term is the constant $-b$. From the

FIGURE 1–7
Log–log plot of XYZ data

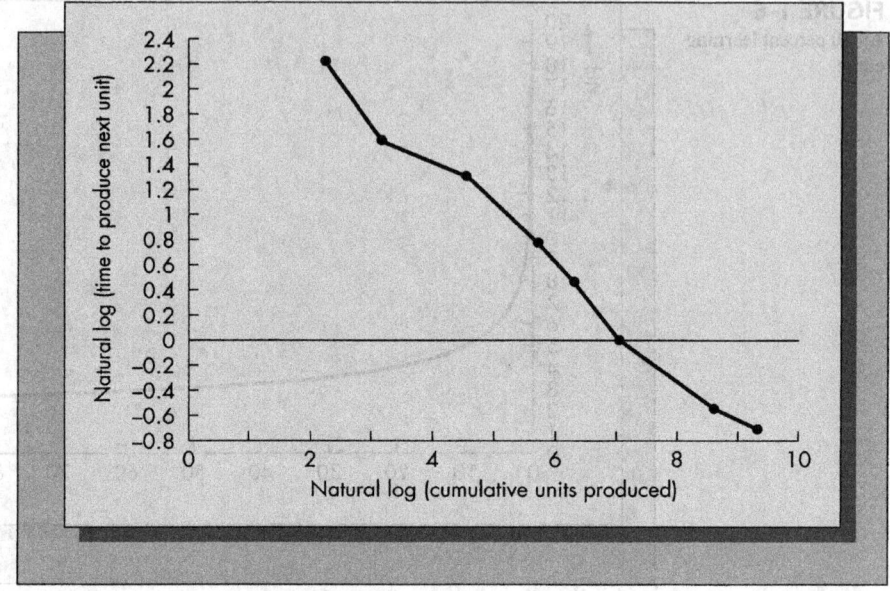

equation for b on page 33 we have that

$$\ln(L) = -b \ln(2) = (-.42276)(.6931) = -.293.$$

It follows that $L = \exp(-.293) = .746$.

Hence, these data show that the learning effect for the production of the transducers can be accurately described by a 75 percent learning curve. This curve can be used to predict the number of labor hours that will be required for continued production of these particular transducers. For example, substituting $u = 50{,}000$ into the relationship

$$Y(u) = 22.88 u^{-.42276}$$

gives a value of $Y(50{,}000) = .236$ hour. One must interpret such results with caution, however. A learning curve relationship may not be valid indefinitely. Eventually the product will reach the end of its natural life cycle, which could occur before 50,000 units have been produced in this example. Alternatively, there could be some absolute limit on the number of labor hours required to produce one unit that, because of the nature of the manufacturing process, can never be improved. Even with these limitations in mind, learning curves can be a valuable planning tool when properly used.

Experience Curves

Learning curves are a means of calibrating the decline in marginal labor hours as workers become more familiar with a particular task or as greater efficiency is introduced into the production process. Experience curves measure the effect that accumulated experience with production of a product or family of products has on overall cost and price. Experience curves are most valuable in industries that are undergoing major changes, such as the microelectronics industry, rather than very mature industries in which most radical changes have already been made, such as the automobile industry. The steady decline in the prices of integrated circuits (ICs) is a classic example of an experience curve. Figure 1–8 (Noyce, 1977) shows the average price per unit as a function of the industry's accumulated experience, in millions of units of production, during the period 1964 to 1972. This graph is shown on log–log scale and the points fall very close to a straight line. This case represents a 72 percent experience curve. That

FIGURE 1–8
Prices of integrated circuits during the period 1964–1972

Source: Robert N. Noyce, "Microelectronics," in *Scientific American*, September 1977.
© 1977 by Scientific American, Inc. All rights reserved. Reprinted with permission of the publisher.

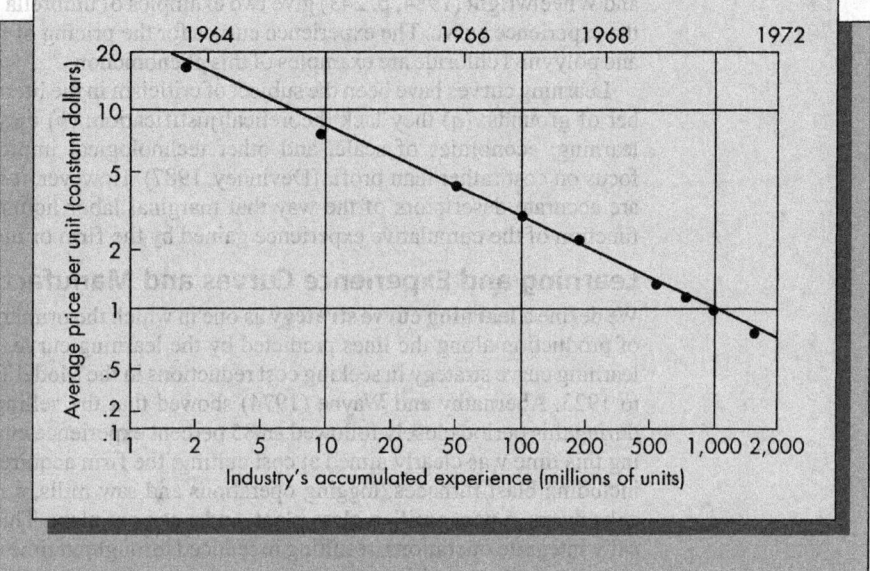

FIGURE 1–9
"Kinked" experience curve due to umbrella pricing

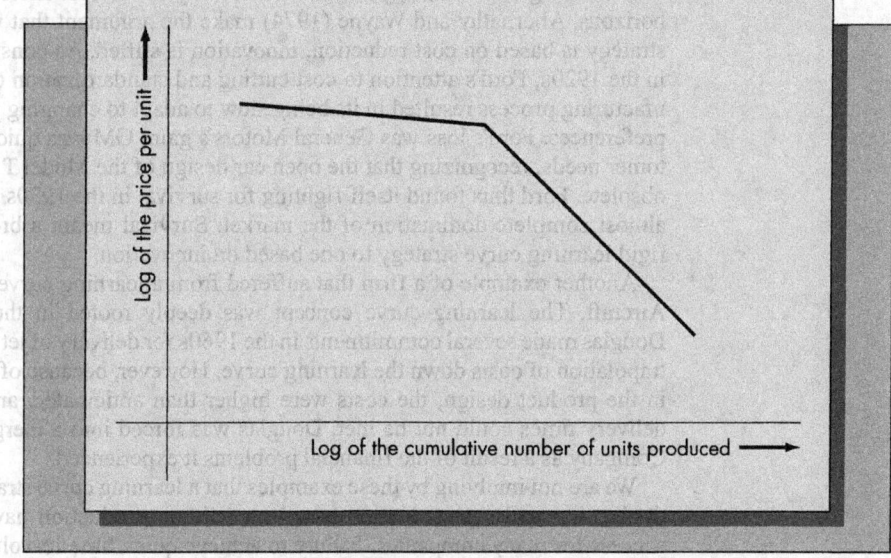

is, the average price per unit declines to about 72 percent of its previous value for each doubling of the cumulative production of ICs throughout the industry.

Experience curves are generally measured in terms of cost per unit of production. In most circumstances, the price of a product or family of products closely tracks the cost of production. However, in some cases umbrella pricing occurs. That is, prices remain fairly stable during a period in which production costs decline. Later, as competitive pressures of the marketplace take hold, prices decline more rapidly than costs until they catch up. This can cause a kink in the experience curve when price rather than cost is measured against cumulative volume. This type of phenomenon is pictured in Figure 1–9. Hayes and Wheelwright (1984, p. 243) give two examples of umbrella pricing and its effect on the experience curve. The experience curves for the pricing of free-standing gas ranges and polyvinyl chloride are examples of this phenomenon.

Learning curves have been the subject of criticism in the literature recently on a number of grounds: (a) they lack theoretical justification; (b) they confuse the effects of learning, economies of scale, and other technological improvements; and (c) they focus on cost rather than profit (Devinney, 1987). However, it is clear that such curves are accurate descriptors of the way that marginal labor hours and costs decline as a function of the cumulative experience gained by the firm or industry.

Learning and Experience Curves and Manufacturing Strategy

We define a **learning curve strategy** as one in which the primary goal is to reduce costs of production along the lines predicted by the learning curve. Ford Motors adopted a learning curve strategy in seeking cost reductions in the Model T during the period 1909 to 1923. Abernathy and Wayne (1974) showed that the selling price of the Model T during this period closely followed an 85 percent experience curve. Ford's strategy during this time was clearly aimed at cost cutting; the firm acquired or built new facilities including blast furnaces, logging operations and saw mills, a railroad, weaving mills, coke ovens, a paper mill, a glass plant, and a cement plant. This allowed Ford to vertically integrate operations, resulting in reduced throughput time and inventory levels—a strategy similar in spirit to the just-in-time philosophy discussed earlier in this chapter.

A learning curve strategy may not necessarily be the best choice over long planning horizons. Abernathy and Wayne (1974) make the argument that when manufacturing strategy is based on cost reduction, innovation is stifled. As consumer tastes changed in the 1920s, Ford's attention to cost cutting and standardization of the Model T manufacturing process resulted in its being slow to adapt to changing patterns of customer preferences. Ford's loss was General Motors's gain. GM was quick to respond to customer needs, recognizing that the open car design of the Model T would soon become obsolete. Ford thus found itself fighting for survival in the 1930s after having enjoyed almost complete domination of the market. Survival meant a break from the earlier rigid learning curve strategy to one based on innovation.

Another example of a firm that suffered from a learning curve strategy is Douglas Aircraft. The learning curve concept was deeply rooted in the airframe industry. Douglas made several commitments in the 1960s for delivery of jet aircraft based on extrapolation of costs down the learning curve. However, because of unforeseen changes in the product design, the costs were higher than anticipated, and commitments for delivery times could not be met. Douglas was forced into a merger with McDonnell Company as a result of the financial problems it experienced.

We are not implying by these examples that a learning curve strategy is wrong. Standardization and cost reduction based on volume production have been the keys to success for many companies. Failure to achieve quick time-to-volume can spell disaster in a highly competitive marketplace. What we are saying is that the learning curve strategy must be balanced with sufficient flexibility to respond to changes in the marketplace. Standardization must not stifle innovation and flexibility.

Problems for Section 1.10

29. What are the factors that contribute to the learning curve/experience curve phenomenon?
30. What is a "learning curve strategy"? Describe how this strategy led to Ford's success up until the mid-1920s and Ford's problems after that time.

31. What are some of the pitfalls that can occur when using learning curves and experience curves to predict costs? Refer to the experience of Douglas Aircraft.
32. Consider the example of XYZ Corporation presented in this section. If the learning curve remains accurate, how long will it take to produce the 100,000th unit?
33. A start-up firm has kept careful records of the time required to manufacture its product, a shutoff valve used in gasoline pipelines.

Cumulative Number of Units Produced	Number of Hours Required for Next Unit
50	3.3
100	2.2
400	1.0
600	0.8
1,000	0.5
10,000	0.2

   a. Compute the logarithms of the numbers in each column. (Use natural logs.)
   b. Graph the ln(hours) against the ln(cumulative units) and eyeball a straight-line fit of the data. Using your approximate fit, estimate a and b.
   c. Using the results of part (b), estimate the time required to produce the first unit and the appropriate percentage learning curve that fits these data.
   d. Repeat parts (b) and (c), but use an exact least squares fit of the logarithms computed in part (a).
34. Consider the learning curve derived in Problem 30. How much time will be required to produce the 100,000th unit, assuming the learning curve remains accurate?
35. Consider the experience curve plotted in Figure 1–10. What percentage experience curve does this represent?

FIGURE 1–10
(for Problem 32)

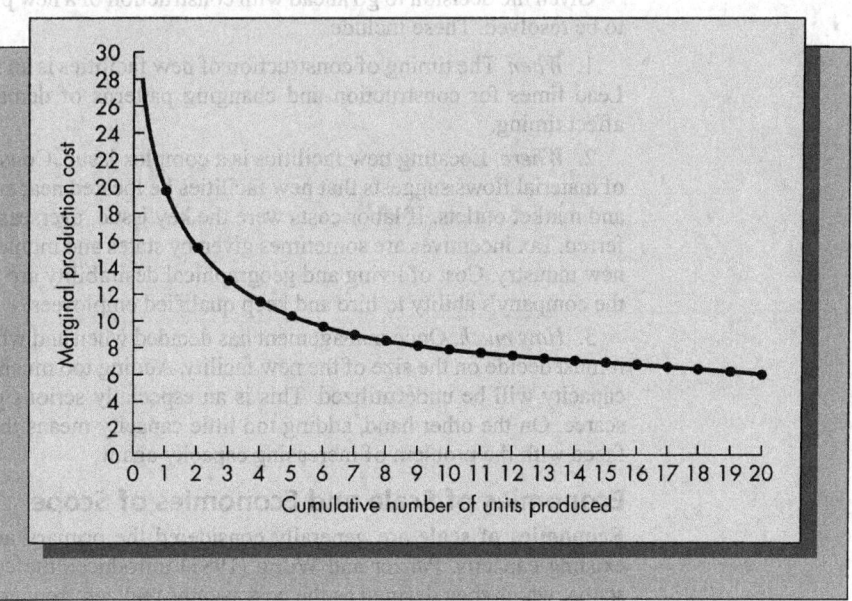

36. Discuss the limitations of learning and experience curves.
37. An analyst predicts that an 80 percent experience curve should be an accurate predictor of the cost of producing a new product. Suppose that the cost of the first unit is $1,000. What would the analyst predict is the cost of producing the
    a. 100th unit?
    b. 10,000th unit?

1.11 CAPACITY GROWTH PLANNING: A LONG-TERM STRATEGIC PROBLEM

The capacity of a plant is the number of units that the plant can produce in a given time. Capacity policy plays a key role in determining the firm's competitive position in the marketplace. A capacity strategy must take into account a variety of factors, including

- Predicted patterns of demand.
- Costs of constructing and operating new facilities.
- New process technology.
- Competitors' strategy.

Capacity planning is an extremely complex issue. Each time a company considers expanding existing productive capacity, it must sift through a myriad of possibilities. First, the decision must be made whether to increase capacity by modifying existing facilities. From an overhead point of view, this is an attractive alternative. It is cheaper to effect major changes in existing processes and plants than to construct new facilities. However, such a strategy ultimately could be penny wise and pound foolish. There is substantial evidence that plants that have focus are the most productive. Diminishing returns quickly set in if the firm tries to push the productive capacity of a single location beyond its optimal value.

Given the decision to go ahead with construction of a new plant, many issues remain to be resolved. These include

1. *When.* The timing of construction of new facilities is an important consideration. Lead times for construction and changing patterns of demand are two factors that affect timing.

2. *Where.* Locating new facilities is a complex issue. Consideration of the logistics of material flows suggests that new facilities be located near suppliers of raw materials and market outlets. If labor costs were the key issue, overseas locations might be preferred. Tax incentives are sometimes given by states and municipalities trying to attract new industry. Cost of living and geographical desirability are factors that would affect the company's ability to hire and keep qualified employees.

3. *How much.* Once management has decided when and where to add new capacity, it must decide on the size of the new facility. Adding too much capacity means that the capacity will be underutilized. This is an especially serious problem when capital is scarce. On the other hand, adding too little capacity means that the firm will soon be faced with the problem of increasing capacity again.

Economies of Scale and Economies of Scope

Economies of scale are generally considered the primary advantages of expanding existing capacity. Panzer and Willig (1981) introduced the concept of **economies of scope,** which they defined as the cost savings realized from combining the production of two or more product lines at a single location. The idea is that the manufacturing processes for these product lines may share some of the same equipment and personnel so that the cost of production at one location could be less than at two or more different locations.

The notion of economies of scope extends beyond the direct cost savings that the firm can realize by combining the production of two or more products at a single location. It is often necessary to duplicate a variety of support functions at different locations. These functions include information storage and retrieval systems and clerical and support staff. Such activities are easier to coordinate if they reside at the same location. The firm also can realize economies of scope by locating different facilities in the same geographic region. In this way employees can, if necessary, call upon the talents of key personnel at a nearby location.

Goldhar and Jelinek (1983) argue that considerations of economies of scope support investment in new manufacturing technology. Flexible manufacturing systems and computer-integrated manufacturing result in "efficiencies wrought by variety, not volume." These types of systems, argue the authors, allow the firm to produce multiple products in small lot sizes more cheaply using the same multipurpose equipment. (Flexible manufacturing systems are discussed in greater detail in Chapter 11.)

Management must weigh the benefits that the firm might realize by combining product lines at a single location against the disadvantages of lack of focus discussed previously. Too many product lines produced at the same facility could cause the various manufacturing operations to interfere with each other. The proper sizing and diversity of the functions of a single plant must be balanced so that the firm can realize economies of scope without allowing the plant to lose its essential focus.

Make or Buy: A Prototype Capacity Expansion Problem

A classic problem faced by the firm is known as the **make-or-buy decision.** The firm can purchase the product from an outside source for c_1 per unit, but can produce it internally for a lower unit price, $c_2 < c_1$. However, in order to produce the product internally, the company must invest K to expand production capacity. Which strategy should the firm adopt?

The make-or-buy problem contains many of the elements of the general capacity expansion problem. It clarifies the essential trade-off of investment and economies of scale. The total cost of the firm to produce x units is $K + c_2 x$. This is equivalent to $K/x + c_2$ per unit. As x increases, the cost per unit of production decreases, since K/x is a decreasing function of x. The cost to purchase outside is c_1 per unit, independent of the quantity ordered. By graphing the total costs of both internal production and external purchasing, we can find the point at which the costs are equal. This is known as the break-even quantity. The break-even curves are pictured in Figure 1–11.

The break-even quantity solves

$$K + c_2 x = c_1 x,$$

giving $x = K/(c_1 - c_2)$.

Example 1.2 A large international computer manufacturer is designing a new model of personal computer and must decide whether to produce the keyboards internally or to purchase them from an outside supplier. The supplier is willing to sell the keyboards for $50 each, but the manufacturer estimates that the firm can produce the keyboards for $35 each. Management estimates that expanding the current plant and purchasing the necessary equipment to make the keyboards would cost $8 million. Should they undertake the expansion?

FIGURE 1–11
Break-even curves

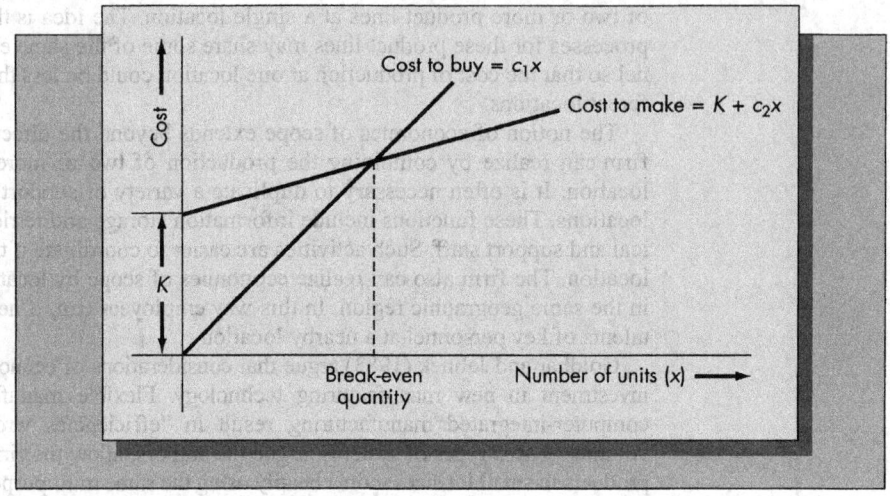

The break-even quantity is

$$x = 8{,}000{,}000/(50 - 35) = 533{,}333.$$

Hence, the firm would have to sell at least 533,333 keyboards in order to justify the $8 million investment required for the expansion.

Break-even curves such as this are useful for getting a quick ballpark estimate of the desirability of a capacity addition. Their primary limitation is that they are static. They do not consider the dynamic aspects of the capacity problem, which cannot be ignored in most cases. These include changes in the anticipated pattern of demand and considerations of the time value of money. Even as static models, break-even curves are only rough approximations. They ignore the learning effects of production; that is, the marginal production cost should decrease as the number of units produced increases. (Learning curves are discussed in detail in Section 1.10.) Depending on the structure of the production function, it may be economical to produce some units internally and purchase some units outside. Manne (1967) discusses the implications of some of these issues.

Dynamic Capacity Expansion Policy

Capacity decisions must be made in a dynamic environment. In particular, the dynamics of the changing demand pattern determine when the firm should invest in new capacity. Two competing objectives in capacity planning are

1. Maximizing market share
2. Maximizing capacity utilization

A firm that bases its long-term strategy on maximization of capacity utilization runs the risk of incurring shortages in periods of higher-than-anticipated demand. An alternative strategy to increasing productive capacity is to produce to inventory and let the inventory absorb demand fluctuations. However, this can be very risky. Inventories can become obsolete, and holding costs can become a financial burden.

Alternatively, a firm may assume the strategy of maintaining a "capacity cushion." This capacity cushion is excess capacity that the firm can use to respond to sudden demand surges; it puts the firm in a position to capture a larger portion of the marketplace if the opportunity arises.

Consider the case where the demand exhibits an increasing linear trend. Two policies, (a) and (b), are represented in Figure 1–12. In both cases the firm is acquiring new capacity at equally spaced intervals $x, 2x, 3x, \ldots$, and increasing the capacity by the same amount at each of these times. However, in case (a) capacity leads demand, meaning that the firm maintains excess capacity at all times; whereas in case (b), the capacity lags the demand, meaning that the existing capacity is fully utilized at all times. Following policy (a) or (b) results in the time path of excess capacity (or capacity shortfall, if appropriate) given in Figure 1–13.

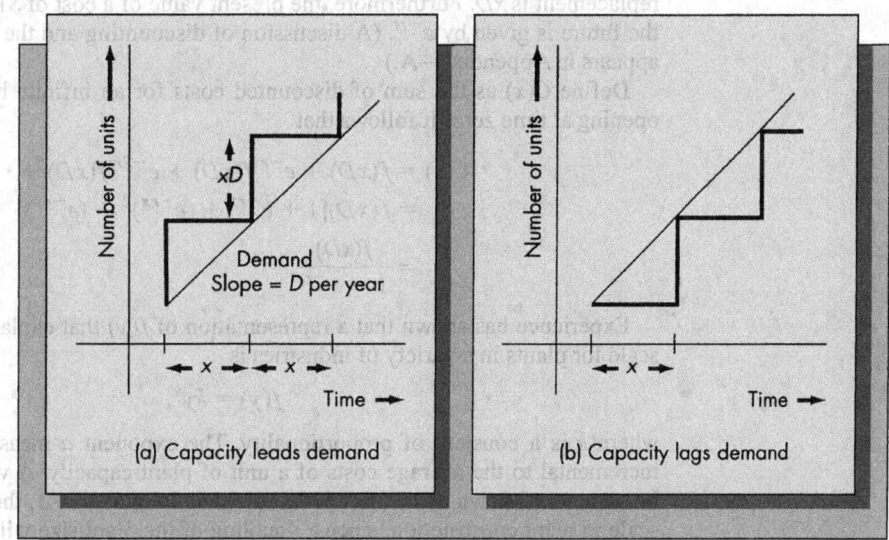

FIGURE 1–12
Capacity planning strategies

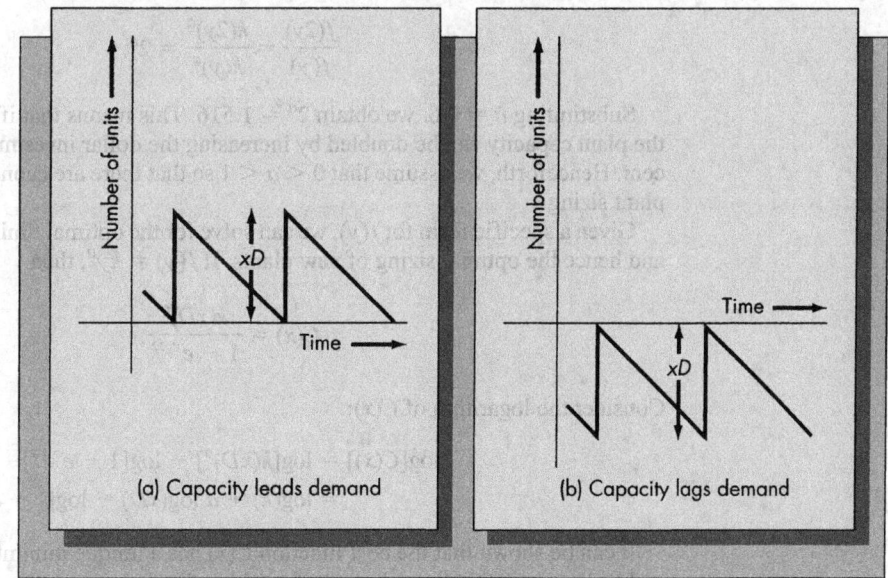

FIGURE 1–13
Time path of excess or deficient capacity

Consider the following specific model that appears in Manne (1967). Define

$D =$ Annual increase in demand.
$x =$ Time interval between introduction of successive plants.
$r =$ Annual discount rate, compounded continuously.
$f(y) =$ Cost of opening a plant of capacity y.

From Figure 1–12a (which is the strategy assumed in the model), we see that if the time interval for plant replacement is x, it must be true that the plant size at each replacement is xD. Furthermore, the present value of a cost of \$1 incurred t years into the future is given by e^{-rt}. (A discussion of discounting and the time value of money appears in Appendix 1–A.)

Define $C(x)$ as the sum of discounted costs for an infinite horizon given a plant opening at time zero. It follows that

$$C(x) = f(xD) + e^{-rx}f(xD) + e^{-2rx}f(xD) + \cdots$$
$$= f(xD)[1 + e^{-rx} + (e^{-rx})^2 + (e^{-rx})^3 + \cdots]$$
$$= \frac{f(xD)}{1 - e^{-rx}}.$$

Experience has shown that a representation of $f(y)$ that explains the economies of scale for plants in a variety of industries is

$$f(y) = ky^a,$$

where k is a constant of proportionality. The exponent a measures the ratio of the incremental to the average costs of a unit of plant capacity. A value of 0.6 seems to be common (known as the six-tenths rule). As long as $a < 1$, there are economies of scale in plant construction, since a doubling of the plant size will result in less than a doubling of the construction costs. To see this, consider the ratio

$$\frac{f(2y)}{f(y)} = \frac{k(2y)^a}{k(y)^a} = 2^a.$$

Substituting $a = 0.6$, we obtain $2^a = 1.516$. This means that if $a = 0.6$ is accurate, the plant capacity can be doubled by increasing the dollar investment by about 52 percent. Henceforth, we assume that $0 < a < 1$ so that there are economies of scale in the plant sizing.

Given a specific form for $f(y)$, we can solve for the optimal timing of plant additions and hence the optimal sizing of new plants. If $f(y) = ky^a$, then

$$C(x) = \frac{k(xD)^a}{1 - e^{-rx}}.$$

Consider the logarithm of $C(x)$:

$$\log[C(x)] = \log[k(xD)^a] - \log[1 - e^{-rx}]$$
$$= \log(k) + a\log(xD) - \log[1 - e^{-rx}].$$

It can be shown that the cost function $C(x)$ has a unique minimum with respect to x and furthermore that the value of x for which the derivative of $\log[C(x)]$ is zero is the

FIGURE 1–14
The function
$u/(e^u - 1)$

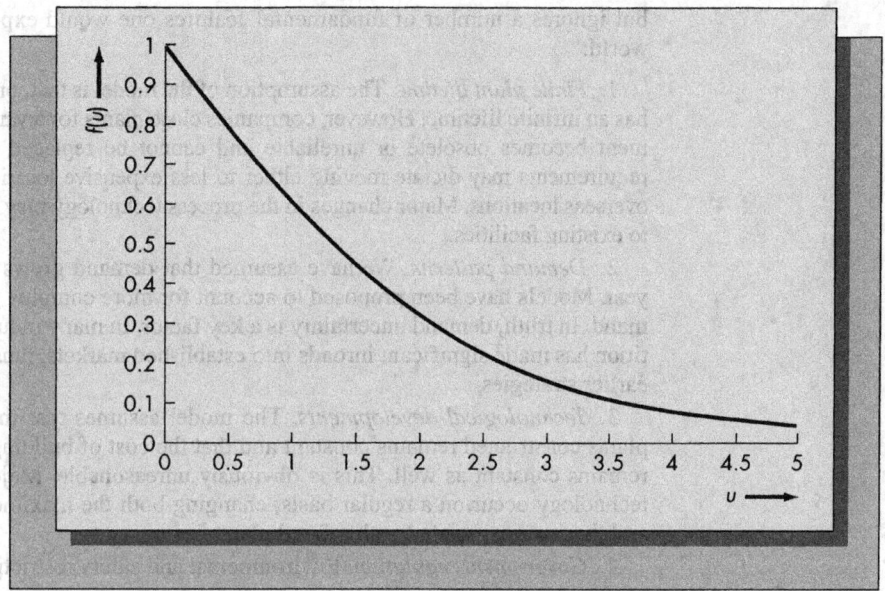

value of x that minimizes $C(x)$. It is easy to show[1] that the optimal solution satisfies

$$\frac{rx}{e^{rx} - 1} = a.$$

The function $f(u) = u/(e^u - 1)$ appears in Figure 1–14, where $u = rx$. By locating the value of a on the ordinate axis, one can find the optimal value of u on the abscissa axis.

Example 1.3   A chemicals firm is planning for an increase of production capacity. The firm has estimated that the cost of adding new capacity obeys the law

$$f(y) = .0107y^{.62},$$

where cost is measured in millions of dollars and capacity is measured in tons per year. For example, substituting $y = 20,000$ tons gives $f(y) = \$4.97$ million plant cost. Furthermore, suppose that the demand is growing at a constant rate of 5,000 tons per year and future costs are discounted using a 16 percent interest rate. From Figure 1–14 we see that, if $a = .62$, the value of u is approximately 0.9. Solving for x, we obtain the optimal timing of new plant openings:

$$x = u/r = .9/.16 = 5.625 \text{ years}.$$

The optimal value of the plant capacity should be $xD = (5.625)(5,000) = 28,125$ tons. Substituting $y = 28,125$ into the equation for $f(y)$ gives the cost of each plant at the optimal solution as \$6.135 million.

Much of the research into the capacity expansion problem consists of extensions of models of this type. This particular model could be helpful in some circumstances

---

[1] $\dfrac{d \log[C(x)]}{dx} = \dfrac{aD}{xD} - \dfrac{(-e^{-rx})(-r)}{1 - e^{-rx}} = \dfrac{a}{x} - \dfrac{r}{e^{rx} - 1} = 0,$

which gives $\dfrac{rx}{e^{rx} - 1} = a.$

but ignores a number of fundamental features one would expect to find in the real world:

1. *Finite plant lifetime.* The assumption of the model is that, once constructed, a plant has an infinite lifetime. However, companies close plants for a variety of reasons: Equipment becomes obsolete or unreliable and cannot be replaced easily. Labor costs or requirements may dictate moving either to less expensive locations domestically or to overseas locations. Major changes in the process technology may not be easily adaptable to existing facilities.

2. *Demand patterns.* We have assumed that demand grows at a constant rate per year. Models have been proposed to account for more complex growth patterns of demand. In truth, demand uncertainty is a key factor. In many industries, foreign competition has made significant inroads into established markets, thus forcing rethinking of earlier strategies.

3. *Technological developments.* The model assumes that the capacity of all new plants constructed remains constant and that the cost of building a plant of given size remains constant as well. This is obviously unreasonable. Major changes in process technology occur on a regular basis, changing both the maximum size of new plants and the costs associated with a fixed plant size.

4. *Government regulation.* Environmental and safety restrictions may limit choices of plant location and scale.

5. *Overhead costs.* Most capacity expansion and location models do not explicitly account for the costs of overhead. During the energy crunch in the late 1970s, costs of energy overhead soared, wreaking havoc with plant overhead budgets.

6. *Tax incentives.* The financial implications of the sizing and location of new facilities must be considered in the context of tax planning. Tax incentives are offered by local or state municipalities to major corporations considering sites for the construction of new facilities.

An interesting question is whether models of this type really capture the way that companies have made capacity expansion decisions in the past. There is some preliminary evidence that they do not. Lieberman (1987) attempted to assess the factors that motivated firms to construct new chemical plants during the period 1957 to 1982. He found that the size of new plants increased by about 8 percent per year independent of market conditions. In periods of high demand, firms constructed more plants. This preliminary study indicates that the rational thinking that leads to models such as the one developed in this section does not accurately reflect the way that companies make plant-sizing decisions. His results suggest that firms build the largest plants possible with the existing technology. (Given sufficient economies of scale, however, this policy may theoretically be optimal.)

Issues in Plant Location

This section has been concerned with capacity expansion decisions, specifically, determining the amount and timing of new capacity additions. A related issue is the **location of the new facility.** Deciding where to locate a plant is a complex problem. Many factors must be carefully considered by management before making the final choice.

The following information about the plant itself is relevant to the location decision:

1. *Size of the plant.* This includes the required acreage, the number of square feet of space needed for the building structure, and constraints that might arise as a result of special needs.

2. *Product lines to be produced.*
3. *Process technology to be used.*
4. *Labor force requirements.* These include both the number of workers required and the specification of the particular skills needed.
5. *Transportation needs.* Depending on the nature of the product produced and the requirements for raw materials, the plant may have to be located near major interstate highways or rail lines.
6. *Utilities requirements.* These include special needs for power, water, sewage, or fossil fuels such as natural gas. Plants that have unusual power needs should be located in areas where energy is less expensive or near sources of hydroelectric power.
7. *Environmental issues.* Because of government regulations, there will be few allowable locations if the plant produces significant waste products.
8. *Interaction with other plants.* If the plant is a satellite of existing facilities, it is likely that management would want to locate the new plant near the others.
9. *International considerations.* Whether to locate a new facility domestically or overseas is a very sensitive issue. Although labor costs may be lower in some locations, such as the Far East, tariffs, import quotas, inventory pipeline costs, and market responsiveness also must be considered.
10. *Tax treatment.* Tax consideration is an important variable in the location decision. Favorable tax treatment is given by some countries, such as Ireland, to encourage new industry. There are also significant differences in state tax laws designed to attract domestic manufacturers.

Mathematical models are useful for assisting with many operational decisions. However, they generally are of only limited value for determining a suitable location for a new plant. Because so many factors and constraints enter into the decision process, such decisions are generally made based on the inputs of one or more of the company's divisions, and the decision process can span several years. (Mathematical techniques for making location decisions will be explored in Chapter 11, on facilities layout and location.) Schmenner (1982) has examined the decision process at a number of the *Fortune* 500 companies. His results showed that in most firms, the decision of where to locate a new facility was made either by the corporate staff or by the CEO, even though the request for new facilities might have originated at the division level. The degree of decision-making autonomy enjoyed at the division level depended on the firm's management style.

Based on a sample survey, Schmenner reported that the major factors that influenced new facilities location decisions were the following:

1. *Labor costs.* This was a primary concern for industries such as apparel, leather, furniture, and consumer electronics. It was less of a concern for capital-intensive industries.
2. *Unionization.* A motivating factor for a firm considering expanding an existing facility, as opposed to one considering building a new facility, is the potential for eliminating union influence in the new facility. A fresh labor force may be more difficult to organize.
3. *Proximity to markets.* When transportation costs account for a major portion of the cost of goods sold, locating new plants near existing markets is essential.
4. *Proximity to supplies and resources.* The decision about where to locate plants in certain industries is based on the location of resources. For example, firms producing wood or paper products must be located near forests and firms producing processed food, near farms.

5. *Proximity to other facilities.* Many companies tend to place manufacturing divisions and corporate facilities in the same geographic area. For example, IBM originated in Westchester County in New York, and located many of its divisions in that state. By locating key personnel near each other, the firm has been able to realize economies of scope.
6. *Quality of life in the region.* When other issues do not dictate the choice of a location, choosing a site that will be attractive to employees may help in recruiting key personnel. This is especially true in high-tech industries that must compete for workers with particular skills.

Problems for Section 1.11

38. A start-up company, Macrotech, plans to produce a device to translate Morse code to a written message on a home computer and to send written messages in Morse code over the airwaves. The device is primarily of interest to ham radio enthusiasts. The president, Ron Lodel, estimates that it would require a $30,000 initial investment. Each unit costs him $20 to produce and each sells for $85.

    a. How many units must be sold in order for the firm to recover its initial investment?
    b. What is the total revenue at the break-even volume?
    c. If the price were increased to $100 each, find the break-even volume.

39. For Problem 35, suppose that sales are expected to be 100 units in the first year and increase at a rate of 40 percent per year. How many years will it take to recoup the $30,000 initial investment? Assume that each unit sells for $85.

40. A domestic producer of baby carriages, Pramble, buys the wheels from a company in the north of England. Currently the wheels cost $4 each, but for a number of reasons the price will double. In order to produce the wheels themselves, Pramble would have to add to existing facilities at a cost of $800,000. It estimates that its unit cost of production would be $3.50. At the current time, the company sells 10,000 carriages annually. (Assume that there are four wheels per carriage.)

    a. At the current sales rate, how long would it take to pay back the investment required for the expansion?
    b. If sales are expected to increase at a rate of 15 percent per year, how long will it take to pay back the expansion?

41. Based on past experience, a chemicals firm estimates that the cost of new capacity additions obeys the law
$$f(y) = .0205 y^{.58}$$
where y is measured in tons per year and $f(y)$ in millions of dollars. Demand is growing at the rate of 3,000 tons per year, and the accounting department recommends a rate of 12 percent per year for discounting future costs.

    a. Determine the optimal timing of plant additions and the optimal size of each addition.
    b. What is the cost of each addition?
    c. What is the present value of the cost of the next four additions? Assume an addition has just been made for the purposes of your calculation. (Refer to Appendix 1–A for a discussion of cost discounting.)

42. A major oil company is considering the optimal timing for the construction of new refineries. From past experience, each doubling of the size of a refinery at a single location results in an increase in the construction costs of about 68 percent. Furthermore, a plant size of 10,000 barrels per day costs $6 million. Assume that the demand for the oil is increasing at a constant rate of two million barrels yearly and the discount rate for future costs is 15 percent.

   a. Find the values of k and a assuming a relationship of the form $f(y) = ky^a$. Assume that y is in units of barrels per day.
   b. Determine the optimal timing of plant additions and the optimal size of each plant.
   c. Suppose that the largest single refinery that can be built with current technology is 15,000 barrels per day. Determine the optimal timing of plant additions and the optimal size of each plant in this case. (Assume 365 days per year for your calculations.)

1.12 Summary

This chapter discussed the importance of **operations strategy** and its relationship to the overall business strategy of the firm. Operations continues to grow in importance in the firm. While a larger portion of direct manufacturing continues to move off-shore, the importance of the manufacturing function should not be underestimated. The success of the operations strategy can be measured along several dimensions. These include the obvious measures of cost and product characteristics, but also include quality, delivery speed, delivery reliability, and flexibility.

The classical view of manufacturing strategy, due primarily to Wickham Skinner, considers the following four dimensions of strategy: **time horizon, focus, evaluation, and consistency.** Different types of decisions relate to different time frames. A plant should be designed with a specific focus in mind, whether it be to minimize unit cost or to maximize product quality. Several evaluation criteria may be applied to analyze the effectiveness of a strategy.

We hear more and more frequently that we are part of a global community. When buying products today, we are less concerned with the country of origin than with the characteristics of the product. How many consumers of cell phones are even aware that Nokia is headquartered in Finland, Ericsson in Sweden, and Motorola in the United States? An interesting question explored by Michael Porter is: Why do some industries seem to thrive in some countries? While the answer is complex, Porter suggests that the following four factors are most important: *factor conditions; demand conditions; related and supporting industries;* and *firm strategy, structure, and rivalry.*

Changing the way that one does things can be difficult. Even more difficult is changing the way that a company does things. For that reason, **business process engineering (BPR)** is a painful process, even when it works. The most dramatic successes of BPR have come in service functions, but the concept can be applied to any environment. It is the process of rethinking how and why things are done in a certain way. Intelligently done, BPR can lead to dramatic improvements. However, it can also be a time-consuming and costly process.

Just-in-time (JIT) is a philosophy that grew from the kanban system developed by Toyota. At the heart of the approach is the elimination of waste. Systems are put in place to reduce material flows to small batches to avoid large buildups of work-in-process inventories. While JIT developed on the factory floor, it is a concept that has been applied to the purchasing function as well. Successful application of JIT purchasing requires the development of long-term relationships, and usually requires close proximity to suppliers. The mechanics of JIT are discussed in more detail in Chapter 8.

Being able to get to the market quickly with products that people want in the volumes that the marketplace requires is crucial if one wants to be a market leader. **Time-based competition** means that the time from product conception to its appearance in the marketplace must be reduced. To do so, one performs as many tasks concurrently as possible. In many instances, time to market is less important than time to volume. Being the first to the market may not mean much if one cannot meet product demand.

The dramatic successes of the Japanese during the 1970s and 1980s were to a large extent due to the outstanding **quality** of their manufactured products. Two Americans, Deming and Juran, visited Japan in the early 1950s and played an important role in making the Japanese aware of the importance of producing quality products. The quality movement in the United States has resulted in a much greater awareness of the importance of quality, recognition for outstanding achievement in this arena via the Malcolm Baldrige Award, and initiation of important programs such as quality circles and the six-sigma program at Motorola. (Both the statistical and the organizational issues concerning quality are discussed in detail in Chapter 12.)

It is important to understand both **product and process life cycles.** Both go through the four cycles of start-up, rapid growth, maturation, and stabilization or decline. It is also important to understand which types of processes are appropriate for which types of products and industries. To this end, Hayes and Wheelwright have developed the concept of the product–process matrix.

Learning and experience curves are useful in modeling the decline in labor hours or the decline in product costs as experience is gained in the production of an item or family of items. These curves have been shown to obey an exponential law, and can be useful predictors of the cost or time required for production. (Moore's Law, due to Gordon Moore, a founder of Intel, predicted the doubling of chip performance every 18 months. This is an example of an experience curve, and the prediction has continued to be accurate to the present day.)

We discussed two methods for assisting with **capacity expansion** decisions. Break-even curves provide a means of determining the sales volume necessary to justify investing in new or existing facilities. A simple model for a dynamic expansion policy is presented that gives the optimal timing and sizing of new facilities assuming constant demand growth and discounting of future costs. We also discussed issues that arise in trying to decide where to locate new facilities. This problem is very complex in that there are many factors that relate to the decision of where to locate production, design, and management facilities.

Additional Problems for Chapter 1

43. What is a production and operations strategy? Discuss the elements in common with marketing and financial strategies and the elements that are different.
44. What is the difference between the product life cycle and the process life cycle? In what way are these concepts related?
45. Suppose that the Mendenhall Corporation, a producer of women's handbags, has determined that a 73 percent experience curve accurately describes the evolution of its production costs for a new line. If the first unit costs $100 to produce, what should the 10,000th unit cost based on the experience curve?
46. Delon's Department Store sells several of its own brands of clothes and several well-known designer brands as well. Delon's is considering building a plant in

Malaysia to produce silk ties. The plant will cost the firm $5.5 million. The plant will be able to produce the ties for $1.20 each. On the other hand, Delon's can subcontract to have the ties produced and pay $3.00 each. How many ties will Delon's have to sell worldwide to break even on its investment in the new plant?

47. A Japanese steel manufacturer is considering expanding operations. From experience, it estimates that new capacity additions obey the law

$$f(y) = .00345 y^{.51},$$

where the cost $f(y)$ is measured in millions of dollars and y is measured in tons of steel produced. If the demand for steel is assumed to grow at the constant rate of 8,000 tons per year and future costs are discounted using a 10 percent discount rate, what is the optimal number of years between new plant openings?

The following problems are designed to be solved by spreadsheet.

48. Consider the following break-even problem: the cost of producing Q units, $c(Q)$, is described by the curve

$$c(Q) = 48Q[1 - \exp(-.08Q)],$$

where Q is in hundreds of units of items produced and $c(Q)$ is in thousands of dollars.

a. Graph the function $c(Q)$. What is its shape? What economic phenomenon gives rise to a cumulative cost curve of this shape?

b. At what production level does the cumulative production cost equal $1,000,000?

c. Suppose that these units can be purchased from an outside supplier at a cost of $800 each, but the firm must invest $850,000 to build a facility that would be able to produce these units at a cost $c(Q)$. At what cumulative volume of production does it make sense to invest in the facility?

49. Maintenance costs for a new facility are expected to be $112,000 for the first year of operation. It is anticipated that these costs will increase at a rate of 8 percent per year. Assuming a rate of return of 10 percent, what is the present value of the stream of maintenance costs over the next 30 years?

50. Suppose the supplier of keyboards described in Example 1.2 is willing to offer the following incremental quantity discount schedule:

Cost per Keyboard	Order Quantity
$50	$Q \leq 100{,}000$
$45	$100{,}000 < Q \leq 500{,}000$
$40	$500{,}000 < Q$

Determine the cost to the firm for order quantities in increments of 20,000 for $Q = 200{,}000$ to $Q = 1{,}000{,}000$, and compare that to the cost to the firm of producing internally for these same values of Q. What is the break-even order quantity?

Appendix 1-A

PRESENT WORTH CALCULATIONS

Including the time value of money in the decision process is common when considering alternative investment strategies. The idea is that a dollar received today has greater value than one received a year from now. For example, if a dollar were placed in a simple passbook account paying 5 percent, it would be worth $1.05 in one year. More generally, if it were invested at a rate of return of r (expressed as a decimal), it would be worth $1 + r$ in a year, $(1 + r)^2$ in two years, and so on.

In the same way, a cost of $1 incurred in a year has a present value of less than $1 today. For example, at 5 percent interest, how much would one need to place in an account today so that the total principal plus interest would equal $1 in a year? The answer is $1/(1.05) = 0.9524$. Similarly, the present value of a $1 cost incurred in two years at 5 percent is $1/(1.05)^2 = 0.9070$. In general, the present value of a cost of $1 incurred in t years assuming a rate of return r is $(1 + r)^{-t}$.

These calculations assume that there is no compounding. Compounding means that one earns interest on the interest, so to speak. For example, 5 percent compounded semiannually means that one earns 2.5 percent on $1 after six months and 2.5 percent on the original $1 plus interest earned in the first six months. Hence, the total return is

$$(1.025)(1.025) = \$1.050625$$

after one year, or slightly more than 5 percent. If the interest were compounded quarterly, the dollar would be worth

$$(1 + .05/4)^4 = 1.0509453$$

at the end of the year. The logical extension of this idea is continuous compounding. One dollar invested at 5 percent compounded continuously would be worth

$$\lim_{n \to \infty} (1 + .05/n)^n = e^{.05}$$
$$= 1.05127$$

at the end of a year. The number $e = 2.7172818\ldots$ is defined as

$$e = \lim_{n \to \infty} (1 + 1/n)^n.$$

Notice that continuous compounding only increases the effective simple interest rate from 5 percent to 5.127 percent.

More generally, C invested at a rate of r for t years compounded continuously is worth Ce^{rt} at the end of t years.

Reversing the argument, the present value of a cost of C incurred in t years assuming continuous compounding at a discount rate r is Ce^{-rt}. A stream of costs $C_1, C_2, \ldots, C_n$ incurred at times $t_1, t_2, \ldots, t_n$ has present value

$$\sum_{i=1}^{n} C_i e^{-rt_i}.$$

A comprehensive treatment of discounting and its relationship to the capacity expansion problem can be found in Freidenfelds (1981).

Bibliography

Abernathy, W. J., and P. L. Townsend. "Technology, Productivity, and Process Change." *Technological Forecasting and Social Change* 7 (1975), pp. 379–96.

Abernathy, W. J., and K. Wayne. "Limits of the Learning Curve." *Harvard Business Review* 52 (September–October 1974), pp. 109–19.

Becker, G. S. Quoted in *Business Week*, January 27, 1986, p. 12.

Bell, D. *The Coming of the Post-Industrial Society: A Venture in Social Forecasting*. New York: Basic Books, 1987.

Blackburn, J. D. *Time-Based Competition: The Next Battleground in American Manufacturing*. New York: McGraw-Hill/Irwin, 1991.

Business Week. October 22, 1990, pp. 94–95.

Business Week. "The Quality Imperative." October 25, 1991.

Cohen, S. S., and J. Zysman. *Manufacturing Matters: The Myth of the Post-Industrial Economy*. New York: Basic Books, 1987.

Davis, D. "Beating the Clock." *Electronic Business*, May 1989.

Devinney, T. M. "Entry and Learning." *Management Science* 33 (1987), pp. 102–12.

Dhalla, N. K., and S. Yuspeh. "Forget about the Product Life Cycle Concept." Harvard Business Review 54 (January–February 1976), pp. 102–12.

The Economist. "Reshoring Manufacturing: Coming Home." January 2013. Retrieved from http://www.economist.com/news/special-report/21569570-growing-number-american-companies-are-moving-their-manufacturing-back-united

Fallon, M. *San Jose Mercury News*, September 30, 1985, p. 11D.

Faux, J. "Manufacturing Key to America's Future." Presentation to the Industrial Union Council Legislative Conference, Economic Policy Institute, 7 pages, February 4, 2003.

Freeland, J. R. "A Survey of Just-in-Time Purchasing Practices in the United States." *Production and Inventory Management Journal*, Second Quarter 1991, pp. 43–50

Freidenfelds, J. *Capacity Expansion: Analysis of Simple Models with Applications*. New York: Elsevier North Holland, 1981.

Goldhar, J. P., and M. Jelinek. "Plan for Economies of Scope." *Harvard Business Review* 61 (1983), pp. 141–48.

Hagenbaugh, B. "U.S. Manufacturing Jobs Fading Away Fast." *USA Today*, December 12, 2002.

Hammer, M. S., and J. Champy. *Reengineering the Corporation: A Manifesto for Business Resolution*. New York: Harper Business, 1993.

Hammer, M. S., and S. A. Stanton. *The Reengineering Revolution*. New York: Harper Business, 1995.

Hayes, R. H., and S. Wheelwright. "Link Manufacturing Profess and Product Life Cycles." *Harvard Business Review* 57 (January–February 1979), pp. 133–40.

Hayes, R. H., and S. Wheelwright. *Restoring Our Competitive Edge: Competing through Manufacturing*. New York: John Wiley & Sons, 1984.

Hutzel, T. and D. Lippert. Reshoring 101: Rebuilding U.S. Manufacturing through Right Sizing and Right Shoring. Retrieved from http://www.mainstreammanagement.com/pdf/rebuilding-us-manufacturing.pdf, 2012.

Jones, P., and L. Kahaner. *Say It and Live It. The Fifty Corporate Mission Statements That Hit the Mark*. New York: Currency Doubleday, 1995.

Koerner, B. I. "Made in America: Small Businesses Buck the Offshoring Trend." *Wired*, March 2011, pp. 104–111.

Krugman, P. *Peddling Prosperity: Economic Sense and Nonsense in the Age of Diminished Expectations*. New York: W. W. Norton and Company, 1994.

Lieberman, M. "Scale Economies, Factory Focus, and Optimal Plant Size." Paper present at Stanford Graduate School of Business, July 22, 1987.

Manne, A. S., ed. *Investments for Capacity Expansion: Size, Location, and Time Phasing*. Cambridge, MA: MIT Press, 1967.

Noyce, R. N. "Microelectronics." *Scientific American*, September 1977.

Panzer, J. C., and R. O. Willing. "Economies of Scope." *American Economic Review*, 1981, pp. 268–72.

Pisano, G.P. and W.C. Shih. *Producing Prosperity: Why America Needs a Manufacturing Renaissance*. Harvard Business Review Press, Boston, Massachusetts, 2012.

Port, O. "Customers Move into the Driver's Seat." *Business Week*. October 4, 1999, pp. 103–06.

Porter, M. E. and J. W. Rivkin. "Choosing the United States." *Harvard Business Review*, pp. 80–93, March 2012.

Shen, Y. "Selection Incentives in a Performance-Based Contracting System." *Health Services Research*. 38 (2003), pp. 535–552.

Skinner, W. *Manufacturing in the Corporate Strategy*. New York: John Wiley & Sons, 1978.

Stasey, R., and C. J. McNair. *Crossroads: A JIT Success Story*. New York: McGraw-Hill/Irwin, 1990.

Vandermerwe, S. and J. Rada. "Servitization of Business: Adding Value by Adding Services." *European Management Journal* 6 (1988), pp. 314–324.

Wills, F. "Bully for Taurus." *Business Month*, February 1990, p. 13.

Wise, R. and P. Baumgartner. "Go Downstream: The New Profit Imperative in Manufacturing." *Harvard Business Review* 77 (1999), pp. 133–141.

Womack, J. P., D. T. Jones, and D. Roos. *The Machine That Changed the World*. New York: Harper Perennial, 1990.

Chapter Two

Forecasting

"It's hard to make predictions, especially about the future."
—Neils Bohr

Chapter Overview

Purpose

To present and illustrate the most important methods for forecasting demand in the context of operations planning.

Key Points

1. *Characteristics of forecasts.*
   - They are almost always going to be wrong.
   - A good forecast also gives some measure of error.
   - Forecasting aggregate units is generally easier than forecasting individual units.
   - Forecasts made further out into the future are less accurate.
   - A forecasting technique should not be used to the exclusion of known information.
2. *Subjective forecasting.* Refers to methods that measure either individual or group opinion. The better known subjective forecasting methods include:
   - Sales force composites.
   - Customer surveys.
   - Jury of executive opinion.
   - The Delphi method.
3. *Objective forecasting methods (time series methods and regression).* Using *objective forecasting* methods, one makes forecasts based on past history. *Time series forecasting* uses only the past history of the series to be forecasted, while *regression models* often incorporate the past history of other series. In time series forecasting, the goal is to find predictable and repeatable patterns in past data. Based on the identified pattern, different methods are appropriate. Time series methods have the advantage of easily being incorporated into a computer program for automatic forecasting and updating. Repeatable patterns that we consider include increasing or decreasing linear trend, curvilinear trend (including exponential growth), and seasonal fluctuations. When using regression, one constructs a causal model that predicts one phenomenon (the dependent variable) based on the evolution of one or more other phenomenon (the independent variables). An example would be predicting the start or end of a recession based on housing starts (housing starts are considered to be a leading economic indicator of the health of the economy).

4. *Evaluation of forecasting methods.* The forecast error in any period, e_t, is the difference between the forecast for period t and the actual value of the series realized for period t ($e_t = F_t - D_t$). Three common measures of forecast error are MAD (average of the absolute errors over n periods), MSE (the average of the sum of the squared errors over n periods), and MAPE (the average of the percentage errors over n periods).

5. *Methods for forecasting stationary time series.* We consider two forecasting methods when the underlying pattern of the series is stationary over time: moving averages and exponential smoothing. A *moving average* is simply the arithmetic average of the N most recent observations. *Exponential smoothing* forecasts rely on a weighted average of the most recent observation and the previous forecast. The weight applied to the most recent observation is α, where $0 < \alpha < 1$, and the weight applied to the last forecast is $1 - \alpha$. Both methods are commonly used in practice, but the exponential smoothing method is favored in inventory control applications—especially in large systems—because it requires much less data storage than does moving averages.

6. *Methods for forecasting series with trend.* When there is an upward or downward linear trend in the data, two common forecasting methods are *linear regression* and double exponential smoothing via *Holt's method*. Linear regression is used to fit a straight line to past data based on the method of least squares, and Holt's method uses separate exponential smoothing equations to forecast the intercept and the slope of the series each period.

7. *Methods for forecasting seasonal series.* A seasonal time series is one that has a regular repeating pattern over the same time frame. Typically, the time frame would be a year, and the periods would be weeks or months. The simplest approach for forecasting seasonal series is based on multiplicative seasonal factors. A multiplicative seasonal factor is a number that indicates the relative value of the series in any period compared to the average value over a year. Suppose a season consists of 12 months. A seasonal factor of 1.25 for a given month means that the demand in that month is 25 percent higher than the mean monthly demand. *Winter's method* is a more complex method based on triple exponential smoothing. Three distinct smoothing equations are used to forecast the intercept, the slope, and the seasonal factors each period.

8. *Box-Jenkins models.* George Box and Gwilym Jenkins developed forecasting methods based largely on a statistical analysis of the autoregressive function of a time series. Autoregression seeks to discover repeating patterns in data by considering the correlation of observations of the series with other observations separated by fixed number of periods. These models have proven to be very powerful for forecasting some economic time series, but they require large data sets (at least 72 observations) and a knowledgeable user. We provide a brief review of these powerful methods.

9. *Other considerations.* In addition to Box-Jenkins methods, when large data sets are available, filtering methods borrowed from electrical engineering can often provide excellent forecasts for economic time series. Two of the better known filters are Kalman Filters and Wiener Filters. Neither of these methods are amenable to automatic forecasting. Monte Carlo simulation is another technique that can be useful for building a forecasting model. Finally, we discuss forecasting demand in the context of a lost sales inventory system.

Families plan vacations around their schedules, and for that reason America's theme parks tend to be very crowded during holidays and school breaks. On June 18, 2011, Universal Studios Theme Parks opened its new Harry Potter section at Universal Orlando Resort in Orlando, FL, which continues to be a major attraction for tourists. If you were planning on taking your family to a theme park such as Universal Studios, when would be the best time to go to avoid the long lines? One might think that Thanksgiving and Christmas would be good choices, as most people are home with families on these holidays. Not so! In fact, these two days (along with New Year's Day) are the busiest days of the year. The period between Thanksgiving and Christmas as well as the periods after New Year's Day and before Halloween are the slowest times, and Universal Orlando Resort recommends that visitors come at these times to avoid longer lines.

As was so eloquently stated by Charles F. Kettering, "My concern is with the future since I plan to spend the rest of my life there." But the future can never be known, so we make forecasts. We forecast traffic patterns and plan routes accordingly. We forecast which foods will be best in a particular restaurant, and order accordingly. We choose universities to attend based on forecasting our experiences there and the doors that a degree from that university will open. We make hundreds of forecasts every day, some carefully thought out, some made almost unconsciously. Forecasting plays a central role in all of our lives.

In the same way, forecasting plays a central role in the operations function of a firm. All business planning is based on forecasts. Sales of existing and new products, requirements and availabilities of raw materials, changing skills of workers, interest rates, capacity requirements, and international politics are only a few of the factors likely to affect the future success of a firm.

The functional areas of the firm that make the most use of forecasting methods are marketing and production. Marketing is responsible for forecasting sales of both new and existing product lines. Sales forecasts are the primary driver for the S&OP (sales and operations planning) function, which will be discussed in detail in Chapter 3. In some circumstances, the forecasts prepared for marketing purposes may not be appropriate or sufficient for operations planning. For example, to determine suitable stocking levels for spare parts, one must know schedules for planned replacements and be able to forecast unplanned replacements. Also it could be that the S&OP planning function might be producing forecasts for aggregate units, while forecasts for individual SKU's (stock-keeping units) might be required.

We have seen firms benefit from good forecasting and pay the price for poor forecasting. During the 1960s, consumer tastes in automobiles slowly shifted from large, heavy gas guzzlers to smaller, more fuel efficient automobiles. Detroit, slow to respond to this change, suffered when the OPEC oil embargo hit in the late 1970s and tastes shifted more dramatically to smaller cars. Compaq Computer became a market leader in the early 1980s by properly forecasting consumer demand for a portable version of the IBM PC, which gained a popularity that far exceeded expectations. Forecasting played a role in Ford Motors's early success and later demise. Henry Ford saw that the consumer wanted a simpler, less expensive car that was easier to maintain than most manufacturers were offering in the early 1900s. His Model T dominated the industry. However, Ford did not see that consumers would tire of the open Model T design. Ford's failure to forecast consumer desires for other designs nearly resulted in the end of a firm that had monopolized the industry only a few years before.

Seeing trends is the first step towards profiting from those trends. As an example, consider the trend towards greater use of renewable energy. Renewable energy sources include wind power, sun power, tidal power, geothermal power, etc. If energy can be generated and stored using renewable methods, this energy can be used to power electric cars, thus cutting down on gasoline consumption.

Some companies were able to see this trend and take advantage of it. In particular, the use of solar cells has grown dramatically in recent years. While Apple Corporation has received a great deal of publicity for its fantastic successes in mobile computing, solar cell installations have actually been growing at a comparable rate. The residential use of solar cells in the United States grew 33 percent in Q1 2013 compared to Q1 2012. Markets in Asia are expected to grow more rapidly than in the United States, thus assuring a steady market growth in this segment. Manufacturers that saw this trend developing are now reaping the rewards of their foresight.

Can all events be accurately forecasted? The answer is clearly no. Consider the experiment of tossing a coin. Assuming that it is a fair coin and the act of tossing does not introduce bias, the best you can say is that the probability of getting heads is 50 percent on any single toss. No one has been able to consistently top the 50 percent prediction rate for such an experiment over a long period of time. Many real phenomena are accurately described by a type of coin-flipping experiment. Games of chance played at casinos are random. By tipping the probabilities in its favor, the house is always guaranteed to win over the long term. There is evidence that daily prices of stocks follow a purely random process, much like a coin-flipping experiment. Studies have shown that professional money managers rarely outperform stock portfolios generated purely at random.

In production and operations management, we are primarily interested in forecasting product demand. Because demand is likely to be random in most circumstances, can forecasting methods provide any value? In most cases, the answer is yes. Although some portions of the demand process may be unpredictable, other portions may be predictable. Trends, cycles, and seasonal variation may be present, all of which give us an advantage over trying to predict the outcome of a coin toss. In this chapter we consider methods for predicting future values of a series based on past observations.

2.1 THE TIME HORIZON IN FORECASTING

We may classify forecasting problems along several dimensions. One is the time horizon. Figure 2–1 is a schematic showing the three time horizons associated with forecasting and typical forecasting problems encountered in operations planning associated with each. Short-term forecasting is crucial for day-to-day planning. Short-term forecasts, typically measured in days or weeks, are required for inventory management, production plans that may be derived from a materials requirements planning system (to be discussed in detail in Chapter 8), and resource requirements planning. Shift scheduling may require forecasts of workers' availabilities and preferences.

The intermediate term is measured in weeks or months. Sales patterns for product families, requirements and availabilities of workers, and resource requirements are typical intermediate-term forecasting problems encountered in operations management.

FIGURE 2–1
Forecast horizons in operation planning

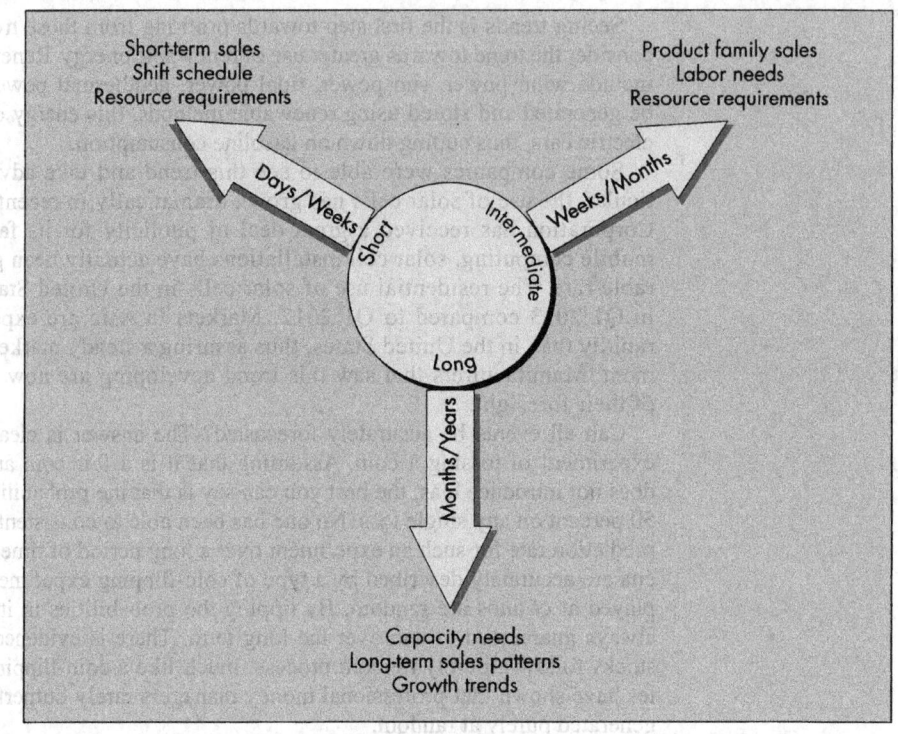

Long-term production and manufacturing decisions, discussed in Chapter 1, are part of the overall firm's manufacturing strategy. One example is long-term planning of capacity needs. When demands are expected to increase, the firm must plan for the construction of new facilities and/or the retrofitting of existing facilities with new technologies. Capacity planning decisions may require downsizing in some circumstances. For example, General Motors Corporation historically commanded about 45 percent of the domestic car market. However, in the 1990s that percentage dropped to 35 percent. As a result, GM was forced to significantly curtail its manufacturing operations to remain profitable.

2.2 CHARACTERISTICS OF FORECASTS

1. *They are usually wrong.* As strange as it may sound, this is probably the most ignored and most significant property of almost all forecasting methods. Forecasts, once determined, are often treated as known information. Resource requirements and production schedules may require modifications if the forecast of demand proves to be inaccurate. The planning system should be sufficiently robust to be able to react to unanticipated forecast errors.

2. *A good forecast* is more than a single number. Given that forecasts are generally wrong, a good forecast also includes some measure of the anticipated forecast error. This could be in the form of a range, or an error measure such as the variance of the distribution of the forecast error.

3. *Aggregate forecasts are more accurate.* Recall from statistics that the variance of the average of a collection of independent identically distributed random variables is lower than the variance of each of the random variables; that is, the variance of the sample mean is smaller than the population variance. This same phenomenon is true in forecasting as well. On a percentage basis, the error made in forecasting sales for an entire product line is generally less than the error made in forecasting sales for an individual item. This phenomenon, known as risk pooling, will be discussed in the inventory control context in Chapter 5.

4. *The longer the forecast horizon, the less accurate the forecast will be.* This property is quite intuitive. One can predict tomorrow's value of the Dow Jones Industrial Average more accurately than next year's value.

5. *Forecasts should not be used to the exclusion of known information.* A particular technique may result in reasonably accurate forecasts in most circumstances. However, there may be information available concerning the future demand that is not presented in the past history of the series. For example, the company may be planning a special promotional sale for a particular item so that the demand will probably be higher than normal. This information must be manually factored into the forecast.

2.3 SUBJECTIVE FORECASTING METHODS

We classify forecasting methods as either subjective or objective. A subjective forecasting method is based on human judgment. There are several techniques for soliciting opinions for forecasting purposes:

1. *Sales force composites.* In forecasting product demand, a good source of subjective information is the company sales force. The sales force has direct contact with consumers and is therefore in a good position to see changes in their preferences. To develop a sales force composite forecast, members of the sales force submit sales estimates of the products they will sell in the coming year. These estimates might be individual numbers or several numbers, such as pessimistic, most likely, and optimistic estimates. Sales managers would then be responsible for aggregating individual estimates to arrive at overall forecasts for each geographic region or product group. Sales force composites may be inaccurate when compensation of sales personnel is based on meeting a quota. In that case, there is clearly an incentive for the sales force to lowball its estimates.

2. *Customer surveys.* Customer surveys can signal future trends and shifting preference patterns. To be effective, however, surveys and sampling plans must be carefully designed to guarantee that the resulting data are statistically unbiased and representative of the customer base. Poorly designed questionnaires or an invalid sampling scheme may result in the wrong conclusions.

3. *Jury of executive opinion.* When there is no past history, as with new products, expert opinion may be the only source of information for preparing forecasts. The approach here is to systematically combine the opinions of experts to derive a forecast. For new product planning, opinions of personnel in the functional areas of marketing, finance, and operations should be solicited. Combining individual forecasts may be done in several ways. One is to have the individual responsible for preparing the forecast interview the executives directly and develop a forecast from the results of the interviews. Another is to require the executives to meet as a group and come to a consensus.

4. *The Delphi method.* The Delphi method, like the jury of executive opinion method, is based on soliciting the opinions of experts. The difference lies in the manner in which individual opinions are combined. (The method is named for the Delphic oracle of ancient Greece, who purportedly had the power to predict the future.) The Delphi method attempts to eliminate some of the inherent shortcomings of group dynamics, in which the personalities of some group members overshadow those of other members. The method requires a group of experts to express their opinions, preferably by individual sample survey. The opinions are then compiled and a summary of the results is returned to the experts, with special attention to those opinions that are significantly different from the group averages. The experts are asked if they wish to reconsider their original opinions in light of the group response. The process is repeated until (ideally) an overall group consensus is reached.

As with any particular technique, the Delphi method has advantages and disadvantages. Its primary advantage is that it provides a means of assessing individual opinion without the usual concerns of personal interactions. On the negative side, the method is highly sensitive to the care in the formulation of the questionnaire. Because discussions are intentionally excluded from the process, the experts have no mechanism for resolving ambiguous questions. Furthermore, it is not necessarily true that a group consensus will ever be reached. An interesting case study of a successful application of the Delphi method can be found in Helmer and Rescher (1959).

2.4 OBJECTIVE FORECASTING METHODS

Objective forecasting methods are those in which the forecast is derived from an analysis of data. A **time series** method is one that uses only past values of the phenomenon we are predicting. **Causal models** are ones that use data from sources other than the series being predicted; that is, there may be other variables with values that are *linked* in some way to what is being forecasted. We discuss these first.

Causal Models

Let Y represent the phenomenon we wish to forecast and $X_1, X_2, \ldots, X_n$ be n variables that we believe to be related to Y. Then a causal model is one in which the forecast for Y is some function of these variables, say,

$$Y = f(X_1, X_2, \ldots, X_n).$$

Econometric models are special causal models in which the relationship between Y and $(X_1, X_2, \ldots, X_n)$ is linear. That is,

$$Y = \alpha_0 + \alpha_1 X_1 + \alpha_2 X_2 + \cdots + \alpha_n X_n$$

for some constants $(\alpha_1, \ldots, \alpha_n)$. The method of least squares is most commonly used to find estimators for the constants. (We discuss the method in Appendix 2–B for the case of one independent variable.)

Let us consider a simple example of a causal forecasting model. A realtor is trying to estimate his income for the succeeding year. In the past he has found that his income is close to being proportional to the total number of housing sales in his territory. He also has noticed that there has typically been a close relationship between housing sales and interest rates for home mortgages. He might construct a model of the form

$$Y_t = \alpha_0 + \alpha_1 X_{t-1},$$

where Y_t is the number of sales in year t and X_{t-1} is the interest rate in year $t - 1$. Based on past data he would then determine the least squares estimators for the constants α_0 and α_1. Suppose that the values of these estimators are currently $\alpha_0 = 385.7$ and $\alpha_1 = -1,878$. Hence, the estimated relationship between home sales and mortgage rates is

$$Y_t = 385.7 - 1,878 X_{t-1},$$

where X_{t-1}, the previous year's interest rate, is expressed as a decimal. Then if the current mortgage interest rate is 10 percent, the model would predict that the number of sales the following year in his territory would be $385.7 - 187.8 = 197.9$, or about 198 houses sold.

Causal models of this type are common for predicting economic phenomena such as the gross national product (GNP) and the gross domestic product (GDP). Both MIT and the Wharton School of Business at the University of Pennsylvania have developed large-scale econometric models for making these predictions. Econometric prediction models are typically used by the economics and finance arms of the firm to forecast values of macroeconomic variables such as interest rates and currency exchange rates. Time series methods are more commonly used for operations planning applications.

Time Series Methods

Time series methods are often called naive methods, as they require no information other than the past values of the variable being predicted. *Time series* is just a fancy term for a collection of observations of some economic or physical phenomenon drawn at discrete points in time, usually equally spaced. The idea is that information can be inferred from the pattern of past observations and can be used to forecast future values of the series.

In time series analysis we attempt to isolate the patterns that arise most often. These include the following:

1. *Trend.* Trend refers to the tendency of a time series to exhibit a stable pattern of growth or decline. We distinguish between linear trend (the pattern described by a straight line) and nonlinear trend (the pattern described by a nonlinear function, such as a quadratic or exponential curve). When the pattern of trend is not specified, it is generally understood to be linear.

2. *Seasonality.* A seasonal pattern is one that repeats at fixed intervals. In time series we generally think of the pattern repeating every year, although daily, weekly, and monthly seasonal patterns are common as well. Fashion wear, ice cream, and heating oil exhibit a yearly seasonal pattern. Consumption of electricity exhibits a strong daily seasonal pattern.

3. *Cycles.* Cyclic variation is similar to seasonality, except that the length and the magnitude of the cycle may vary. One associates cycles with long-term economic variations (that is, business cycles) that may be present in addition to seasonal fluctuations.

Snapshot Application

ADVANCED FORECASTING, INC., SERVES THE SEMICONDUCTOR INDUSTRY

Advanced Forecasting, Inc. (AFI), is a Cupertino-based firm that specializes in providing forecasts for semiconductor sales and sales of related industries, such as semiconductor equipment and suppliers. The firm has had a history of accurately predicting the turning points in the sales patterns of semiconductors for more than a decade. Forecasts are determined from quantitative models (such as the ones discussed in this chapter). Although the actual models used are proprietary, forecasts are based on basic economic factors related to the semiconductor industry. According to the firm's founder Dr. Moshe Handelsman, the problem with most forecaster's predictions is that they are based on subjective opinions and qualitative data. AFI uses a mathematical model to derive its forecasts, which are not second guessed. While the firm is only a small player in the semiconductor forecasting arena, their success has been dramatic. They have consistently been able to predict major shifts in the market for semiconductors, which is a fundamental need for management. According to Jean-Philippe Dauvin, vice president and chief economist for SGS-Thomson Microelectronics: "Our top management pays more attention to Advanced Forecasting's predictions than to any other industry source." Accurate forecasts allow management to deal with important strategic issues such as when production capacity should be expanded, what personnel needs will be, and what the demands will be on marketing and sales. The success of AFI demonstrates that quantitative-based forecasting can provide consistently accurate forecasts and, over the long term, are far more reliable than subjective methods.

Source: Advanced Forecasting, Inc., Website, http://www.adv-forecast.com/afi/.

---

4. *Randomness.* A pure random series is one in which there is no recognizable pattern to the data. One can generate patterns purely at random that often appear to have structure. An example of this is the methodology of stock market chartists who impose forms on random patterns of stock market price data. On the other side of the coin, data that appear to be random could have a very definite structure. Truly random data that fluctuate around a fixed mean form what is called a horizontal pattern.

Examples of time series exhibiting some of these patterns are given in Figure 2–2.

Problems for Sections 2.1–2.4

1. Name the four components of time series (i.e., the four distinct patterns exhibited by time series).
2. What distinguishes seasonality from cycles in time series analysis?
3. What is the appropriate type of forecasting method to use in each of the following scenarios:

    a. Holiday Inn, Inc., is attempting to predict the demand next year for motel rooms, based on a history of demand observations.

    b. Standard Brands has developed a new type of outdoor paint. The company wishes to forecast sales based on new housing starts.

    c. IBM is trying to ascertain the cost of a stock-out of a critical tape drive component. They do so by sample survey of managers at various national spare parts centers. The surveys are sent back to the managers for a reassessment, and the process is repeated until a consensus is reached.

FIGURE 2–2
Time series patterns

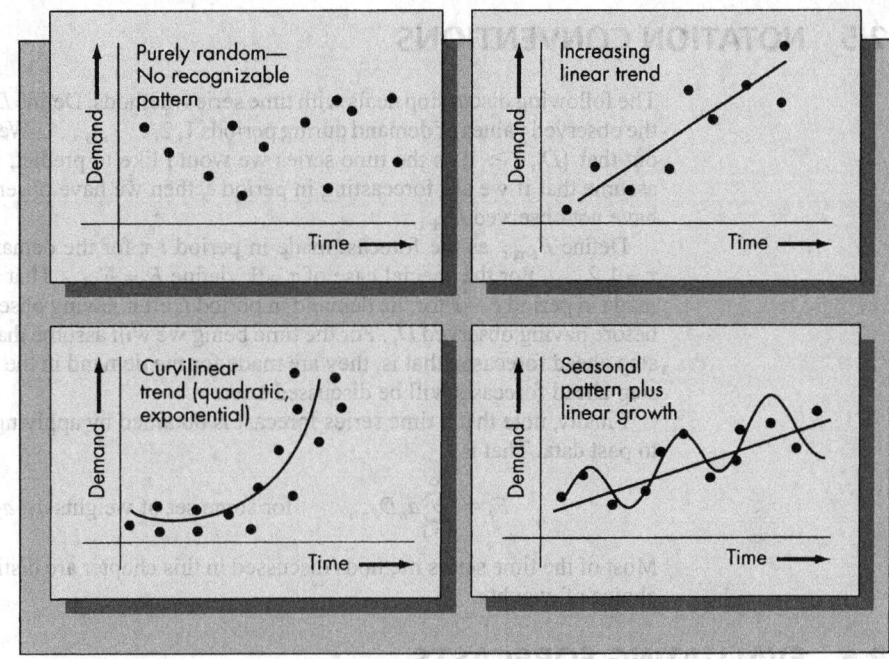

4. Discuss the role of forecasting for the following functions of the firm:
    a. Marketing
    b. Accounting
    c. Finance
    d. Production
5. Distinguish between the following types of forecasts:
    a. Aggregate versus single item.
    b. Short-term versus long-term.
    c. Causal versus naive.
6. What is the advantage of the Delphi method over the jury of executive opinion method? What do these methods have in common?
7. Consider the problem of choosing an appropriate college to attend when you were a high school senior. What forecasting concerns did you have when you made that decision? In particular, list the short-term, intermediate-term, and long-term forecasts you might have considered in making your final decision. What objective sources of data might you have used to provide you with better forecasts in each case?
8. Discuss the following quotation from an inventory control manager: "It's not my fault we ran out of those parts. The demand forecast was wrong."
9. Discuss the following statement: "Economists are predicting that interest rates will continue to be under 10 percent for at least 15 years."

2.5 NOTATION CONVENTIONS

The following discussion deals with time series methods. Define $D_1, D_2, \ldots, D_t, \ldots$ as the observed values of demand during periods $1, 2, \ldots, t, \ldots$. We will assume throughout that $\{D_t, t \geq 1\}$ is the time series we would like to predict. Furthermore, we will assume that if we are forecasting in period t, then we have observed $D_t, D_{t-1}, \ldots$ but have not observed D_{t+1}.

Define $F_{t-\tau, t}$ as the forecast made in period $t-\tau$ for the demand in period t, where $\tau = 1, 2, \ldots$. For the special case of $\tau = 1$, define $F_t = F_{t-1, t}$. That is, F_t is the forecast made in period $t-1$ for the demand in period t, after having observed $D_{t-1}, D_{t-2} \ldots$, but before having observed D_t. For the time being we will assume that all forecasts are one step ahead forecasts; that is, they are made for the demand in the next period. Multiple step ahead forecasts will be discussed later.

Finally, note that a time series forecast is obtained by applying some set of weights to past data. That is,

$$F_t = \sum_{n=1}^{\infty} a_n D_{t-n} \quad \text{for some set of weights } a_1, a_2, \ldots.$$

Most of the time series methods discussed in this chapter are distinguished only by the choice of weights.

2.6 EVALUATING FORECASTS

Define the forecast error in period t, e_t, as the difference between the forecast value for that period and the actual demand for that period. For multiple-step-ahead forecasts,

$$e_t = F_{t-\tau, t} - D_t,$$

and for one-step-ahead forecasts,

$$e_t = F_t - D_t.$$

Let $e_1, e_2, \ldots, e_n$ be the forecast errors observed over n periods. Two common measures of forecast accuracy during these n periods are the mean absolute deviation (MAD) and the mean squared error (MSE), given by the following formulas:

$$\text{MAD} = (1/n) \sum_{i=1}^{n} |e_i|$$

$$\text{MSE} = (1/n) \sum_{i=1}^{n} e_i^2$$

Note that the MSE is similar to the variance of a random sample. The MAD is often the preferred method of measuring the forecast error because it does not require squaring. Furthermore, when forecast errors are normally distributed, as is generally assumed, an estimate of the standard deviation of the forecast error, σ_e, is given by 1.25 times the MAD.

Although the MAD and the MSE are the two most common measures of forecast accuracy, other measures are used as well. One that is not dependent on the magnitude of the values of demand is known as the mean absolute percentage error (MAPE) and is given by the formula

$$\text{MAPE} = \left[(1/n) \sum_{i=1}^{n} |e_i / D_i| \right] \times 100.$$

Example 2.1

Artel, a manufacturer of static random access memories (SRAMs), has production plants in Austin, Texas, and Sacramento, California. The managers of these plants are asked to forecast production yields (measured in percent) one week ahead for their plants. Based on six weekly forecasts, the firm's management wishes to determine which manager is more successful at predicting his plant's yields. The results of their predictions are given in the following spreadsheet.

Week	P1	O1	|E1|	E1^2	|E1/O1|	P2	O2	|E2|	E2^2	|E2/O2|
1	92	88	4	16	0.04545	96	91	5	25	0.05495
2	87	88	1	1	0.01136	89	89	0	0	0
3	95	97	2	4	0.02062	92	90	2	4	0.02222
4	90	83	7	49	0.08434	93	90	3	9	0.03333
5	88	91	3	9	0.03297	90	86	4	16	0.04651
6	93	93	0	0	0	85	89	4	16	0.04494

Cell Formulas

Cell	Formula	Copied to
D2	=ABS(B2-C2)	D3:D7
E2	=ABS(D2/C2)	E3:E7

(Similar formulas and copies for cells H2 and I2)

B10	=AVERAGE(D2:D7)
B11	=AVERAGE(I2:I7)
B13	=AVERAGE(E2:E7)
B14	=AVERAGE(J2:J7)
B16	=AVERAGE(F2:F7)
B17	=AVERAGE(K2:K7)

Interpret P1 as the forecast made by the manager of plant 1 at the beginning of each week, O1 as the yield observed at the end of each week in plant 1, and E1 as the difference between the predicted and the observed yields. The same definitions apply to plant 2.

Let us compare the performance of these managers using the three measures MAD, MSE, and MAPE as defined previously. To compute the MAD we simply average the observed absolute errors:

$$MAD_1 = 17/6 = 2.83$$
$$MAD_2 = 18/6 = 3.00.$$

Based on the MADs, the first manager has a slight edge. To compute the MSE in each case, square the observed errors and average the results to obtain

$$MSE_1 = 79/6 = 13.17$$
$$MSE_2 = 70/6 = 11.67.$$

The second manager's forecasts have a lower MSE than the first, even though the MADs go the other way. Why the switch? The reason that the first manager now looks worse is that the MSE is more sensitive to one large error than is the MAD. Notice that the largest observed error of 7 was incurred by manager 1.

Let us now compare their performances based on the MAPE. To compute the MAPE we average the ratios of the errors and the observed yields:

$$MAPE_1 = .0325$$
$$MAPE_2 = .0336.$$

Using the MAD or the MAPE, the first manager has a very slight edge, but using the MSE, the second manager looks better. The forecasting abilities of the two managers would seem to be very similar. Who is declared the "winner" depends on which method of evaluation management chooses.

FIGURE 2–3
Forecast errors over time

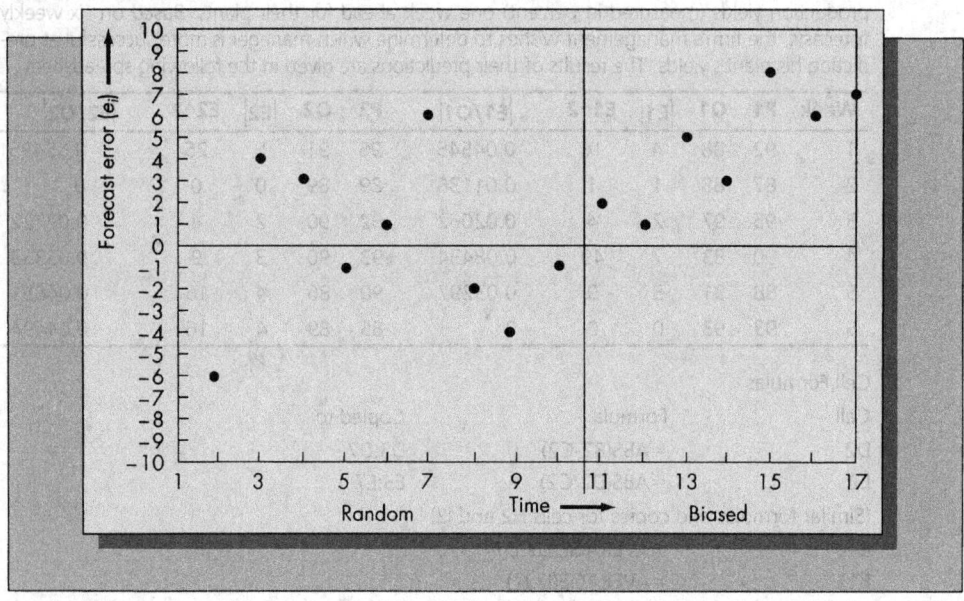

A desirable property of forecasts is that they should be unbiased. Mathematically, that means that $E(e_i) = 0$. One way of tracking a forecast method is to graph the values of the forecast error e_i over time. If the method is unbiased, forecast errors should fluctuate randomly above and below zero. An example is presented in Figure 2–3.

An alternative to a graphical method is to compute the cumulative sum of the forecast errors, Σe_i. If the value of this sum deviates too far from zero (either above or below), it is an indication that the forecasting method is biased. At the end of this chapter we discuss a smoothing technique that also can be used to signal a bias in the forecasts. Statistical control charts also are used to identify unusually large values of the forecast error. (Statistical control charts are discussed in Chapter 12.)

Problems for Section 2.6

10. In *Dave Pelz's Short Game Bible*, the author attempts to characterize the skill of a golfer from a specific distance in terms of the ratio of the error in the shot and the intended shot distance. For example, a five iron that is hit 175 yards and is 20 yards off target would have an accuracy rating of $20/175 = .114$, while a sand wedge hit 60 yards that is 10 yards off target would have an accuracy rating of $10/60 = .1667$ (the lower the rating, the better). To what evaluation method discussed in this section is this most similar? Why does this evaluation method make more sense in golf than absolute or squared errors?

Snapshot Application

PFIZER BETS BIG ON FORECASTS OF DRUG SALES

One of Pfizer's most successful products is Lipitor. Lipitor, the first statin for reducing blood cholesterol, generated annual gross sales in excess of $12 billion. Not only was Lipitor the best selling statin, it was the most profitable pharmaceutical ever sold until its patent expired in November 2011. At that point, generic versions of the drug that cost less entered the market, and Lipitor's sales dropped dramatically. Pfizer was forced to lower prices to compete with generics and saw their profit margin sink considerably. To counteract this loss of a valuable revenue stream, a common strategy for drug companies is something called "evergreening." Evergreening means that the company plans on bringing a new and more effective drug to the market to counter the anticipated losses when the patent runs out. In Pfizer's case, this drug was torcetrapib. Torcetrapib not only decreased LDL (bad cholesterol), but increased the levels of HDL (good cholesterol). In order to make the transition as smooth as possible, Pfizer would have to have sufficient production capacity on line in 2011. Pfizer began production of torcetrapib as early as 2005 at a new $90 million plant in Loughberg, Ireland. This was reportedly a state of the art facility.

Unfortunately, things did not go as planned for Pfizer. After investing $800 million in the development of torcetrapib, Pfizer informed the United States Food and Drug Administration that it was suspending Phase 3 clinical trials. It was at that point that Pfizer discovered serious side effects with the drug. They had to make the painful decision to discontinue their efforts after investing nearly a billion dollars. To Pfizer's credit, it is rare that a drug must be pulled from the market as late as Phase 3. Still, Pfizer's failure to accurately forecast the outcomes of the trials resulted in serious losses.

Source: Bala et al. (2011). "Competition, Capacity, and 'Evergreening'". Unpublished manuscript. Indian School of Business.

11. A forecasting method used to predict can opener sales applies the following set of weights to the last five periods of data: .1, .1, .2, .2, .4 (with .4 being applied to the most recent observation). Observed values of can opener sales are

Period:	1	2	3	4	5	6	7	8
Observation:	18	22	26	33	14	28	30	52

Determine the following:

a. The one-step-ahead forecast for period 9.

b. The one-step-ahead forecast that was made for period 6.

12. A simple forecasting method for weekly sales of flash drives used by a local computer dealer is to form the average of the two most recent sales figures. Suppose sales for the drives for the past 12 weeks were

Week:	1	2	3	4	5	6	7	8	9	10	11	12
Sales:	86	75	72	83	132	65	110	90	67	92	98	73

a. Determine the one-step-ahead forecasts made for periods 3 through 12 using this method.

b. Determine the forecast errors for these periods.

c. Compute the MAD, the MSE, and the MAPE based on the forecast errors computed in part (b).

13. Two forecasting methods have been used to evaluate the same economic time series. The results are

Forecast from Method 1	Forecast from Method 2	Realized Value of the Series
223	210	256
289	320	340
430	390	375
134	112	110
190	150	225
550	490	525

Compare the effectiveness of these methods by computing the MSE, the MAD, and the MAPE. Do each of the measures of forecasting accuracy indicate that the same forecasting technique is best? If not, why?

14. What does the term *biased* mean in reference to a particular forecasting technique?

15. What is the estimate of the standard deviation of forecast error obtained from the data in Problem 12?

2.7 METHODS FOR FORECASTING STATIONARY SERIES

In this section we will discuss two popular techniques, moving averages and exponential smoothing, for forecasting stationary time series. A stationary time series is one in which each observation can be represented by a constant plus a random fluctuation. In symbols,

$$D_t = \mu + \epsilon_t,$$

where μ is an unknown constant corresponding to the mean of the series and ϵ_t is a random error with mean zero and variance σ^2.

The methods we consider in this section are more precisely known as single or simple exponential smoothing and single or simple moving averages. In addition, single moving averages also include weighted moving averages, which we do not discuss. For convenience, we will not use the modifiers single and simple in what follows. The meaning of the terms will be clear from the context.

Moving Averages

A simple but popular forecasting method is the method of moving averages. A moving average of order N is simply the arithmetic average of the most recent N observations. For the time being we restrict attention to one-step-ahead forecasts. Then F_t, the forecast made in period $t - 1$ for period t, is given by

$$F_t = (1/N) \sum_{i=t-N}^{t-1} D_i = (1/N)(D_{t-1} + D_{t-2} + \cdots + D_{t-N}).$$

In words, this says that the mean of the N most recent observations is used as the forecast for the next period. We will use the notation MA(N) for N-period moving averages.

Example 2.2

Quarterly data for the failures of certain aircraft engines at a local military base during the last two years are 200, 250, 175, 186, 225, 285, 305, 190. Both three-quarter and six-quarter moving averages are used to forecast the numbers of engine failures. Determine the one-step-ahead

2.7 Methods for Forecasting Stationary Series

forecasts for periods 4 through 8 using three-period moving averages, and the one-step-ahead forecasts for periods 7 and 8 using six-period moving averages.

Solution

The three-period moving-average forecast for period 4 is obtained by averaging the first three data points.

$$F_4 = (1/3)(200 + 250 + 175) = 208.$$

The three-period moving-average forecast for period 5 is

$$F_5 = (1/3)(250 + 175 + 186) = 204.$$

The six-period moving-average forecast for period 7 is

$$F_7 = (1/6)(200 + 250 + 175 + 186 + 225 + 285) = 220.$$

Other forecasts are computed in a similar fashion. Arranging the forecasts and the associated forecast errors in a spreadsheet, we obtain

Quarter	Engine Failures	MA(3)	Error	MA(6)	Error
1	200				
2	250				
3	175				
4	186	208.33	22.33		
5	225	203.67	−21.33		
6	285	195.33	−89.67		
7	305	232.00	−73.00	220.17	−84.83
8	190	271.67	81.67	237.67	47.67

Cell Formulas

Cell	Formula	Copied to
C4	=1/3*SUM(B2:B4)	C5:C8
E7	=1/6*SUM(B2:B7)	E8
D5	=C5-B5	D6:D8
F8	=E8-B8	F9

An interesting question is, how does one obtain multiple-step-ahead forecasts? For example, suppose in Example 2.2 that we are interested in using MA(3) in period 3 to forecast for period 6. Because the moving-average method is based on the assumption that the demand series is stationary, the forecast made in period 3 for *any* future period will be the same. That is, the multiple-step-ahead and the one-step-ahead forecasts are identical (although the one-step-ahead forecast will generally be more accurate). Hence, the MA(3) forecast made in period 3 for period 6 is 208. In fact, the MA(3) forecast made in period 3 for any period beyond period 3 is 208 as well.

An apparent disadvantage of the moving-average technique is that one must recompute the average of the last N observations each time a new demand observation becomes available. For large N this could be tedious. However, recalculation of the full N-period average is not necessary every period, since

$$F_{t+1} = (1/N) \sum_{i=t-N+1}^{t} D_i = (1/N)\left[D_t + \sum_{i=t-N}^{t-1} D_i - D_{t-N}\right]$$

$$= F_t + (1/N)[D_t - D_{t-N}]$$

This means that for one-step-ahead forecasting, we need only compute the difference between the most recent demand and the demand N periods old in order to update the forecast. However, we still need to keep track of all N past observations. Why?

Moving Average Lags behind the Trend

Consider a demand process in which there is a definite trend. For example, suppose that the observed demand is 2, 4, 6, 8, 10, 12, 14, 16, 18, 20, 22, 24. Consider the one-step-ahead MA(3) and MA(6) forecasts for this series.

Period	Demand	MA(3)	MA(6)
1	2		
2	4		
3	6		
4	8	4	
5	10	6	
6	12	8	
7	14	10	7
8	16	12	9
9	18	14	11
10	20	16	13
11	22	18	15
12	24	20	17

The demand and the forecasts for the respective periods are pictured in Figure 2–4. Notice that both the MA(3) and the MA(6) forecasts lag behind the trend. Furthermore, MA(6) has a greater lag. This implies that the use of simple moving averages is not an appropriate forecasting method when there is a trend in the series.

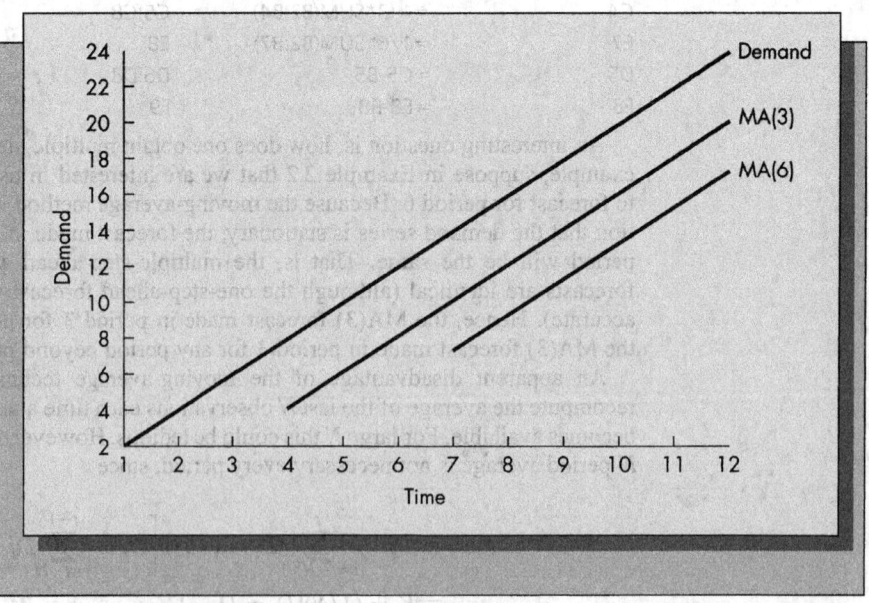

FIGURE 2–4
Moving-average forecasts lag behind a trend

Problems on Moving Averages

Problems 16 through 21 are based on the following data. Observations of the demand for a certain part stocked at a parts supply depot during the calendar year 2013 were

Month	Demand	Month	Demand
January	89	July	223
February	57	August	286
March	144	September	212
April	221	October	275
May	177	November	188
June	280	December	312

16. Determine the one-step-ahead forecasts for the demand for January 2014 using 3-, 6-, and 12-month moving averages.
17. Using a four-month moving average, determine the one-step-ahead forecasts for July through December 2013.
18. Using a four-month moving average, determine the two-step-ahead forecast for July through December 2013. (Hint: The two-step-ahead forecast for July is based on the observed demands in February through May.)
19. Compute the MAD for the forecasts obtained in Problems 17 and 18. Which method gave better results? Based on forecasting theory, which method should have given better results?
20. Compute the one-step-ahead three-month and six-month moving-average forecasts for July through December. What effect does increasing N from 3 to 6 have on the forecasts?
21. What would an MA(1) forecasting method mean? Compare the accuracy of MA(1) and MA(4) forecasts for July through December 2013.

Exponential Smoothing

Another very popular forecasting method for stationary time series is exponential smoothing. The current forecast is the weighted average of the last forecast and the current value of demand. That is,

New forecast = α(Current observation of demand) + $(1 - \alpha)$(Last forecast).

In symbols,

$$F_t = \alpha D_{t-1} + (1 - \alpha)F_{t-1},$$

where $0 < \alpha \leq 1$ is the smoothing constant, which determines the relative weight placed on the current observation of demand. Interpret $(1 - \alpha)$ as the weight placed on past observations of demand. By a simple rearrangement of terms, the exponential smoothing equation for F_t can be written

$$F_t = F_{t-1} - \alpha(F_{t-1} - D_{t-1})$$
$$= F_{t-1} - \alpha e_{t-1}.$$

Written this way, we see that exponential smoothing can be interpreted as follows: the forecast in any period t is the forecast in period $t - 1$ minus some fraction of the observed forecast error in period $t - 1$. Notice that if we forecast high in period $t - 1$, e_{t-1} is positive and the adjustment is to decrease the forecast. Similarly, if we forecast low in period $t - 1$, the error is negative, and the adjustment is to increase the current forecast.

As before, F_t is the one-step-ahead forecast for period t made in period $t - 1$. Notice that since

$$F_{t-1} = \alpha D_{t-2} + (1 - \alpha)F_{t-2},$$

we can substitute above to obtain

$$F_t = \alpha D_{t-1} + \alpha(1 - \alpha)D_{t-2} + (1 - \alpha)^2 F_{t-2}.$$

We can now substitute for F_{t-2} in the same fashion. If we continue in this way, we obtain the infinite expansion for F_t,

$$F_t = \sum_{i=0}^{\infty} \alpha(1 - \alpha)^i D_{t-i-1} = \sum_{i=0}^{\infty} a_i D_{t-i-1},$$

where the weights are $a_0 > a_1 > a_2 > \cdots > a_i = \alpha(1 - \alpha)^i$, and

$$\sum_{i=0}^{\infty} a_i = \sum_{i=0}^{\infty} \alpha(1 - \alpha)^i = \alpha \sum_{i=0}^{\infty} (1 - \alpha)^i = \alpha \times 1/[1 - (1 - \alpha)] = 1.$$

Hence, exponential smoothing applies a declining set of weights to all past data. The weights are graphed as a function of i in Figure 2–5.

In fact, we could fit the continuous exponential curve $g(i) = \alpha \exp(-\alpha i)$ to these weights, which is why the method is called exponential smoothing. The smoothing constant α plays essentially the same role here as the value of N does in moving

FIGURE 2–5
Weights in exponential smoothing

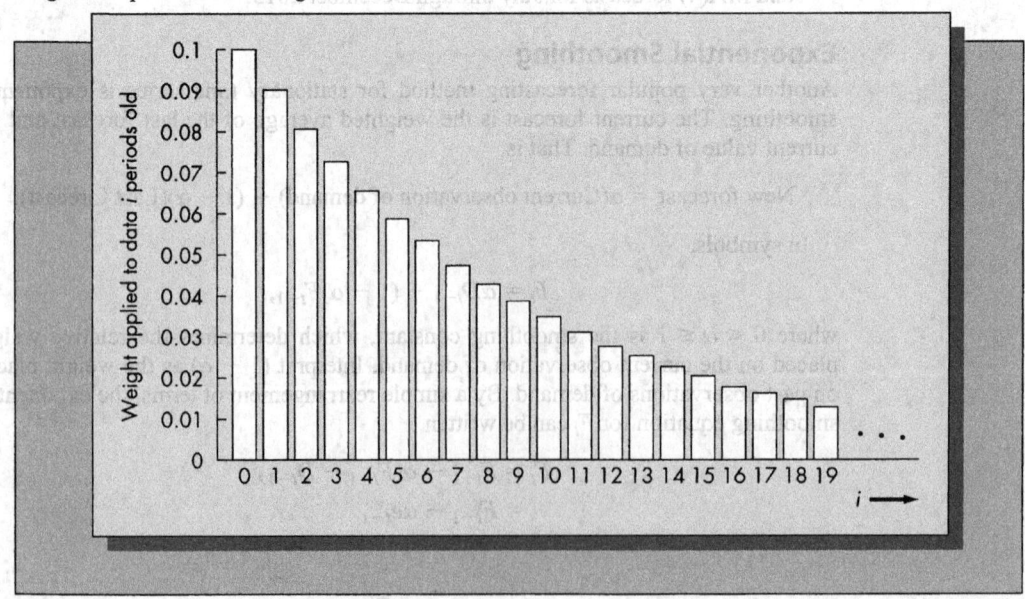

averages. If α is large, more weight is placed on the current observation of demand and less weight on past observations, which results in forecasts that will react quickly to changes in the demand pattern but may have much greater variation from period to period. If α is small, then more weight is placed on past data and the forecasts are more stable.

When using an automatic forecasting technique to predict demand for a production application, stable forecasts (that is, forecasts that do not vary a great deal from period to period) are very desirable. Demand forecasts are used as the starting point for production planning and scheduling. Substantial revision in these forecasts can wreak havoc with employee work schedules, component bills of materials, and external purchase orders. For this reason, a value of α between .1 and .2 is generally recommended for production applications. (See, for example, Brown, 1962.)

Multiple-step-ahead forecasts are handled the same way for simple exponential smoothing as for moving averages; that is, the one-step-ahead and the multiple-step-ahead forecasts are the same.

Example 2.3 Consider Example 2.2 in which moving averages were used to predict aircraft engine failures. The observed numbers of failures over a two-year period were 200, 250, 175, 186, 225, 285, 305, 190. We will now forecast using exponential smoothing. In order to get the method started, let us assume that the forecast for period 1 was 200. Suppose that $\alpha = .1$. The one-step-ahead forecast for period 2 is

$$F_2 = \alpha D_1 + (1 - \alpha)F_1 = (.1)(200) + (.9)(200) = 200.$$

Similarly,

$$F_3 = \alpha D_2 + (1 - \alpha)F_2 = (.1)(250) + (.9)(200) = 205.$$

Other one-step-ahead forecasts are computed in the same fashion. The observed numbers of failures and the one-step-ahead forecasts for each quarter are the following:

Quarter	Failures	Forecast
1	200	200 (by assumption)
2	250	200
3	175	205
4	186	202
5	225	201
6	285	203
7	305	211
8	190	220

Notice the effect of the smoothing constant. Although the original series shows high variance, the forecasts are quite stable. Repeat the calculations with a value of $\alpha = .4$. There will be much greater variation in the forecasts.

Because exponential smoothing requires that at each stage we have the previous forecast, it is not obvious how to get the method started. We could assume that the initial forecast is equal to the initial value of demand, as we did in Example 2.3. However, this approach has a serious drawback. Exponential smoothing puts substantial weight on past observations, so the initial value of demand will have an unreasonably large effect on early forecasts. This problem can be overcome by

FIGURE 2-6
Exponential smoothing for different values of alpha

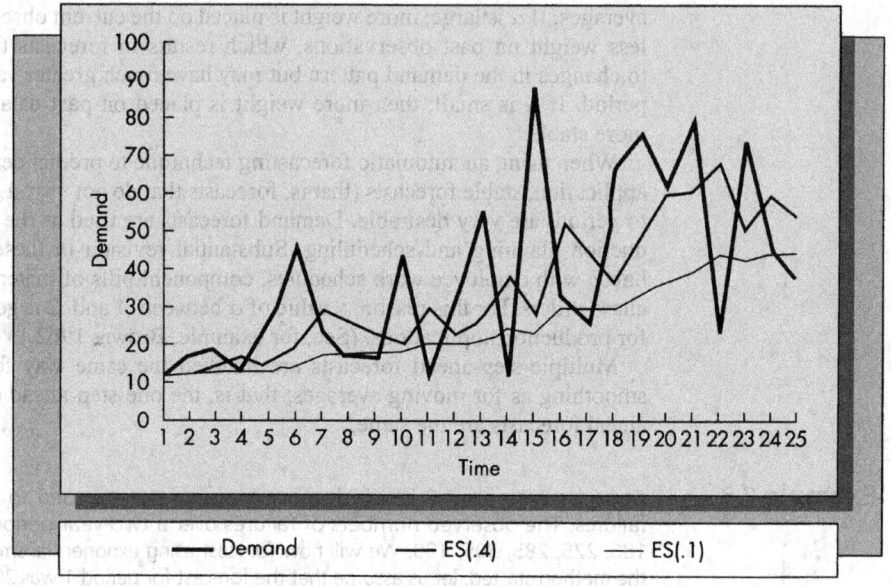

allowing the process to evolve for a reasonable number of periods (say 10 or more) and using the arithmetic average of the demand during those periods as the initial forecast.

In order to appreciate the effect of the smoothing constant, we have graphed a particularly erratic series in Figure 2–6, along with the resulting forecasts using values of $\alpha = .1$ and $\alpha = .4$. Notice that for $\alpha = .1$ the predicted value of demand results in a relatively smooth pattern, whereas for $\alpha = .4$, the predicted value exhibits significantly greater variation. Although smoothing with the larger value of α does a better job of tracking the series, the stability afforded by a smaller smoothing constant is very desirable for planning purposes.

Example 2.3 (continued)

Consider again the problem of forecasting aircraft engine failures. Suppose that we were interested in comparing the performance of MA(3) with the exponential smoothing forecasts obtained earlier (ES(.1)). The first period for which we have a forecast using MA(3) is period 4, so we will make the comparison for periods 4 through 8 only.

Quarter	Failures	Forecast	
1	200	200.00	
2	250	200.00	(by assumption)
3	175	205.00	
4	186	202.00	
5	225	200.40	
6	285	202.86	
7	305	211.07	
8	190	220.47	

Cell Formulas

Cell	Formula	Copied to
C3	=SUM(B$12*B2,(1-B$12)*C2)	C4:C9

The arithmetic average of the absolute errors, the MAD, is 57.6 for the three-period moving average and 49.2 for exponential smoothing. The respective values of the MSE are 4,215.6 and 3,458.4. Based on this comparison only, one might conclude that exponential smoothing is a superior method for this series. This is not necessarily true, however.

In Example 2.3 we compared exponential smoothing with $\alpha = .1$ and a moving average with $N = 3$. How do we know that those parameter settings are consistent? The MA(3) forecasts exhibit much greater variability than the ES(.1) forecasts do, suggesting that $\alpha = .1$ and $N = 3$ are not consistent values of these parameters.

Determining consistent values of α and N can be done in two ways. One is to equate the average age of the data used in making the forecast. A moving-average forecast consists of equal weights of $1/N$ applied to the last N observations. Multiplying the weight placed on each observation by its "age," we get the average age of data for moving averages as

$$\text{Average age} = (1/N)(1 + 2 + 3 + \cdots + N) = (1/N)(N)(N+1)/2$$
$$= (N+1)/2.$$

For exponential smoothing, the weight applied to data i periods old is $\alpha(1-\alpha)^{i-1}$. Assume that we have an infinite history of past observations of demand. Hence, the average age of data in an exponential smoothing forecast is

$$\text{Average age} = \sum_{i=1}^{\infty} i\alpha(1-\alpha)^{i-1} = 1/\alpha.$$

We omit the details of this calculation.

Equating the average age of data for the two methods, we obtain

$$\frac{N+1}{2} = \frac{1}{\alpha},$$

which is equivalent to

$$\alpha = 2/(N+1) \quad \text{or} \quad N = \frac{2-\alpha}{\alpha}.$$

Hence, we see that we would have needed a value of $N = 19$ for $\alpha = .1$ or a value of $\alpha = .5$ for $N = 3$ in order for the methods to be consistent in the sense of average age of data.

In Appendix 2–A of this chapter, we derive the mean and variance of the forecast error for both moving averages and exponential smoothing in terms of the variance of each individual observation, assuming that the underlying demand process is stationary. We show that both methods are unbiased; that is, the expected value of the forecast error is zero. Furthermore, by equating the expressions for the variances of the forecast error, one obtains the same relationship between α and N as by equating the average age of data. This means that if both exponential smoothing and moving averages are used to predict the same stationary demand pattern, forecast errors are normally distributed, and $\alpha = 2/(N+1)$, then both methods will have exactly the same distribution of forecast errors. (However, this does *not* mean that the forecasts obtained by the two methods are the same.)

Multiple-Step-Ahead Forecasts

Thus far, we have talked only about one-step-ahead forecasts. That is, we have assumed that a forecast in period t is for the demand in period $t + 1$. However, there are cases where we are interested in making a forecast for more than one step ahead. For example, a retailer planning for the Christmas season might need to make a forecast for December sales in June in order to have enough time to prepare. Since the underlying model assumed for both moving averages and exponential smoothing is stationary (i.e., not changing in time), the one-step-ahead and multiple-step-ahead forecasts for moving averages and exponential smoothing are the same. That is, a forecast made in June for July sales is the same as a forecast made in June for December sales. (In the case of the retailer, the assumption of stationarity would probably be wrong, since December sales would likely be greater than a typical month's sales. That would suggest that these methods would *not* be appropriate in this case.)

Comparison of Exponential Smoothing and Moving Averages

There are several similarities and several differences between exponential smoothing and moving averages.

Similarities

1. Both methods are derived with the assumption that the underlying demand process is stationary (that is, can be represented by a constant plus a random fluctuation with zero mean). However, we should keep in mind that although the methods are appropriate for stationary time series, we don't necessarily believe that the series are stationary forever. By adjusting the values of N and α we can make the two methods more or less responsive to shifts in the underlying pattern of the data.

2. Both methods depend on the specification of a single parameter. For moving averages the parameter is N, the number of periods in the moving average, and for exponential smoothing the parameter is α, the smoothing constant. Small values of N or large values of α result in forecasts that put greater weight on current data, and large values of N and small values of α put greater weight on past data. Small N and large α may be more responsive to changes in the demand process, but will result in forecast errors with higher variance.

3. Both methods will lag behind a trend if one exists.

4. When $\alpha = 2/(N + 1)$, both methods have the same distribution of forecast error. This means that they should have roughly the same level of accuracy, but it does *not* mean that they will give the same forecasts.

Differences

1. The exponential smoothing forecast is a weighted average of *all* past data points (as long as the smoothing constant is strictly less than 1). The moving-average forecast is a weighted average of only the last N periods of data. This can be an important advantage for moving averages. An outlier (an observation that is not representative of the sample population) is washed out of the moving-average forecast after N periods, but remains forever in the exponential smoothing forecast.

2. In order to use moving averages, one must save all N past data points. In order to use exponential smoothing, one need only save the last forecast. This is the most significant advantage of the exponential smoothing method and one reason for its popularity in practice. In order to appreciate the consequence of this difference, consider a system in which the demand for 300,000 inventory items is forecasted each month using a 12-month moving average. The forecasting module alone requires saving $300,000 \times 12 = 3,600,000$ pieces of information. If exponential smoothing were used, only 300,000 pieces of information need to be saved. This issue is less important today than it has been, as the cost of information storage has decreased enormously in recent years. However, it is still easier to manage a system that requires less data. It is primarily for this reason that exponential smoothing appears to be more popular than moving averages for production-planning applications.

Problems for Section 2.7

22. Handy, Inc., produces a solar-powered electronic calculator that has experienced the following monthly sales history for the first four months of the year, in thousands of units:

January	23.3	March	30.3
February	72.3	April	15.5

    a. If the forecast for January was 25, determine the one-step-ahead forecasts for February through May using exponential smoothing with a smoothing constant of $\alpha = .15$.

    b. Repeat the calculation in part (a) for a value of $\alpha = .40$. What difference in the forecasts do you observe?

    c. Compute the MSEs for the forecasts you obtained in parts (a) and (b) for February through April. Which value of α gave more accurate forecasts, based on the MSE?

23. Compare and contrast exponential smoothing when α is small (near zero) and when α is large (near 1).

24. Observed weekly sales of ball peen hammers at the town hardware store over an eight-week period have been 14, 9, 30, 22, 34, 12, 19, 23.

    a. Suppose that three-week moving averages are used to forecast sales. Determine the one-step-ahead forecasts for weeks 4 through 8.

    b. Suppose that exponential smoothing is used with a smoothing constant of $\alpha = .15$. Find the exponential smoothing forecasts for weeks 4 through 8. [To get the method started, use the same forecast for week 4 as you used in part (a).]

    c. Based on the MAD, which method did better?

    d. What is the exponential smoothing forecast made at the end of week 6 for the sales in week 12?

25. Determine the following:

    a. The value of α consistent with $N = 6$ in moving averages.

    b. The value of N consistent with $\alpha = .05$.

    c. The value of α that results in a variance of forecast error, σ_e^2, 10 percent higher than the variance of each observation, σ^2 (refer to the formulas derived in Appendix 2–A).

26. Referring to the data in Problem 22, what is the exponential smoothing forecast made at the end of March for the sales in July? Assume $\alpha = .15$.

27. For the data for Problems 16 through 21, use the arithmetic average of the first six months of data as a baseline to initialize the exponential smoothing.

    a. Determine the one-step-ahead exponential smoothing forecasts for August through December, assuming $\alpha = .20$.

    b. Compare the accuracy of the forecasts obtained in part (a) with the one-step-ahead six-month moving-average forecasts determined in Problem 20.

    c. Comment on the reasons for the result you obtained in part (b).

Snapshot Application

SPORT OBERMEYER SLASHES COSTS WITH IMPROVED FORECASTING[1]

Sport Obermeyer is a leading supplier in the U.S. fashion ski apparel market. The firm, was founded in 1950 by engineer/ski instructor Klaus Obermeyer. Virtually all the firm's offerings are redesigned annually to incorporate changes in style, fabrics, and colors. For more than 50 years, the firm was able to successfully meet demands by producing during the summer months after receiving firm orders from customers.

During the 1990s, things changed and problems developed. First, volumes increased. There was insufficient capacity among suppliers to produce the required volume in the summer. Second, the firm developed a complex global supply chain strategy (see Section 6.10) to reduce costs. A parka sold in the United States might be sewn in China from fabrics and parts from Japan, South Korea, and Germany. Together these changes lengthened the production lead time, thus requiring the firm to commit to production before orders were placed by customers.

The firm undertook several "quick response" initiatives to reduce lead times. These included encouraging some customers to place orders earlier, locating raw materials near the Far East production facility, and instituting an air freight system to expedite delivery from the Far East to its Denver distribution center. Even with these changes in place, the problem of stockouts and markdowns due to oversupply were not solved. The company still had to commit about half the production based on forecasts. In the fashion industry, there is often no statistical history on which to base forecasts, and forecast errors can be huge. Products that outsell original forecasts by a factor of 2 or undersell original forecasts by a factor of 10 are common.

Sport Obermeyer needed some help with forecasting to avoid expensive miscalculations. The customary procedure was to base the forecasts on a consensus of members of the buying committee. The problem with consensus forecasting is that the dominant personalities in a group carry more weight. A forecast obtained in this way might represent only the opinion of one person. To overcome this problem, the research team (Fisher et al., 1994) recommended that members of the committee supply *individual* forecasts.

The dispersion among individual forecasts turned out to be a reliable indicator of forecast accuracy. When committee members' forecasts were close, forecasts were more accurate. This provided a mechanism for signaling the products whose sales were likely to be poorly forecast. This did not solve the problem of poorly forecast items, but it allowed the firm to commit first to production of items whose forecasts were likely to be accurate. By the time production had to begin on the problem items, information on early sales patterns would be available.

The team noticed that retailers were remarkably similar. That meant that even if only the first 20 percent of orders for a product were in, that information could dramatically improve forecasts. Production plans for these "trouble" items could now be committed with greater confidence. In this way, the firm could separate products into two categories: reactive and nonreactive. The nonreactive items are those for which the forecast is likely to be accurate. These are produced early in the season. The reactive items are those whose forecasts are updated later in the season from early sales figures. The firm's experience was that stockout and markdown costs were reduced from 10.2 percent of sales to 1.8 percent of sales on items that could be produced reactively. Sport Obermeyer was able to produce 30 percent of its season's volume reactively and experienced a cost reduction of about 5 percent of sales.

What are the lessons here? One is that even in cases where there is no statistical history, statistical methodology can be successfully applied to improve forecasting accuracy. Another is not to assume that things should be done a certain way. Sport Obermeyer assumed that consensus forecasting was the best approach. In fact, by requiring the buying committee to reach a consensus, valuable information was being ignored. The *differences* among individual forecasts proved to be important.

---

[1]This application is based on the work of a team from the Wharton School and the Harvard Business School. The results are reported in Fisher et al. (1994).

2.8 TREND-BASED METHODS

Both exponential smoothing and moving-average forecasts will lag behind a trend if one exists. We will consider two forecasting methods that specifically account for a trend in the data: regression analysis and Holt's method. Regression analysis is a method that fits a straight line to a set of data. Holt's method is a type of double exponential smoothing that allows for simultaneous smoothing on the series and on the trend.

Regression Analysis

Let $(x_1, y_1), (x_2, y_2), \ldots, (x_n, y_n)$ be n paired data points for the two variables X and Y. Assume that y_i is the observed value of Y when x_i is the observed value of X. Refer to Y as the dependent variable and X as the independent variable. We believe that a relationship exists between X and Y that can be represented by the straight line

$$\hat{Y} = a + bX.$$

Interpret $\hat{Y}$ as the predicted value of Y. The goal is to find the values of a and b so that the line $\hat{Y} = a + bX$ gives the best fit of the data. The values of a and b are chosen so that the sum of the squared distances between the regression line and the data points is minimized (see Figure 2–7). In Appendix 2–B we derive the optimal values of a and b in terms of the given data.

When applying regression analysis to the forecasting problem, the independent variable often corresponds to time and the dependent variable to the series to be forecast. Assume that $D_1, D_2, \ldots, D_n$ are the values of the demand at times $1, 2, \ldots, n$. Then it is shown in Appendix 2–B that the optimal values of a and b are given by

$$b = \frac{S_{xy}}{S_{xx}}$$

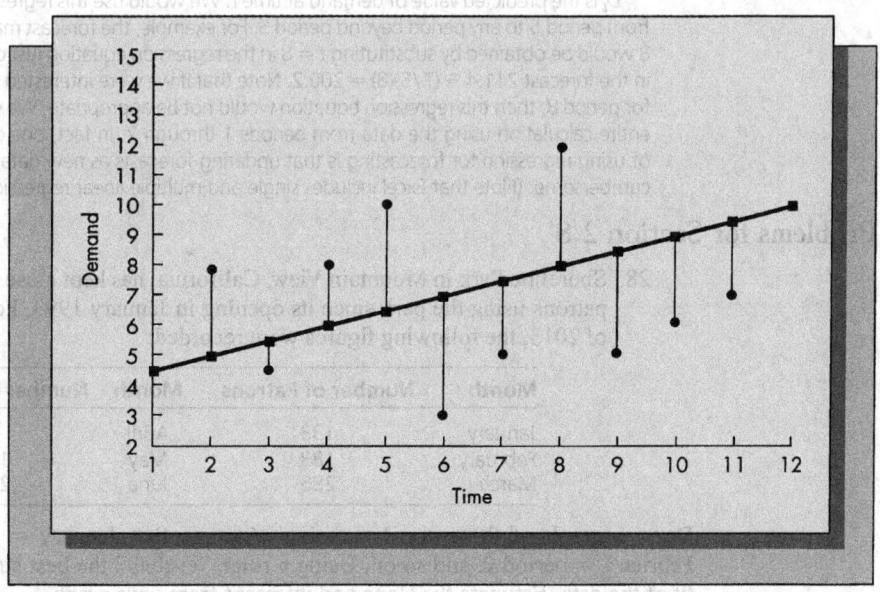

FIGURE 2–7
An example of a regression line

and
$$a = \bar{D} - b(n+1)/2,$$
where
$$S_{xy} = n\sum_{i=1}^{n} iD_i - \frac{n(n+1)}{2}\sum_{i=1}^{n} D_i,$$
$$S_{xx} = \frac{n^2(n+1)(2n+1)}{6} - \frac{n^2(n+1)^2}{4},$$

and $\bar{D}$ is the arithmetic average of the observed demands during periods $1, 2, \ldots, n$.

Example 2.4   We will apply regression analysis to the problem, treated in Examples 2.2 and 2.3, of predicting aircraft engine failures. Recall that the demand for aircraft engines during the last eight quarters was 200, 250, 175, 186, 225, 285, 305, 190. Suppose that we use the first five periods as a baseline in order to estimate our regression parameters. Then

$$S_{xy} = 5[200 + (250)(2) + (175)(3) + (186)(4) + (225)(5)]$$
$$- [(5)(6)/2][200 + 250 + 175 + 186 + 225]$$
$$= -70.$$

$$S_{xx} = (25)(6)(11)/6 - (25)(36)/4 = 50.$$

Then
$$b = S_{xy}/S_{xx} = -70/50 = -7/5,$$
$$a = 207.2 - (-7/5)(3) = 211.4.$$

It follows that the regression equation based on five periods of data is
$$\hat{D}_t = 211.4 - (7/5)t.$$

$\hat{D}_t$ is the predicted value of demand at time t. We would use this regression equation to forecast from period 5 to any period beyond period 5. For example, the forecast made in period 5 for period 8 would be obtained by substituting $t = 8$ in the regression equation just given, which would result in the forecast $211.4 - (7/5)(8) = 200.2$. Note that if we were interested in forecasting in period 7 for period 8, then this regression equation would not be appropriate. We would have to repeat the entire calculation using the data from periods 1 through 7. In fact, one of the serious drawbacks of using regression for forecasting is that updating forecasts as new data become available is very cumbersome. (Note that Excel includes single and multiple linear regression capabilities.)

Problems for Section 2.8

28. Shoreline Park in Mountain View, California, has kept close tabs on the number of patrons using the park since its opening in January 1993. For the first six months of 2013, the following figures were recorded:

Month	Number of Patrons	Month	Number of Patrons
January	133	April	640
February	183	May	1,876
March	285	June	2,550

   a. Draw a graph of these six data points. Assume that January = period 1, February = period 2, and so on. Using a ruler, "eyeball" the best straight-line fit of the data. Estimate the slope and intercept from your graph.

b. Compute the exact values of the intercept a and the slope b from the regression equations.
c. What are the forecasts obtained for July through December 2013 from the regression equation determined in part (b)?
d. Comment on the results you obtained in part (c). Specifically, how confident would you be about the accuracy of the forecasts that you obtained?

29. The Mountain View Department of Parks and Recreation must project the total use of Shoreline Park for calendar year 2014.
a. Determine the forecast for the total number of people using the park in 2014 based on the regression equation.
b. Determine the forecast for the same quantity using a six-month moving average.
c. Draw a graph of the most likely shape of the curve describing the park's usage by month during the calendar year, and predict the same quantity using your graph. Is your prediction closer to the answer you obtained for part (a) or part (b)? Discuss your results.

Double Exponential Smoothing Using Holt's Method

Holt's method is a type of double exponential smoothing designed to track time series with linear trend. The method requires the specification of two smoothing constants, α and β, and uses two smoothing equations: one for the value of the series (the intercept) and one for the trend (the slope). The equations are

$$S_t = \alpha D_t + (1 - \alpha)(S_{t-1} + G_{t-1}),$$
$$G_t = \beta(S_t - S_{t-1}) + (1 - \beta)G_{t-1}.$$

Interpret S_t as the value of the intercept at time t and G_t as the value of the slope at time t. The first equation is very similar to that used for simple exponential smoothing. When the most current observation of demand, D_t, becomes available, it is averaged with the prior forecast of the current demand, which is the previous intercept, S_{t-1}, plus 1 times the previous slope, G_{t-1}. The second equation can be explained as follows. Our new estimate of the intercept, S_t, causes us to revise our estimate of the slope to $S_t - S_{t-1}$. This value is then averaged with the previous estimate of the slope, G_{t-1}. The smoothing constants may be the same, but for most applications more stability is given to the slope estimate (implying $\beta \leq \alpha$).

The τ-step-ahead forecast made in period t, which is denoted by $F_{t,\,t+\tau}$, is given by

$$F_{t,\,t+\tau} = S_t + \tau G_t.$$

Example 2.5 Let us apply Holt's method to the problem of developing one-step-ahead forecasts for the aircraft engine failure data. Recall that the original series was 200, 250, 175, 186, 225, 285, 305, 190. Assume that both α and β are equal to .1. In order to get the method started, we need estimates of both the intercept and the slope at time zero. Suppose that these are $S_0 = 200$ and $G_0 = 10$. Then we obtain

$$S_1 = (.1)(200) + (.9)(200 + 10) = 209.0$$
$$G_1 = (.1)(209 - 200) + (.9)(10) = 9.9$$
$$S_2 = (.1)(250) + (.9)(209 + 9.9) = 222.0$$
$$G_2 = (.1)(222 - 209) + (.9)(9.9) = 10.2$$
$$S_3 = (.1)(175) + (.9)(222 + 10.2) = 226.5$$
$$G_3 = (.1)(226.5 - 222) + (.9)(10.2) = 9.6$$

and so on.

Comparing the one-step-ahead forecasts to the actual numbers of failures for periods 4 through 8, we obtain the following:

Period	Actual	S	G	Forecast	|Error|
1	200	200.00	10.00	200.00	0.00
2	250	209.00	9.90	218.90	31.10
3	175	222.01	10.21	232.22	57.22
4	186	226.50	9.64	236.14	50.14
5	225	231.12	9.14	240.26	15.26
6	285	238.74	8.98	247.72	37.28
7	305	251.45	9.36	260.81	44.19
8	190	265.23	9.80	275.02	85.02

$\alpha = 0.1$
$\beta = 0.1$
$S_0 = 200$
$G_0 = 10$

Cell Formulas

Cell	Formula	Copied to
C3	SUM(B$12*B2,(1-B$12)*(C2+D2))	C4:C9
D3	SUM(B$13*(C3-C2),(1-B$13)*(D2))	D4:D9
E3	C3+D3	E4:E9
F3	ABS(B3-E3)	F4:F9

Averaging the numbers in the final column, we obtain a MAD of 46.4. Notice that this is lower than that for simple exponential smoothing or moving averages. Holt's method does better for this series because it is explicitly designed to track the trend in the data, whereas simple exponential smoothing and moving averages are not. Note that the forecasts in the given table are one-step-ahead forecasts. Suppose you needed to forecast the demand in period 2 for period 5. This forecast is $F_{2,5} = S_2 + (3)G_2 = 222 + (3)(10.2) = 252.6$.

The initialization problem also arises in getting Holt's method started. The best approach is to establish some set of initial periods as a baseline and use regression analysis to determine estimates of the slope and intercept using the baseline data.

Both Holt's method and regression are designed to handle series that exhibit trend. However, with Holt's method it is far easier to update forecasts as new observations become available.

More Problems for Section 2.8

30. For the data in Problem 28, use the results of the regression equation to estimate the slope and intercept of the series at the end of June. Use these numbers as the initial values of slope and intercept required in Holt's method. Assume that $\alpha = .15, \beta = .10$ for all calculations.

    a. Suppose that the actual number of visitors using the park in July was 2,150 and the number in August was 2,660. Use Holt's method to update the estimates of the slope and intercept based on these observations.

    b. What are the one-step-ahead and two-step-ahead forecasts that Holt's method gives for the number of park visitors in September and October?

    c. What is the forecast made at the end of July for the number of park attendees in December?

31. Because of serious flooding, the park was closed for most of December 1993. During that time only 53 people visited. Comment on the effect this observation would have on predictions of future use of the park. If you were in charge of forecasting the park's usage, how would you deal with this data point?

32. Discuss some of the problems that could arise when using either regression analysis or Holt's method for obtaining multiple-step-ahead forecasts.

2.9 METHODS FOR SEASONAL SERIES

This section considers forecasting methods for seasonal problems. A seasonal series is one that has a pattern that repeats every N periods for some value of N (which is at least 3). A typical seasonal series is pictured in Figure 2–8.

We refer to the number of periods before the pattern begins to repeat as the length of the season (N in the picture). Note that this is different from the popular usage of the word *season* as a time of year. In order to use a seasonal model, one must be able to specify the length of the season.

There are several ways to represent seasonality. The most common is to assume that there exists a set of multipliers c_t, for $1 \leq t \leq N$, with the property that $\Sigma\, c_t = N$. The multiplier c_t represents the average amount that the demand in the tth period of the season is above or below the overall average. For example, if $c_3 = 1.25$ and $c_5 = .60$, then, on average, the demand in the third period of the season is 25 percent above the average demand and the demand in the fifth period of the season is 40 percent below the average demand. These multipliers are known as seasonal factors.

Seasonal Factors for Stationary Series

In this part of the section we present a simple method of computing seasonal factors for a time series with seasonal variation and no trend. In the next part of this section we consider a method that is likely to be more accurate when there is also trend. Both methods require a minimum of two seasons of data.

The method is as follows:

1. Compute the sample mean of all the data.
2. Divide each observation by the sample mean. This gives seasonal factors for each period of observed data.
3. Average the factors for like periods within each season. That is, average all the factors corresponding to the first period of a season, all the factors corresponding to the

FIGURE 2–8
A seasonal demand series

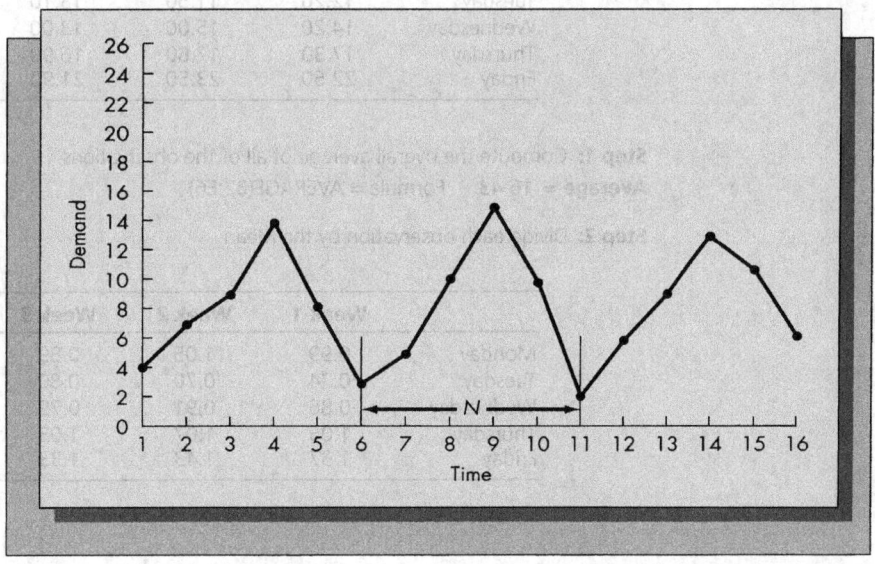

second period of a season, and so on. The resulting averages are the N seasonal factors. They will always add to exactly N.

Example 2.6 The County Transportation Department needs to determine usage factors by day of the week for a popular toll bridge connecting different parts of the city. In the current study, they are considering only working days. Suppose that the numbers of cars using the bridge each working day over the past four weeks were (in thousands of cars)

	Week 1	Week 2	Week 3	Week 4
Monday	16.2	17.3	14.6	16.1
Tuesday	12.2	11.5	13.1	11.8
Wednesday	14.2	15.0	13.0	12.9
Thursday	17.3	17.6	16.9	16.6
Friday	22.5	23.5	21.9	24.3

Find the seasonal factors corresponding to daily usage of the bridge.

Solution To solve this problem we

1. Compute the arithmetic average of all of the observations (20 in this case).
2. Divide each observation by the average computed in step 1. This will give 20 factors.
3. Average factors corresponding to the same period of each season. That is, average all factors for Mondays, all factors for Tuesdays, and so on. This will give five seasonal factors: one for each day of the week. Note that these factors will sum to five.
4. Forecasts for the numbers of cars using the bridge by day of the week are obtained by multiplying the seasonal factors computed in step 3 by the average value computed in step 1.

These steps are summarized in the spreadsheet below.

	Week 1	Week 2	Week 3	Week 4
Monday	16.20	17.30	14.60	16.10
Tuesday	12.20	11.50	13.10	11.80
Wednesday	14.20	15.00	13.00	12.90
Thursday	17.30	17.60	16.90	16.60
Friday	22.50	23.50	21.90	24.30

Step 1: Compute the overall average of all of the observations
Average = 16.43   Formula = AVERAGE(B2:E6)

Step 2: Divide each observation by the Mean

	Week 1	Week 2	Week 3	Week 4
Monday	0.99	1.05	0.89	0.98
Tuesday	0.74	0.70	0.80	0.72
Wednesday	0.86	0.91	0.79	0.79
Thursday	1.05	1.07	1.03	1.01
Friday	1.37	1.43	1.33	1.48

2.9 Methods for Seasonal Series

Step 3: Average Factors corresponding to the same day of the week

	Seasonal Factor
Monday	0.98
Tuesday	0.74
Wednesday	0.84
Thursday	1.04
Friday	1.40

Note that these factors sum to exactly five.

Step 4: Build the forecasts by multiplying the mean, 16.425, by the appropriate factor

	Forecast
Monday	16.05
Tuesday	12.15
Wednesday	13.78
Thursday	17.10
Friday	23.05

Cell Formulas

Cell	Formula	Copied to
B10	AVERAGE(B2:E6)	
B14	B2/$B$10	B15:B18
C14	C2/$C$10	C15:C18
(Similar formulas and copies for cells D14 and E14)		
B22	AVERAGE(B14:E14)	B23:B26
B30	$B$10*B22	B31:B34

Note: Example 2.6

Determining the Deseasonalized Series

In cases where there is both seasonal variation and trend, a useful technique is to form the deseasonalized series by removing the seasonal variation from the original series. To illustrate this, consider the following simple example which consists of two seasons of data.

Example 2.7

Period	Demand
1	10
2	20
3	26
4	17
5	12
6	23
7	30
8	22

Following the steps described above, the reader should satisfy himself or herself that we obtain the following four seasonal factors in this case:

0.550
1.075
1.400
0.975

To obtain the deseasonalized series, one simply divides each observation by the appropriate seasonal factor. For this example, that's 10/.550, 20/1.075, etc. In this case one obtains

Period	Demand	Deseasonalized Demand
1	10	18.182
2	20	18.605
3	26	18.571
4	17	17.436
5	12	21.818
6	23	21.395
7	30	21.429
8	22	22.564

Notice that the deseasonalized demand shows a clear trend. To forecast the deseasonalized series one could use any of the trend based methods discussed earlier in this chapter. Suppose that we fit a simple linear regression to this data where time is the independent variable as described in Section 2.8. Doing so one obtains the regression fit of this data as $y_t = 16.91 + 0.686t$. To forecast, one first applies the regression to forecast the deseasonalized series, and then re-seasonalizes by multiplying by the appropriate factor. For example, if one wishes to forecast for periods 9 through 12, the regression equation gives the following forecasts for the deseasonalized series: 23.08, 23.77, 24.46, 25.14. The final forecasts are obtained by multiplying by the appropriate seasonal factors, giving the final forecasts for periods 9 through 12 as 12.70, 25.55, 34.24, and 25.51.

Problems for Section 2.9

33. Sales of walking shorts at Hugo's Department Store in downtown Rolla appear to exhibit a seasonal pattern. The proprietor of the store, Wally Hugo, has kept careful records of the sales of several of his popular items, including walking shorts. During the past two years the monthly sales of the shorts have been

	Year 1	Year 2		Year 1	Year 2
Jan.	12	16	July	112	130
Feb.	18	14	Aug.	90	83
March	36	46	Sep.	66	52
April	53	48	Oct.	45	49
May	79	88	Nov.	23	14
June	134	160	Dec.	21	26

Assuming no trend in shorts sales over the two years, obtain estimates for the monthly seasonal factors.

34. A popular brand of tennis shoe has had the following demand history by quarters over a three-year period.

Snapshot Application

NATE SILVER PERFECTLY FORECASTS 2012 PRESIDENTIAL ELECTION

In a stunning victory, President Barack Obama won re-election in 2012 with 332 electoral votes versus Governor Romney's 206. This was in stark contrast to the Romney victory confidently predicted by Republican pundits just days before the election. Perhaps this was a result of a Gallup poll weeks before the election that showed Romney with a lead in the popular vote. However, American presidents are not elected by popular vote. They are elected by the Electoral College, which vote on a state by state basis. Even though several past Presidents have won the election while losing the popular vote, this was not the case in 2012.

A statistician named Nate Silver predicted the outcome of the election exactly. He based his forecasts on careful analysis of state by state (and even county by county) polls. His methodology had previously proven very successful in baseball. He also accurately predicted the outcome of the 2008 presidential election in which he was correct in 49 out of 50 states. But in 2012 he was correct in all fifty states, predicting not only an Obama victory with probability exceeding 90 percent, but predicting the number of electoral votes for each candidate exactly.

Silver's striking successes points to the importance in using sound analytics for forecasting. His is not an isolated case, however. Reports abound about such methods being successfully applied in many other contexts. (Note that a group from Princeton University, applying similar methods, was also able to accurately predict the outcome of the 2012 election.)

Year 1	Demand	Year 2	Demand	Year 3	Demand
1	12	1	16	1	14
2	25	2	32	2	45
3	76	3	71	3	84
4	52	4	62	4	47

a. Determine the seasonal factors for each quarter.
b. Based on the result of part (a), determine the deseasonalized demand series.
c. Predict the demand for each quarter of Year 4 for the deseasonalized series from a six-quarter moving average.
d. Using the results from parts (a) and (c), predict the demand for the shoes for each quarter of Year 4.

Winters's Method for Seasonal Problems

The moving-average method just described can be used to predict a seasonal series with or without a trend. However, as new data become available, the method requires that all seasonal factors be recalculated from scratch. Winters's method is a type of triple exponential smoothing, and this has the important advantage of being easy to update as new data become available.

We assume a model of the form

$$D_t = (\mu + G_t)c_t + \epsilon_t.$$

Interpret μ as the base signal or intercept at time $t = 0$ excluding seasonality, G_t as the trend or slope component, c_t as the multiplicative seasonal component in period t, and finally ϵ_t as the error term. Because the seasonal factor multiplies both the base level and the trend term, we are assuming that the underlying series has a form similar to that pictured in Figure 2–10.

Again assume that the length of the season is exactly N periods and that the seasonal factors are the same each season and have the property that $\Sigma\, c_t = N$. Three exponential

FIGURE 2–10
Seasonal series with increasing trend

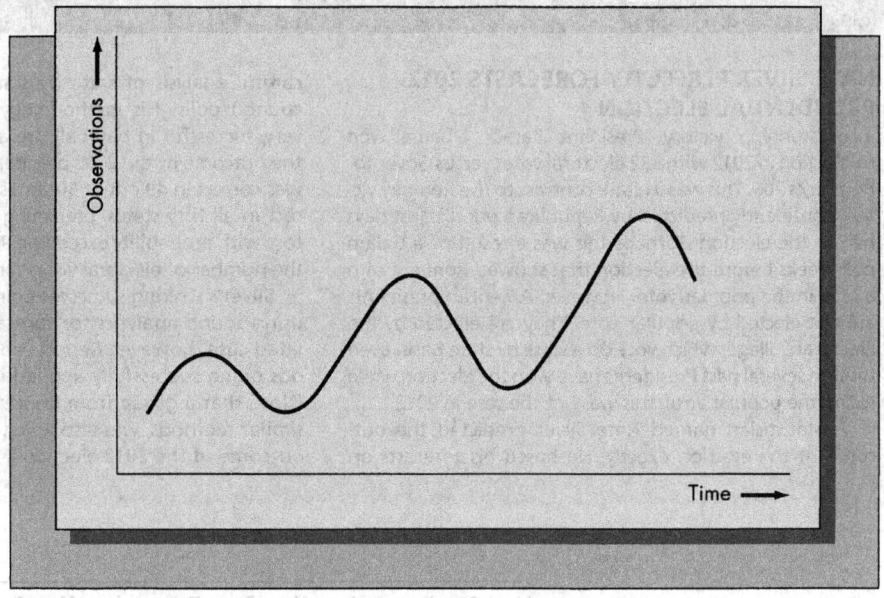

smoothing equations are used each period to update estimates of deseasonalized series, the seasonal factors, and the trend. These equations may have different smoothing constants, which we will label α, β, and γ.

1. *The series.* The current level of the deseasonalized series, S_t, is given by

$$S_t = \alpha(D_t/c_{t-N}) + (1 - \alpha)(S_{t-1} + G_{t-1}).$$

Notice what this equation does. By dividing by the appropriate seasonal factor, we are deseasonalizing the newest demand observation. This is then averaged with the current forecast for the deseasonalized series, as in Holt's method.

2. *The trend.* The trend is updated in a fashion similar to Holt's method.

$$G_t = \beta[S_t - S_{t-1}] + (1 - \beta)G_{t-1}.$$

3. *The seasonal factors.*

$$c_t = \gamma(D_t/S_t) + (1 - \gamma)c_{t-N}.$$

The ratio of the most recent demand observation over the current estimate of the deseasonalized demand gives the current estimate of the seasonal factor. This is then averaged with the previous best estimate of the seasonal factor, c_{t-N}. Each time that a seasonal factor is updated, it is necessary to norm the most recent N factors to add to N.

Finally, the forecast made in period t for any future period $t + \tau$ is given by

$$F_{t, t+\tau} = (S_t + \tau G_t)c_{t+\tau-N}.$$

Note that this forecasting equation assumes that $t \leq N$. If $N < \tau \leq 2N$, the appropriate seasonal factor would be $c_{t+\tau-2N}$; if $2N < \tau \leq 3N$, the appropriate seasonal factor would be $c_{t+\tau-3N}$; and so on.

Initialization Procedure

In order to get the method started, we need to obtain initial estimates for the series, the slope, and the seasonal factors. Winters suggests that a minimum of two seasons of data be available for initialization. Let us assume that exactly two seasons of data are available; that is, $2N$ data points. Suppose that the current period is $t = 0$, so that the past observations are labeled $D_{-2N+1}, D_{-2N+2}, \ldots, D_0$.

1. Calculate the sample means for the two separate seasons of data.

$$V_1 = \frac{1}{N} \sum_{j=-2N+1}^{-N} D_j$$

$$V_2 = \frac{1}{N} \sum_{j=-N+1}^{0} D_j$$

2. Define $G_0 = (V_2 - V_1)/N$ as the initial slope estimate. If $m > 2$ seasons of data are available for initialization, then compute $V_1, \ldots, V_m$ as in step 1 and define $G_0 = (V_m - V_1)/[(m-1)N]$. If we locate V_1 at the center of the first season of data [at period $(-3N+1)/2$] and V_2 at the center of the second season of data [at period $(-N+1)/2$], then G_0 is simply the slope of the line connecting V_1 and V_2 (refer to Figure 2–11).

3. Set $S_0 = V_2 + G_0[(N-1)/2]$. This estimates the value of the series at time $t = 0$. Note that S_0 is the value assumed by the line connecting V_1 and V_2 at $t = 0$ (see Figure 2–11).

4. *a.* The initial seasonal factors are computed for each period in which data are available and then averaged to obtain one set of seasonal factors. The initial seasonal factors are obtained by dividing each of the initial observations by the corresponding

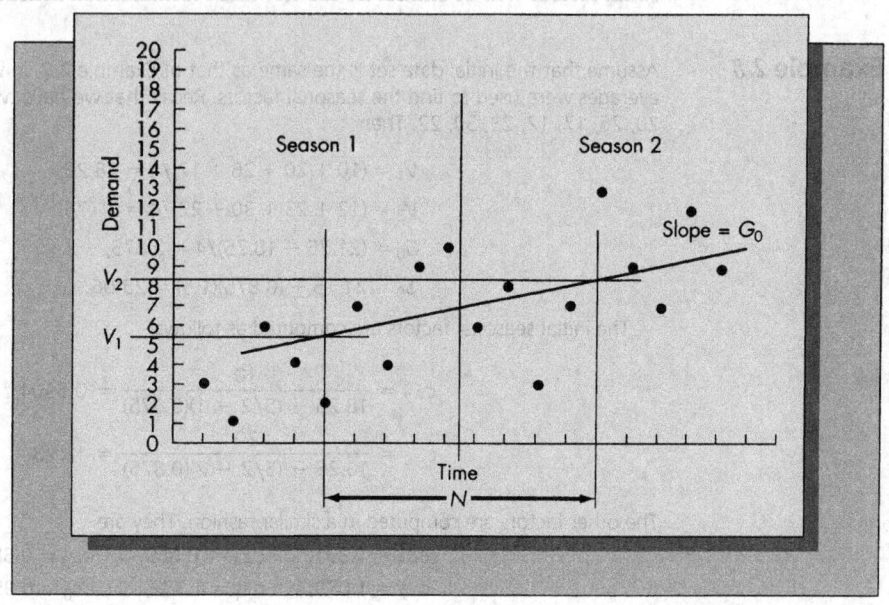

FIGURE 2–11
Initialization for Winters's method

point along the line connecting V_1 and V_2. This can be done graphically or by using the following formula:

$$c_t = \frac{D_t}{V_i - [(N+1)/2 - j]G_0} \quad \text{for } -2N + 1 \leq t \leq 0,$$

where $i = 1$ for the first season, $i = 2$ for the second season, and j is the period of the season. That is, $j = 1$ for $t = -2N + 1$ and $t = -N + 1$; $j = 2$ for $t = -2N + 2$ and $t = -N + 2$; and so on.

b. Average the seasonal factors. Assuming exactly two seasons of initial data, we obtain

$$c_{-N+1} = \frac{c_{-2N+1} + c_{-N+1}}{2}, \ldots, c_0 = \frac{c_{-N} + c_0}{2}.$$

c. Normalize the seasonal factors.

$$c_j = \left[\frac{c_j}{\sum_{i=0}^{-N+1} c_i} \right] \cdot N \quad \text{for } -N + 1 \leq j \leq 0.$$

This initialization procedure just discussed is the one suggested by Winters. It is not the only means of initializing the system. Seasonal factors could be determined by the method of moving averages discussed in the first part of this section. Another alternative would be to fit a linear regression to the baseline data and use the resulting slope and intercept values, as was done in Holt's method, to obtain S_0 and G_0. The seasonal factors would be obtained by dividing each demand observation in the baseline period by the corresponding value on the regression line, averaging like periods, and norming. The actual values of the initial estimates of the intercept, the slope, and the seasonal factors will be similar no matter which initialization scheme is employed.

Example 2.8   Assume that the initial data set is the same as that of Example 2.7, in which centered moving averages were used to find the seasonal factors. Recall that we have two seasons of data: 10, 20, 26, 17, 12, 23, 30, 22. Then

$$V_1 = (10 + 20 + 26 + 17)/4 = 18.25,$$
$$V_2 = (12 + 23 + 30 + 22)/4 = 21.75,$$
$$G_0 = (21.75 - 18.25)/4 = 0.875,$$
$$S_0 = 21.75 + (0.875)(1.5) = 23.06.$$

The initial seasonal factors are computed as follows:

$$c_{-7} = \frac{10}{18.25 - (5/2 - 1)(0.875)} = 0.5904,$$

$$c_{-6} = \frac{20}{18.25 - (5/2 - 2)(0.875)} = 1.123.$$

The other factors are computed in a similar fashion. They are

$$c_{-5} = 1.391, \quad c_{-4} = 0.869, \quad c_{-3} = 0.5872,$$
$$c_{-2} = 1.079, \quad c_{-1} = 1.352, \quad c_0 = 0.9539.$$

We then average c_{-7} and c_{-3}, c_{-6} and c_{-2}, and so on, to obtain the four seasonal factors:

$$c_{-3} = 0.5888, \quad c_{-2} = 1.1010, \quad c_{-1} = 1.3720, \quad c_0 = 0.9115.$$

Finally, norming the factors to ensure that the sum is 4 results in

$$c_{-3} = 0.5900, \quad c_{-2} = 1.1100, \quad c_{-1} = 1.3800, \quad c_0 = 0.9200.$$

Notice how closely these factors agree with those obtained from the moving-average method. Suppose that we wish to forecast the following year's demand at time $t = 0$. The forecasting equation is

$$F_{t,t+\tau} = (S_t + \tau G_t)c_{t+\tau-N},$$

which results in

$$F_{0,1} = (S_0 + G_0)c_{-3} = (23.06 + 0.875)(0.59) = 14.12,$$
$$F_{0,2} = (S_0 + 2G_0)c_{-2} = [23.06 + (2)(0.875)](1.11) = 27.54,$$
$$F_{0,3} = 35.44,$$
$$F_{0,4} = 24.38.$$

Now, suppose that at time $t = 1$ we observe a demand of $D_1 = 16$. We now need to update our equations. Assume that $\alpha = .2$, $\beta = .1$, and $\gamma = .1$. Then

$$S_1 = \alpha(D_1/c_{-3}) + (1 - \alpha)(S_0 + G_0)$$
$$= (0.2)(16/.59) + (0.8)(23.06 + 0.875) = 24.57,$$
$$G_1 = \beta(S_1 - S_0) + (1 - \beta)G_0$$
$$= (0.1)(24.57 - 23.06) + (0.9)(0.875) = 0.9385,$$
$$c_1 = \gamma(D_1/S_1) + (1 - \gamma)c_{-3}$$
$$= (0.1)(16/24.57) + (0.9)(0.59) = 0.5961.$$

At this point, we would renorm c_{-2}, c_{-1}, c_0, and the new value of c_1 to add to 4. Because the sum is 4.0061, it is close enough (the norming would result in rounding c_1 down to .59 once again).

Forecasting from period 1, we obtain

$$F_{1,2} = (S_1 + G_1)c_{-2} = (24.57 + 0.9385)(1.11) = 28.3144,$$
$$F_{1,3} = (S_1 + 2G_1)c_{-1} = [24.57 + (2)(0.9385)](1.38) = 36.4969,$$

and so on.

Now suppose that we have observed one full year of demand, given by $D_1 = 16$, $D_2 = 33$, $D_3 = 34$, and $D_4 = 26$. Each time a new observation becomes available, the intercept, slope, and most current seasonal factor estimates are updated. One obtains

$$S_2 = 26.35, \quad S_3 = 26.83, \quad S_4 = 27.89,$$
$$G_2 = 1.0227, \quad G_3 = 0.9678, \quad G_4 = 0.9770,$$
$$c_2 = 1.124, \quad c_3 = 1.369, \quad c_4 = 0.9212.$$

As c_1, c_2, c_3, and c_4 sum to 4.01, normalization is not necessary. Suppose that we were interested in the forecast made in period 4 for period 10. The forecasting equation is

$$F_{t,t+\tau} = (S_t + \tau G_t)c_{t+\tau-2N},$$

which results in

$$F_{4,10} = (S_4 + 6G_4)c_2 = [27.89 + 6(0.9770)](1.124) = 37.94.$$

An important consideration is the choice of the smoothing constants α, β, and γ to be used in Winters's method. The issues here are the same as those discussed for simple exponential smoothing and Holt's method. Large values of the smoothing constants will result in more responsive but less stable forecasts. One method for setting α, β, and γ is to experiment with various values of the parameters that retrospectively give the best fit of previous forecasts to the observed history of the series. Because one must test many combinations of the three constants, the calculations are tedious. Furthermore, there is no guarantee that the best values of the smoothing constants based on past data will be the best values for future forecasts. The most conservative approach is to guarantee stable forecasts by choosing the smoothing constants to be between 0.1 and 0.2.

More Problems for Section 2.9

35. Consider the data for Problem 34.
    a. Using the data from Years 2 and 3, determine initial values of the intercept, slope, and seasonal factors for Winters's method.
    b. Assume that the observed demand for the first quarter of Year 4 was 18. Using $\alpha = .2$, $\beta = .15$, and $\gamma = .10$, update the estimates of the series, the slope, and the seasonal factors.
    c. What are the forecasts made at the end of the first quarter of Year 4 for the remaining three quarters of Year 4?

36. Suppose the observed quarterly demand for Year 4 was 18, 51, 86, 66. Compare the accuracy of the forecasts obtained for the last three quarters of Year 4 in Problems 34(d) and 35(c) by computing both the MAD and the MSE.

37. Determine updated estimates of the slope, the intercept, and the seasonal factors for the end of Year 4 based on the observations given in Problem 36. Using these updated estimates, determine the forecasts that Winters's method gives for all of Year 6 made at the end of Year 4. Use the values of the smoothing constants given in Problem 35(b).

2.10 BOX-JENKINS MODELS

The forecasting models introduced in this section are significantly more sophisticated than those previously discussed in this chapter. The goal is to present the basic concepts of Box-Jenkins analysis so that the reader can appreciate the power of these methods. However, an in-depth coverage is beyond the scope of this book. The methods are named for two well-known statisticians, George E. Box and Gwilym M. Jenkins formerly from the University of Wisconsin and University of Lancaster, respectively. The approach they developed is based on exploiting the autocorrelation structure of a time series. While Box-Jenkins methods are based on statistical relationships in a time series, much of the basic theory goes back to the famous book by Norbert Wiener (1949), and before.

Box-Jenkins models are also known as ARIMA models. ARIMA is an acronym for autoregressive integrated moving average. The autocorrelation function plays a central role in the development of these models, and is the feature that distinguishes ARIMA models from the other methods discussed in this chapter. As we have assumed throughout this chapter, denote the time series of interest as $D_1, D_2, \ldots$. We will assume initially that the series is stationary. That is, $E(D_i) = \mu$ and $\text{Var}(D_i) = \sigma^2$ for all $i = 1, 2, \ldots$. Practically speaking, *stationarity* means that there is no growth or decline in the series, and variation remains relatively constant. It is important to note that stationarity does not imply independence. Hence, it is possible that values of D_i and D_j are dependent random variables when $i \neq j$ even though their marginal density functions are the same. It is this dependence we wish to exploit. (Note: A more precise way to characterize stationarity is that the joint distribution of $D_t, D_{t+1}, \ldots, D_{t+k}$ is the same as the joint distribution of $D_{t+m}, D_{t+m+1}, \ldots, D_{t+m+k}$ at any time t and pair of positive integers m and k.)

The assumption of stationarity implies that the marginal distributions of any two observations separated by the same time interval are the same. That is, D_t and D_{t+1} have the same joint distribution as D_{t+m} and D_{t+m+1} for any $m \geq 1$. This implies that the covariance of D_t and D_{t+1} is exactly the same as the covariance of D_{t+m} and D_{t+m+1}. Hence, the covariance of any two observations depends only on the number of periods separating them. In this context, the covariance is also known as the autocovariance, since we are comparing two values of the same series separated by a fixed lag.

Let Cov (D_{t+m}, D_{t+m+k}) be the covariance of D_{t+m} and D_{t+m+k} given by

$$\text{Cov}(D_{t+m}, D_{t+m+k}) = E(D_{t+m}D_{t+m+k}) - E(D_{t+m})E(D_{t+m+k}) \quad \text{for any integer } k \geq 1.$$

The correlation coefficient of these two random variables is given by

$$\rho_k = \frac{\text{Cov}(D_{t+m}, D_{t+m+k})}{\sqrt{\text{Var}(D_{t+m})}\sqrt{\text{Var}(D_{t+m+k})}}.$$

This is often referred to as the autocorrelation coefficient of lag k, since it refers to the correlation between all values of the series separated by k periods. These autocorrelation coefficients are typically computed for several values of k. It is these autocorrelation coefficients that will play the key role in building ARIMA models.

The autocorrelation coefficients are estimated from a history of the series. In order to guarantee reliable estimators, Box and Jenkins (1970) suggest that one have at least 72 data points of past history of the series. Hence, these models are only meaningful when one has a substantial and reliable history of the series being studied.

Estimating the Autocorrelation Function

Let $D_1, D_2, \ldots, D_n$ be a history of observations of a time series. The autocorrelation coefficient of lag k is estimated from the following formula:

$$r_k = \frac{\sum_{t=k+1}^{n}(D_t - \overline{D})(D_{t-k} - \overline{D})}{\sum_{t=1}^{n}(D_t - \overline{D})^2},$$

where $\overline{D}$ is the sample mean (that is, the average) of the observed values of the series. Refer to the r_k as sample autocorrelation coefficients. This calculation is typically done for 10 or 15 values of k. For most of the time series discussed earlier in the chapter, one identifies the appropriate patterns by just looking at a graph of the data. This is not the case here, however.

Example 2.9   If observations are completely random (i.e., form a white noise process), then we would expect that there would be no significant autocorrelations among the observed values of the series. To test this, we generated a time series using the random number generator built into Excel. This series appears in Table 2–1. Each value is 100 times the RAND function. The reader can check that the sample autocorrelations for lags of 1 to 10 periods for these 36 observations are

TABLE 2–1
Time Series with 36 Values Generated by a Random Number Generator (White Noise Series)

Period	Value	Period	Value	Period	Value
1	42	13	47	25	88
2	93	14	52	26	73
3	17	15	28	27	60
4	5	16	58	28	56
5	38	17	41	29	49
6	2	18	47	30	51
7	67	19	48	31	59
8	66	20	50	32	80
9	11	21	81	33	40
10	65	22	93	34	60
11	88	23	45	35	20
12	91	24	24	36	35

$r_1 = 0.098$
$r_2 = -0.118$
$r_3 = 0.018$
$r_4 = -0.080$
$r_5 = 0.0752$
$r_6 = 0.006$
$r_7 = -0.270$
$r_8 = -0.207$
$r_9 = 0.117$
$r_{10} = 0.136$

If we had an infinite number of observations and a perfect white noise series, we would expect that all of the autocorrelations would be zero. However, since we only have a finite series, there will be statistical variation resulting in nonzero values of the autocorrelations. The question is whether these values are significantly different from zero. (The data from Table 2–1 appear in Figure 2–12 and the autocorrelations in Figure 2–13.)

FIGURE 2–12
Plot of data in Table 2–1

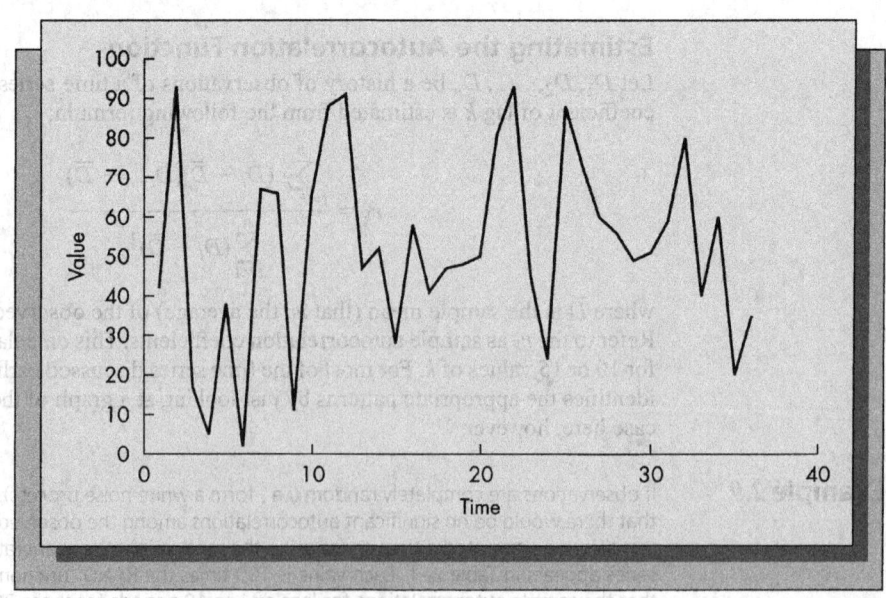

FIGURE 2–13
Plot of autocorrelations of series in Figure 2–12

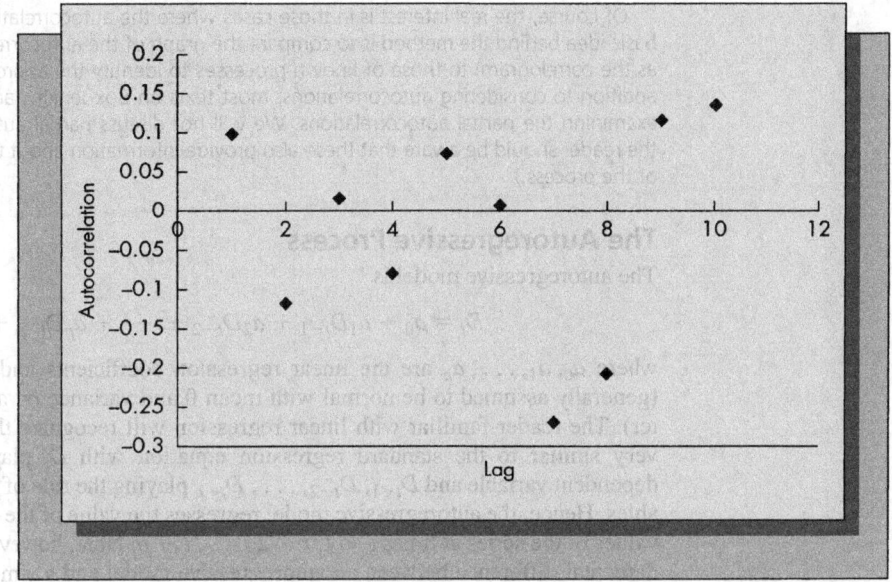

Several statistical tests have been proposed to answer this question. One is the Box-Pierce Q statistic, computed from the formula

$$Q = n \sum_{k=1}^{h} r_k^2,$$

where h is the maximum length of the lag being considered, and n is the number of observations in the series. Under the null hypothesis that the series is white noise, the Q statistic has the chi-square distribution with $(h - m)$ degrees of freedom, where m is the number of parameters in the model that has been fitted to the data. This test can be applied to any set of data not necessarily fitted to a specific model by setting $m = 0$.

Applying the formula for the Q statistic to the preceding autocorrelations, we obtain a value of $Q = 6.62$. Comparing this to the critical values of the chi-square statistic in Table 2–2 with 10 degrees of freedom (df), we see that this value is substantially smaller than any value in the table (for example, the value for a right tail probability of .1 at 10 degrees of freedom is 15.99). Hence, we could not reject the null hypothesis that the data form a white noise process, and we conclude that the autocorrelations are not significant.

TABLE 2–2
Partial Table of Critical Values of the Chi-Square Statistic

	Tail Value Probability		
df	0.1	0.05	0.01
1	2.70	3.84	6.63
2	4.60	5.99	9.21
3	6.25	7.81	11.34
4	7.77	9.48	13.27
5	9.23	11.07	15.08
6	10.64	12.59	16.81
7	12.01	14.06	18.47
8	13.36	15.50	20.09
9	14.68	16.91	21.66
10	15.99	18.30	23.20

Of course, the real interest is in those cases where the autocorrelations are significant. The basic idea behind the method is to compare the graph of the autocorrelation function (known as the correlogram) to those of known processes to identify the appropriate model. (Note: In addition to considering autocorrelations, most texts on Box-Jenkins analysis also recommend examining the partial autocorrelations. We will not discuss partial autocorrelations here, but the reader should be aware that these also provide information about the underlying structure of the process.)

The Autoregressive Process

The autoregressive model is

$$D_t = a_0 + a_1 D_{t-1} + a_2 D_{t-2} + \cdots + a_p D_{t-p} + \epsilon_t,$$

where $a_0, a_1, \ldots, a_p$ are the linear regression coefficients and ϵ_t is the error term (generally assumed to be normal with mean 0 and variance σ^2 as earlier in the chapter). The reader familiar with linear regression will recognize this equation as being very similar to the standard regression equation with D_t playing the role of the dependent variable and $D_{t-1}, D_{t-2}, \ldots, D_{t-p}$ playing the role of the independent variables. Hence, the autoregressive model regresses the value of the series at time t on the values of the series at times $t-1, t-2, \ldots, t-p$. Note, however, that there is a fundamental difference between an autoregressive model and a simple linear regression, since in this case it is likely that the variables are correlated. We will use the notation AR(p) to represent this model.

Consider a basic AR(1) model,

$$D_t = a_0 + a_1 D_{t-1} + \epsilon_t.$$

In order for the process to be stable, we require $|a_1| < 1$. If $a_1 > 0$, it means that successive values of the series are positively correlated—that is, large values tend to be followed by large values, and small values tend to be followed by small values. This means that the series will be relatively smooth. If $a_1 < 0$, then the opposite is true, so the series will appear much spikier. The difference is illustrated in a realization of two AR(1) processes in Figure 2-14. (Figure 2-14 was generated in Excel using the built-in RAND function and the normal variate generator given in Problem 5.34 with $a_0 = 10$ and $\sigma = 30$.)

Of course, it is unlikely one can recognize an AR(1) process by simply examining a graph of the raw data. Rather, one would examine the autocorrelation function. It is easy to show that the autocorrelation function for an AR(1) process (see Nelson, 1973, page 39, for example) is

$$\rho_j = a_1^j.$$

The autocorrelation functions for the two cases illustrated in Figure 2-14 are given in Figure 2-15. If the sample autocorrelation function of a series has a pattern resembling one of those in Figure 2-15, it would suggest that an AR(1) process is appropriate. The theoretical autocorrelation functions for higher-order AR processes can be more complex. [In the case of AR(2), the patterns are either similar to one of the two pictured in Figure 2-15 or follow a damped sine wave.] In practice, one would rarely include more than one or two AR terms in the model. Determining the autocorrelation structure for higher-order AR processes is not difficult. One must solve a series of linear equations known as the Yule-Walker equations. We will not elaborate further here, but refer the interested reader to Box and Jenkins (1970).

FIGURE 2–14
Realizations of an AR(1) process with $a_1 = 0.9$ and $a_1 = -0.9$, respectively.

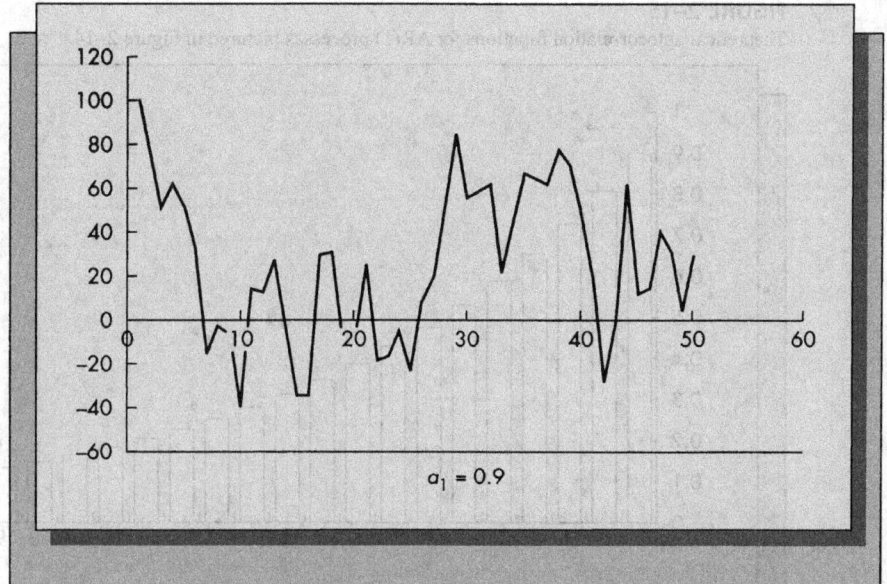

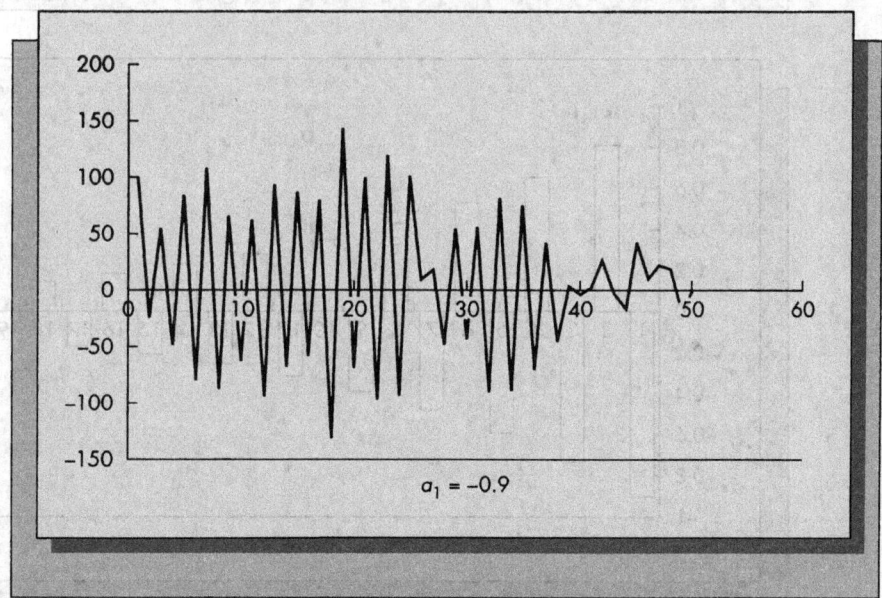

The Moving-Average Process

The moving-average process provides another means of describing a stationary stochastic process used to model time series. The term *moving average* as used here should not be confused with the moving average discussed earlier in this chapter in Section 2.7. In that case, the moving average was an average of past values of the series. In this case, the moving average is a weighted average of past forecast errors.

FIGURE 2–15
Theoretical autocorrelation functions for AR(1) processes pictured in Figure 2–14.

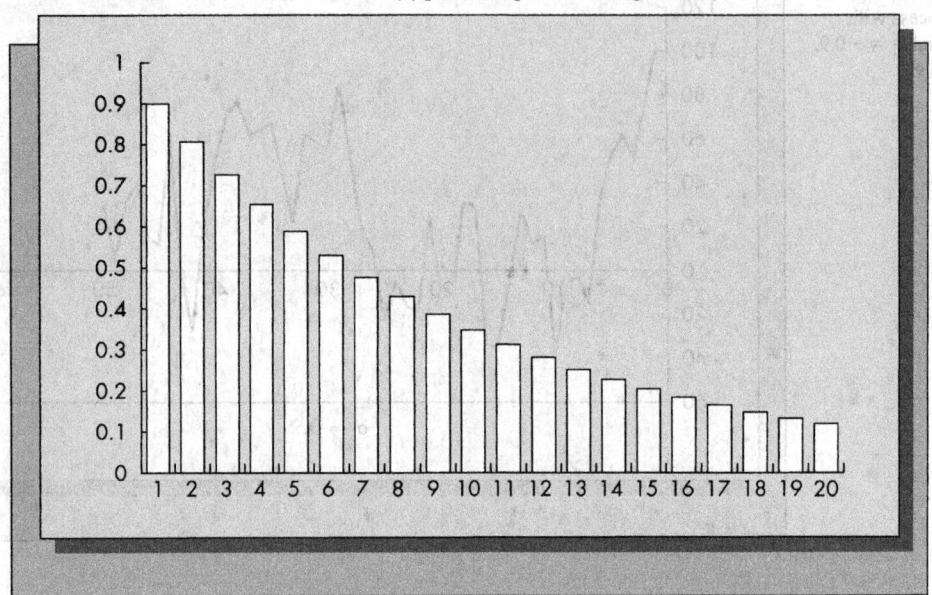

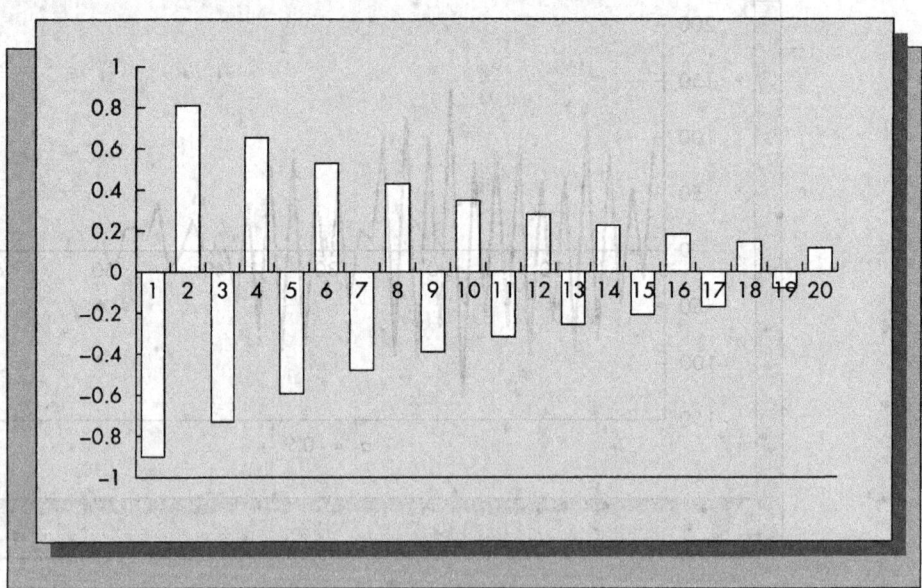

The general moving-average process has the form

$$D_t = b_0 - b_1\epsilon_{t-1} - b_2\epsilon_{t-2} - \cdots - b_q\epsilon_{t-q} + \epsilon_t.$$

[The weights $b_1, b_2, \ldots, b_q$ are shown with negative signs by convention.] We will denote this model as MA(q). The intuition behind the moving-average process is not as straightforward as the autoregressive process, but the two are related. Consider the first-order AR(1) process, $D_t = a_0 + a_1 D_{t-1} + \epsilon_t$. By back-substituting for D_{t-1}, $D_{t-2}, \ldots$, we see that the AR(1) process can also be written as

$$D_t = a_0 \sum_{i=0}^{\infty} a_1^i + a_1 \epsilon_{t-1} + a_1^2 \epsilon_{t-2} + \cdots + \epsilon_t,$$

which is easily recognized as an MA(∞) process.

The reader will better understand the power of MA processes when we examine the autocorrelation function. Consider first the simplest MA process, namely, an MA(1) process. In this case,

$$D_t = b_0 - b_1 \epsilon_{t-1} + \epsilon_t.$$

The autocorrelation structure for this case is very simple:

$$\rho_1 = \frac{-b_1}{1 + b_1^2},$$

$$\rho_2 = \rho_3 = \cdots = 0.$$

Hence, an MA(1) process has only one significant autocorrelation at lag 1. In general, MA(1) processes tend to have spiky patterns independent of the sign of b_1, because successive errors are assumed to be uncorrelated. Figure 2–16 shows realizations of an MA(1) process with b_1 equal to -0.9 and 0.9, respectively. Finding the autocorrelation structure for higher-order MA processes is a challenging mathematical problem, requiring the solution of a collection of nonlinear equations. Again, we refer the interested reader to Box and Jenkins (1970). The main characteristic identifying an MA(q) process is that only the first q autocorrelations are nonzero.

Mixtures: ARMA Models

The real power in Box-Jenkins methodology comes in being able to mix both AR and MA terms. Any model that contains one or more AR terms and one or more MA terms is known as an ARMA model, for autoregressive moving average. An ARMA(p, q) model contains p autoregressive terms and q moving-average terms. For example, one would write an ARMA(1,1) model as

$$D_t = c + a_1 D_{t-1} - b_1 \epsilon_{t-1} + \epsilon_t.$$

The ARMA(1,1) model is quite powerful, and can describe many real processes accurately. It requires identification of the two parameters a_1 and b_1. The ARMA(1, 1) process is equivalent to an MA(∞) process and also equivalent to an AR(∞) process, thus showing the power that can be achieved with a parsimonious model. The autocorrelation function of the ARMA(1,1) process has characteristics of both the MA(1) and AR(1) processes. The autocorrelation at lag 1 is determined primarily by the MA(1) term, while autocorrelations at lags greater than 1 are determined by the AR(1) term.

ARIMA Models

Thus far we have assumed that the underlying stochastic process generating the time series is stationary. However, in many real problems, patterns such as trend or seasonality are present, which imply nonstationarity. The Box-Jenkins approach would be of limited utility if it were unable to address such situations. Fortunately, there is a simple technique for converting many nonstationary processes into stationary processes.

FIGURE 2–16
Realizations of an MA(1) process with $b_1 = -0.9$ and $b_1 = 0.9$, respectively

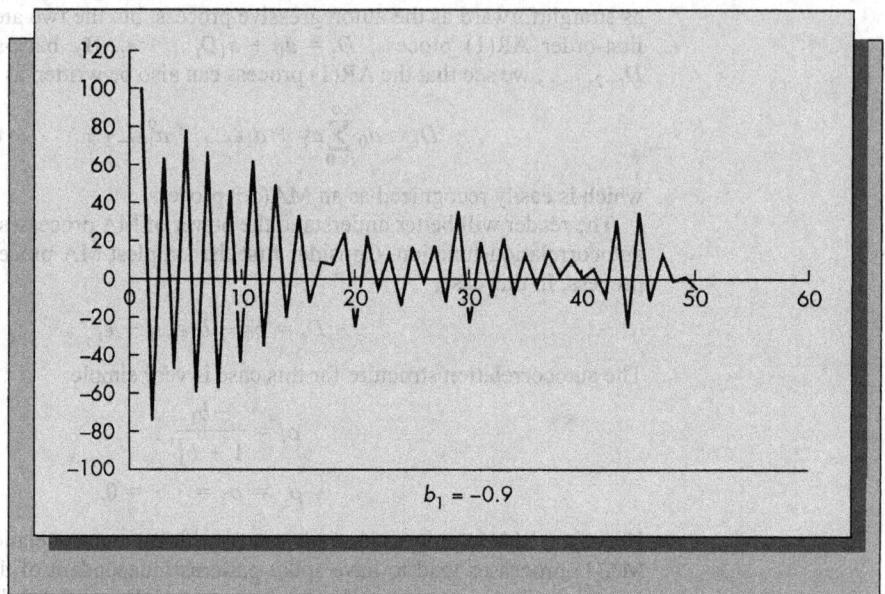

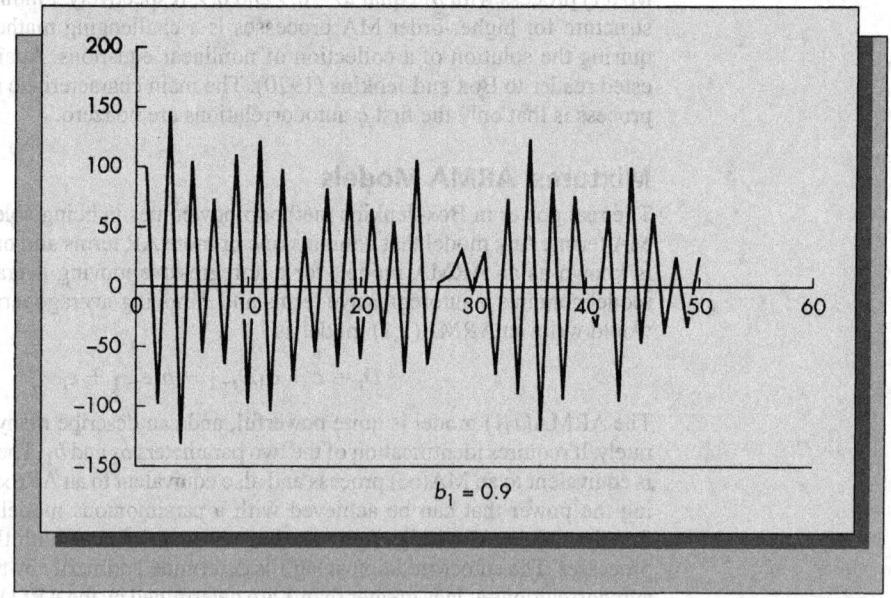

Consider first a process with a linear trend, such as the one pictured in Figure 2–7. Simple methods for dealing with linear trends were discussed in Section 2.8 of this chapter. How can a process with a linear trend be converted to one with no trend? The answer turns out to be surprisingly simple. Suppose our original process D_t has a linear trend. Consider the new process U_t given by

$$U_t = D_t - D_{t-1}.$$

The process U_t tracks the slope of the original process. If the original process had a linear trend, then the slope should be relatively constant, implying that U_t would be stationary. In the same way, if the original process increased or decreased according to a quadratic function, differencing the first difference process (forming a second difference) will result in a stationary process. Differencing is the discrete analogue of a derivative. Going from the process U_t back to the original process D_t requires summing values of U_t, which is the discrete analogue of integration. For that reason, when differencing is introduced, we use the term *integration* to describe it. An ARMA model based on data derived from differencing is denoted ARIMA, which stands for autoregressive integrated moving average.

A common notation is $U_t = \nabla D_t$. If two levels of differencing were required to achieve stationarity, then one would need a double summation to retrieve the original series. In the case of two levels of differencing,

$$\nabla^2 D_t = D_t - D_{t-1} - (D_{t-1} - D_{t-2}) = D_t - 2D_{t-1} + D_{t-2}.$$

Differencing can also be used to remove seasonality from a time series. Suppose that a seasonal pattern repeats every 12 months. Then defining

$$U_t = \nabla^{12} D_t = D_t - D_{t-12}$$

would result in a process with no seasonality.

An ARIMA process has three constants associated with it: p for the number of autoregressive terms, d for the order of differencing, and q for the number of moving-average terms. The general ARIMA process would be denoted ARIMA(p, d, q). Thus, for example, ARMA(1,1) can also be denoted ARIMA(1,0,1). While these parameters can be any nonnegative integers, it is very rare that any of the values of p, d, or q would exceed 2. Thus, virtually all the ARIMA models one finds in practice correspond to values of 0, 1, or 2 for the parameters p, d, and q. While this might seem limiting, these few cases cover an enormous range of practical forecasting scenarios.

It is important to note that observations are lost when differencing. For example, if one uses a single level of differencing ($U_t = D_t - D_{t-1}$), the first difference process, U_t, will have one less observation than the original series. Similarly, each level of differencing will reduce the sample size by 1. Seasonal differencing effectively reduces the data set by the length of the season. Another way to represent the differencing operation is via the backshift operator. That is,

$$BD_t = D_{t-1},$$

which means that one would represent the first difference process as

$$U_t = D_t - D_{t-1} = D_t - BD_t = (1 - B)D_t.$$

The backshift operator can also be used to simplify the notation for AR, MA, and ARMA models. Consider the simple AR(1) process given by $D_t = a_0 + a_1 D_{t-1} + \epsilon_t$. Writing this in the form $D_t - a_1 D_{t-1} = a_0 + \epsilon_t$ reduces the process to the alternate notation $(1 - a_1 B)D_t = a_0 + \epsilon_t$. Similarly, the reader should check that the MA(1) model using the backshift operator is $D_t = b_0 + (1 - b_1 B)e_t$.

Using ARIMA Models for Forecasting

Given an ARIMA model, how does one go about using it to provide forecasts of future values of the series? The approach is similar to that discussed earlier in this chapter for the simpler methods. For example, a forecast based on a simple AR(p) model is a weighted average of past p observations of the series. A forecast based on an MA(q) model is a weighted average of the past q forecast errors. And finally, one must take into account the level of differencing and any transformations made on the original data.

As an example, consider an ARIMA (1, 1, 1) model (that is, a model having one level of differencing, one moving-average term, and one autoregressive term). This can be represented using the backshift notation as

$$(1 - B)(1 + a_1 B)D_t = c + (1 - b_1 B)\epsilon_t,$$

or as

$$(1 + a_1 B)\nabla D_t = c + (1 - b_1 B)\epsilon_t.$$

Writing out the model without backshift notation we have

$$D_t = c + (1 + a_1)D_{t-1} - a_1 D_{t-2} + \epsilon_t - b_1 \epsilon_{t-1}.$$

Let us suppose this model has been fitted to a time series with the result that $c = 15$, $a_1 = 0.24$, and $b_1 = 0.70$. Suppose that the last five values of the time series used to fit this model were 31.68, 29.10, 43.15, 56.74, and 62.44 based on a total of 76 observations. The first period in which one can forecast is period 77. The one-step-ahead forecast for period 77 made at the end of period 76 is

$$\hat{D}_{77} = 15 + (1 + 0.24)D_{76} - 0.24 D_{75} - 0.70 \epsilon_{76}.$$

$\hat{D}_{77}$ is the conditional expected value of D_{77} having observed the demand in periods 1, 2, ..., 76. Since this is the first forecast made for this series, there is no observed previous value of the error, and the final term drops out. Hence, the one-step-ahead forecast made in period 76 for the demand in period 77 is $15 + (1.24)(62.44) - (0.24)(56.74) = 78.81$. Now, suppose we observed a value of 70 for the series in period 77. That means that the forecast error observed in period 77 is $\epsilon_{77} = 78.81 - 70 = 8.81$. The one-step-ahead forecast for period 78 made in period 77 would be $15 + (1.24)(70) - 0.24(62.44) - 0.70(8.81) = 86.25$.

When using an ARIMA model for multiple-step-ahead forecasts, the operative rule is to use the forecasts for the unobserved demand and use zero for the unobserved errors. Thus in the preceding example, a two-step-ahead forecast made at the end of period 76 for demand in period 78 would be based on the assumption that the observed demand in period 77 was the one-step-ahead forecast, 86.25. The observed forecast error for period 77 would be assumed to be zero.

Summary of the Steps Required for Building ARIMA Models

There are four major steps required for building Box-Jenkins forecasting models.

1. *Data transformations.* The Box-Jenkins methodology is predicated on starting with a stationary time series. To be certain that the series is indeed stationary, several preliminary steps might be required. We know that differencing eliminates trend and seasonality. However, if the mean of the series is relatively fixed, it still may be the case that the variance is not constant, thus possibly requiring a transformation of the data (for example, stock market data are often transformed by the logarithm).

2. *Model identification.* This step refers to determining exactly which ARIMA model seems to be most appropriate. Proper model identification is both art and science. It is difficult, if not impossible, to identify the appropriate model by only examining the series itself. It is far more effective to study the sample autocorrelations and

partial autocorrelations to discern patterns that match those of known processes. In some cases, the autocorrelation structure will point to a simple AR or MA process, but it is more common that some mixture of these terms would be required to get the best fit. However, one must not add terms willy-nilly. The operative concept is parsimony—that is, use the most economical model that adequately describes the data.

3. *Parameter estimation.* Once the appropriate model has been identified, the optimal values of the model parameters (i.e., $a_0, a_1, \ldots, a_p$ and $b_0, b_1, \ldots, b_q$) must be determined. Typically, this is done via either least squares fitting methods or the method of maximum likelihood. In either case, this step is done by a computer program.

4. *Forecasting.* Once the model has been identified and the optimal parameter values determined, the model provides forecasts of future values of the series. Box-Jenkins models are most effective in providing one-step-ahead forecasts, but can also provide multiple-step-ahead forecasts as well.

5. *Evaluation.* The pattern of residuals (forecast errors) can provide useful information regarding the quality of the model. The residuals should form a white noise (i.e., random) process with zero mean. Residuals should be normally distributed as well. When there are patterns in the residuals, it suggests that the forecasting model can be improved.

Case Study. *Using Box-Jenkins Methodology to Predict Monthly International Airline Passenger Totals*

This study is based on data that appeared originally in Brown (1962), but was analyzed using ARIMA methods in Box and Jenkins (1970). It illustrates the basic steps in transforming data and building ARIMA models. The data represent the monthly international airline sales from the period January 1949 to December 1960. The raw data appear in Table 2–3 and are pictured in Figure 2–17. From the figure, it is clear that there are several nonstationarities in this data. First, there is clearly an increasing linear trend. Second, there is seasonality, with a pattern repeating yearly. Third, there is increasing variance over time. In cases where the mean and variance increase at a comparable rate (which would occur if the series is

TABLE 2–3
International Airline Passengers: Monthly Totals (Thousands of Passengers), January 1949–December 1960*

Source: From Box and Jenkins (1970), p. 531.

	Jan.	Feb.	Mar.	Apr.	May	June	July	Aug.	Sept.	Oct.	Nov.	Dec.
1949	112	118	132	129	121	135	148	148	136	119	104	118
1950	115	126	141	135	125	149	170	170	158	133	114	140
1951	145	150	178	163	172	178	199	199	184	162	146	166
1952	171	180	193	181	183	218	230	242	209	191	172	194
1953	196	196	236	235	229	243	264	272	237	211	180	201
1954	204	188	235	227	234	264	302	293	259	229	203	229
1955	242	233	267	269	270	315	364	347	312	274	237	278
1956	284	277	317	313	318	374	413	405	355	306	271	306
1957	315	301	356	348	355	422	465	467	404	347	305	336
1958	340	318	362	348	363	435	491	550	404	359	310	337
1959	360	342	406	396	420	472	548	559	463	407	362	405
1960	417	391	419	461	472	535	622	606	508	461	390	432

*144 observations.

FIGURE 2–17
International airline passengers (thousands)

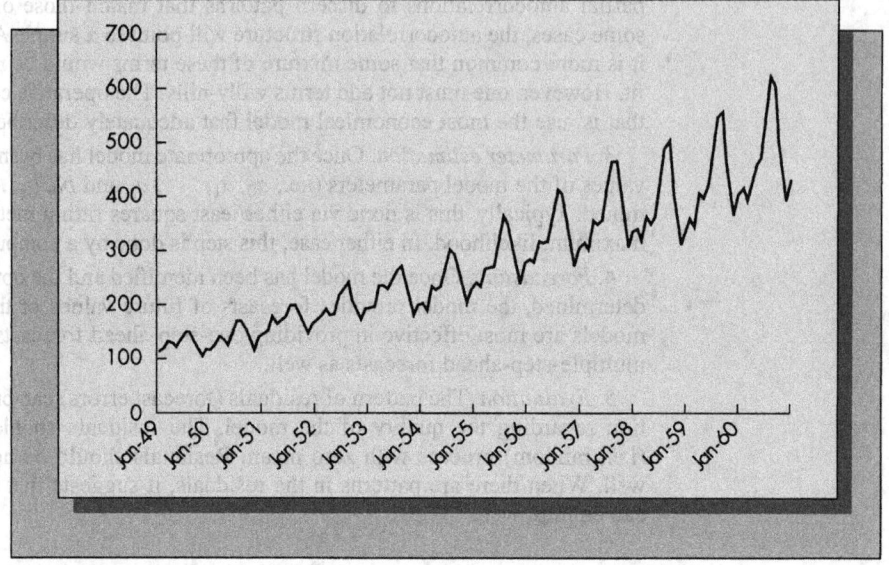

FIGURE 2–18
Natural log of international airline passengers

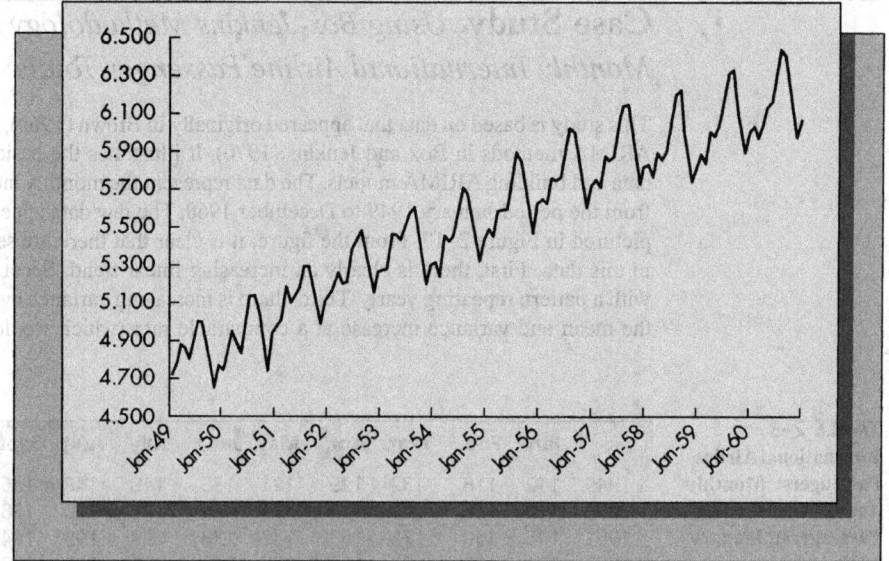

increasing by a fixed percentage), a logarithmic transformation will usually eliminate the nonstationarity due to increasing variance. (Changing variance is known as heteroscedasticity, and constant variance is known as homoscedasticity.) Applying a natural log transformation to the data yields a homoscedastic series as shown in Figure 2–18.

Next, we need to apply two levels of differencing to eliminate both trend and seasonality. The trend is eliminated by applying a single level of differencing and the seasonality by applying 12 periods of differencing. After these three transformations are applied to the original data, the resulting data appear in Figure 2–19. Note now the transformed data

FIGURE 2–19
Natural log of airline data with single and seasonal differencing

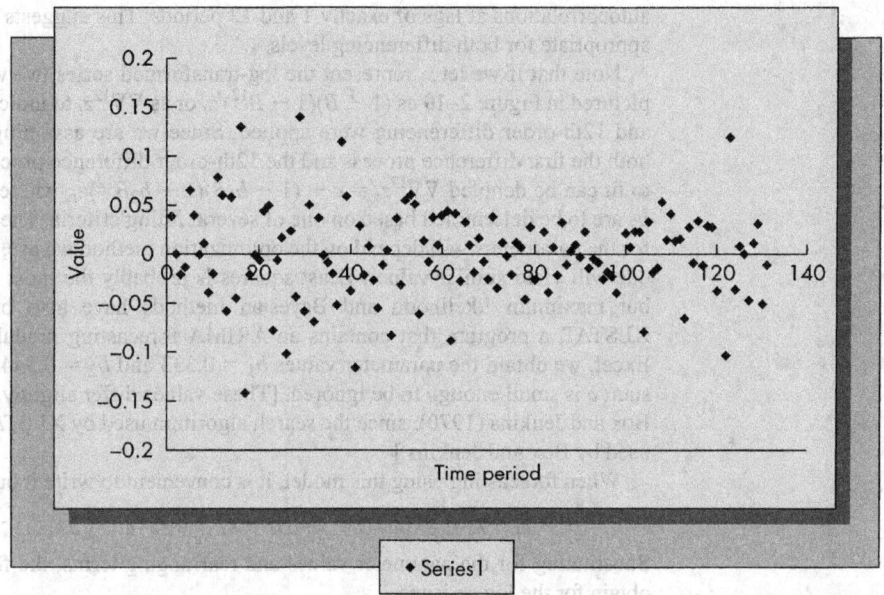

appear to form a random white noise process centered at zero showing neither trend nor seasonality.

It is to this set of data that we wish to fit an ARMA model. To do so, we determine the sample autocorrelations. While this can be accomplished with many of the software programs available for forecasting (including general statistical packages, such as SAS), we have done the calculations directly in Excel using the formulas for sample autocorrelations given earlier. The autocorrelations for lags of 1 to 12 periods for the series pictured in Figure 2–19 appear in Table 2–4.

Although not explicitly discussed in this section, when both seasonal differencing and period-to-period differencing are applied simultaneously, one must determine an ARMA model for each level of differencing. That is, one would like to find an ARMA model corresponding to the single level of differencing and to the seasonal level of differencing. Thus, when examining the autocorrelation function, we look for patterns at lags of 1 period and patterns at lags of 12 periods. From Table 2–4 it is clear that there are significant

TABLE 2–4
Autocorrelations for the Transformed Airline Data Pictured in Figure 2–19 (after taking logarithms and two levels of differencing)

Lag	Autocorrelation	Lag	Autocorrelation	Lag	Autocorrelation
1	−0.34	13	0.15	25	−0.10
2	0.11	14	−0.06	26	0.05
3	−0.20	15	0.15	27	−0.03
4	0.02	16	−0.14	28	0.05
5	0.06	17	0.07	29	−0.02
6	0.03	18	0.02	30	−0.05
7	−0.06	19	−0.01	31	−0.05
8	0.00	20	−0.12	32	0.20
9	0.18	21	0.04	33	−0.12
10	−0.08	22	−0.09	34	0.08
11	0.06	23	0.22	35	−0.15
12	−0.39	24	−0.02	36	−0.01

autocorrelations at lags of exactly 1 and 12 periods. This suggests that MA(1) models are appropriate for both differencing levels.

Note that if we let z_t represent the log-transformed series, we would denote the series pictured in Figure 2–19 as $(1 - B)(1 - B^{12})z_t$ or as $\nabla\nabla^{12}z_t$ to indicate that both first-order and 12th-order differencing were applied. Since we are assuming an MA(1) model for both the first difference process and the 12th-order difference process, the model we wish to fit can be denoted $\nabla\nabla^{12}z_t = c + (1 - b_1B)(1 - b_2B^{12})\epsilon_t$, where the parameters b_1 and b_2 are to be determined based on one of several fitting criteria. The exact values we obtain for the parameters will depend on the optimization method we use, but generally all methods will yield similar values. Least squares is probably the most common method used, but maximum likelihood and Bayesian methods have also been suggested. Using XLSTAT, a program that contains an ARIMA forecasting module and is embedded in Excel, we obtain the parameter values $b_1 = 0.333$ and $b_2 = 0.544$. The value of the constant c is small enough to be ignored. [These values differ slightly from those reported in Box and Jenkins (1970), since the search algorithm used by XLSTAT differs from the one used by Box and Jenkins.]

When forecasting using this model, it is convenient to write it out explicitly in the form

$$z_t - z_{t-1} - (z_{t-12} - z_{t-13}) = \epsilon_t - b_1\epsilon_{t-1} - b_2(\epsilon_{t-12} - b_1\epsilon_{t-13}).$$

Substituting for the parameter values and rearranging terms, the forecasting equation we obtain for the log series is

$$z_t = z_{t-1} + z_{t-12} - z_{t-13} + \epsilon_t - 0.333\epsilon_{t-1} - 0.544\epsilon_{t-12} + 0.181\epsilon_{t-13}.$$

To forecast the original series, D_t, we apply the antilog to z_t, namely, $D_t = \exp(z_t)$. Because of the two levels of differencing, period 14 is the first period for which we can determine a forecast. In Figure 2–20, we show the original series starting at period 14 and the one-step-ahead forecast using the preceding ARIMA model. Note how closely the ARIMA forecast tracks the original series.

FIGURE 2–20
Observed versus predicted number of airline sales

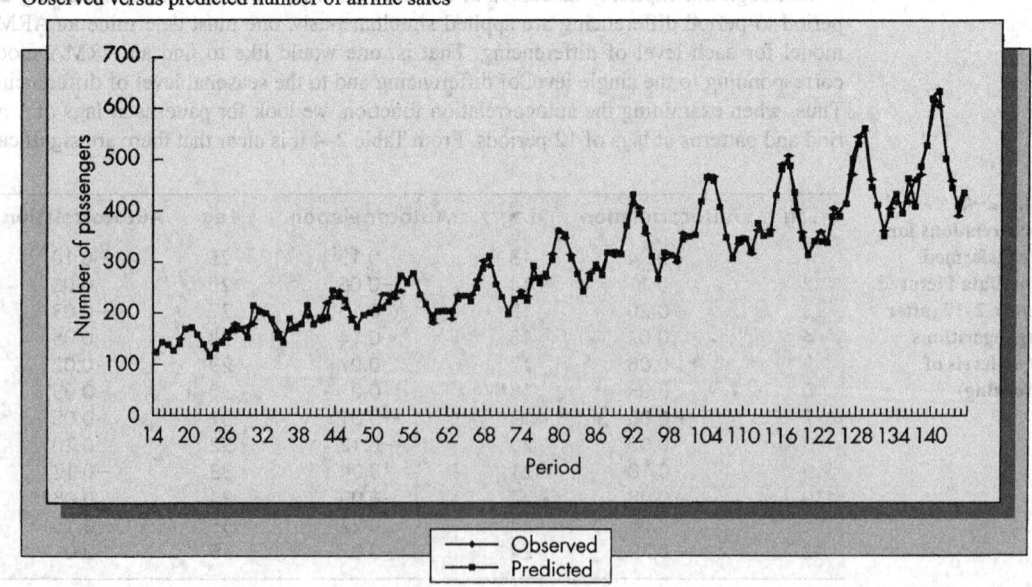

Snapshot Application

A SIMPLE ARIMA MODEL PREDICTS THE PERFORMANCE OF THE U.S. ECONOMY

In years past, a very complex and very large regression model known as the FRB-MIT-PENN (FMP) model (for Federal Reserve Bank—Massachusetts Institute of Technology—University of Pennsylvania) was used to predict several basic measures of the U.S. economy. This model required massive amounts of data and past history. Nelson (1972) employed the ARIMA methodology outlined in this section to obtain predictors for many of the same fundamental measures of the U.S. economy considered in the FMP model. These include gross national product, consumer's expenditures on durable goods, nonfarm inventory investment, and several others.

Perhaps the most interesting case is the prediction of the gross national product. The ARIMA model he obtained is surprisingly simple:

$$z_t = z_{t-1} + 0.615(z_{t-1} - z_{t-2}) + 2.76 + \epsilon_t,$$

which is easily seen to be an AR(1) model with one level of differencing. What is most impressive and surprising is that the forecast errors obtained from this and Nelson's other ARIMA models had lower forecast errors in predicting future values of these measures than did the complex FMP model. Again, this points to the power of these methods in providing accurate forecasts in a variety of scenarios.

Box-Jenkins Modeling—A Critique

The preceding case study highlights the power of ARIMA models. However, one must be aware that there are only a limited number of situations in which one would or could use them. An important requirement is that one must have a substantial history of time series in question. Typical recommendations vary between 50 and 100 observations of past history, and that is for a nonseasonal series. When seasonality is present, the requirement is more severe. In some sense, each season of data is comparable to a single observation.

In the operations context, one would be hard-pressed to find many applications where that much history is available. Style goods, for example, are typically managed with a very small amount of data, if any; for example, recall the Sport Obermeyer Snapshot Application in this chapter. Even when enough data are available, it may not make sense to invest the amount of time and energy required to develop an ARIMA model. Consider forecasting usage rates in a Wal-Mart store, for example, where one must manage tens of thousands of SKUs. ARIMA models are most useful for forecasting economic series with substantial history (such as GNP) or continuous processes (such as chemical processes or stock market prices). In the latter case, one can conceivably choose a small enough time bucket to generate any number of observations.

Another shortcoming of ARIMA models is that they are not easily updated. If the problem parameters change, one must redo the analysis to find a new model, or at least rerun the software to find new optimal values of the parameters.

Even with all of these shortcomings, Box-Jenkins methods are very powerful. In the right situation, they can result in much more accurate short-term forecasts than any of the other methods discussed in this chapter.

Problems for Section 2.10

38. Consider the white noise process data in Table 2–1. Enter this data into Excel and generate the sample autocorrelations for lags of 1 to 10 periods, using the formula for the sample autocorrelations (r_k). Alternatively, if you have access to an ARIMA computing module, generate these autocorrelations using your software.

39. Use the random number generator in Excel and the normal variate generator given in Problem 5.34 to generate a sample path for an AR(1) process such as the ones shown in Figure 2–14 for $a_1 = 0.7$. Compute the sample autocorrelation function for the process you generated, and check that the correlogram has the same structure as shown in Figure 2–15a.

40. Use the random number generator in Excel and the normal variate generator given in Problem 5.34 to generate a sample path for an MA(1) process such as the ones shown in Figure 2–16 for $b_1 = 0.7$. Compute the sample autocorrelation function for the process you generated, and check that the correlogram shows only one significant autocorrelation at a lag of one period. What does the value of this autocorrelation appear to be?

41. Use the random number generator in Excel and the normal variate generator given in Problem 5.34 to generate a sample path for an ARMA(1,1) process. Use $a_1 = 0.8$ and $b_1 = -0.6$. Compute the sample autocorrelation function for this process.

42. Consider an ARIMA(2,1,1) process. Write out the resulting model using
    a. Backshift notation with the backshift operator B.
    b. Backshift notation with the operator ∇.
    c. No backshift notation.

43. Consider an ARIMA(0,2,2) process. Write out the resulting model using
    a. Backshift notation with the backshift operator B.
    b. Backshift notation with the operator ∇.
    c. No backshift notation.

44. Using back-substitution, show that an ARMA(1, 1) model may be written as either an AR(∞) or an MA(∞) model.

45. Consider the seasonal time series pictured in Figure 2–8. What level of differencing would be required to make this series stationary?

46. The U.S. Federal Reserve in St. Louis stores a host of economic data on its Web site at http://research.stlouisfed.org/fred2/categories/106. Download the following time series from this Web site:
    a. U.S. GNP.
    b. Annual Federal Funds rate.
    c. Consumer price index.

    In each case, use a minimum of 50 data points over a period not including the most recent 25 years. Graph the data points, and determine first the level of differencing that appears to be required. Once you have obtained a stationary process, use the methods outlined in this section to arrive at an appropriate ARIMA model for each case. Compare the most recent 25 years of observations with the predictions obtained from your model using both one-step-ahead and two-step-ahead forecasts.

2.11 PRACTICAL CONSIDERATIONS

Model Identification and Monitoring

Determining the proper model depends both on the characteristics of the history of observations and on the context in which the forecasts are required. When historical data are available, they should be examined carefully in order to determine if obvious patterns exist, such as trend or seasonal fluctuations. Usually, these patterns can be spotted by graphing the data. Statistical tests, such as significance of regression, can be used to verify the existence of a trend, for example. Identifying complex relationships requires more sophisticated methods. The *sample autocorrelation function* can reveal intricate relationships that simple graphical methods cannot as we saw in Section 2.10.

Once a model has been chosen, forecasts should be monitored regularly to see if the model is appropriate or if some unforeseen change has occurred in the series. As we indicated, a forecasting method should not be biased. That is, the expected value of the forecast error should be zero. In addition to the methods mentioned in Section 2.6, one means of monitoring the bias is the *tracking signal* developed by Trigg (1964). Following earlier notation, let e_t be the observed error in period t and $|e_t|$ the absolute value of the observed error. The smoothed values of the error and the absolute error are given by

$$E_t = \beta e_t + (1 - \beta)E_{t-1},$$
$$M_t = \beta |e_t| + (1 - \beta)M_{t-1}.$$

The tracking signal is the ratio

$$T_t = \left| \frac{E_t}{M_t} \right|.$$

If forecasts are unbiased, the smoothed error E_t should be small compared to the smoothed absolute error M_t. Hence, a large value of the tracking signal indicates biased forecasts, which suggest that the forecasting model is inappropriate. The value of T_t that signals a significant bias depends on the smoothing constant β. For example, Trigg (1964) claims that a value of T_t exceeding 0.51 indicates nonrandom errors for a β of .1. The tracking signal also can be used directly as a variable smoothing constant. This is considered in Problem 55.

Simple versus Complex Time Series Methods

The literature on forecasting is voluminous. In this chapter we have touched only on a number of fairly simple techniques. The reader is undoubtedly asking himself or herself, do these methods actually work? The results from the literature suggest that the simplest methods are often as accurate as sophisticated ones. Armstrong (1984) reviews 25 years of forecasting case studies with the goal of ascertaining whether or not sophisticated methods work better. In comparing the results of 39 case studies, he found that in 20 cases sophisticated methods performed about as well as simple ones, in 11 cases they outperformed simple methods, and in 7 cases they performed significantly worse.

A more sophisticated forecasting method is one that requires the estimation of a larger number of parameters from the data. Trouble can arise when these parameters are estimated incorrectly. To give some idea of the nature of this problem, consider a comparison of simple moving averages and regression analysis for the following series: 7, 12, 9, 23, 27. Suppose that we are interested in forecasting at the end of period 5 for the demand in period 15 (that is, we require $F_{5,15}$). The five-period moving-average forecast made at the end of period 5 is 15.6, and this would be the forecast for period 15. The least squares fit of the data is $\hat{D}_t = 0.3 + 5.1t$. Substituting $t = 15$, we obtain the regression forecast of 76.8. In Figure 2–21 we picture the realization of the demand through period 15. Notice what has happened. The apparent trend that existed in the first five periods was extrapolated to period 15 by the regression equation. However, there really was no significant trend in this particular

FIGURE 2–21
The difficulty with long-term forecasts

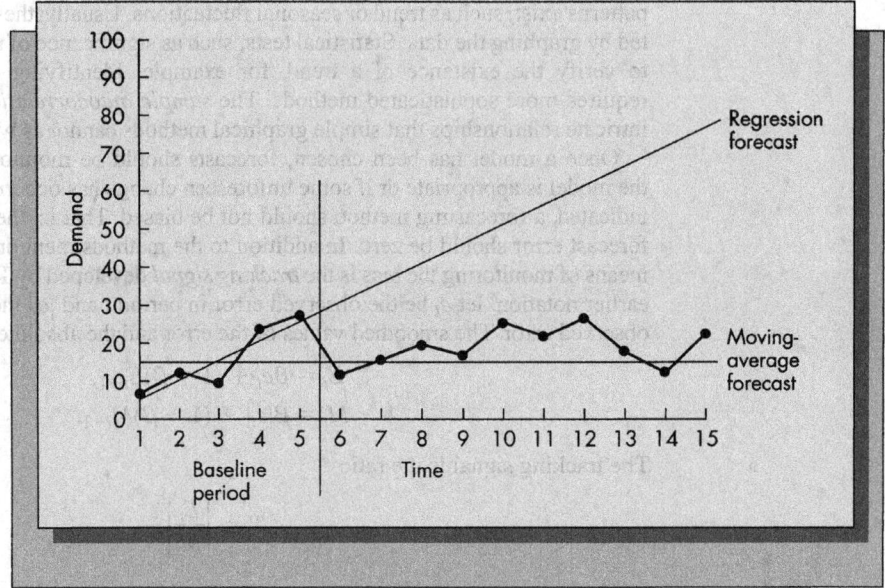

case. The more complex model gave *significantly* poorer results for the long-term forecast.

There is some evidence that the arithmetic average of forecasts obtained from different methods is more accurate than a single method (see Makridakis and Winkler, 1983). This is perhaps because often a single method is unable to capture the underlying signal in the data and different models capture different aspects of the signal. (See a discussion of this phenomenon following Armstrong, 1984.)

What do these observations tell us about the application of forecasting techniques to production planning? At the aggregate level of planning, forecast accuracy is extremely important and multiple-step-ahead forecasts play an integral role in the planning of workforce and production levels. For that reason, blind reliance on time series methods is not advised at this level. At a lower level in the system, such as routine inventory management for spare parts, the use of simple time series methods such as moving averages or exponential smoothing makes a great deal of sense. At the individual item level, short-term forecasts for a large number of items are required, and monitoring the forecast for each item is impractical at best. The risk of severe errors is minimized if simple methods are used.

2.12 OVERVIEW OF ADVANCED TOPICS IN FORECASTING

Simulation as a Forecasting Tool

Computer simulation is a powerful technique for tackling complex problems. A computer simulation is a description of a problem reduced to a computer program. The program is designed to re-create the key aspects of the dynamics of a real situation. When a problem is too complex to model mathematically, simulation is a popular alternative. By rerunning the program under different starting conditions and/or different scenarios, one can, by a kind of trial-and-error process, discover the best strategy for managing a system.

Simulation is a common tool for modeling manufacturing planning problems such as complex material flow problems in the plant. It is less commonly used as a forecasting tool. Compaq Computer, a successful producer of personal computers based in Houston, Texas, has experimented with a powerful simulation-based forecasting tool for assisting with the process of new product introductions (McWilliams, 1995). The program recommends the optimal timing and pricing of new product introductions by incorporating forecasts of component availability and price changes, fluctuating demand for a given feature or price, and the impact of rival models.

Using this tool, Compaq decided to delay announcement of several new Pentium-based models in late 1994. This strategy "went against everything the company believed." Compaq's basic strategy had always been to be a technology leader, but its forecasting tool suggested that corporate customers were not quite ready to switch to Pentium-based machines at the end of 1994. The strategy proved to be very profitable for Compaq, which subsequently posted record earnings.

Forecasting Demand in the Presence of Lost Sales

Retailers rely heavily on forecasting. Basic items (items that don't change appreciably from season to season, such as men's dress shirts) generally have substantial sales history, arguing for the use of time series methods to forecast demand. However, there is an important difference between what is observed and what one wants to forecast. The goal is to forecast *demand,* but one only observes *sales*. What's the difference? Suppose a customer wants to buy a blouse in a certain size and color and finds it's not available on the shelf? What will she do? Perhaps she will place a special order with a salesperson, but, more likely, she will just leave the store and try to find the product somewhere else. This is known as a lost sale. The difficulty is that most retailers have no way to track lost sales. Thus, they observe sales but need to estimate demand.

As an example, consider an item that is restocked to 10 units at the beginning of each week. Suppose that over the past 15 weeks the sales history for the item was 7, 5, 10, 10, 8, 3, 6, 10, 10, 9, 5, 0, 10, 10, 4. Consider those weeks in which sales were 10 units. What were the demands in those weeks? The answer is that we don't know. We only know that it was *at least* 10. If you computed the sample mean and sample variance of these numbers, they would underestimate the true mean and variance of demand.

How does one go about forecasting demand in this situation? In the parlance of classical statistics, this is known as a censored sample. That means that we know the values of demand for only a portion of the sample. For the other portion of the sample, we know only a lower bound on the demand. Special statistical methods that incorporate censoring give significantly improved estimates of the population mean and variance in this case. These methods can be embedded into sequential forecasting schemes, such as exponential smoothing, to provide significantly improved forecasts.

Nahmias (1994) considered the problem of forecasting in the presence of lost sales when the true demand distribution was normal. He compared the method of maximum likelihood for censored samples and a new method, either of which could be incorporated into exponential smoothing routines. He also showed that both of these methods would result in substantially improved forecasts of both the mean and the variation of the demand.

To see how dramatic this difference can be, consider a situation in which the true weekly demand for a product is a normal random variable with mean 100 and standard deviation 30. Suppose that items are stocked up to 110 units at the start of each week. Exponential smoothing is used to obtain two sets of forecasts: the first accounts for lost sales (includes censoring) and the second does not (does not including censoring). Figures 2–22 and 2–23 show the estimators for the mean and the standard

FIGURE 2–22
Tracking the mean when lost sales are present

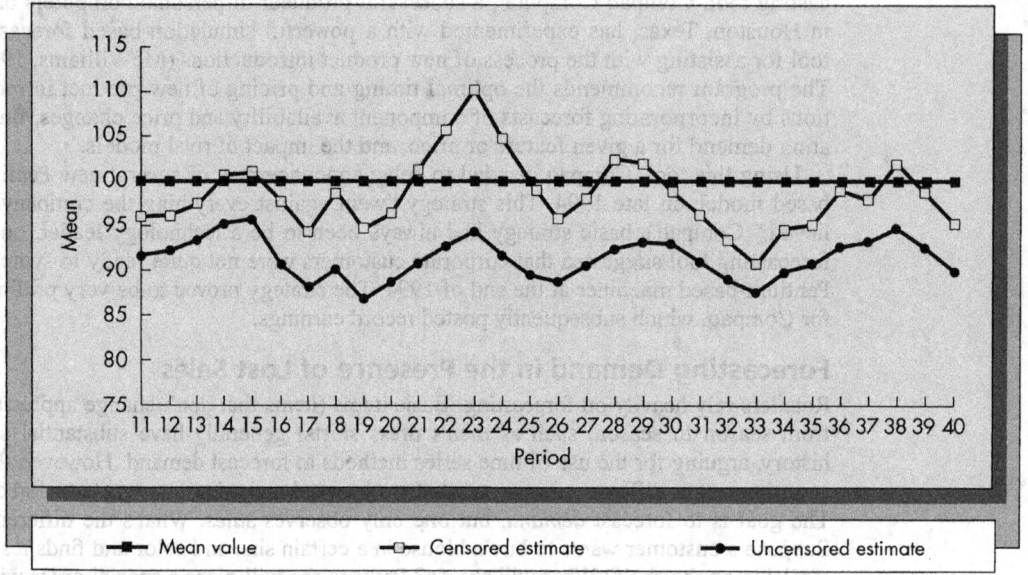

FIGURE 2–23
Tracking the standard deviation when lost sales are present

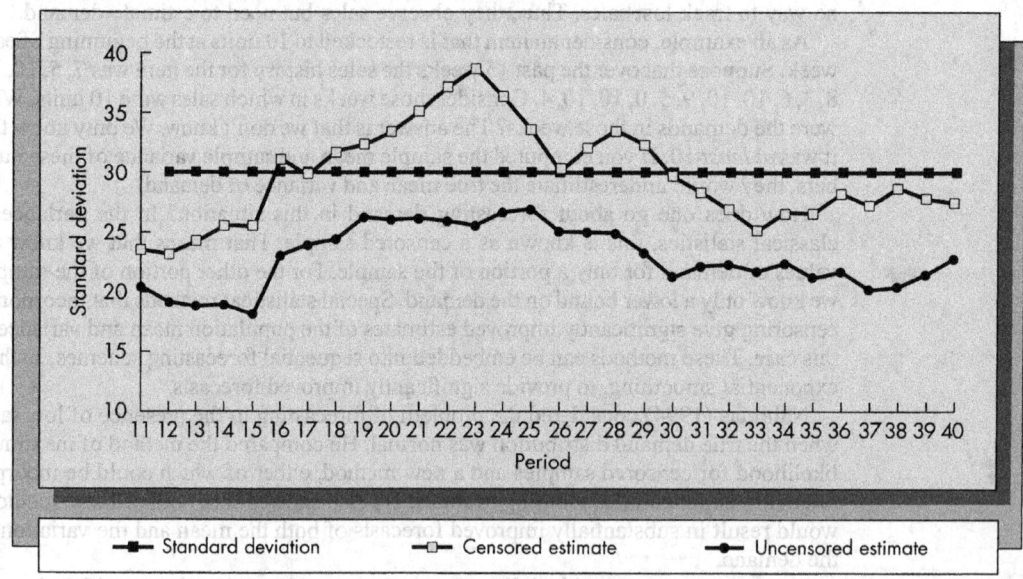

deviation, respectively, with and without censoring. Notice the severe low bias when lost sales are ignored in both cases. That means that by not correctly accounting for the difference between sales and demand, one underestimates both the mean and the variance of the demand. Since both the mean and the variance of demand are inputs for determining optimal stocking levels, these levels could be severely underestimated.

2.13 LINKING FORECASTING AND INVENTORY MANAGEMENT

Inventory control under demand uncertainty will be treated in detail in Chapter 5. In practice, inventory management and demand forecasting are closely linked. The forecasting method could be any one of the methods discussed in this chapter. One of the inputs required for inventory control models is the distribution of the demand over a period or over an order replenishment lead time. Is there a link between the distribution of forecast errors and the distribution of demand? The answer is that there is such a link. The forecast error distribution plays a key role in the correct application of inventory models in practice.

The first issue is to decide on the appropriate form of the distribution of demand. Most commercial systems assume that the demand distribution is normal. That means we need only estimate the mean μ and the standard deviation σ to specify the entire distribution. (Statistical methods, known as goodness-of-fit techniques, can be applied to test the accuracy of the normality assumption.) Whether or not the inventory system is linked to a forecasting system, we must have a history of observations of demand to obtain statistical estimates of the mean and variance. (When no history of demand exists, personal judgment must be substituted for statistical estimation. Methods for aggregating subjective judgment are discussed in Section 2.3.)

In the beginning of Chapter 5, we discuss how one would estimate the mean and the variance of demand directly from a history of demand observations. In practice, however, we don't generally use a long history of observations, because we believe that the underlying demand distribution does not remain constant indefinitely. That is why we adjust the N for moving averages or the α for exponential smoothing to balance stability and responsiveness. If that is the case, what is the appropriate variance estimator one should use?

In Appendix 2–A, we show that for simple moving averages of order N, the variance of forecast error, σ_e^2, is given by

$$\sigma_e^2 = \sigma^2 \left(\frac{N+1}{N} \right)$$

and for exponential smoothing the variance of forecast error is

$$\sigma_e^2 = \sigma^2 \left(\frac{2}{2-\alpha} \right).$$

Notice that in both cases, the value of σ_e^2 *exceeds* the value of σ^2. Also notice that as N gets large and as α gets small, the values of σ_e and σ grow close. These cases occur when one uses the entire history of demand observations to make a forecast. In Chapter 5 one of the inputs needed to determine safety stocks for inventory is the distribution of demand. The problem is, if we have estimators for both σ_e and σ, which should be used as the standard deviation estimator for setting safety stocks?

The obvious answer is that we should use the estimator for σ, since this represents the standard deviation of demand. The correct answer, however, is that we should use σ_e. The reason is that the process of forecasting introduces sampling error into the estimation process, and this sampling error is accounted for in the value of σ_e. The forecasting error variance is higher than the demand variance because the forecast is based on only a limited portion of the demand history.

We also can provide an intuitive explanation. If a forecast is used to estimate the mean demand, we keep safety stocks in order to protect against the error in this forecast.

Hence, the distribution of forecast errors is more relevant than the distribution of demands. This is an important practical point that has been the source of much confusion in the literature. We will return to this issue in Chapter 5 and discuss its relevance in the context of safety stock calculations.

Most inventory control systems use the method suggested by R. G. Brown (1959 and 1962) to estimate the value of σ_e. (In fact, it appears that Brown was the first to recognize the importance of the distribution of forecast errors in inventory management applications.) The method requires estimating the MAD of forecast errors using exponential smoothing. This is accomplished using the smoothing equation

$$\text{MAD}_t = \alpha |F_t - D_t| + (1 - \alpha)\text{MAD}_{t-1}$$

The MAD is converted to an estimate of the standard deviation of forecast error by multiplying by 1.25. That is, the estimator for σ_e obtained at time t is

$$\hat{\sigma}_e = 1.25 \, \text{MAD}_t.$$

A small value of α, generally between 0.1 and 0.2, is used to ensure stability in the MAD estimator. This approach to estimating the MAD works for any of the forecasting methods discussed in this chapter. Safety stocks are then computed using this estimator for σ_e.

Case Study. Predicting the Growth of Facebook

Facebook, founded by Mark Zuckerberg in 2004, is the quintessential social network and one of the true phenomena of the early 21st century. While Myspace, another social network, was founded a year earlier than Facebook, it never enjoyed the kind of success experienced by Facebook. Consider the problem of forecasting the number of Facebook users in 2013 based on data up until 2011. The following chart tracks the numbers of Facebook users from the year of its founding in 2004 to early 2011:

Date	Users (in millions)	Month Number
12/04	1	12
12/05	5.5	24
12/06	12	36
4/07	20	40
10/07	50	46
08/08	100	56
01/09	150	61
02/09	175	62
04/09	200	64
07/09	250	67
09/09	300	69
12/09	350	72
02/10	450	74
07/10	500	79
09/10	550	81
01/11	600	85
02/11	650	86

Note that the dates are not evenly spaced. One way to graph this data, which will also be useful in analyzing it, is to convert the dates to numbers of months elapsed from an arbitrary starting point. If we define month 1 as January 2004, then the dates in column 1 translate to the number of months elapsed in column 3.

Treating numbers of months as the independent variable, the graph of numbers of users versus months elapsed appears in the graph below:

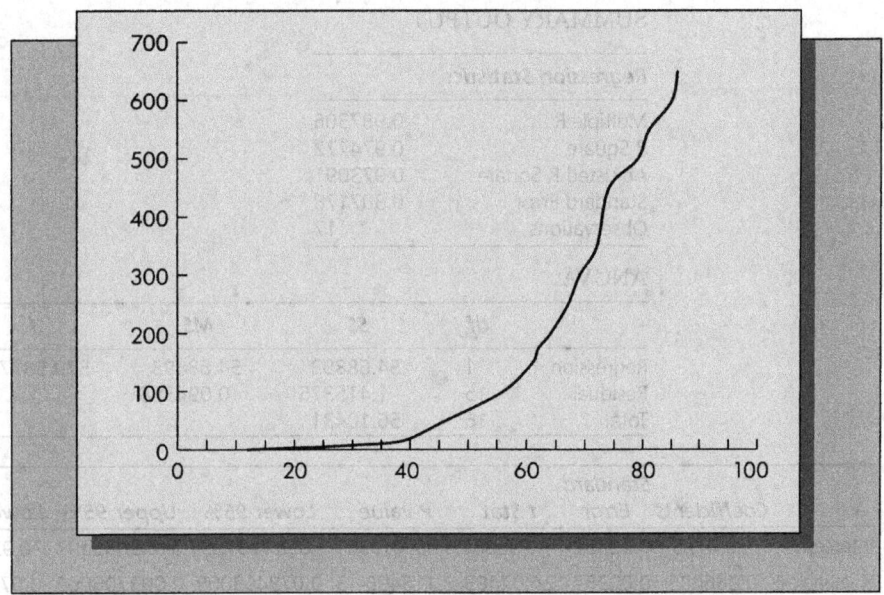

The graph seems to show exponential growth. To test this hypothesis, we consider graphing the natural logarithm of the numbers of users versus elapsed numbers of months. Doing so results in the following graph:

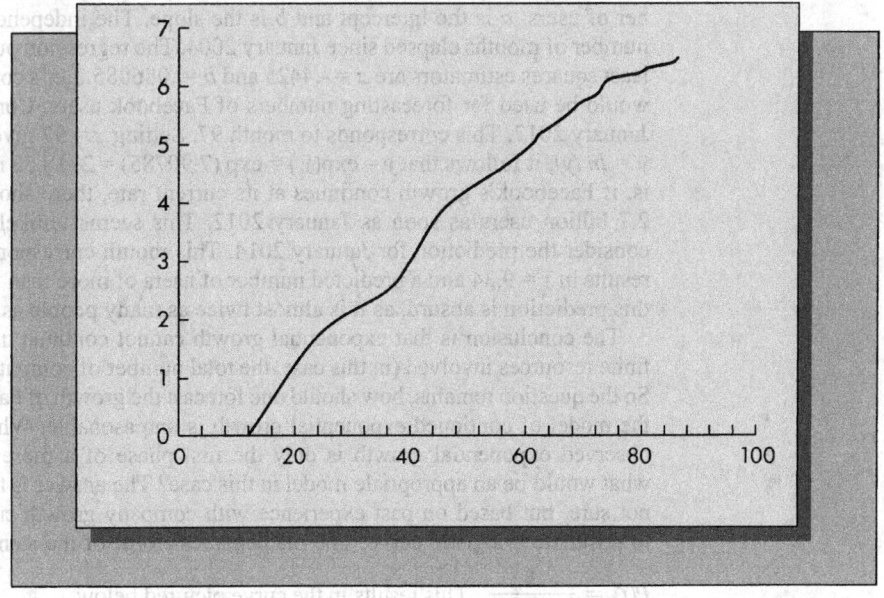

The fact that the graph of the natural logs is almost linear means that the assumption of exponential growth is an accurate one. Fitting a simple linear regression to this curve results in the following:

SUMMARY OUTPUT

Regression Statistics

Multiple R	0.987306
R Square	0.974772
Adjusted R Square	0.973091
Standard Error	0.307178
Observations	17

ANOVA

	df	SS	MS	F	Significance F
Regression	1	54.68893	54.68893	579.5877578	2.11649E-13
Residual	15	1.415375	0.094358		
Total	16	56.10431			

	Coefficients	Standard Error	t Stat	P-value	Lower 95%	Upper 95%	Lower 95.0%	Upper 95.0%
Intercept	−0.4425	0.22592	−1.95867	0.069013361	−0.924037859	0.039035397	−0.924037859	0.039035397
X Variable 1	0.086085	0.00357	24.07463	2.11649E-13	0.078463009	0.093706009	0.078463009	0.093706009

This Excel output shows that the logs follow a straight line relationship very closely. In fact, it's rare to see an R square value of more than .97, so this fit is extremely strong. Let's see what numbers of users would be projected by this model.

The regression model is $\bar{y} = a + bx$ where $\bar{y}$ represents the logarithm of the number of users, a is the intercept and b is the slope. The independent variable, x, is the number of months elapsed since January 2004. The regression output indicates that the least squares estimators are $a = -.4425$ and $b = .086085$. Let's consider how this model would be used for forecasting numbers of Facebook users. Consider the forecast for January 2012. This corresponds to month 97. Setting $x = 97$ gives $\bar{y} = 7.90785$. Since $\bar{y} = \ln(y)$, it follows that $y = \exp(\bar{y}) = \exp(7.90785) = 2718.53$ millions of users. That is, if Facebook's growth continues at its current rate, there should be approximately 2.7 billion users as soon as January 2012. This seems unlikely, but possible. Let's consider the prediction for January 2014. This month corresponds to $x = 121$, which results in $\bar{y} = 9.34$ and a predicted number of users of more than 11 billion! Obviously, this prediction is absurd, as it is almost twice as many people as there are on earth.

The conclusion is that exponential growth cannot continue indefinitely if there are finite resources involved (in this case, the total number of computer users on the Earth). So the question remains, how should one forecast the growth of Facebook users? Clearly the model of continued exponential growth is unreasonable. What is likely is that the observed exponential growth is only the first phase of a more complex model. But what would be an appropriate model in this case? The answer is that at this point we're not sure, but based on past experience with company growth curves, it is reasonable to postulate a logistic curve. The mathematical form of the standard logistic curve is

$P(t) = \dfrac{1}{1 + e^{-t}}$. This results in the curve pictured below.

2.13 Linking Forecasting and Inventory Management

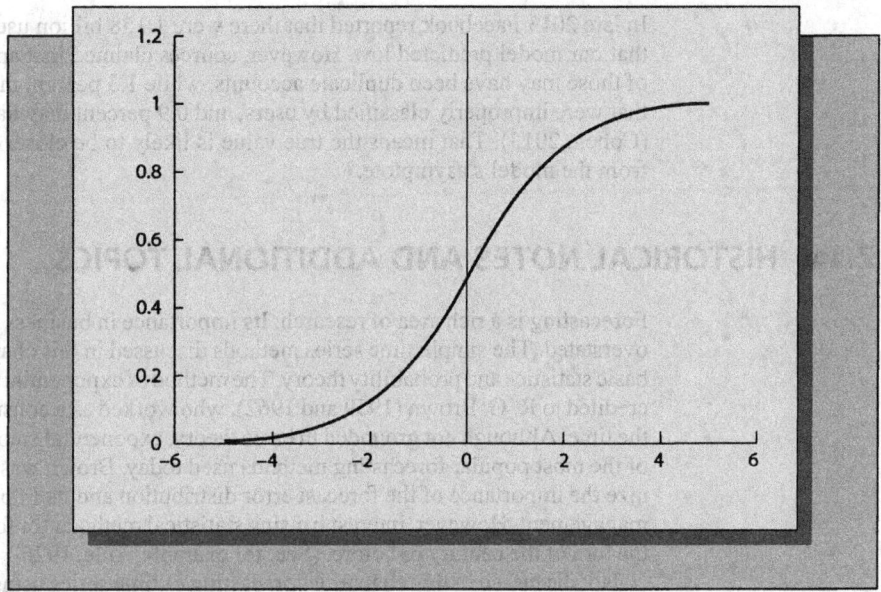

The goal is to try to provide the best fit of this curve to the original Facebook data. Since we're not sure where the point of inflection occurs, our estimate at this stage is probably not going to be very accurate. However, we can do a lot better than simply extrapolating from an exponential growth curve. In order to fit a logistic curve to a set of data, we need to know a few things. First, where in the data set is the inflection point? Second, what is likely to be the value of the asymptote (which is one for the standard curve)? And finally, what is the appropriate time scale?

Consider estimating the asymptote. This is probably not going to be very accurate since we don't know where the inflection point is. From the original graph, it does appear that the inflection point occurs somewhere near month 80. The number of users in month 80 is approximately 525 million. This would imply a value of the asymptote of approximately (2)(525 million) = 1.05 billion. This would be our best guess of where the total numbers of Facebook users would top out in the coming years.

We also need to transform the time scale. If we assume in our original curve that the first half of the logistic curve corresponds to months 20 to 80, this would be the same as 5 to 0 in the standard logistic curve above. The reader should satisfy him or herself that this would correspond to the transformation of the time scale following the equation $u = 12*t + 80$. (Check the values of u and t at -5, 0, and 5 to verify this transformation.) Furthermore, if the asymptote is K rather than 1, we scale the function by multiplying by K. Applying these two transformations, the appropriate logistic curve to fit our original data would be

$$P(u) = \frac{K}{1 + \exp(-(u - 80)/12))}$$

where u corresponds to number of elapsed months, and $K = 1.05 \times 10^9$. Consider the forecast for January 2012 based on this model. Substituting $u = 97$ gives a forecast of $P(u) = 0.845$ billion users. This certainly seems reasonable. According to the logistic model, we would expect that the number of users will be close to the postulated maximum of 1.05 billion by month 140, which corresponds to August of 2015.

In late 2013 Facebook reported that there were 1.158 billion users. If true, this implies that our model predicted low. However, sources claimed that approximately 5 percent of those may have been duplicate accounts, while 1.3 percent may have been accounts that were improperly classified by users, and 0.9 percent may have been fake accounts (Cohen, 2013). That means the true value is likely to be closer to 1.07 billion, not far from the model's asymptote.

2.14 HISTORICAL NOTES AND ADDITIONAL TOPICS

Forecasting is a rich area of research. Its importance in business applications cannot be overstated. The simple time series methods discussed in this chapter have their roots in basic statistics and probability theory. The method of exponential smoothing is generally credited to R. G. Brown (1959 and 1962), who worked as a consultant to A. D. Little at the time. Although not grounded in basic theory, exponential smoothing is probably one of the most popular forecasting methods used today. Brown was also the first to recognize the importance of the forecast error distribution and its implications for inventory management. However, interest in using statistical methods for forecasting goes back to the turn of the century or before. (See, for example, Yule, 1926.)

Not discussed in this chapter is forecasting of time series using spectral analysis and state space methods. These methods are highly sophisticated and require substantial structure to exist in the data. They often rely on the use of the autocorrelation function, and in that sense are similar conceptually to Box-Jenkins methods discussed briefly in Section 2.10. The groundbreaking work in this area is due to Norbert Wiener (1949) and Rudolph Kalman (1960). However, there have been few applications of these methods to forecasting economic time series. Most applications have been in the area of signal processing in electrical engineering. [Davenport and Root (1958) provide a good summary of the fundamental concepts in this area.]

The *Kalman filter* is a type of exponential smoothing technique in which the value of the smoothing constant changes with time and is chosen in some sort of optimal fashion. The idea of adjusting the value of the smoothing constant based on some measure of prior performance of the model has been used in a number of ad hoc ways. A typical approach is the one suggested by Trigg and Leach (1967), which requires the calculation of the tracking signal. The tracking signal is then used as the value of the smoothing constant for the next forecast. The idea is that when the tracking signal is large, it suggests that the time series has undergone a shift; a larger value of the smoothing constant should be more responsive to a sudden shift in the underlying signal. Other methods have also been suggested. We have intentionally not included an explicit discussion of adaptive response rate methods for one reason: there is little evidence that they work in the context of predicting economic time series. Most studies that compare the effectiveness of different forecasting methods for many different series show no advantage for adaptive response rate models. (See, for example, Armstrong, 1984.) The method of Trigg and Leach is discussed in more detail in Problem 55.

With the sixth edition, we have included a reasonably self-contained discussion of Box-Jenkins ARIMA models. The basic ideas behind these methods, such as the autocorrelation structure of a process, go back many years. However, Box and Jenkins (1970) were the first to put these ideas together into a comprehensive step-by-step approach for building ARIMA models for short-term forecasting. Readers may find

2.15 Summary

This chapter provided an introduction to a number of the more popular time series forecasting techniques as well as a brief discussion of other methods, including the Delphi method and causal models. A *moving-average* forecast is obtained by computing the arithmetic average of the N most recent observations of demand. An *exponential smoothing* forecast is obtained by computing the weighted average of the current observation of demand and the most recent forecast of that demand. The weight applied to the current observation is α and the weight applied to the last forecast (that is, the past observations) is $1 - \alpha$. Small N and large α result in responsive forecasts, and large N and small α result in stable forecasts. Although the two methods have similar properties, exponential smoothing is generally preferred because it requires storing only the previous forecast, whereas moving averages requires storing the last N demand observations.

When there is a trend in the series, both moving averages and exponential smoothing lag behind the trend. We discussed two time series techniques that are designed to track the trend. One is *regression analysis*, which uses least squares to fit a straight line to the data, and the other is *Holt's method*, which is a type of double exponential smoothing. Holt's method has the advantage that forecasts are easier to update as new demand observations become available.

We also discussed techniques for seasonal series. We employed *classical decomposition* to show how simple moving averages could be used to estimate seasonal factors and obtain the deseasonalized series when there is a trend and showed how seasonal factors could be estimated quickly when there is no trend. The extension of Holt's method to deal with seasonal problems, called *Winters's method*, is a type of triple exponential smoothing technique.

Section 2.12 provided a brief overview of advanced methods that are beyond the scope of this text. The final section discussed the relationship between forecasting and inventory control. The key point, which will be elaborated on in Chapter 5, is that the standard deviation of forecast error is the appropriate measure of variation for computing safety stocks.

Additional Problems on Forecasting

47. John Kittle, an independent insurance agent, uses a five-year moving average to forecast the number of claims made in a single year for one of the large insurance companies he sells for. He has just discovered that a clerk in his employ incorrectly entered the number of claims made four years ago as 1,400 when it should have been 1,200.

    a. What adjustment should Mr. Kittle make in next year's forecast to take into account the corrected value of the number of claims four years ago?

    b. Suppose that Mr. Kittle used simple exponential smoothing with $\alpha = .2$ instead of moving averages to determine his forecast. What adjustment is now required in next year's forecast? (Note that you do not need to know the value of the forecast for next year in order to solve this problem.)

48. A method of estimating the MAD discussed in Section 2.13 recomputes it each time a new demand is observed according to the following formula:

$$\text{MAD}_t = \alpha|e_t| + (1 - \alpha)\text{MAD}_{t-1}.$$

Consider the one-step-ahead forecasts for aircraft engine failures for quarters 2 through 8 obtained in Example 2.3. Assume an initial value of the MAD = 50 in period 1. Using the same value of α, what values of the MAD does this method give for periods 2 through 8? Discuss the advantages and disadvantages of this approach vis-à-vis direct computation of the MAD.

49. Herman Hahn is attempting to set up an integrated forecasting and inventory control system for his hardware store, Hahn's Hardware. When Herman indicates that outdoor lights are a seasonal item on the computer, he is prompted by the program to input the seasonal factors by quarter.

Unfortunately, Herman has not kept any historical data, but he estimates that first-quarter demand for the lights is about 30 percent below average, the second-quarter demand about 20 percent below average, third-quarter demand about average, and fourth-quarter demand about 50 percent above average. What should he input for the seasonal factors?

50. Irwin Richards, a publisher of business textbooks, publishes in the areas of management, marketing, accounting, production, finance, and economics. The president of the firm is interested in getting a relative measure of the sizes of books in the various fields. Over the past three years, the average numbers of pages of books published in each area were

	Year 1	Year 2	Year 3
Management	835	956	774
Marketing	620	540	575
Accounting	440	490	525
Production	695	680	624
Finance	380	425	410
Economics	1,220	1,040	1,312

Using the quick and dirty methods discussed in Section 2.9, find multiplicative factors for each area giving the percentage above or below the mean number of pages.

51. Over a two-year period, the Topper Company sold the following numbers of lawn mowers:

Month:	1	2	3	4	5	6	7	8	9	10	11	12
Sales:	238	220	195	245	345	380	270	220	280	120	110	85

Month:	13	14	15	16	17	18	19	20	21	22	23	24
Sales:	135	145	185	219	240	420	520	410	380	320	290	240

a. In column A input the numbers 1 to 24 representing the months and in column B the observed monthly sales. Compute the three-month moving-average forecast and place this in the third column. Be sure to align your forecast with the period *for* which you are forecasting (the average of sales for months 1, 2, and 3 should be placed in row 4; the average of sales for months 2, 3, and 4 in row 5; and so on.) In the fourth column, compute the forecast error for each month in which you have obtained a forecast.

b. In columns 5, 6, and 7 compute the absolute error, the squared error, and the absolute percentage error. Using these results, find the MAD, MSE, and MAPE for the MA(3) forecasts for months 4 through 24.

c. Repeat parts (a) and (b) for six-month moving averages. (These calculations should appear in columns 8 through 12.) Which method, MA(3) or MA(6), was more accurate for these data?

52. Repeat the calculations in Problem 51 using simple exponential smoothing, and allow the smoothing constant α to be a variable. That is, the smoothing constant should be a cell location. By experimenting with different values of α, determine the value that appears to minimize the

   a. MAD
   b. MSE
   c. MAPE

   Assume that the forecast for month 1 is 225.

53. Baby It's You, a maker of baby foods, has found a high correlation between the aggregate company sales (in $100,000) and the number of births nationally the preceding year. Suppose that the sales and the birth figures during the past eight years are

	Year							
	1	2	3	4	5	6	7	8
Sales (in $100,000)	6.1	6.4	8.3	8.8	5.1	9.2	7.3	12.5
U.S. births (in millions)	2.9	3.4	3.5	3.1	3.8	2.8	4.2	3.7

   a. Assuming that U.S. births represent the independent variable and sales the dependent variable, determine a regression equation for predicting sales based on births. Use years 2 through 8 as your baseline. (Hint: You will require the general regression formulas appearing in Appendix 2–B to solve this problem.)

   b. Suppose that births are forecasted to be 3.3 million in year 9. What forecast for sales revenue in year 10 do you obtain using the results of part (a)?

   c. Suppose that simple exponential smoothing with $\alpha = .15$ is used to predict the number of births. Use the average of years 1 to 4 as your initial forecast for period 5, and determine an exponentially smoothed forecast for U.S. births in year 9.

   d. Combine the results in parts (a), (b), and (c) to obtain a forecast for the sum of total aggregate sales in years 9 and 10.

54. Hy and Murray are planning to set up an ice cream stand in Shoreline Park, described in Problem 28. After six months of operation, the observed sales of ice cream (in dollars) and the number of park attendees are

	Month					
	1	2	3	4	5	6
Ice cream sales	325	335	172	645	770	950
Park attendees	880	976	440	1,823	1,885	2,436

a. Determine a regression equation treating ice cream sales as the dependent variable and time as the independent variable. Based on this regression equation, what should the dollar sales of ice cream be in two years (month 30)? How confident are you about this forecast? Explain your answer.

b. Determine a regression equation treating ice cream sales as the dependent variable and park attendees as the independent variable. (Hint: You will require the general regression equations in Appendix 2–B in order to solve this part.)

c. Suppose that park attendance is expected to follow a logistic curve (see Figure 2–24).

   The park department expects the attendance to peak out at about 6,000 attendees per month. Plot the data of park attendees by month and "eyeball" a logistics curve fit of the data using 6,000 as your maximum value. Based on your curve and the regression equation determined in part (b), predict ice cream sales for months 12 through 18.

55. A suggested method for determining the "right" value of the smoothing constant α in exponential smoothing is to retrospectively determine the α value that results in the minimum forecast error for some set of historical data. Comment on the appropriateness of this method and some of the potential problems that could result.

56. Lakeroad, a manufacturer of hard disks for personal computers, was founded in 1981 and has sold the following numbers of disks:

Year	Number Sold (in 000s)	Year	Number Sold (in 000s)
1981	0.2	1985	34.5
1982	4.3	1986	68.2
1983	8.8	1987	85.0
1984	18.6	1988	58.0

FIGURE 2–24
Logistic curve (for Problem 52)

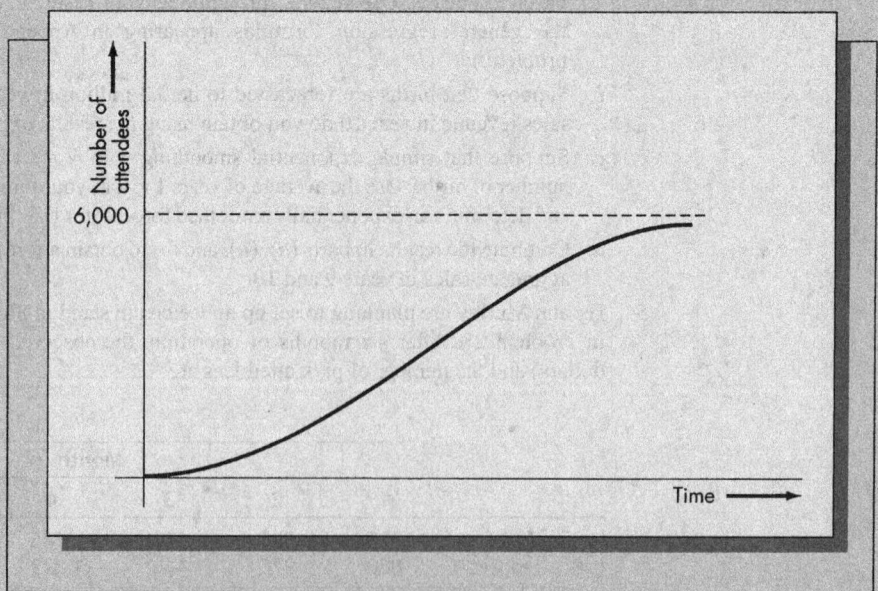

a. Suppose the firm uses Holt's method for forecasting sales. Assume $S_0 = 0$ and $G_0 = 8$. Using $\alpha = .2$ and $\beta = .2$, find one-step-ahead forecasts for 1982 through 1989 and compute the MAD and MSE for the forecasts during this period. What is the sales forecast for the year 2000 made at the end of 1988? Based on the results of 1988, why might this forecast be very inaccurate?

b. By experimenting with various values of α and β, determine the values of the smoothing constants that appear to give the most accurate forecasts.

57. Trigg and Leach (1967) suggest the following adaptive response-rate exponential smoothing method. Along with smoothing the original series, also smooth the error e_t and the absolute error $|e_t|$ according to the equations

$$E_t = \beta e_t + (1 - \beta)E_{t-1},$$
$$M_t = \beta |e_t| + (1 - \beta)M_{t-1}$$

and define the smoothing constant to be used in forecasting the series in period t as

$$\alpha_t = \left|\frac{E_t}{M_t}\right|.$$

The forecast made in period t for period $t + 1$ is obtained by the usual exponential smoothing equation, using α_t as the smoothing constant. That is,

$$F_{t+1} = \alpha_t D_t + (1 - \alpha_t)F_t.$$

The idea behind the approach is that when E_t is close in magnitude to M_t, it suggests that the forecasts are biased. In that case, a larger value of the smoothing constant results that makes the exponential smoothing more responsive to sudden changes in the series.

a. Apply the Trigg-Leach method to the data in Problem 22. Using the MAD, compare the accuracy of these forecasts with the simple exponential smoothing forecasts obtained in Problem 22. Assume that $E_1 = e_1$ (the observed error in January) and $M_1 = |e_1|$. Use $\beta = .1$.

b. For what types of time series will the Trigg-Leach adaptive response rate give more accurate forecasts, and under what circumstances will it give less accurate forecasts? Comment on the advisability of using such a method for situations in which forecasts are not closely monitored.

58. The owner of a small brewery in Milwaukee, Wisconsin, is using Winters's method to forecast his quarterly beer sales. He has been using smoothing constants of $\alpha = .2$, $\beta = .2$, and $\gamma = .2$. He has currently obtained the following values of the various slope, intercept, and seasonal factors: $S_{10} = 120$, $G_{10} = 14$, $c_{10} = 1.2$, $c_9 = 1.1$, $c_8 = .8$, and $c_7 = .9$.

a. Determine the forecast for beer sales in quarter 11.

b. Suppose that the actual sales turn out to be 128 in quarter 11. Find S_{11} and G_{11}, and find the updated values of the seasonal factors. Also determine the forecast made at the end of quarter 11 for quarter 13.

59. The U.S. gross national product (GNP) in billions of dollars during the period 1964 to 1984 was as follows:

Year	GNP	Year	GNP
1964	649.8	1975	1,598.4
1965	705.1	1976	1,782.8
1966	772.0	1977	1,990.5
1967	816.4	1978	2,249.7
1968	892.7	1979	2,508.2
1969	963.9	1980	2,732.0
1970	1,015.5	1981	3,052.6
1971	1,102.7	1982	3,166.0
1972	1,212.8	1983	3,401.6
1973	1,359.3	1984	3,774.7
1974	1,472.8		

Source: *Economic Report of the President*, February 1986.

a. Use Holt's method to predict the GNP. Determine a regression fit of the data for the period 1964 to 1974 to estimate the initial values of the slope and intercept. (Hint: If you are doing the regression by hand, transform the years by subtracting 1963 from each value to make the calculations less cumbersome.) Using Holt's method, determine forecasts for 1975 to 1984. Assume that $\alpha = .2$ and $\beta = .1$. Compute the MAD and the MSE of the one-step-ahead forecasts for the period 1975 to 1984.

b. Determine the percentage increase in GNP from 1964 to 1984 and graph the resulting series. Use a six-year moving average and simple exponential smoothing with $\alpha = .2$ to obtain one-step-ahead forecasts of this series for the period 1975 to 1984. (Use the arithmetic average of the observations from 1964 to 1974 to initialize the exponential smoothing.)

In both cases (i.e., MA and ES forecasts), convert your forecasts of the percentage increase for the following year to a forecast of the GNP itself and compute the MAD and the MSE of the resulting forecasts. Compare the accuracy of these methods with that of part (*a*).

c. Discuss the problem of predicting GNP. What methods other than the ones used in parts (*a*) and (*b*) might give better predictions of this series?

Appendix 2–A

Forecast Errors for Moving Averages and Exponential Smoothing

The forecast error e_t is the difference between the forecast for period t and the actual demand for that period. In this appendix we will derive the distribution of the forecast error for both moving averages and exponential smoothing.

The demand is assumed to be generated by the process

$$D_t = \mu + \epsilon_t,$$

where ϵ_t is normal with mean zero and variance σ^2.

CASE 1. MOVING AVERAGES

Consider first the case in which forecasts are generated by moving averages. Then the forecast error is $e_t = F_t - D_t$, where F_t is given by

$$F_t = \frac{1}{N} \sum_{i=t-N}^{t-1} D_i.$$

It follows that

$$E(F_t - D_t) = (1/N) \sum_{i=t-N}^{t-1} E(D_i) - E(D_t) = (1/N)(N\mu) - \mu = 0.$$

This proves that when demand is stationary, moving-average forecasts are unbiased. Also,

$$\text{Var}(F_t - D_t) = \text{Var}(F_t) + \text{Var}(D_t)$$

$$= (1/N^2) \sum_{i=t-N}^{t-1} \text{Var}(D_i) + \text{Var}(D_t)$$

$$= (1/N^2)(N\sigma^2) + \sigma^2$$

$$= \sigma^2(1 + 1/N) = \sigma^2[(N+1)/N].$$

It follows that the standard deviation of the forecast error, σ_e, is

$$\sigma_e = \sigma \sqrt{\frac{N+1}{N}}.$$

This is the standard deviation of the forecast error for simple moving averages in terms of the standard deviation of each observation.

Having derived the mean and the variance of the forecast error, we still need to specify the *form* of the forecast error distribution. By assumption, the values of D_t form a sequence of independent, identically distributed, normal random variables. Since F_t is a linear combination of $D_{t-1}, D_{t-2}, \ldots, D_{t-N}$, it follows that F_t is normally distributed and independent of D_t. It now follows that e_t is normal as well. Hence, the distribution of e_t is completely specified by its mean and variance.

As the expected value of the forecast error is zero, we say the method is unbiased. Notice that this is a result of the assumption that the demand process is stationary. Consider the variance of the forecast error. The value of N that minimizes σ_e is $N = +\infty$. This means that the variance is minimized if the forecast is the average of all the past data. However, our intuition tells us that we can do better if we use more recent data to make our forecast. The discrepancy arises because we really do not believe our assumption that the demand process is stationary for all time. A smaller value of N will allow the moving-average method to react more quickly to unforeseen changes in the demand process.

CASE 2. EXPONENTIAL SMOOTHING

Now consider the case in which forecasts are generated by exponential smoothing. In this case F_t may be represented by the weighted infinite sum of past values of demand.

$$F_t = \alpha D_{t-1} + \alpha(1-\alpha)D_{t-2} + \alpha(1-\alpha)^2 D_{t-3} + \cdots,$$
$$E(F_t) = \mu[\alpha + \alpha(1-\alpha) + \alpha(1-\alpha)^2 + \cdots] = \mu.$$

Notice that this means that $E(e_t) = 0$, so that both exponential smoothing and moving averages are unbiased forecasting methods when the underlying demand process is a constant plus a random term.

$$\text{Var}(F_t) = \alpha^2 \sigma^2 + (1-\alpha)^2 \alpha^2 \sigma^2 + \cdots$$
$$= \sigma^2 \alpha^2 \sum_{n=0}^{\infty} (1-\alpha)^{2n}.$$

It can be shown that

$$\sum_{n=0}^{\infty} (1-\alpha)^{2n} = \frac{1}{1-(1-\alpha)^2}$$

so that

$$\text{Var}(F_t) = \frac{\sigma^2 \alpha^2}{1-(1-\alpha)^2} = \frac{\sigma^2 \alpha}{2-\alpha}.$$

Since

$$\text{Var}(e_t) = \text{Var}(F_t) + \text{Var}(D_t),$$
$$\text{Var}(e_t) = \sigma^2[\alpha/(2-\alpha) + 1] = \sigma^2[2/(2-\alpha)],$$

or

$$\sigma_e = \sigma \sqrt{\frac{2}{2-\alpha}}.$$

This is the standard deviation of the forecast error for simple exponential smoothing in terms of the standard deviation of each observation. The distribution of the forecast error for exponential smoothing is normal for essentially the same reasons as stated above for moving averages.

Notice that if we equate the variances of the forecast error for exponential smoothing and moving averages, we obtain

$$2/(2-\alpha) = (N+1)/N$$

or $\alpha = 2/(N+1)$, which is exactly the same result as we obtained by equating the average age of data for the two methods.

Appendix 2–B

Derivation of the Equations for the Slope and Intercept for Regression Analysis

In this appendix we derive the equations for the optimal values of a and b for the regression model. Assume that the data are $(x_1, y_1), (x_2, y_2), \ldots, (x_n, y_n)$, and the regression model to be fitted is $Y = a + bX$. Define

$$g(a, b) = \sum_{i=1}^{n} [y_i - (a + bx_i)]^2.$$

Interpret $g(a, b)$ as the sum of the squares of the distances from the line $a + bx$ to the data points y_i. The object of the analysis is to choose a and b to minimize $g(a, b)$. This is accomplished where

$$\frac{\partial g}{\partial a} = \frac{\partial g}{\partial b} = 0.$$

That is,

$$\frac{\partial g}{\partial a} = -\sum_{i=1}^{n} 2[y_i - (a + bx_i)] = 0,$$

$$\frac{\partial g}{\partial b} = -\sum_{i=1}^{n} 2x_i[y_i - (a + bx_i)] = 0,$$

which results in the two equations

$$an + b\sum_{i=1}^{n} x_i = \sum_{i=1}^{n} y_i, \tag{1}$$

$$a\sum_{i=1}^{n} x_i + b\sum_{i=1}^{n} x_i^2 = \sum_{i=1}^{n} x_i y_i. \tag{2}$$

These are two linear equations in the unknowns a and b. Multiplying Equation (1) by $\sum x_i$ and Equation (2) by n gives

$$an\sum_{i=1}^{n} x_i + b\left(\sum_{i=1}^{n} x_i\right)^2 = \left(\sum_{i=1}^{n} x_i\right)\left(\sum_{i=1}^{n} y_i\right), \tag{3}$$

$$an\sum_{i=1}^{n} x_i + bn\sum_{i=1}^{n} x_i^2 = n\sum_{i=1}^{n} x_i y_i. \tag{4}$$

Subtracting Equation (3) from Equation (4) results in

$$b\left[n\sum_{i=1}^{n} x_i^2 - \left(\sum_{i=1}^{n} x_i\right)^2\right] = n\sum_{i=1}^{n} x_i y_i - \left(\sum_{i=1}^{n} x_i\right)\left(\sum_{i=1}^{n} y_i\right). \tag{5}$$

Define $S_{xy} = n\sum x_i y_i - (\sum x_i)(\sum y_i)$ and $S_{xx} = n\sum x_i^2 - (\sum x_i)^2$. It follows that Equation (5) may be written $bS_{xx} = S_{xy}$, which gives

$$b = \frac{S_{xy}}{S_{xx}}. \tag{6}$$

From Equation (1) we have

$$an = \sum_{i=1}^{n} y_i - b\sum_{i=1}^{n} x_i$$

or

$$a = \bar{y} - b\bar{x}, \tag{7}$$

where $\bar{y} = (1/n)\sum y_i$ and $\bar{x} = (1/n)\sum x_i$.

These formulas can be specialized to the forecasting problem when the independent variable is assumed to be time. In that case, the data are of the form $(1, D_1), (2, D_2), \ldots, (n, D_n)$, and the forecasting equation is of the form $\hat{D}_t = a + bt$. The various formulas can be simplified as follows:

$$\sum x_i = 1 + 2 + 3 + \cdots + n = \frac{n(n + 1)}{2};$$

$$\sum x_i^2 = 1 + 4 + 9 + \cdots + n^2 = \frac{n(n + 1)(2n + 1)}{6}.$$

Hence, we can write

$$S_{xy} = n \sum_{i=1}^{n} iD_i - n(n+1)/2 \sum_{i=1}^{n} D_i,$$

$$S_{xx} = \frac{n^2(n+1)(2n+1)}{6} - \frac{n^2(n+1)^2}{4}.$$

$$b = \frac{S_{xy}}{S_{xx}}$$

$$a = \bar{D} - \frac{b(n+1)}{2}$$

Appendix 2–C

Glossary of Notation for Chapter 2

a = Estimate of the intercept in regression analysis.

α = Smoothing constant used for single exponential smoothing. One of the smoothing constants used for Holt's method or one of the smoothing constants used for Winters's method.

b = Estimate of the slope in regression analysis.

β = Second smoothing constant used for either Holt's method or Winters's method.

c_t = Seasonal factor for the tth period of a season.

γ = Third smoothing constant used for Winters's method.

D_t = Demand in period t. Refers to the series whose values are to be forecasted.

$e_t = F_t - D_t$ = (Observed) forecasting error in period t.

ϵ_t = Random variable representing the random component of the demand.

F_t = One-step-ahead forecast made in period $t - 1$ for demand in period t.

$F_{t,t+\tau}$ = τ-step-ahead forecast made in period t for the demand in period $t + \tau$.

G_t = Smoothed value of the slope for Holt's and Winters's methods.

μ = Mean of the demand process.

MAD = Mean absolute deviation = $(1/n) \sum_{i=1}^{n} |e_i|$.

MAPE = Mean absolute percentage error = $(1/n) \sum_{i=1}^{n} |e_i/D_i| \times 100$.

MSE = Mean squared error = $(1/n) \sum_{i=1}^{n} e_i^2$.

S_t = Smoothed value of the series (intercept) for Holt's and Winters's methods.

σ^2 = Variance of the demand process.

T_t = Value of the tracking signal in period t (refer to Problem 57).

Bibliography

Armstrong, J. S. "Forecasting by Extrapolation: Conclusions from Twenty-Five Years of Research." *Interfaces* 14 (1984), pp. 52–66.

Box, G. E. P., and G. M. Jenkins. *Time Series Analysis, Forecasting, and Control.* San Francisco: Holden Day, 1970.

Brown, R. G. *Statistical Forecasting for Inventory Control.* New York: McGraw-Hill, 1959.

Brown, R. G. *Smoothing, Forecasting, and Prediction of Discrete Time Series.* Englewood Cliffs, NJ: Prentice Hall, 1962.

Cohen, D. "Facebook Has 1.15B Monthly Active Users, But How Many Are Invalid?" *AllFacebook* (www.allfacebook.com), accessed September 3, 2013.

Davenport, W. B., and W. L. Root. *An Introduction to the Theory of Random Signals and Noise*. New York: McGraw-Hill, 1958.

Draper, N. R., and H. Smith. *Applied Regression Analysis*. New York: John Wiley & Sons, 1968.

Fisher, M. L.; J. H. Hammond; W. R. Obermeyer; and A. Raman, "Making Supply Meet Demand in an Uncertain World." *Harvard Business Review*, May–June 1994, pp. 221–40.

Helmer, O., and N. Rescher. "On the Epistemology of the Inexact Sciences." *Management Science* 6 (1959), pp. 25–52.

Kalman, R. E. "A New Approach to Linear Filtering and Prediction Problems." *Journal of Basic Engineering*, Ser. D 82, 1960, pp. 35–44.

Makridakis, S.; S. C. Wheelwright; and R. J. Hyndman. *Forecasting: Methods and Applications*. 3rd ed. New York: John Wiley & Sons, 1998.

Makridakis, S., and R. L. Winkler. "Averages of Forecasts." *Management Science* 29 (1983), pp. 987–96.

McWilliams, G. "At Compaq, a Desktop Crystal Ball." *Business Week*, March 20, 1995, pp. 96–97.

Nahmias, S. "Demand Estimation in Lost Sales Inventory Systems." *Naval Research Logistics* 41 (1994), pp. 739–57.

Nelson, C. R. "The Prediction Performance of the FRB-MIT-PENN Model of the U.S. Economy." *The American Economic Review* 62, no. 5 (December 1972), pp. 902–917.

Nelson, C. R. *Applied Time Series Analysis for Managerial Forecasting*. San Francisco: Holden Day, 1973.

Trigg, D. W. "Monitoring a Forecasting System." *Operational Research Quarterly* 15 (1964), pp. 271–74.

Trigg, D. W., and A. G. Leach. "Exponential Smoothing with Adaptive Response Rate." *Operational Research Quarterly* 18 (1967), pp. 53–59.

Wiener, N. *Extrapolation, Interpolation, and Smoothing of Stationary Time Series*. Cambridge, MA: MIT Press, 1949.

Yule, G. U. "Why Do We Sometimes Get Nonsense Correlations between Time Series? A Study of Sampling and the Nature of Time Series." *Journal of the Royal Statistical Society* 89 (1926), pp. 1–64.

Chapter Three

Sales and Operations Planning

"In preparing for battle I have always found that plans are useless, but planning is indispensable."

—Dwight D. Eisenhower

Chapter Overview

Purpose

To present the process by which companies go from technical forecasts to aggregate level sales and operations plans.

Key Points

1. *The sales and operations planning (S&OP) process.* This chapter could also be called Macro Planning, since the purpose of an S&OP process is to develop top-down sales and operations plans for the entire firm, or for some subset of the firm such as a product line or particular plant. The key goals of the process are to (a) make aggregate level plans that all divisions as well as suppliers can work to; (b) resolve the inherent tensions between sales and operations divisions; and (c) anticipate and escalate strategic challenges in matching supply with demand for the firm.

2. *Key Performance Indicators.* Inherent in any S&OP process are a set of metrics, or key performance indicators (KPIs), that the firm uses to judge the performance of the different divisions. Effective KPIs measure important factors, are relatively easy to compute, and are actionable, in the sense that those being measured by it can also effect its change. Operational KPIs may be efficiency or effectiveness focused and must be aligned with the strategic goals of the firm.

3. *The role of uncertainty.* It is important to explicitly recognize the role of uncertainty in planning. For a firm producing a wide range of products, or providing a service, uncertainty can be particularly problematic in planning, and management techniques must be adjusted accordingly. Furthermore, different types of uncertainty require different types of management responses. The S&OP process needs to explicitly acknowledge possible major sources of uncertainty and plan for them appropriately.

4. *Costs in aggregate operations plans.* The following are key costs to be considered in developing aggregate operations plans.

   - *Smoothing costs.* The cost of changing production and/or workforce levels.
   - *Holding costs.* The opportunity cost of dollars invested in inventory.
   - *Shortage costs.* The costs associated with back-ordered or lost demand.
   - *Labor costs.* These include direct labor costs on regular time, overtime, subcontracting costs, and idle time costs.

5. *Solving aggregate planning problems.* Approximate solutions to aggregate planning problems can be found graphically and exact solutions via linear programming. A level plan has constant production or workforce levels over the planning horizon, while a chase strategy keeps zero inventory and minimizes holding and shortage costs. A linear programming formulation assumes that all costs are linear and typically does not take into account management policy, such as avoiding hiring and firing as much as possible.

6. *Disaggregating plans.* While aggregate planning is useful for providing approximate solutions for macro planning at the firm level, the question is whether these aggregate plans provide any guidance for planning at the lower levels of the firm. A disaggregation scheme is a mean of taking an aggregate plan and breaking it down to get more detailed plans at lower levels of the firm.

As we go through life, we make both micro and macro decisions. Micro decisions might be what to eat for breakfast, what route to take to work, what auto service to use, or which movie to rent. Macro decisions are the kind that change the course of one's life: where to live, what to major in, which job to take, whom to marry. A company also must make both micro and macro decisions every day. Some macro decisions are highly strategic in nature, such as process technology or market entry choices, and were discussed in Chapter 1. Other macro decisions are more tactical, such as planning companywide workforce and production levels or setting sales target. In this chapter we explore tactical decisions made at the macro level in the context of a process known as **sales and operations planning** or **S&OP** for short.

S&OP begins with demand forecasts and turns them into targets for both sales and operations plans; techniques for demand forecasting were presented in Chapter 2. However, a firm will not want to just use such forecasts blindly. They may want to produce more than is forecast if stock-outs are unacceptable or if they are planning a major promotion; they may want to produce less than is forecast if overstocks are costly or they see the product winding down in its lifecycle. Such decisions must be made at a high strategic level and must involve both the sales and the operations staff.

One of the key goals in S&OP is to resolve the fundamental tension between sales and operations divisions in an organization. Sales divisions are typically measured on revenue; they want the product 100% available with as many different varieties as possible. Meanwhile, operations divisions are typically measured on cost; they want to keep both capacity and inventory costs low, which means limiting overproduction and product varieties. The best way to resolve these inherent tensions is with a formal S&OP process that gets the heads of sales and operations together in a room with other high level executives. This chapter explores what such processes look like.

Core to the S&OP process is a review of divisional **Key Performance Indicators** (KPIs). Section 3.2 reviews key challenges in KPI selection and key types of operational KPIs. One the fundamental challenges in KPI selection is in making sure the

KPI is both sufficiently high-level to be well aligned with the corporate strategy while being sufficiently low-level so that it provides a meaningful guide to behavior for those who are being evaluated by it.

The S&OP process would be a lot simpler if demand were certain; however, as noted in Chapter 2, it is not and therefore forecasts are generally wrong. In fact, there are a range of uncertainties that must be considered in the planning process from **known unknowns** to **unknown unknowns**, terms which will be formally defined in Section 3.3. Part of an S&OP process must include decisions around how to plan for and mitigate risk or uncertainty.

An important part of S&OP is **aggregate planning**, which might also be called macro production planning. It addresses the problem of deciding how many employees the firm should retain and, for a manufacturing firm, the quantity and the mix of products to be produced. Macro planning is not limited to manufacturing firms. Service organizations must determine employee staffing needs as well. For example, airlines must plan staffing levels for flight attendants and pilots, and hospitals must plan staffing levels for nurses. Macro planning strategies are a fundamental part of the firm's overall business strategy. Some firms operate on the philosophy that costs can be controlled only by making frequent changes in the size and/or composition of the workforce. The aerospace industry in California in the 1970s adopted this strategy. As government contracts shifted from one producer to another, so did the technical workforce. Other firms have a reputation for retaining employees, even in bad times. Traditionally, IBM and AT&T were two well-known examples.

Aggregate planning methodology is designed to translate demand forecasts into a blueprint for planning staffing and production levels for the firm over a predetermined planning horizon. Aggregate planning methodology is not limited to top-level planning. Although generally considered to be a macro planning tool for determining overall workforce and production levels, large companies may find aggregate planning useful at the plant level as well. Production planning may be viewed as a hierarchical process in which purchasing, production, and staffing decisions must be made at several levels in the firm. Aggregate planning methods may be applied at almost any level, although the concept is one of managing groups of items rather than single items.

This chapter outlines the S&OP process. Core to the process are KPIs, thus this chapter briefly reviews principles involved in setting KPIs. The chapter also describes the types of uncertainty that must be planned for in the process and how they are best addressed. Core to the operations component of any S&OP process is determining an aggregate production plan for capacity and inventory. This chapter reviews several techniques for determining aggregate production plans. Some of these are heuristic (i.e., approximate) and some are optimal. We hope to convey to the reader an understanding of the issues involved in S&OP, a knowledge of the basic tools available for providing production plans, and an appreciation of the difficulties associated with such planning in the real world.

3.1 The S&OP Process

The S&OP process is designed to produce a plan that all divisions within in the organization, as well as suppliers to the organization, can work to. The process is also sometimes referred to as sales, inventory, and operations planning (SIOP) to emphasize the important role that inventory can play as a buffer between sales planning and operations planning.

In any organization, demand is a function of sales effort and pricing and supply is a function of operations effort and capacity. Therefore, in order to best balance supply with demand a strategic approach must be applied. As defined by Grimson and Pyke (2007), "S&OP is a business process that links the corporate strategic plan to daily operations plans and enables companies to balance demand and supply for their products."

One of the key words in Grimson and Pike's definition of S&OP is that it is a "business process." That is, it a consistent set of steps that a company follows on a regular basis. Each business will apply its process slightly differently but some common elements include the following:

1. *Strategically focused.* As discussed above, finding the appropriate balance for supply and demand requires knowledge of the company's strategic plan. Typically c-level executives are involved in S&OP planning to ensure that the company's strategy is appropriately represented.

2. *Cross-functional team.* Because the S&OP process must balance the interests of different parts of the organization, the team performing the process must be both cross-functional and balanced.

3. *Aggregated.* It is typically not possible to forecast at the individual stock keeping unit (SKU) level. Thus S&OP processes typically work with aggregated units of production, such as product families. One natural unit of aggregation is sales dollars, but of course there is not a one-to-one mapping from sales dollars to units produced.

4. *Time fences.* The agreed sales and operations plan will typically be only fixed for a relatively short period (e.g., a week or month) and forecasts for future time periods will typically be assumed to be flexible within a given range. Oftentimes fences are used to show when the level of certainty changes and can be referred to as frozen (i.e., fixed), slushy (somewhat fixed), and liquid (highly flexible) time periods.

There are a number of key inputs required for the S&OP process as follows:

1. *Technical demand forecast.* Advanced forecasting techniques such as those discussed in Chapter 2 are used to understand raw demand.

2. *Sales plans.* The Marketing and Sales divisions will use the technical forecasts and their own promotion and marketing plans to provide a sales forecast.

3. *Operations plans.* Operations will produce a production plan that includes plans for capacity, supply, and inventory.

4. *Innovation plans.* The planned role out of new products and future product innovation must be considered in the context of sales and operations plans.

5. *Financial plans.* Any public company must announce earnings forecasts, typically with a breakdown of how such earnings are to be achieved. Because negative market surprises can affect a company's ability to raise capital, the sales and operations plans must also consider the financial forecasts. Further, in many smaller companies cash flow constraints must also be considered in the planning process.

The basic S&OP process must iterate between these five key inputs above to resolve tensions and unforeseen constraints (e.g., a supplier who cannot deliver until six weeks from today) to finalize the sales and operations plans for the company. It is then left to the sales and operations divisions of the company to execute on these plans, such as disaggregating sales dollars into actual production units.

FIGURE 3-1
S&OP Overview: Source: Smits and English (2010)

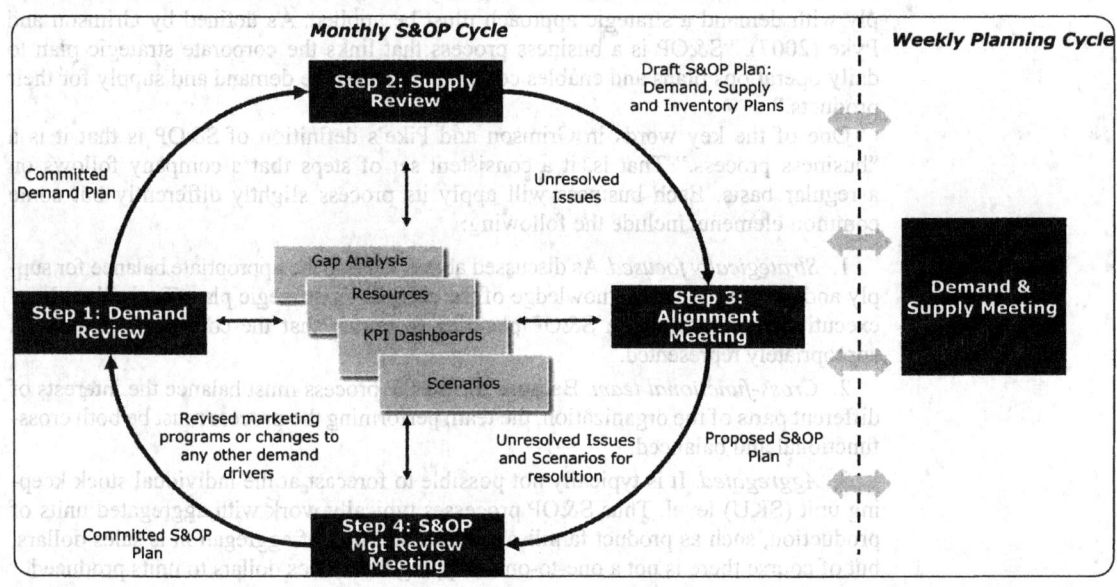

One sample iterative process is shown in Figure 3–1, which has been produced for Heineken by Smits and English (2010). Notice how the outcome of the S&OP meeting is a committed S&OP plan for the following month. Key uncertainties are shown as "scenarios" in the above.

Typically the chief executive officer (CEO) leads the S&OP meeting and makes the key decisions with respect to trade-offs (Sheldon, 2006). A well run meeting is focused on decision making, rather than information dissemination, and all participants are expected to have studied the materials that are prepared ahead of time by the different divisions. The vice president of sales and/or marketing will be present and is the process owner for the demand plan. The vice president of operations and/or supply chain management will also be present and is the process owner for the operations plan. The chief financial officer (CFO) will attend and prepares the financial plan, which measures performance for the master business plan. The master scheduler prepares documents and is the process owner for weekly schedules (which are not typically part of the S&OP process). In a larger organization this will take place at the divisional level, although the CEO may well attend at least semi-regularly divisional S&OP meetings.

A standard agenda for a monthly S&OP meeting is the following:

- Review of last 30 days—Accuracy of financial, demand, and operations plans (typically by product family)
- Review of 30- to 60-day plan expectations—Risks for each plan

Snapshot Application

Heineken International was founded in 1864 by Gerard Adriaan Heineken in Amsterdam and has a global network of distributors and 125 breweries in more than 70 countries. Heineken's corporate strategy is "to be a leading brewer in each of the markets in which it operates and to have the world's most prominent brand portfolio (with Heineken as leading premium beer)." Supply chain planning within the beer supply chain is complicated by the fact that most beers, including Heineken, are produced in batches. In fact, Heineken has a highly prescribed process for its brewing that all producers must follow to ensure global consistency in taste. It also has a robust S&OP process, which it implements in all of its subsidiaries. The key mantra for this process, pictured in Figure 3–1, is "one single plan." This process is described as follows:

> The global beer market is a dynamic environment with changing markets, strong competition, and changing customer preferences. Heineken realized that a Global Sales and Operations Planning (S&OP) program would become a key enabler in supporting aggressive expansion targets, and would become necessary to support a retail globalization landscape, which is applying increasing pressures on costs and service. Heineken's S&OP process integrates finance, marketing, sales, and supply chain departments with the objective of aligning the organization towards a synchronized operating plan globally. This program is supported by a very strong project management approach which has been designed to provide enough consistency across regions, yet provide enough flexibility to embrace and benefit from local cultural differences. (Smits & English, 2010)

Notice how this description matches with the general description of S&OP given above yet leaves some flexibility in terms of the actual running of meeting to allow for local customs to apply. The benefits Heineken has realized from their S&OP process are better cross-functional decisions; an enabler of growth; higher capacity utilization; lower supply chain costs; and reduced working capital (Rooijen, 2011).

- Review 90- to 120-day risks as required
- Review balance of 12-month horizon for exceptions (Sheldon, 2006)

Typically, an S&OP plan is considered fixed (with agreed windows of flexibility for later time periods) and, therefore, the operations division must plan for uncertainty within its own execution plan. Common strategies for dealing with uncertainty include the following:

1. *Buffering*: Maintaining excess resources (inventory, capacity, or time) to cover for fluctuations in supply or demand. Such buffering is an explicit component of planning under uncertainty, such as the inventory models considered in Chapter 5.

2. *Pooling*: Sharing buffers to cover multiple sources of variability (e.g., demand from different markets). This will be covered in more detail in Section 6.7.

3. *Contingency planning*: Establishing a preset course of action for an anticipated scenario. This may involve strategies such as bringing on a backup supplier or sourcing from the spot market. This is best done explicitly in the S&OP process.

Heineken Netherlands positions the S&OP process within their planning framework as given in Figure 3–2.

FIGURE 3-2
Planning and Control Framework for Heineken Netherlands.
Source: Every Angle (2013)

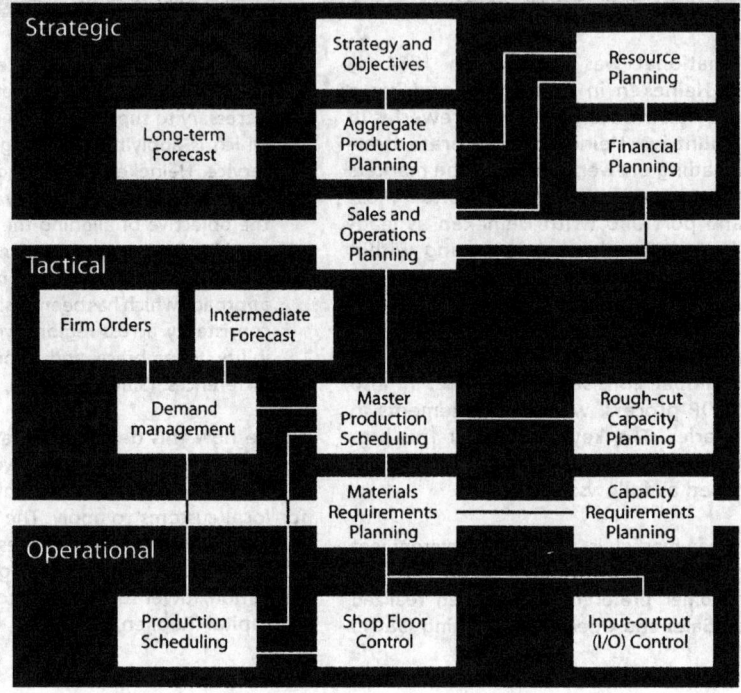

Notice how in Figure 3–2, S&OP straddles the strategy and tactical portions of the planning framework. Many of the other planning topics, such as the master production schedule and materials requirements planning, will be covered in Chapter 8.

Problems for Section 3.1

1. Why don't the head of sales or the head of operations chair the S&OP meeting?
2. Why do you think it is important that the CFO attends the S&OP meeting?
3. Describe the likely key tensions between the sales and operations divisions of a small manufacturer that mostly produces to the local market. Now describe them for a global organization that sells in many regions and outsources most of its production to China.
4. Why is S&OP described as an iterative process?
5. What are the trade-offs between having long fixed or frozen periods versus short fixed or frozen periods as outputs of the S&OP process?
6. What are the trade-offs between using revenue dollars versus sales quantities as the units in the aggregate S&OP plan.

3.2 Key Performance Indicators

One of the quantitative inputs to the S&OP process will be the key performance indicators (KPIs) for the divisions and the organization. The CFO is present at the meeting to present key financial performance measurements such as net profit and return on investment. However, as discussed in Chapter 1, such financial measures tend to emphasize short-term goals. This issue is often counteracted by the **balanced score card approach**, which provides a more well-rounded performance measurement approach covering a wider scope of metrics than pure finance measures. The balanced score card approach was developed by Kaplan and Norton (1992) and represents performance measures designed to reflect strategy and communicate a vision to the organization. There are four standard perspectives for the approach, although many organizations have adapted these for their own use; these perspectives are (a) customer; (b) internal; (c) innovation and learning; and (d) financial. Figure 3–3 depicts these perspectives.

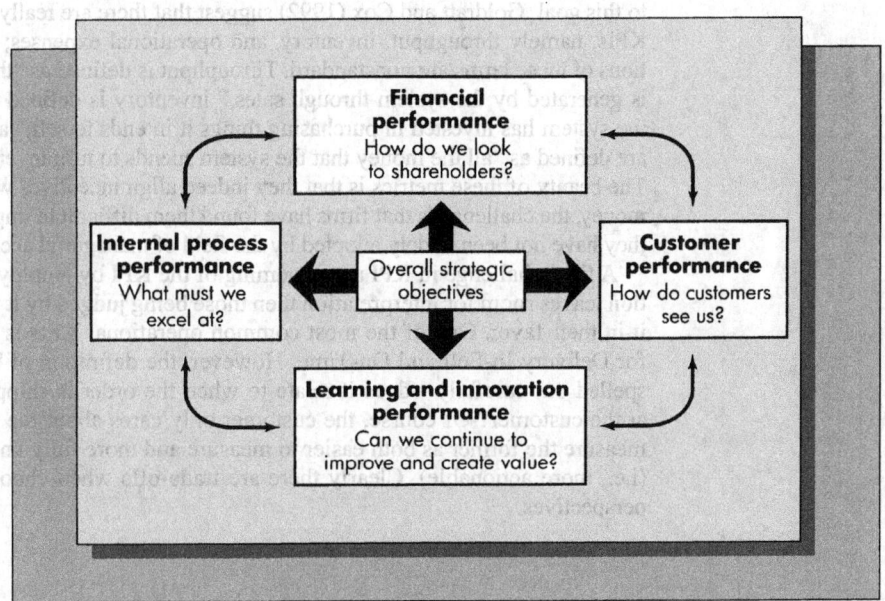

FIGURE 3–3
Perspectives for the Balanced Scorecard Approach; Source: Kaplan and Norton (1992)

Operational metrics typically sit within internal process measures. There are two key types of operational KPIs, namely **efficiency** related KPIs, which are a measure of resource utilization (e.g., time, cost, materials, etc.) and **effectiveness** related KPIs, which are a measure of how well the process meets or exceeds customer requirements (e.g., defects, complaints, satisfaction score, etc.). Which of these are most important will depend on the product-line strategy, with efficiency being the most important for products that compete on cost and effectiveness being the most important for high-margin products that compete on innovation or fashion dimensions.

Some evaluation criteria for the merits of a KPI (ABB, 2010) are: (a) *Importance*—Are you measuring the things that really matter? (b) *Ease*—Does the measurement 'flow' from the activity being monitored? (c) *Actionable*—Can the metric initiate appropriate actions? The KPI must be well understood by employees if it is to be both measured accurately and to incentivize behavior correctly. One of the key challenges in choosing KPIs is in achieving organizational alignment. KPIs must be aligned to the strategic plan in order to monitor the essential performance results implied by the vision and mission statements and to monitor current strategic goals or objectives. It is then recommended that they be cascaded down to the business processes to maintain alignment. Finally, the KPIs may be assigned to business units once they have been associated with business processes. Going the opposite direction starting from business units is more likely to result in misaligned KPIs. In general, a high level KPI (e.g., monthly profit) is easier to align but if employees don't feel that they can control the KPI then they may disengage. This is the reason for the recommendation that KPIs be "actionable" in the above.

In the book *The Goal* by Goldratt and Cox (1992) it is stated that "The goal of a firm is to make money." Many of the issues described in the book arise from misaligned KPIs to this goal. Goldratt and Cox (1992) suggest that there are really only three operational KPIs, namely throughput, inventory, and operational expenses; however, their definitions of these terms are nonstandard. Throughput is defined as "the rate at which money is generated by the system through sales," inventory is defined as "all the money that the system has invested in purchasing things it intends to sell," and operating expenses are defined as "all the money that the system spends to turn inventory into throughput." The beauty of these metrics is that they indeed align incentives with the goal of making money, the challenge is that firms have found them difficult to implement in practice and they have not been widely adopted by the field of managerial accounting.

A final challenge in KPI use is gaming of the KPI by employees. If the KPI definition leaves room for interpretation then those being judged by it will typically interpret it in their favor. One of the most common operational KPIs is DIFOT, which stands for Delivery In-Full and On-Time. However, the definition of "on-time" needs to be spelled out carefully—does it relate to when the order is shipped or when it arrives at the customer? Of course, the customer only cares about the latter, but many firms measure the former as both easier to measure and more fully under operations control (i.e., more actionable). Clearly there are trade-offs when choosing between the two perspectives.

Problems for Section 3.2

7. In some S&OP processes all divisions are measured by the same set of KPIs. What are the advantages and disadvantages to this approach?

8. Give two efficiency-related KPIs and two effectiveness-related KPIs that you believe Wal-Mart is likely to use to evaluate its suppliers? Its in-store managers?

9. What types of organizations are likely to face the largest challenges in achieving alignment between operational KPIs and strategic priorities?

10. Evaluate the following metrics along the three dimensions of importance, ease, and actionablity: DIFOT, ROI, machine utilization, and number of customer complaints.

11. Do you think efficiency-related KPIs or effectiveness-related KPIs will be easier for employees to "game" in practice? Explain your answer.

12. Why do you think that the KPIs proposed by Goldratt and Cox (1992) have not been very widely implemented?

3.3 THE ROLE OF UNCERTAINTY

One of the key challenges in sales and operations planning is the effective management of uncertainty or risk. In a survey by IBM of 400 Supply Chain Executives (IBM, 2009) risk was identified as the second most important key challenge that comprise the Chief Supply Chain Officer agenda; it was identified by 60 percent of respondents as important "to a very great extent" or "to a significant extent" (the challenge that was ranked highest was supply chain visibility). Because S&OP is the highest level of tactical planning in the organization it must explicitly acknowledge major sources of uncertainty and explicitly work to manage and/or mitigate risk.

De Meyer et al. (2002) highlight four different types of uncertainty. While they particularly focus on project management, the categorization also applies to S&OP processes and operational risks.

1. *Variation*. Variation is anything that causes the system to depart from regular, predictable behavior that may be described by a probability distribution (see Appendix 5–A). Typical sources for variation include variability in customer orders, differential worker skill levels, and variability in quality or lead times.

2. *Foreseen uncertainty*. Foreseen uncertainty, or "known unknowns" as they are often called, are risks that can be foreseen and planned for. They are typically described by a probability of occurrence and have a larger impact than variation as described above. Typical sources include supply breakdowns, design changes, natural disasters, labor strikes, etc.

3. *Unforeseen uncertainty*. Unforeseen uncertainty, or "unknown unknowns," are risks that could not be predicted ahead of time or that are considered too unlikely to make contingency plans for. Typical sources include natural disasters of unusual scale or in regions where they do not typically occur (e.g., an earthquake on the eastern coast of the United States) or competitor innovations that were not anticipated. These are the so-called "black swan" events of Taleb (2007).

4. *Chaos*. Chaos is unforeseen uncertainty where the event not only affects the operations but also the fundamental goal of the project or company. For example, in the wake of the New Zealand city of Christchurch's 2010 earthquake, a number of local beverage manufacturers offered to switch to bottling water instead of regular products. Not only was the earthquake unforeseen because the fault rupture occurred along a previously unknown east-west fault line that is thought to not have moved for at least 16,000 years, but the goal for the beverage manufacturers shifted from profit from beverage sales to humanitarian aid.

Each of the above forms of uncertainty must be dealt with and planned for in different ways. However, all require a firm to have effective management and communication processes.

Variation is the type of uncertainty most commonly dealt with by operations analysts and managers and will be described in more detail in Section 5.1a. Because variation is considered routine and within an operations manager purview to anticipate and plan for, it is not usually much discussed during the S&OP process. Strategies used by operations to mitigate variation include holding inventory, deliberately maintaining excess capacity, or incurring deliberate delays in order fulfillment. Foreseen uncertainty is best dealt with specific contingency plans, risk mitigation processes, and clear ownership responsibility for processes. It is foreseen uncertainty that is best dealt with explicitly within the S&OP process. For example, if it is known that a supplier is currently struggling with labor issues, then it should be discussed at the S&OP meeting what plans should be put in place for the event that the supplier's workforce goes on strike.

Unforeseen uncertainty may be mitigated by generic contingency plans and good leadership while chaos requires strong leadership and crisis management processes. By definition, neither unforeseen uncertainty nor chaos may be explicitly planned for in the S&OP process. However, an organization with strong cross-functional ties, which good S&OP processes foster, is going to manage such occurrences better than a siloed organization with little cross-functional planning.

Problems for Section 3.3

13. Why does the S&OP process typically not explicitly recognize variation even though it is a fact of life for both operations and sales divisions?
14. Classify the following risks into variation, foreseen uncertainty, unforeseen uncertainty, and chaos:
    a. A hurricane on the U.S. East Coast floods a regional warehouse destroying a large amount of stock.
    b. A machine on the plant floor breaks down for an hour.
    c. Bad weather on the weekend causes an increase in demand for umbrellas.
    d. A cool summer causes a decrease in demand for air conditioners for that season.
    e. The excavation process for a new manufacturing plant in the U.S. Midwest uncovers an archaeological find of such significance that no building can take place on that site and a new site for the plant must be found.
    f. Competitors to the iPad launch smaller tablet computers before the iPad mini is ready to launch, thus negatively affecting demand for the iPad.
    g. The Second World War caused auto manufacturers to switch to producing military vehicles.
    h. A drug is found to have dangerous side effects following its launch.
    i. The transportation disruptions, including the grounding of all airplanes, following the attacks on September 11, 2001 severed many supply chains.
15. List two examples each of variation, foreseen uncertainty, and unforeseen uncertainty that you have personally experienced in your studies.
16. Give an example of chaos, either from your own experience or from others, within the educational domain.

3.4 AGGREGATE PLANNING OF CAPACITY

The operations division is responsible for determining an aggregate plan for capacity usage throughout the planning horizon. This plan uses the agreed upon set of sales forecasts that comes out of the S&OP meeting. Such a forecast is expressed in terms of aggregate production units or dollars. The operations division must then determine aggregate production quantities and the levels of resources required to achieve these production goals. In practice, this translates to finding the number of workers that should be employed and the number of aggregate units to be produced in each of the planning periods $1, 2, \ldots, T$. The objective of such aggregate planning is to balance the advantages of producing to meet demand as closely as possible against the disturbance caused by changing the levels of production and/or the workforce levels.

As just noted, aggregate planning methodology requires the assumption that demand is known with certainty. This is simultaneously a weakness and a strength of the approach. It is a weakness because it does not provide any buffer against unanticipated forecast errors. However, most inventory models that allow for random demand require that the average demand be constant over time. Aggregate planning allows the manager to focus on the systematic changes that are generally not present in models that assume random demand. By assuming deterministic demand, the effects of seasonal fluctuations and business cycles can be incorporated into the planning function. As discussed in Section 3.1, variation caused by demand uncertainty may be buffered using inventory, capacity, or customer delays.

Costs in Aggregate Capacity Planning

As with most of the optimization problems considered in production management, the goal of the analysis is to choose the aggregate plan that minimizes cost. It is important to identify and measure those specific costs that are affected by the planning decision.

1. *Smoothing costs.* Smoothing costs are those costs that accrue as a result of changing the production levels from one period to the next. In the aggregate planning context, the most salient smoothing cost is the cost of changing the size of the workforce. Increasing the size of the workforce requires time and expense to advertise positions, interview prospective employees, and train new hires. Decreasing the size of the workforces means that workers must be laid off. Severance pay is thus one cost of decreasing the size of the workforce. However, there are other costs associated with firing workers that may be harder to measure.

Firing workers could have far-reaching consequences. Firms that hire and fire frequently develop a poor public image. This could adversely affect sales and discourage potential employees from joining the company. It may adversely affect employee morale. Furthermore, workers that are laid off might not simply wait around for business to pick up. Firing workers can have a detrimental effect on the future size of the labor force if those workers obtain employment in other industries. Finally, most companies are simply not at liberty to hire and fire at will. Labor agreements restrict the freedom of management to freely alter workforce levels.

Most of the models that we consider assume that the costs of increasing and decreasing the size of the workforce are linear functions of the number of employees that are hired or fired. That is, there is a constant dollar amount charged for each employee hired or fired. The assumption on linearity is probably reasonable up to a point. As the supply of labor becomes scarce, there may be additional costs required to hire more workers, and the costs of laying off workers may go up substantially if the number of workers laid off is too large. A typical cost function for changing the size of the workforce appears in Figure 3–4.

2. *Holding costs.* Holding costs are the costs that accrue as a result of having capital tied up in inventory. If the firm can decrease its inventory, the money saved could be invested elsewhere with a return that will vary with the industry and with the specific company. (A more complete discussion of holding costs is deferred to Chapter 4.) Holding costs are almost always assumed to be linear in the number of units being held at a particular point in time. We will assume for the purposes of the aggregate planning analysis that the holding cost is expressed in terms of dollars per unit held per planning period. We also will assume that holding costs are charged against the inventory remaining on hand at the *end* of the planning period. This assumption is made for

FIGURE 3–4
Cost of changing the size of the workforce

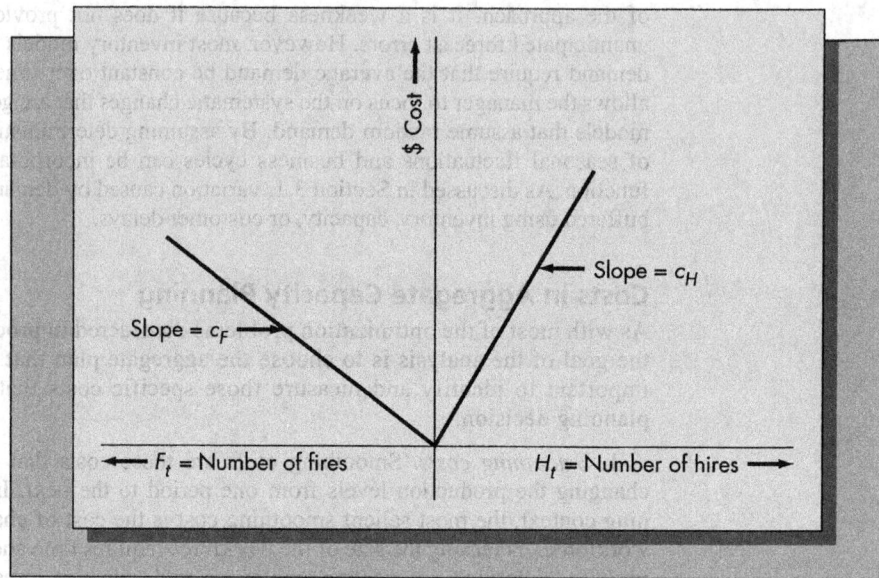

convenience only. Holding costs could be charged against starting inventory or average inventory as well.

3. *Shortage costs.* Holding costs are charged against the aggregate inventory as long as it is positive. In some situations it may be necessary to incur shortages, which are represented by a negative level of inventory. Shortages can occur when forecasted demand exceeds the capacity of the production facility or when demands are higher than anticipated. For the purposes of aggregate planning, it is generally assumed that excess demand is backlogged and filled in a future period. In a highly competitive situation, however, it is possible that excess demand is lost and the customer goes elsewhere. This case, which is known as lost sales, is more appropriate in the management of single items and is more common in a retail than in a manufacturing context.

As with holding costs, shortage costs are generally assumed to be linear. Convex functions also can accurately describe shortage costs, but linear functions seem to be the most common. Figure 3–5 shows a typical holding/shortage cost function.

4. *Regular time costs.* These costs involve the cost of producing one unit of output during regular working hours. Included in this category are the actual payroll costs of regular employees working on regular time, the direct and indirect costs of materials, and other manufacturing expenses. When all production is carried out on regular time, regular payroll costs become a "sunk cost," because the number of units produced must equal the number of units demanded over any planning horizon of sufficient length. If there is no overtime or worker idle time, regular payroll costs do not have to be included in the evaluation of different strategies.

5. *Overtime and subcontracting costs.* Overtime and subcontracting costs are the costs of production of units not produced on regular time. Overtime refers to production by regular-time employees beyond the normal workday, and subcontracting refers to the production of items by an outside supplier. Again, it is generally assumed that both of these costs are linear.

6. *Idle time costs.* The complete formulation of the aggregate planning problem also includes a cost for underutilization of the workforce, or idle time. In most contexts,

FIGURE 3–5
Holding and back-order costs

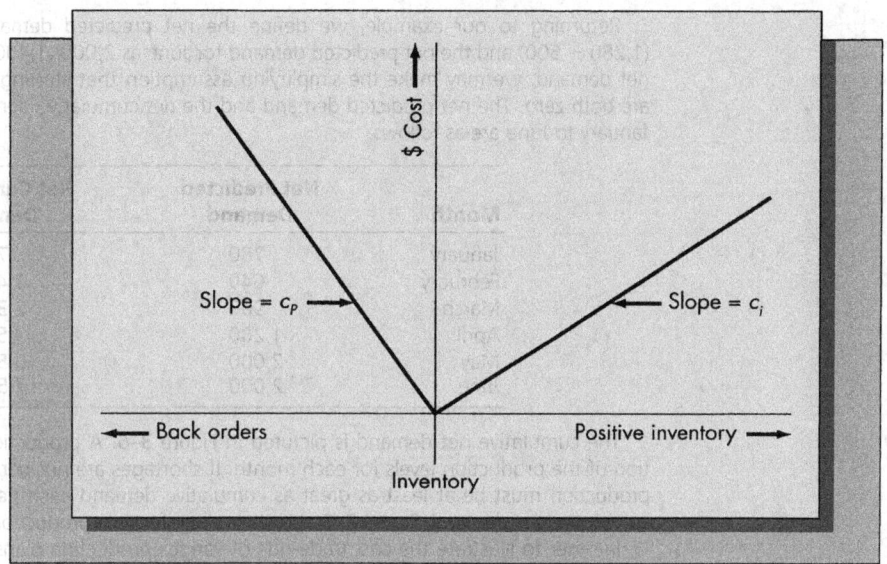

the idle time cost is zero, as the direct costs of idle time would be taken into account in labor costs and lower production levels. However, idle time could have other consequences for the firm. For example, if the aggregate units are input to another process, idle time on the line could result in higher costs to the subsequent process. In such cases, one would explicitly include a positive idle cost.

When planning is done at a relatively high level of the firm, the effects of intangible factors are more pronounced. Any solution to the aggregate planning problem obtained from a cost-based model must be considered carefully in the context of company policy. An optimal solution to a mathematical model might result in a policy that requires frequent hiring and firing of personnel. Such a policy may be infeasible because of prior contract agreements, or undesirable because of the potential negative effects on the firm's public image.

A Prototype Problem

We will illustrate the various techniques for solving aggregate planning problems with the following example.

Example 3.1

Densepack is to plan workforce and production levels for the six-month period January to June. The firm produces a line of disk drives for mainframe computers that are plug compatible with several computers produced by major manufacturers. Forecast demands over the next six months for a particular line of drives produced in the Milpitas, California, plant are 1,280, 640, 900, 1,200, 2,000, and 1,400. There are currently (end of December) 300 workers employed in the Milpitas plant. Ending inventory in December is expected to be 500 units, and the firm would like to have 600 units on hand at the end of June.

There are several ways to incorporate the starting and the ending inventory constraints into the formulation. The most convenient is simply to modify the values of the predicted demand. Define net predicted demand in period 1 as the predicted demand minus initial inventory. If there is a minimum ending inventory constraint, then this amount should be added to the demand in period T. Minimum buffer inventories also can be handled by modifying the predicted demand. If there is a minimum buffer inventory in every period, this amount should be added to the first period's demand. If there is a minimum buffer inventory in only one period, this amount should be added to that period's demand and subtracted from the next period's demand. Actual ending inventories should be computed using the original demand pattern, however.

142 Chapter Three Sales and Operations Planning

Returning to our example, we define the net predicted demand for January as 780 (1,280 − 500) and the net predicted demand for June as 2,000 (1,400 + 600). By considering net demand, we may make the simplifying assumption that starting and ending inventories are both zero. The net predicted demand and the net cumulative demand for the six months January to June are as follows:

Month	Net Predicted Demand	Net Cumulative Demand
January	780	780
February	640	1,420
March	900	2,320
April	1,200	3,520
May	2,000	5,520
June	2,000	7,520

The cumulative net demand is pictured in Figure 3–6. A production plan is the specification of the production levels for each month. If shortages are not permitted, then cumulative production must be at least as great as cumulative demand each period. In addition to the cumulative net demand, Figure 3–6 also shows one feasible production plan.

In order to illustrate the cost trade-offs of various production plans, we will assume in the example that there are only three costs to be considered: cost of hiring workers, cost of firing workers, and cost of holding inventory. Define

c_H = Cost of hiring one worker = $500,

c_F = Cost of firing one worker = $1,000,

c_I = Cost of holding one unit of inventory for one month = $80.

We require a means of translating aggregate production in units to workforce levels. Because not all months have an equal number of working days, we will use a day as an indivisible unit of measure and define

K = Number of aggregate units produced by one worker in one day.

FIGURE 3–6
A feasible aggregate plan for Densepack

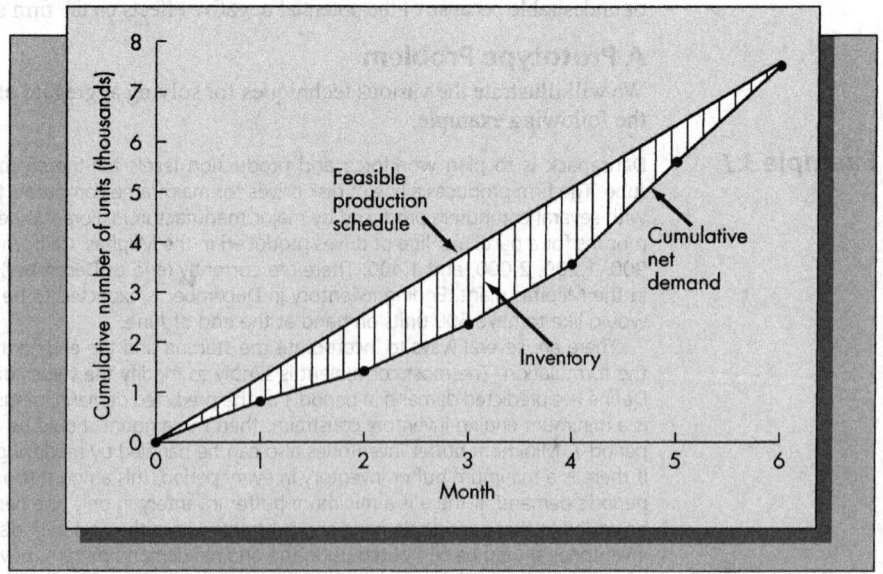

In the past, the plant manager observed that over 22 working days, with the workforce level constant at 76 workers, the firm produced 245 disk drives. That means that on average the production rate was $245/22 = 11.1364$ drives per day when there were 76 workers employed at the plant. It follows that one worker produced an average of $11.1364/76 = 0.14653$ drive in one day. Hence, $K = 0.14653$ for this example.

The final data needed to evaluate a plan for this example is the number of working days per month. In what follows we assume this to be 20, 24, 18, 26, 22, and 15 for January to June, respectively.

Chase, Level, and Mixed Strategies

Two extremes in capacity planning are the *zero inventory plan*, also known as a *chase strategy*, and the *constant workforce plan*, also known as a *level strategy*. Under the zero inventory plan the workforce is changed each month in order to produce enough units to most closely match the demand pattern. Capacity is adjusted up and down (i.e., workers are hired and fired) to achieve this matching. Under the constant workforce plan, capacity is kept constant during the planning period (i.e., no workers are hired or fired) and instead inventory is kept between periods; capacity is set to the minimum possible to ensure no shortages in any period.

For Example 3–1, a zero inventory plan hires at total of 755 workers, fires a total 145 workers, and achieves a total cost of $572,900 (calculations are not shown and are left as a reader's exercise). The best constant workforce plan sets capacity to 411 workers each month (hiring 111 at the beginning of January) with no further hiring or firing, has a total inventory cost of $524,960, and a total cost of $580,460 once the initial workers are considered (calculations again left to the reader). While the zero inventory plan has slightly lower costs it is unlikely to be practical because there may be constraints on the total capacity of the plant or on the maximum change that is possible from one month to the next.

The zero inventory plan and constant workforce strategies are pure strategies: they are designed to achieve one objective. They are useful in enhancing intuition and for ballpark calculations. However, with more flexibility, small modifications can result in dramatically lower costs. Such plans are described as *mixed strategies*. Optimal mixed strategies are typically found using linear programming formulations, which can incorporate a variety of additional practical constraints. Linear programming formulations are the subject of the next section.

Problems for Sections 3.4

17. A local machine shop employs 60 workers who have a variety of skills. The shop accepts one-time orders and also maintains a number of regular clients. Discuss some of the difficulties with using the aggregate planning methodology in this context.

18. A large manufacturer of household consumer goods is considering integrating an aggregate planning model into its manufacturing strategy. Two of the company vice presidents disagree strongly as to the value of the approach. What arguments might each of the vice presidents use to support his or her point of view?

19. Describe the following costs and discuss the difficulties that arise in attempting to measure them in a real operating environment.

    a. Smoothing costs
    b. Holding costs
    c. Payroll costs

Snapshot Application

HP ENTERPRISE SERVICES USES OPTIMIZATION FOR WORKFORCE PLANNING

The S&OP planning problem discussed in this chapter includes optimization of several of the firm's functions, including production planning and workforce planning. In practice, the workforce planning problem is much more difficult than the problem framed in this chapter, since it is often the case that both the supply and demand for workers is uncertain. This means that both demand and supply are likely to be random variables, thus making the problem potentially very complex. HP Enterprise Services (HPES) is a part of the HP Corporation that focuses on global business and technology. These services are provided by more than 100,000 employees located in over 60 countries. To provide an optimal solution to HPES' planning problem is probably not realistic due to the scale of the problem. Traditional operations research methods such as Markov Decision Process modeling or large scale mixed integer programming (two methods that have been proposed in the literature) quickly become computationally unwieldy.

A group of researchers (Santos, et. al. (2013)) suggested a two stage approach for solving this problem. The first stage (supply and demand consolidation) indicates those jobs for which an employee is fully qualified. For those employees that are partially qualified, they develop a transition table that provides scores which indicate the degree of qualification. Supply uncertainty in this context is primarily due to employee attrition, which can be 30% or more in some locations. Under ideal circumstances, the firm would like to be able to match job requirements with those employees that are 100% qualified. However, such a stringent rule results in poor demand fulfilment levels. Rather, the group designed a flexible matching scheme based concepts developed for the analytical hierarchy process, a tool that allows one to determine appropriate weights in a multi-criteria decision problem.

The second stage of the analysis is to build a mixed integer programming (MIP) module to allocate workers to jobs. This is done in stages: first, available employees are allocated to jobs. Second, employees that are currently committed to jobs, but will be freed up at some future time are allocated. If neither of these schemes covers the job requirements, then new hires are recommended. Finally, if positions are still unfilled, a "gap" is declared. As noted above, mixed integer optimization can be very demanding computationally, so the authors employ a heuristic for this phase. Gaps are quite common, so procedures are recommended to deal with them.

HP first implemented this approach at its facility in Bangalore, India in 2009. Resource utilization rates improved from approximately 75% to approximately 90% as a result of this planning tool. HP is now in the process of implementing this system on a worldwide scale.

Source: Santos, C., et al. "HP Enterprise Services Uses Optimization for Resource Planning". *Interfaces* 43 (2013), pp. 152–169.

---

20. Discuss the following statement: "Since we use a rolling production schedule, I really don't need to know the demand beyond next month."
21. St. Clair County Hospital is attempting to assess its needs for nurses over the coming four months (January to April). The need for nurses depends on both the numbers and the types of patients in the hospital. Based on a study conducted by consultants, the hospital has determined that the following ratios of nurses to patients are required:

Patient Type	Numbers of Nurses Required per Patient	Patient Forecasts			
		Jan.	Feb.	Mar.	Apr.
Major surgery	0.4	28	21	16	18
Minor surgery	0.1	12	25	45	32
Maternity	0.5	22	43	90	26
Critical care	0.6	75	45	60	30
Other	0.3	80	94	73	77

a. How many nurses should be working each month to most closely match patient forecasts?
b. Suppose the hospital does not want to change its policy of not increasing the nursing staff size by more than 10 percent in any month. Suggest a schedule of nurse staffing over the four months that meets this requirement and also meets the need for nurses each month.

22. Give an example of an environment where a chase strategy would be highly disruptive. Now give one where a level strategy would be highly disruptive.
23. Is a chase or level strategy more appropriate for aggregate planning in an air conditioning manufacturing plant where demand is highly seasonal and the workforce is relatively skilled? Explain your answer.

3.5 SOLVING AGGREGATE PLANNING PROBLEMS

Linear programming is a term used to describe a general class of optimization problems. The objective is to determine values of n nonnegative real variables in order to maximize or minimize a linear function of these variables that is subject to m linear constraints of these variables.[1] The primary advantage in formulating a problem as a linear program is that optimal solutions can be found very efficiently by the simplex method.

When all cost functions are linear, there is a linear programming formulation of the general aggregate planning problem. Because of the efficiency of commercial linear programming codes, this means that (essentially) optimal solutions can be obtained for very large problems.[2]

Cost Parameters and Given Information

The following values are assumed to be known:

c_H = Cost of hiring one worker,
c_F = Cost of firing one worker,
c_I = Cost of holding one unit of stock for one period,
c_R = Cost of producing one unit on regular time,
c_O = Incremental cost of producing one unit on overtime,
c_U = Idle cost per unit of production,
c_S = Cost to subcontract one unit of production,
n_t = Number of production days in period t,
K = Number of aggregate units produced by one worker in one day,
I_0 = Initial inventory on hand at the start of the planning horizon,
W_0 = Initial workforce at the start of the planning horizon,
D_t = Forecast of demand in period t.

The cost parameters also may be time dependent; that is, they may change with t. Time-dependent cost parameters could be useful for modeling changes in the costs of hiring or firing due, for example, to shortages in the labor pool, or changes in the costs of production and/or storage due to shortages in the supply of resources, or changes in interest rates.

---
[1] An overview of linear programming can be found in Supplement 1, which follows this chapter.
[2] The qualifier is included because rounding may give suboptimal solutions. There will be more about this point later.

Problem Variables

The following are the problem variables:

W_t = Workforce level in period t,
P_t = Production level in period t,
I_t = Inventory level in period t,
H_t = Number of workers hired in period t,
F_t = Number of workers fired in period t,
O_t = Overtime production in units,
U_t = Worker idle time in units ("undertime"),
S_t = Number of units subcontracted from outside.

The overtime and idle time variables are determined in the following way. The term Kn_t represents the number of units produced by one worker in period t, so that Kn_tW_t would be the number of units produced by the entire workforce in period t. However, we do not require that $Kn_tW_t = P_t$. If $P_t > Kn_tW_t$, then the number of units produced exceeds what the workforce can produce on regular time. This means that the difference is being produced on overtime, so that the number of units produced on overtime is exactly $O_t = P_t - Kn_tW_t$. If $P_t < Kn_tW_t$, then the workforce is producing less than it should be on regular time, which means that there is worker idle time. The idle time is measured in units of production rather than in time, and is given by $U_t = Kn_tW_t - P_t$.

Problem Constraints

Three sets of constraints are required for the linear programming formulation. They are included to ensure that conservation of labor and conservation of units are satisfied.

1. Conservation of workforce constraints.

$$W_t = W_{t-1} + H_t - F_t \quad \text{for } 1 \leq t \leq T.$$
Number = Number + Number − Number
of workers   of workers   hired   fired
in t in $t-1$ in t in t

2. Conservation of units constraints.

$$I_t = I_{t-1} + P_t + S_t - D_t \quad \text{for } 1 \leq t \leq T.$$
Inventory = Inventory + Number + Number − Demand
in t in $t-1$ of units   of units   in t
                          produced   subcontracted
                          in t in t

3. Constraints relating production levels to workforce levels.

$$P_t = Kn_tW_t + O_t - U_t \quad \text{for } 1 \leq t \leq T.$$
Number = Number + Number − Number
of units   of units   of units   of units
produced   produced   produced   of idle
in t by regular on over-   production
           workforce   time in t in t
           in t

In addition to these constraints, linear programming requires that all problem variables be nonnegative. These constraints and the nonnegativity constraints are the minimum that must be present in any formulation. Notice that (1), (2), and (3) constitute $3T$ constraints, rather than 3 constraints, where T is the length of the forecast horizon.

The formulation also requires specification of the initial inventory, I_0, and the initial workforce, W_0, and may include specification of the ending inventory in the final period, I_T.

The objective function includes all the costs defined earlier. The linear programming formulation is to choose values of the problem variables $W_t, P_t, I_t, H_t, F_t, O_t, U_t,$ and S_t to

$$\text{Minimize} \sum_{t=1}^{T} (c_H H_t + c_F F_t + c_I I_t + c_R P_t + c_O O_t + c_U U_t + c_S S_t)$$

subject to

$$W_t = W_{t-1} + H_t - F_t \quad \text{for } 1 \leq t \leq T \quad \text{(A)}$$
(conservation of workforce),

$$P_t = K n_t W_t + O_t - U_t \quad \text{for } 1 \leq t \leq T \quad \text{(B)}$$
(production and workforce)

$$I_t = I_{t-1} + P_t + S_t - D_t \quad \text{for } 1 \leq t \leq T \text{ (inventory balance)}, \quad \text{(C)}$$

$$H_t, F_t, I_t, O_t, U_t, S_t, W_t, P_t \geq 0 \text{ (nonnegativity)}, \quad \text{(D)}$$

plus any additional constraints that define the values of starting inventory, starting workforce, ending inventory, or any other variables with values that are fixed in advance.

Rounding the Variables

In general, the optimal values of the problem variables will not be integers. However, fractional values for many of the variables do not make sense. These variables include the size of the workforce, the number of workers hired each period, and the number of workers fired each period, and also may include the number of units produced each period. (It is possible that fractional numbers of units could be produced in some applications.) One way to deal with this problem is to require in advance that some or all of the problem variables assume only integer values. Unfortunately, this makes the solution algorithm considerably more complex. The resulting problem, known as an integer linear programming problem, requires much more computational effort to solve than does ordinary linear programming. For a moderate-sized problem, solving the problem as an integer linear program is certainly a reasonable alternative.

If an integer programming code is unavailable or if the problem is simply too large to solve by integer programming, linear programming still provides a workable solution. However, after the linear programming solution is obtained, some of the problem variables must be rounded to integer values. Simply rounding off each variable to the closest integer may lead to an infeasible solution and/or one in which production and workforce levels are inconsistent. It is not obvious what is the best way to round the variables. We recommend the following conservative approach: round the values of the numbers of workers in each period t to W_t, the next larger integer. Once the values of W_t are determined, the values of the other variables, $H_t, F_t,$ and P_t, can be found along with the cost of the resulting plan.

Conservative rounding will always result in a feasible solution, but will rarely give the optimal solution. The conservative solution generally can be improved by trial-and-error experimentation.

There is no guarantee that if a problem can be formulated as a linear program, the final solution makes sense in the context of the problem. In the aggregate planning problem, it does not make sense that there should be both overtime production and idle time in the same period, and it does not make sense that workers should be hired and fired in the same period. This means that either one or both of the variables O_t and U_t must be zero, and either one or both of the variables H_t and F_t must be zero for each t, $1 \leq t \leq T$. This requirement can be included explicitly in the problem formulation by adding the constraints

$$O_t U_t = 0 \quad \text{for } 1 \leq t \leq T,$$
$$H_t F_t = 0 \quad \text{for } 1 \leq t \leq T,$$

since if the product of two variables is zero it means that at least one must be zero. Unfortunately, these constraints are not linear, as they involve a product of problem variables. However, it turns out that it is not necessary to explicitly include these constraints, because the optimal solution to a linear programming problem always occurs at an extreme point of the feasible region. It can be shown that every extreme point solution automatically has this property. If this were not the case, the linear programming solution would be meaningless.

Extensions

Linear programming also can be used to solve somewhat more general versions of the aggregate planning problem. Uncertainty of demand can be accounted for indirectly by assuming that there is a minimum buffer inventory B_t each period. In that case we would include the constraints

$$I_t \geq B_t \quad \text{for } 1 \leq t \leq T.$$

The constants B_t would have to be specified in advance. Upper bounds on the number of workers hired and the number of workers fired each period could be included in a similar way. Capacity constraints on the amount of production each period could easily be represented by the set of constraints:

$$P_t \leq C_t \quad \text{for } 1 \leq t \leq T.$$

The linear programming formulation introduced in this section assumed that inventory levels would never go negative. However, in some cases it might be desirable or even necessary to allow demand to exceed supply, for example, if forecast demand exceeded production capacity over some set of planning periods. In order to treat backlogging of excess demand, the inventory level I_t must be expressed as the difference between two nonnegative variables, say I_t^+ and I_t^-, satisfying

$$I_t = I_t^+ - I_t^-,$$
$$I_t^+ \geq 0, \quad I_t^- \geq 0.$$

The holding cost would now be charged against I_t^+ and the penalty cost for back orders (say c_P) against I_t^-. However, notice that for the solution to be sensible, it must be true that I_t^+ and I_t^- are not both positive in the same period t. As with the overtime and idle time and the hiring and firing variables, the properties of linear programming will guarantee that this holds without having to explicitly include the constraint $I_t^+ I_t^- = 0$ in the formulation.

FIGURE 3–7
A convex piecewise-linear function

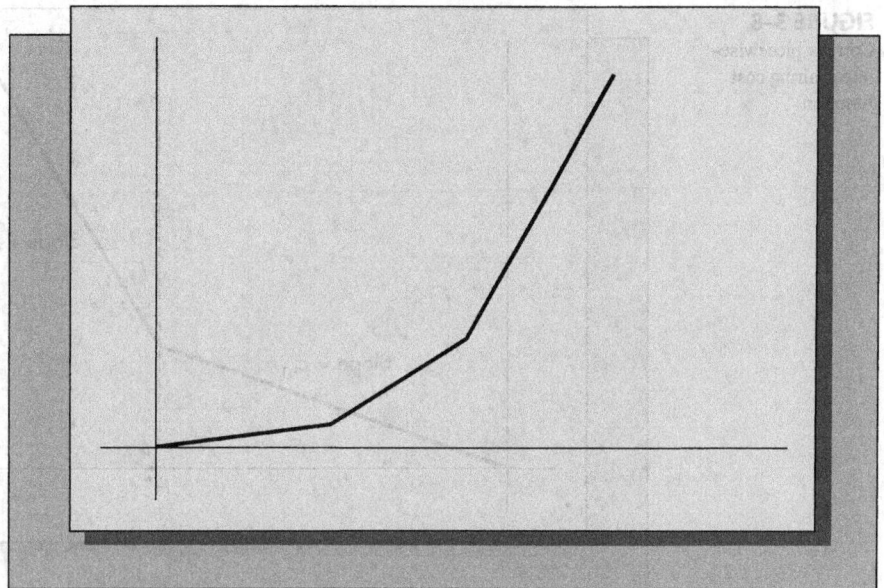

In the development of the linear programming model, we stated the requirement that all the cost functions must be linear. This is not strictly correct. Linear programming also can be used when the cost functions are *convex piecewise-linear functions*.

A convex function is one with an increasing slope. A piecewise-linear function is one that is composed of straight-line segments. Hence, a convex piecewise-linear function is a function composed of straight lines that have increasing slopes. A typical example is presented in Figure 3–7.

In practice, it is likely that some or all of the cost functions for aggregate planning are convex. For example, if Figure 3–7 represents the cost of hiring workers, then the marginal cost of hiring one additional worker increases with the number of workers that have already been hired. This is probably more accurate than assuming that the cost of hiring one additional worker is a constant independent of the number of workers previously hired. As more workers are hired, the available labor pool shrinks and more effort must be expended to hire the remaining available workers.

In order to see exactly how convex piecewise-linear functions would be incorporated into the linear programming formulation, we will consider a very simple case. Suppose that the cost of hiring new workers is represented by the function pictured in Figure 3–8. According to the figure, it costs c_{H1} to hire each worker until H^* workers are hired, and it costs c_{H2} for each worker hired beyond H^* workers, with $c_{H1} < c_{H2}$. The variable H_t, the number of workers hired in period t, must be expressed as the sum of two variables:

$$H_t = H_{1t} + H_{2t}.$$

Interpret H_{1t} as the number of workers hired up to H^* and H_{2t} as the number of workers hired beyond H^* in period t. The cost of hiring is now represented in the objective function as

$$\sum_{t=1}^{T} (c_{H1}H_{1t} + c_{H2}H_{2t}),$$

FIGURE 3–8
Convex piecewise-linear hiring cost function

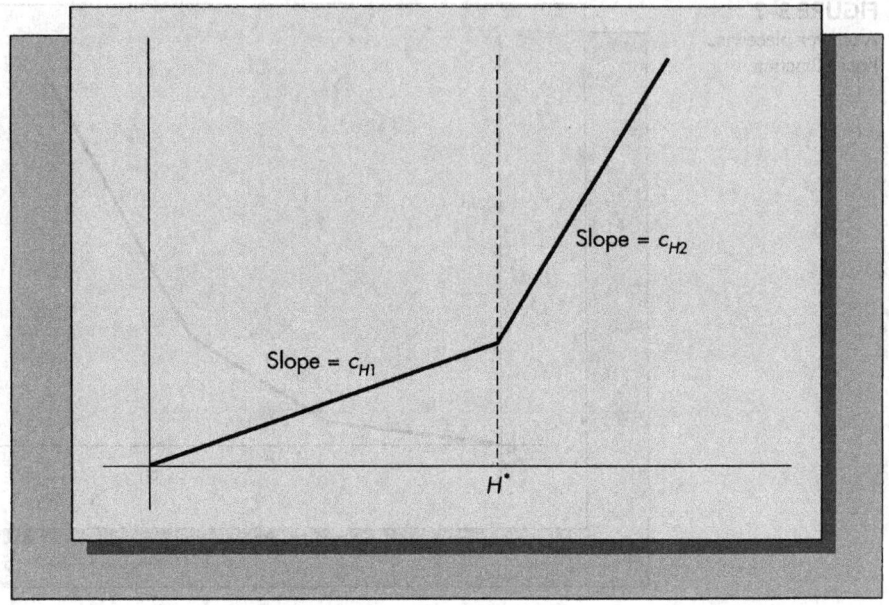

and the additional constraints

$$H_t = H_{1t} + H_{2t}$$
$$0 \leq H_{1t} \leq H^*$$
$$0 \leq H_{2t}$$

must also be included.

In order for the final solution to make sense, it can never be the case that $H_{1t} < H^*$ and $H_{2t} > 0$ for some t. (Why?) However, because linear programming searches for the minimum cost solution, it will force H_{1t} to its maximum value before allowing H_{2t} to become positive, since $c_{H1} < c_{H2}$. This is the reason that the cost functions must be convex. This approach can easily be extended to more than two linear segments and to any of the other cost functions present in the objective function. The technique is known as separable convex programming and is discussed in greater detail in Hillier and Lieberman (1990).

We will demonstrate the use of linear programming by finding the optimal solution to the example presented in Section 3.4. As there is no subcontracting, overtime, or idle time allowed, and the cost coefficients are constant with respect to time, the objective function is simply

$$\text{Minimize} \left(500 \sum_{t=1}^{6} H_t + 1{,}000 \sum_{t=1}^{6} F_t + 80 \sum_{t=1}^{6} I_t \right).$$

The boundary conditions comprise the specifications of the initial inventory of 500 units, the initial workforce of 300 workers, and the ending inventory of 600 units. These are best handled by including a separate additional constraint for each boundary condition.

The constraints are obtained by substituting $t = 1, \ldots, 6$ into Equations (A), (B), and (C). The full set of constraints expressed in standard linear programming format (with all problem variables on the left-hand side and nonnegative constants on the right-hand side) is as follows:

$$
\begin{aligned}
W_1 - W_0 - H_1 + F_1 &= 0, \\
W_2 - W_1 - H_2 + F_2 &= 0, \\
W_3 - W_2 - H_3 + F_3 &= 0, \\
W_4 - W_3 - H_4 + F_4 &= 0, \\
W_5 - W_4 - H_5 + F_5 &= 0, \\
W_6 - W_5 - H_6 + F_6 &= 0;
\end{aligned}
\quad \text{(A)}
$$

$$
\begin{aligned}
P_1 - I_1 + I_0 &= 1{,}280, \\
P_2 - I_2 + I_1 &= 640, \\
P_3 - I_3 + I_2 &= 900, \\
P_4 - I_4 + I_3 &= 1{,}200, \\
P_5 - I_5 + I_4 &= 2{,}000, \\
P_6 - I_6 + I_5 &= 1{,}400;
\end{aligned}
\quad \text{(B)}
$$

$$
\begin{aligned}
P_1 - 2.931 W_1 &= 0, \\
P_2 - 3.517 W_2 &= 0, \\
P_3 - 2.638 W_3 &= 0, \\
P_4 - 3.810 W_4 &= 0, \\
P_5 - 3.224 W_5 &= 0, \\
P_6 - 2.198 W_6 &= 0;
\end{aligned}
\quad \text{(C)}
$$

$$W_1, \ldots, W_6, P_1, \ldots, P_6, I_1, \ldots, I_6, F_1, \ldots, F_6, H_1, \ldots, H_6 \geq 0; \quad \text{(D)}$$

$$
\begin{aligned}
W_0 &= 300, \\
I_0 &= 500, \\
I_6 &= 600.
\end{aligned}
\quad \text{(E)}
$$

The values in equations (C) come from multiplying the value of K, number of aggregate units per worker, found earlier by the number of working days in the month, which shows this formulation in Excel.

	A	B	C	D	E	F	G	H	I	J
1	Cost of hiring	$500								
2	Cost of firing	$1,000								
3	Holding cost	$80								
4	K	0.14653								
5	Ending inv	600								
6										
7	Month	Hired	Fired	Inventory	Workers	Production		Worker	Inventory	Adjusted
8		(H_t)	(F_t)	(I_t)	(W_t)	(P_t)		balance	balance	Demand
9	Start			500	300					
10	January	0.00	27.02	20.00	272.98	800.00		0	1280	1280
11	February	0.00	0.00	340.00	272.98	960.00		0	640	640
12	March	0.00	0.00	160.00	272.98	720.00		0	900	900
13	April	0.00	0.00	0.00	272.98	1040.00		0	1200	1200
14	May	464.80	0.00	378.38	737.78	2378.38		0	2000	2000
15	June	0.00	0.00	600.00	737.78	1621.62		0	1400	1400
16	Totals	464.80	27.02	1498.38						
17										
18	Month	Days	Units per	Production						
19		(n_t)	worker	balance						
20	January	20	2.931	0						
21	February	24	3.517	0						
22	March	18	2.638	0						
23	April	26	3.810	0						
24	May	22	3.224	0						
25	June	15	2.198	0						
26										
27	Total cost	$379,292.22								

Cell Formulas

Cell	Formula	Copied to
B4	=245/22/76	
H9	=E9-E8-B9+C9	H10:H14
I9	=F9-D9+D8	I10:I14
C20	=B20*$B$4	C21:C25
D20	=F10-C20*E10	D21:D25
B16	=SUM(B10:B15)	C16:D16
B27	=$B$1*$B$16+$B$2*$C$16+$B$3*$D$16	

The Solver window for this problem is as follows.

Solver Parameters

Set Objective: $B$27

To: ◯ Max   ◉ Min   ◯ Value Of: 0

By Changing Variable Cells:
$B$10:$F$15

Subject to the Constraints:
```
$D$15 = $B$5
$D$20:$D$25 = 0
$H$10:$H$15 = 0
$I$10:$I$15 = $J$10:$J$15
```

☑ Make Unconstrained Variables Non-Negative

Select a Solving Method: Simplex LP

Solving Method

Select the GRG Nonlinear engine for Solver Problems that are smooth nonlinear. Select the LP Simplex engine for linear Solver Problems, and select the Evolutionary engine for Solver problems that are non-smooth.

TABLE 3–1 Aggregate Plan for Densepack Obtained from Rounding the Linear Programming Solution

A	B	C	D	E	F	G	H	I
Month	Number of Workers	Number Hired	Number Fired	Number of Units per Worker	Number of Units Produced (B × E)	Cumulative Production	Cumulative Net Demand	Ending Inventory (G − H)
January	273		27	2.931	800	800	780	20
February	273			3.517	960	1,760	1,420	340
March	273			2.638	720	2,480	2,320	160
April	273			3.810	1,040	3,520	3,520	0
May	738	465		3.224	2,379	5,899	5,520	379
June	738			2.198	1,622	7,521	7,520	1
Totals		465	27					900

The value of the objective function at the optimal solution is 379,292.22, which is *considerably* less than that achieved with either the zero inventory plan or the constant workforce plan. However, this cost is based on fractional values of the variables. The actual cost will be slightly higher after rounding.

Following the rounding procedure recommended earlier, we will round all the values of W_t to the next higher integer. That gives $W_1 = \cdots = W_4 = 273$ and $W_5 = W_6 = 738$. This determines the values of the other problem variables. This means that the firm should fire 27 workers in January and hire 465 workers in May. The complete solution is given in Table 3–6.

Again, because column H in Table 3–1 corresponds to net demand, we add the 600 units of ending inventory in June, giving a total inventory of $900 + 600 = 1,500$ units. Hence, the total cost of this plan is $(500)(465) + (1,000)(27) + (80)(1,500) = \$379,500$, which represents a substantial savings over both the zero inventory plan and the constant workforce plan.

The results of the linear programming analysis suggest another plan that might be more suitable for the company. Because the optimal strategy is to decrease the workforce in January and build it back up again in May, a reasonable alternative might be to not fire the 27 workers in January and to hire fewer workers in May. In this case, the most efficient method for finding the correct number of workers to hire in May is to simply re-solve the linear program, but without the variables $F_1, \ldots, F_6$, as no firing of workers means that these variables are forced to zero. (If you wish to avoid reentering the problem into the computer, simply append the old formulation with the constraints $F_1 = 0, F_2 = 0, \ldots, F_6 = 0$.) The optimal number of workers to hire in May turns out to be 374 if no workers are fired, and the cost of the plan is approximately $386,120. This is only slightly more expensive than the optimal plan, and has the important advantage of not requiring the firing of any workers.

Problems for Section 3.5

24. Mr. Meadows Cookie Company makes a variety of chocolate chip cookies in the plant in Albion, Michigan. Based on orders received and forecasts of buying habits, it is estimated that the demand for the next four months is 850,

1,260, 510, and 980, expressed in thousands of cookies. During a 46-day period when there were 120 workers, the company produced 1.7 million cookies. Assume that the number of workdays over the four months are respectively 26, 24, 20, and 16. There are currently 100 workers employed, and there is no starting inventory of cookies.

   a. What is the minimum constant workforce required to meet demand over the next four months?

   b. Assume that c_I = 10 cents per cookie per month, c_H = $100, and c_F = $200. Evaluate the cost of the plan derived in part (a).

   c. Formulate as a linear program. Be sure to define all variables and include the required constraints.

   d. Solve for the optimal solution.

25. Harold Grey owns a small farm in the Salinas Valley that grows apricots. The apricots are dried on the premises and sold to a number of large supermarket chains. Based on past experience and committed contracts, he estimates that sales over the next five years in thousands of packages will be as follows:

Year	Forecasted Demand (thousands of packages)
1	300
2	120
3	200
4	110
5	135

Assume that each worker stays on the job for at least one year, and that Grey currently has three workers on the payroll. He estimates that he will have 20,000 packages on hand at the end of the current year. Assume that, on the average, each worker is paid $25,000 per year and is responsible for producing 30,000 packages. Inventory costs have been estimated to be 4 cents per package per year, and shortages are not allowed.

Based on the effort of interviewing and training new workers, Farmer Grey estimates that it costs $500 for each worker hired. Severance pay amounts to $1,000 per worker.

   a. Assuming that shortages are not allowed, determine the minimum constant workforce that he will need over the next five years.

   b. Evaluate the cost of the plan found in part (a).

   c. Formulate this as a linear program.

   d. Solve the problem and round-off the solution and determine the cost of the resulting plan.

26. A local semiconductor firm, Superchip, is planning its workforce and production levels over the next year. The firm makes a variety of microprocessors and uses sales dollars as its aggregate production measure. Based on orders received

and sales forecasts provided by the marketing department, the estimate of dollar sales for the next year by month is as follows:

Month	Production Days	Predicted Demand (in $10,000)
January	22	340
February	16	380
March	21	220
April	19	100
May	23	490
June	20	625
July	24	375
August	12	310
September	19	175
October	22	145
November	20	120
December	16	165

Inventory holding costs are based on a 25 percent annual interest charge. It is anticipated that there will be 675 workers on the payroll at the end of the current year and inventories will amount to $120,000. The firm would like to have at least $100,000 of inventory at the end of December next year. It is estimated that each worker accounts for an average of $60,000 of production per year (assume that one year consists of 250 working days). The cost of hiring a new worker is $200, and the cost of laying off a worker is $400.

    a. Formulate this as a linear program.

    b. Solve the problem. Round the variables in the resulting solution and determine the cost of the plan you obtain.

27. Consider Mr. Meadows Cookie Company, described in Problem 24. Suppose that the cost of hiring workers each period is $100 for each worker until 20 workers are hired, $400 for each worker when between 21 and 50 workers are hired, and $700 for each worker hired beyond 50.

    a. Write down the complete linear programming formulation of the revised problem.

    b. Solve the revised problem for the optimal solution. What difference does the new hiring cost function make in the solution?

28. Leather-All produces a line of handmade leather products. At the present time, the company is producing only belts, handbags, and attaché cases. The predicted demand for these three types of items over a six-month planning horizon is as follows:

Month	Number of Working Days	Belts	Handbags	Attaché Cases
1	22	2,500	1,250	240
2	20	2,800	680	380
3	19	2,000	1,625	110
4	24	3,400	745	75
5	21	3,000	835	126
6	17	1,600	375	45

The belts require an average of two hours to produce, the handbags three hours, and the attaché cases six hours. All the workers have the skill to work on any item. Leather-All has 46 employees who each has a share in the firm and cannot be fired. There are an additional 30 locals that are available and can be hired for short periods at higher cost. Regular employees earn $8.50 per hour on regular time and $14.00 per hour on overtime. Regular time comprises a seven-hour workday, and the regular employees will work as much overtime as is available. The additional workers are hired for $11.00 per hour and are kept on the payroll for at least one full month. Costs of hiring and firing are negligible.

Because of the competitive nature of the industry, Leather-All does not want to incur any demand back orders.

  a. Using worker hours as an aggregate measure of production, convert the forecasted demands to demands in terms of aggregate units.

  b. What would be the size of the workforce needed to satisfy the demand for the coming six months on regular time only? Would it be to the company's advantage to bring the permanent workforce up to this level? Why or why not?

  c. Formulate the problem of optimizing Leather-All's hiring schedule as a linear program. Define all problem variables and include whatever constraints are necessary.

  d. Solve the problem formulated in part (*a*) for the optimal solution. Round all the relevant variables and determine the cost of the resulting plan.

3.6 DISAGGREGATING PLANS

Aggregate

As we saw earlier in this chapter, aggregate planning may be done at several levels of the firm. Example 3.1 considered a single plant, and showed how one might define an aggregate unit to include the six different items produced at that plant. Aggregate planning might be done for a single plant, a product family, a group of families, or for the firm as a whole.

There are two views of production planning: bottom-up or top-down. The bottom-up approach means that one would start with individual item production plans. These plans could then be aggregated up the chain of products to produce aggregate plans. The top-down approach, which is the one treated in this chapter, is to start with an aggregate plan at a high level. These plans would then have to be "disaggregated" to produce detailed production plans at the plant and individual item levels.

It is not clear that disaggregation is an issue in all circumstances. If the aggregate plan is used only for macro planning purposes, and not for planning at the detail level, then one need not worry about disaggregation. However, if it is important that individual item production plans and aggregate plans be consistent, then it might be necessary to consider disaggregation schemes.

The disaggregation problem is similar to the classic problem of resource allocation. Consider how resources are allocated in a university, for example. A university receives revenues from tuition, gifts, interest on the endowment, and research grants. Costs include salaries, maintenance, and capital expenditures. Once an annual budget is determined, each school (arts and science, engineering, business, law, etc.) and each budget center (staff, maintenance, buildings and grounds, etc.) would have to be allocated its share. Budget centers would have to allocate funds to each of their subgroups. For example, each school would allocate funds to individual departments, and departments would allocate funds to faculty and staff in that department.

In the manufacturing context, a disaggregation scheme is just a means of allocating aggregate units to individual items. Just as funds are allocated on several levels in the university, aggregate units might have to be disaggregated at several levels of the firm. This is the idea behind hierarchical production planning championed by several researchers at MIT and reported in detail in Bitran and Hax (1981) and Hax and Candea (1984).

We will discuss one possible approach to the disaggregation problem from Bitran and Hax (1981). Suppose that X^* represents the number of aggregate units of production for a particular planning period. Further, suppose that X^* represents an aggregation of n different items ($Y_1, Y_2, \ldots, Y_n$). The question is how to divide up (i.e., disaggregate) X^* among the n items. We know that holding costs are already included in the determination of X^*, so we need not include them again in the disaggregation scheme. Suppose that K_j represents the fixed cost of setting up for production of Y_j, and λ_j is the annual usage rate for item j. A reasonable optimization criterion in this context is to choose $Y_1, Y_2, \ldots, Y_n$ to minimize the average annual cost of setting up for production. As we will see in Chapter 4, the average annual setup cost for item j is $K_j \lambda_j / Y_j$. Hence, disaggregation requires solving the following mathematical programming problem:

$$\text{Minimise} \sum_{j=1}^{J} \frac{K_j \lambda_j}{Y_j}$$

subject to

$$\sum_{j=1}^{J} Y_j = X^*$$

and

$$a_j \leq Y_j \leq b_j \quad \text{for } 1 \leq j \leq J.$$

The upper and lower bounds on Y_j account for possible side constraints on the production level for item j.

A number of feasibility issues need to be addressed before the family run sizes Y_j are further disaggregated into lots for individual items. The objective is to schedule the lots for individual items within a family so that they run out at the scheduled setup time for the family. In this way, items within the same family can be produced within the same production setup.

Snapshot Application

WELCH'S USES AGGREGATE PLANNING FOR PRODUCTION SCHEDULING

Welch's is a make-to-stock food manufacturer based in Concord, Massachusetts. They are probably best known for grape jelly and grape juices, but they produce a wide variety of processed foods. Allen and Schuster (1994) describe an aggregate planning model for Welch's primary production facility.

The characteristics of the production system for which their system was designed are

- Dynamic, uncertain demand, resulting in changing buffer stock requirements.
- Make-to-stock environment.
- Dedicated production lines.
- Production lines that each produces two or more families of products.
- Large setup times and setup costs for families, as opposed to low setup times and costs for individual items.

The two primary objectives of the production system as described by the authors are to smooth peak demands through time so as not to exceed production capacity and to allocate production requirements among the families to balance family holding and setup costs. The planning is done with a six-month time horizon for demand forecasting. The six-month period is divided into two portions: the next four weeks and the remaining five months. Detailed plans are developed for the near term, including regular and overtime production allocation.

The model has two primary components: a family planning model, which finds the optimal timing and sizing of family production runs, and a disaggregation planning model, which takes the results of family planning and determines lot sizes for individual items within families.

The authors also discuss several implementation issues specific to Welch's environment. Product run lengths must be tied to the existing eight-hour shift structure. To do so; they recommend that production run lengths be expressed as multiples of one-quarter shift (two hours).

The model was implemented on a personal computer. Computing times are very moderate. Solution techniques include a mixed integer mathematical program and a linear programming formulation with relaxation (that is, rounding of variables to integer values).

This case demonstrates that the concepts discussed in this chapter can be useful in a real production planning environment. Although the system described here is not based on any of the specific models discussed in this chapter, this application shows that aggregation and disaggregation are useful concepts. Hierarchical aggregation for production scheduling is a valuable planning tool.

The concept of disaggregating the aggregate plan along organizational lines in a fashion that is consistent with the aggregation scheme is an appealing one. Whether or not the methods discussed in this section provide a workable link between aggregate plans and detailed item schedules remains to be seen.

Another approach to the disaggregation problem has been explored by Chung and Krajewski (1984). They develop a mathematical programming formulation of the problem. Inputs to the program include aggregate plans for each product family. This includes setup time, setup status, total production level for the family, inventory level, workforce level, overtime, and regular time availability. The goal of the analysis is to specify lot sizes and timing of production runs for each individual item, consistent with the aggregate information for the product family. Although such a formulation provides a potential link between the aggregate plan and the master production schedule, the resulting mathematical program requires many inputs and can result in a very large mixed integer problem that could be very time-consuming to solve.

Problems for Section 3.6

29. What does "disaggregation of aggregate plans" mean?
30. Discuss the following quotation made by a production manager: "Aggregate planning is useless to me because the results have nothing to do with my master production schedule."

3.7 SALES AND OPERATION PLANNING ON A GLOBAL SCALE

Globalization of manufacturing operations is commonplace. Many major corporations are now classified as multinationals; manufacturing and distribution activities routinely cross international borders. With the globalization of both sources of production and markets, firms must rethink production planning strategies. One issue explored in this chapter was smoothing of production plans over time; costs of increasing or decreasing workforce levels (and, hence, production levels) play a major role in the optimization of any aggregate plan. When formulating global production strategies, other smoothing issues arise. Exchange rates, costs of direct labor, and tax structure are just some of the differences among countries that must be factored into a global strategy.

Why the increased interest in global operations? In short, cost and competitiveness. According to McGrath and Bequillard (1989):

> The benefits of a properly executed international manufacturing strategy can be very substantial. A well developed strategy can have a direct impact on the financial performance and ultimately be reflected in increased profitability. In the electronic industry, there are examples of companies attributing 5% to 15% reduction in cost of goods sold, 10% to 20% increase in sales, 50% to 150% improvement in asset utilization, and 30% to 100% increase in inventory turnover to their internationalization of manufacturing.

Cohen et al. (1989) outline some of the issues that a firm must consider when planning production levels on a worldwide basis. These include

- In order to achieve the kinds of economies of scale required to be competitive today, multinational plants and vendors must be managed as a global system.
- Duties and tariffs are based on material flows. Their impact must be factored into decisions regarding shipments of raw material, intermediate product, and finished product across national boundaries.
- Exchange rates fluctuate randomly and affect production costs and pricing decisions in countries where the product is produced and sold.
- Corporate tax rates vary widely from one country to another.
- Global sourcing must take into account longer lead times, lower unit costs, and access to new technologies.
- Strategies for market penetration, local content rules, and quotas constrain product flow across borders.
- Product designs may vary by national market.
- Centralized control of multinational enterprises creates difficulties for several reasons, and decentralized control requires coordination.
- Cultural, language, and skill differences can be significant.

Determining optimal globalized manufacturing strategies is clearly a daunting problem for any multinational firm. One can formulate and solve mathematical models similar to the linear programming formulations of the aggregate planning models presented in this chapter, but the results of these models must always be balanced against judgment and experience. Cohen et al. (1989) consider such a model. They assume multiple products, plants, markets, raw materials, vendors, vendor supply contract alternatives, time periods, and countries. Their formulation is a large-scale mixed integer, nonlinear program.

One issue not treated in their model is that of exchange rate fluctuations and their effect on both pricing and production planning. Pricing, in particular, is traditionally done by adding a markup to unit costs in the home market. This completely ignores the issue of exchange rate fluctuations and can lead to unreasonable prices in some countries. For example, this issue has arisen at Caterpillar Tractor (Caterpillar Tractor Company, 1985). In this case, dealers all over the world were billed in U.S. dollars based on U.S. production costs. When the dollar was strong relative to other currencies, retail prices charged to overseas customers were not competitive in local markets. Caterpillar found itself losing market share abroad as a result. In the early 1980s the firm switched to a locally competitive pricing strategy to counteract this problem.

The notion that manufacturing capacity can be used as a hedge against exchange rate fluctuations has been explored by several researchers. Kogut and Kulatilaka (1994), for example, develop a mathematical model for determining when it is optimal to switch production from one location to another. Since the cost of switching is assumed to be positive, there must be a sufficiently large difference in exchange rates before switching is recommended. As an example, they consider a situation where a firm can produce its product in either the United States or Germany. If production is currently being done in one location, the model provides a means of determining if it is economical to switch locations based on the relative strengths of the euro and dollar. While such models are in the early stages of development, they provide a means of rationalizing international production planning strategies. Similar issues have been explored by Huchzermeier and Cohen (1996) as well.

3.8 HISTORICAL NOTES

The aggregate planning problem was conceived in an important series of papers that appeared in the mid-1950s. The first, Holt, Modigliani, and Simon (1955), discussed the structure of the problem and introduced the quadratic cost approach, and the later study of Holt, Modigliani, and Muth (1956) concentrated on the computational aspects of the model. A complete description of the method and its application to production planning for a paint company is presented in Holt, Modigliani, Muth, and Simon (1960).

It should be recognized that the text by Holt et al. (1960) represents a landmark work in the application of quantitative methods to production planning problems. The authors developed a solution method that results in a set of formulas that are easy to implement and they actually undertook the implementation of the method. The work details the application of the approach to a large manufacturer of household paints in the Pittsburgh area. The analysis was implemented in the company but a subsequent visit to the firm indicated that serious problems arose when the linear decision rule was followed, primarily because of the firm's policy of not firing workers when the model indicated that they should be fired.

That production planning problems could be formulated as linear programs appears to have been known in the early 1950s. Bowman (1956) discussed the use of a transportation model for production planning. The particular linear programming formulation of the aggregate planning problem discussed in Section 3.5 is essentially the same as the one developed by Hansmann and Hess (1960). Other linear programming formulations of the production planning problem generally involve multiple products or more complex cost structures (see, for example, Newson, 1975a and 1975b).

More recent work on the aggregate planning problem has focused on aggregation and disaggregation issues (Axsater, 1981; Bitran and Hax, 1981; and Zoller, 1971), the incorporation of learning curves into linear decision rules (Ebert, 1976), extensions to allow for multiple products (Bergstrom and Smith, 1970), and inclusion of marketing and/or financial variables (Damon and Schramm, 1972, and Leitch, 1974).

Taubert (1968) considers a technique he refers to as the search decision rule. The method requires developing a computer simulation model of the system and searching the response surface using standard search techniques to obtain a (not necessarily optimal) solution. Taubert's approach, which was described in detail in Buffa and Taubert (1972), gives results that are comparable to those of Holt, Modigliani, Muth, and Simon (1960) for the case of the paint company.

Kamien and Li (1990) developed a mathematical model to examine the effects of subcontracting on aggregate planning decisions. The authors show that under certain circumstances it is preferred to producing in-house, and provides an additional means of smoothing production and workforce levels.

3.9 Summary

Modern firms take a much less siloed approach to planning than firms of the past. They have come to realize that large benefits can accrue from a collaborative approach among the different divisions including operations, sales and marketing, and finance. A well designed S&OP process can manage the inherent tensions between these divisions and make trade-offs from a strategic perspective. The key output from an operational perspective of this process is a fixed sales plan that the operations division can plan to.

A common component of the S&OP process will be reviewing divisional KPIs. Because KPIs have such a large impact on employee incentives they need to be carefully chosen. The primary challenge in KPI selection is to ensure that the KPI is *aligned* with the strategic imperatives of the firm while still remaining *actionable* as far as the person being measured by it is concerned. It is also important to try to mitigate opportunities for gaming of KPIs by employees.

The key output from the S&OP process is a fixed forecast and therefore planning for routine uncertainty in these numbers is typically left to the operations division. While risk pooling (see Chapter 6) can be used to mitigate some of the uncertainty, there will always be natural variation that must be buffered. Such buffering can take the form of inventory, spare capacity, or time in the form of customer lead times. This sort of buffering typically takes place outside the S&OP process and will be discussed in later chapters in this text.

At a higher level than routine variation are more major risks that are discussed within the S&OP process. Such *known unknowns* should have contingency plans and/or mitigation strategies associated with them. They may be demand-side risks, such as new product introductions by competitors or demand shocks caused by extreme weather, or they may be supply-side risks such as supplier failure or major quality issues. An effective S&OP can anticipate such risks and set strategies for dealing with them that are in line with the company strategy. This may include the explicit relaxing of certain KPIs that become less relevant when working under exceptional circumstances.

Determining optimal production levels for all products produced by a large firm can be an enormous undertaking. *Aggregate planning* addresses this problem by assuming that individual items can be grouped together. However, finding an effective aggregating scheme can be difficult and often revenue dollars are used for simplicity. One particular aggregating scheme that has been suggested is *items, families,* and *types*. Items (or stock keeping units, SKUs), represent the finest level of detail, are identified by separate part numbers, bar codes, and/or radio frequency ID (RFID) tags when appropriate. Families are groups of items that share a common manufacturing setup, and types are natural groups of families. This particular aggregation scheme is fairly general but there is no guarantee that it will work in every application.

As mentioned above, once the strategies for dealing with uncertainty have been determined, most firms assume *determinist demand* in coming up with an aggregate production plan. Indeed, fixed demand forecasts over a specified planning horizon are required input. This assumption is not made for the sake of realism, but to allow the analysis to focus on the changes in the demand that are systematic rather than random. The goal of the analysis is to determine for each period the number of workers that should be employed, the production that should occur, and the inventory that should be carried over for each period.

The objective of an aggregate production plan is to minimize costs of production, payroll, holding, and changing the size of the workforce or capacity. The costs of making changes are generally referred to as *smoothing costs*. The aggregate planning models discussed in this chapter assume that all the costs are *linear functions*. This assumption is probably a reasonable approximation for most real systems within a given reasonable range of values. It is unlikely that the primary problem with applying a linear programming formulation to a real situation will be that the shape of the cost function is incorrect; it is more likely that the primary difficulty will be in correctly estimating the costs and other required input information.

Aggregate production plans will be of little use to the firm if they cannot be coordinated with detailed item schedules (i.e., the master production schedule). The problem of *disaggregating aggregate plans* is a difficult one, but one that must be addressed if the aggregate plans are to have value to the firm. There have been some mathematical programming formulations of the disaggregating problem suggested in the literature but these disaggregation schemes have yet to be proven in practice.

Additional Problems on Aggregate Planning

31. An aggregate planning model is being considered for the following applications. Suggest an aggregate measure of production and discuss the difficulties of applying aggregate planning in each case.

    a. Planning for the size of the faculty in a university.

    b. Determining workforce requirements for a travel agency.

    c. Planning workforce and production levels in a fish-processing plant that produces canned sardines, anchovies, kippers, and smoked oysters.

32. A local firm manufactures children's toys. The projected demand over the next four months for one particular model of toy robot is

Month	Workdays	Forecasted Demand (in aggregate units)
July	23	3,825
August	16	7,245
September	20	2,770
October	22	4,440

Assume that a normal workday is eight hours. Hiring costs are $350 per worker and firing costs (including severance pay) are $850 per worker. Holding costs are $4.00 per aggregate unit held per month. Assume that it requires an average of 1 hour and 40 minutes for one worker to assemble one toy. Shortages are not permitted. Assume that the ending inventory for June was 600 of these toys and the manager wishes to have at least 800 units on hand at the end of October. Assume that the current workforce level is 35 workers. Find the optimal plan by formulating as a linear program.

33. The Paris Paint Company is in the process of planning labor force requirements and production levels for the next four quarters. The marketing department has provided production with the following forecasts of demand for Paris Paint over the next year:

Quarter	Demand Forecast (in thousands of gallons)
1	380
2	630
3	220
4	160

Assume that there are currently 280 employees with the company. Employees are hired for at least one full quarter. Hiring costs amount to $1,200 per employee and firing costs are $2,500 per employee. Inventory costs are $1 per gallon per quarter. It is estimated that one worker produces 1,000 gallons of paint each quarter.

Assume that Paris currently has 80,000 gallons of paint in inventory and would like to end the year with an inventory of at least 20,000 gallons.

a. Determine the minimum constant workforce plan for Paris Paint and the cost of the plan. Assume that stock-outs are not allowed.

b. If Paris were able to back-order excess demand at a cost of $2 per gallon per quarter, determine a minimum constant workforce plan that holds less inventory than the plan you found in part (a), but incurs stock-outs in quarter 2. Determine the cost of the new plan.

c. Formulate this as a linear program. Assume that stock-outs are not allowed.

d. Solve the linear program. Round the variables and determine the cost of the resulting plan.

34. Consider the problem of Paris Paint presented in Problem 33. Suppose that the plant has the capacity to employ a maximum of 370 workers. Suppose that regular-time employee costs are $12.50 per hour. Assume seven-hour days, five-day weeks, and four-week months. Overtime is paid on a time-and-a-half basis. Subcontracting is available at a cost of $7 per gallon of paint produced. Overtime is limited to three hours per employee per day, and no more than 100,000 gallons can be subcontracted in any quarter.

a. Formulate as a linear program.

b. Solve the linear program. Round the variables and determine the cost of the resulting plan.

35. The Mr. Meadows Cookie Company can obtain accurate forecasts for 12 months based on firm orders. These forecasts and the number of workdays per month are as follows:

Month	Demand Forecast (in thousands of cookies)	Workdays
1	850	26
2	1,260	24
3	510	20
4	980	18
5	770	22
6	850	23
7	1,050	14
8	1,550	21
9	1,350	23
10	1,000	24
11	970	21
12	680	13

During a 46-day period when there were 120 workers, the firm produced 1,700,000 cookies. Assume that there are 100 workers employed at the beginning of month 1 and zero starting inventory.

a. Find the minimum constant workforce needed to meet monthly demand.
b. Assume $c_I = \$0.10$ per cookie per month, $c_H = \$100$, and $c_F = \$200$. Add columns that give the cumulative on-hand inventory and inventory cost. What is the total cost of the constant workforce plan?
c. Solve for the optimal plan using linear programming. Compare your solution to b.

36. The Yeasty Brewing Company produces a popular local beer known as Iron Stomach. Beer sales are somewhat seasonal, and Yeasty is planning its production and workforce levels on March 31 for the next six months. The demand forecasts are as follows:

Month	Production Days	Forecasted Demand (in hundreds of cases)
April	11	85
May	22	93
June	20	122
July	23	176
August	16	140
September	20	63

As of March 31, Yeasty had 86 workers on the payroll. Over a period of 26 working days when there were 100 workers on the payroll, Yeasty produced 12,000 cases of beer. The cost to hire each worker is $125 and the cost of laying off each worker is $300. Holding costs amount to 75 cents per case per month.

As of March 31, Yeasty expects to have 4,500 cases of beer in stock, and it wants to maintain a minimum buffer inventory of 1,000 cases each month. It plans to start October with 3,000 cases on hand.

a. Based on this information, find the minimum constant workforce plan for Yeasty over the six months, and determine hiring, firing, and holding costs associated with that plan.
b. Suppose that it takes one month to train a new worker. How will that affect your solution?
c. Suppose that the maximum number of workers that the company can expect to be able to hire in one month is 10. How will that affect your solution to part (*a*)?
d. Formulate the problem levels as a linear program. [You may ignore the conditions in parts (*b*) and (*c*).]
e. Solve the resulting linear program. Round the appropriate variables and determine the cost of your solution.
f. Suppose Yeasty does not wish to fire any workers. What is the optimal plan subject to this constraint?

37. A local canning company sells canned vegetables to a supermarket chain in the Minneapolis area. A typical case of canned vegetables requires an average of 0.2 day of labor to produce. The aggregate inventory on hand at the end of June is 800 cases. The demand for the vegetables can be accurately predicted for about 18 months based on orders received by the firm. The predicted demands for the next 18 months are as follows:

Month	Forecasted Demand (hundreds of cases)	Workdays	Month	Forecasted Demand (hundreds of cases)	Workdays
July	23	21	April	29	20
August	28	14	May	33	22
September	42	20	June	31	21
October	26	23	July	20	18
November	29	18	August	16	14
December	58	10	September	33	20
January	19	20	October	35	23
February	17	14	November	28	18
March	25	20	December	50	10

The firm currently has 25 workers. The cost of hiring and training a new worker is $1,000, and the cost to lay off one worker is $1,500. The firm estimates a cost of $2.80 to store a case of vegetables for a month. They would like to have 1,500 cases in inventory at the end of the 18-month planning horizon.

a. Develop a spreadsheet to find the minimum constant workforce aggregate plan and determine the total cost of that plan.
b. Develop a spreadsheet to find a plan that hires and fires workers monthly in order to minimize inventory costs. Determine the total cost of that plan as well.

Appendix 3-A

Glossary of Notation for Chapter 3

α = Smoothing constant for production and demand used in Bowman's model.
β = Smoothing constant for inventory used in Bowman's model.
c_F = Cost of firing one worker.
c_H = Cost of hiring one worker.
c_I = Cost of holding one unit of stock for one period.
c_O = Cost of producing one unit on overtime.
c_P = Penalty cost for back orders.
c_R = Cost of producing one unit on regular time.
c_S = Cost to subcontract one unit of production.
c_U = Idle cost per unit of production.
D_t = Forecast of demand in period t.
F_t = Number of workers fired in period t.
H_t = Number of workers hired in period t.
I_t = Inventory level in period t.
K = Number of aggregate units produced by one worker in one day.
λ_j = Annual demand for family j (refer to Section 3.9).
n_t = Number of production days in period t.
O_t = Overtime production in units.
P_t = Production level in period t.
S_t = Number of units subcontracted from outside.
T = Number of periods in the planning horizon.
U_t = Worker idle time in units ("undertime").
W_t = Workforce level in period t.

Bibliography

ABB Group. "Key Performance Indicators: Identifying and using key metrics for performance." PowerPoint accessed from http://www.abb.com/Search.aspx?q=pr&abbcontext=products&num=10&filetype=mspowerpoint&filter=0&start=10

Allen, S. J., and E. W. Schuster. "Practical Production Scheduling with Capacity Constraints and Dynamic Demand: Family Planning and Disaggregation." *Production and Inventory Management Journal* 35 (1994), pp. 15–20.

Axsater, S. "Aggregation of Product Data for Hierarchical Production Planning." *Operations Research* 29 (1981), pp. 744–56.

Bergstron, G. L., and B. E. Smith. "Multi-Item Production Planning—An Extension of the HMMS Rules." *Management Science* 16 (1970), pp. 100–103.

Bitran, G. R., and A. Hax. "Disaggregation and Resource Allocation Using Convex Knapsack Problems with Bounded Variables." *Management Science* 27 (1981), pp. 431–41.

Buffa, E. S., and W. H. Taubert. *Production-Inventory Systems: Planning and Control.* Rev. ed. New York: McGraw-Hill/Irwin, 1972.

Chopra, S. and P. Meindl. *Supply Chain Management: Strategy, Planning & Operation.* 3rd ed. Upper Saddle River, NJ: Prentice Hall, 2006.

Chung, C., and L. J. Krajewski. "Planning Horizons for Master Production Scheduling." *Journal of Operations Management* (1984), pp. 389–406.

De Meyer, A., C. H. Loch, and M. T. Pich. "Managing Project Uncertainty: From Variation to Chaos." *MIT Sloan Management Review* (2002).

Damon, W. W., and R. Schramm. "A Simultaneous Decision Model for Production, Marketing, and Finance." *Management Science* 19 (1972), pp. 16–72.

Ebert, R. J. "Aggregate Planning with Learning Curve Productivity." *Management Science* 23 (1976), pp. 171–82.

Erenguc, S., and S. Tufekci. "A Transportation Type Aggregate Production Model with Bounds on Inventory and Backordering." *European Journal of Operations Research* 35 (1988), pp. 414–25.

EveryAngle Software. Accessed from http://www.everyangle.com/downloads/customer-cases/en/customercase_heineken.pdf

Goldratt, E. M. and J. Cox. *The Goal: A Process of Ongoing Improvement.* 2nd Revised Edition. Great Barrington, MA: North River Press, 1992.

Grimson, J. A., and D. F. Pyke. "Sales and operations planning: an exploratory study and framework." *International Journal of Logistics Management* 18 (2007), pp. 322–346.

Hansmann, F., and S. W. Hess. "A Linear Programming Approach to Production and Employment Scheduling." *Management Technology* 1 (1960), pp. 46–51.

Hax, A. C., and D. Candea. *Production and Inventory Management.* Englewood Cliffs, NJ: Prentice Hall, 1984.

Hax, A. C., and H. C. Meal., "Hierarchical Integration of Production Planning and Scheduling." In *TIMS Studies in Management Science.* Volume 1, *Logistics,* ed. M. Geisler. New York: Elsevier, 1975.

Hiller, F. S., and G. J. Lieberman. *Introduction to Operations Research.* 5th ed. San Francisco: Holden Day, 1990.

Holt, C. C., F. Modigliani, and J. F. Muth. "Derivation of a Linear Decision Rule for Production and Employment." *Management Science* 2 (1956), pp. 159–77.

Holt, C. C., F. Modigliani, J. F. Muth, and H. A. Simon. *Planning Production, Inventories, and Workforce.* Englewood Cliffs, NJ: Prentice Hall, 1960.

Holt, C. C., F. Modigliani; and H. A. Simon. "A Linear Decision Rule for Employment and Production Scheduling." *Management Science* 2 (1955), pp. 1–30.

Hopp, W. J., and M. L. Spearman. *Factory Physics.* (1996). Boston, MA: McGraw Hill.

IBM. "IBM Global Chief Supply Chain Officer Study." Accessed from http://www-935.ibm.com/services/us/gbs/bus/html/gbs-csco-study.html

Jordan, W. C., and S. C. Graves. "Principles on the benefits of manufacturing process flexibility." *Management Science* 41 (1995), pp. 577–594.

Kaplan, R. S., and D. P. Norton. "The Balanced Scorecard: Measures that Drive Performance." *Harvard Business Review* (1992), pp. 71–80.

Kamien, M. I., and L. Li. "Subcontracting, Coordination, and Flexibility, and Production Smoothing Aggregate Planning." *Management Science* 36 (1990), pp. 1352–63.

Leitch, R. A. "Marketing Strategy and Optimal Production Schedule." *Management Science* 20 (1974), pp. 903–11.

Newson, E. F. P. "Multi-Item Lost Size Scheduling by Heuristic, Part 1: With Fixed Resources." *Management Science* 21 (1975a), pp. 1186–93.

Newson, E. F. P. "Multi-Item Lost Size Scheduling by Heuristic, Part 2: With Fixed Resources." *Management Science* 21 (1975b), pp. 1194–1205.

Rooijen, H. "Connecting our supply chain to our customers. Accessed from http://www.heinekeninternational.com/content/live/files%202011/investors/6.%20Henk%20van%20Rooijen.pdf

Santos, C., et al. "HP Enterprise Services Uses Optimization for Resource Planning." *Interfaces* 43 (2013), pp. 152–169.

Sheldon, D. H. *World Class Sales & Operations Planning.* Ft. Lauderdale, FL: J Ross Publishing and APICS, 2006.

Smits, J. and M. English. "The Journey to Worldclass S&OP at Heineken." Accessed from http://supply-chain.org/node/17283

Taleb, N. N. *The Black Swan: The Impact of the Highly Improbable.* New York: Random House, 2007.

Taubert, W. H. "A Search Decision Rule for the Aggregate Scheduling Problem." *Management Science* 14 (1968), pp. B343–53.

Vollmann, T. E., W. L. Berry, and D. C. Whybark. *Manufacturing, Planning, and Control Systems.* 3rd ed. New York: McGraw-Hill/Irwin, 1992.

Zoller, K. "Optimal Disaggregation of Aggregate Production Plans." *Management Science* 17 (1971), pp. B53–49.

Chapter **Four**

Inventory Control Subject to Known Demand

"We want to turn our inventory faster than our people."
—James Sinegal

Chapter Overview

Purpose

To consider methods for controlling individual item inventories when product demand is assumed to follow a known pattern (that is, demand forecast error is zero).

Key Points

1. *Classification of inventories*
   - *Raw materials.* These are resources required for production or processing.
   - *Components.* These could be raw materials or subassemblies that will later be included into a final product.
   - *Work-in-process (WIP).* These are inventories that are in the plant waiting for processing.
   - *Finished goods.* These are items that have completed the production process and are waiting to be shipped out.
2. *Why hold inventory?*
   - *Economies of scale.* It is probably cheaper to order or produce in large batches than in small batches.
   - *Uncertainties.* Demand uncertainty, lead time uncertainty, and supply uncertainty all provide reasons for holding inventory.
   - *Speculation.* Inventories may be held in anticipation of a rise in their value or cost.
   - *Transportation.* Refers to pipeline inventories that are in transit from one location to another.
   - *Smoothing.* As noted in Chapter 3, inventories provide a means of smoothing out an irregular demand pattern.
   - *Logistics.* System constraints that may require holding inventories.
   - *Control costs.* Holding inventory can lower the costs necessary to monitor a system. (For example, it may be less expensive to order yearly and hold the units than to order weekly and closely monitor orders and deliveries.)

3. Characteristics of inventory systems
   - *Patterns of demand.* The two patterns are (a) constant versus variable and (b) known versus uncertain.
   - *Replenishment lead times.* The time between placement of an order (or initiation of production) until the order arrives (or is completed).
   - *Review times.* The points in time that current inventory levels are checked.
   - *Treatment of excess demand.* When demand exceeds supply, excess demand may be either backlogged or lost.
4. Relevant costs
   - *Holding costs.* These include the opportunity cost of lost investment revenue, physical storage costs, insurance, breakage and pilferage, and obsolescence.
   - *Order costs.* These generally consist of two components: a fixed component and a variable component. The fixed component is incurred whenever a positive order is placed (or a production run is initiated), and the variable component is a unit cost paid for each unit ordered or produced.
   - *Penalty costs.* These are incurred when demand exceeds supply. In this case excess demand may be back-ordered (to be filled at a later time) or lost. Lost demand results in lost profit, and back orders require record keeping and in both cases, one risks losing customer goodwill.
5. *The basic EOQ model.* The EOQ model dates back to 1915 and forms the basis for all the inventory control models developed subsequently. It treats the basic trade-off between the fixed cost of ordering and the variable cost of holding. If h represents the holding cost per unit time and K the fixed cost of setup, then we show that the order quantity that minimizes costs per unit time is $Q = \sqrt{2K\lambda/h}$, where λ is the rate of demand. This formula is very robust for several reasons: (a) It is a very accurate approximation for the optimal order quantity when demand is uncertain (treated in Chapter 5), and (b) we show that deviations from the optimal Q generally result in modest cost errors. For example, a 25 percent error in Q results in an average annual holding and setup cost error of only 2.5 percent.
6. *The EOQ with finite production rate.* This is an extension of the basic EOQ model to take into account that when items are produced internally rather than ordered from an outside supplier, the rate of production is finite rather than infinite, as would be required in the simple EOQ model. We show that the optimal size of a production run now follows the formula $Q = \sqrt{2K\lambda/h'}$ where $h' = h(1 - \lambda/P)$ and P is the rate of production ($P > \lambda$). Note that since $h' < h$, the batch size when the production rate is taken into account exceeds the batch size obtained by the EOQ formula.
7. *Quantity discounts.* We consider two types of quantity discounts: all-units and incremental discounts. In the case of all-units discounts, the discount is applied to all the units in the order, while in the case of incremental discounts, the discount is applied to only the units above the break point. The all-units case is by far the most common in practice, but one does encounter incremental discounts in industry. In the case of all-units discounts, the optimization procedure requires searching for the lowest point on a broken annual cost curve. In the incremental discounts case, the annual cost curve is continuous, but has discontinuous derivatives.

8. *Resource-constrained multiple product systems.* Consider a retail store that orders many different items, but cannot exceed a fixed budget. If we optimize the order quantity of each item separately, then each item should be ordered according to its EOQ value. However, suppose doing so exceeds the budget. In this section, a model is developed that explicitly takes into account the budget constraint and adjusts the EOQ values accordingly. In most cases, the optimal solution subject to the budget constraint requires an iterative search of the Lagrange multiplier. However, when the condition $c_1/h_1 = c_2/h_2 = \cdots = c_n/h_n$ is met, the optimal order quantities are a simple scaling of the optimal EOQ values. Note that this problem is mathematically identical to one in which the constraint is on available space rather than available budget.

9. *EOQ models for production planning.* Suppose that n distinct products are produced on a single production line or machine. Assume we know the holding costs, order costs, demand rates, and production rates for each of the items. The goal is to determine the optimal sequence to produce the items, and the optimal batch size for each of the items to meet the demand and minimize costs. Note that simply setting a batch size for each item equal to its EOQ value (that is, optimal lot size with a finite production rate), is likely to be suboptimal since it is likely to result in stock-outs. The problem is handled by considering the optimal cycle time, T, where we assume we produce exactly one lot of each item each cycle. The optimal size of the production run for item j is simply $Q_j = \lambda_j T$, where T is the optimal cycle time. Finding T is nontrivial, however.

The current investment in inventories in the United States is enormous. In the third quarter of 2007, the total dollar investment was estimated to be $1.57 trillion.[1] Figure 4–1 shows investment in inventories broken down by sectors of the economy. The inventory models we will be discussing in this chapter and in Chapter 5 can be applied

FIGURE 4–1
Breakdown of the total investment in inventories in the U.S. economy (2007)

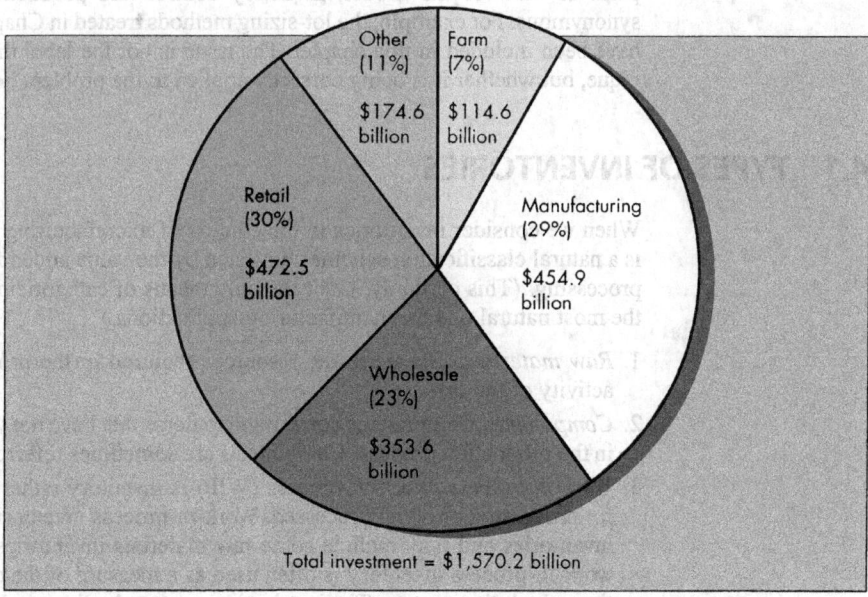

[1] *Survey of Current Business* (July 2007).

to all the sectors of the economy shown in Figure 4–1, but are most applicable to the manufacturing, wholesale, and retail sectors, which compose approximately 82 percent of the total. The trillion-dollar investment in inventories accounts for between 20 and 25 percent of the total annual GNP. Clearly there is enormous potential for improving the efficiency of our economy by intelligently controlling inventories. Companies that use scientific inventory control methods have a significant competitive advantage in the marketplace.

A major portion of this text is devoted to presenting and analyzing several mathematical models that can assist with controlling the replenishment of inventories. Both Chapters 4 and 5 assume that the demand for the item is external to the system. In most cases, this means that the inventory is being acquired or produced to meet the needs of a customer. In a manufacturing environment, however, demands for certain parts are the result of production schedules for higher-level assemblies; the production-lot-sizing decisions at one level of the system result in the demand patterns at other levels. The interaction of components, subassemblies, and final products plays an important role in determining future demand. Systems of this type are referred to as *materials requirements planning* (MRP) systems or dependent demand systems. MRP is treated in detail in Chapter 8.

The fundamental problem of inventory management can be succinctly described by the two questions (1) When should an order be placed? and (2) How much should be ordered? The complexity of the resulting model depends upon the assumptions one makes about the various parameters of the system. The major distinction is between models that assume known demand (this chapter) and those that assume random demand (Chapter 5), although, as we will see, the form of the cost functions and the assumptions one makes about physical characteristics of the system also play an important role in determining the complexity of the resulting model.

In general, the models that we discuss can be used interchangeably to describe either replenishment from an outside vendor or internal production. This means that from the point of view of the model, inventory control and production planning are often synonymous. For example, the lot-sizing methods treated in Chapter 8 could just as well have been included in this chapter. The issue is not the label that is placed on a technique, but whether it is being correctly applied to the problem being addressed.

4.1 TYPES OF INVENTORIES

When we consider inventories in the context of manufacturing and distribution, there is a natural classification scheme suggested by the value added from manufacturing or processing. (This certainly is not the only means of categorizing inventories, but it is the most natural one for manufacturing applications.)

1. *Raw materials.* These are the resources required in the production or processing activity of the firm.
2. *Components.* Components correspond to items that have not yet reached completion in the production process. Components are sometimes referred to as subassemblies.
3. *Work-in-process.* Work-in-process (WIP) is inventory either waiting in the system for processing or being processed. Work-in-process inventories include component inventories and may include some raw materials inventories as well. The level of work-in-process inventory is often used as a measure of the efficiency of a production scheduling system. The just-in-time approach, discussed in detail in Chapter 8, is aimed at reducing WIP to a minimum.

4. *Finished goods.* Also known as end items, these are the final products of the production process. During production, value is added to the inventory at each level of the manufacturing operation, culminating with finished goods.

The appropriate label to place on inventory depends upon the context. For example, components for some operations might be the end products for others.

4.2 MOTIVATION FOR HOLDING INVENTORIES

1. *Economies of scale.* Consider a company that produces a line of similar items, such as air filters for automobiles. Each production run of a particular size of filter requires that the production line be reconfigured and the machines recalibrated. Because the company must invest substantial time and money in setting up to produce each filter size, enough filters should be produced at each setup to justify this cost. This means that it could be economical to produce a relatively large number of items in each production run and store them for future use. This allows the firm to amortize fixed setup costs over a larger number of units.[2]

2. *Uncertainties.* Uncertainty often plays a major role in motivating a firm to store inventories. Uncertainty of external demand is the most important. For example, a retailer stocks different items so that he or she can be responsive to consumer preferences. If a customer requests an item that is not available immediately, it is likely that the customer will go elsewhere. Worse, the customer may never return. Inventory provides a buffer against the uncertainty of demand.

Other uncertainties provide a motivation for holding inventories as well. One is the uncertainty of the lead time. Lead time is defined as the amount of time that elapses from the point that an order is placed until it arrives. In the production planning context, interpret the lead time as the time required to produce the item. Even when future demand can be predicted accurately, the company needs to hold buffer stocks to ensure a smooth flow of production or continued sales when replenishment lead times are uncertain.

A third significant source of uncertainty is the supply. The OPEC oil embargo of the late 1970s is an example of the chaos that can result when supply lines are threatened. Two industries that relied (and continue to rely) heavily on oil and gasoline are the electric utilities and the airlines. Firms in these and other industries risked having to curtail operations because of fuel shortages.

Additional uncertainties that could motivate a firm to store inventory include the uncertainty in the supply of labor, the price of resources, and the cost of capital.

3. *Speculation.* If the value of an item or natural resource is expected to increase, it may be more economical to purchase large quantities at current prices and store the items for future use than to pay the higher prices at a future date. In the early 1970s, for example, the Westinghouse Corporation sustained severe losses on its contracts to build nuclear plants for several electric utility companies because it guaranteed to supply the uranium necessary to operate the plants at a fixed price. Unfortunately for Westinghouse, the price of the uranium skyrocketed between the time the contracts were signed and the time the plants were built.

Other industries require large quantities of costly commodities that have experienced considerable fluctuation in price. For example, silver is required for the production of photographic film. By correctly anticipating a major price increase in

---

[2] This argument assumes that the setup cost is a fixed constant. In some circumstances it can be reduced, thus justifying smaller lot sizes. This forms the basis of the just-in-time philosophy discussed in detail in Chapter 8.

silver, a major producer of photographic film, such as Kodak, could purchase and store large quantities of silver in advance of the increase and realize substantial savings.

The speculative motive also can be a factor for a firm facing the possibility of a labor strike. The cost of production could increase significantly when there is a severe shortage of labor.

4. *Transportation.* In-transit or *pipeline* inventories exist because transportation times are positive. When transportation times are long, as is the case when transporting oil from the Middle East to the United States, the investment in pipeline inventories can be substantial. One of the disadvantages of producing overseas is the increased transportation time, and hence the increase in pipeline inventories. This factor has been instrumental in motivating some firms to establish production operations domestically.

5. *Smoothing.* Changes in the demand pattern for a product can be deterministic or random. Seasonality is an example of a deterministic variation, while unanticipated changes in economic conditions can result in random variation. Producing and storing inventory in anticipation of peak demand can help to alleviate the disruptions caused by changing production rates and workforce levels. Smoothing costs and planning for anticipated swings in the demand were considered in the aggregate planning models in Chapter 3.

6. *Logistics.* We use the term *logistics* to describe reasons for holding inventory different from those already outlined. Certain constraints can arise in the purchasing, production, or distribution of items that force the system to maintain inventory. One such case is an item that must be purchased in minimum quantities. Another is the logistics of manufacture; it is virtually impossible to reduce all inventories to zero and expect any continuity in a manufacturing process.

7. *Control costs.* An important issue, and one that often is overlooked, is the cost of maintaining the inventory control system. A system in which more inventory is carried does not require the same level of control as one in which inventory levels are kept to a bare minimum. It can be less costly to the firm in the long run to maintain large inventories of inexpensive items than to expend worker time to keep detailed records for these items. Even though control costs could be a major factor in determining the suitability of a particular technique or system, they are rarely factored into the types of inventory models we will be discussing.

4.3 CHARACTERISTICS OF INVENTORY SYSTEMS

1. *Demand.* The assumptions one makes about the pattern and characteristics of the demand often turn out to be the most significant in determining the complexity of the resulting control model.

   a. *Constant versus variable.* The simplest inventory models assume that the rate of demand is a constant. The economic order quantity (EOQ) model and its extensions are based on this assumption. Variable demand arises in a variety of contexts, including aggregate planning (Chapter 3) and materials requirements planning (Chapter 8).

   b. *Known versus random.* It is possible for demand to be constant in expectation but still be random. Synonyms for random are *uncertain* and *stochastic*. Virtually all stochastic demand models assume that the average demand rate is constant. Random demand models are generally both more realistic and more complex than their deterministic counterparts.

2. *Lead time.* If items are ordered from the outside, the lead time is defined as the amount of time that elapses from the instant that an order is placed until it arrives. If items are produced internally, however, then interpret lead time as the amount of time required to produce a batch of items. We will use the Greek letter τ to represent lead time, which is expressed in the same units of time as demand. That is, if demand is expressed in units per year, then lead time should be expressed in years.

3. *Review time.* In some systems the current level of inventory is known at all times. This is an accurate assumption when demand transactions are recorded as they occur. One example of a system in which inventory levels are known at all times is a modern supermarket with a visual scanning device at the checkout stand that is linked to a storewide inventory database. As an item is passed through the scanner, the transaction is recorded in the database, and the inventory level is decreased by one unit. We will refer to this case as *continuous review*. In the other case, referred to as *periodic review*, inventory levels are known only at discrete points in time. An example of periodic review is a small grocery store in which physical stock-taking is required to determine the current levels of on-hand inventory.

4. *Excess demand.* Another important distinguishing characteristic is how the system reacts to excess demand (that is, demand that cannot be filled immediately from stock). The two most common assumptions are that excess demand is either back-ordered (held over to be satisfied at a future time) or lost (generally satisfied from outside the system). Other possibilities include partial back-ordering (part of the demand is back-ordered and part of the demand is lost) or customer impatience (if the customer's order is not filled within a fixed amount of time, he or she cancels). The vast majority of inventory models, especially the ones that are used in practice, assume full back-ordering of excess demand.

5. *Changing inventory.* In some cases the inventory undergoes changes over time that may affect its utility. Some items have a limited shelf life, such as food, and others may become obsolete, such as automotive spare parts. Mathematical models that incorporate the effects of perishability or obsolescence are generally quite complex and beyond the scope of this text. A brief discussion can be found in Section 5.8.

4.4 RELEVANT COSTS

Because we are interested in optimizing the inventory system, we must determine an appropriate optimization or performance criterion. Virtually all inventory models use cost minimization as the optimization criterion. An alternative performance criterion might be profit maximization. However, cost minimization and profit maximization are essentially equivalent criteria for most inventory control problems. Although different systems have different characteristics, virtually all inventory costs can be placed into one of three categories: holding cost, order cost, or penalty cost. We discuss each in turn.

Holding Cost

The **holding cost,** also known as the carrying cost or the inventory cost, is the sum of all costs that are proportional to the amount of inventory physically on hand at any point in time. The components of the holding cost include a variety of seemingly unrelated items. Some of these are

- Cost of providing the physical space to store the items.
- Taxes and insurance.
- Breakage, spoilage, deterioration, and obsolescence.
- Opportunity cost of alternative investment.

The last item often turns out to be the most significant in computing holding costs for most applications. Inventory and cash are in some sense equivalent. Capital must be invested to either purchase or produce inventory, and decreasing inventory levels results in increased capital. This capital could be invested by the company either internally, in its own operation, or externally.

What is the interest rate that could be earned on this capital? You and I can place our money in a simple passbook account with an interest rate of 2 percent, or possibly a long-term certificate of deposit with a return of maybe 5 percent. We could earn somewhat more by investing in high-yield bond funds or buying short-term industrial paper or second deeds of trust.

In general, however, most companies must earn higher rates of return on their investments than do individuals in order to remain profitable. The value of the interest rate that corresponds to the opportunity cost of alternative investment is related to (but not the same as) a number of standard accounting measures, including the internal rate of return, the return on assets, and the hurdle rate (the minimum rate that would make an investment attractive to the firm). Finding the right interest rate for the opportunity cost of alternative investment is very difficult. Its value is estimated by the firm's accounting department and is usually an amalgam of the accounting measures listed earlier. For convenience, we will use the term *cost of capital* to refer to this component of the holding cost. We may think of the holding cost as an aggregated interest rate comprised of the four components we listed. For example,

$$
\begin{aligned}
28\% &= \text{Cost of capital} \\
2\% &= \text{Taxes and insurance} \\
6\% &= \text{Cost of storage} \\
\underline{1\%} &= \text{Breakage and spoilage} \\
37\% &= \text{Total interest charge}
\end{aligned}
$$

This would be interpreted as follows: We would assess a charge of 37 cents for every dollar that we have invested in inventory during a one-year period. However, as we generally measure inventory in units rather than in dollars, it is convenient to express the holding cost in terms of dollars per unit per year rather than dollars per dollar per year. Let c be the dollar value of one unit of inventory, I be the annual interest rate, and h be the holding cost in terms of dollars per unit per year. Then we have the relationship

$$h = Ic.$$

Hence, in this example, an item valued at $180 would have an annual holding cost of $h = (0.37)(\$180) = \$66.60$. If we held 300 of these items for five years, the total holding cost over the five years would be

$$(5)(300)(66.60) = \$99,900.$$

This example raises an interesting question. Suppose that during the five-year period the inventory level did not stay fixed at 300 but varied on a continuous basis. We would expect inventory levels to change over time. Inventory levels decrease when items are used to satisfy demand and increase when units are produced or new orders arrive. How would the holding cost be computed in such a case? In particular, suppose the inventory level $I(t)$ during some interval (t_1, t_2) behaves as in Figure 4–2.

The holding cost incurred at any point in time is proportional to the inventory level at that point in time. In general, the total holding cost incurred from a time t_1 to a time t_2 is h multiplied by the area under the curve described by $I(t)$. The *average* inventory

FIGURE 4–2
Inventory as a function of time

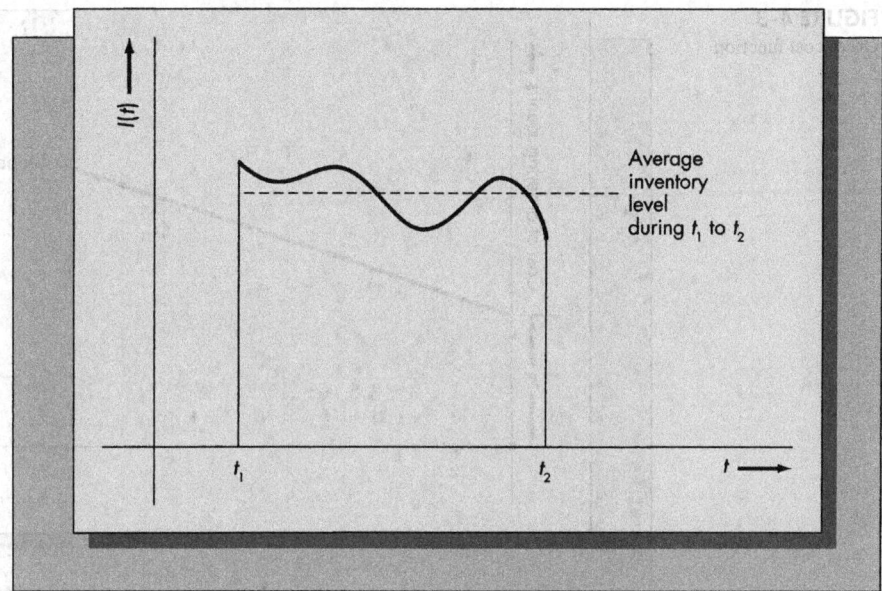

level during the period (t_1, t_2) is the area under the curve divided by $t_2 - t_1$. For the cases considered in this chapter, simple geometry can be used to find the area under the inventory level curve. When $I(t)$ is described by a straight line, its average value is obvious. In cases such as that pictured in Figure 4–2, in which the curve of $I(t)$ is complex, the average inventory level would be determined by computing the integral of $I(t)$ over the interval (t_1, t_2) and dividing by $t_2 - t_1$.

Order Cost

The holding cost includes all those costs that are proportional to the amount of inventory on hand, whereas the **order cost** depends on the amount of inventory that is ordered or produced.

In most applications, the order cost has two components: a fixed and a variable component. The fixed cost, K, is incurred independent of the size of the order as long as it is not zero. The variable cost, c, is incurred on a per-unit basis. We also refer to K as the setup cost and c as the proportional order cost. Define $C(x)$ as the cost of ordering (or producing) x units. It follows that

$$C(x) = \begin{cases} 0 & \text{if } x = 0, \\ K + cx & \text{if } x > 0. \end{cases}$$

The order cost function is pictured in Figure 4–3.

When estimating the setup cost, one should include *only* those costs that are relevant to the current ordering decision. For example, the cost of maintaining the purchasing department of the company is *not* relevant to daily ordering decisions and should not be factored into the estimation of the setup cost. This is an overhead cost that is independent of the decision of whether or not an order should be placed. The appropriate costs comprising K would be the bookkeeping expense associated with the order, the fixed costs independent of the size of the order that might be required by the vendor, costs of order generation and receiving, and handling costs.

FIGURE 4–3
Order cost function

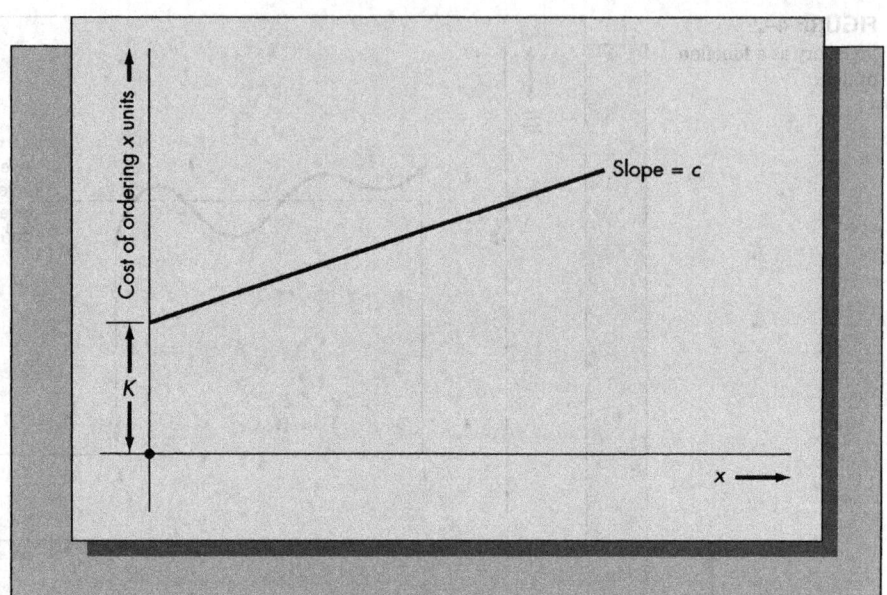

Penalty Cost

The **penalty cost,** also known as the shortage cost or the stock-out cost, is the cost of not having sufficient stock on hand to satisfy a demand *when it occurs*. This cost has a different interpretation depending on whether excess demand is back-ordered (orders that cannot be filled immediately are held on the books until the next shipment arrives) or lost (known as lost sales). In the back-order case, the penalty cost includes whatever bookkeeping and/or delay costs might be involved. In the lost-sales case, it includes the lost profit that would have been made from the sale. In either case, it would also include the *loss-of-goodwill* cost, which is a measure of customer satisfaction. Estimating the loss-of-goodwill component of the penalty cost can be very difficult in practice.

We use the symbol p to denote penalty cost and assume that p is charged on a per-unit basis. That is, each time a demand occurs that cannot be satisfied immediately, a cost p is incurred independent of how long it takes to eventually fill the demand. An alternative means of accounting for shortages is to charge the penalty cost on a per-unit-per-unit-time basis (as we did with the holding cost). This approach is appropriate if the time that a back order stays on the books is important, for example, if a back order results in stopping a production line because of the unavailability of a part. The models considered in this chapter assume that penalty costs are charged on a per-unit basis only. Penalty cost models are not considered in this chapter. Penalty costs are included in Chapter 5, but models incorporating a time-weighted penalty cost are not.

We present those inventory models that have had the greatest impact in the user community. Many of the techniques discussed in both this chapter and in Chapter 5 form the basis for commercial inventory control systems or in-house systems. In most cases, the models are simple enough that optimal operating policies can be calculated by hand, but they are often complex enough to capture the essential trade-offs in inventory management.

Problems for Sections 4.1–4.4

1. What are the two questions that inventory control addresses?
2. Discuss the cost penalties incurred by a firm that holds too much inventory and one that holds too little inventory.
3. ABC, Inc., produces a line of touring bicycles. Specifically, what are the four types of inventories (raw materials, components, work-in-process, and finished goods) that would arise in the production of this item?
4. I Carry rents trucks for moving and hauling. Each truck costs the company an average of $8,000, and the inventory of trucks varies monthly depending on the number that are rented out. During the first eight months of last year, I Carry had the following ending inventory of trucks on hand:

Month	Number of Trucks	Month	Number of Trucks
January	26	May	13
February	38	June	9
March	31	July	16
April	22	August	5

I Carry uses a 20 percent annual interest rate to represent the cost of capital. Yearly costs of storage amount to 3 percent of the value of each truck, and the cost of liability insurance is 2 percent.

a. Determine the total handling cost incurred by I Carry during the period January to August. Assume for the purposes of your calculation that the holding cost incurred in a month is proportional to the inventory on hand at the end of the month.

b. Assuming that these eight months are representative, estimate the average annual cost of holding trucks.

5. Stationery Supplies is considering installing an inventory control system in its store in Provo, Utah. The store carries about 1,400 different inventory items and has annual gross sales of about $80,000. The inventory control system would cost $12,500 to install and about $2,000 per year in additional supplies, time, and maintenance. If the savings to the store from the system can be represented as a fixed percentage of annual sales, what would that percentage have to be in order for the system to pay for itself in five years or less?

6. For Stationery Supplies, discussed in Problem 5, list and discuss all the uncertainties that would motivate the store to maintain inventories of its 1,400 items.

7. Stationery Supplies orders plastic erasers from a company in Nürnberg, Germany. It takes six weeks to ship the erasers from Germany to Utah. Stationery Supplies maintains a standing order of 200 erasers every six months (shipped on the first of January and the first of July).

a. Assuming the ordering policy the store is using does not result in large buildups of inventory or long-term stock-outs, what is the annual demand for erasers?

b. Draw a graph of the pipeline inventory (that is, the inventory ordered but not received) of the erasers during one year. What is the average pipeline inventory of erasers during the year?

c. Express the replenishment lead time in years and multiply the annual demand you obtained in part (a) by the lead time. What do you notice about the result that you obtain?

8. Penalty costs can be assessed only against the number of units of demand that cannot be satisfied, or against the number of units weighted by the amount of time that an order stays on the books. Consider the following history of supply and demand transactions for a particular part:

Month	Number of Items Received	Demand during Month
January	200	520
February	175	1,640
March	750	670
April	950	425
May	500	280
June	2,050	550

Assume that starting inventory at the beginning of January is 480 units.

a. Determine the ending inventory each month. Assume that excess demands are back-ordered.

b. Assume that each time a unit is demanded that cannot be supplied immediately, a one-time charge of $10 is made. Determine the stock-out cost incurred during the six months (1) if excess demand at the end of each month is lost, and (2) if excess demand at the end of each month is back-ordered.

c. Suppose that each stock-out costs $10 per unit per month that the demand remains unfilled. If demands are filled on a first-come, first-served basis, what is the total stock-out cost incurred during the six months using this type of cost criterion? (Assume that the demand occurs at the beginning of the month for purposes of your calculation.) Notice that you must assume that excess demands are back-ordered for this case to make any sense.

d. Discuss under what circumstances the cost criterion used in part (b) might be appropriate and under what circumstances the cost criterion used in part (c) might be appropriate.

9. HAL Ltd. produces a line of high-capacity disk drives for mainframe computers. The housings for the drives are produced in Hamilton, Ontario, and shipped to the main plant in Toronto. HAL uses the drive housings at a fairly steady rate of 720 per year. Suppose that the housings are shipped in trucks that can hold 40 housings at one time. It is estimated that the fixed cost of loading the housings onto the truck and unloading them on the other end is $300 for shipments of 120 or fewer housings (i.e., three or fewer truckloads). Each trip made by a single truck costs the company $160 in driver time, gasoline, oil, insurance, and wear and tear on the truck.

a. Compute the annual costs of transportation and loading and unloading the housings for the following policies: (1) shipping one truck per week, (2) shipping one full truckload as often as needed, and (3) shipping three full truckloads as often as needed.

b. For what reasons might the policy in part (a) with the highest annual cost be more desirable from a systems point of view than the policy having the lowest annual cost?

4.5 THE EOQ MODEL

The **EOQ model** (or *economic order quantity model*) is the simplest and most fundamental of all inventory models. It describes the important trade-off between fixed order costs and holding costs, and is the basis for the analysis of more complex systems.

The Basic Model

Assumptions:

1. The demand rate is known and is a constant λ units per unit time. (The unit of time may be days, weeks, months, etc. In what follows we assume that the default unit of time is a year. However, the analysis is valid for other time units as long as all relevant variables are expressed in the same units.)
2. Shortages are not permitted.
3. There is no order lead time. (This assumption will be relaxed.)
4. The costs include
   a. Setup cost at K per positive order placed.
   b. Proportional order cost at c per unit ordered.
   c. Holding cost at h per unit held per unit time.

Assume with no loss in generality that the on-hand inventory at time zero is zero. Shortages are not allowed, so we must place an order at time zero. Let Q be the size of the order. It follows that the on-hand inventory level increases instantaneously from zero to Q at time $t = 0$.

Consider the next time an order is to be placed. At this time, either the inventory is positive or it is again zero. A little reflection shows that we can reduce the holding costs by waiting until the inventory level drops to zero before ordering again. At the instant that on-hand inventory equals zero, the situation looks exactly the same as it did at time $t = 0$. If it was optimal to place an order for Q units at that time, then it is still optimal to order Q units. It follows that the function that describes the changes in stock levels over time is the familiar sawtooth pattern of Figure 4–4.

The objective is to choose Q to minimize the average cost per unit time. Unless otherwise stated, we will assume that a unit of time is a year, so that we minimize the average annual cost. Other units of time, such as days, weeks, or months, are also acceptable, as long as all time-related variables are expressed in the same units. One might think that the appropriate optimization criterion would be to minimize the *total* cost in a cycle. However, this ignores the fact that the cycle length itself is a function of Q and must be explicitly included in the formulation.

Next, we derive an expression for the average annual cost as a function of the lot size Q. In each cycle, the total fixed plus proportional order cost is $C(Q) = K + cQ$. In order to obtain the order cost per unit time, we divide by the cycle length T. As Q units are consumed each cycle at a rate λ, it follows that $T = Q/\lambda$. This result also can be obtained by noting that the slope of the inventory curve pictured in Figure 4–4, $-\lambda$, equals the ratio $-Q/T$.

Consider the holding cost. Because the inventory level decreases linearly from Q to 0 each cycle, the average inventory level during one order cycle is $Q/2$. Because all cycles are identical, the average inventory level over a time horizon composed

FIGURE 4–4
Inventory levels for the EOQ model

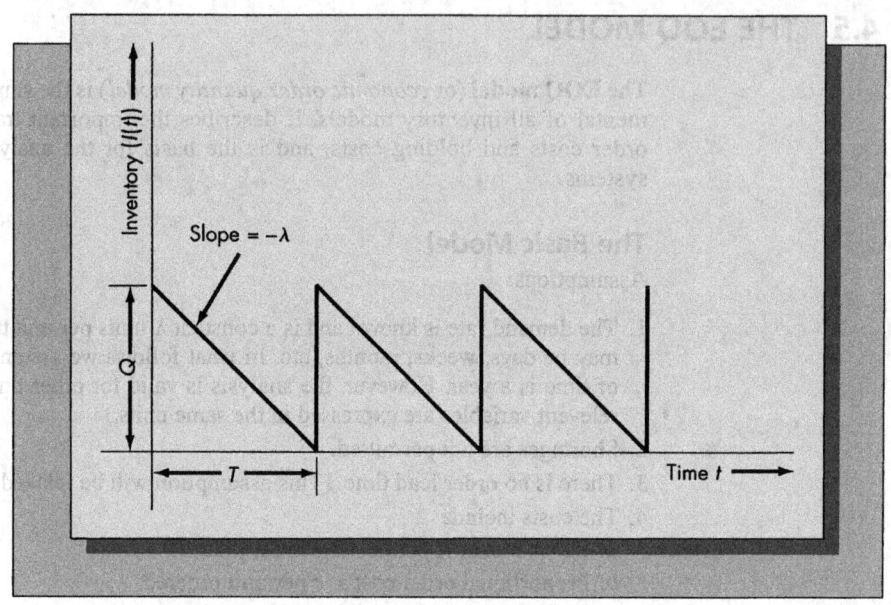

of many cycles is also $Q/2$. It follows that the average annual cost, say $G(Q)$, is given by

$$G(Q) = \frac{K + cQ}{T} + \frac{hQ}{2} = \frac{K + cQ}{Q/\lambda} + \frac{hQ}{2}$$

$$= \frac{K\lambda}{Q} + \lambda c + \frac{hQ}{2}.$$

The three terms composing $G(Q)$ are annual setup cost, annual purchase cost, and annual holding cost, respectively.

We now wish to find Q to minimize $G(Q)$. Consider the shape of the curve $G(Q)$. We have that

$$G'(Q) = -K\lambda/Q^2 + h/2$$

and

$$G''(Q) = 2K\lambda/Q^3 > 0 \quad \text{for } Q > 0.$$

Since $G''(Q) > 0$, it follows that $G(Q)$ is a convex function of Q. Furthermore, since $G'(0) = -\infty$ and $G'(\infty) = h/2$, it follows that $G(Q)$ behaves as pictured in Figure 4–5.

The optimal value of Q occurs where $G'(Q) = 0$. This is true when $Q^2 = 2K\lambda/h$, which gives

$$Q^* = \sqrt{\frac{2K\lambda}{h}}.$$

Q^* is known as the economic order quantity (EOQ). There are a number of interesting points to note:

1. In Figure 4–5, the curves corresponding to the fixed order cost component $K\lambda/Q$ and the holding cost component $hQ/2$ also are included. Notice that Q^* is the value of

FIGURE 4–5
The average annual cost function $G(Q)$

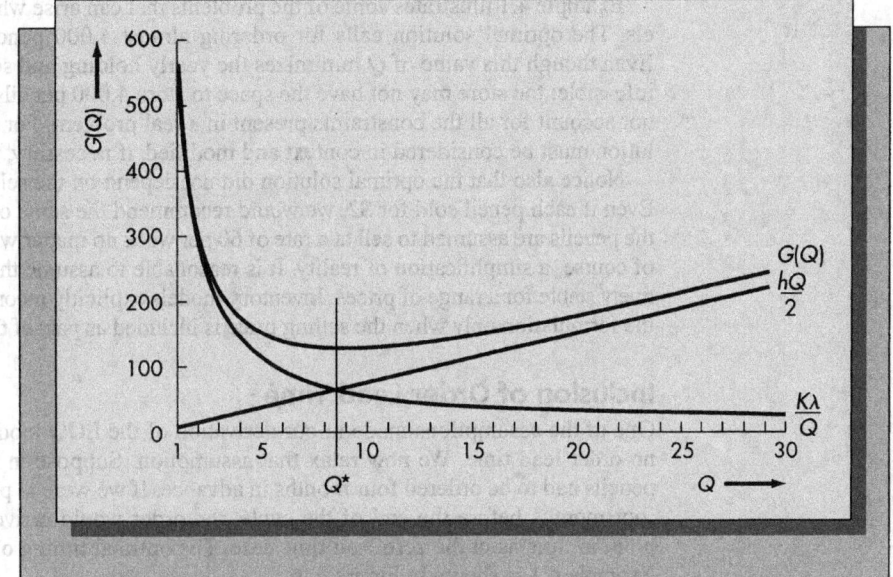

Q where the two curves intersect. (If you equate $hQ/2$ and $K\lambda/Q$ and solve for Q, you will obtain the EOQ formula.) In general, the minimum of the sum of two functions will *not* occur at the intersection of the two functions. It is an interesting coincidence that it does in this case.

2. Notice that the proportional order cost component, c, does not appear explicitly in the expression for Q^*. This is because the term λc appearing in the definition of $G(Q)$ is independent of Q. As all feasible policies must replenish inventory at the rate of demand, the proportional order cost incurred per unit time is λc independent of Q. Because λc is a constant, we generally ignore it when computing average costs. Notice that c does affect the value of Q^* indirectly, as h appears in the EOQ formula and $h = Ic$.

Example 4.1   Number 2 pencils at the campus bookstore are sold at a fairly steady rate of 60 per week. The pencils cost the bookstore 2 cents each and sell for 15 cents each. It costs the bookstore $12 to initiate an order, and holding costs are based on an annual interest rate of 25 percent. Determine the optimal number of pencils for the bookstore to purchase and the time between placement of orders. What are the yearly holding and setup costs for this item?

Solution   First, we convert the demand to a yearly rate so that it is consistent with the interest charge, which is given on an annual basis. (Alternatively, we could have converted the annual interest rate to a weekly interest rate.) The annual demand rate is $\lambda = (60)(52) = 3{,}120$. The holding cost h is the product of the annual interest rate and the variable cost of the item. Hence, $h = (0.25)(0.02) = 0.005$. Substituting into the EOQ formula, we obtain

$$Q^* = \sqrt{\frac{2K\lambda}{h}} = \sqrt{\frac{(2)(12)(3{,}120)}{0.005}} = 3{,}870.$$

The cycle time is $T = Q/\lambda = 3{,}870/3{,}120 = 1.24$ years. The average annual holding cost is $h(Q/2) = 0.005(3{,}870/2) = \$9.675$. The average annual setup cost is $K\lambda/Q$, which is also $\$9.675$.

Example 4.1 illustrates some of the problems that can arise when using simple models. The optimal solution calls for ordering almost 4,000 pencils every 15 months. Even though this value of Q minimizes the yearly holding and setup costs, it could be infeasible: the store may not have the space to store 4,000 pencils. Simple models cannot account for all the constraints present in a real problem. For that reason, every solution must be considered in context and modified, if necessary, to fit the application.

Notice also that the optimal solution did not depend on the selling price of 15 cents. Even if each pencil sold for $2, we would recommend the same order quantity, because the pencils are assumed to sell at a rate of 60 per week no matter what their price. This is, of course, a simplification of reality. It is reasonable to assume that the demand is relatively stable for a range of prices. Inventory models explicitly incorporate selling price in the formulation only when the selling price is included as part of the optimization.

Inclusion of Order Lead Time

One of the assumptions made in our derivation of the EOQ model was that there was no order lead time. We now relax that assumption. Suppose in Example 4.1 that the pencils had to be ordered four months in advance. If we were to place the order exactly four months before the end of the cycle, the order would arrive at exactly the same point in time as in the zero lead time case. The optimal timing of order placement for Example 4.1 is shown in Figure 4–6.

Rather than say that an order should be placed so far in advance of the end of a cycle, it is more convenient to indicate reordering in terms of the on-hand inventory. Define R, the reorder point, as the level of on-hand inventory at the instant an order should be placed. From Figure 4–6, we see that R is the product of the lead time and the demand rate ($R = \lambda\tau$). For the example, $R = (3{,}120)(0.3333) = 1{,}040$. Notice that we converted the lead time to years before multiplying. *Always express all relevant variables in the same units of time.*

Determining the reorder point is more difficult when the lead time exceeds a cycle. Consider an item with an EOQ of 25, a demand rate of 500 units per year, and a lead time of six weeks. The cycle time is $T = 25/500 = 0.05$ year, or 2.6 weeks. Forming

FIGURE 4–6
Reorder point calculation for Example 4.1

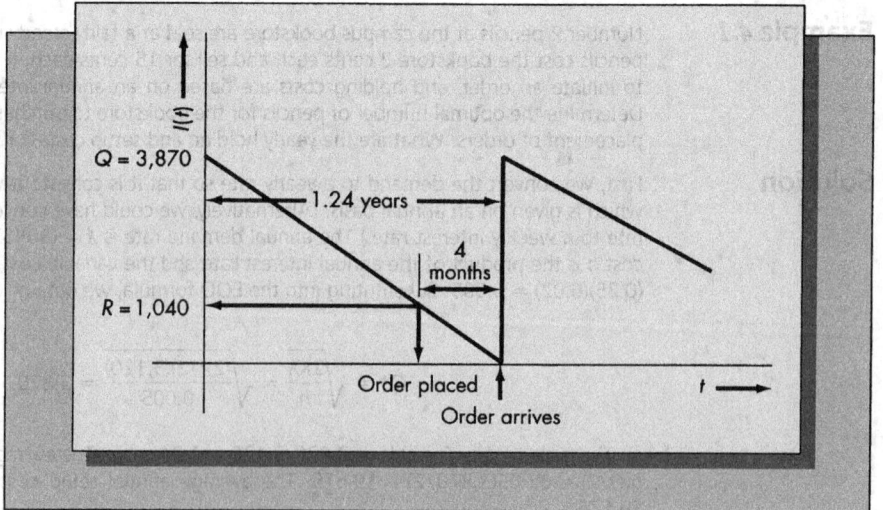

FIGURE 4–7
Reorder point calculation for lead times exceeding one cycle

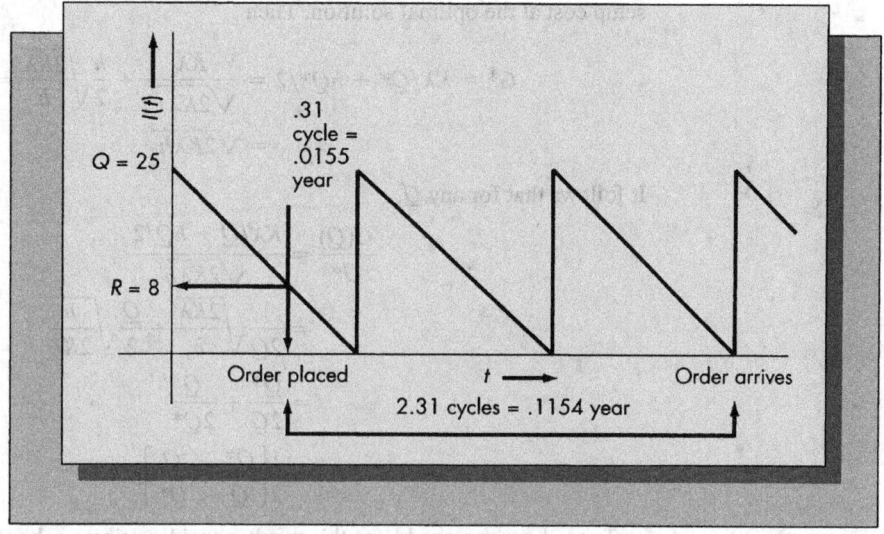

the ratio of τ/T, we obtain 2.31. This means that there are exactly 2.31 cycles in the lead time. Every order must be placed 2.31 cycles in advance (see Figure 4–7).

Notice that for the purpose of computing the reorder point, this is exactly the same as placing the order *0.31 cycle in advance.* This is true because the level of on-hand inventory is the same whether we are at a point 2.31 or 0.31 cycle before the arrival of an order. In this case, 0.31 cycle is 0.0155 year, thus giving a reorder point of $R = (0.0155)(500) = 7.75 \approx 8$. In general, when $\tau > T$, use the following procedure:

a. Form the ratio τ/T.
b. Consider only the fractional remainder of the ratio. Multiply this fractional remainder by the cycle length to convert back to years.
c. Multiply the result of step (b) by the demand rate to obtain the reorder point.

Sensitivity

In this part we examine the issue of how sensitive the annual cost function is to errors in the calculation of Q. Consider Example 4.1. Suppose that the bookstore orders pencils in batches of 1,000, rather than 3,870 as the optimal solution indicates. What additional cost is it incurring by using a suboptimal solution? To answer the question, we consider the average annual cost function $G(Q)$. By substituting $Q = 1,000$, we can find the average annual cost for this lot size and compare it to the optimal cost to determine the magnitude of the penalty. We have

$$G(Q) = K\lambda/Q + hQ/2 = (12)(3,120)/1,000 + (0.005)(1,000)/2 = \$39.94,$$

which is considerably larger than the optimal cost of $19.35.

One can find the cost penalty for suboptimal solutions in this manner for any particular problem. However, it is more instructive and more convenient to obtain a universal solution to the sensitivity problem. We do so by deriving an expression for the ratio of the suboptimal cost over the optimal cost as a function of the ratio of the optimal and suboptimal order quantities. Let G^* be the average annual holding and setup cost at the optimal solution. Then

$$G^* = K\lambda/Q^* + hQ^*/2 = \frac{K\lambda}{\sqrt{2K\lambda/h}} + \frac{h}{2}\sqrt{\frac{2K\lambda}{h}} = 2\sqrt{\frac{K\lambda h}{2}}$$

$$= \sqrt{2K\lambda h}.$$

It follows that for any Q,

$$\frac{G(Q)}{G^*} = \frac{K\lambda/Q + hQ/2}{\sqrt{2K\lambda h}}$$

$$= \frac{1}{2Q}\sqrt{\frac{2K\lambda}{h}} + \frac{Q}{2}\sqrt{\frac{h}{2K\lambda}}$$

$$= \frac{Q^*}{2Q} + \frac{Q}{2Q^*}$$

$$= \frac{1}{2}\left[\frac{Q^*}{Q} + \frac{Q}{Q^*}\right].$$

To see how one would use this result, consider using a suboptimal lot size in Example 4.1. The optimal solution was $Q^* = 3,870$, and we wished to evaluate the cost error of using $Q = 1,000$. Forming the ratio Q^*/Q gives 3.87. Hence, $G(Q)/G^* = (0.5)(3.87 + 1/3.87) = (0.5)(4.128) = 2.06$. This says that the average annual holding and setup cost with $Q = 1,000$ is 2.06 times the optimal average annual holding and setup cost.

In general, the cost function $G(Q)$ is relatively insensitive to errors in Q. For example, if Q is twice as large as it should be, Q/Q^* is 2 and G/G^* is 1.25. Hence, an error of 100 percent in the value of Q results in an error of only 25 percent in the annual holding and setup cost. Notice that you obtain the same result if Q is half Q^*, since $Q^*/Q = 2$. However, this does *not* imply that the average annual cost function is symmetric. In fact, suppose that the order quantity differed from the optimal by ΔQ units. A value of $Q = Q^* + \Delta Q$ would result in a *lower* average annual cost than a value of $Q = Q^* - \Delta Q$.

EOQ and JIT

Largely as a result of the success of Toyota's kanban system, a new philosophy is emerging about the role and importance of inventories in manufacturing environments. This philosophy, known as *just-in-time* (JIT), says that excess work-in-process inventories are not desirable, and inventories should be reduced to the bare essentials. (We discuss the just-in-time philosophy in more detail in Chapter 1 and the mechanics of kanban in Chapter 8.) EOQ is the result of traditional thinking about inventories and scale economies in economics. Are the EOQ and JIT approaches at odds with each other?

Proponents argue that an essential part of implementing JIT is reducing setup times, and hence setup costs. As setup costs decrease, traditional EOQ theory says that lot sizes should be reduced. In this sense, the two ways of thinking are compatible. However, there are times when they may not be. We believe that there is substantial value to the JIT approach that may not be incorporated easily into a mathematical model. Quality problems can be identified and rectified before inventories of defective parts accumulate. Plants can be more flexible if they are not burdened with excess in-process inventories. Certainly Toyota's success with the JIT approach, as evidenced by substantially lower inventory costs per car than are typical for U.S. auto manufacturers, is a testament to the value of JIT.

However, we believe that every new approach must be incorporated carefully into the firm's business and not adopted blindly without evaluating its consequences and appropriateness. JIT, although an important development in material management, is not always the best approach. The principles underlying EOQ (and MRP, discussed in Chapter 8) are sound and should not be ignored. The following example illustrates this point.

Example 4.2 The Rahway, New Jersey, plant of Metalcase, a manufacturer of office furniture, produces metal desks at a rate of 200 per month. Each desk requires 40 Phillips head metal screws purchased from a supplier in North Carolina. The screws cost 3 cents each. Fixed delivery charges and costs of receiving and storing shipments of the screws amount to about $100 per shipment, independently of the size of the shipment. The firm uses a 25 percent interest rate to determine holding costs. Metalcase would like to establish a standing order with the supplier and is considering several alternatives. What standing order size should they use?

Solution First we compute the EOQ. The annual demand for screws is

$$(200)(12)(40) = 96{,}000.$$

The annual holding cost per screw is $(0.25)(0.03) = 0.0075$. From the EOQ formula, the optimal lot size is

$$Q^* = \sqrt{\frac{(2)(100)(96{,}000)}{0.0075}} = 50{,}597.$$

Note that the cycle time is $T = Q/\lambda = 50{,}597/96{,}000 = 0.53$ year or about once every six months. Hence the optimal policy calls for replenishment of the screws about twice a year. A JIT approach would be to order the screws as frequently as possible to minimize the inventory held at the plant. Implementing such an approach might suggest a policy of weekly deliveries. Such a policy makes little sense in this context, however. This policy would require 52 deliveries per year, incurring setup costs of $5,200 annually. The EOQ solution gives a total annual cost of both setups and holding of less than $400. For a low-value item such as this with high fixed order costs, small lot sizes in accordance with JIT are inappropriate. The point is that no single approach should be blindly adopted for all situations. The success of a method in one context does not ensure its appropriateness in all other contexts.

Problems for Section 4.5

10. A specialty coffeehouse sells Colombian coffee at a fairly steady rate of 280 pounds annually. The beans are purchased from a local supplier for $2.40 per pound. The coffeehouse estimates that it costs $45 in paperwork and labor to place an order for the coffee, and holding costs are based on a 20 percent annual interest rate.
    a. Determine the optimal order quantity for Colombian coffee.
    b. What is the time between placement of orders?
    c. What is the average annual cost of holding and setup due to this item?
    d. If replenishment lead time is three weeks, determine the reorder level based on the on-hand inventory.

11. For the situation described in Problem 10, draw a graph of the amount of inventory on order. Using your graph, determine the average amount of inventory on order. Also compute the demand during the replenishment lead time. How do these two quantities differ?

12. A large automobile repair shop installs about 1,250 mufflers per year, 18 percent of which are for imported cars. All the imported-car mufflers are purchased from a single local supplier at a cost of $18.50 each. The shop uses a holding cost based on a 25 percent annual interest rate. The setup cost for placing an order is estimated to be $28.

    a. Determine the optimal number of imported-car mufflers the shop should purchase each time an order is placed, and the time between placement of orders.

    b. If the replenishment lead time is six weeks, what is the reorder point based on the level of on-hand inventory?

    c. The current reorder policy is to buy imported-car mufflers only once a year. What are the additional holding and setup costs incurred by this policy?

13. Consider the coffeehouse discussed in Problem 10. Suppose that its setup cost for ordering was really only $15. Determine the error made in calculating the annual cost of holding and setup incurred as a result of its using the wrong value of K. (Note that this implies that its current order policy is suboptimal.)

14. A local machine shop buys hex nuts and molly screws from the same supplier. The hex nuts cost 15 cents each and the molly screws cost 38 cents each. A setup cost of $100 is assumed for all orders. This includes the cost of tracking and receiving the orders. Holding costs are based on a 25 percent annual interest rate. The shop uses an average of 20,000 hex nuts and 14,000 molly screws annually.

    a. Determine the optimal size of the orders of hex nuts and molly screws, and the optimal time between placement of orders of these two items.

    b. If both items are ordered and received simultaneously, the setup cost of $100 applies to the combined order. Compare the average annual cost of holding and setup if these items are ordered separately; if they are both ordered when the hex nuts would normally be ordered; and if they are both ordered when the molly screws would normally be ordered.

15. David's Delicatessen flies in Hebrew National salamis regularly to satisfy a growing demand for the salamis in Silicon Valley. The owner, David Gold, estimates that the demand for the salamis is pretty steady at 175 per month. The salamis cost Gold $1.85 each. The fixed cost of calling his brother in New York and having the salamis flown in is $200. It takes three weeks to receive an order. Gold's accountant, Irving Wu, recommends an annual cost of capital of 22 percent, a cost of shelf space of 3 percent of the value of the item, and a cost of 2 percent of the value for taxes and insurance.

    a. How many salamis should Gold have flown in and how often should he order them?

    b. How many salamis should Gold have on hand when he phones his brother to send another shipment?

    c. Suppose that the salamis sell for $3 each. Are these salamis a profitable item for Gold? If so, what annual profit can he expect to realize from this item? (Assume that he operates the system optimally.)

    d. If the salamis have a shelf life of only 4 weeks, what is the trouble with the policy that you derived in part (a)? What policy would Gold have to use in that case? Is the item still profitable?

16. In view of the results derived in the section on sensitivity analysis, discuss the following quotation of an inventory control manager: "If my lot sizes are going to be off the mark, I'd rather miss on the high side than on the low side."

4.6 EXTENSION TO A FINITE PRODUCTION RATE

An implicit assumption of the simple EOQ model is that the items are obtained from an outside supplier. When that is the case, it is reasonable to assume that the entire lot is delivered at the same time. However, if we wish to use the EOQ formula when the units are produced internally, then we are effectively assuming that the production rate is infinite. When the production rate is much larger than the demand rate, this assumption is probably satisfactory as an approximation. However, if the rate of production is comparable to the rate of demand, the simple EOQ formula will lead to incorrect results.

Assume that items are produced at a rate P during a production run. We require that $P > \lambda$ for feasibility. All other assumptions will be identical to those made in the derivation of the simple EOQ. When units are produced internally, the curve describing inventory levels as a function of time is slightly different from the sawtooth pattern of Figure 4–4. The change in the inventory level over time for the finite production rate case is shown in Figure 4–8.

Let Q be the size of each production run. Let T, the cycle length, be the time between successive production startups. Write $T = T_1 + T_2$, where T_1 is uptime (production time) and T_2 is downtime. Note that the maximum level of on-hand inventory during a cycle is *not* Q.

The number of units consumed each cycle is λT, which must be the same as the number of units produced each cycle, which is simply Q. It follows that $Q = \lambda T$, or $T = Q/\lambda$. Define H as the maximum level of on-hand inventory. As items are produced at a rate P for a time T_1, it follows that $Q = PT_1$, or $T_1 = Q/P$. From Figure 4–8 we see that $H/T_1 = P - \lambda$. This follows from the definition of the slope as the rise over the run. Substituting $T_1 = Q/P$ and solving for H gives $H = Q(1 - \lambda/P)$.

We now determine an expression for the average annual cost function. Because the average inventory level is $H/2$, it follows that

$$G(Q) = \frac{K}{T} + \frac{hH}{2} = \frac{K\lambda}{Q} + \frac{hQ}{2}(1 - \lambda/P).$$

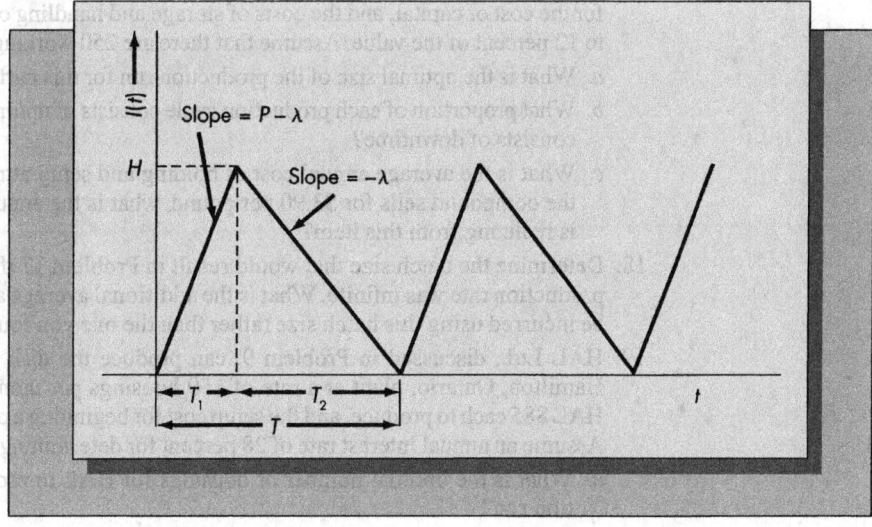

FIGURE 4–8
Inventory levels for finite production rate model

Notice that if we define $h' = h(1 - \lambda/P)$, then this $G(Q)$ is identical to that of the infinite production rate case with h' substituted for h. It follows that

$$Q^* = \sqrt{\frac{2K\lambda}{h'}}.$$

Example 4.3   A local company produces an erasable programmable read-only memory (EPROM) for several industrial clients. It has experienced a relatively flat demand of 2,500 units per year for the product. The EPROM is produced at a rate of 10,000 units per year. The accounting department has estimated that it costs $50 to initiate a production run, each unit costs the company $2 to manufacture, and the cost of holding is based on a 30 percent annual interest rate. Determine the optimal size of a production run, the length of each production run, and the average annual cost of holding and setup. What is the maximum level of the on-hand inventory of the EPROMs?

Solution   First, we compute $h = (0.3)(2) = 0.6$ per unit per year. The modified holding cost is $h' = h(1 - \lambda/P) = (0.6)(1 - 2,500/10,000) = 0.45$. Substituting into the EOQ formula and using h' for h, we obtain $Q^* = 745$. Note that the simple EOQ equals 645, all out 14 percent less.

The time between production runs is $T = Q/\lambda = 745/2,500 = 0.298$ year. The uptime each cycle is $T_1 = Q/P = 745/10,000 = 0.0745$ year, and the downtime each cycle is $T_2 = T - T_1 = 0.2235$ year.

The average annual cost of holding and setup is

$$G(Q^*) = \frac{K\lambda}{Q^*} + \frac{h'Q^*}{2} = \frac{(50)(2,500)}{745} + \frac{(0.45)(745)}{2} = 335.41.$$

The maximum level of on-hand inventory is $H = Q^*(1 - \lambda/P) = 559$ units.

Problems for Section 4.6

17. The Wod Chemical Company produces a chemical compound that is used as a lawn fertilizer. The compound can be produced at a rate of 10,000 pounds per day. Annual demand for the compound is 0.6 million pounds per year. The fixed cost of setting up for a production run of the chemical is $1,500, and the variable cost of production is $3.50 per pound. The company uses an interest rate of 22 percent to account for the cost of capital, and the costs of storage and handling of the chemical amount to 12 percent of the value. Assume that there are 250 working days in a year.

    a. What is the optimal size of the production run for this particular compound?

    b. What proportion of each production cycle consists of uptime and what proportion consists of downtime?

    c. What is the average annual cost of holding and setup attributed to this item? If the compound sells for $3.90 per pound, what is the annual profit the company is realizing from this item?

18. Determine the batch size that would result in Problem 17 if you assumed that the production rate was infinite. What is the additional average annual cost that would be incurred using this batch size rather than the one you found in Problem 17?

19. HAL Ltd., discussed in Problem 9, can produce the disk drive housings in the Hamilton, Ontario, plant at a rate of 150 housings per month. The housings cost HAL $85 each to produce, and the setup cost for beginning a production run is $700. Assume an annual interest rate of 28 percent for determining the holding cost.

    a. What is the optimal number of housings for HAL to produce in each production run?

b. Find the time between initiation of production runs, the time devoted to production, and the downtime each production cycle.

c. What is the maximum dollar investment in housings that HAL has at any point in time?

20. Filter Systems produces air filters for domestic and foreign cars. One filter, part number JJ39877, is supplied on an exclusive contract basis to Oil Changers at a constant 200 units monthly. Filter Systems can produce this filter at a rate of 50 per hour. Setup time to change the settings on the equipment is 1.5 hours. Worker time (including overhead) is charged at the rate of $55 per hour, and plant idle time during setups is estimated to cost the firm $100 per hour in lost profit.

Filter Systems has established a 22 percent annual interest charge for determining holding cost. Each filter costs the company $2.50 to produce; they are sold for $5.50 each to Oil Changers. Assume 6-hour days, 20 working days per month, and 12 months per year for your calculations.

a. How many JJ39877 filters should Filter Systems produce in each production run of this particular part to minimize annual holding and setup costs?

b. Assuming that it produces the optimal number of filters in each run, what is the maximum level of on-hand inventory of these filters that the firm has at any point in time?

c. What percentage of the working time does the company produce these particular filters, assuming that the policy in part (a) is used?

4.7 QUANTITY DISCOUNT MODELS

We have assumed up until this point that the cost c of each unit is independent of the size of the order. Often, however, the supplier is willing to charge less per unit for larger orders. The purpose of the discount is to encourage the customer to buy the product in larger batches. Such quantity discounts are common for many consumer goods.

Although many different types of discount schedules exist, there are two that seem to be the most popular: all-units and incremental. In each case we assume that there are one or more breakpoints defining changes in the unit cost. However, there are two possibilities: either the discount is applied to all the units in an order (all-units), or it is applied only to the additional units beyond the breakpoint (incremental). The all-units case is more common.

Example 4.4

The Weighty Trash Bag Company has the following price schedule for its large trash can liners. For orders of less than 500 bags, the company charges 30 cents per bag; for orders of 500 or more but fewer than 1,000 bags, it charges 29 cents per bag; and for orders of 1,000 or more, it charges 28 cents per bag. In this case the breakpoints occur at 500 and 1,000. The discount schedule is all-units because the discount is applied to all of the units in an order. The order cost function $C(Q)$ is defined as

$$C(Q) = \begin{cases} 0.30Q & \text{for} \quad 0 \leq Q < 500, \\ 0.29Q & \text{for} \quad 500 \leq Q < 1{,}000, \\ 0.28Q & \text{for} \quad 1{,}000 \leq Q \end{cases}$$

The function $C(Q)$ is pictured in Figure 4–9. In Figure 4–10, we consider the same breakpoints, but assume an incremental quantity discount schedule.

Note that the average cost per unit with an all-units schedule will be less than the average cost per unit with the corresponding incremental schedule.

FIGURE 4–9
All-units discount order cost function

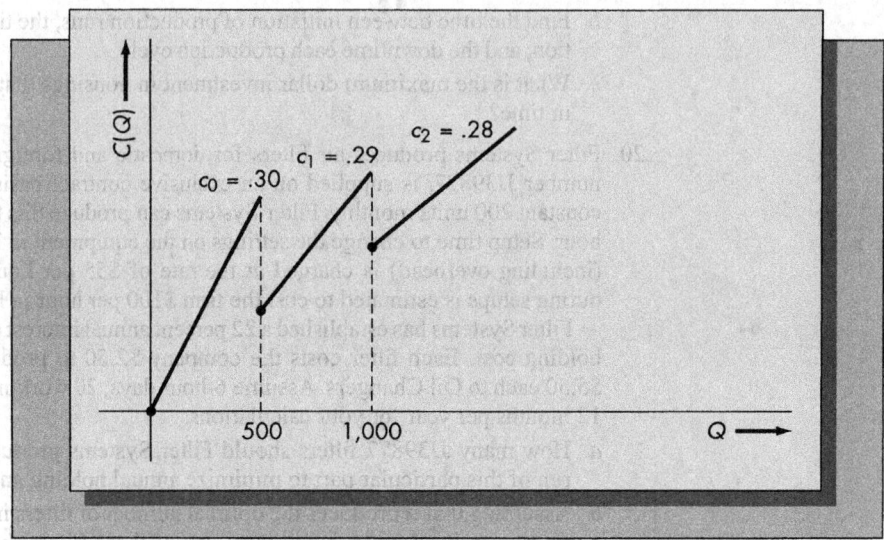

FIGURE 4–10
Incremental discount order cost function

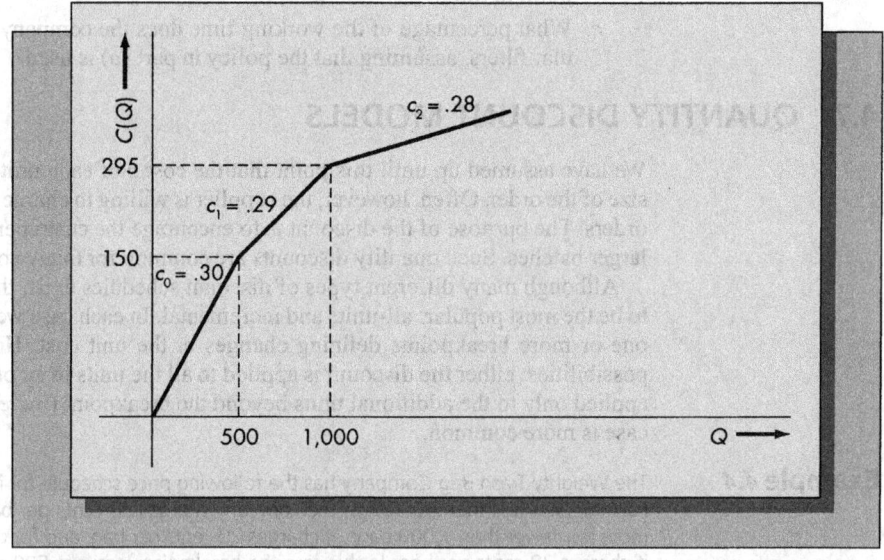

The all-units schedule appears irrational in some respects. In Example 4.4, 499 bags would cost $149.70, whereas 500 bags would cost only $145.00. Why would Weighty actually charge less for a larger order? One reason would be to provide an incentive for the purchaser to buy more. If you were considering buying 400 bags, you might choose to move up to the breakpoint to obtain the discount. Furthermore, it is possible that Weighty has stored its bags in lots of 100, so that its savings in handling costs might more than compensate for the lower total cost.

Optimal Policy for All-Units Discount Schedule

We will illustrate the solution technique using Example 4.4. Assume that the company considering what standing order to place with Weighty uses trash bags at a fairly constant rate of 600 per year. The accounting department estimates that the fixed cost of placing an order is $8, and holding costs are based on a 20 percent annual interest rate. From Example 4.4, $c_0 = 0.30$, $c_1 = 0.29$, and $c_2 = 0.28$ are the respective unit costs.

The first step toward finding a solution is to compute the EOQ values corresponding to each of the unit costs, which we will label $Q^{(0)}$, $Q^{(1)}$, and $Q^{(2)}$, respectively.

$$Q^{(0)} = \sqrt{\frac{2K\lambda}{Ic_0}} = \sqrt{\frac{(2)(8)(600)}{(0.2)(0.30)}} = 400,$$

$$Q^{(1)} = \sqrt{\frac{2K\lambda}{Ic_1}} = \sqrt{\frac{(2)(8)(600)}{(0.2)(0.29)}} = 406,$$

$$Q^{(2)} = \sqrt{\frac{2K\lambda}{Ic_2}} = \sqrt{\frac{(2)(8)(600)}{(0.2)(0.28)}} = 414.$$

We say that the EOQ value is realizable if it falls within the interval that corresponds to the unit cost used to compute it. Since $0 \leq 400 < 500$, Q^0 is realizable. However, neither $Q^{(1)}$ nor $Q^{(2)}$ is realizable ($Q^{(1)}$ would have to have been between 500 and 1,000, and $Q^{(2)}$ would have to have been 1,000 or more). Each EOQ value corresponds to the minimum of a different annual cost curve. In this example, if $Q^{(2)}$ were realizable, it would necessarily have to have been the optimal solution, as it corresponds to the lowest point on the lowest curve. The three average annual cost curves for this example appear in Figure 4–11. Because each curve is valid only for certain values of Q, the average annual cost function is given by the discontinuous curve shown in heavy shading. The goal of the analysis is to find the minimum of this discontinuous curve.

There are three candidates for the optimal solution: 400, 500, and 1,000. In general, the optimal solution will be either the largest realizable EOQ or one of the breakpoints that exceeds it. The optimal solution is the lot size with the lowest average annual cost.

FIGURE 4–11
All-units discount average annual cost function

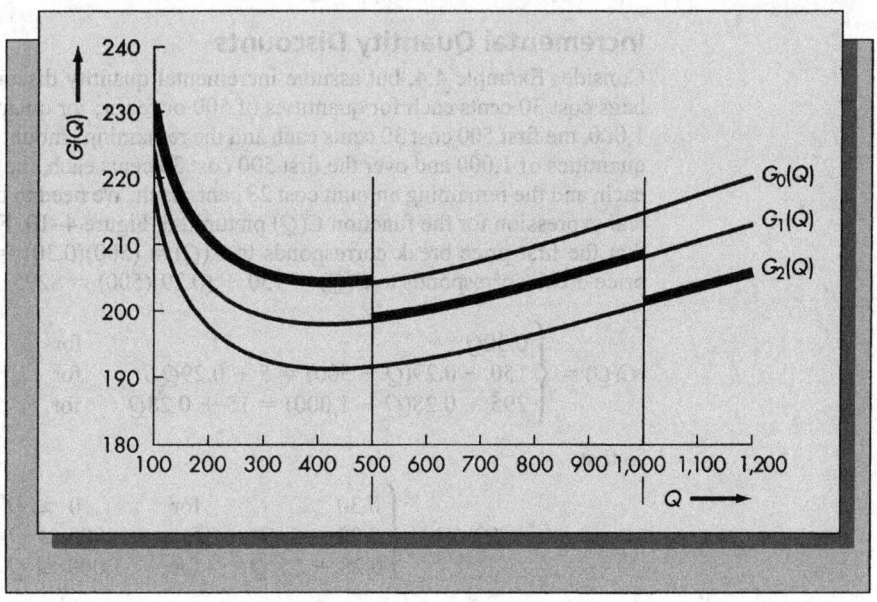

4.7 Quantity Discount Models

The average annual cost functions are given by

$$G_j(Q) = \lambda c_j + \lambda K/Q + I c_j Q/2 \quad \text{for } j = 0, 1, \text{ and } 2.$$

The broken curve pictured in Figure 4–11, $G(Q)$, is defined as

$$G(Q) = \begin{cases} G_0(Q) & \text{for} & 0 \le Q < 500, \\ G_1(Q) & \text{for} & 500 \le Q < 1{,}000, \\ G_2(Q) & \text{for} & 1{,}000 \le Q. \end{cases}$$

Substituting Q equals 400, 500, and 1,000, and using the appropriate values of c_j, we obtain

$$G(400) = G_0(400)$$
$$= (600)(0.30) + (600)(8)/400 + (0.2)(0.30)(400)/2 = \$204.00$$

$$G(500) = G_1(500)$$
$$= (600)(0.29) + (600)(8)/500 + (0.2)(0.29)(500)/2 = \$198.10$$

$$G(1{,}000) = G_2(1{,}000)$$
$$= (600)(0.28) + (600)(8)/1{,}000 + (0.2)(0.28)(1{,}000)/2 = \$200.80.$$

Hence, we conclude that the optimal solution is to place a standing order for 500 units with Weighty at an average annual cost of \$198.10.

Summary of the Solution Technique for All-Units Discounts

1. Determine the largest realizable EOQ value. The most efficient way to do this is to compute the EOQ for the lowest price first, and continue with the next higher price. Stop when the first EOQ value is realizable (that is, within the correct interval).
2. Compare the value of the average annual cost at the largest realizable EOQ and at all the price breakpoints that are greater than the largest realizable EOQ. The optimal Q is the point at which the average annual cost is a minimum.

Incremental Quantity Discounts

Consider Example 4.4, but assume incremental quantity discounts. That is, the trash bags cost 30 cents each for quantities of 500 or fewer; for quantities between 500 and 1,000, the first 500 cost 30 cents each and the remaining amount cost 29 cents each; for quantities of 1,000 and over the first 500 cost 30 cents each, the next 500 cost 29 cents each, and the remaining amount cost 28 cents each. We need to determine a mathematical expression for the function $C(Q)$ pictured in Figure 4–10. From the figure, we see that the first price break corresponds to $C(Q) = (500)(0.30) = \$150$ and the second price break corresponds to $C(Q) = 150 + (0.29)(500) = \$295$. It follows that

$$C(Q) = \begin{cases} 0.30Q & \text{for} & 0 \le Q < 500, \\ 150 + 0.29(Q - 500) = 5 + 0.29Q & \text{for} & 500 \le Q < 1{,}000, \\ 295 + 0.28(Q - 1{,}000) = 15 + 0.28Q & \text{for} & 1{,}000 \le Q. \end{cases}$$

so that

$$C(Q)/Q = \begin{cases} 0.30 & \text{for} & 0 \le Q < 500, \\ 0.29 + 5/Q & \text{for} & 500 \le Q < 1{,}000, \\ 0.28 + 15/Q & \text{for} & 1{,}000 \le Q. \end{cases}$$

FIGURE 4–12
Average annual cost function for incremental discount schedule

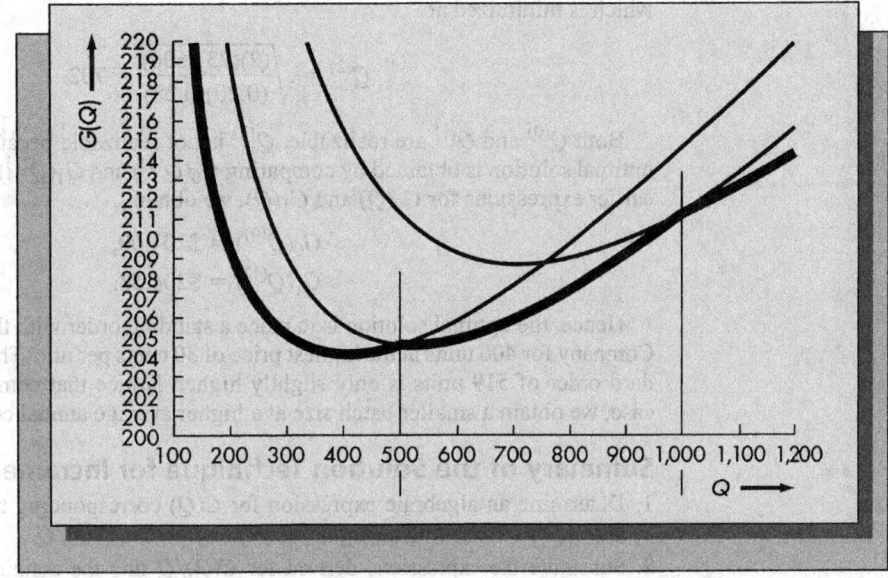

The average annual cost function, $G(Q)$, is

$$G(Q) = \lambda C(Q)/Q + K\lambda/Q + I[C(Q)/Q]Q/2.$$

In this example, $G(Q)$ will have three different algebraic representations $[G_0(Q), G_1(Q),$ and $G_2(Q)]$ depending upon into which interval Q falls. Because $C(Q)$ is continuous, $G(Q)$ also will be continuous. The function $G(Q)$ appears in Figure 4–12.

The optimal solution occurs at the minimum of one of the average annual cost curves. The solution is obtained by substituting the three expressions for $C(Q)/Q$ in the defining equation for $G(Q)$, computing the three minima of the curves, determining which of these minima fall into the correct interval, and, finally, comparing the average annual costs at the realizable values. We have that

$$G_0(Q) = (600)(0.30) + (8)(600)/Q + (0.20)(0.30)Q/2$$

which is minimized at

$$Q^{(0)} = \sqrt{\frac{2K\lambda}{Ic_0}} = \sqrt{\frac{(2)(8)(600)}{(0.20)(0.30)}} = 400;$$

$$G_1(Q) = (600)(0.29 + 5/Q) + (8)(600)/Q + (0.20)(0.29 + 5/Q)(Q/2)$$
$$= (0.29)(600) + (13)(600)/Q + (0.20)(0.29)Q/2 + (0.20)(5)/2$$

which is minimized at

$$Q^{(1)} = \sqrt{\frac{(2)(13)(600)}{(0.20)(0.29)}} = 519;$$

and finally

$$G_2(Q) = (600)(0.28 + 15/Q) + (8)(600)/Q + (0.20)(0.28 + 15/Q)Q/2$$
$$= (0.28)(600) + (23)(600)/Q + (0.20)(0.28)Q/2 + (0.20)(15)/2$$

which is minimized at

$$Q^{(2)} = \sqrt{\frac{(2)(23)(600)}{(0.20)(0.28)}} = 702.$$

Both $Q^{(0)}$ and $Q^{(1)}$ are realizable. $Q^{(2)}$ is not realizable because $Q^{(2)} < 1,000$. The optimal solution is obtained by comparing $G_0(Q^{(0)})$ and $G_1(Q^{(1)})$. Substituting into the earlier expressions for $G_0(Q)$ and $G_1(Q)$, we obtain

$$G_0(Q^{(0)}) = \$204.00,$$
$$G_1(Q^{(1)}) = \$204.58.$$

Hence, the optimal solution is to place a standing order with the Weighty Trash Bag Company for 400 units at the highest price of 30 cents per unit. The cost of using a standard order of 519 units is only slightly higher. Notice that compared to the all-units case, we obtain a smaller batch size at a higher average annual cost.

Summary of the Solution Technique for Incremental Discounts

1. Determine an algebraic expression for $C(Q)$ corresponding to each price interval. Use that to determine an algebraic expression for $C(Q)/Q$.
2. Substitute the expressions derived for $C(Q)/Q$ into the defining equation for $G(Q)$. Compute the minimum value of Q corresponding to each price interval separately.
3. Determine which minima computed in (2) are realizable (that is, fall into the correct interval). Compare the values of the average annual costs at the realizable EOQ values and pick the lowest.

Other Discount Schedules

Although all-units and incremental discount schedules are the most common, there are a variety of other discount schedules as well. One example is the carload discount schedule pictured in Figure 4–13.

FIGURE 4–13
Order cost function for carload discount schedule

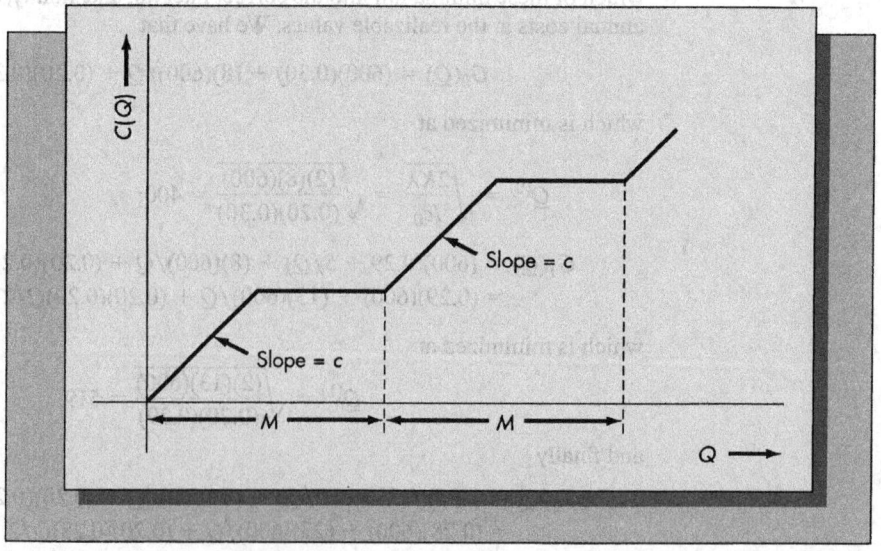

Chapter Four Inventory Control Subject to Known Demand

The rationale behind the carload discount schedule is the following. A carload consists of M units. The supplier charges a constant c per unit up until you have paid for the cost of a full carload, at which point there is no charge for the remaining units in that carload. Once the first carload is full, you again pay c per unit until the second carload is full, and so forth.

Determining optimal policies for the carload or other discount schedules could be extremely difficult. Each discount schedule has a unique solution procedure. Some can be extremely complex.

Problems for Section 4.7

21. Your local grocery store stocks rolls of bathroom tissue in single packages and in more economical 12-packs. You are trying to decide which to buy. The single package costs 45 cents and the 12-pack costs $5. You consume bathroom tissue at a fairly steady rate of one roll every three months. Your opportunity cost of money is computed assuming an interest rate of 25 percent and a fixed cost of $1 for the additional time it takes you to buy bathroom tissue when you go shopping. (We are assuming that you shop often enough so that you don't require a special trip when you run out.)

    a. How many single rolls should you be buying in order to minimize the annual holding and setup costs of purchasing bathroom tissue?

    b. Determine if it is more economical to purchase the bathroom tissue in 12-packs.

    c. Are there reasons other than those discussed in the problem that would motivate you not to buy the bathroom tissue in 12-packs?

22. A purchasing agent for a particular type of silicon wafer used in the production of semiconductors must decide among three sources. Source A will sell the silicon wafers for $2.50 per wafer, independently of the number of wafers ordered. Source B will sell the wafers for $2.40 each but will not consider an order for fewer than 3,000 wafers, and Source C will sell the wafers for $2.30 each but will not accept an order for fewer than 4,000 wafers. Assume an order setup cost of $100 and an annual requirement of 20,000 wafers. Assume a 20 percent annual interest rate for holding cost calculations.

    a. Which source should be used, and what is the size of the standing order?

    b. What is the optimal value of the holding and setup costs for wafers when the optimal source is used?

    c. If the replenishment lead time for wafers is three months, determine the reorder point based on the on-hand level of inventory of wafers.

23. Assume that two years have passed, and the purchasing agent mentioned in Problem 22 must recompute the optimal number of wafers to purchase and from which source to purchase them. Source B has decided to accept any size offer, but sells the wafers for $2.55 each for orders of up to 3,000 wafers and $2.25 each for the incremental amount ordered over 3,000 wafers. Source A still has the same price schedule, and Source C went out of business. Now which source should be used?

24. In the calculation of an optimal policy for an all-units discount schedule, you first compute the EOQ values for each of the three order costs, and you obtain: $Q^{(0)} = 800$, $Q^{(1)} = 875$, and $Q^{(2)} = 925$. The all-units discount schedule has breakpoints at 750 and 900. Based on this information only, can you determine what the optimal order quantity is? Explain your answer.

Snapshot Application

SMARTOPS ASSISTS IN DESIGNING CATERPILLAR'S INVENTORY CONTROL SYSTEM

The Caterpillar Corporation is one of the world's leading manufacturers of construction and mining equipment, diesel and natural gas engines, and gas turbines. Caterpillar posted annual sales of nearly $66 billion in 2012, and is a Fortune 100 company. In 1997, management embarked on a project aimed at improving product availability and inventory turns. In 2001, the project team was expanded to include both internal Caterpillar personnel and two analysts from SmartOps, David Alberti and SmartOps founder Sridhar Tayur. The team was charged with examining the following questions: (1) What product availability is possible at what cost and what inventory levels? (2) How much inventory reduction is possible? (3) What mix and deployment of inventory is necessary to achieve the firm's service objectives?

The team focused its attention on backhoe loaders produced by the company's Clayton, North Carolina, facility. A key part of their focus was on lead times. These include both lead times for products being shipped from the plant, and for materials and equipment shipped into the plant from suppliers. While lead times coming out of the plant were relatively short (typically one week), the lead times of products coming from suppliers could be quite long, and also tended to have high variance. The team developed a comprehensive model of the entire inventory supply chain. Inputs to the model included inventory stocking locations, historical forecast errors for different seasons and different products, subassemblies and bill of materials for each product, lead times, and inventory review times. The model developed took into account the multi-echelon (that is, multi-level) nature of the system.

In order to provide an accurate picture of the system, the analysts differentiated three types of orders placed by dealers: (a) sold orders based on firm sales to customers, (b) orders by dealers placed for the purpose of replenishing inventory, and (c) orders placed by dealers to replenish stock of machines rented to customers. Note that replenishment lead times for each of these demand types are different: four to six weeks for sold orders, six weeks for inventory replenishment, and fourteen weeks for replenishment of rental equipment.

The model provided a comprehensive picture of the important service versus inventory trade-offs Caterpillar could expect from the Clayton plant. For example, the team found that the Clayton plant could achieve a consistent 45 and 30 day product availability to dealers with 50 percent less finished goods inventory. However, to achieve a 14 or 10 day availability the finished goods inventory would have to be increased by approximately 90 percent. They also found that current service levels could be maintained with a total supply chain inventory reduction of 30–50 percent by repositioning inventory from finished goods to components.

After careful consideration of the trade-offs involved, management made the following changes to the system: (1) total inventory in the supply chain was reduced by 16 percent, (2) the mean time for orders was reduced by 20 percent and the variance reduced by 50 percent, and (3) order fulfillment was increased 2 percent.

The analysis provided by the team allowed management to better understand that there were no simple answers to their inventory management problems. The Caterpillar supply chain was very complex with interaction among the multiple levels. Seeing what trade-offs were possible allowed management to set priorities which ultimately resulted in lower inventory costs and higher levels of service to the customer.

Source: Keene, et al. "Caterpillar's Building Construction Products Division Improves and Stabilizes Product Availability" *Interfaces* 36 (2006), pp. 283–295.

25. Parasol Systems sells motherboards for personal computers. For quantities up through 25, the firm charges $350 per board; for quantities between 26 and 50, it charges $315 for each board purchased beyond 25; and it charges $285 each for the additional quantities over 50. A large communications firm expects to require these motherboards for the next 10 years at a rate of at least 140 per year. Order setup costs are $30 and holding costs are based on an 18 percent annual interest rate. What should be the size of the standing order?

*4.8 RESOURCE-CONSTRAINED MULTIPLE PRODUCT SYSTEMS

The EOQ model and its extensions apply only to single inventory items. However, these models are often used in companies stocking many different items. Although we could certainly compute optimal order quantities separately for each of the different items, there could exist constraints that would make the resulting solution infeasible. In Example 4.1, the optimal solution called for purchasing 3,870 pencils every 1.24 years. The bookstore, however, may not have allocated enough space to store that many pencils, nor enough money to purchase that many at one time.

Example 4.5

Three items are produced in a small fabrication shop. The shop management has established the requirement that the shop never have more than $30,000 invested in the inventory of these items at one time. The management uses a 25 percent annual interest charge to compute the holding cost. The relevant cost and demand parameters are given in the following table. What lot sizes should the shop be producing so that they do not exceed the budget?

	Item		
	1	2	3
Demand rate λ_j	1,850	1,150	800
Variable cost c_j	50	350	85
Setup cost K_j	100	150	50

Solution

If the budget is not exceeded when using the EOQ values of these three items, then the EOQs are optimal. Hence, the first step is to compute the EOQ values for all items to determine whether or not the constraint is active.

$$EOQ_1 = \sqrt{\frac{(2)(100)(1,850)}{(0.25)(50)}} = 172,$$

$$EOQ_2 = \sqrt{\frac{(2)(150)(1,150)}{(0.25)(350)}} = 63,$$

$$EOQ_3 = \sqrt{\frac{(2)(50)(800)}{(0.25)(85)}} = 61.$$

If the EOQ value for each item is used, the maximum investment in inventory would be

$$(172)(50) + (63)(350) + (61)(85) = \$35,835.[3]$$

Because the EOQ solution violates the constraint, we need to reduce these lot sizes. But how?

The optimal solution turns out to be very easy to find in this case. We merely multiply each EOQ value by the ratio (30,000)/(35,835) = 0.8372. In order to guarantee that we do not exceed the $30,000 budget, we round each value *down* (adjustments can be made subsequently). Letting Q_1^*, Q_2^*, and Q_3^* be the optimal values, we obtain

$$Q_1^* = (172)(0.8372) \approx 144,$$
$$Q_2^* = (63)(0.8372) \approx 52,$$
$$Q_3^* = (61)(0.8372) \approx 51,$$

where ≈ should be interpreted as rounding to the next lower integer in this case.

The total budget required for these lot sizes is $29,735. The remaining $265 can now be used to increase the lot sizes of products 1 and 3 slightly. (For example, $Q_1^* = 147$, $Q_3^* = 52$ results in a budget of $29,970.)

[3] We are assuming for the purposes of this section that the three products are ordered simultaneously. By staggering order cycles, it is possible to meet the constraint with larger lot sizes. We will not consider that case here.

In general, budget- or space-constrained problems are not solved so easily. Suppose that n items have unit costs of $c_1, c_2, \ldots, c_n$, respectively, and the total budget available for them is C. Then the budget constraint can be written

$$c_1 Q_1 + c_2 Q_2 + \cdots + c_n Q_n \leq C.$$

Let

$$\text{EOQ}_i = \sqrt{\frac{2K_i \lambda_i}{h_i}} \quad \text{for } i = 1, \ldots, n,$$

where K_i, h_i, and λ_i are the respective cost and demand parameters.

There are two possibilities: either the constraint is active or it is not. If the constraint is not active, then

$$\sum_{i=1}^{n} c_i \text{EOQ}_i \leq C,$$

and the optimal solution is $Q_i = \text{EOQ}_i$. If the constraint is active, then

$$\sum_{i=1}^{n} c_i \text{EOQ}_i > C,$$

and the EOQ solution is no longer feasible. If we include the following assumption, the solution to the active case is relatively easy to find:

Assumption: $c_1/h_1 = c_2/h_2 = \cdots = c_n/h_n$.

If this assumption holds and the constraint is active, we prove in Appendix 4–A that the optimal solution is

$$Q_i^* = m \text{EOQ}_i,$$

where the multiplier m solves

$$m = C \Big/ \left[\sum_{i=1}^{n} (c_i \text{EOQ}_i) \right].$$

Since $c_i/h_i = c_i/(I_i c_i) = 1/I_i$, the condition that the ratios be equal is equivalent to the requirement that the same interest rate be used to compute the holding cost for each item, which is reasonable in most circumstances.

Suppose that the constraint is on the available space. Let w_i be the space consumed by one unit of product i for $i = 1, 2, \ldots, n$ (this could be floor space measured, say, in square feet, or volume measured in cubic feet), and let W be the total space available. Then the space constraint is of the form

$$w_1 Q_1 + w_2 Q_2 + \cdots + w_n Q_n \leq W.$$

This is mathematically of the same form as the budget constraint, so the same analysis applies. However, our condition for a simple solution now is that the ratios w_i/h_i are equal. That is, the space consumed by an item should be proportional to its holding cost. When the interest rate is fixed, this is equivalent to the requirement that the space consumed should be proportional to the value of the item. This requirement would probably be too restrictive in most cases. For example, fountain pens take up far less space than legal pads, but are more expensive.

230 Chapter Four *Inventory Control Subject to Known Demand*

Let us now consider the problem in which the constraint is active, but the proportionality assumption is not met. This problem is far more complex than that just solved. It requires formulating the *Lagrangian* function. The details of the formulation of this problem can be found in Appendix 4–A. As we show, the optimal lot sizes are now of the form

$$Q_i^* = \sqrt{\frac{2K_i\lambda_i}{h_i + 2\theta w_i}},$$

where θ is a constant chosen so that

$$\sum_{i=1}^{n} w_i Q_i^* = W.$$

The constant θ, known as the Lagrange multiplier, reduces the lot sizes by increasing the effective holding cost. The correct value of θ can be found by trial and error or by a search technique such as interval bisection. Note that $\theta > 0$, so that the search can be limited to positive numbers only. The value of θ can be interpreted as the decrease in the average annual cost that would result from adding an additional unit of resource. In this case, it would represent the marginal benefit of an additional square foot of space.

Example 4.6   Consider the fabrication shop of Example 4.5. In addition to the budget constraint, suppose that there are only 2,000 square feet of floor space available. Assume that the three products consume respectively 9, 12, and 18 square feet per unit.

First, we check to see if the EOQ solution is feasible. Setting $w_1 = 9$, $w_2 = 12$, and $w_3 = 18$, we find that

$$\sum EOQ_i w_i = (172)(9) + (63)(12) + (61)(18) = 3,402,$$

which is obviously infeasible. Next, we check if the budget-constrained solution provides a feasible solution to the space-constrained problem. The budget-constrained solution requires $(147)(9) + (52)(12) + (52)(18) = 2,883$ square feet of space, which is also infeasible.

The next step is to compute the ratios w_i/h_i for $1 \leq i \leq 3$. These ratios turn out to be 0.72, 0.14, and 0.85, respectively. Because their values are different, the simple solution obtained by a proportional scaling of the EOQ values will not be optimal. Hence, we must determine the value of the Lagrange multiplier θ.

We can determine upper and lower bounds on the optimal value of θ by assuming equal ratios. If the ratios were equal, the multiplier, m, would be

$$m = W/\sum(EOQ_i w_i) = 2,000/3,402 = 0.5879,$$

which would give the three lot sizes as 101, 37, and 36, respectively. The three values of θ that result in these lot sizes are respectively $\theta = 1.32$, $\theta = 6.86$, and $\theta = 2.33$. (These values were obtained by setting the given expression for Q_i^* equal to the lot sizes 101, 37, and 36, and solving for θ.)

The true value of θ will be between 1.32 and 6.86. If we start with $\theta = 3.5$, we obtain $Q_1^* = 70$, $Q_2^* = 45$, and $Q_3^* = 23$, and $\sum w_i Q_i^* = (70)(9) + (45)(12) + (23)(18) = 1,584$, which implies $\theta < 3.5$. After considerable experimentation, we finally find that the optimal value of $\theta = 1.75$, and $Q_1^* = 92$, $Q_2^* = 51$, and $Q_3^* = 31$, giving $\sum w_i Q_i^* = 1,998$. Notice that these lot sizes are in very different proportions from the ones obtained assuming a constant multiplier. Searching for the optimal value of the Lagrange multiplier, although tedious to do by hand, can be accomplished very efficiently using a computer. Spreadsheets are a useful means for effecting such calculations.

We have only touched on some of the complications that could arise when applying EOQ-type models to a realistic system with multiple products. Often, real problems are far too complex to be expressed accurately as a solvable mathematical model. For this reason, simple models such as the ones presented in this and subsequent chapters are used by practitioners. However, any solution recommended by a mathematical model must be considered in the context of the system in which it is to be used.

Problems for Section 4.8

26. A local outdoor vegetable stand has exactly 1,000 square feet of space to display three vegetables: tomatoes, lettuce, and zucchini. The appropriate data for these items are given in the following table.

	Item		
	Tomatoes	Lettuce	Zucchini
Annual demand (in pounds)	850	1,280	630
Cost per pound	$0.29	$0.45	$0.25

    The setup cost for replenishment of the vegetables is $100 in each case, and the space consumed by each vegetable is proportional to its costs, with tomatoes requiring 0.5 square foot per pound. The annual interest rate used for computing holding costs is 25 percent. What are the optimal quantities that should be purchased of these three vegetables?

27. Suppose that the vegetables discussed in Problem 26 are purchased at different times. In what way could that have an effect on the order policy that the stand owner should use?

28. Suppose that in Problem 26 the space consumed by each vegetable is not proportional to its cost. In particular, suppose that one pound of lettuce required 0.4 square foot of space and one pound of zucchini required 1 square foot of space. Determine upper and lower bounds on the optimal values of the order quantities in this case. Test different values of the Lagrange multiplier to find the optimal values of the order quantities. (A spreadsheet is ideally suited for this kind of calculation. If you solve the problem using a spreadsheet, place the Lagrange multiplier in a cell so that its value can be changed easily.)

4.9 EOQ MODELS FOR PRODUCTION PLANNING

Simple lot-sizing models have been successfully applied to a variety of manufacturing problems. In this section we consider an extension of the EOQ model with a finite production rate, discussed in Section 4.6, to the problem of producing n products on a single machine. Following the notation used in this chapter, let

$\lambda_j =$ Demand rate for product j,

$P_j =$ Production rate for product j,

$h_j =$ Holding cost per unit per unit time for product j,

$K_j =$ Cost of setting up the production facility to produce product j.

The goal is to determine the optimal procedure for producing n products on the machine to minimize the cost of holding and setups, and to guarantee that no stock-outs occur during the production cycle.

We require the assumption that

$$\sum_{j=1}^{n} \lambda_j/P_j \leq 1.$$

This assumption is needed to ensure that the facility has sufficient capacity to satisfy the demand for all products. Notice that this is stronger than the assumption made in Section 4.6 that $\lambda_j < P_j$ for each j. To see why this assumption is necessary, consider the case of two products with identical demand and production rates. In each cycle one would produce product 1 first, then product 2. Clearly $P_1 \geq 2\lambda_1$ and $P_2 \geq 2\lambda_2$, so that enough could be produced to meet the total demand for both products each cycle. This translates to $\lambda_1/P_1 \leq 0.5$ and $\lambda_2/P_2 \leq 0.5$, giving a value of the sum less than or equal to one. Similar reasoning holds for more than two products with nonidentical demand and production rates.

We also will assume that the policy used is a *rotation cycle policy*. That means that in each cycle there is exactly one setup for each product, and products are produced in the same sequence in each production cycle. The importance of this assumption will be discussed further at the end of the section.

At first, one might think that the optimal solution is to sequentially produce lot sizes for each product optimized by treating each product in isolation. From Section 4.6, this would result in a lot size for product j of

$$Q_j = \sqrt{\frac{2K_j \lambda_j}{h'_j}},$$

where $h'_j = h_j(1 - \lambda_j/P_j)$. The problem with this approach is that because we have only a single production facility, it is likely that some of the lot sizes Q_j will not be large enough to meet the demand between production runs for product j, thus resulting in stock-outs.

Let T be the cycle time. During time T we assume that exactly one lot of each product is produced. In order that the lot for product j will be large enough to meet the demand occurring during time T, it follows that the lot size must be

$$Q_j = \lambda_j T.$$

From Section 4.6, the average annual cost associated with product j can be written in the form

$$G(Q_j) = K_j \lambda_j / Q_j + h'_j Q_j / 2.$$

The average annual cost for all products is the sum

$$\sum_{j=1}^{n} G(Q_j) = \sum_{j=1}^{n} K_j \lambda_j / Q_j + h'_j Q_j / 2.$$

Substituting $T = Q_j/\lambda_j$, we obtain the average annual cost associated with the n products in terms of the cycle time T as

$$G(T) = \sum_{j=1}^{n} [K_j/T + h'_j \lambda_j T/2].$$

4.9 EOQ Models for Production Planning

The goal is to find T to minimize $G(T)$. The necessary condition for an optimal T is

$$\frac{dG(T)}{dT} = 0.$$

Setting the first derivative with respect to T to zero gives

$$\sum_{j=1}^{n}[-K_j/T^2 + h'_j\lambda_j/2] = 0.$$

Solving for T, we obtain the optimal cycle time T^* as

$$T^* = \sqrt{\frac{2\sum_{j=1}^{n} K_j}{\sum_{j=1}^{n} h'_j\lambda_j}}.$$

If setup times are a factor, we must check that there is enough time each cycle to account for both setup times and production of the n products. Let s_j be the setup time for product j. Ensuring that the total time required for setups and production each cycle does not exceed T leads to the constraint

$$\sum_{j=1}^{n}(s_j + Q_j/P_j) \leq T.$$

Using the fact that $Q_j = \lambda_j T$, this condition translates to

$$\sum_{j=1}^{n}(s_j + \lambda_j T/P_j) \leq T,$$

which gives, after rearranging terms,

$$T \geq \frac{\sum_{j=1}^{n} s_j}{1 - \sum_{j=1}^{n}(\lambda_j/P_j)} = T_{\min}.$$

Because $T_{\min}$ cannot be exceeded without compromising feasibility, the optimal solution is to choose the cycle time T equal to the *larger* of T^* and $T_{\min}$.

Example 4.7 Bali produces several styles of men's and women's shoes at a single facility near Bergamo, Italy. The leather for both the uppers and the soles of the shoes is cut on a single machine. This Bergamo plant is responsible for seven styles and several colors in each style. (The colors are not considered different products for our purposes, because no setup is required when switching colors.) Bali would like to schedule cutting for the shoes using a rotation policy that meets all demand and minimizes setup and holding costs. Setup costs are proportional to setup times.

TABLE 4–1
Relevant Data for Example 4.7

Style	Annual Demand (units/year)	Production Rate (units/year)	Setup Time (hours)	Variable Cost ($/unit)
Women's pump	4,520	35,800	3.2	$40
Women's loafer	6,600	62,600	2.5	26
Women's boot	2,340	41,000	4.4	52
Women's sandal	2,600	71,000	1.8	18
Men's wingtip	8,800	46,800	5.1	38
Men's loafer	6,200	71,200	3.1	28
Men's oxford	5,200	56,000	4.4	31

The firm estimates that setup costs amount to an average of $110 per hour, based on the cost of worker time and the cost of forced machine idle time during setups. Holding costs are based on a 22 percent annual interest charge.

The relevant data for this problem appear in Table 4–1.

Solution

The first step is to verify that the problem is feasible. To do so we compute $\Sigma \lambda_j/P_j$. The reader should verify that this sum is equal to 0.69355. Because this is less than one, there will be a feasible solution. Next we compute the value of T^*, but to do so we need to do several intermediate calculations.

First, we compute setup costs. Setup costs are assumed to be $110 times setup times. Second, we compute modified holding costs (h'_j). This is done by multiplying the cost of each product by the annual interest rate (0.22) times the factor $1 - \lambda_j/P_j$. These calculations give

Setup Costs (K_j)	Modified Holding Costs (h'_j)
352	7.69
275	5.12
484	10.79
198	3.81
561	6.79
341	5.62
484	6.19

The sum of the setup costs is 2,695, and the sum of the products of the modified holding costs and the annual demands is 230,458.4. Substituting these figures into the formula for T^* gives the optimal cycle time as 0.1529 year. Assuming a 250-day work year, this means that the rotation cycle should repeat roughly every 38 working days. The optimal lot size for each of the shoes is found by multiplying the cycle time by the demand rate for each item. The reader should check that the following lot sizes result:

Style	Optimal Lot Sizes for Each Production Run
Women's pump	691
Women's loafer	1,009
Women's boot	358
Women's sandal	398
Men's wingtip	1,346
Men's loafer	948
Men's oxford	795

The plant would cut the soles and uppers in these lot sizes in sequence (although the sequence does not necessarily have to be this one) and would repeat the rotation cycle roughly every 38 days (0.1529 year). However, this solution can be implemented only if T^* is at least T_{min}. To determine T_{min} we must express the setup times in years. Assuming 8 working hours per day and 250 working days per year, one would divide the setup times given in hours by 2,000 (250 times 8). The reader should check that the resulting value of T_{min} is 0.04, thus making T^* feasible and, hence, optimal.

The total average annual cost of holding and setups at an optimal policy can be found by computing the value of $G(T)$ when $T = T^*$. It is $35,244.44. It is interesting to note that if the plant manager chooses to implement this policy, the facility will be idle for a substantial portion of each rotation cycle. The total uptime each rotation cycle is found by dividing the lot sizes by the production rates for each style and summing the results. It turns out to be 0.106 year. Hence, the optimal rotation policy that minimizes total holding and setup costs results in the cutting operation remaining idle about one-third of the time.

The reader should be aware that the relatively simple solution to this problem was the result of two assumptions. One was that the setup costs were not sequence dependent. In Example 4.7, it is possible that the time required to change over from one shoe style to another could depend on the styles. For example, a changeover from a woman's style to a man's style probably takes longer than from one woman's style to another. A second assumption was that the plant used a rotation cycle policy. That is, in each cycle Bali does a single production run of each style. When demand rates and setup costs differ widely, it might be advantageous to do two or more production runs of a product in a cycle. This more general problem has not, to our knowledge, been solved. A discussion of these and related issues can be found in Maxwell (1964). Magee and Boodman (1967) provide some heuristic ways of dealing with the more general problem.

Problems for Section 4.9

29. A metal fabrication shop has a single punch press. There are currently three parts that the shop has agreed to produce that require the press, and it appears that they will be supplying these parts well into the future. You may assume that the press is the critical resource for these parts, so that we need not worry about the interaction of the press with the other machines in the shop. The relevant information here is

Part Number	Annual Contracted Amount (demand)	Setup Cost	Cost (per unit)	Production Rate (per year)
1	2,500	$80	$16	45,000
2	5,500	120	18	40,000
3	1,450	60	22	26,000

Holding costs are based on an 18 percent annual interest rate, and the products are to be produced in sequence on a rotation cycle. Setup times can be considered negligible.

a. What is the optimal time between setups for part number 1?

b. What percentage of the time is the punch press idle, assuming an optimal rotation cycle policy?

c. What are the optimal lot sizes of each part put through the press at an optimal solution?

d. What is the total annual cost of holding and setup for these items on the punch press, assuming an optimal rotation cycle?

30. Tomlinson Furniture has a single lathe for turning the wood for various furniture pieces, including bedposts, rounded table legs, and other items. Four forms are turned on the lathe and produced in lots for inventory. To simplify scheduling, one lot of each type will be produced in a cycle, which may include idle time. The four products and the relevant information concerning them appears in the following table.

Piece	Monthly Requirements	Setup Time (hours)	Unit Cost	Production Rate (units/day)
J–55R	125	1.2	$20	140
H–223	140	0.8	35	220
K–18R	45	2.2	12	100
Z–344	240	3.1	45	165

Worker time for setups is valued at $85 per hour, and holding costs are based on a 20 percent annual interest charge. Assume 20 working days per month and 12 months per year for your calculations.

a. Determine the optimal length of the rotation cycle.
b. What are the optimal lot sizes for each product?
c. What are the percentages of uptime and downtime for the lathe, assuming that it is not used for any other purpose?
d. Draw a graph showing the change in the inventory level over a typical cycle for each product.
e. Discuss why the solution you obtained might not be feasible for the firm, or why it might not be desirable even when it is feasible.

4.10 POWER-OF-TWO POLICIES

The inventory models treated in this chapter form the basis of more complex cases. In almost every case treated here, we were able to find relatively straightforward algebraic solutions. However, even when demand is assumed known, there exist several extensions of these basic models whose optimal solutions may be difficult or impossible to find. In those cases, effective approximations are very valuable. Here, we discuss an approach that has proven to be successful in a variety of deterministic environments. The idea is based on choosing the best replenishment interval from a set of possible intervals proportional to powers of two. While the analysis of power-of-two policies in complex environments is beyond the scope of this book, we can illustrate the idea in the context of the basic EOQ model.

From Section 4.5, we know that the order quantity that minimizes average annual holding and setup costs when demand is fixed at λ units per unit time is the EOQ given by

$$Q^* = \sqrt{\frac{2K\lambda}{h}},$$

and the optimal time between placement of orders, say T^*, is given by

$$T^* = Q^*/\lambda = \sqrt{\frac{2K}{\lambda h}}.$$

It is possible, and even likely, that optimal order intervals are inconvenient. For example, the optimal solution might call for ordering every 3.393 weeks. However, one might only want to place orders at the beginning of a day or a week. To account for this, suppose that we impose the constraint that ordering must occur in some multiple of a base time, T_L. To find the optimal solution under the constraint that the order interval must be a multiple of T_L, one would simply compare the costs at the two closest multiples of T_L to T^* and pick the order interval with the lower cost. [That is, find k for which $kT_L \leq T^* \leq (k+1)T_L$ and choose the reorder interval to be either kT_L or $(k+1)T_L$ depending on which results in a lower average annual cost.]

Now suppose we add the additional restriction that the order interval must be a power of two times T_L. That is, the order interval must be of the form $2^k T_L$ for some integer $k \geq 0$. While it is unlikely one would impose such a restriction in the context of the simple EOQ problem, the ultimate goal is to explore these policies for more complex problems whose optimal solutions are hard to find. The question we wish to address is: Under such a restriction (known as a power-of-two policy), what is the worst cost error we will incur relative to that of the optimal reorder interval T^*? On the surface, it appears that such a restriction would result in serious errors. As k increases, the distance between successive powers of two grows rapidly. For example, if $k = 12$, $2^k = 4{,}096$ and $2^{k+1} = 8{,}192$, a very wide interval. If $T^* = 6{,}000$ and $T_L = 1$, for example, it seems that forcing the order interval to be either 4,096 or 8,192 would result in a large cost error (as the error in T is nearly 30 percent in either direction). However, this turns out not to be the case. In fact, we can prove that the cost error in every case is bounded by slightly more than 6 percent. While the result seems unintuitive at first, recall that the average annual cost function is relatively insensitive to errors in Q, as we saw in Section 4.5. Since Q and T are proportional, a similar cost insensitivity holds with respect to T.

We know from Section 4.5 that the average annual holding and setup cost as a function of the order quantity, Q, is given by

$$G(Q) = \frac{K\lambda}{Q} + \frac{hQ}{2}.$$

Since $Q = \lambda T$, the average annual cost can also be expressed in terms of the reorder interval, T, as

$$G(T) = \frac{K}{T} + \frac{h\lambda T}{2}.$$

In the case of a power-of-two policy, we wish to find the value of k that minimizes $G(2^k T_L)$. Since $G(T)$ is a continuous convex function of T, it follows that $G(2^k T_L)$ is a discrete convex function of k. That means that the optimal value of k, say k^*, satisfies

$$k^* = \min\{k : G(2^{k+1}T_L) \geq G(2^k T_L)\}.$$

Substituting for $G(T)$, the optimality condition becomes

$$\frac{K}{2^{k+1}T_L} - \frac{K}{2^k T_L} \geq \frac{h\lambda 2^k T_L}{2} - \frac{h\lambda 2^{k+1} T_L}{2}$$

which can easily be seen to reduce to

$$\frac{K/2}{2^k T_L} \leq h\lambda 2^{k-1} T_L.$$

Rearranging terms gives

$$2^k \geq \frac{1}{T_L}\sqrt{\frac{K}{h\lambda}},$$

or

$$2^k T_L \geq \frac{1}{\sqrt{2}} T^*.$$

We assume that $T^* \geq T_L$, which means that $\sqrt{2}T^* > T_L$. Hence, to summarize, we seek the smallest value of k that satisfies the simultaneous inequalities

$$\frac{1}{\sqrt{2}} T^* \leq 2^k T_L \leq \sqrt{2} T^*.$$

Note that this implies that as long as $T^* \geq T_L$, the optimal power-of-two solution will always lie between $.707T^*$ and $1.41T^*$. The next question is: What is the worst-case cost error of this policy? Since $Q = \lambda T$, if $T = T^*/\sqrt{2}$, then $Q = Q^*/\sqrt{2}$, and similarly if $T = \sqrt{2}T^*$, then $Q = \sqrt{2}Q^*$. It follows that the worst-case cost error of the power-of-two policy is given by

$$\frac{G(Q)}{G(Q^*)} = \frac{1}{2}\left(\frac{Q^*}{Q} + \frac{Q}{Q^*}\right) = \frac{1}{2}\left(\frac{1}{\sqrt{2}} + \sqrt{2}\right) = 1.0607,$$

or slightly more than 6 percent. (Because of symmetry, we obtain the same result when $Q = Q^*/\sqrt{2}$ or when $Q = \sqrt{2}Q^*$.)

The real "power" of power-of-two policies occurs when trying to solve more complex problems whose optimal policies are difficult to find. Consider the following scenario. A single warehouse is the sole supplier of N retailers. The demand rate experienced by each retailer is known and constant. As with the simple EOQ problem, assume that shortages at both the warehouse and the retailers are not permitted. There are fixed costs for ordering at both the warehouse and the retailers, and holding costs at these locations. These costs do not necessarily need to be the same. It is assumed that there is no lead time for placement or arrival of orders.

Unlike the simple EOQ problem, determining an optimal policy (that is, one that minimizes long-run average costs) for this problem could be extremely difficult, or even close to impossible. In many cases, even the form of an optimal policy may not be known. Clearly, effective approximations are very important.

One approximation for this problem is a so-called nested policy. In this case, a retailer would automatically order whenever the warehouse does, and possibly at other times as well. Although nested policies can have arbitrarily large cost errors, various adaptations of power-of-two policies can be shown to have 94 percent or even 98 percent guaranteed effectiveness. Power-of-two approximations have also been shown to be equally effective in serial production systems, and more complex arborescent assembly systems. We refer the interested reader to Roundy (1985) and Muckstadt and Roundy (1993).

Case Study. Betty Buys a Business

Betty Robinson decided it was time for a change. She had been a social worker for 10 years, and although she found the work rewarding, it was time for something else. So, when Herbie's Hut came up for sale, she made some inquiries.

Herbie's Hut was a small gift shop and toy store in her old neighborhood of Skokie, a Chicago suburb. Herb Gold had been running the business for 40 years, but it was a demanding job and he decided it was time to hang it up. The business was pretty steady, so Herb figured that there would buyers. He was delighted to hear from Betty, whom he had known as a child growing up in the neighborhood. The money was less important to Herb than making sure the store was in good hands. He had a good feeling about Betty, so he agreed to let the business go for a modest price.

After Betty purchased the business, she decided to remodel the store. Herbie's Hut would reopen as Betty's Best. Skylights, new wallpaper, and a fresh layout gave the store a sprightlier look that reflected Betty's personality. During this time, Betty took a careful look at the stock that came with the purchase. She noticed that several items were severely understocked. Two of those were ID bracelets and Lego sets. She spoke with Herb about it and he apologized. These were popular items and he hadn't had a chance to reorder them.

Betty was concerned that she might run out of these items quickly and that it would hurt her reputation. When she called the suppliers she realized that she had no idea how much to order. She asked Herb and he said that his rule of thumb was to order about one month's supply. This sounded reasonable to Betty; she could figure out what a month's supply was from the store's sales records, which Herb graciously turned over to her.

The store stocked hundreds of different items. It occurred to Betty that if she reordered every item monthly, she would be spending a lot of time processing orders. Betty thought that perhaps there was a better way. She consulted her boyfriend Bob who had an MBA degree. Bob fished up his old class notes and showed Betty the EOQ formula, $\sqrt{\frac{2K\lambda}{h}}$, which was supposed to be used for determining order sizes. "What are these symbols supposed be?" asked Betty. Bob had reviewed his notes and explained that K is the fixed cost of each order, a Greek letter (λ) is the sales rate, and h is the cost of holding. Betty still wasn't sure what it all meant.

"Let's take an item you need to order now and see how this works out," suggested Bob. So they considered the bracelets.

"First, what's the process you would go through to place a new order?" asked Bob. "Well," replied Betty, "I would call the supplier to place the order, and when it arrived I would unpack the shipment, possibly put some of the items on display, and store the rest." "How long does that take?" inquired Bob. "I don't know," she responded, "maybe a couple of hours. Also, that supplier charges a fixed cost of $50 per order in addition to the cost of each bracelet." Figuring Betty's time at $50 per hour Bob computed a total fixed cost of $(2)(50) + 50 = \$150$.

"Ok. Let's look at the sales rate," said Bob. Based on Herb's records, she estimated that he had sold an average of about 75 bracelets a month. That would give the value of λ. Finally, they needed to estimate the holding cost. Bob had spent some time thinking about this. "Holding cost can be thought of in two ways. The symbol h refers to the cost of holding a single unit of inventory for some fixed time, typically one year. It can also be thought of as an interest rate, which is then multiplied by the unit cost of the item. I think the most appropriate value of the interest rate is the rate of return you expect to earn in this business. I did a little research on the web and it seems that for businesses of this type, a 15 percent annual return on investment seems to be about right. We'll use that to figure the holding cost." Since Betty's cost of each bracelet was $30, this resulted in an annual holding cost of $h = (.15)(30) = \$4.50$ annually.

Since the holding cost was based on an annual interest rate, the sales rate had to be yearly as well. This translated to an annual sales rate of $(12)(75) = 900$. Plugging these numbers into the formula gave a lot size of $\sqrt{\frac{(2)(150)(900)}{4.5}} = 245$. This made more sense to Betty than ordering 75 bracelets every month. This translates to a little more than a three month supply.

Once Betty got the idea, it didn't take her long to set up a spreadsheet for all the items in the store. For example, a similar analysis of the Lego sets resulted in an EOQ value of 80 Lego sets. That seemed all well and good until her first order arrived.

Uh oh, she thought, these things are pretty bulky. They filled up almost half of her backroom storage area. She realized that there was a little more to figuring out the right lot sizes than just applying the EOQ formula.

Betty asked Bob what she should do about the fact that the Lego order took up so much space. "Well, I'm not sure," answered Bob. "I guess you shouldn't order so many Lego sets." "Well thanks for nothing, genius." Betty responded. "I know that now, but just how many should I order?"

So Bob did his research, and found out this was a tougher problem than figuring the EOQ. As a first cut, Bob read that if the value of each item were proportional to the space it consumed, the solution would be pretty simple. Realizing that this was only an approximation, he figured it would be better than nothing, and would hopefully satisfy Betty.

"Ok," Bob said, "let's consider your spreadsheet that computes the EOQ values for all of the items in the store. Now let's add a column to the spreadsheet that indicates the cubic feet of space consumed by each item. Multiply the two for each item and add up the total."

This was an easy calculation once Betty was able to approximate the space requirements for each of the items. Multiplying the two columns and adding resulted in a total space requirement of 120,000 cubic feet. Betty had only 50,000 cubic feet of storage space, so Bob suggested that each of the order quantities be reduced by multiplying by the constant $50,000/120,000 = .4167$. "If you reduce all of your order quantities by around 60 percent, you shouldn't run of the space," Bob recommended.

"Bob, that's great! That will be a big help," said Betty. Betty added another column to her spreadsheet that reduced all of the lot sizes by 60 percent. But as she started looking at the numbers, something bothered her.

"You know, Bob, this will solve my space problem, but there's something about it that doesn't make sense to me. Reducing the lot size of the Lego sets from 80 to 32 sounds about right, but why should I reduce the lot size for the bracelets? They hardly take up any room at all."

Jeez, she's absolutely right on the money about that, thought Bob. You really wanted to reduce the lot sizes of the bulky items a lot more than the small items. But how do you do that? Bob consulted his friend Phil, who has a PhD in operations research. Phil explained that this was a nontrivial optimization problem that involved finding the value of something called the Lagrange multiplier. Given Betty's spreadsheet, this was a piece of cake for Phil. Once the calculation was completed, the lot sizes for the bulky items were indeed reduced much more than those of the smaller items.

By applying a few basic concepts from inventory control, Betty was able to get a handle on the problem of managing her stock. Her willingness to apply scientific principles meant that Betty was well on her way to creating a successful business.

4.11 HISTORICAL NOTES AND ADDITIONAL TOPICS

The interest in using mathematical models to control the replenishment of inventories dates back to the early part of the 20th century. Ford Harris (1915) is generally credited with the development of the simple EOQ model. R. H. Wilson (1934) is also recognized for his analysis of the model. The procedure we suggest for the all-units quantity discount model appears to be due to Churchman, Ackoff, and Arnoff (1957), and the incremental discount model appears to be due to Hadley and Whitin (1963). Kenneth Arrow provides an excellent discussion of the economic motives for holding inventories in Chapter 1 of Arrow, Karlin, and Scarf (1958).

Hadley and Whitin (1963) also seem to have been the first to consider budget- and space-constrained problems, although several researchers have studied the problem subsequently. Rosenblatt (1981) derives results similar to those of Section 4.8 and considers several extensions not treated in this section.

Academic interest in inventory management problems took a sudden upturn in the late 1950s and early 1960s with the publication of a number of texts in addition to those just mentioned, including Whitin (1957); Magee and Boodman (1967); Bowman and Fetter (1961); Fetter and Dalleck (1961); Hanssmann (1961); Star and Miller (1962); Wagner (1962); and Scarf, Gilford, and Shelly (1963).

By and large, the vast majority of the published research on inventory systems since the 1960s has been on stochastic models, which will be the subject of Chapter 5. Extensions of the EOQ model have been considered more recently by Barbosa and Friedman (1978) and Schwarz and Schrage (1971), for example.

4.12 Summary

This chapter presented several popular models used to control inventories when the demand is known. We discussed the various *economic motives for holding inventories*, which include economies of scale, uncertainties, speculation, and logistics. In addition, we mentioned some of the *physical characteristics of inventory systems* that are important in determining the complexity and applicability of the models to real problems. These include demand, lead time, review time, back-order/lost-sales assumptions, and the changes that take place in the inventory over time.

There are three significant classes of costs in inventory management. These are *holding or carrying costs, order or setup costs,* and *penalty cost* for not meeting demand. The holding cost is usually expressed as the product of an interest rate and the cost of the item.

The grandfather of all inventory control models is the simple *EOQ model,* in which demand is assumed to be constant, no stock-outs are permitted, and only holding and order costs are present. The optimal batch size is given by the classic square root formula. The first extension of the EOQ model we considered was to the case in which items are produced internally at a finite production rate. We showed that the optimal batch size in this case could be obtained from the EOQ formula with a modified holding cost.

Two types of *quantity discounts* were considered: *all-units,* in which the discounted price is valid on all the units in an order, and *incremental,* in which the discount is applied only to the additional units beyond the breakpoint. The optimal solution to the all-units case will often occur at a breakpoint, whereas the optimal solution to the incremental case will almost never occur at a breakpoint.

In most real systems, the inventory manager cannot ignore the interactions that exist between products. These interactions impose *constraints* on the system; these might arise because of limitations in the space available to store inventory or in the budget available to purchase items. We considered both cases, and showed that when the ratio of the item value or space consumed by the item over the holding cost is the same for all items, a solution to the constrained problem can be obtained easily. When this condition is not met, the formulation requires introducing a *Lagrange multiplier.* The correct value of the Lagrangian multiplier can be found by trial and error or by some type of search. The presence of the multiplier reduces lot sizes by effectively increasing holding costs.

The finite production rate model of Section 4.6 was extended to multiple products under the assumption that all the products are produced on a single machine. Assuming a *rotation cycle policy* in which one lot of each product is produced each cycle, we showed how to determine the cycle time minimizing the sum of annual setup and holding costs for all products. Rotation cycles provide a straightforward way to schedule production on one machine, but may be suboptimal when demand or production rates differ widely or setup costs are sequence dependent.

The chapter concluded with a brief overview of several commercial inventory control systems. There are dozens of products available ranging in price from under $100 to tens of thousands of dollars. Many of the products designed to run on personal computers are parts of integrated accounting systems. Most of these products do not include item forecasting, lot sizing, and reorder point calculations.

Additional Problems on Deterministic Inventory Models

31. Peet's Coffees in Menlo Park, California, sells Melitta Number 101 coffee filters at a fairly steady rate of about 60 boxes of filters monthly. The filters are ordered from a supplier in Trenton, New Jersey. Peet's manager is interested in applying some inventory theory to determine the best replenishment strategy for the filters.

    Peet's pays $2.80 per box of filters and estimates that fixed costs of employee time for placing and receiving orders amount to about $20. Peet's uses a 22 percent annual interest rate to compute holding costs.

    a. How large a standing order should Peet's have with its supplier in Trenton, and how often should these orders be placed?

    b. Suppose that it takes three weeks to receive a shipment. What inventory of filters should be on hand when an order is placed?

    c. What are the average annual holding and fixed costs associated with these filters, assuming they adopt an optimal policy?

    d. The Peet's store in Menlo Park is rather small. In what way might this affect the solution you recommended in part (a)?

32. A local supermarket sells a popular brand of shampoo at a fairly steady rate of 380 bottles per month. The cost of each bottle to the supermarket is 45 cents, and the cost of placing an order has been estimated at $8.50. Assume that holding costs are based on a 25 percent annual interest rate. Stock-outs of the shampoo are not allowed.

    a. Determine the optimal lot size the supermarket should order and the time between placements of orders for this product.

    b. If the procurement lead time is two months, find the reorder point based on the on-hand inventory.

    c. If the item sells for 99 cents, what is the annual profit (exclusive of overhead and labor costs) from this item?

33. Diskup produces a variety of personal computer products. High-density 3.5-inch disks are produced at a rate of 1,800 per day and are shipped out at a rate of 800 per day. The disks are produced in batches. Each disk costs the company 20 cents, and the holding costs are based on an 18 percent annual interest rate. Shortages are not permitted. Each production run of a disk type requires recalibration of the equipment. The company estimates that this step costs $180.

    a. Find the optimal size of each production run and the time between runs.

    b. What fraction of the time is the company producing high-density 3.5-inch disks?

    c. What is the maximum dollar investment in inventory that the company has in these disks?

34. Berry Computer is considering moving some of its operations overseas in order to reduce labor costs. In the United States, its main circuit board costs Berry $75 per unit to produce, while overseas it costs only $65 to produce. Holding costs are based on a 20 percent annual interest rate, and the demand has been a fairly steady 200 units per week. Assume that setup costs are $200 both locally and overseas. Production lead times are one month locally and six months overseas.

    a. Determine the average annual costs of production, holding, and setup at each location, assuming that an optimal solution is employed in each case. Based on these results only, which location is preferable?

    b. Determine the value of the pipeline inventory in each case. (The pipeline inventory is the inventory on order.) Does comparison of the pipeline inventories alter the conclusion reached in part (a)?

c. Might considerations other than cost favor local over overseas production?

35. A large producer of household products purchases a glyceride used in one of its deodorant soaps from outside of the company. It uses the glyceride at a fairly steady rate of 40 pounds per month, and the company uses a 23 percent annual interest rate to compute holding costs. The chemical can be purchased from two suppliers, A and B. A offers the following all-units discount schedule:

Order Size	Price per Pound
$0 \leq Q < 500$	$1.30
$500 \leq Q < 1{,}000$	1.20
$1{,}000 \leq Q$	1.10

whereas B offers the following incremental discount schedule: $1.25 per pound for all orders less than or equal to 700 pounds, and $1.05 per pound for all incremental amounts over 700 pounds. Assume that the cost of order processing for each case is $150. Which supplier should be used?

36. The president of Value Filters became very enthusiastic about using EOQs to plan the sizes of her production runs, and instituted lot sizing based on EOQ values before she could properly estimate costs. For one particular filter line, which had an annual demand of 1,800 units per year and which was valued at $2.40 per unit, she assumed a holding cost based on a 30 percent annual interest rate and a setup cost of $100. Some time later, after the cost accounting department had time to perform an analysis, it found that the appropriate value of the interest rate was closer to 20 percent and the setup cost was about $40. What was the additional average annual cost of holding and setup incurred from the use of the wrong costs?

37. Consider the carload discount schedule pictured in Figure 4–13 (page 225). Suppose $M = 500$ units, $C = \$10$ per unit, and a full carload of 500 units costs $3,000.

   a. Develop a graph of the average cost per unit, $C(Q)/Q$, assuming this schedule.
   b. Suppose that the units are consumed at a rate of 800 per week, order setup cost is $2,500, and holding costs are based on an annual interest charge of 22 percent. Graph the function $G(Q) = \lambda C(Q)/Q + K\lambda/Q + I(C(Q)/Q)Q/2$ and find the optimal value of Q. (Assume that 1 year = 50 weeks.)
   c. Repeat part (b) for $\lambda = 1{,}000$ per week and $K = \$1{,}500$.

38. Harold Gwynne is considering starting a sandwich-making business from his dormitory room in order to earn some extra income. However, he has only a limited budget of $100 to make his initial purchases. Harold divides his needs into three areas: breads, meats and cheeses, and condiments. He estimates that he will be able to use all the products he purchases before they spoil, so perishability is not a relevant issue. The demand and cost parameters are as follows.

	Breads	Meats and Cheeses	Condiments
Weekly demand	6 packages	12 packages	2 pounds
Cost per unit	$0.85	$3.50	$1.25
Fixed order cost	$12	$8	$10

244 Chapter Four *Inventory Control Subject to Known Demand*

The choice of these fixed costs is based on the fact that these items are purchased at different locations in town. They include the cost of Harold's time in making the purchase. Assume that holding costs are based on an annual interest rate of 25 percent.

a. Find the optimal quantities that Harold should purchase of each type of product so that he does not exceed his budget.

b. If Harold could purchase all the items at the same location, would that alter your solution? Why?

39. Mike's Garage, a local automotive service and repair shop, uses oil filters at a fairly steady rate of 2,400 per year. Mike estimates that the cost of his time to make and process an order is about $50. It takes one month for the supplier to deliver the oil filters to the garage, and each one costs Mike $5. Mike uses an annual interest rate of 25 percent to compute his holding cost.

a. Determine the optimal number of oil filters that Mike should purchase, and the optimal time between placement of orders.

b. Determine the level of on-hand inventory at the time a reorder should be placed.

c. Assuming that Mike uses an optimal inventory control policy for oil filters, what is the annual cost of holding and order setup for this item?

40. An import/export firm has leased 20,000 cubic feet of storage space to store six items that it imports from the Far East. The relevant data for the six items it plans to store in the warehouse are

Item	Annual Demand (units)	Cost per Unit	Space per Unit (feet^3)
DVD	800	$200.00	12
32-inch flat screen TV	1,600	150.00	18
Blank DVD's (box of 10)	8,000	30.00	3
Blank CD's (box of 50)	12,000	18.00	2
Compact stereo	400	250.00	24
Telephone	1,200	12.50	3

Setup costs for each product amount to $2,000 per order, and holding costs are based on a 25 percent annual interest rate. Find the optimal order quantities for these six items so that the storage space is never exceeded. (Hint: Use a cell location for the Lagrange multiplier and experiment with different values until the storage constraint is satisfied as closely as possible.)

41. A manufacturer of greeting cards must determine the size of production runs for a certain popular line of cards. The demand for these cards has been a fairly steady 2 million per year, and the manufacturer is currently producing the cards in batch sizes of 50,000. The cost of setting up for each production run is $400.

Assume that for each card the material cost is 35 cents, the labor cost is 15 cents, and the distribution cost is 5 cents. The accounting department of the firm has established an interest rate to represent the opportunity cost of alternative investment and storage costs at 20 percent of the value of each card.

a. What is the optimal value of the EOQ for this line of greeting cards?

b. Determine the additional annual cost resulting from using the wrong production lot size.

42. Suppose that in Problem 41 the firm decides to account for the fact that the production rate of the cards is not infinite. Determine the optimal size of each production run assuming that cards are produced at the rate of 75,000 per week.

43. Pies 'R' Us bakes its own pies on the premises in a large oven that holds 100 pies. They sell the pies at a fairly steady rate of 86 per month. The pies cost $2 each to make. Prior to each baking, the oven must be cleaned out, which requires one hour's time for four workers, each of whom is paid $8 per hour. Inventory costs are based on an 18 percent annual interest rate. The pies have a shelf life of three months.

   a. How many pies should be baked for each production run? What is the annual cost of setup and holding for the pies?

   b. The owner of Pies 'R' Us is thinking about buying a new oven that requires one-half the cleaning time of the old oven and has a capacity twice as large as the old one. What is the optimal number of pies to be baked each time in the new oven?

   c. The net cost of the new oven (after trading in the old oven) is $350. How many years would it take for the new oven to pay for itself?

44. The Kirei-Hana Japanese Steak House in San Francisco consumes 3,000 pounds of sirloin steak each month. Yama Hirai, the new restaurant manager, recently completed an MBA degree. He learned that the steak was replenished using an EOQ value of 2,000 pounds. The EOQ value was computed assuming an interest rate of 36 percent per year. Assume that the current cost of the sirloin steak to the steak house is $4 per pound.

   a. What is the setup cost used in determining the EOQ value?

   Mr. Hirai received an offer from a meat wholesaler in which a discount of 5 percent would be given if the steak house purchased the steak in quantities of 3,000 pounds or more.

   b. Should Mr. Hirai accept the offer from the wholesaler? If so, how much can be saved?

   c. Because of Mr. Hirai's language problems, he apparently misunderstood the offer. In fact, the 5 percent discount is applied only to the amounts ordered over 3,000 pounds. Should this offer be accepted, and if so, how much is now saved?

45. Green's Buttons of Rolla, Missouri, supplies all the New Jersey Fabrics stores with eight different styles of buttons for men's dress shirts. The plastic injection molding machine can produce only one button style at a time and substantial time is required to reconfigure the machine for different button styles. As Green's has contracted to supply fixed quantities of buttons for the next three years, its demand can be treated as fixed and known. The relevant data for this problem appear in the following table.

Button Type	Annual Sales	Production Rate (units/day)	Setup Time (hours)	Variable Cost
A	25,900	4,500	6	$0.003
B	42,000	5,500	4	0.002
C	14,400	3,300	8	0.008
D	46,000	3,200	4	0.002
E	12,500	1,800	3	0.010
F	75,000	3,900	6	0.005
G	30,000	2,900	1	0.004
H	18,900	1,200	3	0.007

Assume 250 working days per year. Green's accounting department has established an 18 percent annual interest rate for the cost of capital and a 3 percent annual interest rate to account for storage space. Setup costs are $20 per hour required to reconfigure the equipment for a new style. Suppose that the firm decides to use a rotation cycle policy for production of the buttons.

a. What is the optimal rotation cycle time?
b. How large should the lots be?
c. What is the average annual cost of holding and setups at the optimal solution?
d. What contractual obligations might Green's have with New Jersey Fabrics that would prevent them from implementing the policy you determined in parts (a) and (b)? More specifically, if Green's agreed to make three shipments per year for each button style, what production policy would you recommend?

Appendix 4–A

Mathematical Derivations for Multiproduct Constrained EOQ Systems

Consider the standard multiproduct EOQ system with a budget constraint, which was discussed in Section 4.8. Mathematically, the problem is to find values of the variables $Q_1, Q_2, \ldots, Q_n$ to

$$\text{Minimize} \sum_{i=1}^{n} \left[\frac{h_i Q_i}{2} + \frac{K_i \lambda_i}{Q_i} \right]$$

subject to

$$\sum_{i=1}^{n} c_i Q_i \leq C.$$

Let EOQ_i be the respective unconstrained EOQ values. Then there are two possibilities:

$$\sum_{i=1}^{n} c_i EOQ_i \leq C, \qquad (1)$$

$$\sum_{i=1}^{n} c_i EOQ_i > C. \qquad (2)$$

If Equation (1) holds, the optimal solution is the trivial solution; namely, set $Q_i = EOQ_i$. If Equation (2) holds, then we are guaranteed that the constraint is binding at the optimal solution. That means that the constraint may be written

$$\sum_{i=1}^{n} c_i Q_i = C.$$

In this case, we introduce the Lagrange multiplier θ, and the problem is now to find $Q_1, Q_2, \ldots, Q_n$, and θ to solve the unconstrained problem:

$$\text{Minimize } G(Q_1, Q_2, \ldots, Q_n, \theta) = \sum_{i=1}^{n}\left(\frac{h_i Q_i}{2} + \frac{K_i \lambda_i}{Q_i}\right) + \theta \sum_{i=1}^{n}(c_i Q_i - C).$$

Necessary conditions for optimality are that

$$\frac{\partial G}{\partial Q_i} = 0 \quad \text{for } i = 1, \ldots, n$$

and

$$\frac{\partial G}{\partial \theta} = 0.$$

The first n conditions give

$$\frac{h_i}{2} - \frac{K_i \lambda_i}{Q_i^2} + \theta c_i = 0 \quad \text{for } i = 1, \ldots, n.$$

Rearranging terms, we get

$$Q_i = \sqrt{\frac{2 K_i \lambda_i}{h_i + 2\theta c_i}} \quad \text{for } i = 1, \ldots, n,$$

and we also have the final condition

$$\sum_{i=1}^{n} c_i Q_i = C.$$

Now consider the case where $c_i/h_i = c/h$ independent of i. By dividing the numerator and the denominator by h_i, we may write

$$Q_i = \sqrt{\frac{2 K_i \lambda_i}{h_i}} \sqrt{\frac{1}{1 + 2\theta c/h}}$$

$$= \text{EOQ}_i \sqrt{\frac{1}{1 + 2\theta c/h}}$$

$$= \text{EOQ}_i m,$$

where

$$m = \sqrt{\frac{1}{1 + 2\theta c/h}}.$$

Substituting this expression for Q_i into the constraint gives

$$\sum_{i=1}^{n} c_i \text{EOQ}_i m = C$$

or

$$m = \frac{C}{\sum_{i=1}^{n} c_i \text{EOQ}_i}.$$

Appendix 4–B

Glossary of Notation for Chapter 4

c = Proportional order cost.
EOQ = Economic order quantity (optimal lot size).
$G(Q)$ = Average annual cost associated with lot size Q.
h = Holding cost per unit time.
h' = Modified holding cost for finite production rate model.
I = Annual interest rate used to compute holding cost.
K = Setup cost or fixed order cost.
λ = Demand rate (units per unit time).
P = Production rate for finite production rate model.
Q = Lot size or size of the order.
s_i = Setup time for product i (refer to Section 4.9).
T = Cycle time; time between placement of successive orders.
τ = Order lead time.
θ = Lagrange multiplier for space-constrained model (refer to Section 4.8).
w_i = Space consumed by one unit of product i (refer to Section 4.8).
W = Total space available (refer to Section 4.8).

Bibliography

Arrow, K. A.; S. Karlin; and H. Scarf, eds. *Studies in the Mathematical Theory of Inventory Production*. Stanford, CA: Stanford University Press, 1958.

Barbosa, L. C., and M. Friedman. "Deterministic Inventory Lot Size Models—A General Root Law." *Management Science* 23 (1978), pp. 820–29.

Bowman, E. H., and R. B. Fetter. *Analysis for Production Management*. New York: McGraw-Hill/Irwin, 1961.

Churchman, C. W.; R. L. Ackoff; and E. L. Arnoff. *Introduction to Operations Research*. New York: John Wiley & Sons, 1957.

Donnelly, H. "Technology Awards: Recognizing Retailing's Best." *Stores* 76, no. 10 (1994), pp. 52–56.

Fetter, R. B., and W. C. Dalleck. *Decision Models for Inventory Management*. New York: McGraw-Hill/Irwin, 1961.

Hadley, G. J., and T. M. Whitin. *Analysis of Inventory Systems*. Englewood Cliffs, NJ: Prentice Hall, 1963.

Hanssmann, F. "A Survey of Inventory Theory from the Operations Research Viewpoint." In *Progress in Operations Research* 1, ed. R. L. Ackoff. New York: John Wiley & Sons, 1961.

Harris, F. W. *Operations and Cost* (Factory Management Series). Chicago: Shaw, 1915.

Magee, J. F., and D. M. Boodman. *Production Planning and Inventory Control*. 2nd ed. New York: McGraw-Hill, 1967.

Maxwell, W. L. "The Scheduling of Economic Lot Sizes." *Naval Research Logistics Quarterly* 11 (1964), pp. 89–124.

Muckstadt, J. A., and R. O. Roundy. "Analysis of Multi-Stage Production Systems." Chapter 2 in *Logistics of Production and Inventory,* eds. S. C. Graves, A. H. G. Rinnooy Kan, and P. H. Zipkin. Volume 4 of *Handbooks in Operations Research and Management Science,* Amsterdam: North-Holland, 1993.

Rosenblatt, M. J. "Multi-Item Inventory System with Budgetary Constraint: A Comparison between the Lagrangian and the Fixed Cycle Approach." *International Journal of Production Research* 19 (1981), pp. 331–39.

Roundy, R. O. "98%-Effective Integer-Ratio Lot-Sizing for One Warehouse Multi-Retailer Systems." *Management Science* 31 (1985), pp. 1416–30.

Scarf, H. E.; D. M. Gilford; and M. W. Shelly. *Multistage Inventory Models and Techniques*. Stanford, CA: Stanford University Press, 1963.

Schwarz, L. B., and L. Schrage. "Optimal and Systems Myopic Policies for Multiechelon Production/Inventory Assembly Systems." *Management Science* 21 (1971), pp. 1285–94.

Starr, M. K., and D. W. Miller. *Inventory Control: Theory and Practice*. Englewood Cliffs, NJ: Prentice Hall, 1962.

Wagner, H. M. *Statistical Management of Inventory Systems*. New York: John Wiley & Sons, 1962.

Whitin, T. M. *The Theory of Inventory Management*. Rev. ed. Princeton, NJ: Princeton University Press, 1957.

Wilson, R. H. "A Scientific Routine for Stock Control." *Harvard Business Review* 13 (1934), pp. 116–28.

Chapter Five

Inventory Control Subject to Uncertain Demand

"Knowing what you've got, knowing what you need, knowing what you don't—that's inventory control."
—Frank Wheeler in *Revolutionary Road*

Chapter Overview

Purpose

To understand how one deals with uncertainty (randomness) in the demand when computing replenishment policies for a single inventory item.

Key Points

1. *What is uncertainty and when should it be assumed?* Uncertainty means that demand is a random variable. A random variable is defined by its probability distribution, which is generally estimated from a past history of demands. In practice, it is common to assume that demand follows a normal distribution. When demand is assumed normal, one only needs to estimate the mean, μ, and variance, σ^2. Clearly, demand is uncertain to a greater or lesser extent in all real-world applications. What value, then, does the analysis of Chapters 3 and 4 have, where demand was assumed known? Chapter 3 focused on *systematic* or predictable changes in the demand pattern, such as peaks and valleys. Chapter 4 results for single items are useful if the variance of demand is low relative to the mean. In this chapter we consider items whose primary variation is due to uncertainty rather than predictable causes.

   If demand is described by a random variable, it is unclear what the optimization criterion should be, since the cost function is a random variable as well. To handle this, we assume that the objective is to minimize *expected* costs. The use of the expectation operator is justified by the law of large numbers from probability, since an inventory control problem invariably spans many planning periods. The law of large numbers guarantees that the arithmetic average of the incurred costs and the expected costs grow close as the number of planning periods gets large.

2. *The newsvendor model.* Consider a news vendor that decides each morning how many papers to buy to sell during the day. Since daily demand is highly variable, it is modeled with a random variable, D. Suppose that Q is the number of papers he purchases. If Q is too large, he is left with unsold papers, and if Q is too small, some demands go unfilled. If we let c_o be the unit overage cost, and c_u be the

250 Chapter Five *Inventory Control Subject to Uncertain Demand*

unit underage cost, then we show that the optimal number of papers he should purchase at the start of a day, say Q^*, satisfies:

$$F(Q^*) = c_u/(c_u + c_o)$$

where $F(Q^*)$ is the cumulative distribution function of D evaluated at Q^* (which is the same as the probability that demand is less than or equal to Q^*).

3. *Lot size–reorder point systems.* The newsvendor model is appropriate for a problem that essentially restarts from scratch every period. Yesterday's newspaper has no value in the market, save for the possible scrap value of the paper itself. However, most inventory control situations that one encounters in the real world are not like this. Unsold items continue to have value in the marketplace for many periods. For these cases we use an approach that is essentially an extension of the EOQ model of Chapter 4.

The lot size–reorder point system relies on the assumption that inventories are reviewed continuously rather than periodically. That is, the state of the system is known at all times. The system consists of two decision variables: Q and R. Q is the order size and R is the reorder point. That is, when the inventory of stock on hand reaches R, an order for Q units is placed. The model also allows for a positive order lead time, τ. It is the demand over the lead time that is the key uncertainty in the problem, since the lead time is the response time of the system. Let D represent the demand over the lead time, and let $F(t)$ be the cumulative distribution function of D. Cost parameters include a fixed order cost K, a unit penalty cost for unsatisfied demand p, and a per unit per unit time holding cost h. Interpret λ as the average annual demand rate (that is, the expected demand over a year). Then we show in this section that the optimal values of Q and R satisfy the following two simultaneous nonlinear equations:

$$Q = \sqrt{\frac{2\lambda[K + pn(R)]}{h}}$$

$$1 - F(R) = Qh/p\lambda.$$

The solution to these equations requires a back-and-forth iterative solution method. We provide details of the method only when the lead time demand distribution is normal. Convergence generally occurs quickly. A quick and dirty approximation is to set $Q = \text{EOQ}$ and solve for R in the second equation. This will give good results in most cases.

4. *Service levels in (Q, R) systems.* We assume two types of service: Type 1 service is the probability of not stocking out in the lead time and is represented by the symbol α. Type 2 service is the proportion of demands that are filled from stock (also known as the fill rate) and is represented by the symbol β. Finding the optimal (Q, R) subject to a Type 1 service objective is very easy. One merely finds R from $F(R) = \alpha$ and sets $Q = \text{EOQ}$. Unfortunately, what one generally means by service is the Type 2 criterion, and finding (Q, R) in that case is more difficult. For Type 2 service, we only consider the normal distribution. The solution requires using standardized loss tables, $L(z)$, which are supplied in the back of the book. As with the cost model, setting $Q = \text{EOQ}$ and solving for R will usually give good results if one does not want to bother with an iterative procedure.

In this chapter, we consider the link between inventory control and forecasting, and how one typically updates estimates of the mean and standard deviation of demand using exponential smoothing. The section concludes with a discussion of lead time variability, and how that additional uncertainty is taken into account.

5. *Periodic review systems under uncertainty.* The newsvendor model treats a product that perishes quickly (after one period). However, periodic review models also make sense when unsold product can be used in future periods. In this case the form of the optimal policy is known as an (s, S) policy. Let u be the starting inventory in any period. Then the (s, S) policy is

If $u \leq s$, order to S (that is, order $S - u$).
If $u > s$, don't order.

Unfortunately, finding the optimal values of (s, S) each period is much more difficult than finding the optimal (Q, R) policy, and is beyond the scope of this book. We also briefly discuss service levels in periodic review systems.

6. *Multiproduct systems.* Virtually all inventory control problems occurring in the operations planning context involve multiple products. One issue that arises in multiproduct systems is determining the amount of effort one should expend managing each item. Clearly, some items are more valuable to the business than others. The ABC classification system is one means of ranking items. Items are sequenced in decreasing order of annual dollar volume of sales or usage. Ordering the items in this way, and graphing the cumulative dollar volume gives an exponentially increasing curve known as a Pareto curve. Typically, 20 percent of the items account for 80 percent of the annual dollar volume (A items), the next 30 percent of the items typically account for the next 15 percent of the dollar volume (B items), and the final 50 percent of the items account for the final 5 percent of the dollar volume (C items). A items should receive the most attention. Their inventory levels should be reviewed often, and they should carry a high service level. B items do not need such close scrutiny, and C items are typically ordered infrequently in large quantities.

7. *Other issues.* The discussion of stochastic inventory models in this chapter barely reveals the tip of the iceberg in terms of the vast quantity of research done on this topic. Two important areas of research are multi-echelon inventory systems, and perishable inventory systems. A multi-echelon inventory system is one in which items are stored at multiple locations linked by a network. Supply chains, discussed in detail in Chapter 6, are such a system. Another important area of research are items that change during storage, thus affecting their useful lifetime. One class of such items are perishable items. Perishable items have a fixed lifetime known in advance, and include food, pharmaceuticals and photographic film. A related problem is managing items subject to obsolescence. Obsolescence differs from perishability in that the useful lifetime of an item subject to obsolescence cannot be predicted in advance. Mathematical models for analyzing such problems are quite complex and well beyond the scope of this book.

The management of uncertainty plays an important role in the success of any firm. What are the sources of uncertainty that affect a firm? A partial list includes uncertainty in consumer preferences and trends in the market, uncertainty in the availability and cost of labor and resources, uncertainty in vendor resupply times, uncertainty in weather and its ramifications on operations logistics, uncertainty of financial variables such as stock prices and interest rates, and uncertainty of demand for products and services.

Before the terrible tragedy of September 11, 2001, many of us would arrive at the airport no more than 30 or 40 minutes before the scheduled departure time of our flight. Now we might arrive two hours before the flight. Increased airport security has not only increased the average time required, it has increased the uncertainty of this time. To compensate for this increased uncertainty, we arrive far in advance of our scheduled departure time to provide a larger buffer time. This same principle will apply when managing inventories.

The uncertainty of demand and its effect on inventory management strategies are the subjects of this chapter. When a quantity is uncertain, it means that we cannot predict its value exactly in advance. For example, a department store cannot exactly predict the sales of a particular item on any given day. An airline cannot exactly predict the number of people that will choose to fly on any given flight. How, then, can these firms choose the number of items to keep in inventory or the number of flights to schedule on any given route?

Although exact sales of an item or numbers of seats booked on a plane cannot be predicted in advance, one's past experience can provide useful information for planning. As shown in Section 5.1, previous observations of any random phenomenon can be used to estimate its *probability distribution*. By properly quantifying the consequences of incorrect decisions, a well-thought-out mathematical model of the system being studied will result in intelligent strategies. When uncertainty is present, the objective is almost always to minimize expected cost or maximize expected profits.

Demand uncertainty plays a key role in many industries, but some are more susceptible to business cycles than others. The world economy saw one of the worst recessions in recent times in 2008. The stock market eventually dropped to about half of its high in 2007 and unemployment levels soared. The retailing industry in particular is very sensitive to the vicissitudes of consumer demand. Low cost providers such as Costco and Walmart fared well, but high-end retailers such as Nordstrom and Bloomingdales suffered. Matching supply and demand becomes even more critical in times of recession.

As some level of demand uncertainty seems to characterize almost all inventory management problems in practice, one might question the value of the deterministic inventory control models discussed in Chapter 4. There are two reasons for studying deterministic models. One is that they provide a basis for understanding the fundamental trade-offs encountered in inventory management. Another is that they may be good approximations depending on the degree of uncertainty in the demand.

To better understand the second point, let D be the demand for an item over a given period of time. We express D as the sum of two parts, D_{Det} and D_{Ran}. That is,

$$D = D_{\text{Det}} + D_{\text{Ran}},$$

where

D_{Det} = Deterministic component of demand,

D_{Ran} = Random component of demand.

There are a number of circumstances under which it would be appropriate to treat D as being deterministic even though D_{Ran} is not zero. Some of these are

1. When the variance of the random component, D_{Ran}, is small relative to the magnitude of D.
2. When the predictable variation is more important than the random variation.
3. When the problem structure is too complex to include an explicit representation of randomness in the model.

An example of circumstance 2 occurs in the aggregate planning problem. Although the forecast error of the aggregate demands over the planning horizon may not be zero, we are more concerned with planning for the anticipated changes in the demand than for the unanticipated changes. An example of circumstance 3 occurs in material requirements planning (treated in detail in Chapter 7). The intricacies of the relationships among various component levels and end items make it difficult to incorporate demand uncertainty into the analysis.

However, for many items, the random component of the demand is too significant to ignore. As long as the expected demand per unit time is relatively constant and the problem structure not too complex, explicit treatment of demand uncertainty is desirable. In this chapter we will examine several of the most important stochastic inventory models and the key issues surrounding uncertainty.[1]

Overview of Models Treated in This Chapter

Inventory control models subject to uncertainty are basically of two types: (1) **periodic review** and (2) **continuous review.** (Recall the discussion at the start of Chapter 4. Periodic review means that the inventory level is known at discrete points in time only, and continuous review means that the inventory level is known at all times.) Periodic review models may be for one planning period or for multiple planning periods. For one-period models, the objective is to properly balance the costs of overage (ordering too much) and underage (ordering too little). Single-period models are useful in several contexts: planning for initial shipment sizes for high-fashion items, ordering policies for food products that perish quickly, or determining run sizes for items with short useful lifetimes, such as newspapers. Because of this last application, the single-period stochastic inventory model has come to be known as the **newsvendor model.** The newsvendor model will be the first one considered in this chapter.

From this writer's experience, the vast majority of computer-based inventory control systems on the market use some variant of the continuous review models treated in the remainder of this chapter. They are, in a sense, extensions of the EOQ model to incorporate uncertainty. Their popularity in practice is attributable to several factors. First, the policies are easy to compute and easy to implement. Second, the models accurately describe most systems in which there is ongoing replenishment of inventory items under uncertainty. A detailed discussion of service levels is included as well. Because estimating penalty costs is difficult in practice, service level approaches are more frequently implemented than penalty cost approaches.

Multiperiod stochastic inventory models dominate the professional literature on inventory theory. There are enough results in this fascinating research area to compose a

---

[1] For those unfamiliar with it, the word *stochastic* is merely a synonym for *random*.

5.1 THE NATURE OF RANDOMNESS

In order to clarify what the terms *randomness* and *uncertainty* mean in the context of inventory control, we begin with an example.

Example 5.1 On consecutive Sundays, Mac, the owner of a local newsstand, purchases a number of copies of *The Computer Journal*, a popular weekly magazine. He pays 25 cents for each copy and sells each for 75 cents. Copies he has not sold during the week can be returned to his supplier for 10 cents each. The supplier is able to salvage the paper for printing future issues. Mac has kept careful records of the demand each week for the *Journal*. (This includes the number of copies actually sold plus the number of customer requests that could not be satisfied.) The observed demands during each of the last 52 weeks were

15	19	9	12	9	22	4	7	8	11
14	11	6	11	9	18	10	0	14	12
8	9	5	4	4	17	18	14	15	8
6	7	12	15	15	19	9	10	9	16
8	11	11	18	15	17	19	14	14	17
13	12								

There is no discernible pattern to these data, so it is difficult to predict the demand for the *Journal* in any given week. However, we can represent the demand experience of this item as a frequency histogram, which gives the number of times each weekly demand occurrence was observed during the year. The histogram for this demand pattern appears in Figure 5–1.

One uses the frequency histogram to estimate the probability that the number of copies of the *Journal* sold in any week is a specific value. These probability estimates are obtained by dividing the number of times that each demand occurrence was observed during the year by 52. For example, the probability that demand is 10 is estimated to be 2/52 = .0385, and the

FIGURE 5–1
Frequency histogram for a 52-week history of sales of *The Computer Journal* at Mac's

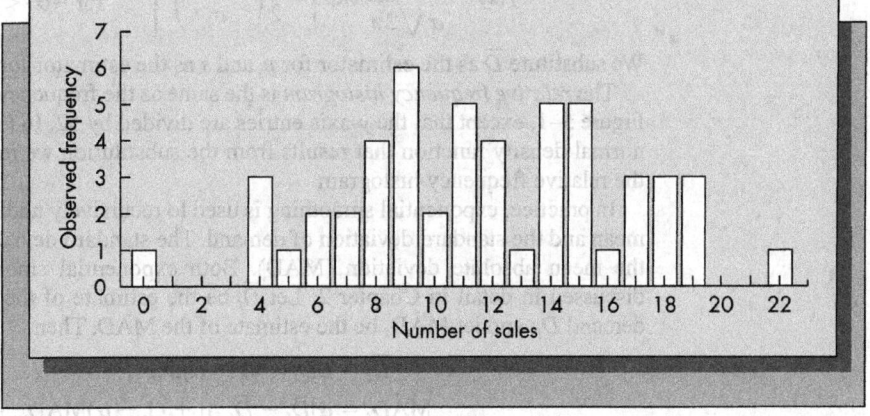

probability that the demand is 15 is 5/52 = .0962. The collection of all the probabilities is known as the *empirical probability distribution*. Cumulative probabilities also can be estimated in a similar way. For example, the probability that there are nine or fewer copies of the *Journal* sold in any week is $(1 + 0 + 0 + 0 + 3 + 1 + 2 + 2 + 4 + 6) = 19/52 = .3654$.

Although empirical probabilities can be used in subsequent analysis, they are inconvenient for a number of reasons. First, they require maintaining a record of the demand history for every item. This can be costly and cumbersome. Second, the distribution must be expressed (in this case) as 23 different probabilities. Other items may have an even wider range of past values. Finally, it is more difficult to compute optimal inventory policies with empirical distributions.

For these reasons, we generally approximate the demand history using a continuous distribution. The form of the distribution chosen depends upon the history of past demand and its ease of use. By far the most popular distribution for inventory applications is the normal. One reason is the frequency with which it seems to accurately model demand fluctuations. Another is its convenience. The normal model of demand must be used with care, however, as it admits the possibility of negative values. When using the normal distribution to describe a nonnegative phenomenon such as demand, the likelihood of a negative observation should be sufficiently small (less than .01 should suffice for most applications) so as not to be a factor.

A normal distribution is determined by two parameters: the mean μ and the variance σ^2. These can be estimated from a history of demand by the sample mean $\overline{D}$ and the sample variance s^2. Let $D_1, D_2, \ldots, D_n$ be n past observations of demand. Then

$$\overline{D} = \frac{1}{n} \sum_{i=1}^{n} D_i,$$

$$s^2 = \frac{1}{n-1} \sum_{i=1}^{n} (D_i - \overline{D})^2.$$

For the data pictured in Figure 5–1 we obtain

$$\overline{D} = 11.73,$$
$$s = 4.74.$$

The normal density function, $f(x)$, is given by the formula

$$f(x) = \frac{1}{\sigma\sqrt{2\pi}} \exp\left[-\frac{1}{2}\left(\frac{x-\mu}{\sigma}\right)^2\right] \quad \text{for } -\infty < x < +\infty.$$

We substitute $\overline{D}$ as the estimator for μ and s as the estimator for σ.

The *relative frequency histogram* is the same as the frequency histogram pictured in Figure 5–1, except that the y-axis entries are divided by 52. In Figure 5–2 we show the normal density function that results from the substitution we made, superimposed on the relative frequency histogram.

In practice, exponential smoothing is used to recursively update the estimates of the mean and the standard deviation of demand. The standard deviation is estimated using the mean absolute deviation (MAD). Both exponential smoothing and MAD are discussed in detail in Chapter 2. Let $\overline{D}_t$ be the estimate of the mean after observing demand D_t, and let MAD_t be the estimate of the MAD. Then

$$\overline{D}_t = \alpha D_t + (1-\alpha)\overline{D}_{t-1},$$
$$\text{MAD}_t = \alpha|D_t - \overline{D}_{t-1}| + (1-\alpha)\text{MAD}_{t-1},$$

FIGURE 5–2
Frequency histogram and normal approximation

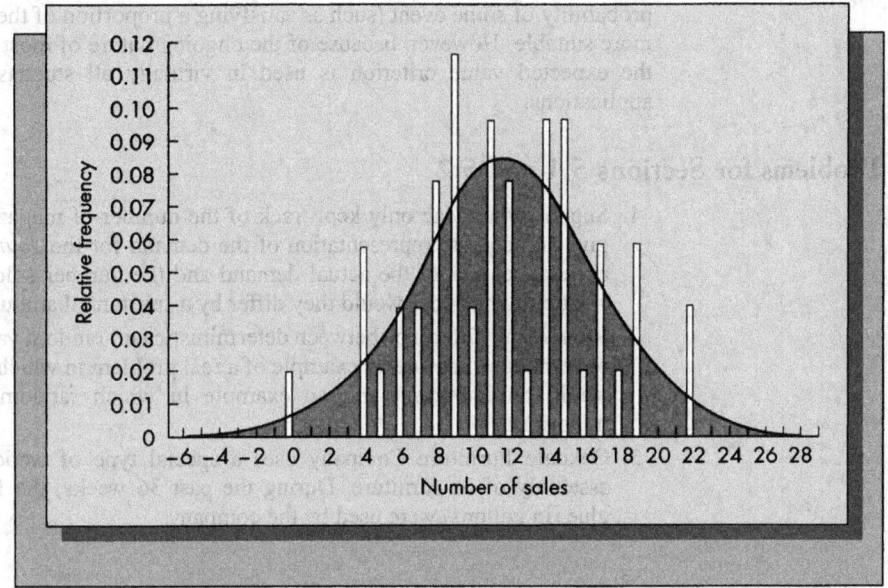

where $0 < \alpha < 1$ is the smoothing constant. For normally distributed demand

$$\sigma \approx 1.25 * \text{MAD}.$$

A smoothing constant of $\alpha \approx .1$ is generally used to ensure stability in the estimates (see Chapter 2 for a more complete discussion of the issues surrounding the choice of the smoothing constant).

5.2 OPTIMIZATION CRITERION

In general, optimization in production problems means finding a control rule that achieves minimum cost. However, when demand is random, the cost incurred is itself random, and it is no longer obvious what the optimization criterion should be. Virtually all stochastic optimization techniques applied to inventory control assume that the goal is to minimize *expected* costs.

The motivation for using the expected value criterion is that inventory control problems are generally ongoing problems. Decisions are made repetitively. The law of large numbers from probability theory says that the arithmetic average of many observations of a random variable will converge to the expected value of that random variable. In the context of the inventory problem, if we follow a control rule that minimizes expected costs, then the arithmetic average of the actual costs incurred over many periods will also be a minimum.

In certain circumstances, the expected value may not be the best optimization criterion. When a product is acquired only once and not on an ongoing basis, it is not clear that minimizing expected costs is appropriate. In such a case, maximizing the probability of some event (such as satisfying a proportion of the demand) is generally more suitable. However, because of the ongoing nature of most production problems, the expected value criterion is used in virtually all stochastic inventory control applications.

Problems for Sections 5.1 and 5.2

1. Suppose that Mac only kept track of the number of magazines sold. Would this give an accurate representation of the demand for the *Journal*? Under what circumstances would the actual demand and the number sold be close, and under what circumstances would they differ by a substantial amount?

2. What is the difference between deterministic and random variations in the pattern of demands? Provide an example of a real problem in which predictable variation would be important and an example in which random variation would be important.

3. Oakdale Furniture Company uses a special type of woodworking glue in the assembly of its furniture. During the past 36 weeks, the following amounts of glue (in gallons) were used by the company:

25	38	26	31	21	46	29	19	35	39	24	21
17	42	46	19	50	40	43	34	31	51	36	32
18	29	22	21	24	39	46	31	33	34	30	30

a. Compute the mean and the standard deviation of this sample.

b. Consider the following class intervals for the number of gallons used each week:

Less than 20.
20–27.
28–33.
34–37.
38–43.
More than 43.

Determine the proportion of data points that fall into each of these intervals. Compare these proportions to the probabilities that a normal variate with the mean and the standard deviation you computed in part (*a*) falls into each of these intervals. Based on the comparison of the observed proportions and those obtained from assuming a normal distribution, would you conclude that the normal distribution provides an adequate fit of these data? (This procedure is essentially the same as a chi-square goodness-of-fit test.)

c. Assume that the numbers of gallons of glue used each week are independent random variables, having the normal distribution with mean and standard deviation computed in part (*a*). What is the probability that the total number of gallons used in six weeks does not exceed 200 gallons? (Hint: The mean of a sum of random variables is the sum of the means and the *variance* of a sum of *independent* random variables is the sum of the variances.)

4. In Problem 3, what other probability distributions might accurately describe Oakdale's weekly usage of glue?
5. Rather than keeping track of each demand observation, Betty Sucasas, a member of the marketing staff with a large company that produces a line of switches, has kept only grouped data. For switch C9660Q, used in small power supplies, she has observed the following numbers of units of the switch shipped over the last year.

Units Shipped	Number of Weeks
0–2,000	3
2,001–5,000	6
5,001–9,000	12
9,001–12,000	17
12,001–18,000	10
18,001–20,000	4

Based on these observations, estimate the mean and the standard deviation of the weekly shipments. (Hint: This is known as grouped data. For the purposes of your calculation, assume that all observations occur at the midpoint of each interval.)

6. *a.* Consider the Oakdale Furniture Company described in Problem 3. Under what circumstances might the major portion of the usage of the glue be predictable?

b. If the demand were predictable, would you want to use a probability law to describe it? Under what circumstances might the use of a probability model of demand be justified even if the demand could be predicted exactly?

5.3 THE NEWSVENDOR MODEL

Let us return to Example 5.1, in which Mac wishes to determine the number of copies of *The Computer Journal* he should purchase each Sunday. A study of the historical data showed that the demand during any week is a random variable that is approximately normally distributed, with mean 11.73 and standard deviation 4.74. Each copy is purchased for 25 cents and sold for 75 cents, and he is paid 10 cents for each unsold copy by his supplier. One obvious solution is that he should buy enough to meet the mean demand, which is approximately 12 copies. There is something wrong with this solution. Suppose Mac purchases a copy that he does not sell. His out-of-pocket expense is 25 cents − 10 cents = 15 cents. Suppose, on the other hand, that he is unable to meet the demand of a customer. In that case, he loses 75 cents − 25 cents = 50 cents profit. Hence, there is a significantly greater penalty for not having enough than there is for having too much. If he only buys enough to satisfy mean demand, he will stock-out with the same frequency that he has an oversupply. Our intuition tells us that he should buy more than the mean, but how much more? This question is answered in this section.

Notation

This problem is an example of the newsvendor model, in which a single product is to be ordered at the beginning of a period and can be used only to satisfy demand during that period. Assume that all relevant costs can be determined on the basis of ending inventory. Define

c_o = Cost per unit of positive inventory remaining at the end of the period (known as the *overage cost*).

c_u = Cost per unit of unsatisfied demand. This can be thought of as a cost per unit of negative ending inventory (known as the *underage cost*).

In the development of the model, we will assume that the demand D is a continuous nonnegative random variable with density function $f(x)$ and cumulative distribution function $F(x)$. [A brief review of probability theory is given in Appendix 5–A. In particular, both $F(x)$ and $f(x)$ are defined there.]

The *decision variable* Q is the number of units to be purchased at the beginning of the period. The goal of the analysis is to determine Q to minimize the expected costs incurred at the end of the period.

Development of the Cost Function

A general outline for analyzing most stochastic inventory problems is the following:

1. Develop an expression for the cost incurred as a function of both the random variable D and the decision variable Q.
2. Determine the expected value of this expression with respect to the density function or probability function of demand.
3. Determine the value of Q that minimizes the expected cost function.

Define $G(Q, D)$ as the total overage and underage cost incurred at the end of the period when Q units are ordered at the start of the period and D is the demand. If Q units are purchased and D is the demand, $Q - D$ units are left at the end of the period as long as $Q \geq D$. If $Q < D$, then $Q - D$ is negative and the number of units remaining on hand at the end of the period is 0. Notice that

$$\max\{Q - D, 0\} = \begin{cases} Q - D & \text{if } Q \geq D, \\ 0 & \text{if } Q \leq D. \end{cases}$$

In the same way, $\max\{D - Q, 0\}$ represents the excess demand over the supply, or the unsatisfied demand remaining at the end of the period. For any realization of the random variable D, either one or the other of these terms will be zero.

Hence, it now follows that

$$G(Q, D) = c_o \max(0, Q - D) + c_u \max(0, D - Q).$$

Next, we derive the expected cost function. Define

$$G(Q) = E(G(Q, D)).$$

Using the rules outlined in Appendix 5–A for taking the expected value of a function of a random variable, we obtain

$$G(Q) = c_o \int_0^\infty \max(0, Q - x) f(x)\, dx + c_u \int_0^\infty \max(0, x - Q) f(x)\, dx$$

$$= c_o \int_0^Q (Q - x) f(x)\, dx + c_u \int_Q^\infty (x - Q) f(x)\, dx.$$

Determining the Optimal Policy

We would like to determine the value of Q that minimizes the expected cost $G(Q)$. In order to do so, it is necessary to obtain an accurate description of the function $G(Q)$. We have that

$$\frac{dG(Q)}{dQ} = c_o \int_0^Q 1 f(x)\, dx + c_u \int_Q^\infty (-1) f(x)\, dx$$

$$= c_o F(Q) - c_u(1 - F(Q)).$$

(This is a result of Leibniz's rule, which indicates how one differentiates integrals. Leibniz's rule is stated in Appendix 5–A.)

It follows that

$$\frac{d^2 G(Q)}{dQ^2} = (c_o + c_u) f(Q) \geq 0 \quad \text{for all } Q \geq 0.$$

Because the second derivative is nonnegative, the function $G(Q)$ is said to be *convex* (bowl shaped). We can obtain additional insight into the shape of $G(Q)$ by further analysis. Note that

$$\left. \frac{dG(Q)}{dQ} \right|_{Q=0} = c_o F(0) - c_u(1 - F(0))$$

$$= -c_u < 0 \quad \text{since } F(0) = 0.$$

Since the slope is negative at $Q = 0$, $G(Q)$ is decreasing at $Q = 0$. The function $G(Q)$ is pictured in Figure 5–3.

It follows that the optimal solution, say Q^*, occurs where the first derivative of $G(Q)$ equals zero. That is,

$$G'(Q^*) = (c_o + c_u) F(Q^*) - c_u = 0.$$

FIGURE 5–3
Expected cost function for newsvendor model

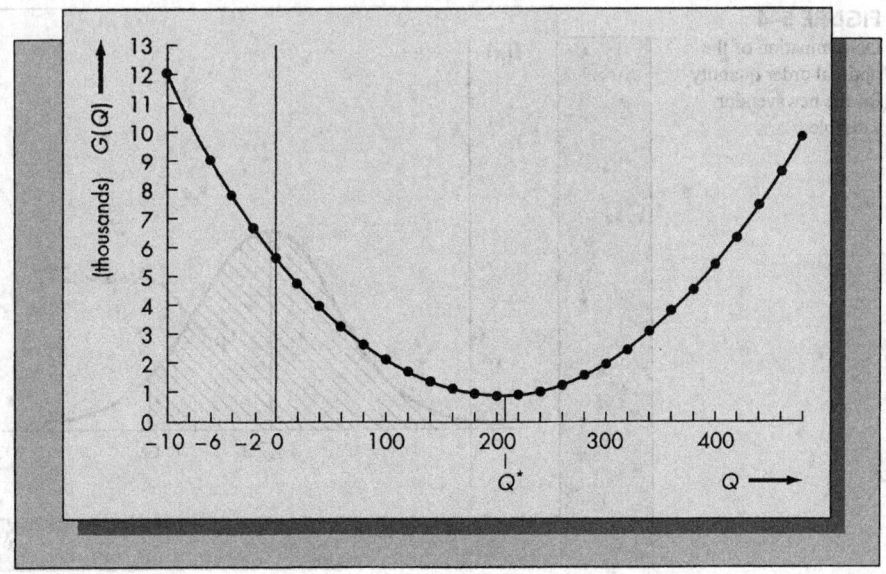

Rearranging terms gives

$$F(Q^*) = c_u/(c_o + c_u).$$

We refer to the right-hand side of the last equation as the *critical ratio*. Because c_u and c_o are positive numbers, the critical ratio is strictly between zero and one. This implies that for a continuous demand distribution this equation is always solvable.

As $F(Q^*)$ is defined as the probability that the demand does not exceed Q^*, the critical ratio is the probability of satisfying all the demand during the period if Q^* units are purchased at the start of the period. It is important to understand that this is *not* the same as the proportion of satisfied demands. When underage and overage costs are equal, the critical ratio is exactly one-half. In that case Q^* corresponds to the *median* of the demand distribution. When the demand density is symmetric (such as the normal density), the mean and the median are the same.

Example 5.1 (continued)

Consider the example of Mac's newsstand. From past experience, we saw that the weekly demand for the *Journal* is approximately normally distributed with mean $\mu = 11.73$ and standard deviation $\sigma = 4.74$. Because Mac purchases the magazines for 25 cents and can salvage unsold copies for 10 cents, his overage cost is $c_o = 25 - 10 = 15$ cents. His underage cost is the profit on each sale, so that $c_u = 75 - 25 = 50$ cents. The critical ratio is $c_u/(c_o + c_u) = 0.50/0.65 = .77$. Hence, he should purchase enough copies to satisfy all the weekly demand with probability .77. The optimal Q^* is the 77th percentile of the demand distribution (see Figure 5–4).

Using either Table A–1 or Table A–4 at the back of the book, we obtain a standardized value of $z = 0.74$. The optimal Q is

$$Q^* = \sigma z + \mu = (4.74)(0.74) + 11.73$$
$$= 15.24 \approx 15.$$

Hence, he should purchase 15 copies every week.

FIGURE 5–4
Determination of the optimal order quantity for the newsvendor example

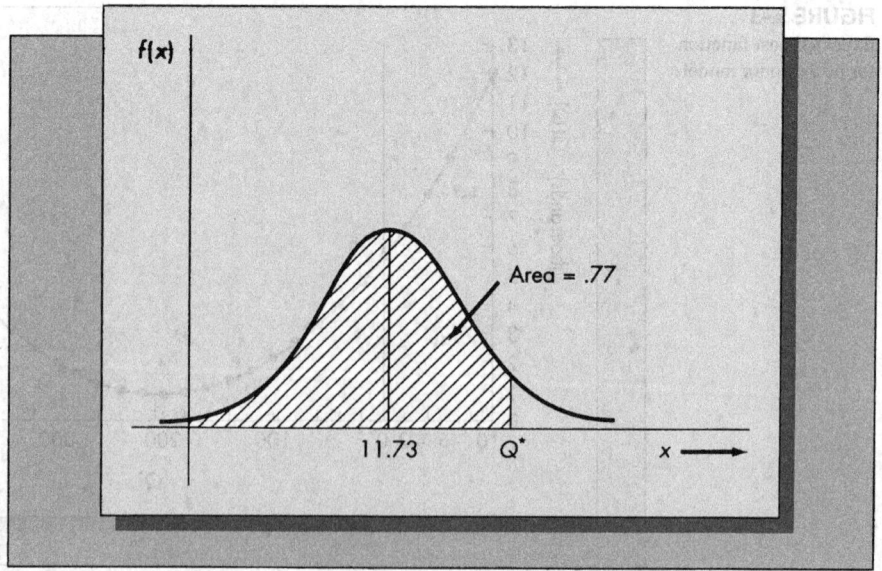

Optimal Policy for Discrete Demand

Our derivation of the newsvendor formula was based on the assumption that the demand in the period was described by a continuous probability distribution. We noted a number of reasons for the desirability of working with continuous distributions. However, in some cases, and particularly when the mean demand is small, it may not be possible to obtain an accurate representation of the observed pattern of demand using a continuous distribution. For example, the normal approximation of the 52-week history of the demand for the *Journal* pictured in Figure 5–2 may not be considered sufficiently accurate for our purposes.

The procedure for finding the optimal solution to the newsvendor problem when the demand is assumed to be discrete is a natural generalization of the continuous case. In the continuous case, the optimal solution is the value of Q that makes the distribution function equal to the critical ratio $c_u/(c_u + c_o)$. In the discrete case, the distribution function increases by jumps; it is unlikely that any of its values exactly equal the critical ratio. The critical ratio will generally fall between two values of $F(Q)$. The optimal solution procedure is to locate the critical ratio between two values of $F(Q)$ and choose the Q corresponding to the *higher* value. (The fact that you always round Q up rather than simply round it off can be easily proven mathematically. This is different from assuming that units are ordered in discrete amounts but demand is continuous, in which case Q is rounded to the closest integer, as we did earlier.)

Example 5.2 We will solve the problem faced by Mac's newsstand using the empirical distribution derived from a one-year history of the demand, rather than the normal approximation of that demand history. The empirical probabilities are obtained from Figure 5–1 by dividing each of the heights by 52. We obtain

Q	f(Q)	F(Q)	Q	f(Q)	F(Q)
0	1/52	1/52 (.0192)	12	4/52	30/52 (.5769)
1	0	1/52 (.0192)	13	1/52	31/52 (.5962)
2	0	1/52 (.0192)	14	5/52	36/52 (.6923)
3	0	1/52 (.0192)	15	5/52	41/52 (.7885)
4	3/52	4/52 (.0769)	16	1/52	42/52 (.8077)
5	1/52	5/52 (.0962)	17	3/52	45/52 (.8654)
6	2/52	7/52 (.1346)	18	3/52	48/52 (.9231)
7	2/52	9/52 (.1731)	19	3/52	51/52 (.9808)
8	4/52	13/52 (.2500)	20	0	51/52 (.9808)
9	6/52	19/52 (.3654)	21	0	51/52 (.9808)
10	2/52	21/52 (.4038)	22	1/52	52/52 (1.0000)
11	5/52	26/52 (.5000)			

The critical ratio for this problem was .77, which corresponds to a value of $F(Q)$ between $Q = 14$ and $Q = 15$. Because we round up, the optimal solution is $Q^* = 15$. Notice that this is exactly the same order quantity obtained using the normal approximation.

Extension to Include Starting Inventory

In the derivation of the newsvendor model, we assumed that the starting inventory at the beginning of the period was zero. Suppose now that the starting inventory is some value u and $u > 0$. The optimal policy for this case is a simple modification of the case $u = 0$. Note that this extension would not apply to newspapers, but would be appropriate for a product with a shelf life that exceeds one period.

Snapshot Application

USING INVENTORY MODELS TO MANAGE THE SEED-CORN SUPPLY CHAIN AT SYNGENTA

Each year farmers plant tens of thousands of acres of corn worldwide to meet the demands of a growing population. Companies such as Minnesota-based Syngenta Seeds supply seed to these farmers. In the United States alone, the market for corn seed is approximately $2.3 billion annually. Syngenta is one of eight firms that accounts for 73 percent of this market. Where do Syngenta and its competitors obtain this seed? The answer is that it is produced by growing corn and harvesting the seeds. Corn grown for the purpose of harvesting seed is known as seed-corn.

The problem of determining how much seed-corn to plant is complicated by several factors. One is that there are hundreds of different seed hybrids. Some hybrids do better in warmer, more humid climates, while others do better in cooler, dryer climates. The color, texture, sugar content, and so forth, of the corn produced by different hybrids varies as well. Farmers will not reuse a hybrid that yielded disappointing results. Hence, annual demand is hard to predict. In addition to facing uncertain demand, seed-corn producers also face uncertain yields. Their seed-corn plantings are subject to the same set of risks faced by all farmers: frost, draught, and heat spells.

Syngenta must decide each season how much seed-corn to plant. Since demand for the seeds is uncertain, the problem sounds like a straightforward application of the newsvendor model with uncertain demand and uncertain supply. However, Syngenta's decision problem has an additional feature that makes it more complicated than an ordinary newsvendor problem. Syngenta, along with many of its competitors, plants seed-corn in both northern and southern hemispheres. Since the hemispheric seasons run counter to each other, the plantings are done at different times of the year. In particular, the seed-corn is planted in the spring season in each hemisphere, so that the South American planting occurs about six months after the North American planting. This gives the company a second chance to increase production levels in South America to make up for shortfalls in North America, or decrease production levels in South America when there are surpluses in North America.

The problem of planning the size of the seed-corn planting was tackled by a team of researchers from the University of Iowa in collaboration with a vice president in charge of supply at Syngenta.[1] Using discrete approximations of the demand and yield distributions, they were able to formulate the planning problem as a linear program, so that it could be solved on a firmwide scale. A retrospective analysis showed that the company could have saved upwards of $5 million using the model. Also, the analysts were able to identify a systematic bias in the forecasts for seed generated by the firm that resulted in consistent overproduction. The mathematical model is now used to help guide the firm on its planting decisions each year.

[1] Jones, P. C.; Kegler, G.; Lowe, T. J.; and Traub, R. D. "Managing the Seed-Corn Supply Chain at Syngenta," *Interfaces* 33 (1), January–February 2003, pp. 80–90.

Consider the expected cost function $G(Q)$, pictured in Figure 5–3. If $u > 0$, it just means that we are starting at some point other than 0. We still want to be at Q^* after ordering, as that is still the lowest point on the cost curve. If $u < Q^*$, this is accomplished by ordering $Q^* - u$. If $u > Q^*$, we are past where we want to be on the curve. Ordering any additional inventory merely moves us up the cost curve, which results in higher costs. In this case it is optimal to simply not order.

Hence the optimal policy when there is a starting inventory of $u > 0$ is

Order $Q^* - u$ if $u < Q^*$.
Do not order if $u \geq Q^*$.

Note that Q^* should be interpreted as the order-up-to point rather than the order quantity when $u > 0$. It is also known as a target or base stock level.

Example 5.2 (continued) Let us suppose that in Example 5.2, Mac has received 6 copies of the *Journal* at the beginning of the week from another supplier. The optimal policy still calls for having 15 copies on hand after ordering, so now he would order the difference $15 - 6 = 9$ copies. (Set $Q^* = 15$ and $u = 6$ to get the order quantity of $Q^* - u = 9$.)

Extension to Multiple Planning Periods

The underlying assumption made in the derivation of the newsvendor model was that the item "perished" quickly and could not be used to satisfy demand in subsequent periods. In most industrial and retail environments, however, products are durable and inventory left at the end of a period can be stored and used to satisfy future demand.

This means that the ending inventory in any period becomes the starting inventory in the next period. Previously, we indicated how the optimal policy is modified when starting inventory is present. However, when the number of periods remaining exceeds one, the value of Q^* also must be modified. In particular, the interpretation of both c_o and c_u will be different. We consider only the case in which there are infinitely many periods remaining. The optimal value of the order-up-to point when a finite number of periods remain will fall between the one-period and the infinite-period solutions.

In our derivation and subsequent analysis of the EOQ formula in Chapter 4, we saw that the variable order cost c only entered into the optimization to determine the holding cost ($h = Ic$). In addition, we saw that all feasible operating policies incurred the same average annual cost of replenishment, λc. It turns out that essentially the same thing applies in the infinite horizon newsvendor problem. As long as excess demand is back-ordered, all feasible policies will just order the demand over any long period of time. Similarly, as long as excess demand is back-ordered, the number of units sold will just be equal to the demand over any long period of time. Hence, both c_u and c_o will be independent of both the proportional order cost c and the selling price of the item. Interpret c_u as the loss-of-goodwill cost and c_o as the holding cost in this case. That this is the correct interpretation of the underage and overage costs is established rigorously in Appendix 5–B.

Example 5.3

Let us return to Mac's newsstand, described in Examples 5.1 and 5.2. Suppose that Mac is considering how to replenish the inventory of a very popular paperback thesaurus that is ordered monthly. Copies of the thesaurus unsold at the end of a month are still kept on the shelves for future sales. Assume that customers who request copies of the thesaurus when they are out of stock will wait until the following month. Mac buys the thesaurus for $1.15 and sells it for $2.75. Mac estimates a loss-of-goodwill cost of 50 cents each time a demand for a thesaurus must be back-ordered. Monthly demand for the book is fairly closely approximated by a normal distribution with mean 18 and standard deviation 6. Mac uses a 20 percent annual interest rate to determine his holding cost. How many copies of the thesaurus should he purchase at the beginning of each month?

Solution

The overage cost in this case is just the cost of holding, which is $(1.15)(0.20)/12 = 0.0192$. The underage cost is just the loss-of-goodwill cost, which is assumed to be 50 cents. Hence, the critical ratio is $0.5/(0.5 + 0.0192) = .9630$. From Table A–1 at the back of this book, this corresponds to a z value of 1.79. The optimal value of the order-up-to point $Q^* = \sigma z + \mu = (6)(1.79) + 18 = 28.74 \approx 29$.

Example 5.3 (continued)

Assume that a local bookstore also stocks the thesaurus and that customers will purchase the thesaurus there if Mac is out of stock. In this case excess demands are lost rather than back-ordered. The order-up-to point will be different from that obtained assuming full back-ordering of demand. In Appendix 5–B we show that in the lost sales case the underage cost should be interpreted as the loss-of-goodwill cost plus the lost profit. The overage cost should still be interpreted as the holding cost only. Hence, the lost sales solution for this example gives $c_u = 0.5 + 1.6 = 2.1$. The critical ratio is $2.1/(2.1 + 0.0192) = .9909$, giving a z value of 2.36. The optimal value of Q in the lost sales case is $Q^* = \sigma z + \mu = (6)(2.36) + 18 = 32.16 \approx 32$.

Although the multiperiod solution appears to be sufficiently general to cover many types of real problems, it suffers from one serious limitation: there is no fixed cost of ordering. This means that the optimal policy, which is to order up to Q^*, requires that ordering take place in every period. In most real systems, however, there are fixed costs associated with ordering, and it is not optimal to place orders each period. Unfortunately, if we include a fixed charge for placing an order, it becomes extremely difficult to determine optimal operating policies. For this reason, we approach the problem of random demand when a fixed charge for ordering is present in a different way. We will assume that inventory levels are reviewed continuously and develop a generalization of the EOQ analysis presented in Chapter 4. This analysis is presented in Section 5.4.

Problems for Section 5.3

7. A newsvendor keeps careful records of the number of papers he sells each day and the various costs that are relevant to his decision regarding the optimal number of newspapers to purchase. For what reason might his results be inaccurate? What would he need to do in order to accurately measure the daily demand for newspapers?

8. Billy's Bakery bakes fresh bagels each morning. The daily demand for bagels is a random variable with a distribution estimated from prior experience given by

Number of Bagels Sold in One Day	Probability
0	.05
5	.10
10	.10
15	.20
20	.25
25	.15
30	.10
35	.05

The bagels cost Billy's 8 cents to make, and they are sold for 35 cents each. Bagels unsold at the end of the day are purchased by a nearby charity soup kitchen for 3 cents each.

   a. Based on the given discrete distribution, how many bagels should Billy's bake at the start of each day? (Your answer should be a multiple of 5.)

   b. If you were to approximate the discrete distribution with a normal distribution, would you expect the resulting solution to be close to the answer that you obtained in part (a)? Why or why not?

   c. Determine the optimal number of bagels to bake each day using a normal approximation. (Hint: You must compute the mean μ and the variance σ^2 of the demand from the given discrete distribution.)

9. The Crestview Printing Company prints a particularly popular Christmas card once a year and distributes the cards to stationery and gift shops throughout the United States. It costs Crestview 50 cents to print each card, and the company receives 65 cents for each card sold.

   Because the cards have the current year printed on them, those cards that are not sold are generally discarded. Based on past experience and forecasts of current buying patterns, the probability distribution of the number of cards to be sold nationwide for the next Christmas season is estimated to be

Quantity Sold	Probability
100,000–150,000	.10
150,001–200,000	.15
200,001–250,000	.25
250,001–300,000	.20
300,001–350,000	.15
350,001–400,000	.10
400,001–450,000	.05

Determine the number of cards that Crestview should print this year.

10. Happy Henry's car dealer sells an imported car called the EX123. Once every three months, a shipment of the cars is made to Happy Henry's. Emergency shipments can be made between these three-month intervals to resupply the cars when inventory falls short of demand. The emergency shipments require two weeks, and buyers are willing to wait this long for the cars, but will generally go elsewhere before the next three-month shipment is due.

From experience, it appears that the demand for the EX123 over a three-month interval is normally distributed with a mean of 60 and a variance of 36. The cost of holding an EX123 for one year is $500. Emergency shipments cost $250 per car over and above normal shipping costs.

   a. How many cars should Happy Henry's be purchasing every three months?

   b. Repeat the calculations, assuming that excess demands are back-ordered from one three-month period to the next. Assume a loss-of-goodwill cost of $100 for customers having to wait until the next three-month period and a cost of $50 per customer for bookkeeping expenses.

   c. Repeat the calculations, assuming that when Happy Henry's is out of stock of EX123s, the customer will purchase the car elsewhere. In this case, assume that the cars cost Henry an average of $10,000 and sell for an average of $13,500. Ignore loss-of-goodwill costs for this calculation.

11. Irwin's sells a particular model of fan, with most of the sales being made in the summer months. Irwin's makes a one-time purchase of the fans prior to each summer season at a cost of $40 each and sells each fan for $60. Any fans unsold at the end of the summer season are marked down to $29 and sold in a special fall sale. Virtually all marked-down fans are sold. The following is the number of sales of fans during the past 10 summers: 30, 50, 30, 60, 10, 40, 30, 30, 20, 40.

   a. Estimate the mean and the variance of the demand for fans each summer.

   b. Assume that the demand for fans each summer follows a normal distribution, with mean and variance given by what you obtained in part (*a*). Determine the optimal number of fans for Irwin's to buy prior to each summer season.

   c. Based on the observed 10 values of the prior demand, construct an empirical probability distribution of summer demand and determine the optimal number of fans for Irwin's to buy based on the empirical distribution.

   d. Based on your results for parts (*b*) and (*c*), would you say that the normal distribution provides an adequate approximation?

12. The buyer for Needless Markup, a famous "high end" department store, must decide on the quantity of a high-priced woman's handbag to procure in Italy for the following Christmas season. The unit cost of the handbag to the store is $28.50 and the handbag will sell for $150.00. Any handbags not sold by the end of the season are purchased by a discount firm for $20.00. In addition, the store accountants estimate that there is a cost of $0.40 for each dollar tied up in inventory, as this dollar invested elsewhere could have yielded a gross profit. Assume that this cost is attached to unsold bags only.

   a. Suppose that the sales of the bags are equally likely to be anywhere from 50 to 250 handbags during the season. Based on this, how many bags should the buyer purchase? (Hint: This means that the correct distribution of demand is uniform. You may solve this problem assuming either a discrete or a continuous uniform distribution.)

   b. A detailed analysis of past data shows that the number of bags sold is better described by a normal distribution, with mean 150 and standard deviation 20. Now what is the optimal number of bags to be purchased?

   c. The expected demand was the same in parts (a) and (b), but the optimal order quantities should have been different. What accounted for this difference?

5.4 LOT SIZE–REORDER POINT SYSTEMS

The form of the optimal solution for the simple EOQ model with a positive lead time analyzed in Chapter 4 is: When the level of on-hand inventory hits R, place an order for Q units. In that model the only independent decision variable was Q, the order quantity. The value of R was determined from Q, λ, and τ. In what follows, we also assume that the operating policy is of the (Q, R) form. However, when generalizing the EOQ analysis to allow for random demand, we treat Q and R as independent decision variables.

The multiperiod newsvendor model was unrealistic for two reasons: it did not include a setup cost for placing an order and it did not allow for a positive lead time. In most real systems, however, both a setup cost and a lead time are present. For these reasons, the kinds of models discussed in this section are used much more often in practice and, in fact, form the basis for the policies used in many commercial inventory systems.

Note that Q in this section is the amount ordered, whereas Q in Section 5.3 was the order-up-to point.

We make the following assumptions:

1. The system is continuous review. That is, demands are recorded as they occur, and the level of on-hand inventory is known at all times.
2. Demand is random and stationary. That means that although we cannot predict the value of demand, the *expected* value of demand over any time interval of fixed length is constant. Assume that the expected demand rate is λ units per year.
3. There is a fixed positive lead time τ for placing an order.
4. The following costs are assumed:

   Setup cost at $\$K$ per order.
   Holding cost at $\$h$ per unit held per year.
   Proportional order cost of $\$c$ per item.
   Stock-out cost of $\$p$ per unit of unsatisfied demand. This is also called the shortage cost or the penalty cost.

FIGURE 5–5
Changes in inventory over time for continuous-review (Q, R) system

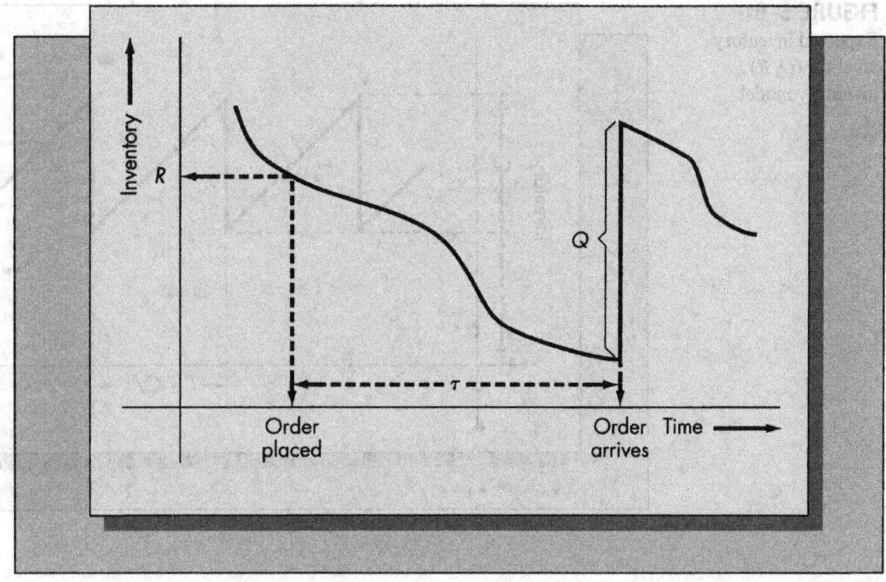

Describing Demand

In the newsvendor problem, the appropriate random variable is the demand during the period. One period is the amount of time required to effect a change in the on-hand inventory level. This is known as the response time of the system. In the context of our current problem, the response time is the reorder lead time τ. Hence, the random variable of interest is the demand during the lead time. We will assume that the demand during the lead time is a continuous random variable D with probability density function (or pdf) $f(x)$ and cumulative distribution function (or cdf) $F(x)$. Let $\mu = E(D)$ and $\sigma = \sqrt{\mathrm{var}(D)}$ be the mean and the standard deviation of demand during the lead time.

Decision Variables

There are two decision variables for this problem, Q and R, where Q is the lot size or order quantity and R is the reorder level in units of inventory.[2] Unlike the EOQ model, this problem treats Q and R as independent decision variables. The policy is implemented as follows: when the level of on-hand inventory reaches R, an order for Q units is placed that will arrive in τ units of time. The operation of this system is pictured in Figure 5–5.

Derivation of the Expected Cost Function

The analytical approach we will use to solve this problem is, in principle, the same as that used in the derivation of the newsvendor model. Namely, we will derive an expression for the expected average annual cost in terms of the decision variables (Q, R) and search for the optimal values of (Q, R) to minimize this cost.

---

[2] When lead times are very long, it may happen that an order should be placed again before a prior order arrives. In that case, the reorder decision variable R should be interpreted as the inventory position (on-hand plus on-order) when a reorder is placed, rather than the inventory level.

FIGURE 5–6
Expected inventory level for (Q, R) inventory model

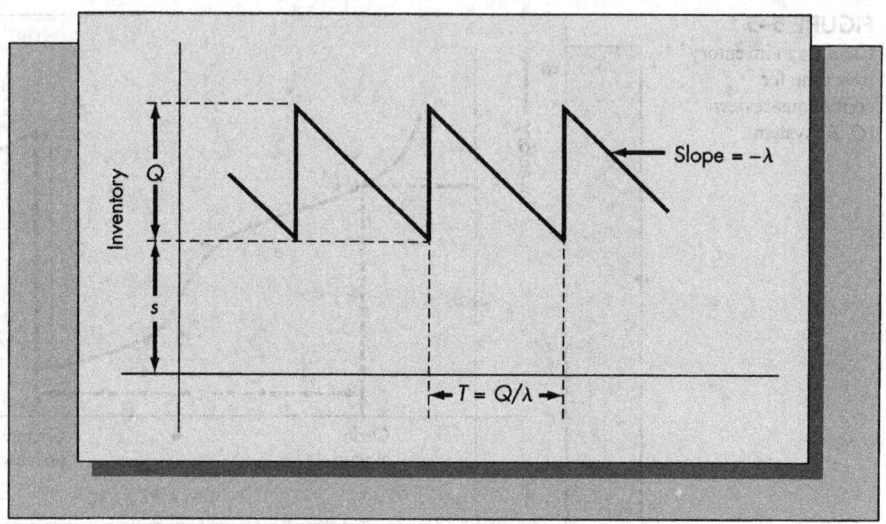

The Holding Cost

We assume that the mean rate of demand is λ units per year. The expected inventory level varies linearly between s and $Q + s$. We call s the safety stock; it is defined as the expected level of on-hand inventory just before an order arrives, and is given by the formula $s = R - \lambda\tau$. The expected inventory level curve appears in Figure 5–6.

We estimate the holding cost from the average of the expected inventory curve. The average of the function pictured in Figure 5–6 is $s + Q/2 = R - \lambda\tau + Q/2$. An important point to note here is that this computation is only an approximation. When computing the average inventory level, we include both the cases when inventory is positive and the cases when it is negative. However, the holding cost should *not* be charged against the inventory level when it is negative, so that we are underestimating the true value of expected holding cost. An exact expression for the true average inventory is quite complex and has been derived only for certain specific demand distributions. In most real systems, however, the proportion of time spent out of stock is generally small, so this approximation should be reasonably accurate.

Setup Cost

A cycle is defined as the time between the arrival of successive orders of size Q. Consistent with the notation used in Chapter 4, let T represent the expected cycle length. Because the setup cost is incurred exactly once each cycle, we need to obtain an expression for the average length of a cycle in order to accurately estimate the setup cost per unit of time.

There are a number of ways to derive an expression for the expected cycle length. From Figure 5–6, we see that the distance between successive arrivals of orders is Q/λ. Another argument is the following. The expected demand during T is clearly λT. However, because the number of units that are entering inventory each cycle is Q and there is conservation of units, the number of units demanded each cycle on average also must be Q. Setting $Q = \lambda T$ and solving for T gives the same result.

It follows, therefore, that the average setup cost incurred per unit time is $K/T = K\lambda/Q$.

Penalty Cost

From Figure 5–5 we see that the only portion of the cycle during which the system is exposed to shortages is between the time that an order is placed and the time that it arrives (the lead time). The number of units of excess demand is simply the amount by which the demand over the lead time, D, exceeds the reorder level, R. It follows that the expected number of shortages that occur in one cycle is given by the expression

$$E(\max(D - R, 0)) = \int_R^\infty (x - R)f(x)\, dx,$$

which is defined as $n(R)$.

Note that this is essentially the same expression that we derived for the expected number of stock-outs in the newsvendor model. As $n(R)$ represents the expected number of stock-outs incurred in a cycle, it follows that the expected number of stock-outs incurred per unit of time is $n(R)/T = \lambda n(R)/Q$.

Proportional Ordering Cost Component

Over a long period of time, the number of units that enter inventory and the number that leave inventory must be the same. This means that every feasible policy will necessarily order a number of units equal to the demand over any long interval of time. That is, every feasible policy, on average, will replenish inventory at the rate of demand. It follows that the expected proportional order cost per unit of time is λc. Because this term is independent of the decision variables Q and R, it does not affect the optimization. We will henceforth ignore it.

It should be pointed out, however, that the proportional order cost will generally be part of the optimization in an indirect way. The holding cost h is usually computed by multiplying an appropriate value of the annual interest rate I by the value of the item c. For convenience we use the symbol h to represent the holding cost, but keep in mind that it could also be written in the form Ic.

The Cost Function

Define $G(Q, R)$ as the expected average annual cost of holding, setup, and shortages. Combining the expressions derived for each of these terms gives

$$G(Q, R) = h(Q/2 + R - \lambda\tau) + K\lambda/Q + p\lambda n(R)/Q.$$

The objective is to choose Q and R to minimize $G(Q, R)$. We present the details of the optimization in Appendix 5–C. As shown, the optimal solution is to iteratively solve the two equations

$$Q = \sqrt{\frac{2\lambda[K + pn(R)]}{h}} \tag{1}$$

$$1 - F(R) = Qh/p\lambda. \tag{2}$$

The solution procedure requires iterating between Equations (1) and (2) until two successive values of Q and R are (essentially) the same. The procedure is started by using $Q_0 = $ EOQ (as defined in Chapter 4). One then finds R_0 from Equation (2). That value of R is used to compute $n(R)$, which is substituted into Equation (1) to find Q_1, which is then substituted into Equation (2) to find R_1, and so on. Convergence generally occurs within two or three iterations. When units are integral, the computations should be continued until successive values of both Q and R are within a single unit of their previous values. When units are continuous, a convergence requirement of less than one unit may be required depending upon the level of accuracy desired.

When the demand is normally distributed, $n(R)$ is computed by using the standardized loss function. The standardized loss function $L(z)$ is defined as

$$L(z) = \int_z^\infty (t-z)\phi(t)\, dt$$

where $\phi(t)$ is the standard normal density. If lead time demand is normal with mean μ and standard deviation σ, then it can be shown that

$$n(R) = \sigma L\left(\frac{R-\mu}{\sigma}\right) = \sigma L(z).$$

The standardized variate z is equal to $(R-\mu)/\sigma$. Calculations of the optimal policy are carried out using Table A–4 at the back of this book.[3]

Example 5.4

Harvey's Specialty Shop is a popular spot that specializes in international gourmet foods. One of the items that Harvey sells is a popular mustard that he purchases from an English company. The mustard costs Harvey $10 a jar and requires a six-month lead time for replenishment of stock. Harvey uses a 20 percent annual interest rate to compute holding costs and estimates that if a customer requests the mustard when he is out of stock, the loss-of-goodwill cost is $25 a jar. Bookkeeping expenses for placing an order amount to about $50. During the six-month replenishment lead time, Harvey estimates that he sells an average of 100 jars, but there is substantial variation from one six-month period to the next. He estimates that the standard deviation of demand during each six-month period is 25. Assume that demand is described by a normal distribution. How should Harvey control the replenishment of the mustard?

Solution

We wish to find the optimal values of the reorder point R and the lot size Q. In order to get the calculation started we need to find the EOQ. However, this requires knowledge of the annual rate of demand, which does not seem to be specified. But notice that if the order lead time is six months and the mean lead time demand is 100, that implies that the mean yearly demand is 200, giving a value of $\lambda = 200$. It follows that the EOQ = $\sqrt{2K\lambda/h} = \sqrt{(2)(50)(200)/(0.2)(10)} = 100$.

The next step is to find R_0 from Equation (2). Substituting $Q = 100$, we obtain

$$1 - F(R_0) = Q_0 h/p\lambda = (100)(2)/(25)(200) = .04.$$

From Table A–4 we find that the z value corresponding to a right tail of .04 is $z = 1.75$. Solving $R = \sigma z + \mu$ gives $R = (25)(1.75) + 100 = 144$. Furthermore, $z = 1.75$ results in $L(z) = 0.0162$. Hence, $n(R) = \sigma L(z) = (25)(0.0162) = 0.405$.

We can now find Q_1 from Equation (1):

$$Q_1 = \sqrt{\frac{(2)(200)}{2}[50 + (25)(0.405)]} = 110.$$

This value of Q is compared with the previous one, which is 100. They are not close enough to stop. Substituting $Q = 110$ into Equation (2) results in $1 - F(R_1) = (110)(2)/(25)(200) = .044$. Table A–4 now gives $z = 1.70$ and $L(z) = 0.0183$. Furthermore, $R_1 = (25)(1.70) + 100 = 143$. We

---

[3] Note that in rare cases Equations (1) and (2) may not be solvable. This can occur when the penalty cost p is small compared to the holding cost h. The result is either diverging values of Q and R or the right side of Equation (2) having a value exceeding 1 at some point in the calculation. In this case, the recommended solution is to set Q = EOQ and $R = R_0$ as long as the right side of Equation (2) is less than 1. This often leads to negative safety stock, discussed later in this chapter.

now obtain $n(R_1) = (25)(0.0183) = 0.4575$, and $Q_2 = \sqrt{(200)[50 + (25)(0.4575)]} = 110.85 \approx 111$. Substituting $Q_2 = 111$ into Equation (2) gives $1 - F(R_2) = .0444$, $z = 1.70$, and $R_2 = R_1 = 143$. Because both Q_2 and R_2 are within one unit of Q_1 and R_1, we may terminate computations.

We conclude that the optimal values of Q and R are $(Q, R) = (111, 143)$. Hence, each time that Harvey's inventory of this type of mustard hits 143 jars, he should place an order for 111 jars.

Example 5.4 (continued)

For the same example, determine the following:

1. Safety stock.
2. The average annual holding, setup, and penalty costs associated with the inventory control of the mustard.
3. The average time between placement of orders.
4. The proportion of order cycles in which no stock-outs occur.
5. The proportion of demands that are not met.

Solution

1. The safety stock is $s = R - \mu = 143 - 100 = 43$ jars.
2. We will compute average annual holding, setup, and penalty costs separately.

    The holding cost is $h[Q/2 + R - \mu] = 2[111/2 + 143 - 100] = \$197$ per year.
    The setup cost is $K\lambda/Q = (50)(200)/111 = \$90.09$ per year.
    The stock-out cost is $p\lambda n(R)/Q = (25)(200)(0.4575)/111 = \$20.61$ per year.

    Hence, the total average annual cost associated with the inventory control of the mustard, assuming an optimal control policy, is \$307.70 per year.

3. $T = Q/\lambda = 111/200 = 0.556$ year $= 6.7$ months.
4. Here we need to compute the probability that no stock-out occurs in the lead time. This is the same as the probability that the lead time demand does not exceed the reorder point. We have $P\{D \leq R\} = F(R) = 1 - .044 = .956$. We conclude that there will be no stock-outs in 95.6 percent of the order cycles.
5. The expected demand per cycle must be Q (see the argument in the derivation of the expected setup cost). The expected number of stock-outs per cycle is $n(R)$. Hence, the proportion of demands that stock out is $n(R)/Q = 0.4575/111 = .004$. Another way of stating this result is that on average 99.6 percent of the demands are satisfied as they occur.

It should be noted in ending this section that Equations (1) and (2) are derived under the assumption that all excess demand is back-ordered. That is, when an item is demanded that is not immediately available, the demand is filled at a later time. However, in many competitive situations, such as retailing, a more accurate assumption is that excess demand is lost. This case is known as *lost sales*. As long as the likelihood of being out of stock is relatively small, Equations (1) and (2) will give adequate solutions to both lost sales and back-order situations. If this is not the case, a slight modification to Equation (2) is required. The lost-sales version of Equation (2) is

$$1 - F(R) = Qh/(Qh + p\lambda). \qquad (2')$$

The effect of solving Equations (1) and (2') simultaneously rather than Equations (1) and (2) will be to increase the value of R slightly and decrease the value of Q slightly.

Inventory Level versus Inventory Position

An implicit assumption required in the analysis of (Q, R) policies was that each time an order of Q units arrives, it increases the inventory level to a value greater than the reorder point R. If this were not the case, one would never reach R, and one would never order again. This will happen if the demand during the lead time exceeds Q, which is certainly

Snapshot Application

INVENTORY MANAGEMENT SOFTWARE FOR THE SMALL BUSINESS

The software for PC-based inventory management continues to grow at an increasing rate. As personal computers have become more powerful, the inventory management needs of larger businesses can be handled by software designed to run on PCs. One example is an inventory system called inFlow, which can handle inventories stored at multiple locations. It is relatively expensive at $299. A less expensive alternative is Inventoria, which costs $79.99, which might be more appropriate for single location businesses, such as one-off retail stores. Another choice for small businesses is Small Business Inventory Control, which has the advantage of allowing the user to enter items into the system via barcode scanning. At $99, this package is also relatively inexpensive. Some other choices include iMagic Inventory, Inventory Power, Inventory Tracker Plus, Inventory Executive System, and many others. Each of the packages have certain advantages, including compatibility with other software systems, additional features such as financial functions, single versus multiple locations, industry specific applications, etc. Of course, inventory management modules are also available in large ERP systems, such as those sold by United States-based Oracle Corporation and German-based SAS.

An application that makes use of the most modern hardware and software is ShopKeep POS. ShopKeep is designed to run on the Apple iPad, and all of the records are stored in the cloud. This means that inventory data can be accessed from any iPad in the system at any time. One customer, The Bean, a small chain of coffee shops based in New York City, ported their inventory control function from a Windows-based system to ShopKeep, running on iPads and iPhones. The system gives them the opportunity to run reports from any iPad that's connected to the system. According to owner Ike Estavo, one of the most useful functions of ShopKeep is identifying the most profitable items per square foot of display space.

The personal computer has become ubiquitous since the first edition of this book was published in 1989. The huge growth in personal computers has been accompanied by an explosion in software choices for almost every conceivable application. Inventory control is no exception. A challenge for operations managers is to choose wisely among the multitude of applications, only a few of which are mentioned here. One must be able to pick the level of generality and complexity that's appropriate to the particular application. But no matter what software package is chosen, it is vitally important to understand the basic principles of inventory management discussed here. Hoping that the software will solve one's problem without really understanding the key elements of that problem is a big mistake.

Source: The information discussed here was obtained from the websites of the vendors mentioned.

---

possible. On the surface, this seems like a serious flaw in the approach, but it isn't. To avoid this problem, one bases the reorder decision on the inventory position rather than on the inventory level. The inventory position is defined as the total stock on hand plus on order. The inventory position varies from R to $R + Q$ as shown in Figure 5–7.

FIGURE 5–7
Inventory level versus inventory position

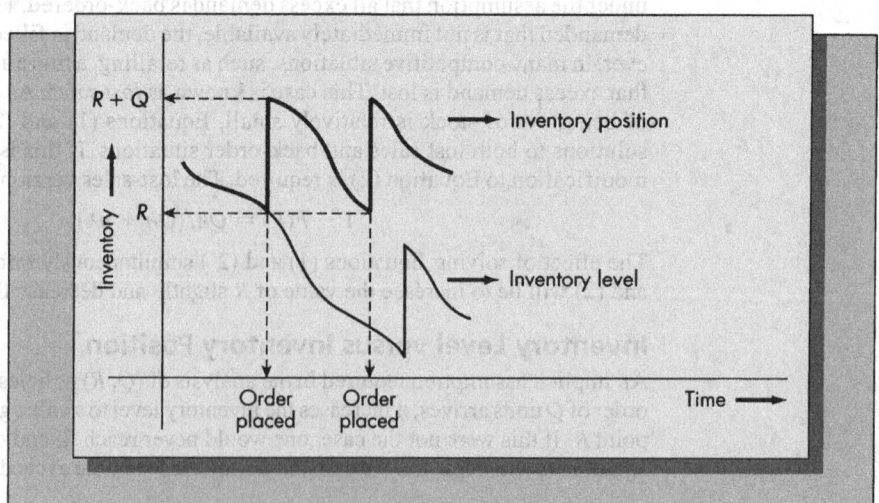

5.5 SERVICE LEVELS IN (Q, R) SYSTEMS

Although the inventory model described in Section 5.4 is quite realistic for describing many real systems, managers often have a difficult time determining an exact value for the stock-out cost p. In many cases, the stock-out cost includes intangible components such as loss of goodwill and potential delays to other parts of the system. A common substitute for a stock-out cost is a service level. Although there are a number of different definitions of service, it generally refers to the probability that a demand or a collection of demands is met. Service levels can be applied in both periodic review and (Q, R) systems. The application of service levels to periodic-review systems will be discussed in Section 5.6. Service levels for continuous-review systems are considered here.

Two types of service are considered, labeled Type 1 and Type 2, respectively.

Type 1 Service

In this case we specify the probability of not stocking out in the lead time. We will use the symbol α to represent this probability. As specification of α completely determines the value of R, the computation of R and Q can be decoupled. The computation of the optimal (Q, R) values subject to a Type 1 service constraint is very straightforward.

    a. Determine R to satisfy the equation $F(R) = \alpha$.
    b. Set $Q = \text{EOQ}$.

Interpret α as the proportion of cycles in which no stock-out occurs. A Type 1 service objective is appropriate when a shortage occurrence has the same consequence independent of its time or amount. One example would be where a production line is stopped whether 1 unit or 100 units are short. However, Type 1 service is not how service is interpreted in most applications. Usually when we say we would like to provide 95 percent service, we mean that we would like to be able to fill 95 percent of the demands when they occur, not fill all the demands in 95 percent of the order cycles. Also, as different items have different cycle lengths, this measure will not be consistent among different products, making the proper choice of α difficult.

Type 2 Service

Type 2 service measures the proportion of demands that are met from stock. We will use the symbol β to represent this proportion. As we saw in part 5 of Example 5.4, $n(R)/Q$ is the average fraction of demands that stock out each cycle. Hence, specification of β results in the constraint $n(R)/Q = 1 - \beta$.

This constraint is more complex than the one arising from Type 1 service, as it involves both Q and R. It turns out that although the EOQ is not optimal in this case, it usually gives pretty good results. If we use the EOQ to estimate the lot size, then we would find R to solve $n(R) = \text{EOQ}(1 - \beta)$.

Example 5.5   Consider again Harvey's Specialty Shop, described in Example 5.4. Harvey feels uncomfortable with the assumption that the stock-out cost is $25 and decides to use a service level criterion instead. Suppose that he chooses to use a 98 percent service objective.

1. *Type 1 service.* If we assume an α of .98, then we find R to solve $F(R) = 0.98$. From Table A–1 or A–4, we obtain $z = 2.05$. Setting $R = \sigma z + \mu$ gives $R = 151$.

2. *Type 2 service.* Here $\beta = 0.98$. We are required to solve the equation

$$n(R) = \text{EOQ}(1 - \beta),$$

which is equivalent to

$$L(z) = \text{EOQ}(1 - \beta)/\sigma.$$

Substituting EOQ = 100 and $\beta = .98$, we obtain

$$L(z) = (100)(0.02)/25 = 0.08.$$

From Table A-4 of the unit normal partial expectations, we obtain $z = 1.02$. Setting $R = \sigma z + \mu$ gives $R = 126$. Notice that the same values of α and β give *considerably* different values of R.

In order to understand more clearly the difference between these two measures of service, consider the following example. Suppose that we have tracked the demands and stock-outs over 10 consecutive order cycles with the following results:

Order Cycle	Demand	Stock-Outs
1	180	0
2	75	0
3	235	45
4	140	0
5	180	0
6	200	10
7	150	0
8	90	0
9	160	0
10	40	0

Based on a Type 1 measure of service, we find that the fraction of periods in which there is no stock-out is 8/10 = 80 percent. That is, the probability that all the demands are met in a single order cycle is 0.8, based on these observations. However, the Type 2 service provided here is considerably better. In this example, the total number of demands over the 10 periods is 1,450 (the sum of the numbers in the second column), and the total number of demands that result in a stock-out is 55. Hence, the number of satisfied demands is 1,450 − 55 = 1,395. The proportion of satisfied demands is 1,395/1,450 = .9621, or roughly 96 percent.

The term *fill rate* is often used to describe Type 2 service, and is generally what most managers mean by service. (The fill rate in this example is 96 percent.) We saw in the example that there is a significant difference between the proportion of cycles in which all demands are satisfied (Type 1 service) and the fill rate (Type 2 service). *Even though it is easier to determine the best operating policy satisfying a Type 1 service objective, this policy will not accurately approximate a Type 2 service objective and should not be used in place of it.*

Optimal (Q, R) Policies Subject to Type 2 Constraint

Using the EOQ value to estimate the lot size gives reasonably accurate results when using a fill rate constraint, but the EOQ value is only an approximation of the optimal lot size. A more accurate value of Q can be obtained as follows. Consider the pair of equations (1) and (2) we solved for the optimal values of Q and R when a stock-out cost was present. Solving for p in Equation (2) gives

$$p = Qh/[(1 - F(R))\lambda],$$

which now can be substituted for p in Equation (1), resulting in

$$Q = \sqrt{\frac{2\lambda\{K + Qhn(R)/[(1 - F(R))\lambda]\}}{h}},$$

which is a quadratic equation in Q. It can be shown that the positive root of this equation is

$$Q = \frac{n(R)}{1 - F(R)} + \sqrt{\frac{2K\lambda}{h} + \left(\frac{n(R)}{1 - F(R)}\right)^2} \qquad (3)$$

Equation (3) will be called the SOQ formula (for service level order quantity).[4] This equation is solved simultaneously with

$$n(R) = (1 - \beta)Q \qquad (4)$$

to obtain optimal values of (Q, R) satisfying a Type 2 service constraint.

The reader should note that the version of Equation (4) used in the calculations is in terms of the standardized variate z and is given by

$$L(z) = (1 - \beta)Q/\sigma.$$

The solution procedure is essentially the same as that required to solve Equations (1) and (2) simultaneously. Start with $Q_0 =$ EOQ, find R_0 from (4), use R_0 in (3) to find Q_1, and so on, and stop when two successive values of Q and R are sufficiently close (within one unit is sufficient for most problems).

Example 5.5 (continued)

Returning to Example 5.5, $Q_0 = 100$ and $R_0 = 126$. Furthermore, $n(R_0) = (0.02)(100) = 2$. Using $z = 1.02$ gives $1 - F(R_0) = 0.154$. Continuing with the calculations,

$$Q_1 = \frac{2}{0.154} + \sqrt{(100)^2 + \left(\frac{2}{0.154}\right)^2}$$

$$= 114.$$

Solving Equation (4) gives $n(R_1) = (114)(0.02)$, which is equivalent to

$$L(z) = (114)(0.02)/25 = 0.0912.$$

From Table A–4, $z = 0.95$, so that

$$1 - F(R_1) = 0.171$$

and

$$R_1 = \sigma z + \mu = 124.$$

Carrying the computation one more step gives $Q_2 = 114$ and $R_2 = 124$. As both Q and R are within one unit of their previous values, we terminate computations. Hence, we conclude that the optimal values of Q and R satisfying a 98 percent fill rate constraint are $(Q, R) = (114, 124)$.

Consider the cost error resulting from the EOQ substituted for the SOQ. In order to compare these policies, we compute the average annual holding and setup costs (notice that there is no stock-out cost) for the policies $(Q, R) = (100, 126)$ and $(Q, R) = (114, 124)$.

---

[4] The SOQ formula also could have been derived by more conventional Lagrange multiplier techniques. We include this derivation to demonstrate the relationship between the fill rate objective and the stock-out cost model.

Recall the formulas for average annual holding and setup costs.

$$\text{Holding cost} = h(Q/2 + R - \mu).$$
$$\text{Setup cost} = K\lambda/Q.$$

For (100, 126):

$$\left.\begin{array}{l}\text{Holding cost} = 2(100/2 + 126 - 100) = \$152\\ \text{Setup cost} = (50)(200)/100 \qquad\qquad\ = \$100\end{array}\right\} \text{Total} = \$252$$

For (114, 124):

$$\left.\begin{array}{l}\text{Holding cost} = 2(114/2 + 124 - 100) = \$162\\ \text{Setup cost} = (50)(200)/114 \qquad\qquad\ = \$88\end{array}\right\} \text{Total} = \$250$$

We see that the EOQ approximation gives costs close to the optimal in this case.

Imputed Shortage Cost

Consider the solutions that we obtained for (Q, R) in Example 5.5 when we used a service level criterion rather than a shortage cost. For a Type 2 service of $\beta = 0.98$ we obtained the solution (114, 124). Although no shortage cost was specified, this solution clearly corresponds to *some* value of p. That is, there is some value of p such that the policy (114, 124) satisfies Equations (1) and (2). This particular value of p is known as the imputed shortage cost.

The imputed shortage cost is easy to find. One solves for p in Equation (2) to obtain $p = Qh/[(1 - F(R))\lambda]$. The imputed shortage cost is a useful way to determine whether the value chosen for the service level is appropriate.

Example 5.5 (continued)

Consider again Harvey's Specialty Shop. Using a value of $\alpha = .98$ (Type 1 service), we obtained the policy (100, 151). The imputed shortage cost is $p = (100)(2)/[(0.02)(200)] = \$50$.

Using a value of $\beta = 0.98$ (Type 2 service) we obtained the policy (114, 124). In this case the imputed cost of shortage is $p = (114)(2)/[(0.171)(200)] = \$6.67$.

Scaling of Lead Time Demand

In all previous examples the demand during the lead time was given. However, in most applications demand would be forecast on a periodic basis, such as monthly. In such cases one would need to convert the demand distribution to correspond to the lead time.

Assume that demands follow a normal distribution. Because sums of independent normal random variables are also normally distributed, the form of the distribution of lead time demand is normal. Hence, all that remains is to determine the mean and the standard deviation. Let the periodic demand have mean λ and standard deviation ν, and let τ be the lead time in periods. As both the means and the *variances* (not standard deviations) are additive, the mean demand during lead time is $\mu = \lambda\tau$ and the variance of demand during lead time is $\nu^2\tau$. Hence, the standard deviation of demand during lead time is $\sigma = \nu\sqrt{\tau}$ (although the square root may not always be appropriate).[5]

---

[5] Often in practice it turns out that there is more variation in the demand process than is described by a pure normal distribution. For that reason the standard deviation of demand is generally expressed in the form $\nu\tau^q$ where the correct value of q, generally between 0.5 and 1, must be determined for each item or group of items by an analysis of historical data.

Example 5.6

Weekly demand for a certain type of automotive spark plug in a local repair shop is normally distributed with mean 34 and standard deviation 12. Procurement lead time is six weeks. Determine the lead time demand distribution.

Solution

The demand over the lead time is also normally distributed with mean $(34)(6) = 204$ and standard deviation $(12)\sqrt{6} = 29.39$. These would be the values of μ and σ that one would use for all remaining calculations.

Estimating Sigma When Inventory Control and Forecasting Are Linked

Thus far in this chapter we have assumed that the distribution of demand over the lead time is known. In practice, one assumes a *form* for the distribution, but its parameters must be estimated from real data. Assuming a normal distribution for lead time demand (which is the most common assumption), one needs to estimate the mean and the standard deviation. When a complete history of past data is available, the standard statistical estimates for the mean and the standard deviation (i.e., those suggested in Section 5.1) are fine. However, most forecasting schemes do *not* use all past data. Moving averages use only the past N data values and exponential smoothing places declining weights on past data.

In these cases, it is unclear exactly what are the right estimators for the mean and the standard deviation of demand. This issue was discussed in Section 2.13. The best estimate of the mean is simply the forecast of demand for the next period. For the variance, one should use the estimator for the variance of forecast error. The rationale for this is rarely understood. The variance of forecast error and the variance of demand are *not* the same thing. This was established rigorously in Appendix 2–A.

Why is it appropriate to use the standard deviation of forecast error to estimate σ? The reason is that it is the forecast that we are using to estimate demand. Safety stock is held to protect against errors in forecasting demand. In general, the variance of forecast error will be higher than the variance of demand. This is the result of the additional sampling error introduced by a forecasting scheme that uses only a portion of past data.[6]

R. G. Brown (1959) was apparently the first to recommend using the standard deviation of forecast error in safety stock calculations. The method he recommended, which is still in widespread use today, is to track the MAD (mean absolute deviation) of forecast error using the formula

$$\text{MAD}_t = \alpha \, \text{MAD}_{t-1} + (1 - \alpha)|F_t - D_t|$$

where F_t is the forecast of demand at time t and D_t is the actual observed demand at time t. The estimator for the standard deviation of forecast error at time t is $1.25 \, \text{MAD}_t$. While this method is very popular in commercial inventory control systems, apparently few realize that by using this approach they are estimating not demand variance but forecast error variance, and that these are not the same quantities.

---

[6] In cases where the underlying demand process is nonstationary, that is, where there is trend or seasonality, the variance of demand due to *systematic* changes could be higher than the variance of forecast error. All of our analysis assumes stationary (constant mean and variance) demand patterns, however.

*Lead Time Variability

Thus far, we have assumed that the lead time τ is a known constant. However, lead time uncertainty is common in practice. For example, the time required to transport commodities, such as oil, that are shipped by sea depends upon weather conditions. In general, it is very difficult to incorporate the variability of lead time into the calculation of optimal inventory policies. The problem is that if we assume that successive lead times are independent random variables, then it is possible for lead times to cross; that is, two successive orders would not necessarily be received in the same sequence that they were placed.

Order crossing is unlikely when a single supplier is used. If we are willing to make the simultaneous assumptions that orders do not cross and that successive lead times are independent, the variability of lead time can be easily incorporated into the analysis. Suppose that the lead time τ is a random variable with mean μ_τ and variance σ_τ^2. Furthermore, suppose that demand in any time t has mean λt and variance $\nu^2 t$. Then it can be shown that the demand during lead time has mean and variance[7]

$$\mu = \lambda \mu_\tau,$$
$$\sigma^2 = \mu_\tau \nu^2 + \lambda^2 \sigma_\tau^2.$$

Example 5.7   Harvey Gold, the owner of Harvey's Specialty Shop, orders an unusual olive from the island of Santorini, off the Greek coast. Over the years, Harvey has noticed considerable variability in the time it takes to receive orders of these olives. On average, the order lead time is four months and the standard deviation is six weeks (1.5 months). Monthly demand for the olives is normally distributed with mean 15 (jars) and standard deviation 6.

Setting $\mu_\tau = 4$, $\sigma_\tau = 1.5$, $\lambda = 15$, and $\nu = 6$, we obtain

$$\mu = \mu_\tau \lambda = (4)(15) = 60,$$
$$\sigma^2 = \mu_\tau \nu^2 + \lambda^2 \sigma_\tau^2 = (4)(36) + (225)(2.25) = 650.25.$$

One would proceed with the calculations of optimal inventory policies using $\mu = 60$ and $\sigma^2 = 650.25$ as the mean and the variance of lead time demand.

Calculations in Excel

The standardized loss function, $L(z)$, can be computed in Excel. To do so, write $L(z)$ in the following way:

$$L(z) = \int_z^\infty (t-z)\phi(t)\,dt = \int_z^\infty t\phi(t)\,dt - z(1-\Phi(z)) = \phi(z) - z(1-\Phi(z)).$$

The first equality results from the definition of the cumulative distribution function, and the second equality is a consequence of a well-known property of the standard normal distribution (see, for example, Hadley and Whitin, 1963, p. 444). To program this formula into Excel, use the definition of the standard normal density function, which is

$$\phi(z) = \frac{1}{\sqrt{2\pi}} \exp(-0.5z^2),$$

and the built-in Excel function *normsdist( )*, which returns the value of $\Phi(\ )$. In this way one could compute (Q, R) policies within the spreadsheet. Alternatively, one could build a table of $L(z)$, which can then be embedded into a search routine.

[7] Hadley and Whitin (1963), p. 153.

280 Chapter Five *Inventory Control Subject to Uncertain Demand*

Negative Safety Stock

When the shortage cost or service level is relatively low, it is possible for a negative safety stock situation to arise. Recall that safety stock is the expected inventory on hand at the arrival of an order. If the safety stock is negative, there would be a backorder situation in more than 50 percent of the order cycles (that is, the Type 1 service would be under 50 percent). When this occurs, the optimal z value is negative, and the optimal $L(z)$ value would exceed $L(0) = .3989$. We illustrate with an example.

Example 5.8   Consider once again Harvey's Specialty Shop from Examples 5.4 to 5.7. Harvey sells a high-end espresso machine, an expensive and bulky item. For this reason, Harvey attaches a very high holding cost of $50 per year to each machine. Harvey sells about 20 of these yearly, and estimates the variance of yearly demand to be 50. Annual demand follows the normal distribution. Since customers are willing to wait for the machine when he is out of stock, the shortage penalty is low. He estimates it to be $25 per unit. Order lead time is six months. The fixed cost of ordering is $80. Assume that the lot size used for reordering is the EOQ value. Determine the following:

1. Optimal reorder level
2. Safety stock
3. Resulting Type 1 service level
4. Resulting Type 2 service level

Solution

1. We have that $K = \$80$, $p = \$25$, $h = \$50$, and $\lambda = 20$. Scaling lead time demand to 0.5 year, we obtain $\mu = 10$ and $\sigma \sqrt{(50)(0.5)} = 5$. The reader can check that the EOQ rounded to the nearest integer is $Q = 8$. The equation for determining R_0 is

$$1 - F(R_0) = \frac{Q_0 h}{p\lambda} = \frac{(8)(50)}{(25)(20)} = 0.8.$$

Since $1 - F(R_0)$ exceeds 0.5, the resulting z value is negative. In this case $z = -0.84$, $L(z) = 0.9520$, and $R_0 = \sigma z + \mu = (5)(-.84) + 10 = 5.8$, which we round to 6. Hence, the optimal solution based on the EOQ is to order eight units when the on-hand inventory falls to six units.

2. The safety stock is $S = R - \mu = 6 - 10 = -4$.
3. The Type 1 service level is $\alpha = F(R) = .20$ (or 20 percent).
4. The Type 2 service level is $\beta = 1 - n(R)/Q = 1 - \sigma L(z)/Q = 1 - (5)(.9520)/8 = 0.405$ (or 41 percent).

Note: Had we tried to solve this problem for the optimal (Q, R) iteratively using Equations (1) and (2), the equations would have diverged and not yielded a solution. This is a result of having a very low shortage cost compared to the holding cost. Furthermore, if Q were larger, the problem could be unsolvable. For example, if one assumes the setup cost $K = 150$, then EOQ = 11 and $1 - F(R_0) = Q_0 h/p\lambda = (11)(50)/(25)(20) = 1.1$, which is obviously not solvable. Such circumstances are very rare in practice, but, as we see from this example, it is possible for the model to fail. This is a consequence of the fact that the model is not exact. Exact (Q, R) models are beyond the scope of this book, and are known only for certain demand distributions.

Problems for Sections 5.4 and 5.5

13. An automotive warehouse stocks a variety of parts that are sold at neighborhood stores. One particular part, a popular brand of oil filter, is purchased by the warehouse for $1.50 each. It is estimated that the cost of order processing and

receipt is $100 per order. The company uses an inventory carrying charge based on a 28 percent annual interest rate.

The monthly demand for the filter follows a normal distribution with mean 280 and standard deviation 77. Order lead time is assumed to be five months.

Assume that if a filter is demanded when the warehouse is out of stock, then the demand is back-ordered, and the cost assessed for each back-ordered demand is $12.80. Determine the following quantities:

a. The optimal values of the order quantity and the reorder level.

b. The average annual cost of holding, setup, and stock-out associated with this item assuming that an optimal policy is used.

c. Evaluate the cost of uncertainty for this process. That is, compare the average annual cost you obtained in part (*b*) with the average annual cost that would be incurred if the lead time demand had zero variance.

14. Weiss's paint store uses a (Q, R) inventory system to control its stock levels. For a particularly popular white latex paint, historical data show that the distribution of monthly demand is approximately normal, with mean 28 and standard deviation 8. Replenishment lead time for this paint is about 14 weeks. Each can of paint costs the store $6. Although excess demands are back-ordered, the store owner estimates that unfilled demands cost about $10 each in bookkeeping and loss-of-goodwill costs. Fixed costs of replenishment are $15 per order, and holding costs are based on a 30 percent annual rate of interest.

a. What are the optimal lot sizes and reorder points for this brand of paint?

b. What is the optimal safety stock for this paint?

15. After taking a production seminar, Al Weiss, the owner of Weiss's paint store mentioned in Problem 14, decides that his stock-out cost of $10 may not be very accurate and switches to a service level model. He decides to set his lot size by the EOQ formula and determines his reorder point so that there is *no stock-out* in 90 percent of the order cycles.

a. Find the resulting (Q, R) values.

b. Suppose that, unfortunately, he really wanted to satisfy 90 percent of his demands (that is, achieve a 90 percent fill rate). What fill rate did he actually achieve from the policy determined in part (*a*)?

16. Suppose that in Problem 13 the stock-out cost is replaced with a Type 1 service objective of 95 percent. Find the optimal values of (Q, R) in this case.

17. Suppose that in Problem 13 a Type 2 service objective of 95 percent is substituted for the stock-out cost of $12.80. Find the resulting values of Q and R. Also, what is the imputed cost of shortage for this case?

18. Suppose that the warehouse mistakenly used a Type 1 service objective when it really meant to use a Type 2 service objective (see Problems 16 and 17). What is the additional holding cost being incurred each year for this item because of this mistake?

19. Disk Drives Limited (DDL) produces a line of internal Winchester disks for microcomputers. The drives use a 3.5-inch platter that DDL purchases from an outside supplier. Demand data and sales forecasts indicate that the weekly demand for the platters seems to be closely approximated by a normal distribution with mean 38 and variance 130. The platters require a three-week lead time for receipt. DDL has been using a 40 percent annual interest charge to compute holding costs.

The platters cost $18.80 each, order cost is $75.00 per order, and the company is currently using a stock-out cost of $400.00 per platter. (Because the industry is so competitive, stock-outs are very costly.)

a. Because of a prior contractual agreement with the supplier, DDL must purchase the platters in lots of 500. What is the reorder point that it should be using in this case?

b. When DDL renegotiates its contract with the supplier, what lot size should it write into the agreement?

c. How much of a penalty in terms of setup, holding, and stock-out cost is DDL paying for contracting to buy too large a lot?

d. DDL's president is uncomfortable with the $400 stock-out cost and decides to substitute a 99 percent fill rate criterion. If DDL used a lot size equal to the EOQ, what would its reorder point be in this case? Also, find the imputed cost of shortage.

20. Bobbi's Restaurant in Boise, Idaho, is a popular place for weekend brunch. The restaurant serves real maple syrup with french toast and pancakes. Bobbi buys the maple syrup from a company in Maine that requires three weeks for delivery. The syrup costs Bobbi $4 a bottle and may be purchased in any quantity. Fixed costs of ordering amount to about $75 for bookkeeping expenses, and holding costs are based on a 20 percent annual rate. Bobbi estimates that the loss of customer goodwill for not being able to serve the syrup when requested amounts to $25. Based on past experience, the weekly demand for the syrup is normal with mean 12 and variance 16 (in bottles). For the purposes of your calculations, you may assume that there are 52 weeks in a year and that all excess demand is back-ordered.

a. How large an order should Bobbi be placing with her supplier for the maple syrup, and when should those orders be placed?

b. What level of Type 1 service is being provided by the policy you found in part (a)?

c. What level of Type 2 service is being provided by the policy you found in part (a)?

d. What policy should Bobbi use if the stock-out cost is replaced with a Type 1 service objective of 95 percent?

e. What policy should Bobbi use if the stock-out cost is replaced with a Type 2 service objective of 95 percent? (You may assume an EOQ lot size.)

f. Suppose that Bobbi's supplier requires a minimum order size of 500 bottles. Find the reorder level that Bobbi should use if she wishes to satisfy 99 percent of her customer demands for the syrup.

5.6 ADDITIONAL DISCUSSION OF PERIODIC-REVIEW SYSTEMS

(s, S) Policies

In our analysis of the newsvendor problem, we noted that a severe limitation of the model from a practical viewpoint is that there is no setup cost included in the formulation. The (Q, R) model treated in the preceding sections included an order setup cost, but assumed that the inventory levels were reviewed continuously; that is, known at all times. How should the system be managed when there is a setup cost for ordering, but inventory levels are known only at discrete points in time?

The difficulty that arises from trying to implement a continuous-review solution in a periodic-review environment is that the inventory level is likely to overshoot the reorder point R during a period, making it impossible to place an order the instant the inventory reaches R. To overcome this problem, the operating policy is modified slightly. Define two numbers, s and S, to be used as follows: When the level of on-hand inventory is *less than or equal to* s, an order for the difference between the inventory and S is placed. If u is the starting inventory in any period, then the (s, S) policy is

If $u \leq s$, order $S - u$.
If $u > s$, do not order.

Determining optimal values of (s, S) is extremely difficult, and for that reason few real operating systems use optimal (s, S) values. Several approximations have been suggested. One such approximation is to compute a (Q, R) policy using the methods described earlier, and set $s = R$ and $S = R + Q$. This approximation will give reasonable results in many cases, and is probably the most commonly used. The reader interested in a comprehensive comparison of several approximate (s, S) policies should refer to Porteus (1985).

*Service Levels in Periodic-Review Systems

Service levels also may be used when inventory levels are reviewed periodically. Consider first a Type 1 service objective. That is, we wish to find the order-up-to point Q so that all the demand is satisfied in a given percentage of the periods. Suppose that the value of Type 1 service is α. Then Q should solve the equation

$$F(Q) = \alpha.$$

This follows because $F(Q)$ is the probability that the demand during the period does not exceed Q. Notice that one simply substitutes α for the critical ratio in the newsvendor model. To find Q to satisfy a Type 2 service objective of β, it is necessary to obtain an expression for the fraction of demands that stock out each period. Using essentially the same notation as that used for (Q, R) systems, define

$$n(Q) = \int_Q^\infty (x - Q)f(x)\,dx.$$

Note that $n(Q)$, which represents the expected number of demands that stock out at the end of the period, is the same as the term multiplying c_u in the expression for the expected cost function for the newsvendor model discussed in Section 5.3. As the demand per period is μ, it follows that the proportion of demands that stock out each period is $n(Q)/\mu$. Hence, the value of Q that meets a fill rate objective of β solves

$$n(Q) = (1 - \beta)\mu.$$

The specification of either a Type 1 or Type 2 service objective completely determines the order quantity, independent of the cost parameters.

Example 5.9 Mac, the owner of the newsstand described in Example 5.1, wishes to use a Type 1 service level of 90 percent to control his replenishment of *The Computer Journal*. The z value corresponding to the 90th percentile of the unit normal is $z = 1.28$. Hence,

$$Q^* = \sigma z + \mu = (4.74)(1.28) + 11.73 = 17.8 \approx 18.$$

Using a Type 2 service of 90 percent, we obtain

$$n(Q) = (1 - \beta)\mu = (0.1)(11.73) = 1.173.$$

It follows that $L(z) = n(Q)/\sigma = 1.173/4.74 = 0.2475$. From Table A–4 at the back of this book, we find

$$z \approx 0.35;$$

then

$$Q^* = \sigma z + \mu = (4.74)(0.35) + 11.73 = 13.4 \approx 13.$$

As with (Q, R) models, notice the striking difference between the resulting values of Q^* for the same levels of Type 1 and Type 2 service.

Fixed Order Size Model

If a positive order lead time is included, only a slight modification of these equations is required. In particular, the response time of the system is now the order lead time plus one period. Hence, we would now use the distribution of demand over $\tau + T$, where T is the time between inventory reviews.

This periodic review service level model is very useful in retail settings, in particular. It is common in retailing to place orders at fixed points in time to take advantage of bundling multiple orders together.

Example 5.10 Stroheim's is a dry goods store located in downtown Milwaukee, Wisconsin. Stroheim's places orders weekly with their suppliers for all of their reorders. The lead time for men's briefs is 4 days. Stroheim's uses a 95 percent service level. Assuming a Type 1 service, what is the order up to level for the briefs? Assume demands for briefs are uncertain with daily mean demand of 20 and daily standard deviation of 12.

Solution The total response time (review time plus lead time) is $7 + 4 = 11$ days. No matter what the form of the daily demand distribution, the Central Limit Theorem indicates that the demand over 11 days should be close to normal. The parameters are $\mu = (11)(20) = 220$ and $\sigma = 12\sqrt{11} = 39.80$. Hence it follows that for a type 1 service objective of 95 percent, the order-up-to-point should be $Q = \sigma z + \mu = (39.80)(1.645) + 220 = 286$.

If Stroheim's was interested in a Type 2 service objective, the z value would be lower, and the corresponding order up to point would be lower as well. In particular, $n(Q) = (1 - \beta)\mu = (.05)(220) = 11$, and $L(z) = n(Q)/\sigma = 11/39.80 = .2764$, which gives a z value of 0.27 and a corresponding order up to level of 231.

Problems for Section 5.6

21. Consider the Crestview Printing Company mentioned in Problem 9. Suppose that Crestview wishes to produce enough cards to satisfy all Christmas demand with probability 90 percent. How many cards should they print? Suppose the probability is 97 percent. What would you recommend in this case? (Your answer will depend upon the assumption you make concerning the shape of the cumulative distribution function.)

22. Consider Happy Henry's car dealer described in Problem 10.

    a. How many EX123s should Happy Henry's purchase to satisfy all the demand over a three-month interval with probability .95?

    b. How many cars should be purchased if the goal is to satisfy 95 percent of the demands?

Snapshot Application

TROPICANA USES SOPHISTICATED MODELING FOR INVENTORY MANAGEMENT

Tropicana, based in Bradenton, Florida, is one of the world's largest suppliers of citrus-based juice products. The company was founded by an Italian immigrant, Anthony Rossi, in 1947, and was acquired by PepsiCo in 1998. From its production facilities in Florida, Tropicana makes daily rail shipments to its regional distribution centers (DCs).

The focus of this application is the largest DC located in Jersey City, New Jersey, that services the northeast United States and Canada. Shipments from Bradenton to Jersey City require four days: one day for loading, two days in transit, and one day for unloading. This is the order lead time as seen from the DC. Lead time variability is not considered to be a significant issue.

Based on a statistical analysis of past data, Tropicana planners have determined that daily demands on the DC are closely approximated by a normal distribution for each of their products. Product classes are assumed to be independent.

Trains are sent from Florida five times per week; arrivals coincide with each business day at the Jersey City DC. Demand data and inventory levels are reviewed very frequently, a reorder point R triggers replenishment, and lot size Q is defined by the user. Hence, they operate a standard (Q, R) continuous-review system with a positive lead time. The state variable is the inventory position defined as the total amount of stock on hand at, and in transit to, the DC.

Let μ_D and σ_D be the mean and standard deviation of daily demand for a particular product line. According to the theory outlined in this chapter, the mean and standard deviation of demand over the four-day lead time should be

$$\mu = \mu_D \tau = 4\mu_D,$$
$$\sigma = \sigma_D \sqrt{\tau} = 2\sigma_D.$$

However, analysis of Tropicana data showed that the standard deviation of lead time demand is closer to $\sigma_D \tau^{0.7} = 2.64 \sigma_D$.

The firm's objective is to maintain a 99.5 percent Type 2 service level at the DC. Values of (Q, R) are computed using the methodology of this chapter. Planners check the inventory on hand and in transit, and place an order equal to the EOQ, when this value falls below the reorder level, R. This analysis is carried out for a wide range of the company's products and individually determined for each regional DC.

Source: Based on joint work between the author and Tim Rowell of Tropicana.

23. For the problem of controlling the inventory of white latex paint at Weiss's paint store, described in Problem 14, suppose that the paint is reordered on a monthly basis rather than on a continuous basis.

   a. Using the (Q, R) solution you obtained in part (a) of Problem 14, determine appropriate values of (s, S).
   b. Suppose that the demands during the months of January to June were

Month	Demand	Month	Demand
January	37	April	31
February	33	May	14
March	26	June	40

   If the starting inventory in January was 26 cans of paint, determine the number of units of paint ordered in each of the months January to June following the (s, S) policy you found in part (a).

5.7 MULTIPRODUCT SYSTEMS

ABC Analysis

One issue that we have not discussed is the cost of implementing an inventory control system and the trade-offs between the cost of controlling the system and the potential benefits that accrue from that control. In multiproduct inventory systems, not all products are equally profitable. Control costs may be justified in some cases and not in others. For example, spending $200 annually to monitor an item that contributes only $100 a year to profits is clearly not economical.

For this reason, it is important to differentiate profitable from unprofitable items. To do so, we borrow a concept from economics. The economist Vilfredo Pareto, who studied the distribution of wealth in the 19th century, noted that a large portion of the wealth was owned by a small segment of the population. This *Pareto effect* also applies to inventory systems: a large portion of the total dollar volume of sales is often accounted for by a small number of inventory items. Assume that items are ranked in decreasing order of the dollar value of annual sales. The *cumulative* value of sales generally results in a curve much like the one pictured in Figure 5–8.

Typically, the top 20 percent of the items account for about 80 percent of the annual dollar volume of sales, the next 30 percent of the items for the next 15 percent of sales, and the remaining 50 percent for the last 5 percent of dollar volume. These figures are

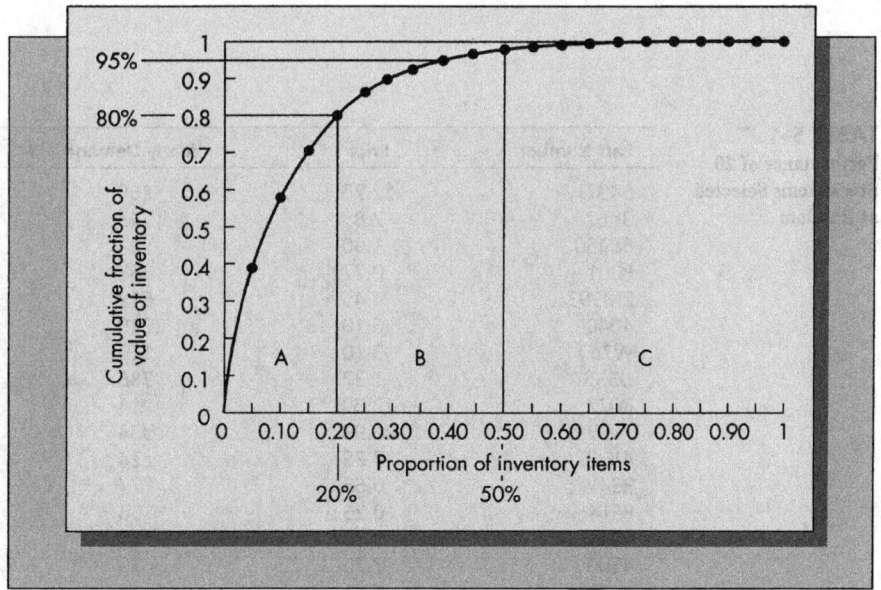

FIGURE 5–8
Pareto curve: Distribution of inventory by value

only approximate and will vary slightly from one system to another. The three item groups are labeled A, B, and C, respectively. When a finer distinction is needed, four or five categories could be used. Even when using only three categories, the percentages used in defining A, B, and C items could be different from the 80 percent, 15 percent, and 5 percent recommended.

Because A items account for the lion's share of the yearly revenue, these items should be watched most closely. Inventory levels for A items should be monitored continuously. More sophisticated forecasting procedures might be used and more care would be taken in the estimation of the various cost parameters required in calculating operating policies. For B items inventories could be reviewed periodically, items could be ordered in groups rather than individually, and somewhat less sophisticated forecasting methods could be used. The minimum degree of control would be applied to C items. For very inexpensive C items with moderate levels of demand, large lot sizes are recommended to minimize the frequency that these items are ordered. For expensive C items with very low demand, the best policy is generally not to hold any inventory. One would simply order these items as they are demanded.

Example 5.10 (continued)

A sample of 20 different stock items from Harvey's Specialty Shop is selected at random. These items vary in price from $0.25 to $24.99 and in average yearly demand from 12 to 786. The results of the sampling are presented in Table 5–1. In Table 5–2 the items are ranked in decreasing order of the annual dollar volume of sales. Notice that only 4 of the 20 stock items account for over 80 percent of the annual dollar volume generated by the entire group. Also notice that there are high-priced items in both categories A and C.

This report was very illuminating to Harvey, who had assumed that R077, a packaged goat cheese from the south of France, was a profitable item because of its cost, and had been virtually ignoring TTR77, a domestic chocolate bar.

TABLE 5–1
Performance of 20 Stock Items Selected at Random

Part Number	Price	Yearly Demand	Dollar Volume
5497J	$2.25	260	$ 585.00
3K62	2.85	43	122.55
88450	1.50	21	31.50
P001	0.77	388	298.76
2M993	4.45	612	2,723.40
4040	6.10	220	1,342.00
W76	3.10	110	341.00
JJ335	1.32	786	1,037.52
R077	12.80	14	179.20
70779	24.99	334	8,346.66
4J65E	7.75	24	186.00
334Y	0.68	77	52.36
8ST4	0.25	56	14.00
16113	3.89	89	346.21
45000	7.70	675	5,197.50
7878	6.22	66	410.52
6193L	0.85	148	125.80
TTR77	0.77	690	531.30
39SS5	1.23	52	63.96
93939	4.05	12	48.60

TABLE 5–2
Twenty Stock Items Ranked in Decreasing Order of Annual Dollar Volume

Part Number	Price	Yearly Demand	Dollar Volume	Cumulative Dollar Volume	
70779	$24.99	334	$8,346.66	$ 8,346.66	A items:
45000	7.70	675	5,197.50	13,544.16	20% of items
2M993	4.45	612	2,723.40	16,267.56	account for 80.1%
4040	6.10	220	1,342.00	17,609.56	of total value.
JJ335	1.32	786	1,037.52	18,647.08	
5497J	2.25	260	585.00	19,232.08	B items:
TTR77	0.77	690	531.30	19,763.38	30% of items
7878	6.22	66	410.52	20,173.90	account for 14.8%
16113	3.89	89	346.21	20,520.11	of total value.
W76	3.10	110	341.00	20,861.11	
P001	0.77	388	298.76	21,159.87	
4J65E	7.75	24	186.00	21,345.87	
R077	12.80	14	179.20	21,525.07	C items:
6193L	0.85	148	125.80	21,650.87	50% of items
3K62	2.85	43	122.55	21,773.42	account for 5.1%
39SS5	1.23	52	63.96	21,837.38	of total value.
334Y	0.68	77	52.36	21,889.74	
93939	4.05	12	48.60	21,938.34	
88450	1.50	21	31.50	21,969.84	
8ST4	0.25	56	14.00	21,983.84	

Exchange Curves

Much of our analysis assumes a single item in isolation and that the relevant cost parameters K, h, and p (or just K and h in the case of service levels) are constants with "correct" values that can be determined. However, it may be more appropriate to think of one or all of the cost parameters as policy variables. The correct values are those that result in a control system with characteristics that meet the needs of the firm and the goals of management. In a typical multiproduct system, the same values of setup cost K and interest rate I are used for all items. We can treat the ratio K/I as a policy variable; if this ratio is large, lot sizes will be larger and the average investment in inventory will be greater. If this ratio is small, the number of annual replenishments will increase.

To see exactly how a typical exchange curve is derived, consider a deterministic system consisting of n products with varying demand rates $\lambda_1, \ldots, \lambda_n$ and item values $c_1, \ldots, c_n$. If EOQ values are used to replenish stock for each item, then

$$Q_i = \sqrt{\frac{2K\lambda_i}{Ic_i}} \quad \text{for } 1 \leq i \leq n.$$

For item i, the cycle time is Q_i/λ_i, so that λ_i/Q_i is the number of replenishments in one year. The total number of replenishments for the entire system is $\Sigma \lambda_i/Q_i$. The average on-hand inventory of item i is $Q_i/2$, and the value of this inventory in dollars is $c_i Q_i/2$. Hence, the total value of the inventory is $\Sigma c_i Q_i/2$.

Each choice of the ratio K/I will result in a different value of the number of replenishments per year and the dollar value of inventory. As K/I is varied, one traces out a curve such as the one pictured in Figure 5–9. An exchange curve such as this one allows management to easily see the trade-off between the dollar investment in inventory and the frequency of stock replenishment.

Exchange curves also can be used to compare various safety stock and service level strategies. As an example, consider a system in which a fill rate constraint is used (i.e., Type 2 service) for all items. Furthermore, suppose that the lead time demand distribution for all items is normal, and each item gets equal service. The dollar value of the safety stock is $\Sigma c_i(R_i - \mu_i)$, and the annual value of back-ordered demand is $\Sigma c_i \lambda_i n(R_i)/Q_i$. A fixed value of the fill rate β will result in a set of values of the control variables $(Q_1, R_1), \ldots, (Q_n, R_n)$, which can be computed by the methods discussed

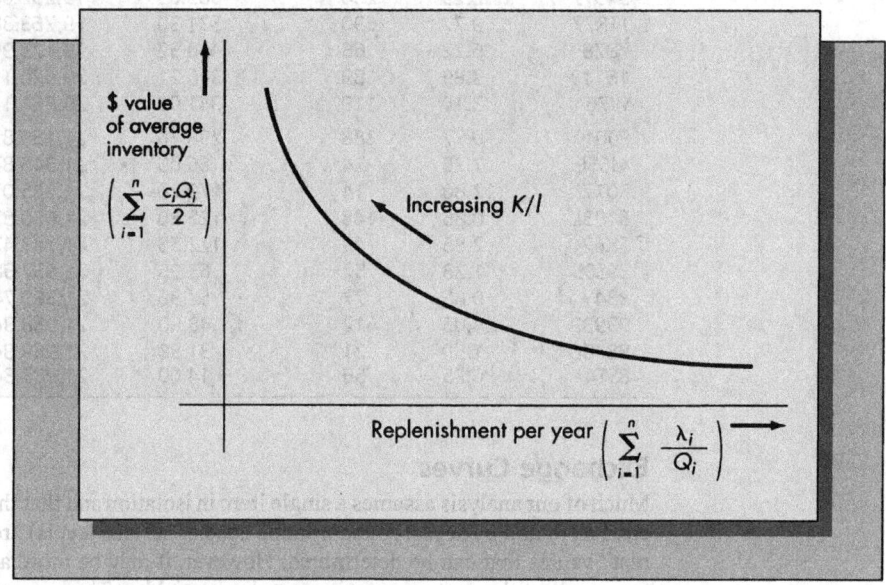

FIGURE 5–9
Exchange curve of replenishment frequency and inventory value

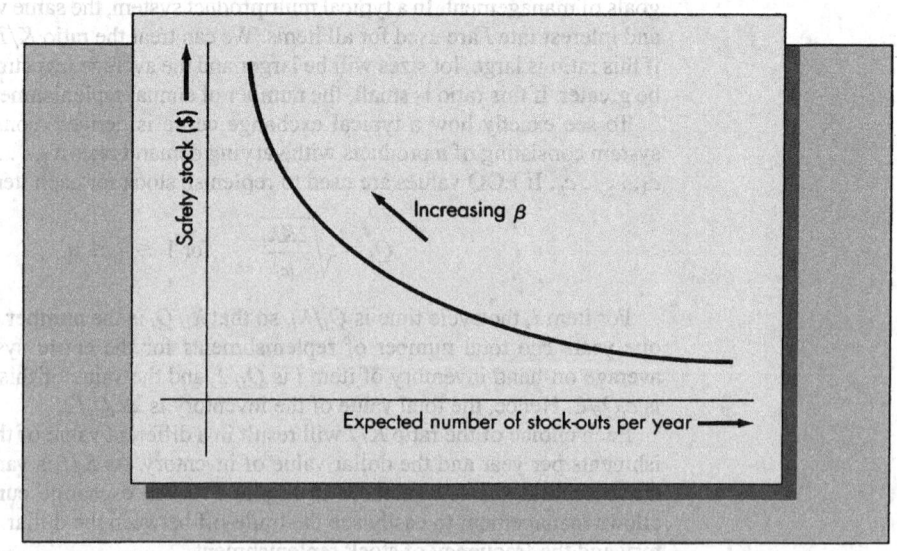

FIGURE 5–10
Exchange curve of the investment in safety stock and β

earlier in the chapter. Each set of (Q, R) values yields a pair of values for the safety stock and the back-ordered demand. As the fill rate is increased, the investment in safety stock increases and the value of back-ordered demand decreases. The exchange curve one would obtain is pictured in Figure 5–10. Such an exchange curve is a useful way for management to assess the dollar impact of various service levels.

Example 5.11 Consider the 20 stock items listed in Tables 5–1 and 5–2. Suppose that Harvey, the owner of Harvey's Specialty Shop, is reconsidering his choices of the setup cost of $50 and interest charge of 20 percent. Harvey uses the EOQ formula to compute lot sizes for the 20 items for a range of values of K/I from 50 to 500. The resulting exchange curve appears in Figure 5–11.

FIGURE 5–11
Exchange curve: Harvey's Specialty Shop

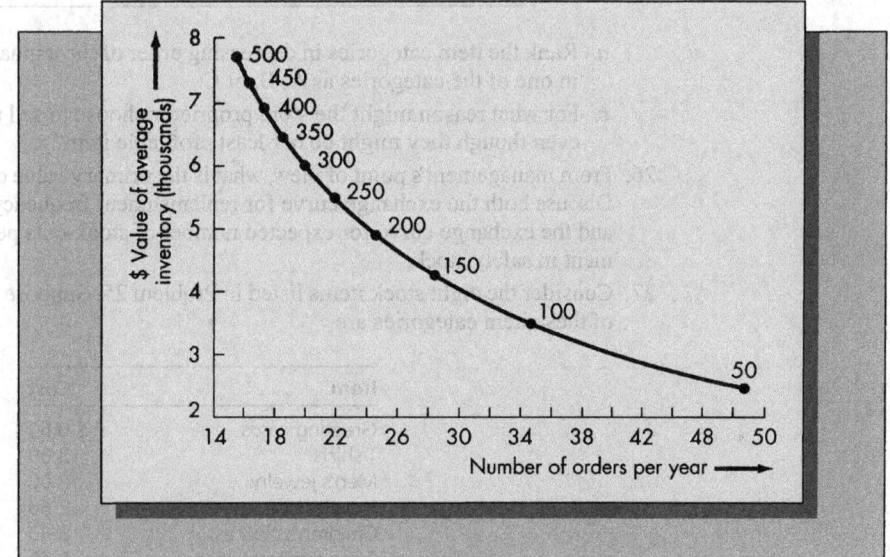

Harvey is currently operating at $K/I = 50/0.2 = 250$, which results in approximately 22 orders per year and an average inventory cost of $5,447 annually. By reducing K/I to 100, the inventory cost for these 20 items is reduced to $3,445 and the order frequency is increased to 34 orders a year. After some thought, Harvey decides that the additional time and bookkeeping expenses required to track an additional 12 orders annually is definitely worth the $2,000 savings in inventory cost. (He is fairly comfortable with the 20 percent interest rate, which means that the true value of his setup cost for ordering is closer to $20 than $50. In this way the exchange curve can assist in determining the correct value of cost parameters that may otherwise be difficult to estimate.) He also considers moving to $K/I = 50$, but decides that the additional savings of about $1,000 are not worth having to process almost 50 orders a year.

Problems for Section 5.7

24. Describe the ABC classification system. What is the purpose of classifying items in this fashion? What would be the primary value of ABC analysis to a retailer? To a manufacturer?

25. Consider the following list of retail items sold in a small neighborhood gift shop.

Item	Annual Volume	Average Profit per Item
Greeting cards	3,870	$ 0.40
T-shirts	1,550	1.25
Men's jewelry	875	4.50
Novelty gifts	2,050	12.25
Children's clothes	575	6.85
Chocolate cookies	7,000	0.10
Earrings	1,285	3.50
Other costume jewelry	1,900	15.00

a. Rank the item categories in decreasing order of the annual profit. Classify each in one of the categories as A, B, or C.

b. For what reason might the store proprietor choose to sell the chocolate cookies even though they might be her least profitable item?

26. From management's point of view, what is the primary value of an exchange curve? Discuss both the exchange curve for replenishment frequency and inventory value and the exchange curve for expected number of stock-outs per year and the investment in safety stock.

27. Consider the eight stock items listed in Problem 25. Suppose that the average costs of these item categories are

Item	Cost
Greeting cards	$ 0.50
T-shirts	3.00
Men's jewelry	8.00
Novelty gifts	12.50
Children's clothes	8.80
Chocolate cookies	0.40
Earrings	4.80
Other costume jewelry	12.00

Compare the total number of replenishments per year and the dollar value of the inventory of these items for the following values of the ratio of K/I: 100, 200, 500, 1,000. From the four points obtained, estimate the exchange curve of replenishment frequency and inventory value.

*5.8 OVERVIEW OF ADVANCED TOPICS

This chapter has treated only a small portion of inventory models available. Considerable research has been devoted to analyzing far more complex stochastic inventory control problems, but most of this research is beyond the scope of our coverage. This section presents a brief overview of two areas not discussed in this chapter that account for a large portion of the recent research on inventory management.

Multi-echelon Systems

Firms involved in the manufacture and distribution of consumer products must take into account the interactions of the various levels in the distribution chain. Typically,

FIGURE 5–12
Typical three-level distribution system

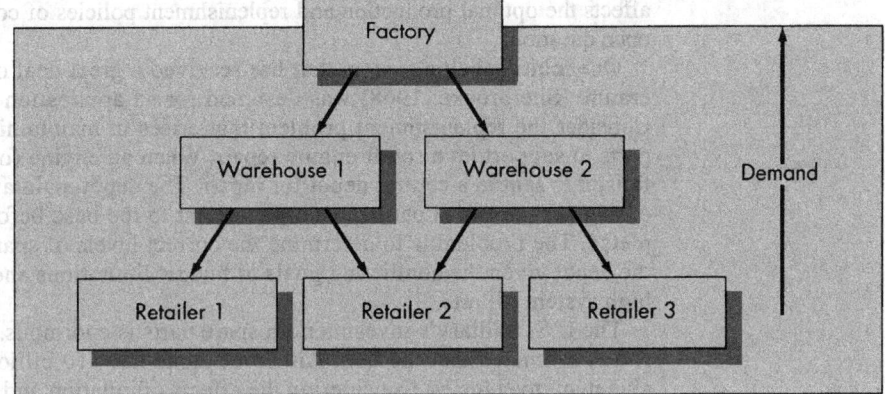

items are produced at one or more factories, shipped to warehouses for intermediate storage, and subsequently shipped to retail outlets to be sold to the consumer. We refer to the levels of the system as *echelons*. For example, the factory–warehouse–retailer three-echelon system is pictured in Figure 5–12.

A system of the type pictured in Figure 5–12 is generally referred to as a *distribution* system. In such a system, the demand arises at the lowest echelon (the retailer in this case) and is transmitted up to the higher echelons. Production plans at the factory must be coordinated with orders placed at the warehouse by the retailers. Another type of multi-echelon system arising in manufacturing contexts is known as an *assembly* system. In an assembly system, components are combined to form subassemblies, which are eventually combined to form end items (that is, final products). A typical assembly system is pictured in Figure 5–13.

In the assembly system, external demand originates at the end-item level only. Demand for the components arises only when "orders" are placed at higher levels of the system, which are the consequence of end-item production schedules. Materials requirements planning methodology is designed to model systems of this type, but does not consider the effect of uncertainty on the final demand. Although there has been some research on this problem, precisely how the uncertainty in the final demand

FIGURE 5–13
Typical three-level assembly system

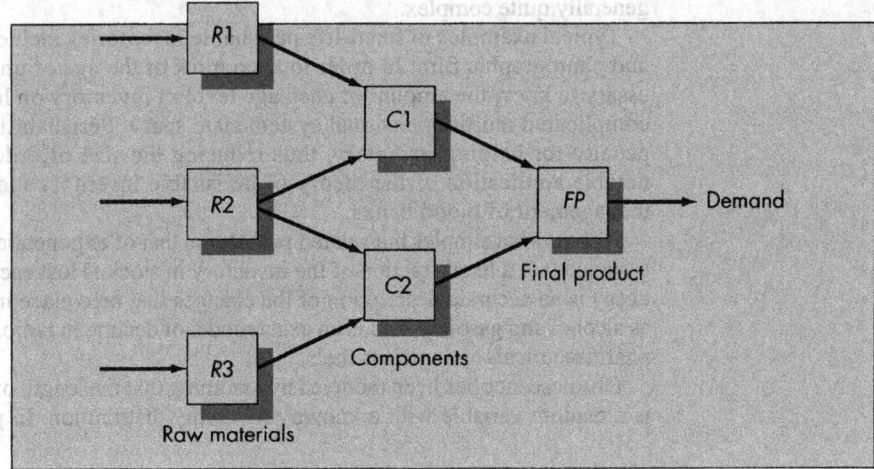

affects the optimal production and replenishment policies of components remains an open question.

One multi-echelon system that has received a great deal of attention in the literature (Sherbrooke, 1968) was designed for an application in military logistics. Consider the replenishment problem that arises in maintaining a supply of spare parts to support jet aircraft engine repair. When an engine (or engine component) fails, it is sent to a central depot for repair. The depot maintains its own inventory of engines, so that it can ship a replacement to the base before the repair is completed. The problem is to determine the correct levels of spares at the base and at the depot given the conflicting goals of budget limitations and the desirability of a high system fill rate.

The U.S. military's investment in spare parts is enormous. As far back as 1968 it was estimated that the U.S. Air Force alone has $10 billion invested in repairable item inventories. Considering the effects of inflation and the sizes of the other armed services, the current investment in repairable items in the U.S. military probably exceeds $100 billion. Mathematical inventory models have made a significant impact on the management of repairable item inventories, both in military and nonmilitary environments.

In the private sector, retailing is an area in which multi-echelon distribution systems are common. Most major retail chains utilize a distribution center (DC) as an intermediate storage point between the manufacturer and the retail store. Determining how to allocate inventory between the DC and the stores is an important strategic issue. DC inventory allows "risk pooling" among the stores and facilitates redistribution of store inventories that might grow out of balance. Several commercial computer-based inventory packages are available for retail inventory management, perhaps the best known being Inforem, designed and marketed by IBM. Readers interested in a comprehensive review of the research on the retailer inventory management problem should refer to the recent book by Agrawal and Smith (2008) and Nahmias and Smith (1992).

Perishable Inventory Problems

Although certain types of decay can be accounted for by adjustments to the holding cost, the mathematical models that describe perishability, decay, or obsolescence are generally quite complex.

Typical examples of fixed-life perishable inventories include food, blood, drugs, and photographic film. In order to keep track of the age of units in stock, it is necessary to know the amount of each age level of inventory on hand. This results in a complicated multidimensional system state space. Perishability adds an additional penalty for holding inventory, thus reducing the size of orders placed. The most notable application of the theory of perishable inventory models has been to the management of blood banks.

A somewhat simpler but related problem is that of exponential decay, in which it is assumed that a fixed fraction of the inventory in stock is lost each period. Exponential decay is an accurate description of the changes that take place in volatile liquids such as alcohol and gasoline, and is an exact model of decline in radioactivity of radioactive pharmaceuticals and nuclear fuels.

Obsolescence has been modeled by assuming that the length of the planning horizon is a random variable with a known probability distribution. In practice, such models

Snapshot Application

INTEL USES MULTIECHELON INVENTORY MODELLING TO MANAGE THE SUPPLY CHAIN FOR BOXED CPUS

Intel Corporation, headquartered in Santa Clara, California, is the largest producer of integrated circuits in the world. Intel microprocessors have been the "guts" of most personal computers ever since IBM first adopted the Intel 8088 as the CPU in the original IBM PC in 1981. In 2005, a group at Intel and one outside consultant was charged with the problem of managing the supply chain of its branded boxed CPUs. The division typically sells 100–150 configurations of these products.

The group chose to model the problem as a three echelon inventory system: (1) global supply, (2) boxing sites, and (3) boxed CPU warehouses. The group quickly realized that there were many factors affecting the supply chain, but the primary driver of system effectiveness was demand uncertainty. Predicting demand uncertainty is difficult in this environment since product life cycles are often relatively short, resulting in very little historical data for some products.

Another complicating factor is that the three echelons are far apart geographically, resulting in a very long cumulative lead time for the system. Hence, a make-to-order business model is simply not feasible. For that reason, proper positioning of inventory along the entire supply chain is critical. The mathematical model developed for this application was a nonlinear mathematical programming model that could be solved by standard dynamic programming techniques.

A key issue is metrics. That is, how does one evaluate the quality of the model's results? One metric is the total inventory in the system. This translates to the total dollar investment required by Intel. A second metric is the quality of the service provided to the customer. Both Type 1 and Type 2 service level metrics (as discussed in detail in this chapter) were considered. Intel management chose a modified version of Type 2 service (that is, the fill rate). Their metric was the percentage of an order filled on the date the customer asks for delivery of the product.

The team decided that it was not worth trying to apply their optimization tool to all 150 products, so they embarked on an ABC analysis, and ultimately chose to apply the model only to products with more than 3,000 sales per month and 12,000 sales per quarter. Also, it became clear that in order to be responsive to customer demand, the vast majority of the inventory would be held at the third echelon, namely the boxed CPU warehouses. This inventory has the most value added, so is the most expensive. That expense is offset by the fact that keeping the inventory closer to the customer significantly improves service levels. The system was implemented at Intel in late 2005. Comparisons with pre and post implementation metrics showed that the model resulted in a modest decline in system-wide inventory levels, but significantly improved level of customer service.

An important aspect of this study was the priorities set by the project team. These priorities provide a good blueprint on how to go about a project of this type to maximize the likelihood of implementation. The four goals they set were: (1) keep models and processes simple, (2) make things better now, (3) implement changes in a phased manner, and (4) be clear about what success is.

Source: Wieland, B. et al. "Optimizing Inventory Levels within Intel's Channel Supply Demand Operations." *Interfaces* 42 (2012), pp. 517–527.

are valuable only if the distribution of the useful lifetime of the item can be accurately estimated in advance.

A related problem is the management of style goods, such as fashion items in the garment industry. The style goods problem differs from the inventory models considered in this chapter in that not only is the demand itself uncertain, but the distribution of demand is uncertain as well. This is typical of problems for which there is no prior demand history. The procedures suggested to deal with the style goods problem generally involve some type of Bayesian updating scheme to combine current observations of demand with prior estimates of the demand distribution.

5.9 HISTORICAL NOTES AND ADDITIONAL READINGS

Research on stochastic inventory models was sparked by the national war effort and appears to date back to the 1940s, although the first published material appeared in the early 1950s (see Arrow, Harris, and Marschak, 1951; and Dvorestsky, Kiefer, and Wolfowitz, 1952). The important text by Arrow, Karlin, and Scarf (1958) produced considerable interest in the field.

The model we discuss of a lot size–reorder point system with stock-out cost criterion seems to be attributed to Whitin (1957). The extensions to service levels are attributed to Brown (1967). Brown also treats a variety of other topics of practical importance, including the relationship between forecasting models and inventory control. An excellent discussion of exchange curves and ABC analysis, and more in-depth coverage of a number of the topics we discuss, can be found in Silver and Peterson (1985). Love (1979) provides an excellent summary of many of the issues we treat. Hadley and Whitin (1963) also deal with these topics at a more sophisticated mathematical level.

There has been considerable interest in the development of approximate (s, S) policies. Scarf (1960), and later Iglehart (1963), proved the optimality of (s, S) policies, and Veinott and Wagner (1965) considered methods for computing optimal (s, S) policies. A number of approximation techniques have been suggested. Ehrhardt (1979) considers using regression analysis to fit a grid of optimal policies, whereas Freeland and Porteus (1980) adapt dynamic programming methods to the problem. Porteus (1985) numerically compares the effectiveness of various approximation techniques. Some of the issues regarding lead time uncertainty are treated by Kaplan (1970) and Nahmias (1979), among others.

The original formulation of the standard multi-echelon inventory problem came from Clark and Scarf (1960). Extensions have been developed by a variety of researchers, most notably Bessler and Veinott (1966), and, more recently, Federgruen and Zipkin (1984). Retailer-warehouse systems have been studied by Deuermeyer and Schwarz (1981) and Eppen and Schrage (1981). Schmidt and Nahmias (1985) analyzed an assembly system when demand for the final product is random.

The classic work on the type of multi-echelon model that has become the basis for the inventory control systems implemented in the military was done by Sherbrooke (1968). An extension of Sherbrooke's analysis is considered by Graves (1985). Muckstadt and Thomas (1980) discuss the advantages of implementing multi-echelon models in an industrial environment. A comprehensive review of models for managing repairables can be found in Nahmias (1981).

Interest in perishable inventory control models appears to stem from the problem of blood bank inventory control, although food management has a far greater economic impact. Most of the mathematical models for perishables assume that the inventory is issued from stock on an oldest-first basis (although a notable exception is the study by Cohen and Pekelman, 1978). Nahmias (1982) provides a comprehensive review of the research on perishable inventory control.

The style goods problem has been studied by a variety of researchers. Representative work in this area includes that by Murray and Silver (1966), Hartung (1973), and Hausman and Peterson (1972). Those interested in additional readings on stochastic inventory models should refer to the various review articles in the field. Some of the most notable include those of Scarf (1963), Veinott (1966), and Nahmias (1978). A recent collection of up-to-date reviews can be found in Graves et al. (1992).

5.10 Summary

This chapter presented an overview of several inventory control methods when the demand for the item is random. The *newsvendor model* is based on the assumption that the product has a useful life of exactly one planning period. We assumed that the demand during the period is a continuous random variable with cumulative distribution function $F(x)$, and that there are specified overage and underage costs of c_o and c_u charged against the inventory remaining on hand at the end of the period or the excess demand, respectively. The optimal order quantity Q^* solves the equation

$$F(Q^*) = \frac{c_u}{c_u + c_o}.$$

Extensions to discrete demand and multiple planning periods also were considered.

From a practical standpoint, the newsvendor model has a serious limitation: it does not allow for a positive order setup cost. For that reason, we considered an extension of the EOQ model known as a *lot size–reorder point* model. The key random variable for this case was the demand during the lead time. We showed how optimal values of the decision variables Q and R could be obtained by the iterative solution of two equations. The system operates in the following manner. When the level of on-hand inventory hits R, an order for Q units is placed (which will arrive after the lead time τ). This policy is the basis of many commercial inventory control systems.

Service levels provide an alternative to stock-out costs. Two service levels were considered: Type 1 and Type 2. Type 1 service is the probability of not stocking out in any order cycle, and Type 2 service is the probability of being able to meet a demand when it occurs. Type 2 service, also known as the *fill rate*, is the more natural definition of service for most applications.

Several additional topics for (Q, R) systems also were considered. The *imputed shortage cost* is the effective shortage cost resulting from specification of the service level. Assuming normality, we showed how one transforms the distribution of periodic demand to lead time demand. Finally, we considered the effects of *lead time variability*.

If a setup cost is included in the multiperiod version of the newsvendor problem, the optimal form of the control policy is known as an (s, S) *policy*. This means that if the starting inventory in a period, u, is less than or equal to s, an order for $S - u$ units is placed. An effective approximation for the optimal (s, S) policy can be obtained by solving the problem as if it were continuous review to obtain the corresponding (Q, R) policy, and setting $s = R$ and $S = Q + R$. We also discussed the application of service levels to periodic-review systems.

Most real inventory systems involve the management of more than a single product. We discussed several issues that arise when managing a multiproduct inventory system. One of these is the amount of time and expense that should be allocated to the control of each item. The *ABC system* is a method of classifying items by their annual volume of sales. Another issue concerns the correct choice of the cost parameters used in computing inventory control policies. Because many of the cost parameters used in inventory analysis involve managerial judgment and are not easily measured, it would be useful if management could compare the effects of various parameter settings on the performance of the system. A convenient technique for making these comparisons is via *exchange curves*. We discussed two of the most popular exchange curves: (1) the trade-off between the investment in inventory and the frequency of stock replenishment and (2) the trade-off between the investment in safety stock and service levels.

Additional Problems on Stochastic Inventory Models

28. An artist's supply shop stocks a variety of different items to satisfy the needs of both amateur and professional artists. In each case described, what is the appropriate inventory control model that the store should use to manage the replenishment of the item described? Choose your answer from the following list and be sure to explain your answer in each case:

Simple EOQ	Newsvendor model with service level
Finite production rate	(Q, R) model with stock-out cost
EOQ with quantity discounts	(Q, R) model with Type 1 service level
Resource-constrained EOQ	(Q, R) model with Type 2 service level
Newsvendor model	Other type of model

   a. A highly volatile paint thinner is ordered once every three months. Cans not sold during the three-month period are discarded. The demand for the paint thinner exhibits considerable variation from one three-month period to the next.

   b. A white oil-base paint sells at a fairly regular rate of 600 tubes per month and requires a six-week order lead time. The paint store buys the paint for $1.20 per tube.

   c. Burnt sienna oil paint does not sell as regularly or as heavily as the white. Sales of the burnt sienna vary considerably from one month to the next. The useful lifetime of the paint is about two years, but the store sells almost all the paint prior to the two-year limit.

   d. Synthetic paint brushes are purchased from an East Coast supplier who charges $1.60 for each brush in orders of under 100 and $1.30 for each brush in orders of 100 or greater. The store sells the brushes at a fairly steady rate of 40 per month for $2.80 each.

   e. Camel hair brushes are purchased from the supplier of part (d), who offers a discount schedule similar to the one for the synthetic brushes. The camel hair brushes, however, exhibit considerable sales variation from month to month.

29. Annual demand for number 2 pencils at the campus store is normally distributed with mean 1,000 and standard deviation 250. The store purchases the pencils for 6 cents each and sells them for 20 cents each. There is a two-month lead time from the initiation to the receipt of an order. The store accountant estimates that the cost in employee time for performing the necessary paperwork to initiate and receive an order is $20, and recommends a 22 percent annual interest rate for determining holding cost. The cost of a stock-out is the cost of lost profit plus an additional 20 cents per pencil, which represents the cost of loss of goodwill.

   a. Find the optimal value of the reorder point R assuming that the lot size used is the EOQ.

   b. Find the simultaneous optimal values of Q and R.

   c. Compare the average annual holding, setup, and stock-out costs of the policies determined in parts (a) and (b).

   d. What is the safety stock for this item at the optimal solution?

30. Consider the problem of satisfying the demand for number 2 pencils faced by the campus store mentioned in Problem 29.

    a. Re-solve the problem, substituting a Type 1 service level criterion of 95 percent for the stock-out cost.
    b. Re-solve the problem, substituting a Type 2 service level criterion of 95 percent for the stock-out cost. Assume that Q is given by the EOQ.
    c. Find the simultaneous optimal values of Q and R assuming a Type 2 service level of 95 percent.

31. Answer the following true or false.

    a. The lead time is always less than the cycle time.
    b. The optimal lot size for a Type 1 service objective of X percent is always less than the optimal lot size for a Type 2 service objective of X percent for the same item.
    c. The newsvendor model does not include a fixed order cost.
    d. ABC analysis ranks items according to the annual value of their demand.
    e. For a finite production rate model, the optimal lot size to produce each cycle is equal to the maximum inventory each cycle.

32. One of the products stocked at Weiss's paint store, mentioned in Problem 14, is a certain type of highly volatile paint thinner that, due to chemical changes in the product, has a shelf life of exactly one year. Al Weiss purchases the paint thinner for $20 a gallon can and sells it for $50 a can. The supplier buys back cans not sold during the year for $8 for reprocessing. The demand for this thinner generally varies from 20 to 70 cans a year. Al assumes a holding cost for unsold cans at a 30 percent annual interest rate.

    a. Assuming that all values of the demand from 20 to 70 are equally likely, what is the optimal number of cans of paint thinner for Al to buy each year?
    b. More accurate analysis of the demand shows that a normal distribution gives a better fit of the data. The distribution mean is identical to that used in part (a), and the standard deviation estimator turns out to be 7. What policy do you now obtain?

33. Semicon is a start-up company that produces semiconductors for a variety of applications. The process of burning in the circuits requires large amounts of nitric acid, which has a shelf life of only three months. Semicon estimates that it will need between 1,000 and 3,000 gallons of acid for the next three-month period and assumes that all values in this interval are equally likely. The acid costs them $150 per gallon. The company assumes a 30 percent annual interest rate for the money it has invested in inventory, and the acid costs the company $35 a gallon to store. (Assume that all inventory costs are attached to the end of the three-month period.) Acid that is left over at the end of the three-month period costs $75 per gallon to dispose of. If the company runs out of acid during the three-month period, it can purchase emergency supplies quickly at a price of $600 per gallon.

    a. How many gallons of nitric acid should Semicon purchase? Experience with the marketplace later shows that the demand is closer to a normal distribution, with mean 1,800 and standard deviation 480.

b. Suppose that now Semicon switches to a 94 percent fill rate criterion. How many gallons should now be purchased at the start of each three-month period?

34. *Newsvendor simulator.* In order to solve this problem, your spreadsheet program will need to have a function that produces random numbers [@RAND in Lotus 1-2-3 and RAND ( ) in Excel]. The purpose of this exercise is to construct a simulation of a periodic-review inventory system with random demand. We assume that the reader is familiar with the fundamentals of Monte Carlo simulation.

Your spreadsheet should allow for cell locations for storing values of the holding cost, the penalty cost, the proportional order cost, the order-up-to point, the initial inventory, and the mean and the standard deviation of periodic demand.

An efficient means of generating an observation from a standard normal variate is the formula

$$Z = [-2 \ln(U_1)]^{0.5} \cos(2\pi U_2),$$

where U_1 and U_2 are two independent draws from a (0, 1) uniform distribution. (See, for example, Fishman, 1973.) Note that two independent calls of @RAND are required. Since Z is approximately standard normal, the demand X is given by

$$X = \sigma Z + \mu$$

where μ and σ are the mean and the standard deviation of one period's demand.

A suggested layout of the spreadsheet is

		NEWSVENDOR SIMULATOR				
		Holding cost =		Mean demand =		
		Order cost =		Std. dev. demand =		
		Penalty cost =		Initial inventory =		
				Order-up-to point =		
Period	Starting Inventory	Order Quantity	Demand	Ending Inventory	Holding Cost	Penalty Cost	Order Cost
1							
2							
3							
.							
20							
Totals							

Each time you recalculate, the simulator will generate a different sequence of demands. A set of suggested parameters is

$$h = 2,$$
$$c = 5,$$
$$p = 20,$$
$$\mu = 100,$$
$$\sigma = 20,$$
$$I_0 = 50,$$
Order-up-to point = 150.

35. *Using the simulator for optimization.* You will be able to do this problem only if the program you are using does not restrict the size of the spreadsheet. Assume the parameters given in Problem 34 but use $\sigma = 10$. Extend the spreadsheet from Problem 34 to 1,000 rows or more and compute the average cost per period. If the cost changes substantially as you recalculate the spreadsheet, you need to add additional rows.

    Now, experiment with different values of the order-up-to point to find the one that minimizes the average cost per period. Compare your results to the theoretical optimal solution.

36. *Newsvendor calculator.* Design a spreadsheet to calculate the optimal order-up-to point for a newsvendor problem with normally distributed demands. In order to avoid table look-ups, use the approximation formula

$$Z = 5.0633[F^{0.135} - (1 - F)^{0.135}]$$

for the inverse of the standard normal distribution function. (This formula is from Ramberg and Schmieser, 1972.) The optimal order-up-to point, y^*, is of the form $y^* = \sigma Z + \mu$.

   a. Assume that all parameters are as given in Problem 34. Graph y^* as a function of p, the penalty cost, for $p = 10, 15, \ldots, 100$. By what percentage does y^* increase if p increases from 10 to 20? from 50 to 100?

   b. Repeat part (a) with $\sigma = 35$. Comment on the effect that the variance in demand has on the sensitivity of y^* to p.

37. A large national producer of canned foods plans to purchase 100 combines that are to be customized for its needs. One of the parts used in the combine is a replaceable blade for harvesting corn. Spare blades can be purchased at the time the order is placed for $100 each, but will cost $1,000 each if purchased at a later time because a special production run will be required.

    It is estimated that the number of replacement blades required by a combine over its useful lifetime can be closely approximated by a normal distribution with mean 18 and standard deviation 5.2. The combine maker agrees to buy back unused blades for $20 each. How many spare blades should the company purchase with the combines?

38. Crazy Charlie's, a discount stereo shop, uses simple exponential smoothing with a smoothing constant of $\alpha = .2$ to track the mean and the MAD of monthly item demand. One particular item, a stereo receiver, has experienced the following sales over the last three months: 126, 138, 94.

    Three months ago the computer had stored values of mean = 135 and MAD = 18.5.

    a. Using the exponential smoothing equations given in Section 5.1, determine the current values for the mean and the MAD of monthly demand. (Assume that the stored values were computed *prior* to observing the demand of 126.)

    b. Suppose that the order lead time for this particular item is 10 weeks (2.5 months). Assuming a normal distribution for monthly demand, determine the current estimates for the mean and the standard deviation of lead time demand.

    c. This particular receiver is ordered directly from Japan, and as a result there has been considerable variation in the replenishment lead time from one order cycle to the next. Based on an analysis of past order cycles, it is estimated that the standard deviation of the lead time is 3.3 weeks. All other relevant figures are given in parts (a) and (b). Find the mean and the standard deviation of lead time demand in this case.

d. If Crazy Charlie's uses a Type 1 service objective of 98 percent to control the replenishment of this item, what is the value of the reorder level? (Assume that the lead time demand has a normal distribution.)

39. The home appliance department of a large department store is using a lot size–reorder point system to control the replenishment of a particular model of FM table radio. The store sells an average of 10 radios each week. Weekly demand follows a normal distribution with variance 26.

The store pays $20 for each radio, which it sells for $75. Fixed costs of replenishment amount to $28. The accounting department recommends a 20 percent interest rate for the cost of capital. Storage costs amount to 3 percent and breakage to 2 percent of the value of each item.

If a customer demands the radio when it is out of stock, the customer will generally go elsewhere. Loss-of-goodwill costs are estimated to be about $25 per radio. Replenishment lead time is three months.

a. If lot sizes are based on the EOQ formula, what reorder level should be used for the radios?

b. Find the optimal values of (Q, R).

c. Compare the average annual costs of holding, ordering, and stock-out for the policies that you found in parts (a) and (b).

d. Re-solve the problem using Equations (1) and (2′) rather than (1) and (2). What is the effect of including lost sales explicitly?

40. Re-solve the problem faced by the department store mentioned in Problem 39, replacing the stock-out cost with a 96 percent Type 1 service level.

41. Re-solve the problem faced by the department store mentioned in Problem 39, replacing the stock-out cost with a 96 percent Type 2 service level. What is the imputed shortage cost?

42. Consider the equation giving the expected average annual cost of the policy (Q, R) in a continuous-review inventory control system from Section 5.4:

$$G(Q, R) = h\left(\frac{Q}{2} + r - \lambda T\right) + \frac{K\lambda}{Q} + \frac{P\lambda n(R)}{Q}.$$

Design a spreadsheet to compute $G(Q, R)$ for a range of values of $Q \geq \text{EOQ}$ and $R \geq \mu$. Use the following approximation formula for $L(z)$ to avoid table look-ups:

$$L(z) = \exp(-0.92 - 1.19z - 0.37z^2).$$

(This formula is from Parr, 1972.) Store the problem parameters c, h, p, μ, σ, and λ in cell locations. Visually search through the tabled values of $G(Q, R)$ to discover the minimum value and estimate the optimal (Q, R) values in this manner. Compare your results to the true optimal found from manual calculation.

a. Solve Example 5.4.

b. Solve Problem 13 in this manner.

c. Solve Problem 14 in this manner.

43. The daily demand for a spare engine part is a random variable with a distribution, based on past experience, given by

Number of Demands per Day	Probability
0	.21
1	.38
2	.19
3	.14
4	.08

The part is expected to be obsolete after 400 days. Assume that demands from one day to the next are independent. The parts cost $1,500 each when acquired in advance of the 400-day period and $5,000 each when purchased on an emergency basis during the 400-day period. Holding costs for unused parts are based on a daily interest rate of 0.08 percent. Unused parts can be scrapped for 10 percent of their purchase price. How many parts should be acquired in advance of the 400-day period? (Hint: Let $D_1, D_2, \ldots, D_{400}$ represent the daily demand for the part. Assume each D_i has mean μ and variance σ^2. The central limit theorem says that the total demand for the 400-day period, ΣD_i, is approximately normally distributed with mean 400μ and variance $400\sigma^2$.)

44. Cassorla's Clothes sells a large number of white dress shirts. The shirts, which bear the store label, are shipped from a manufacturer in New York City. Hy Cassorla, the proprietor, says, "I want to be sure that I never run out of dress shirts. I always try to keep at least a two months' supply in stock. When my inventory drops below that level, I order another two-month supply. I've been using that method for 20 years, and it works."

The shirts cost $6 each and sell for $15 each. The cost of processing an order and receiving new goods amounts to $80, and it takes three weeks to receive a shipment. Monthly demand is approximately normally distributed with mean 120 and standard deviation 32. Assume a 20 percent annual interest rate for computing the holding cost.

a. What value of Q and R is Hy Cassorla using to control the inventory of white dress shirts?

b. What fill rate (Type 2 service level) is being achieved with the current policy?

c. Based on a 99 percent fill rate criterion, determine the optimal values of Q and R that he should be using. (Assume four weeks in a month for your calculations.)

d. Determine the difference in the average annual holding and setup costs between the policies in parts (b) and (c).

e. Estimate how much time would be required to pay for a $25,000 inventory control system, assuming that the dress shirts represent 5 percent of Hy's annual business and that similar savings could be realized on the other items as well.

45. The Poisson distribution is discussed in Appendix 5–D at the end of this chapter. Assume that the distribution of bagels sold daily at Billy's Bakery in Problem 8 follows a Poisson distribution with mean 16 per day. Using Table A–3 in the back of the book or the Poisson distribution function built into Excel, determine the optimal number of bagels for Billy's to bake each day.

46. Consider the Crestview Printing Company described in Problem 9. Suppose that sales of cards (in units of 50,000) follow a Poisson distribution with mean 6.3. Using Table A–3 in the back of the book or the Poisson distribution function built into Excel find the optimal number of cards for Crestview to print for the next Christmas season.

47. The Laplace distribution is discussed in Appendix 5–D. As noted there, the Laplace distribution could be a good choice for describing demand for slow-moving items and for fast-moving items with high variation. The cdf of the Laplace distribution is given by

$$F(x) = 0.5[1 + \text{sgn}(x - \mu)](1 - \exp(-|x - \mu|/\theta)),$$

and the inverse of the cdf is given by

$$F^{-1}(p) = \mu - \theta \, \text{sgn}(p - 0.5) \ln(1 - 2|p - 0.5|),$$

where sgn(x) is the sign of x. The mean is μ and the variance is $2\theta^2$. Since the inverse distribution function can be written down explicitly, one does not have to resort to tables to solve newsvendor problems when demand follows the Laplace distribution.

Solve Problem 10, part (a), assuming the demand for the EX123 follows a Laplace distribution with parameters $\mu = 60$ and $\theta = 3\sqrt{2}$ (which will give exactly the same mean and variance).

48. Solve Problem 11 assuming the demand for fans over the selling season follows a Laplace distribution with the same mean and variance as you computed in Problem 11(a).

49. Solve Problem 12(b) assuming the demand for handbags over the selling season follows a Laplace distribution with mean 150 and standard deviation 20.

50. Solve Problem 13 assuming that the lead time demand follows a Laplace distribution with mean and variance equal to that which was computed in Problem 13. What difference do you see in the (Q, R) values as compared to those for the normal case?

51. Solve Problem 14 assuming that the lead time demand follows a Laplace distribution with mean and variance equal to the mean and variance of lead time demand you computed for Problem 14. What difference do you see in the (Q, R) values as compared to those for the normal case?

Appendix 5–A

Notational Conventions and Probability Review

Demand will be denoted by D, which is assumed to be a random variable. The cumulative distribution function (cdf) of demand is $F(x)$ and is defined by

$$F(x) = P\{D \leq x\} \quad \text{for } -\infty < x < +\infty.$$

When D is continuous, the probability density function (pdf) of demand, $f(x)$, is defined by

$$f(x) = \frac{dF(x)}{dx}.$$

When D is discrete, $f(x)$ is the probability function (pf) defined by

$$f(x) = P\{X = x\} = F(x) - F(x - 1).$$

Note that in the continuous case the density function is not a probability and the value of $f(x)$ is not necessarily less than 1, although it is always true that $f(x) \geq 0$ for all x. The expected value of demand, $E(D)$, is defined as

$$E(D) = \int_{-\infty}^{+\infty} xf(x)\, dx$$

in the continuous case, and

$$E(D) = \sum_{x=-\infty}^{+\infty} xf(x)$$

in the discrete case.

We use the symbol μ to represent the expected value of demand $[E(D) = \mu]$. In what follows we assume that D is continuous; similar formulas hold in the discrete case. Let $g(x)$ be any real-valued function of the real variable x. Then

$$E(g(D)) = \int_{-\infty}^{+\infty} g(x)f(x)\, dx.$$

In particular, let $g(D) = \max(0, Q - D)$. Then

$$E(g(D)) = \int_{-\infty}^{+\infty} \max(0, Q - x)f(x)\, dx.$$

Because demand is nonnegative, it must be true that $f(x) = 0$ for $x < 0$. Furthermore, when $x > Q$, $\max(0, Q - x) = 0$, so we may write

$$E(g(D)) = \int_{0}^{Q} (Q - x)f(x)\, dx.$$

In the analysis of the newsvendor model, Leibniz's rule is used to determine the derivative of $G(Q)$. According to Leibniz's rule:

$$\frac{d}{dy}\int_{a_1(y)}^{a_2(y)} h(x, y)\, dx = \int_{a_1(y)}^{a_2(y)} [\partial h(x, y)/\partial y]\, dx + h(a_2(y), y)a_2'(y) - h(a_1(y), y)a_1'(y).$$

Appendix 5-B

Additional Results and Extensions for the Newsvendor Model

1. INTERPRETATION OF THE OVERAGE AND UNDERAGE COSTS FOR THE SINGLE PERIOD PROBLEM

Define

S = Selling price of the item.

c = Variable cost of the item.

h = Holding cost per unit of inventory remaining in stock at the end of the period.

p = Loss-of-goodwill cost plus bookkeeping expense (charged against the number of back orders on the books at the end of the period).

We show how c_u and c_o should be interpreted in terms of these parameters. As earlier, let Q be the order quantity and D the demand during the period. Assume without loss of generality that starting inventory is zero. Then the cost incurred at the end of the period is

$$cQ + h\max(Q - D, 0) + p\max(D - Q, 0) - S\min(Q, D).$$

The expected cost is

$$G(Q) = cQ + h\int_0^Q (Q-x)f(x)\,dx + p\int_Q^\infty (x-Q)f(x)\,dx$$

$$- S\int_0^Q xf(x)\,dx - SQ\int_Q^\infty f(x)\,dx.$$

Using

$$\int_0^Q xf(x)\,dx = \int_0^\infty xf(x)\,dx - \int_Q^\infty xf(x)\,dx = \mu - \int_Q^\infty xf(x)\,dx,$$

the expected cost may be written

$$G(Q) = cQ + h\int_0^Q (Q-x)f(x)\,dx + (p+S)\int_Q^\infty (x-Q)f(x)\,dx - S\mu.$$

The optimal order quantity satisfies

$$G'(Q) = 0$$

or

$$c + hF(Q) - (p+S)(1 - F(Q)) = 0,$$

which results in

$$F(Q) = \frac{p + S - c}{p + S + h}.$$

Setting $c_u = p + S - c$ and $c_o = h + c$ gives the critical ratio in the form $c_u/(c_u + c_o)$.

2. THE NEWSVENDOR COST WHEN DEMAND IS NORMAL

When the one period demand follows a normal distribution, we can obtain an explicit expression for the optimal one period cost for the newsvendor model from Section 5.3. We know that the expected single period cost function is

$$G(Q) = c_o\int_0^Q (Q-t)f(t)\,dt + c_u\int_Q^\infty (t-Q)f(t)\,dt,$$

and the optimal value of Q satisfies

$$F(Q^*) = \frac{c_u}{c_u + c_o}.$$

It is convenient to express $G(Q)$ in a slightly different form. Note that

$$\int_0^Q (Q-t)f(t)\,dt = \int_0^\infty (Q-t)f(t)\,dt - \int_Q^\infty (Q-t)f(t)\,dt = Q - \mu + n(Q)\text{ where}$$

$$n(Q) = \int_Q^\infty (t-Q)f(t)\,dt.$$

It follows that $G(Q)$ can be written in the form

$$G(Q) = c_o(Q - \mu) + (c_u + c_o)n(Q).$$

where μ is the expected demand.

We know from Section 5.4 that one can write an explicit expression for $n(Q)$ when demand is normal. In particular, we showed that $n(Q) = \sigma L(z)$ where $L(z)$ is the standard loss integral. As noted in Section 5.4,

$$L(z) = \phi(z) - z[1 - \Phi(z)].$$

where $\phi(z)$ is the standard normal density, $\Phi(z)$ the standard normal distribution function and $z = (Q - \mu)/\sigma$ is the standardized value of the order quantity Q.

It follows that in the normal case we can write

$$G(Q) = c_o(Q - \mu) + (c_u + c_o)\sigma[\phi(z) - z(1 - \Phi(z)].$$

The standard normal density function can be computed directly, and the cumulative distribution function is available through tables and is a built in function in Excel.

It might also be of interest to know the minimum value of the expected cost. This is the value of the function G when $Q = Q^*$. Note that at $Q = Q^*$ the cumulative distribution function $\Phi(z^*)$ is equal to the critical ratio $c_u/(c_u + c_o)$, which means the complementary cumulative distribution function $1 - \Phi(z^*)$ is equal to the ratio $c_o/(c_u + c_o)$. Also, since $z = (Q - \mu)/\sigma$, it follows that $Q - \mu = \sigma z$. Making these two substitutions in the expression above for $G(Q)$ we obtain

$$G(Q^*) = c_o \sigma z^* + (c_u + c_o)\sigma \left[\phi(z^*) - z^*\left(\frac{c_o}{c_o + c_u}\right)\right] = (c_u + c_o)\sigma\phi(z^*).[1]$$

Note that if one knows z^* no table look up is required to compute this expression since we know that

$$\phi(z) = \frac{1}{\sqrt{2\pi}} e^{-0.5z^2}.$$

The expression for $G(Q^*)$ shows that the optimal newsvendor cost increases linearly in both the underage and overage costs as well as in the standard deviation of demand.

3. EXTENSION TO INFINITE HORIZON ASSUMING FULL BACK-ORDERING OF DEMAND

Let $D_1, D_2, \ldots$ be an infinite sequence of demands. Assume that the demands are independent identically distributed random variables having common distribution function $F(x)$ and density $f(x)$. The policy is to order up to Q each period. As all excess demand is back-ordered, the order quantity in any period is exactly the previous period's demand. The number of units sold will also equal the demand. In order to see this, consider the number of units sold in successive periods:

Number of units sold in period 1 = $\min(Q, D_1)$,

Number of units sold in period 2 = $\max(D_1 - Q, 0) + \min(Q, D_2)$,

Number of units sold in period 3 = $\max(D_2 - Q, 0) + \min(Q, D_3)$,

and so on.

[1] Porteus (2002) has derived essentially the same expression on page 13. I am grateful to Gerard Cachon for helpful discussions on this point.

These relationships follow because back-ordering of excess demand means that the sales are made in the subsequent period. Now, notice that

$$\min(Q, D_i) + \max(D_i - Q, 0) = D_i \quad \text{for } i = 1, 2, \ldots,$$

which follows from considering the cases $Q < D_i$ and $Q \geq D_i$.

Hence, the expected cost over n periods is

$$cQ + (c - S)E(D_1 + D_2 + \ldots + D_{n-1}) - (S)E[\min(Q, D_n)] + nL(Q)$$
$$= cQ + (c - S)(n - 1)\mu - (S)E[\min(Q, D_n)] + nL(Q)$$

where

$$L(Q) = h\int_0^Q (Q - x)f(x)dx + p\int_Q^\infty (x - Q)f(x)\,dx.$$

Dividing by n and letting $n \to \infty$ gives the average cost over infinitely many periods as

$$(c - S)\mu + L(Q).$$

The optimal value of Q occurs where $L'(Q) = 0$, which results in

$$F(Q) = p/(p + h).$$

4. EXTENSION TO INFINITE HORIZON ASSUMING LOST SALES

If excess demand is lost rather than back-ordered, then the previous argument is no longer valid. The number of units sold in period 1 is $\min(Q, D_1)$, which is also the number of units ordered in period 2; the number of units sold in period 2 is $\min(Q, D_2)$ (since there is no back-ordering of excess demand), which is also the number of units ordered in period 3; and so on. As shown in Section 1 of this appendix,

$$E[\min(Q, D)] = \mu - \int_Q^\infty (x - Q)f(x)\,dx.$$

Hence, it follows that the expected cost over n periods is given by

$$cQ + [(n - 1)c - nS]\left[\mu - \int_Q^\infty (x - Q)f(x)\,dx\right] + nL(Q)$$

If we divide by n and let $n \to \infty$, we obtain the following expression for the average cost per period:

$$(c - S)\left[\mu - \int_Q^\infty (x - Q)f(x)\,dx\right] + L(Q).$$

Differentiating with respect to Q and setting the result equal to zero gives the following condition for the optimal Q:

$$F(Q) = \frac{p + S - c}{p + S + h - c}.$$

Setting $c_u = p + S - c$ and $c_o = h$ gives the critical ratio in the form $c_u/(c_u + c_o)$. Hence, we interpret c_u as the cost of the loss of goodwill plus the lost profit per sale, and c_o as the cost of holding only.

Appendix 5–C

Derivation of the Optimal (Q, R) Policy

From Section 5.4, the objective is to find values of the variables Q and R to minimize the function

$$G(Q, R) = h(Q/2 + R - \lambda\tau) + K\lambda/Q + p\lambda n(R)/Q. \tag{1}$$

Because this function is to be minimized with respect to the two variables (Q, R), a necessary condition for optimality is that $\partial G/\partial Q = \partial G/\partial R = 0$. The two resulting equations are

$$\frac{\partial G}{\partial Q} = \frac{h}{2} - \frac{K\lambda}{Q^2} - \frac{p\lambda n(R)}{Q^2} = 0, \tag{2}$$

$$\frac{\partial G}{\partial R} = h + p\lambda n'(R)/Q = 0. \tag{3}$$

Note that since $n(R) = \int_R^\infty (x - R)f(x)\,dx$, one can show that

$$n'(R) = -(1 - F(R)).$$

From Equation (2) we obtain

$$\frac{1}{Q^2}[K\lambda + p\lambda n(R)] = \frac{h}{2}$$

or

$$Q^2 = \frac{2K\lambda + 2p\lambda n(R)}{h},$$

which gives

$$Q = \sqrt{\frac{2\lambda[K + pn(R)]}{h}}. \tag{4}$$

From Equation (3) we obtain

$$h + p\lambda[-(1 - F(R))]/Q = 0,$$

which gives

$$1 - F(R) = Qh/p\lambda. \tag{5}$$

Author's note: We use the term *optimal* somewhat loosely here. Technically speaking, the model that gives rise to these two equations is only approximate for several reasons. For one, the use of the average expected inventory is an approximation, since this is not the same as the expected average inventory (because one should not charge holding costs when inventory goes negative). As we saw in the discussion of negative safety stock in this chapter, there are cases where the right-hand side of Equation (5) can exceed 1, and the model "blows up." This would not be the case for a truly exact model, which is beyond the scope of this book.

Appendix 5–D

Probability Distributions for Inventory Management

In this chapter we have made frequent reference to the normal distribution as a model for demand uncertainty. Although the normal distribution certainly dominates applications, it is not the only choice available. In fact, it could be a poor choice in some circumstances. In this appendix we discuss other distributions for modeling demand uncertainty.

1. THE POISSON DISTRIBUTION AS A MODEL OF DEMAND UNCERTAINTY

One situation in which the normal distribution may be inappropriate is for slow-moving items, that is, ones with small demand rates. Because the normal is an infinite distribution, when the mean is small it is possible that a substantial portion of the density curve extends into the negative half line. This could give poor results for safety stock calculations. A common choice for modeling slow movers is the Poisson distribution. The Poisson is a discrete distribution defined on the positive half line only. Let X have the Poisson distribution with parameter μ. Then

$$f(x) = \frac{e^{-\mu}\mu^x}{x!} \quad \text{for } x = 0, 1, 2, \ldots.$$

(The derivation of the Poisson distribution and its relationship to the exponential distribution are discussed in detail in Section 12.3).

An important feature of the Poisson distribution is that both the mean and the variance are equal to μ (giving $\sigma = \sqrt{\mu}$). Hence, it should be true that the observed standard deviation of periodic demand (or lead time demand) is close to the square root of the mean periodic demand (or lead time demand) for the Poisson to be an appropriate choice. Table A–3 at the back of the book is a table of the complementary cumulative Poisson distribution. This table allows one to compute optimal policies for the newsvendor and the (Q, R) models assuming that demand follows the Poisson distribution.

We show how to find optimal policies for both the newsvendor and the (Q, R) models when demand is Poisson. For the newsvendor case, one simply applies the method outlined in Section 5.3 for discrete demand and obtains the probabilities from Table A–3. We illustrate with an example.

Example 5D.1 Consider Mac's newsstand, discussed in several examples in Chapter 5. A few regular customers have asked Mac to stock a particular stereo magazine. Mac has agreed even though sales have been slow. Based on past data, Mac has found that a Poisson distribution with mean 5 closely fits the weekly sales pattern for the magazine. Mac purchases the magazines for $0.50 and sells them for $1.50. He returns unsold copies to his supplier, who pays Mac $0.10 for each. Find the number of these magazines he should purchase from his supplier each week.

Solution The overage cost is c_o = $0.50 − $0.10 = $0.40 and the underage cost is c_u = $1.50 − $0.50 = $1.00. It follows that the critical ratio is $c_u/(c_o + c_u) = 1/1.4 = .7143$. As Table A–3 gives the complementary cumulative distribution, we subtract table entries from 1 to obtain values of the cumulative distribution function. From the table we see that

$$F(5) = 1 - .5595 = .4405,$$
$$F(6) = 1 - .3840 = .6160,$$
$$F(7) = 1 - .2378 = .7622.$$

Because the critical ratio is between $F(6)$ and $F(7)$, we move to the larger value, thus giving an optimal order quantity of 7 magazines.

It is not difficult to calculate optimal (Q, R) policies when the demand follows a Poisson distribution, but the process requires an iterative solution similar to that for the normal distribution described in Section 5.5. Define $P(x)$ as the complementary cumulative probability of the Poisson. That is,

$$P(x) = \sum_{k=x}^{\infty} f(k).$$

Table A–3 gives values of $P(x)$. It can then be shown that for the Poisson distribution

$$n(R) = \mu P(R) - R P(R + 1),$$

310 Chapter Five Inventory Control Subject to Uncertain Demand

which means that all the information required to compute optimal policies appears in Table A–3.[1] That is, special tables for computing $n(R)$ are not required in this case. This relationship allows one to compute the (Q, R) policy using the pair of equations (1) and (2) from Section 5.4.

Example 5D.2 A department store uses a (Q, R) policy to control its inventories. Sales of a pocket FM radio average 1.4 radios per week. The radio costs the store $50.00, and fixed costs of replenishment amount to $20.00. Holding costs are based on a 20 percent annual interest charge, and the store manager estimates a $12.50 cost of lost profit and loss of goodwill if the radio is demanded when out of stock. Reorder lead time is 2 weeks, and statistical studies have shown that demand over the lead time is accurately described by a Poisson distribution. Find the optimal lot sizes and reorder points for this item.

Solution The relevant parameters for this problem are

$$\lambda = (1.4)(52) = 72.8.$$
$$h = (50)(0.2) = 10.0.$$
$$K = \$20.$$
$$\mu = (1.4)(2) = 2.8.$$
$$p = \$12.50.$$

To start the solution process, we compute the EOQ. It is

$$EOQ = \sqrt{\frac{2K\lambda}{h}} = \sqrt{\frac{(2)(20)(72.8)}{10}} = 17.1.$$

The next step is to find R solving

$$P(R) = Qh/p\lambda.$$

Substituting the EOQ for Q and solving gives $P(R_0) = .1868$. From Table A–3, we see that $R = 4$ results in $P(R) = .3081$ and $R = 5$ results in $P(R) = .1523$. Assuming the conservative strategy of rounding to the *larger* R, we would choose $R = 5$ and $P(R) = .1523$. It now follows that

$$n(R_0) = (2.8)(.1523) - (5)(.0651) = 0.1009.$$

Hence Q_1 is

$$Q_1 = \sqrt{\frac{(2)(72.8)[20 + (12.5)(0.1009)]}{10}} = 17.6.$$

It follows that $P(R_1) = .1934$, giving $R_1 = R_0 = 5$. Hence the solution has converged, because successive R (and, hence, Q) values are the same. The optimal solution is $(Q, R) = (18, 5)$.

2. THE LAPLACE DISTRIBUTION

A continuous distribution, which has been suggested for modeling slow-moving items or ones with more variance in the tails than the normal, is the Laplace distribution. The Laplace distribution has been called the pseudo-exponential distribution, as it is mathematically an exponential distribution with a symmetric mirror image. (The exponential distribution is discussed at length in Chapter 12 in the context of reliability management.)

The mathematical form of the Laplace pdf is

$$f(x) = \frac{1}{2\theta} \exp(-|x - \mu|/\theta) \qquad \text{for } -\infty < x < +\infty.$$

Because the pdf is symmetric around μ, the mean is μ. The variance is $2\theta^2$. The Laplace distribution is also a reasonable model for slow-moving items, and is an

[1] See Hadley and Whitin (1963), p. 441.

alternative to the normal distribution for fast-moving items when there is more spread in the tails of the distribution than the normal distribution gives. As far as inventory applications are concerned, Presutti and Trepp (1970) noticed that it significantly simplified the calculation of the optimal policy for the (Q, R) model.

One can show that for any value of $R > \mu$, the complementary cumulative distribution $(P(R))$ and the loss integral $(n(R))$ are given by

$$P(R) = 0.5 \exp(-[(R - \mu)/\theta])$$
$$n(R) = 0.5\theta \exp(-[(R - \mu)/\theta])$$

so that the ratio $n(R)/P(R) = \theta$, independent of R. This fact results in a very simple solution for the (Q, R) model. Recall that the two equations defining the optimal policy were

$$Q = \sqrt{\frac{2\lambda[K + pm(R)]}{h}}$$

$$P(R) = Qh/p\lambda \qquad \text{[where } P(R) = 1 - F(R)\text{]}.$$

The simplification is achieved by using the SOQ formula presented in Section 5.5. The SOQ representation is an alternative representation for Q that does not include the stock-out cost, p. Using $P(R) = 1 - F(R)$, the SOQ formula is

$$Q = \frac{n(R)}{P(R)} + \sqrt{\frac{2K\lambda}{h} + \left(\frac{n(R)}{P(R)}\right)^2}$$

$$= \theta + \sqrt{\frac{2K\lambda}{h} + \theta^2}$$

independently of R! Hence, the optimal Q and R can be found in a simple one-step calculation. When using a cost model, find the value of $P(R)$ from $P(R) = Qh/p\lambda$. Then, using the representation $P(R) = \exp[-(R - \mu)/\theta]/2$, it follows that $R = -\theta \ln(2P(R)) + \mu$. Using a service level model, one simply uses the formulas for R given in Section 5.5. We illustrate with an example.

Example 5D.3 Consider Example 5D.2, but suppose that we wish to use the Laplace distribution to compute the optimal policy rather than the Poisson distribution. As both the mean and the variance of the lead time demand are 2.8, we set $\mu = 2.8$ and $2\theta^2 = 2.8$, giving $\theta = 1.1832$. It follows that

$$Q = 1.1832 + \sqrt{\frac{(2)(20)(72.8)}{10} + (1.1832)^2} = 18.3.$$

As with Example 5D.2, we obtain $P(R) = .1934$. Using $R = -\theta \ln(2P(R)) + \mu$ and substituting $P(R) = .1934$ gives $R = 3.92$, which we round to 4. Notice that this solution differs slightly from the one we obtained assuming Poisson demand. However, recall that using the Poisson distribution we found that the optimal R was between 4 and 5, which we chose to round to 5 to be conservative.

3. OTHER LEAD TIME DEMAND DISTRIBUTIONS

Many other probability distributions have been recommended for modeling lead time demand. Some of these include the negative binomial distribution, the gamma distribution, the logarithmic distribution, and the Pearson distribution. (See Silver and Peterson,

1985, p. 289, for a list of articles that discuss these distributions in the context of inventory management.) The normal distribution probably accounts for the lion's share of applications, with the Poisson accounting for almost all the rest. We included the Laplace distribution because of the interesting property that optimal (Q, R) policies can be found without an iterative solution, and because it could be a good alternative to the Poisson for low-demand items.

Appendix 5–E

Glossary of Notation for Chapter 5

α = Desired level of Type 1 service.

β = Desired level of Type 2 service.

c_o = Unit overage cost for newsvendor model.

c_u = Unit underage cost for newsvendor model.

D = Random variable corresponding to demand. It is the one-period demand for the newsvendor model and the lead time demand for the (Q, R) model.

EOQ = Economic order quantity.

$F(t)$ = Cumulative distribution function of demand. Values of the standard normal CDF appear in Table A–4 at the end of the book.

$f(t)$ = Probability density function of demand.

$G(Q)$ = Expected one-period cost associated with lot size Q (newsvendor model).

$G(Q, R)$ = Expected average annual cost for the (Q, R) model.

h = Holding cost per unit per unit time.

I = Annual interest rate used to compute holding cost.

K = Setup cost or fixed order cost.

λ = Expected demand rate (units per unit time).

$L(z)$ = Normalized loss function. Used to compute $n(R) = \sigma L(z)$. Tabled values of $L(z)$ appear in Table A–4 at the end of the book.

μ = Mean demand [lead time demand for (Q, R) model].

$n(R)$ = Expected number of stock-outs in the lead time for (Q, R) model.

p = Penalty cost per unit for not satisfying demand.

Q = Lot size or size of the order.

S = Safety stock; $S = R - \lambda\tau$ for (Q, R) model.

SOQ = Service order quantity.

T = Expected cycle time; mean time between placement of successive orders.

τ = Order lead time.

Type 1 service = Proportion of cycles in which all demand is satisfied.

Type 2 service = Proportion of demands satisfied.

Bibliography

Agrawal, N., and S. A. Smith, *Retail Supply Chain Management*. Springer, 2008.

Arrow, K. A.; T. E. Harris; and T. Marschak. "Optimal Inventory Policy." *Econometrica* 19 (1951), pp. 250–72.

Arrow, K. A.; S. Karlin; and H. E. Scarf, eds. *Studies in the Mathematical Theory of Inventory and Production*. Stanford, CA: Stanford University Press, 1958.

Bessler, S. A., and A. F. Veinott, Jr. "Optimal Policy for a Dynamic Multiechelon Inventory Model." *Naval Research Logistics Quarterly* 13 (1966), pp. 355–89.

Brown, R. G. *Statistical Forecasting for Inventory Control*. New York: McGraw-Hill, 1959.

Brown, R. G. *Decision Rules for Inventory Management*. Hinsdale, IL: Dryden Press, 1967.

Clark, A., and H. E. Scarf. "Optimal Policies for a Multiechelon Inventory Problem." *Management Science* 6 (1960), pp. 475–90.

Cohen, M. A., and D. Pekelman. "LIFO Inventory Systems." *Management Science* 24 (1978), pp. 1150–62.

Deuermeyer, B. L., and L. B. Schwarz. "A Model for the Analysis of System Service Level in Warehouse-Retailer Distribution Systems: Identical Retailer Case." In *Multilevel Production/Inventory Control Systems: Theory and Practice*, ed. L. B. Schwarz, pp. 163–94. Amsterdam: North Holland, 1981.

Dvoretsky, A.; J. Kiefer; and J. Wolfowitz. "The Inventory Problem: I. Case of Known Distributions of Demand." *Econometrica* 20 (1952), pp. 187–222.

Ehrhardt, R. "The Power Approximation for Computing (s, S) Inventory Policies." *Management Science* 25 (1979), pp. 777–86.

Eppen, G., and L. Schrage. "Centralized Ordering Policies in a Multi-Warehouse System with Lead Times and Random Demand." In *Multilevel Production/Inventory Control Systems: Theory and Practice*, ed. L. B. Schwarz, pp. 51–68. Amsterdam: North Holland, 1981.

Federgruen, A., and P. Zipkin. "Computational Issues in an Infinite Horizon Multi-Echelon Inventory Model." *Operations Research* 32 (1984), pp. 818–36.

Fishman, G. S. *Concepts and Methods in Discrete Event Digital Simulation*. New York: John Wiley & Sons, 1973.

Freeland, J. R., and E. L. Porteus. "Evaluating the Effectiveness of a New Method of Computing Approximately Optimal (s, S) Inventory Policies." *Operations Research* 28 (1980), pp. 353–64.

Graves, S. C. "A Multiechelon Inventory Model for a Repairable Item with One for One Replenishment." *Management Science* 31 (1985), pp. 1247–56.

Graves, S. C.; A. H. G. Rinnooy Kan; and P. Zipkin, eds. *Handbooks in Operations Research and Management Science*. Volume 4, *Logistics of Production and Inventory*. Amsterdam: Elsevier Science Publishers, 1992.

Hadley, G. J., and T. M. Whitin. *Analysis of Inventory Systems*. Englewood Cliffs, NJ: Prentice Hall, 1963.

Hartung, P. "A Simple Style Goods Inventory Model." *Management Science* 19 (1973), pp. 1452–58.

Hausman, W. H., and R. Peterson. "Multiproduct Production Scheduling for Style Goods with Limited Capacity, Forecast Revisions, and Terminal Delivery." *Management Science* 18 (1972), pp. 370–83.

Iglehart, D. L., "Optimality of (s, S) Inventory Policies in the Infinite Horizon Dynamic Inventory Problem." *Management Science* 9 (1963), pp. 259–67.

Kaplan, R. "A Dynamic Inventory Model with Stochastic Lead Times." *Management Science* 16 (1970), pp. 491–507.

Love, S. F. *Inventory Control*. New York: McGraw-Hill, 1979.

Mohan, S. "EDI's Move to Prime Time Stalled by Cost Perception." *Computerworld* 29 (February 20, 1995), p. 91.

Muckstadt, J. M., and L. J. Thomas. "Are Multiechelon Inventory Models Worth Implementing in Systems with Low Demand Rate Items?" *Management Science* 26 (1980), pp. 483–94.

Murray, G. R., and E. A. Silver. "A Bayesian Analysis of the Style Goods Inventory Problem." *Management Science* 12 (1966), pp. 785–97.

Murray, J. E. "The EDI Explosion." *Purchasing* 118 (February 16, 1995), pp. 28–30.

Nahmias, S. "Inventory Models." In *The Encyclopedia of Computer Science and Technology, Volume 9*, ed. J. Belzer, A. G. Holzman, and A. Kent, pp. 447–83. New York: Marcel Dekker, 1978.

Nahmias, S. "Simple Approximations for a Variety of Dynamic Lead Time Lost-Sales Inventory Models." *Operations Research* 27 (1979), pp. 904–24.

Nahmias, S. "Managing Reparable Item Inventory Systems: A Review." In *Multilevel Production/Inventory Control Systems: Theory and Practice*, ed. L. B. Schwarz, pp. 253–77. Amsterdam: North Holland, 1981.

Nahmias, S. "Perishable Inventory Theory: A Review." *Operations Research* 30 (1982), pp. 680–708.

Nahmias, S., and S. Smith. "Mathematical Models of Retailer Inventory Systems: A Review." In *Perspectives in Operations Management: Essays in Honor of Elwood S. Buffa*, ed. R. K. Sarin. Boston: Kluwer, 1992.

Parr, J. O. "Formula Approximations to Brown's Service Function." *Production and Inventory Management* 13 (1972), pp. 84–86.

Porteus, E. L. *Foundations of Stochastic Inventory Theory*. Stanford, CA: Stanford Business Books, 2002.

Porteus, E. L. "Numerical Comparisons of Inventory Policies for Periodic Review Systems." *Operations Research* 33 (1985), pp. 134–52.

Presutti, V., and R. Trepp. "More Ado about EOQ." *Naval Research Logistics Quarterly* 17 (1970), pp. 243–51.

Ramberg, J. S., and B. W. Schmeiser. "An Approximate Method for Generating Symmetric Random Variables." *Communications of the ACM* 15 (1972), pp. 987–89.

Scarf, H. E. "The Optimality of (s, S) Policies in the Dynamic Inventory Problem." In *Mathematical Methods in the Social Sciences*, ed. K. J. Arrow, S. Karlin, and P. Suppes. Stanford, CA: Stanford University Press, 1960.

Scarf, H. E. "Analytical Techniques in Inventory Theory." In *Multi-Stage Inventory Models and Techniques*, ed. H. E. Scarf, D. M. Gilford, and M. W. Shelly. Stanford, CA: Stanford University Press, 1963.

Schmidt, C. P., and S. Nahmias. "Optimal Policy for a Single Stage Assembly System with Stochastic Demand." *Operations Research* 33 (1985), pp. 1130–45.

Sherbrooke, C. C. "METRIC: Multiechelon Technique for Recoverable Item Control." *Operations Research* 16 (1968), pp. 122–41.

Silver, E. A., and R. Peterson. *Decision Systems for Inventory Management and Production Planning*. 2nd ed. New York: John Wiley & Sons, 1985.

Veinott, A. F. "The Status of Mathematical Inventory Theory." *Management Science* 12 (1966), pp. 745–77.

Veinott, A. F., and H. M. Wagner. "Computing Optimal (s, S) Inventory Policies." *Management Science* 11 (1965), pp. 525–52.

Whitin, T. M. *The Theory of Inventory Management*. Rev. ed. Princeton, NJ: Princeton University Press, 1957.

Chapter Six

Supply Chain Management

"Supply chains cannot tolerate even 24 hours of disruption. So if you lose your place in the supply chain because of wild behavior, you could lose a lot. It would be like pouring cement down one of your oil wells."

—Thomas Friedman

Chapter Overview

Purpose

To understand what a modern supply chain is, how supply chains are organized and managed, and to review the newest developments in this important area.

Key Points

1. *What is a supply chain?* A supply chain is the entire network comprising the activities of a firm that links suppliers, factories, warehouses, stores, and customers. It requires management of goods, money, and information among all the relevant players. While the specific term *supply chain management* (SCM) emerged only in the late 1980s, managing the flow of goods has been an issue since the industrial revolution, and was traditionally simply called logistics.
2. *Supply chain strategy.* For most products it is not possible to have a supply chain that is both low cost and highly responsive. A supply chain strategy must therefore align with the product's positioning in the marketplace. In particular, a product that competes on price must be delivered through a highly efficient supply chain, while for an innovative or high-fashion item it is most important to be able to respond quickly to changes in customer demand.
3. *The role of information in supply chains.* As has been noted, a supply chain involves the transfer of goods, money, and information. Modern supply chain management seeks to eliminate the inefficiencies that arise from poor information flows. One way to ameliorate this problem is vendor-managed inventories, where vendors, rather than retailers, are responsible for keeping inventory on the shelves. Advances in technology have also improved the availability of information in supply chains.
4. *The transportation problem.* The transportation problem is one of the early applications of linear programming. Assume m production facilities (sources) and n demand points (sinks). The unit cost of shipping from every source to every sink is known, and the objective is to determine a shipping plan that satisfies the supply

and demand constraints at minimum cost. The linear programming formulation of the transportation problem has been successfully solved with hundreds of thousands of variables and constraints. A generalization of the transportation problem is the transshipment problem, where intermediate nodes can be used for storage as well as be demand or supply points. Transshipment problems can also be solved with linear programming.

5. *Routing in supply chains.* Consider a delivery truck that must make deliveries to several customers. The objective is to find the optimal sequence of deliveries that minimizes the total distance required. This problem is known as the traveling salesman problem, and turns out to be very difficult to solve optimally. The calculations required to find the optimal solution grow exponentially with the problem size (known mathematically as an NP hard problem). In this section, we present a simple heuristic for obtaining approximate solutions known as the savings method.

6. *Risk pooling.* One key technique for mitigating uncertainty and improving planning is risk pooling. In essence, this principle states that the sum of a number of uncertain variables is inherently less variable than each individual variable, and as such is easier to plan for, schedule, and manage. There are a variety of ways to operationalize risk pooling, including product postponement, regional warehouses, aggregate capacity plans, and flexible capacity.

7. *Designing products for supply chain efficiency.* "Thinking outside the box" has become a cliché. It means looking at a problem in a new way, often not taking constraints at face value. An example of thinking outside the box is postponement in supply chains. The first application of this idea is due to Benetton, a well-known manufacturer of fashion knitwear. Benetton must predict consumers' color preferences in advance of the selling season. Because wool is dyed first and then later weaved into sweaters, the color mix must be decided upon well in advance. If their predictions about consumers' color preferences are wrong (which they invariably are), popular colors would sell out quickly and unpopular colors would sit on the shelves. Their solution was to reverse the order of the weaving and dying operations. Sweaters were woven from undyed wool (gray stock) and then dyed to specific colors as late as possible. This provided Benetton with more time to observe which colors were selling best. Hewlett Packard discovered a similar solution in their printer division. Printers must be configured for local markets due to language and other differences. By producing "gray stock" printers that had all common parts, and then configuring export printers on site in local markets, they were able to delay product differentiation and better balance their inventories.

Another example of designing products for supply chain efficiency is Ikea. Ikea is a Swedish-based firm that sells inexpensive home furnishings. To reduce costs Ikea designs their furniture to be easily stored directly at the retail outlets. This means that customers can take their purchases with them, thus removing the long delays and customization required by more traditional furniture outlets.

8. *Multilevel distribution systems.* Typically in large systems, stock is stored at multiple locations. Distribution centers (DCs) receive stock from plants and factories and then ship to either smaller local DCs or directly to stores. Some of the advantages of employing DCs include economies of scale, tailoring the mix of product to a particular region or culture, and safety stock reduction via risk pooling.

9. *Incentives in the supply chain.* Consider a clothing designer whose goods are sold at a chain of high-end boutiques. The designer contracts the manufacturing to a firm that subcontracts to a plant in China. The Chinese plant manager is paid

a bonus based on the quantity of output. As a result, he provides incentives for his workers to produce as quickly as they can. However, this results in slipshod quality and a high rate of defective pieces. Ultimately, the designer has to answer to the boutique chain that carries her designs. This is an example of misaligned incentives. How could this problem be ameliorated? One possible answer is to have careful inspection at the plant level, and pay the plant manager based on nondefective items only. What this means is that each player in the supply chain needs to have its incentives aligned with what is best for the system as a whole.

10. *Global supply chain management.* Today, most firms are multinational. Products are designed for, and shipped to, a wide variety of markets around the world. As an example, consider the market for automobiles. Fifty years ago, virtually all the automobiles sold in the United States were produced here. Today, that number is probably closer to 50 percent. Global market forces are shaping the new economy. Vast markets, such as China, are now emerging, and the major industrial powers are vying for a share. Technology, cost considerations, and political and macroeconomic forces have driven globalization. Selling in diverse markets presents special problems for supply chain management.

We take a trip to the grocery store at 10 P.M. to get a jar of peanut butter for our child's lunch the next day. Not only is the store open, but there are a large variety of brands, styles, and sizes of peanut butter available. Americans (and residents of most modern countries) take such things for granted. However, there is a complex myriad of activities that must be carefully coordinated to ensure that the peanut butter will be there when we need it. And this goes for clothes, hardware, and all the other consumer goods we purchase. Do we appreciate the fact that many of these goods are produced and shipped all over the world before they make it to our homes? The logistics of coordinating all the activities that afford us this convenience is the essence of supply chain management.

The term *supply chain management* (SCM) seems to have emerged in the late 1980s and continues to gain interest at an increasing rate. The trade literature abounds with book titles and articles relating to some aspect of SCM. Software and consulting firms specializing in SCM solutions are now commonplace. These companies have grown at remarkable rates and include giants SAP and Oracle, which offer SCM solutions as part of comprehensive information retrieval systems. Although the SCM label is somewhat new, the problems considered are not. Nearly all the material in Chapters 2 to 5 involves SCM. So what is different about SCM? The simple answer is that SCM looks at the problem of managing the flow of goods as an integrated system. Many definitions of SCM have been proposed, and it is instructive to examine some of them. The simplest and most straightforward appears at the Stanford Supply Chain Forum (1999) Web site and is probably due to Hau Lee, the head of the Forum. It is

> Supply chain management deals with the management of materials, information and financial flows in a network consisting of suppliers, manufacturers, distributors, and customers.

While short, this definition is fairly complete. It indicates that it is not only the flow of goods that is important, but the flow of information and money as well.

A definition due to Simchi-Levi et al. (1999, p. 1) that focuses on only the flow of goods is

> Supply chain management is a set of approaches utilized to efficiently integrate suppliers, manufacturers, warehouses, and stores, so that merchandise is produced and distributed at the right quantities, to the right locations, and at the right time, in order to minimize systemwide costs while satisfying service level requirements.

FIGURE 6–1
The supply chain umbrella

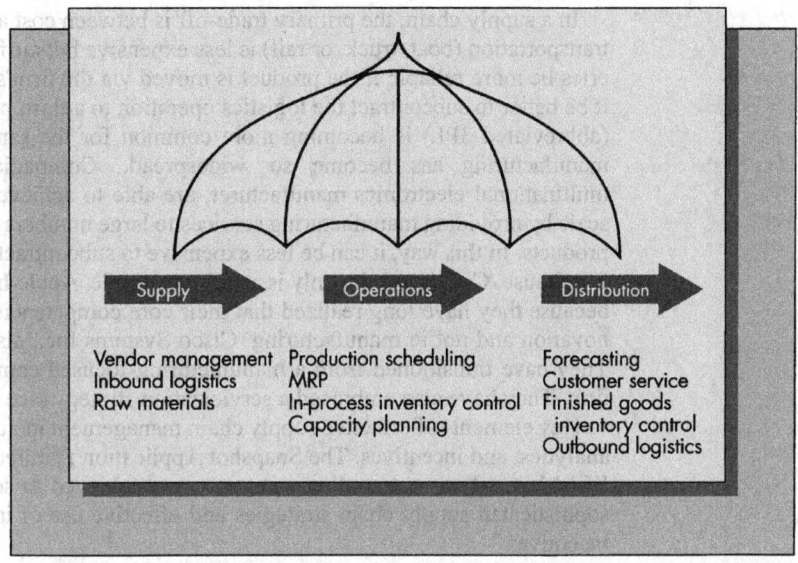

Since this definition focuses on the flow of goods, it implies that SCM is relevant only to manufacturing firms. Is SCM also relevant to service organizations? These days it is well recognized that many aspects of SCM do indeed apply to service organizations, although typically these organizations refer to the *value chain* instead of the supply chain.

Most writers agree that "logistics" deals with essentially the same issues as supply chain management. The term logistics originated in the military and concerned problems of moving personnel and materiel in critical times. It was later adopted by business and became a common moniker for professional societies and academic programs. One might argue that although classical logistics treated the same set of problems as SCM, it did not consider the supply chain as an integrated system (Copacino, 1997). A summary of the "umbrella" of activities composing SCM appears in Figure 6–1.

In a sense, one might consider this entire text to deal with some aspect of SCM if one takes the broad view of the field depicted in Figure 6–1. However, most of the chapters focus on specific topics, like inventory control or job shop scheduling. SCM, on the other hand, treats the entire product delivery system from suppliers of raw materials to distribution channels of finished goods. While important and useful in many contexts, simple formulas such as the EOQ are unlikely to shed much light on effective management of complex supply chains.

The Supply Chain as a Strategic Weapon

Where does the supply chain fit into the overall business strategy of the firm? In Chapter 1, it was noted that an important part of the firm's competitive edge is its strategic positioning in the marketplace. Examples of strategic positioning include being the low-cost provider (such as Hyundai automobiles) or the high-quality provider (such as Mercedes-Benz) or exploiting market segmentation to achieve shares of both markets (as does General Motors with different brands aimed at different market segments). The design of the supply chain also reflects a firm's strategic positioning.

In a supply chain, the primary trade-off is between cost and response time. Ground transportation (boat, truck, or rail) is less expensive but air freight is faster. Will deliveries be more reliable if the product is moved via the firm's internal system or would it be better to subcontract the logistics operation to a third party? Third-party logistics (abbreviated 3PL) is becoming more common for the same reason that third-party manufacturing has become so widespread. Companies such as Foxconn, a multinational electronics manufacturer, are able to achieve significant economies of scale by providing manufacturing services to large numbers of firms producing similar products. In this way, it can be less expensive to subcontract manufacturing than to do it in-house. Cost is not the only issue. For example, Apple Inc. outsources to Foxconn because they have long realized that their core competencies lie in aesthetics and innovation and not in manufacturing. Cisco Systems Inc., also outsources to Foxconn. They have transitioned from a manufacturing-focused company to a design-focused firm. They have also embraced a servicization strategy (see Chapter 1).

Key elements of effective supply chain management include the use of information, analytics, and incentives. The Snapshot Application featured in this section highlights Wal-Mart, whose extraordinary success was achieved to some extent because of its sophisticated supply chain strategies and effective use of information, analytics, and incentives.

As previously mentioned, one of the key challenges in supply chain management is aligning incentives. Much of the research is concerned with developing appropriate contracts to align incentives. Modern technologies make this easier. In fact, it has been almost 20 years since Gibson, the then chairman of Manugistics Inc., stated in a *Wall Street Journal* article that "strategic partnering used to mean stealing revenue or pushing cost onto someone else in the supply chain. You are a pig at the trough if you view it that way. With technology, there are so many efficiencies that can be shared." (*WSJ*, April 12, 1996)

In this chapter we provide the reader with an appreciation of the most important issues encountered in managing complex supply chains. In addition, we present a sampling of the mathematical models (analytics) used in SCM analysis.

6.1 SUPPLY CHAIN STRATEGY

As just discussed, one of the key trade-offs in supply chain design is between cost and speed. It is important to recognize that the best choices on this dimension depend on the product being produced. Fisher (1997) presents a simple framework for this choice. He breaks products into two categories: *functional* or *innovative*, and supply chains into two types: *efficient* versus *responsive*. He argues that functional products should be produced using efficient supply chains while innovative products require responsive supply chains.

A functional product is a commodity-type product that competes primarily on cost. A canonical functional product is Campbell's Soup. Only 5 percent of the products they produce are new each year and most products have been in the market for many years. It has highly predictable demand and long life cycles (particularly relative to lead times). This type of product is best produced using an efficient supply chain where the primary focus is on costs, which include inventory holding, transportation, handling, and manufacturing costs. Large manufacturing batches achieve scale economies, and minimum order quantities reduce handling/order processing costs. Supply chain performance is evaluated using traditional cost measures, such as inventory turns, and factory and transportation utilization.

Snapshot Application

WAL-MART WINS WITH SOLID SUPPLY CHAIN MANAGEMENT

Although there are many examples of companies winning (or losing) because of either good or bad supply chain strategies, perhaps none is more dramatic than the stories of Wal-Mart and Kmart. Both companies were founded in the same year, 1962. In only a few years, Kmart had become a household term, while Wal-Mart was largely unknown except for a few communities in the South. Wal-Mart stores were typically located in rural areas, so they rarely competed head-on with the larger, better-known chains like Sears and Kmart, most of whose stores were located in large cities and surrounding suburbs. In 1987 Kmart's sales were almost twice those of Wal-Mart (about $25 billion annually versus about $15 billion annually). By 1990 Wal-Mart had overtaken Kmart and in 1994 Wal-Mart's annual sales almost tripled Kmart's (about $80 billion versus about $27 billion)! Wal-Mart is now the largest discount retailer in the United States, surpassing Sears as well as Kmart, who have now merged. What could have possibly accounted for this dramatic turn-around?

While one can point to several factors leading to Wal-Mart's success, there is no question that the firm's emphasis on solid supply chain management was one of the most important. According to Duff and Ortega (1995) in comparing the management decisions of Kmart's former CEO, Joseph Antonini, and Wal-Mart's Sam Walton:

> When Mr. Antonini took the reins of Kmart in 1987, he had his hands full . . . Also, his predecessors neglected to implement the sophisticated computer systems that were helping Wal-Mart track and replenish its merchandise swiftly and efficiently.
>
> A self-promoter with a boisterous voice and wide smile, Mr. Antonini invested heavily in national television campaigns and glamorous representatives such as Jaclyn Smith . . . Mr. Walton avoided publicity. And instead of marketing, he became obsessed with operations. He invested tens of millions of dollars in a companywide computer system linking cash registers to headquarters, enabling him to quickly restock goods selling off the shelves. He also invested heavily in trucks and distribution centers. Besides enhancing his control, these moves sharply reduced costs.
>
> Mr. Antonini tried bolstering growth by overseeing the purchase of other types of retailers: the Sports Authority sporting goods chain, OfficeMax office supply stores, Borders bookstores, and Pace Membership Warehouse clubs . . .
>
> But the least visible difference between Wal-Mart and Kmart was beginning to matter a lot. Wal-Mart's incredibly sophisticated distribution inventory and scanner systems meant that customers almost never encountered depleted shelves or price-check delays at the cash register.
>
> The halls of Kmart, meanwhile, were filled with distribution horror stories. Joseph R. Thomas, who oversaw distribution, said that in retrospect, he should have smelled trouble when he found warehouses stuffed full of merchandise on December 15, the height of the Christmas season.

Wal-Mart is the world's largest public corporation, according to the Fortune Global 500 list in 2014, the biggest private employer in the world with over two million employees, and the largest retailer in the world. It has over 11,000 stores in 27 countries, under a total of 55 different names, and continues to expand. Its Chinese operations are growing particularly quickly with 100 stores planned for the next few years and a projected market of 2,000 stores.

Wal-Mart is known for both its sophisticated business analytics and advanced information systems. They have been a leader in vendor-managed inventory, sharing data with suppliers for better decisions, implementing effective cross-docking operations, and lately they have been proponents of sustainable supply chain management. Although much of the information about their systems is proprietary, it is clear that they invest heavily in business intelligence.

There are some important lessons here. When problems arose, Kmart's management responded by putting money into marketing and acquisitions, while Wal-Mart invested in better stores and a better logistics system for making sure that shelves were stocked with what customers wanted. One of the key themes of this book is that operations matter, and indeed effective operations and supply chain management can be a strategic weapon for a firm. While innovative designs can delay the need for effective supply chain management, sooner or later inefficiencies catch up with a firm.

The story of Kmart and Wal-Mart is reminiscent of the story of the American and Japanese auto industries. In the 1950s and 1960s when American auto makers had a virtual monopoly on much of the world's auto market, where did the Big Three put their resources? Into producing better engineered cars at lower cost? No. Into slick marketing campaigns and annual cosmetic makeovers. The Japanese, on the other hand, invested in the latest automotive technology and sophisticated logistics systems such as just-in-time. The rest, as they say, is history.

An innovative product is one that typically has high margin but highly variable demand and short life cycle. An example is Sport Obermeyer's fashion skiwear. Each year, 95 percent of the products are completely new designs and demand forecasts err by as much as 200 percent. There is a short retail season, and cost concerns focus around inventory obsolescence and lost sales (see the Snapshot Application in Chapter 2). This type of product is best produced using a market responsive supply chain, where a premium is paid for flexibility, including faster transportation, lower transportation and factory utilization, and smaller batches. Supply chain performance is best measured not with traditional cost measures but by recognizing that the opportunity costs of lost sales and poor service are key metrics to consider.

Cost and speed are both key measures of supply chain effectiveness. However, Lee (2004) argues that they are not the whole story. He proposes the "Triple A" supply chain, which is *agile*, *adaptable*, and *aligned*. Here agility is defined as the ability to respond to short-term changes in demand or supply quickly. Adaptability is defined as the ability to adjust the supply chain design to accommodate market changes. Finally, alignment relates to the existence of incentives for supply chain partners to improve performance of the entire chain. Further details may be found within his article but clearly these are desirable traits for a supply chain. Like any desirable feature they are not costless, and the cost to implement must be balanced against strategic necessity.

6.2 THE ROLE OF INFORMATION IN THE SUPPLY CHAIN

How often have we heard it said that we are living in the "information age"? The availability of information is increasing at an exponential rate. New sources of information in the form of academic and trade journals, magazines, newsletters, and so on are introduced every day. The explosion of information availability on the Web has been truly phenomenal. Web searches are now the first place many go for information on almost anything.

Knowledge is power. In supply chains, information is power. It provides the decision maker the power to get ahead of the competition, the power to run a business smoothly and efficiently, and the power to succeed in an ever more complex environment. Information plays a key role in the management of the supply chain. As we saw in the earlier chapters of this book, many aspects of operations planning start with the forecast of sales and build a plan for manufacturing or inventory replenishment from that forecast. Forecasts, of course, are based on information.

An excellent example of the role of information in supply chains is the Harvard Business School cases Barilla SpA (A and B) (1994) written by Jan Hammond. In many operations management courses, these cases provide an introduction to the role of information in supply chains. Barilla is an Italian company that specializes in the production of pasta. In the late 1980s, Barilla's head of logistics tried to introduce a new approach to dealing with distributors, which he called just-in-time distribution (JITD). Briefly, the idea was to obtain sales data directly from the distributors (Barilla's customers) and use these data to allow Barilla to determine when and how large the deliveries should be. At that time, Barilla was operating in the traditional fashion. Distributors would independently place weekly orders based on standard reorder point methods. This led to wide swings in the demand on Barilla's factories due to the "bullwhip effect," which is discussed in detail next. The JITD idea met with staunch resistance, both within and outside Barilla.

Snapshot Application

ANHEUSER-BUSCH RE-ENGINEERS THEIR SUPPLY CHAIN

Anheuser-Busch is the leading American brewer, holding close to a half share of U.S. beer sales, and producing iconic brands such as Budweiser and Bud Light. In the late 1990s they undertook a major reorganization of their supply chain (John & Willis, 1998).They found that less than 10 percent of their volume accounted for around 80 percent of the brand and package combinations. Management decided to switch to focused production. Some breweries were dedicated for the efficient production of large volume items, such as Bud and Bud Light. Others were responsible for producing lower volume niche products, such as wheat beers or products targeted at holidays. (Refer to the discussion of the focused factory in Chapter 1.)

By aligning supply chain metrics to the type of product being produced, their decisions were in line with Fisher's recommendations for matching product type with supply chain type. In particular, they made sure that their high-volume breweries were measured by efficiency metrics, such as utilization and volume of output; whereas, their niche product breweries were measured by how effectively they met demand. Previously, benchmarking had been across all breweries, which did not create the correct incentives for either the high volume or niche products.

In addition to focused facilities and supply chains, Anheuser-Busch also undertook a number of initiatives in line with topics covered later in this chapter. In particular, a mixed integer programming model (i.e., supply chain analytics) was used to identify the optimal number and location of distribution points in the supply chain. Contracts with a thousand different trucking companies (across the whole network) were largely replaced by a single contract with a single dedicated carrier, decreasing the complexity of the network. Inventory pooling was used to reduce both risk and cost. Finally, replenishment agreements were renegotiated and vendor-managed inventory agreements were put in place, which improved the alignment of the incentives in the supply chain.

The Barilla sales and marketing organizations, in particular, were most threatened by the proposed changes. Distributors were concerned that their prerogatives would be compromised.

Without going into the details [which can be found in Barilla SpA (B)], management eventually did prevail, and the JITD system was implemented with several of Barilla's largest distributors. The results were striking. Delivery reliability improved, and the variance of orders placed on the factory were substantially reduced. The program proved a win-win for Barilla and its customers.

Barilla's success with its JITD program is one example of what today is known as vendor-managed inventory (VMI). VMI programs have been the mainstay of many successful retailers in the United States. For example, Procter & Gamble has assumed responsibility for keeping track of inventories for several of its major clients, such as Wal-Mart. Years ago, grocery store managements were responsible for keeping track of their inventories. Today, it is commonplace to see, in our local grocery stores, folks checking shelves who are not store employees but employees of the manufacturers. With VMI programs, it becomes the manufacturer's responsibility to keep the shelves stocked. While stock-outs certainly hurt the retailer, they hurt the manufacturer even more. When a product stocks out, customers typically will substitute another, so the store makes the sale anyway. It is the manufacturer that really suffers the penalty of lost sales, so the manufacturer has a strong incentive to keep shelves stocked.

The Bullwhip Effect

Barilla's experience prior to the implementation of their VMI program is one example of the bullwhip effect. It has become a topic of considerable interest among both practitioners and academics alike. The history of bullwhip appears to be the following.

Executives at Procter & Gamble (P&G) were studying replenishment patterns for one of their best-selling products: Pampers disposable diapers. They were surprised to see that the orders placed by distributors had much more variation than sales at retail stores. Furthermore, orders of materials to suppliers had even greater variability. Demand for diapers is pretty steady, so one would assume that variance would be low in the entire supply chain. However, this was clearly not the case. P&G coined the term "bullwhip" effect for this phenomenon. It also has been referred to as the "whiplash" or "whipsaw" effect.

This phenomenon was observed by other firms as well. HP experienced the bullwhip effect in patterns of sales of its printers. Orders placed by a reseller exhibited wider swings than retail sales, and orders placed by the printer division to the company's integrated circuit division had even wider swings. Figure 6–2 shows how variance increases as one moves up the supply chain.

Where does the bullwhip effect come from? One cause stems from a phenomenon discussed in Chapter 8 in MRP systems. Consider a basic two-level MRP system in which the pattern of final demand is fixed and constant. Since items are produced in batches of size Q, the demand pattern one level down is much spikier. The tendency for lower levels in the supply chain to batch orders in this way is one of the root causes of the bullwhip effect.

High levels of inventories, caused in part by the bullwhip effect, are common in the grocery industry as well. To address this problem, the industry has adopted the efficient consumer response (ECR) initiative (see, for example, Crawford, 1994). The total food delivery supply chain, from the point at which products leave the manufacturer to the point when they are stocked on the shelves at the retailer, has an average of over 100 days of supply. The stated goal of the ECR initiative is to save $30 billion annually by streamlining food delivery logistics.

Another example of the bullwhip effect is the popular "beer game" due to Sterman (1989). Participants play the roles of retailers, wholesalers, and manufacturers of beer. Communication among participants is prohibited: each player must make ordering

FIGURE 6–2
Increasing variability of orders up the supply chain

Source: H. L. Lee, P. Padmanabhan, and S. Whang, 1997.

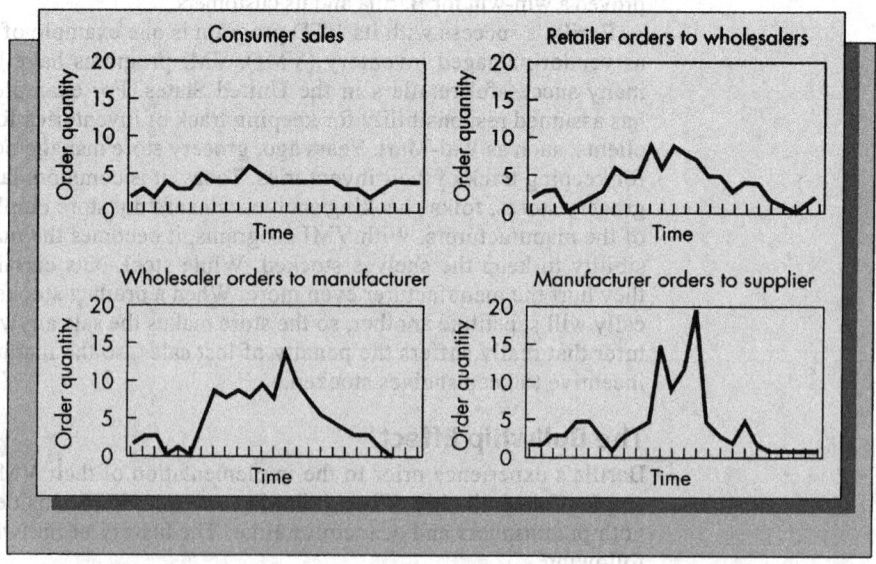

decisions based on what is demanded from the downstream player only. What one observes are wild swings in orders placed downstream even when the original demands are fairly stable. This is a consequence of the bullwhip effect.

The telescoping variation in the demand patterns in a supply chain results in a planning nightmare for many industries. What can be done to alleviate these effects? First, we need to understand the causes of this phenomenon. According to Lee, Padmanabhan and Whang (1997), there are four primary causes of the bullwhip effect:

- Demand forecast updating
- Order batching
- Price fluctuations
- Shortage gaming

We consider each of these effects in turn. *Demand forecasts* at each stage of the supply chain are the result of demands observed one level downstream (as in the beer game). Only at the final stage of the chain (the retailer) are consumer demands observed directly. When each individual in a serial supply chain determines his or her demand forecasts individually, the bullwhip effect results. The retailer builds in safety stocks to protect against uncertainty in consumer demand. These safety stocks cause the retailers' orders to have greater variance than the consumers'. The distributor observes these swings in the orders of the retailer and builds in even larger safety stocks, and so on.

Order batching is the phenomenon we saw in MRP systems that results in smooth demand patterns being translated to spiky demand patterns at lower levels of the product structure. The natural tendency to save fixed costs by ordering less frequently (which is the idea behind the EOQ formula) gives rise to order batching. Given the cost structure at each level, this is certainly a reasonable response.

When prices *fluctuate*, there is a speculative motive for holding inventories. (This was first discussed in the inventory management context by Arrow, 1958, and relates to the motivations for holding cash postulated by the economist John Maynard Keynes.) In the food industry, the majority of transactions from the manufacturer to distributors are made under a "forward buy" arrangement. This refers to the practice of buying in advance of need because of an attractive price offered by manufacturers. Such practices also contribute to the bullwhip effect. Large orders are placed when promotions are offered.

Shortage gaming occurs when product is in short supply and manufacturers place customers on allocation. When customers find out that they may not get all the units they request, they simply inflate orders to make up for the anticipated shortfall. For example, if a computer manufacturer expects to receive only half a request for a CPU in short supply, they can simply double the size of their order. If anticipated demands don't materialize, orders can be canceled. The result is that the manufacturer gets an inflated picture of the real demand for the product. This could have dire consequences for a manufacturer placing large amounts of capital into capacity expansion based on "phantom" demands.

Clearly, the bullwhip effect is not the result of poor planning or irrational behavior on the part of players in the supply chain. Each individual acts to optimize his or her position. What, then, can be done to alleviate the situation? There are several potential remedies, which we will discuss. However, these remedies must take into account that people behave selfishly. The motivation for bullwhip-inducing behavior must be eliminated.

Lee, Padmanabhan, and Whang (1997) recommend four initiatives. They are

1. Information sharing
2. Channel alignment
3. Price stabilization
4. Discouragement of shortage gaming

1. *Information sharing* means that all parties involved share information on point-of-sale (POS) data and base forecasts on these data only. Information sharing can be accomplished by several techniques, one of which is EDI (electronic data interchange), discussed in detail later. The trend toward information sharing is beginning to take hold. Computer manufacturers, for example, are now requiring sell-through data from resellers (these are data on the withdrawal of stocks from the central warehouse). At some point, we expect to see manufacturers linked directly to sources of POS data.

2. *Channel alignment* is the coordination of efforts in the form of pricing, transportation, inventory planning, and ownership between upstream and downstream sites in the supply chain. One of the tendencies that defeats channel alignment is order batching. As we noted earlier, fixed costs motivate order batching. Reducing fixed costs will result in smaller order sizes. One of the important components of fixed costs is the paperwork required to process an order. With new technologies, such as EDI, these costs could be reduced substantially. Another factor motivating large batches is transportation economies of scale. It is cheaper on a per-unit basis to order a full truckload than a partial one. If manufacturers allow customers to order an assortment of items in a single truckload, the motivation to order large batches of single items is reduced. Another trend encouraging small batch ordering is the outsourcing of logistics to third parties. Logistics companies can consolidate loads from multiple suppliers. Outsourcing of logistics (like outsourcing of manufacturing) is expanding rapidly.

3. Pricing promotions motivate customers to buy in large batches and store items for future use; this is very common in the grocery industry. By stabilizing pricing, sales patterns will have less variation. In retailing, the effect of stable pricing is evident by comparing sales patterns at retailers such as Macy's that run frequent promotions and warehouse stores such as Costco that offer everyday low pricing. The warehouse stores experience steadier sales than do the department stores. In fact, for many department stores, promotional sales account for most of their business. Major grocery manufacturers such as P&G, Kraft, and Pillsbury are moving toward a value-pricing strategy and away from promotional pricing for the same reason.

4. One way to minimize excessive orders as a result of shortage gaming is to allocate based on past sales records rather than on orders. This will reduce the tendency of customers to exaggerate orders. Several companies (including General Motors) are moving in this direction.

The bullwhip effect has been observed in a variety of settings and is also theoretically predicted to occur by so-called systems dynamics models (Sterman, 1989). However, a well-designed production system should work to smooth variability, particularly that associated with seasonality. Cachon et al. (2007) perform an empirical study on demand variability across a wide range of U.S. firms. They find that "industries with seasonality tend to smooth production relative to demand, whereas industries without seasonality tend to amplify." They also show that retailers, in particular, tend to perform a smoothing rather than amplifying effect on demand variability.

The study by Cachon et al. is primarily at the industry level, whereas Bray and Mendelson (2012) perform a firm level study that finds "65 percent of firms exhibit a positive overall bullwhip." They confirm the findings of Cachon et al. that in highly seasonal settings the production smoothing effect outweighs the inherent uncertainty amplification caused by demand shocks. Interestingly, they also show that the bullwhip effect is significantly reduced for data after 1995. While much of this can be explained by improved information systems, perhaps the increasing awareness of the bullwhip effect is also a contributing factor. Bray and Mendelson (2012) empirically verify the impressive bullwhip reduction achieved by Caterpillar Inc., which is known to have focused its efforts on initiatives similar to the four outlined above, for bullwhip reduction.

In summary, the bullwhip effect is the consequence of individual agents in the supply chain acting in their own best interests. To mitigate bullwhip effects, several changes must be made. Incentives must be put in place to reduce demand forecast errors, reduce excessive order sizes in allocation situations, and encourage information sharing and system alignment. As these initiatives become policy, everyone, especially the consumer, will benefit from reduced costs and improved supply chain efficiency.

Electronic Commerce

Electronic commerce, or simply e-commerce, is a catch-all term for a wide range of methods for effecting business transactions without the traditional paper-based systems. It includes EDI, e-mail, electronic funds transfers, electronic publishing, image processing, electronic bulletin boards, shared databases, and all manner of Internet-based business systems (Handfield and Nichols, 1999). The point-of-sale barcode system, now ubiquitous in supermarkets and retailers, is another type of e-commerce.

Barcodes were first introduced as a way to speed up supermarket checkouts. The first retail scanning of a barcode appears to be a pack of Wrigley chewing gum in June 1974 (Varchaver, 2004). However, a powerful advantage of barcodes is their role in information gathering. Assuming the check-out operator scans the products correctly, the retailer now has accurate information on sales. The reason for the caveat in the previous sentence is that a major source of data error is operators who scan, for example, one can of mushroom soup and hit times three on the till, rather than separately scanning the mushroom, tomato, and cream of asparagus soups that the customer has actually purchased. Retailers have put significant educational effort into ensuring correct scanning techniques by staff. Further, with the introduction of customer loyalty cards, retailers now have information on individual purchasing behavior and can target promotions to the individual customer.

The internet has fundamentally changed supply chain management. First, it allows easy transmission of information to users within the firms and to customers and trading partners. This includes point-of-sale demand information, purchase orders, and inventory status information. Originally, such information sharing was through electronic data interchange (EDI) systems that allow the transmission of standard business documents in a predetermined format between computers. Dedicated EDI systems have now been mostly replaced by internet-based systems. Cloud computing has also facilitated information sharing and enterprise systems. SAP and Oracle, for example, offer cloud computing options for their systems. One of the key advantages of such systems from a supply chain management perspective is speed. By transmitting information quickly, lead times are reduced. As noted in Chapter 5, it is the uncertainty of demand over the replenishment lead time that results in the need to carry safety stock.

In addition to facilitating information sharing, the internet has also provided both business to consumer (B2C) and business to business (B2B) opportunities. The rise of B2C commerce was rocky with the now infamous dot-com bust in the early 21st century. Many internet-only companies failed at that time; however, Amazon.com, which is now the world's largest online retailer, has thrived. Amazon started as a discount bookseller. By selling from a single location, it could reap the benefits of stock centralization (to be discussed in Section 6.9) and avoid the costly capital investment in brick and mortar stores.

The model for internet-based retailing is essentially the same as that for catalog shopping. Catalog retailers have been around for many years, with Lands' End and L.L.Bean being perhaps the most successful. However, catalogs need to be developed, printed, and mailed regularly, which is quite expensive, especially considering that most catalogs are thrown away. For this reason, the internet has a significant advantage over the traditional mail-order catalog business, and both Lands' End and L.L.Bean have put significant investment into their websites. Further, the move away from paper catalogs has allowed them to reach consumers around the world. Lands' End boasts that they "proudly ship to over 170 countries."

Along with the growth of B2C commerce there has also been a less visible growth of B2B commerce. Hundreds, if not thousands, of firms offer internet-based supply chain solutions. Many tailor their products to specific industry segments, such as PrintingForLess.com (printing) and ShowMeTheParts.com (automotive aftermarket). There are also intermediaries, such as Li & Fung Lmt., who specialize in third party sourcing. While Li & Fung started as a traditional trading company, today they provide access to a network of over 15,000 suppliers in more than 40 economies. This would not be possible without e-commerce.

It is interesting to speculate what effect 3D printing will have on e-commerce. 3D printing, or additive manufacturing, allows the construction of three dimensional objects by a "printer" just as regular printers allow for the production of two dimensional text. Such printers are currently used widely in the production of manufacturing prototypes but less widely in consumer goods. The range of materials that may be printed is limited but increasing. Examples of products produced by 3D printing include custom jewelry and home decor, such as lampshades. In time, instead of buying items from the internet (or store) we may simply buy a design and print it up at home or in our local print shop. Such a development could drastically simplify supply chain management!

RFID Technology

Radio frequency identification (RFID) tags are an emerging technology that will change the way information is stored and transmitted in a supply chain. Unlike barcodes, which are the same across all items of the same stock-keeping unit (SKU), RFID tags can contain item specific information, such as farm of origin (for produce) or date of production.

RFID tags were invented in 1973, but are only now becoming commercially viable. They are microchips powered by batteries (active tags) or radio signals (passive tags).

The passive device is smaller and cheaper and is likely to emerge as the device of choice for inventory management applications. Passive tags receive power from the readers (at which time they are "woken up") and transmit a unique code. Passive tags can only be read at close distances but they provide a simple means of electronic identification.

Passive RFID tags cost between $.07 and $.15 each, which makes them too expensive for small grocery items, such as gum, but practical for larger items, such as jeans. JCPenney announced in 2012 that they were moving to 100 percent RFID tagging of all items in their stores. While their roll out was postponed, at the time of this writing they have moved to item-level tagging in bras, footwear, fashion jewelry, and men's and women's denim. Wal-Mart and American Apparel have also moved to tagging clothing. One of the main advantages of such tagging is in drastically speeding up and improving accuracy in stock-taking, thereby reducing stock-outs and increasing sales. For example, in a pilot program at American Apparel Inc. in 2007, sales increased by 14.3 percent (Bustillo, 2010). When all items are tagged retailers will also see savings in the checkout process because RFID readers can replace the need for item by item barcode scanning.

Beyond retail item tagging, other applications of RFID technology include (1) EZ Pass for paying bridge or highway tolls, (2) tagging of luggage on flights, and (3) tagging of cargo containers at most of the world's ports. As the cost of RFID tags declines, we will see a much wider range of applications in the context of supply chain management. Reconciling shipments against bills-of-lading (i.e., cargo records) or packing and pick lists can be performed quickly and accurately electronically, eliminating the need to perform these functions manually.

Of course, RFID technology has far broader implications than its application to supply chains. For example, Solusat, the Mexican distributor of the VeriChip—a rice-sized microchip that is injected beneath the skin—is marketing its device as an emergency identification. The interest in Mexico for this product is a consequence of the more than 10,000 Mexican children abducted annually. VeriChip manufacturer, Applied Digital Solutions, said it plans to roll out the VeriKid service in other countries, including the United States (Scheeres, 2003). Such applications of RFID technology potentially have enormous benefits, but also can be used in ways to threaten our privacy.

RFID technology is quickly making inroads into many other industries. Potential applications discussed in a recent book on the subject (Schuster, Allen, and Brock, 2007) include the following:

- *Warehousing.* By tagging inventory stored in a warehouse, improved tracking of items and order fulfillment can lead to significant improvements in several measures of customer service.
- *Maintenance.* Maintenance programs require keeping track of the location, suitability, and condition of spare parts. RFID tags can provide significant improvements in monitoring the installed base of parts and components.
- *Pharmaceuticals.* Tracking and tracing pharmaceuticals can help ameliorate the problems of counterfeit drugs and theft in the industry. These problems have been estimated to run to $30 billion annually worldwide.
- *Medical devices.* RFID technology can provide continuous access to the identity, location, and state of medical devices. This has the potential to significantly improve patient care.

- *Animal tracking.* The appearance of mad cow disease (BSE) in the United Kingdom, Canada, and the United States raised an alarm worldwide about food safety. Being able to track individual livestock can be invaluable when trying to trace the source of problems.
- *Shelf-life tracking.* We are all familiar with expiration dates on foods such as dairy products, packaged meats, fish, and canned goods. RFID technology provides the opportunity for "dynamic" shelf-life tracking, that is, updating the shelf-life indicator to take into account environmental conditions such as temperature.
- *Retailing.* It is common for expensive retail items, such as leather jackets, to be tagged with a transmitter that sounds an alarm if removed from the store. Inexpensive RFID chips provide the opportunity to tag almost all retail items, virtually eliminating theft altogether.
- *Defense.* Logistic support has always been a key to securing victory in battle, in both modern and ancient times. It is currently estimated that the U.S. Department of Defense manages an inventory valued at $67 billion. Keeping track of this inventory is obviously a top priority, and RFID technology can go a long way toward accomplishing this goal.

Problems for Sections 6.1 and 6.2

1. Name two products you are familiar with, that are *not* discussed in this chapter, one of which is best classed as functional and the other as innovative.
2. What product characteristics would be necessary for a product to be able to have a supply chain that is simultaneously both efficient and responsive?
3. What is the bullwhip effect? What is the origin of the term?
4. Do you think that eliminating intermediaries would always get rid of the bullwhip effect? Under what circumstances might it not work?
5. Discuss the four initiatives recommended for ameliorating the bullwhip effect in supply chains.
6. Amazon.com is a purely e-commerce company, yet Barnes & Noble maintains both retail bookstores and a significant internet business. What are the advantages and disadvantages of Barnes and Noble's strategy (as contrasted to Amazon's)?
7. What are the key benefits that the internet has provided in aiding efficiency or effectiveness in supply chain management?
8. Give three examples of revenue or cost benefits made possible by RFID tags when contrasted to barcodes.

6.3 THE TRANSPORTATION PROBLEM

With good information comes the opportunity to optimize within the supply chain. The transportation problem is a mathematical model for optimally scheduling the flow of goods from production facilities to distribution centers. Assume that a fixed amount of product must be transported from a group of sources (plants) to a group of sinks (warehouses). The unit cost of transporting from each source to each sink is assumed to be known. The goal is to find the optimal flow paths and the amounts to be shipped on those paths to minimize the total cost of all shipments.

The transportation problem can be viewed as a prototype supply chain problem. Although most real-world problems involving the shipment of goods are more complex, the model provides an illustration of the issues and methods one would encounter in practice.

Example 6.1

The Pear Tablet Corporation produces several types of tablet computers. In 2013, Pear produced tablets with capacities from gigabytes (GB), all 10-inch display. The most popular product is the 64 GB tablet. Pear produces the tablets in three plants located in Sunnyvale, California; Dublin, Ireland; and Bangkok, Thailand. Periodically, shipments are made from these three production facilities to four distribution warehouses located in the United States in Amarillo, Texas; Teaneck, New Jersey; Chicago, Illinois; and Sioux Falls, South Dakota. Over the next month, it has been determined that these warehouses should receive the following proportions of the company's total production of the 64 GB tablets.

Warehouse	Percentage of Total Production
Amarillo	31
Teaneck	30
Chicago	18
Sioux Falls	21

The production quantities at the factories in the next month are expected to be (in thousands of units)

Plant	Anticipated Production (in 1,000s of units)
Sunnyvale	45
Dublin	120
Bangkok	95

Since the total production at the three plants is 260 units, the amounts shipped to the four warehouses will be (rounded to the nearest unit)

Warehouse	Total Shipment Quantity (1,000s)
Amarillo	80
Teaneck	78
Chicago	47
Sioux Falls	55

While the shipping cost may be lower between certain plants and distribution centers, Pear has established shipping routes between every plant and every warehouse. This is in case of unforeseen problems such as a forced shutdown at a plant, unanticipated swings in regional

6.3 The Transportation Problem

demands, or poor weather along some routes. The unit costs for shipping 1,000 units from each plant to each warehouse is given in the following table.

Shipping Costs per 1,000 Units in $					
		TO			
		Amarillo	Teaneck	Chicago	Sioux Falls
FROM	Sunnyvale	250	420	380	280
	Dublin	1,280	990	1,440	1,520
	Bangkok	1,550	1,420	1,660	1,730

The goal is to determine a pattern of shipping that minimizes the total transportation cost from plants to warehouses. The network representation of Pear's distribution problem appears in Figure 6–3.

FIGURE 6–3
Pear Tablet transportation problem

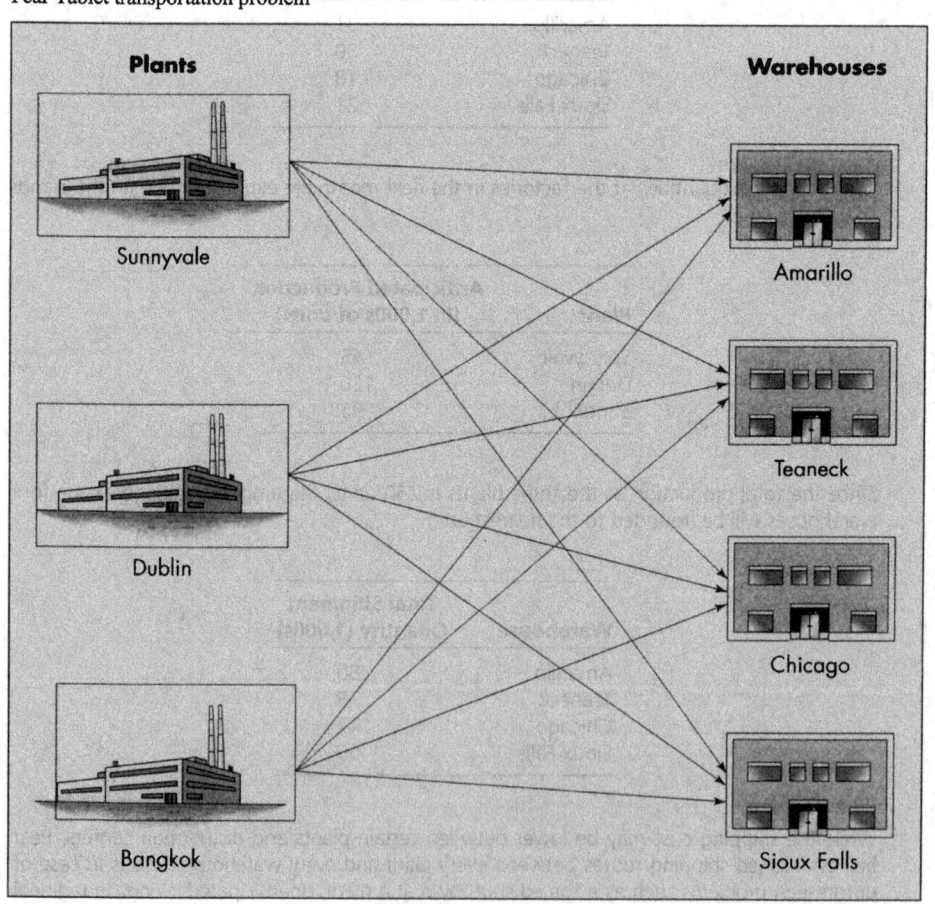

Several heuristics for solving transportation problems have been proposed, such as a greedy heuristic that allocates capacity first to the cheapest options. However, it is unlikely that anyone with a real problem would use a heuristic, since optimal solutions can be found efficiently by linear programming. In fact, because of the special structure of the transportation problem, today's specialized codes can solve problems with millions of variables.

Let m be the number of sources and n the number of sinks. (In Example 6.1, $m = 3$ and $n = 4$.) Recall the definition of the decision variables from Section 6.1:

x_{ij} = flow from source i to sink j for $1 \leq i \leq m$ and $1 \leq j \leq n$,

and define c_{ij} as the cost of shipping one unit from i to j. It follows that the total cost of making all shipments is

$$\sum_{i=1}^{m}\sum_{j=1}^{n} c_{ij} x_{ij}$$

For the case of Pear Company, described in Example 6.1, the objective function is

$$250x_{11} + 420x_{12} + 380x_{13} + 280x_{14} + \cdots + 1{,}730x_{34}.$$

Since many routes are obviously not economical, it is likely that many of the decision variables will equal zero at the optimal solution.

The constraints are designed to ensure that the total amount shipped out of each source equals the amount available at that source, and the amount shipped into any sink equals the amount required at that sink. Since there are m sources and n sinks, there are a total of $m + n$ constraints (excluding nonnegativity constraints). Let a_i be the total amount to be shipped out of source i and b_j the total amount to be shipped into sink j. Then linear programming constraints may be written:

$$\sum_{j=1}^{n} x_{ij} = a_i \quad \text{for } 1 \leq i \leq m$$

$$\sum_{i=1}^{m} x_{ij} = b_j \quad \text{for } 1 \leq j \leq n$$

$$x_{ij} \geq 0 \quad \text{for } 1 \leq i \leq m \text{ and } 1 \leq j \leq n.$$

For the Pear Tablet Company problem, we obtain the following seven constraints:

$x_{11} + x_{12} + x_{13} + x_{14} = 45$ (shipments out of Sunnyvale)
$x_{21} + x_{22} + x_{23} + x_{24} = 120$ (shipments out of Dublin)
$x_{31} + x_{32} + x_{33} + x_{34} = 95$ (shipments out of Bangkok)
$x_{11} + x_{21} + x_{31} = 80$ (shipments into Amarillo)
$x_{12} + x_{22} + x_{32} = 78$ (shipments into Teaneck)
$x_{13} + x_{23} + x_{33} = 47$ (shipments into Chicago)
$x_{14} + x_{24} + x_{34} = 55$ (shipments into Sioux Falls)

and the nonnegativity constraints required in linear programming:

$$x_{ij} \geq 0 \quad \text{for } 1 \leq i \leq 3 \text{ and } 1 \leq j \leq 4.$$

The problem was entered in Excel Solver. The spreadsheet used and the solution appear in Figure 6–4. The solution obtained is

$$x_{14} = 45, \quad x_{21} = 42, \quad x_{22} = 78, \quad x_{31} = 38,$$
$$x_{33} = 47, \quad \text{and} \quad x_{34} = 10,$$

with all other values equaling zero. The total cost of this solution is $297,800.

FIGURE 6-4
Solution of Pear's transportation problem using Excel Solver

	A	B	C	D	E	F	G	H	I	J	K	L	M	N	O	P
1					Solution of Example 6.1 (Pear's Transportation Problem)											
2																
3	Variables	x11	x12	x13	x14	x21	x22	x23	x24	x31	x32	x33	x34	Operator	Value	RHS
4																
5	Values	0	0	0	45	42	78	0	0	38	0	47	10			
6																
7	Objective Coeff	250	420	380	280	1280	990	1440	1520	1550	1420	1660	1730	Min	297800	
8	st															
9	Constraint 1	1	1	1	1									=	45	45
10	Constraint 2					1	1	1	1					=	120	120
11	Constraint 3									1	1	1	1	=	95	95
12	Constraint 4	1				1				1				=	80	80
13	Constraint 5		1				1				1			=	78	78
14	Constraint 6			1				1				1		=	47	47
15	Constraint 7				1				1				1	=	55	55
16																
17																
18			Notes:	Formula for Cell O9: =SUMPRODUCT (B9:M9,$B$5:$M$5). Copied to O10 to O15.												
19				Changing cells for Solver are $B$5:$M$5.												
20																

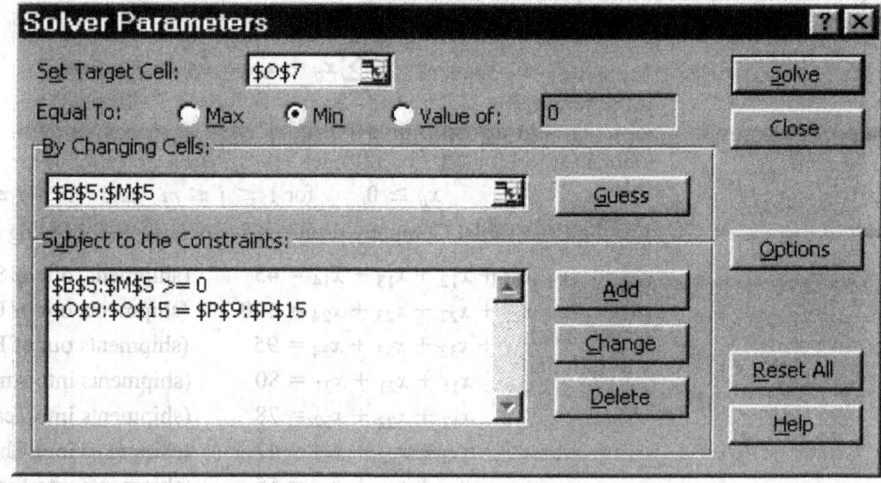

6.4 GENERALIZATIONS OF THE TRANSPORTATION PROBLEM

The Pear Company example is the simplest type of transportation problem. Every link from source to sink is feasible, and the total amount available from the sources exactly equals the total demand at the sinks. Several of these requirements can be relaxed without making the problem significantly more complicated.

Infeasible Routes

Suppose in the example that the firm has decided to eliminate the routes from Dublin to Chicago and from Bangkok to Sioux Falls. This would be accounted for by placing very high costs on these arcs in the network. Traditionally, uppercase M has been used to signify a very high cost. In practice, of course, one would have to assign a number to these locations. As long as that number is much larger than the other costs, an optimal solution will never assign flow to these routes. For the example, suppose we assign costs of $1,000,000 to each of these routes and re-solve the problem. The reader can check that one now obtains the following solution:

$$x_{14} = 45, \quad x_{21} = 32, \quad x_{22} = 78, \quad x_{31} = 48, \quad \text{and} \quad x_{33} = 47,$$

with all other values equaling zero. The cost of the new solution is $298,400, only slightly larger than the cost obtained when all the routes were feasible.

Unbalanced Problems

An unbalanced transportation problem is one in which the total amount shipped from the sources is not equal to the total amount required at the sinks. This can arise if the demand exceeds the supply or vice versa. There are two ways of handling unbalanced problems. One is to add either a dummy row or a dummy column to absorb the excess supply or demand. A second method for solving unbalanced problems is to alter the appropriate set of constraints to either $\leq$ or $\geq$ form. Both methods will be illustrated.

Suppose in Example 6.1 that the demand for the tablets was higher than anticipated. Suppose that the respective requirements at the four warehouses are now Amarillo, 90; Teaneck, 78; Chicago, 55; and Sioux Falls, 55. This means that the total demand is 278 and the total supply is 260. To turn this into a balanced problem, we add an additional fictitious factory to account for the 18-unit shortfall. This can be labeled as a dummy row in the transportation tableau and all entries for that row assigned an arbitrarily large unit cost. Note that when supply exceeds demand and one adds a dummy column, the costs in the dummy column do *not* have to be very large numbers, but they do all have to be the same. (In fact, one can assign zero to all costs in the dummy column.) In the example, we assigned a cost of 10^6 to each cell in the dummy row. The resulting Excel spreadsheet and Solver solution (shown in the row labeled "Values") appear in Figure 6–5. The optimal solution calls for assigning the shortfall to two warehouses: 8 units to Chicago and 10 units to Sioux Falls.

Unbalanced transportation problems also can be formulated as linear programs by using inequality constraints. In the previous example, where there is excess demand, one would use equality for the first three constraints, to be sure that all the supply is shipped, and less than or equal to constraints for the last four, with the slack accounting for the shortfall. The reader should check that one obtains the same solution by doing so as was obtained by adding a dummy row. This method has the advantage of giving an accurate value for the objective function. (In the case where the supply exceeds the demand, the principle is the same, but the details differ. The first three supply constraints are converted to *greater than or equal to* form, while the last four demand constraints are still equality constraints. The slack in the first three constraints corresponds to the excess supply.)

FIGURE 6–5
Solution of Example 6.1 with excess demand and dummy row

	Solution of Example 6.1 with Excess Demand and a Dummy Row																		
Variables	x11	x12	x13	x14	x21	x22	x23	x24	x31	x32	x33	x34	x41	x42	x43	x44	Oper	Value	RHS
Values	0	0	0	45	42	78	0	0	48	0	47	0	0	0	8	10			
Obj Func	250	420	380	280	1280	990	1440	1520	1550	1420	1660	1730	1.E+06	1.E+06	1.E+06	1.E+06	Min	2E+07	
st																			
Constraint 1	1	1	1	1													=	45	60
Constraint 2					1	1	1	1									=	120	130
Constraint 3									1	1	1	1					=	95	95
Constraint 4													1	1	1	1	=	18	18
Constraint 5	1				1				1				1				=	90	90
Constraint 6		1				1				1				1			=	78	78
Constraint 7			1				1				1				1		=	55	55
Constraint 8				1				1				1				1	=	55	55

6.5 MORE GENERAL NETWORK FORMULATIONS

The transportation problem is a special type of network where all nodes are either supply nodes (also called sources) or demand nodes (also called sinks). Linear programming also can be used to solve more complex network distribution problems as well. One example is the *transshipment problem*. In this case, one or more of the nodes in the network are transshipment points rather than supply or demand points. Note that a transshipment node also can be either a supply or a demand node as well (but no node is both a supply and a demand node).

For general network flow problems, we use the following balance of flow rules:

If	Apply the Following Rule at Each Node:
1. Total supply > total demand	Inflow − outflow ≥ supply or demand
2. Total supply < total demand	Inflow − outflow ≤ supply or demand
3. Total supply = total demand	Inflow − outflow = supply or demand

The decision variables are defined in the same way as with the simple transportation problem. That is, x_{ij} represents the total flow from node i to node j. For general network flow problems, we represent the supply as a negative number attached to that node and the demand as a positive number attached to that node. This convention along with the flow rules will result in the correct balance-of-flow equations.

Example 6.2 Consider the example of Pear Tablets. The company has decided to place a warehouse in Sacramento to be used as a transshipment node and has expanded the Chicago facility to also allow for transshipments. Suppose that in addition to being transshipment nodes, both Chicago and Sacramento are also demand nodes. The new network is pictured in Figure 6–6. Note that several of the old routes have been eliminated in the new configuration.

FIGURE 6–6
Pear Tablets problem with transshipment nodes

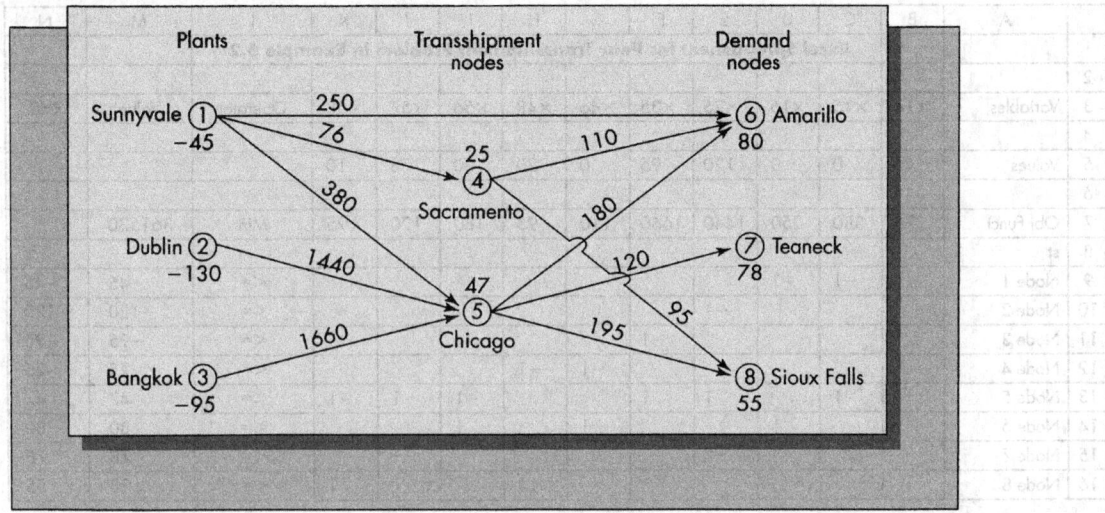

We define a decision variable for each arc in the network. In this case, there are a total of 10 decision variables. The objective function is

Minimize $250x_{16} + 76x_{14} + 380x_{15} + 1{,}440x_{25} + 1{,}660x_{35}$
$+ 110x_{46} + 95x_{48} + 180x_{56} + 120x_{57} + 195x_{58}$

The total supply available is still 260 units, but the demand is 285 units (due to the additional 25 units demanded at Sacramento). Hence, this corresponds to case 2 of the flow rules in which total demand exceeds total supply. Applying rule 2 to each node gives the following eight constraints for this problem:

Node 1: $\quad -x_{14} - x_{15} - x_{16} \leq -45$

Node 2: $\quad -x_{25} \leq -120$

Node 3: $\quad -x_{35} \leq -95$

Node 4: $\quad x_{14} - x_{46} - x_{48} \leq 25$

Node 5: $\quad x_{16} + x_{46} + x_{56} - x_{56} - x_{57} - x_{58} \leq 47$

Node 6: $\quad x_{16} + x_{46} + x_{56} \leq 80$

Node 7: $\quad x_{57} \leq 78$

Node 8: $\quad x_{48} + x_{58} \leq 55$.

For some linear programming codes, all right-hand sides would have to be nonnegative. In those cases, one would multiply the first three constraints by −1. However, this is not required in Excel, so we can enter the constraints just as they appear.

The Excel spreadsheet and solution for Pear's transshipment problem appears in Figure 6–7. Note that the solution calls for shipping all units from the sources. Since this problem had more supply than demand, it is interesting to see where the shortfall occurs. The amount shipped into Sacramento is 45 units (all from Sunnyvale), and the total shipped out of Sacramento is 20 units. Thus, all the demand (25 units) is satisfied in Sacramento. For the other transshipment point, Chicago, the shipments into Chicago are 120 units from Dublin and 95 units from Bangkok, and

FIGURE 6–7
Excel spreadsheet for Pear transshipment problem in Example 6.2

	A	B	C	D	E	F	G	H	I	J	K	L	M	N
1					Excel Spreadsheet for Pear Transshipment Problem in Example 6.2									
2														
3	Variables	x14	x15	x16	x25	x35	x46	x48	x56	x57	x58	Operator	Value	RHS
4														
5	Values	45	0	0	120	95	0	20	80	78	10			
6														
7	Obj Funct	76	380	250	1440	1660	110	95	180	120	195	Min	361530	
8	st													
9	Node 1	−1	−1	−1								<=	−45	−45
10	Node 2			−1								<=	−120	−120
11	Node 3				−1							<=	−95	−95
12	Node 4	1					−1	−1				<=	25	25
13	Node 5		1		1	1			−1	−1	−1	<=	47	47
14	Node 6			1			1					<=	80	80
15	Node 7									1		<=	78	78
16	Node 8							1			1	<=	30	55

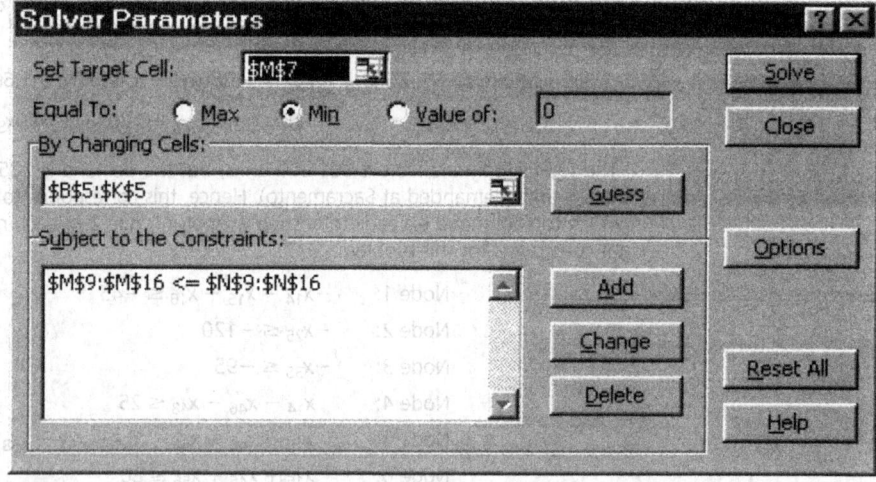

the shipments out of Chicago are 48 units to Amarillo and 120 units to Teaneck. The difference is 120 + 95 − (48 + 120) = 47 units. Hence, there is also no shortage in Chicago. Total shipments into the demand nodes at Amarillo, Teaneck, and Sioux Falls are respectively 80, 78, and 30 units. Hence, all the shortage (25 units) is absorbed at the Sioux Falls location at the optimal solution.

Real networks can be extremely complex by virtue of their sheer magnitude. As Simchi-Levi et al. (1999) note, a typical soft drink distribution system could involve anywhere between 10,000 and 120,000 accounts. Some retailers have thousands of stores and hundreds of thousands of products. For this reason, efficient data aggregation may be required to solve problems of this magnitude. Customer aggregation is generally

Snapshot Application

IBM STREAMLINES ITS SEMICONDUCTOR SUPPLY CHAIN USING SOPHISTICATED MATHEMATICAL MODELS

An important part of IBM's success is its focus on servicization (see Chapter 1). IBM has also been a leader in the use of optimization and other business analytics tools, both selling them as software and services and applying them to their own supply chains. In the mid-1980s they applied such tools to their supply chain for spare parts (Cohen et al., 1990) realizing a 10 percent improvement in parts availability and savings of approximately $20 million annually. More recently, they have applied a combination of optimization and heuristics to improve the planning of their semiconductor supply chain (Degbotse et al., 2013).

IBM has been in the semiconductor business since 1957 and has manufacturing and contract manufacturing facilities in Asia and North America. These facilities make products that range from silicon wafers to complex semiconductor devices. Until the 1990s, IBM facilities were separated by regions. A North American facility would supply component parts to local assembly plants in North America, for example. The regional supply chains were managed and planned independently, in part because enterprise supply chain optimization was not feasible.

Aided by more powerful computers and algorithms, Degbotse et al. (2013) developed a central planning engine to coordinate planning across the extended supply chain. Its purpose is "to determine a production and shipment plan for the enterprise by using limited material inventories and capacity availability to satisfy a prioritized demand statement." Because such a problem is still too large-scale to solve optimally, they used heuristic decomposition and mixed integer programming. They state that the result is "is a unified production, shipping, and distribution plan with no evidence of the original decomposition."

They found the following benefits: (a) on-time deliveries to commit date increased by 15 percent, (b) asset utilization increased by 2–4 percent of costs, and (c) inventory decreased by 25–30 percent. Notice that by coordinating and planning the supply chain as a whole they are effectively pooling the different regions into one centralized system. Further, notice how the benefits include both increased service and decreased costs, rather than a trade-off between the two. This is the ideal outcome for any process improvement.

What is the lesson learned from this case? As supply chains get larger and more complex, more and more sophisticated methods will be required to manage those systems. Generic software products may not be able to provide sufficient power and customization to be effective in such environments. IBM's experience is only one example of how the management of complex supply chain structures can be improved with the aid of the modeling methods discussed in this text.

---

accomplished by combining accounts that are nearby. Combining customers with like or similar zip codes is a common means of geographic aggregation. Product aggregation is discussed in detail in Chapter 3 in the context of manufacturing. Product aggregation rules for a supply chain are likely to be different from those discussed in Chapter 3. For example, one might aggregate products according to where they are picked up or where they are delivered. We refer the interested reader to Simchi-Levi et al. (1999) for a more comprehensive discussion of the practical issues surrounding implementation of supply chain networks.

Mathematical modeling has been used successfully in many supply chain applications. Sophisticated models lie at the heart of several commercial software products such as those offered by Texas-based i2 Technologies. The Snapshot Application for this section discusses a successful application of advanced inventory control models to IBM's supply chain for semiconductors.

Problems for Sections 6.3–6.5

9. Consider Example 6.2 of the Pear Company assuming the following supplies and demands:

Plant	Production	Warehouse	Requirement
Sunnyvale	60	Amarillo	100
Dublin	145	Teaneck	84
Bangkok	125	Chicago	77
		Sioux Falls	69

Use Excel's Solver (or other linear programming code) to determine the optimal solution.

10. Resolve Pear's transportation problem assuming that the following routes are eliminated: Sunnyvale to Teaneck, Dublin to Chicago, and Bangkok to Amarillo. What is the percentage increase in total shipping costs at the optimal solution due to the elimination of these routes?

11. Resolve Pear's transshipment problem assuming that an additional transshipment point is located at Oklahoma City. Assume that the unit costs of shipping from the three plants to Oklahoma City are Sunnyvale, $170; Dublin, $1,200; and Bangkok, $1,600; and the respective costs of shipping from Oklahoma City to the demand nodes are Amarillo, $35; Teaneck, $245; and Sioux Falls, $145. Assume that Oklahoma City is only a transshipment point and has no demand of its own. Find the new shipping pattern with the addition of the new transshipment point and the savings, if any, of introducing this additional node.

12. Major Motors produces its Trans National model in three plants located in Flint, Michigan; Fresno, California; and Monterrey, Mexico. Dealers receive cars from regional distribution centers located in Phoenix, Arizona; Davenport, Iowa; and Columbia, South Carolina. Anticipated production at the plants over the next month (in 100s of cars) is 43 at Flint, 26 at Fresno, and 31 at Monterrey. Based on firm orders and other requests from dealers, Major Motors has decided that it needs to have the following numbers of cars at the regional distribution centers at month's end: Phoenix, 26; Davenport, 28; and Columbia, 30. Suppose that the cost of shipping 100 cars from each plant to each distribution center is given in the following matrix (in $1,000s):

		TO		
		Phoenix	Davenport	Columbia
FROM	Flint	12	8	17
	Fresno	7	14	21
	Monterrey	18	22	31

a. Convert the problem to a balanced problem by adding an appropriate row or column and find the optimal solution using Solver.
b. Now find the optimal solution using Solver and inequality constraints.
c. Do the solutions in (a) and (b) match? Why or why not?
d. Suppose that the route between Monterrey and Columbia is no longer available due to a landslide on a key road in Mexico. Modify the model in (b) and resolve to find the optimal solution. Has the objective value increased or decreased? Explain why.

13. Consider the problem of Major Motors described in Problem 4. In order to be able to deal more effectively with unforeseen events (such as the road closing), Major Motors has established two transshipment points between the factories and the regional distribution centers at Santa Fe, New Mexico, and Jefferson City, Missouri. The cost of shipping 100 cars to the transshipment points is (in $1,000s):

		TO	
		Santa Fe	Jefferson City
F	Flint	8	6
R	Fresno	6	9
O	Monterrey	9	14
M			

while the cost of shipping from the transshipment points to the distribution centers is

		TO		
		Phoenix	Davenport	Columbia
F	Santa Fe	3	8	10
R	Jefferson City	5	5	9
O				
M				

Assuming that none of the direct routes between the factories and the distribution centers is available, find the optimal flow of cars through the transshipment points that minimizes the total shipping costs.

14. Toyco produces a line of Bonnie dolls and accessories at its plants in New York and Baltimore that must be shipped to distribution centers in Chicago and Los Angeles. The company uses Air Freight, Inc., to make its shipments. Suppose that it can ship directly or through Pittsburgh and Denver. The daily production rates at the plants are respectively 5,000 and 7,000 units daily, and the demands at the distribution centers are respectively 3,500 and 8,500 units daily. The costs of shipping 1,000 units are given in the following table. Find the optimal shipping routes and the associated cost.

		TO			
		Pittsburgh	Denver	Chicago	Los Angeles
F	New York	$182	$375	$285	$460
R	Baltimore	77	290	245	575
O	Pittsburgh	—	275	125	380
M	Denver		—	90	110

15. Reconsider Problem 6 if there is a drop in the demand for dolls to 3,000 at Chicago and 7,000 at Los Angeles. Find the optimal shipping pattern in this case. How much of the total decrease in demand of 2,000 units is absorbed at each factory at the optimal solution?
16. Reconsider Problem 6 assuming that the maximum amount that can be shipped from either New York or Baltimore through Pittsburgh is 2,000 units due to the size of the plane available for this route.

6.6 DETERMINING DELIVERY ROUTES IN SUPPLY CHAINS

An important aspect of supply chain logistics is efficiently moving product from one place to another. The transportation and transshipment problems discussed earlier in this chapter deal with this problem at a macro or firmwide level. At a micro level, deliveries to customers also must be planned efficiently. Because of the scale of the problem, efficient delivery schedules can have a very significant impact on the bottom line. As a result, they become an important part of designing the entire supply chain.

Determining optimal delivery schedules turns out to be a very difficult problem in general, rivaling the complexity of job shop scheduling problems discussed in detail in Chapter 8. Vehicle scheduling is closely related to a classical operations research problem known as the traveling salesman problem. The problem is described in the following way. A salesman starts at his home base, labeled city 1. He must then make stops at $n - 1$ other cities, visiting each city exactly once. The problem is to determine the optimal sequence in which to visit the cities to minimize the total distance traveled. Although this problem is easy to state, it turns out to be very hard to solve. If the number of cities is small, it is possible to enumerate all the possible tours. There are $n!$ orderings of n objects.[1] For modest values of n, one can enumerate all the tours and compute their distances directly. For example, for $n = 5$ there are 120 sequences. This number grows very fast, however. For $n = 10$, the number of sequences grows to over 3 million, and for $n = 25$ it grows to more than 1.55×10^{25}. To get some idea of how large this number is, suppose that we could evaluate 1 trillion sequences per second on a supercomputer. Then, for a 25-city problem, it would take nearly 500,000 years to evaluate all the sequences!

Total enumeration is hopeless for solving all but the smallest traveling salesman problems. Problems such as this are known in mathematics as *NP hard*. The NP stands for no polynomial, meaning that the time required to solve such problems is an exponential function of the number of cities rather than a polynomial function. We will not dwell on the traveling salesman problem here, but note that methods of solution have been proposed that are vast improvements over total enumeration. However, finding optimal solutions to even moderate-sized problems is still difficult.

Finding optimal routes in vehicle scheduling is a similar, but more complex, problem. Assume that there is a central depot with one or more delivery vehicles and n customer locations, each having a known requirement. The question is how to assign vehicles to customer locations to meet customer demand and satisfy whatever constraints there might be at minimum cost. More real vehicle scheduling problems are too large and complex to solve optimally.

---

[1] $n!$ is equal to n times $(n - 1)$ times $(n - 2) \ldots$ times 1.

Because optimality may be impossible to achieve, methods for determining "good" solutions are important. We will discuss a simple technique for finding good routes, known as the savings method and developed by Clarke and Wright (1964).

Suppose that there is a single depot from which all vehicles depart and return. Customers' locations and needs are known. Identify the depot as location 0 and the customers as locations 1, 2, ..., n. We assume that there are known costs of traveling from the depot to each customer location, given by

$$c_{0j} = \text{Cost of making one trip from the depot to customer } j.$$

To implement the method, we will also need to know the costs of trips between customers. This means that we will assume that the following constants are known as well:

$$c_{ij} = \text{Cost of making a trip from customer location } i \text{ to customer location } j.$$

For our purposes we consider only the case in which $c_{ij} = c_{ji}$ for all $1 \leq i, j \leq n$. This does not necessarily hold in all situations, however. For example, if there are one-way streets, the distance from i to j may be different from the distance from j to i. The method proceeds as follows: Suppose initially that there is a separate vehicle assigned to each customer location. Then the initial solution consists of n separate routes from the depot to each customer location and back. It follows that the total cost of all round trips for the initial solution is

$$2 \sum_{j=1}^{n} c_{0j}.$$

Now, suppose that we link customers i and j. That is, we go from the depot to i to j and back to the depot again. In doing so, we would save one trip between the depot and location i and one trip between the depot and location j. However, there would be an added cost of c_{ij} for the trip from i to j (or vice versa). Hence, the savings realized by linking i and j is

$$s_{ij} = c_{0i} + c_{0j} - c_{ij}.$$

The method is to compute s_{ij} for all possible pairs of customer locations i and j, and then rank the s_{ij} in decreasing order. One then considers each of the links in descending order of savings and includes link (i, j) in a route if it does not violate feasibility constraints. If including the current link violates feasibility, one goes to the next link on the list and considers including that on a single route. One continues in this manner until the list is exhausted. Whenever link (i, j) is included on a route, the cost savings is s_{ij}.

The total number of calculations of s_{ij} required is

$$\binom{n}{2} = \frac{n!}{2!(n-2)!} = \frac{n(n-1)}{2}.$$

(When c_{ij} and c_{ji} are not equal, twice as many savings terms must be computed.)

6.6 Determining Delivery Routes in Supply Chains

The savings method is feasible to solve by hand for only small values of n. For example, for $n = 10$ there are 45 terms, and for $n = 100$ there are nearly 5,000 terms. However, as long as the constraints are not too complex, the method can be implemented easily on a computer.

We illustrate the method with the following example.

Example 6.3 Whole Grains is a small bakery that supplies five major customers with bread each morning. If we locate the bakery at the origin of a grid [i.e., at the point (0, 0)], then the five customer locations and their daily requirements are

Customer	Location	Daily Requirements (loaves)
1	(15, 30)	85
2	(5, 30)	162
3	(10, 20)	26
4	(5, 5)	140
5	(20, 10)	110

The relative locations of the Whole Grains bakery and its five customers are shown in Figure 6–8. The bakery has several delivery trucks, each having a capacity of 300 loaves. We shall assume that the cost of traveling between any two locations is simply the straight-line or Euclidean distance between the points. The formula for the straight-line distance separating the points (x_1, y_1) and (x_2, y_2) is

$$\sqrt{(x_1 - x_2)^2 + (y_1 - y_2)^2}.$$

The goal is to find a delivery pattern that both meets customer demand and minimizes delivery costs, subject to not exceeding the capacity constraint on the size of the delivery trucks.

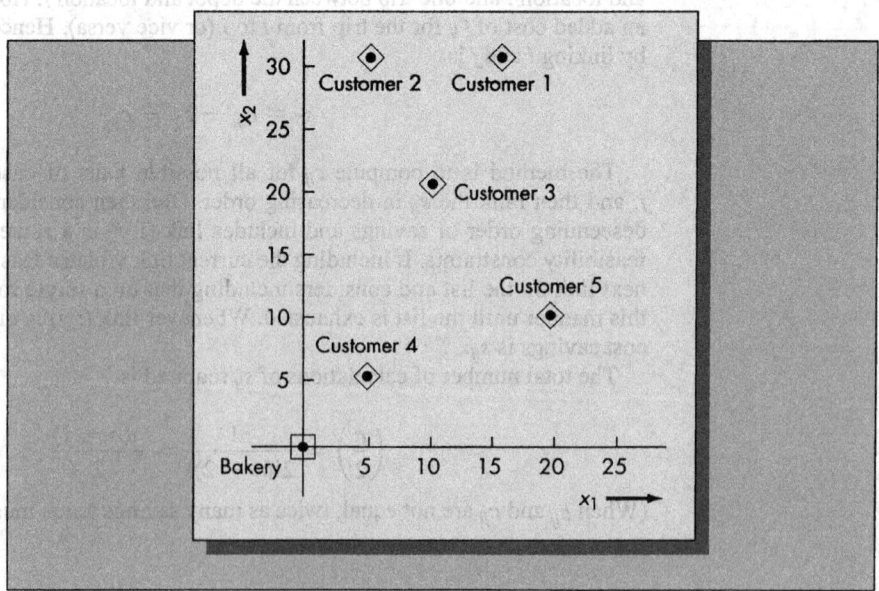

FIGURE 6–8 Customer locations in Example 6.3

Solution

The first step is to compute the cost for each pair (i, j) where i and j vary from 0 to 5. We are assuming that this cost is the straight-line distance between the points representing customer locations. The straight-line distances are given in the following matrix.

Cost Matrix (c_{ij})

		\multicolumn{5}{c}{TO}				
		0	1	2	3	4	5
FROM	0		33.5	30.4	22.4	7.1	22.4
	1			10.0	11.2	26.9	20.6
	2				11.2	25.0	25.0
	3					15.8	14.1
	4						15.8

Next, we compute the savings for all pairs (i, j), $1 \le i < j \le 5$. There are a total of 10 savings terms to compute for this example:

$$s_{12} = c_{01} + c_{02} - c_{12} = 33.5 + 30.4 - 10 = 53.9,$$
$$s_{13} = c_{01} + c_{03} - c_{13} = 33.5 + 22.4 - 11.2 = 44.7.$$

The remaining terms are computed in the same way, with the results

$$s_{14} = 13.7, \quad s_{25} = 27.8,$$
$$s_{15} = 35.3, \quad s_{34} = 13.7,$$
$$s_{23} = 41.6, \quad s_{35} = 30.7,$$
$$s_{24} = 12.5, \quad s_{45} = 13.7.$$

The next step is to rank the customer pairs in decreasing order of their savings values. This results in the ranking

(1, 2), (1, 3), (2, 3), (1, 5), (3, 5), (2, 5), (1, 4), (3, 4), (4, 5), and (2, 4).

Note that (1, 4), (3, 4), and (4, 5) have the same savings. Ties are broken arbitrarily, so these three pairs could have been ranked differently. We now begin combining customers and creating vehicle routes by considering the pairs in ranked order, checking each time that we do not violate the problem constraints. Because (1, 2) is first on the list, we first try linking customers 1 and 2 on the same route. Doing so results in a load of 85 + 162 = 247 loaves. Next, we consider combining 1 and 3, which means including 3 on the same route. This results in a load of 247 + 26 = 273, which is still feasible. Hence, we have now constructed a route consisting of customers 1, 2, and 3. The next pair on the list is (2, 3). However, 2 and 3 are already on the same route. Next on the list is (1, 5). Linking customer 5 to the current route is infeasible, however. As the demand at location 5 is 110 loaves, adding location 5 to the current route would exceed the truck's capacity. The next feasible pair on the list is (4, 5) which we make into a new route. The solution recommended by the savings method consists of two routes, as shown in Figure 6–9.

We should point out that the savings method is only a heuristic. It does not necessarily produce an optimal routing. The problem is that forcing the choice of a highly ranked link may preclude other links that might have slightly lower savings but might be better choices in a global sense by allowing other links to be chosen downstream. Several authors have suggested modifications of the savings method to attempt to overcome this difficulty. The interested reader should refer to Eilon et al. (1971) for a discussion on these methods. However, the authors point out that these modifications do not always result in a more cost-effective solution.

FIGURE 6–9
Vehicle routing found from the savings method for Example 6.3

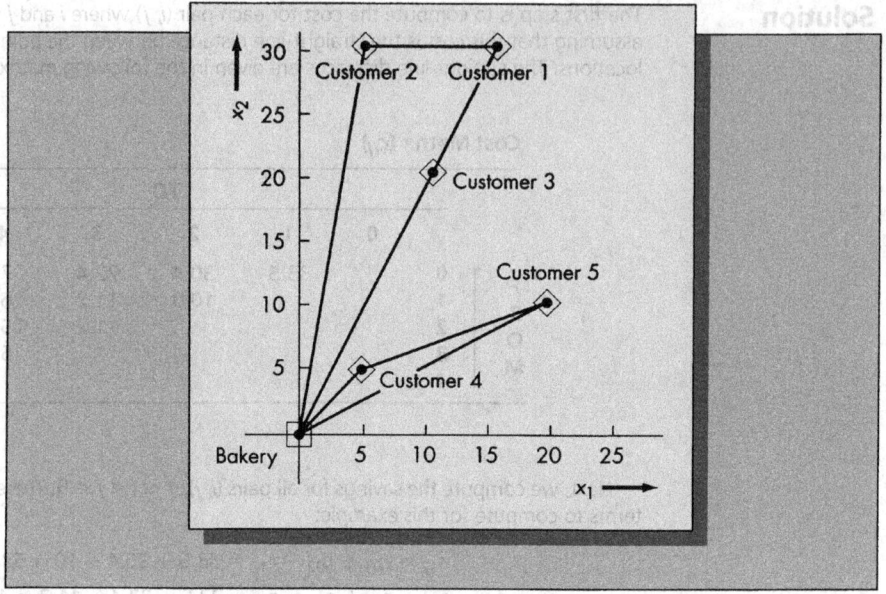

Practical Issues in Vehicle Scheduling

We may classify vehicle scheduling problems as one of two types: arc-based or node-based. Arc-based problems are ones in which the goal is to cover a certain collection of arcs in a network. Typical examples are snow removal and garbage collection. The type of distribution problems we have discussed in this section are node-based problems. The objective is to visit a specified set of locations. Problems also may be a combination of both of these.

Most real vehicle scheduling problems are much more complex than that described in Example 6.3. Schrage (1981) lists 10 features that make real problems difficult to solve. These include the following seven features:

1. *Frequency requirements.* Visits to customers may have to occur at a certain frequency, and that frequency may vary from customer to customer. In our example, bread deliveries are made daily to each customer, so frequency is not an issue. Consider, however, the problem of delivering oil or gas for residential use. The frequency of delivery depends on the usage rate, so delivery frequency will vary from customer to customer.

2. *Time windows.* This refers to the requirement that visits to customer locations be made at specific times. Dial-a-ride systems and postal and bank pickups and deliveries are typical examples.

3. *Time-dependent travel time.* When deliveries are made in urban centers, rush-hour congestion can be an important factor. This is an example of the case in which travel time (and hence the cost associated with a link in the network) depends on the time of day.

4. *Multidimensional capacity constraints.* There may be constraints on weight as well as on volume. This can be a thorny issue, especially when the same vehicles are used to transport a variety of different products.

Snapshot Application

J.B. HUNT SAVES BIG WITH ROUTING AND SCHEDULING ALGORITHM

J.B. Hunt Transport Services, Inc., is one of the largest transportation logistics companies in North America. A significant portion of their business lies in *drayage*, which is the transport of goods from an origin to a destination within the same urban area (i.e., it does not include long haul operations). The term originated from transport by dray horses, but of course trucks are used exclusively for such operations these days. One of the most common types of drayage is the transport of containerized cargo between and among rail ramps and shipping docks.

Pazour and Neubert (2013) describe a routing and scheduling project done for J.B. Hunt Transport to determine cross-town drayage moves between rail ramps. While this scheduling was originally done manually, the size of the fleet and scale of movements had grown too large for this to remain practical. The combination of fleet and movements made for 4.13×10^{32} routes, although not all will be feasible because they ignore availability constraints for ramps and drivers and geographical considerations. Because of the scale of the problem, the authors produced a heuristic to decide the routing of trucks and the scheduling of drivers on the routes.

J.B. Hunt retains a fleet of drivers and also hires third-party drivers to cover overloads. Since third-party drivers are paid by the load, the primary objective of the heuristic is to maximize the number of loads covered by company drivers. However, there may be many solutions with identical numbers of company driver loads; therefore, the heuristic also tries to minimize total empty travel miles, which can cost a significant amount of money in terms of fuel usage and vehicle wear and tear.

The constraints in the optimization are that every load must be covered, either by a company driver or a third-party contractor and every company driver must be assigned a route. The heuristic generates feasible routes that consist of combinations of legs that either move a container across town or move the empty truck to where it is needed. A truck may do twelve or more loads in a day. Third-party contractors are not assigned to routes. Instead, they are assumed to simply do a single container load from an origin to a destination, which is a conservative assumption. The heuristic also considers operational constraints, including the number of loads per driver schedule, driver start times, driver start and end locations, hourly traffic patterns, load time windows, and required driver service hours.

As reported by the authors, the implementation of the cross-town application has positively impacted J.B. Hunt's intermodal drayage operation by automating and enhancing planning work flow for dispatchers, allowing the fleet size to grow without making planning impossible, reducing the number of costly outsourced loads, and significantly improving operational efficiency. J.B. Hunt has documented the annualized cost savings of the cross-town heuristic implementation at $581,000. This is yet another example of the application of sophisticated operations research methods.

5. *Vehicle types*. Large firms may have several vehicle types from which to choose. Vehicle types may differ according to capacity, the cost of operation, and whether the vehicle is constrained to closed trips only (where it must return to the depot after making deliveries). When several types of vehicles are available, the number of feasible alternatives increases dramatically.

6. *Split deliveries*. If one customer has a particular requirement, it could make sense to have more than one vehicle assigned to that customer.

7. Uncertainty. Routing algorithms invariably assume that all the information is known in advance. In truth, however, the time required to cross certain portions of a network could be highly variable, depending on factors such as traffic conditions, weather, and vehicle breakdowns.

Problems for Section 6.6

17. Re-solve Example 6.3 assuming that the capacity of the vehicles is only 250 loaves of bread.

18. Re-solve Example 6.3 assuming that the distance between any two locations is the rectangular distance rather than the Euclidean distance. (See Section 10.7 for a definition of rectangular distance.)

19. Add the following customer locations and requirements to Example 6.3 and re-solve:

Customer	Location	Daily Requirement
6	(12, 12)	78
7	(23, 3)	126

20. Suppose that one wishes to schedule vehicles from a central depot to five customer locations. The cost of making trips between each pair of locations is given in the following matrix. (Assume that the depot is location 0.)

    Cost Matrix (c_{ij})

		\\	\\	TO	\\	\\
		0	1	2	3	4	5
	0		20	75	33	10	30
F	1			35	5	20	15
R	2				18	58	42
O	3					40	20
M	4						25

    Assume that these costs correspond to distances between locations and that each vehicle is constrained to travel no more than 50 miles on each route. Find the routing suggested by the savings method.

21. All-Weather Oil and Gas Company is planning delivery routes to six natural gas customers. The customer locations and gas requirements (in gallons) are given in the following table.

Customer	Location	Requirements (gallons)
1	(5, 14)	550
2	(10, 25)	400
3	(3, 30)	650
4	(35, 12)	250
5	(10, 7)	300

    Assume that the depot is located at the origin of the grid and that the delivery trucks have a capacity of 1,200 gallons. Also assume that the cost of travel between any two locations is the straight-line (Euclidean) distance between them. Find the route schedule obtained from the savings method.

6.7 RISK POOLING

A key strategy for increasing efficiency and mitigating uncertainty in supply chains is known as *risk pooling*. Put simply, risk pooling means that when one adds multiple sources of variability, the whole is inherently less variable. A common measure of relative variability is known as the coefficient of variation (CV). The coefficient of variation of a random variable is the ratio of the standard deviation over the mean. In symbols, if X is a random variable with mean μ and standard deviation σ, then $CV(X) = \frac{\sigma}{\mu}$.

Now, consider n independent sources of variation, represented by the random variables $(X_1, X_2, \ldots, X_n)$. Assume that these are independent and identically distributed and each have mean μ and standard deviation σ. These might represent demands at n stores of a single retailer. Now consider $CV(W)$ where $W = \sum_{i=1}^{n} X_i$ (the sum of the demands at the n stores). Since the random variables are assumed to be independent, it follows that the variance of W is $n\sigma^2$ and hence the standard deviation of W is $\sigma\sqrt{n}$. Since the expected value (that is, the mean) of W is $n\mu$, it follows that the coefficient of variation of W is $CV(W) = \dfrac{\sigma}{\mu\sqrt{n}}$. Clearly this is decreasing in n. Even if the random variables $(X_1, X_2, \ldots, X_n)$ do not have the same distribution, a similar phenomenon will hold. (However, if the demands are positively correlated the relative variation can actually increase.) Pooling is analogous to portfolio diversification in finance. In that case, one seeks financial products (e.g., stocks and bonds) that are negatively correlated and that are of sufficient variety (i.e., large enough n) such that the risk of the total portfolio is decreased. In operations management, the goal is to aggregate sources of uncertainty so that the whole is easier to manage. There are three key versions of risk pooling that will be discussed below.

1. Inventory/location pooling.
2. Product pooling and postponement.
3. Capacity pooling.

Inventory/Location Pooling

If two geographic sources of demand can be served by the same supply then pooling will mean that the aggregate demand will have lower coefficient of variation. This in turn implied that the inventory needed to achieve a target service level will be less. Of course, there are declining marginal returns to pooling so if the coefficient of variation is already low it will have little benefit.

Inventory pooling can either be achieved by a centralized warehouse, which has the disadvantage of moving inventory away from customers, or by *virtual pooling*, where items are transshipped from one location to another for resupply, which may increase transportation costs.

Example 6.4

Consider a toy retailer with warehouses in St. Louis and Kansas City, Missouri. The warehouses stock an identical popular toy delivered to stores in the two cities. Assume a warehouse serves only stores in its city. Weekly demand for St. Louis is normally distributed with mean 2,000, and standard deviation 400 (that is $N(\mu = 2{,}000, \sigma = 400)$). Weekly demand for Kansas City is distributed $N(\mu = 2{,}000, \sigma = 300)$. We assume that the two cities are far enough apart so that demand in the two cities is independent.

The following parameters are seen by both warehouses:

Replenishment lead time in weeks ~ $N(\mu = 2, \sigma = 0.1)$;

Fixed shipping cost of replenishment: $500;

Cost per toy: $10; and

Holding cost per toy 20 percent of toy's value per year.

How many toys should each location order at a time and when should they reorder if they want a 99 percent cycle service level? What if they pool the two locations?

Solution From the EOQ equation of Section 4.5 of Chapter 4, shown in the spreadsheet below, both warehouses should order 7,221 toys at a time. Notice how weekly demand has been converted to yearly demand so it is in the same time units as the holding cost.

	A	B	C	D	E	F	G
1	λ	104280	Demand rate of the item, in units/unit time				
2	K	$500	Fixed cost incurred with each replenishment, in dollars				
3	h	2	Holding cost per unit per unit time				
4	EOQ	7220.8	Economic order quantity				
5	EOQ rounded up	7221					
6							

Cell Formulas
Cell	Formula
B1	=2000*52.14
B3	=0.2*10
B4	=SQRT(2*B2*B1/B3)

From the type-1 service reorder point model of Section 5.5, shown in the spreadsheet below, St. Louis should keep a safety stock of 1,396 toys and Kansas City should keep a safety stock of 1,092 toys (only calculations for St Louis are shown but Kansas City is similar with cell B3 equal to 300 instead of 400).

	A	B	C	D	E	F	G
1	Service level = (1−α)	0.01	Probability of a stockout in a reorder cycle				
2	λ	2000	Demand rate of the item, in units/unit time (E[D])				
3	σ(λ)	400	Standard deviation of the demand per unit time				
4	μ(t)	2	Expected lead time, in unit time				
5	σ(t)	0.1	Standard deviation of the leadtime				
6							
7							
8	Solve for safety stock and reorder point						
9	σ(LTD)	600.00	Standard deviation of demand during lead time, in units				
10	z	2.33	Safety factor				
11	Safety Stock	1395.81	zσ(LTD)				
12	Reorder Point	5395.81	Safety stock + λμ(t)				

Cell Formulas
Cell	Formula
B9	=SQRT(B4*B3*B3+B2*B2*B5*B5)
B10	=NORMSINV(1−B1)
B11	=B10*B9
B12	=B11+B2*B4

If the two warehouses are pooled (either physically or virtually through an information system) then weekly demand becomes 4,000 (=2*2000) and the standard deviation of weekly demand becomes $500(=\sqrt{300^2 + 400^2})$. Substituting these numbers into the above spreadsheets show that the company should order 10,199 toys at a time (a 29 percent reduction) and keep a safety stock of 1,890 toys (a 24 percent reduction).

Thus it can be seen that pooling inventory can result in a significant reduction of inventory in the system. As another illustration consider the following simple scenario. Assume n independent retail locations stock similar items. For example, these could be Macy's department stores located in different cities. Let us further assume that the stock level of a particular item is determined from the newsvendor model. Referring to the discussion in Section 5.5, there are known values of the unit overage cost, c_o, and the unit underage cost, c_u. In Chapter 5 it was proven that the optimal stocking level is the $c_u/(c_u + c_o)$ fractile of the demand distribution. (If we assume that stocking levels are determined based on service levels instead of costs, then the critical ratio *is* the service level and c_o and c_u need not be known.)

To simplify the analysis, let us suppose that the demand for this item follows the same normal distribution at each store with mean μ and standard deviation σ, and the demands are independent from store to store. Let z^* be the value of the standard normal variate that corresponds to a left-tail probability equal to the critical ratio. Then, as is shown in Section 5.3, the optimal policy is to order up to $Q = m + \sigma z^*$ at each location. The safety stock held at each location is σz^*, so the total safety stock in the system is $n\sigma z^*$. Refer to this case as the decentralized system.

Alternatively, suppose that all inventory for this item is held at a single distribution center and shipped overnight on an as-needed basis to the stores. Let's consider the amount of safety stock needed in this case to provide the same level of service as with the decentralized system. Since store demands are independent normal random variables with mean μ and variance σ^2, the aggregated demand from all n stores is also normal, but with mean $n\mu$ and variance $n\sigma^2$. The standard deviation of the aggregated demand therefore has standard deviation $\sigma\sqrt{n}$. This means that to achieve the same level of service, the warehouse needs to stock up to the level Q_w given by $Q_w = n\mu + z^*\sigma\sqrt{n}$. The total safety stock is now $z^*\sigma\sqrt{n}$. This corresponds to a centralized system.

Forming the ratio of the safety stock in the decentralized system over the safety stock in the centralized system gives $z^*\sigma n/z^*\sigma\sqrt{n} = \sqrt{n}$. Hence, the decentralized system will have to hold $\sqrt{n}$ times more safety stock than the centralized system to achieve the same level of service. Even for small values of n, this difference is significant, and for large retailers such as Wal-Mart that have thousands of stores, this difference is enormous.

Of course, this example is a simplification of reality. For most products, it is impractical for every sale to come from a distribution center, and it is impractical for a single distribution center to serve the entire country. Furthermore, the assumption that demands at different stores for the same item are independent is also unlikely to be true. Demands for some items, such as desirable fashion items, are likely to be positively correlated, while others, such as seasonal items like bathing suits, might be negatively correlated. However, even with these caveats, the advantages of centralization are substantial and account for the fact that multilevel distribution systems are widespread in many industries, especially retailing. These results are based on the work of Eppen (1979) (who allowed for correlated demands). This model was extended by Eppen and Schrage (1981) and Erkip, Hausman, and Nahmias (1990) to more general settings.

Several authors have examined the issue of how item characteristics affect the optimal breakdown of DC versus in-store inventory. Muckstadt and Thomas (1980) showed that high-cost, low-demand items derived the greatest benefit from centralized stocking, while Nahmias and Smith (1994) showed how other factors, such as the probability of a lost sale and the frequency of shipments from the DC to the stores, also affect the optimal breakdown between store and DC inventory. A comprehensive review of inventory control models for retailing can be found in Nahmias and Smith (1993), and an excellent collection of articles on general multi-echelon inventory models in Schwarz (1981).

Product Pooling and Postponement

A universal design may be used to pool demand between two product categories. We see the reverse of this effect when products are tailored to a specific market (e.g., boys and girls diapers). The likely negative effect on variability, and hence inventory and production planning, is often overlooked when making such product decisions. One way to mitigate such effects is using delayed differentiation or postponement where the configuration of the final product is delayed as long as possible.

The first application of this principle known to this writer was implemented by Benetton (Signorelli and Heskett, 1984). The Benetton Group is an Italian-based maker of fashion clothes that had, by 1982, become the world leader in the field of knitwear. About 60 percent of the garments sold by the firm are made of wool. Traditionally, wool is dyed before it is knitted. In 1972 Benetton undertook a unique strategy: to dye the garments *after* they were knitted. One might well question this strategy since labor and production costs for garments dyed after manufacture are about 10 percent higher than for garments knitted from dyed thread.

The advantage of reversing the order of the dying and the knitting operations is that it provides additional time before committing to the final mix of colors. This time gives the firm a chance to gain additional data on consumer preferences for colors. Benetton's knitwear included nearly 500 color and style combinations. Undyed garments are referred to as *gray stock*. Keeping inventories of gray stock rather than dyed garments had several advantages. First, if a specific color became more popular than anticipated, Benetton could meet the demand for that color. Second, the company would run less risk of having large unsold stockpiles of garments in unpopular colors. These advantages more than offset the higher costs of dying the knitted garments rather than the raw wool.

How does postponement correlate with inventory management theory? As we saw in Chapter 5, safety stock is retained to protect against demand uncertainty over the replenishment lead time. The lead time for garments of a specific color is reduced by postponing the dying operation. It follows that the uncertainty is reduced as well, thus achieving comparable service levels with less safety stock. Further, because intermediate inventories for different end items are pooled (e.g., all sweaters have the same base garment at Benetton) the inherent demand uncertainty has been reduced.

Postponement has become a key strategy in many diverse industries. Another example discussed in the literature is that of Hewlett-Packard (HP) (Lee, Billington, and Carter, 1994). HP is one of the world's leading producers of inkjet and laser printers, among other products. Printers are sold worldwide. While the basic mechanisms of the printers sold overseas are the same as the American versions, subassemblies, such as power supplies, must be customized for local markets. HP's original strategy was to configure printers for local requirements (i.e., localize them) at the factory. That is, printers with the correct power supplies, plugs, and manuals would be produced at the factory, sorted, and shipped overseas as final products. The result was that HP needed to carry large safety stocks of all printer configurations.

In order to reduce inventories and improve the service provided by the distribution centers (DCs) to retail customers, HP adopted a strategy similar to Benetton's. Printers sent from the factory would be generic or gray stock. Localization would be done at the DC level rather than at the factory. As with Benetton, this had the ultimate effect of reducing necessary safety stocks while improving service. Printers are shipped to overseas DCs by boat, requiring one-month transit time. With local customization of the product, the replenishment lead time for locally configured printers was dramatically reduced. Also, the demand on the factory is now the aggregate of the demands at the DCs, which has relatively smaller variation due to pooling. Lee, Billington, and Carter showed that DC localization for HP Deskjet-Plus printers would lead to an 18 percent reduction in inventories with no reduction in service levels.

According to Harold E. Edmondson, an HP vice president (as quoted in Lee, Billington, and Carter, 1994):

> The results of this model analysis confirmed the effectiveness of the strategy for localizing the printers at remote distribution centers. Such a design strategy has significant benefits in terms of increased flexibility to meet customer demands, as well as savings in both inventory and transportation costs . . . I should add that the design for localization concept is now part of our manufacturing and distribution strategy.

The notion of postponing customization of a product appears to be gaining acceptance. For example, semiconductors are produced in generic form when possible and customized through programming or other means after firm orders are received (Barrone, 1996). Firms in many industries are becoming aware of the risk-pooling and lead time reduction benefits from postponement and local customization of products.

Capacity Pooling

Almost all production systems require capacity that is larger than expected demand to allow for fluctuations in either demand or supply. This excess capacity is called *safety capacity* and forms a buffer against variability, similar to how inventory buffers variation. If capacity can be shifted among products, the different product demands are effectively one pool. In this case, less safety capacity is needed. However, flexible capacity is usually either more expensive or less efficient than dedicated capacity, so such pooling needs to be done carefully. There has been significant research on the "right" level of flexibility for various types of systems.

For manufacturing systems, capacity pooling typically involves investing in more flexible machines. Setup times for changing between product types need to be carefully managed in any nondedicated system. Toyota has led the way in designing equipment to produce multiple products with minimal setup times between different types of products. (Toyota's single minute exchange of dies, SMED, were described in Chapter 1.) For assembly or service system, capacity pooling typically involves cross-training workers. In this case, the workers may be more expensive because they need a higher skill set. Also, there are cognitive limits on how much cross-training one person can absorb.

The good news on capacity pooling is that its benefits can be achieved without a fully flexible system. That is, as shown originally by Jordan and Graves (1995), a little flexibility goes a long way. Consider Figure 6–10, which reproduces Figure 2 in Jordan and Graves (1995). On the right is a fully flexible system where each of 10 plants can produce any of 10 products. Not shown is the fully dedicated system where each product is only produced by one plant. On the left is a strategy known as *chaining* where each product is connected to two plants in such a fashion that the whole system becomes linked. Jordan and Graves (1995) show that such a chain is almost as effective as full flexibility.

Notice that there are many more options for capacity pooling than just the two described above, particularly when capacity corresponds to people rather than machines. For example, instead of training all staff to either work on products (or customer types) 1 and 10 or 1 and 2, as shown in Figure 6–10, some staff may be trained on types 1 and 3, 1 and 4, etc. In addition, some staff may be dedicated to a product or customer type, while others are cross-trained. Such a strategy is called *tailored pairing* by Bassamboo et al. (2010a, 2010b) and is shown to be close to optimal for the systems they consider.

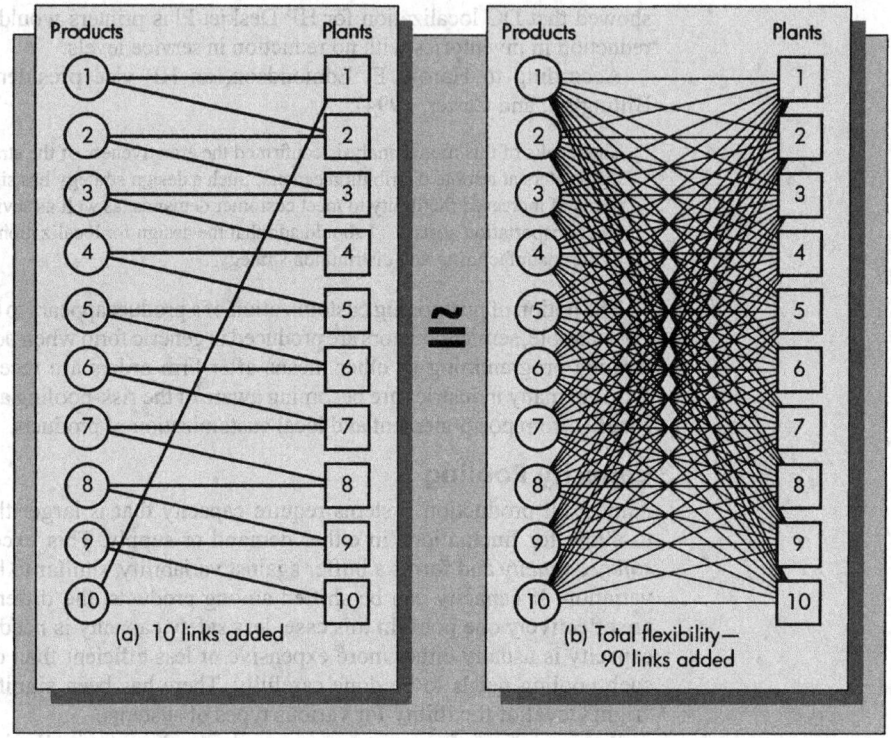

FIGURE 6–10
Flexibility Configurations.

Source: Jordan and Graves (1995)

The key finding in most capacity pooling research is that more pooling is better but there are decreasing returns to scope (i.e., number of types of product pooled). Furthermore, it is important to try to create a circuit with the pooling that encompasses as broad a range of capacity and products as possible. In practice, pooling is constrained by the day-to-day realities of running a production system. But, as we saw above, a little pooling can go a long way.

6.8 DESIGNING PRODUCTS FOR SUPPLY CHAIN EFFICIENCY

Product design was traditionally a function that was totally divorced from more mundane operations management issues. Designers would be concerned primarily with aesthetics and marketability. Little attention would be given to nuts-and-bolts concerns such as manufacturing and logistics at the design stage. As quality and reliability advanced to the forefront, it became clear that product reliability and product design are closely linked. The design for manufacturability (DFM) movement developed out of a need to know why products fail and how those failures could be minimized. Once it was understood that reliability could be factored in at the design stage, the link between design and manufacturing was forged. Another term for DFM is concurrent engineering.

In recent years, firms have realized that the logistics of managing the supply chain can have as much impact on the bottom line as product design and manufacturing. More than ever, we are seeing innovative designs that take supply chain considerations into account. One way of describing this concept is design for logistics (DFL). Another is three-dimensional concurrent engineering (3-DCE), a term adopted by Fine (1998). The three dimensions here are product, process, and supply chains. It carries the concept of concurrent engineering one step further. Concurrent engineering means that product-related issues (functionality, marketability) and process-related issues (how the product is produced, reliability and quality of the final product) are joint considerations in the design phase. Three-dimensional concurrent engineering means that supply chain logistics is also considered in the product design phase.

Two significant ways that logistics considerations enter into the product design phase are

1. Product design for efficient transportation and shipment.
2. Postponement of final product configuration (as discussed earlier).

Products that can be packed, moved, and stored easily streamline both manufacturing and logistics. Buyers prefer products that are easy to store and easy to move. Some products tend to be large and bulky and present a special challenge in this regard. An example is furniture. Swedish-based Ikea certainly did an excellent job of designing products that are modular and easily stored. Furniture is sold in simple-to-assemble kits that allow Ikea retailers to store furniture in the same warehouselike locations at which they are displayed. Simchi-Levi et al. (1999) discuss several other examples of products whose success is partially based on their ease of shipment and storage.

Additional Issues in Supply Chain Design

While products can be better designed for efficient supply chain operation, there are several important issues to consider in the design of the supply chain itself. Fine (1998) refers to supply chain design as the "ultimate core competency." Three important relevant issues are

- The configuration of the supplier base.
- Outsourcing arrangements.
- Channels of distribution.

Configuration of the Supplier Base

The number of suppliers, their locations, and their sizes are important considerations for efficient supply chain design. In recent years, the trend has been to reduce the number of suppliers and develop long-term arrangements with the existing supplier base. An example is the Xerox Corporation. Jacobson and Hillkirk (1986) discuss several reasons for the impressive turnaround of Xerox during the 1980s. One of the company's strategies was to streamline the supply chain on the procurement side by reducing the number of its suppliers from 5,000 to only about 400. Those 00 suppliers included a mix of both overseas and local suppliers. The overseas suppliers were chosen primarily on a cost basis, while the local suppliers could provide more timely deliveries when necessary.

Cooperative efforts between manufacturers and suppliers (as well as manufacturers and retailers on the other end of the chain) have been gaining popularity. Traditionally this relationship was an adversarial one. Today, with the advent of arrangements like vendor-managed inventories, suppliers and manufacturers work closely and often share what was once proprietary data to improve performance on both ends.

Outsourcing Arrangements

Outsourcing of manufacturing has become a popular trend in recent years. Successful contract manufacturers such as Foxxcon experienced rapid growth in the past decade. Many firms are outsourcing supply chain functions as well. Third-party logistics (3PL) is becoming big business. For example, Wal-Mart now outsources a major portion of its logistics operation.

A 3PL agreement might only outsource transport operations or it might also outsource warehousing, purchasing, and inventory management. A new term, 4PL, has been coined to reflect 3PL providers that offer end-to-end logistics support. Originally the term was only applied to firms that manage external 3PL providers (as well as providing full logistics support). However, more common usage allows the 3PL activities to take place internally to the 4PL. In some sense, Amazon.com is a 4PL provider as it sells products for other companies providing both the web interface as well as the pick-and-pack and dispatch operations.

Dreifus (1992) describes a case of a smaller firm that decided to outsource purchasing. The Singer Furniture Company contracted with the Florida-based IMX Corporation to handle its procurements. In the agreement, IMX handles all negotiations from consolidated shipments, takes care of the paperwork, conducts quality-control inspection, and searches for new suppliers in exchange for a fixed commission. In a trial run, IMX suggested a switch from a Taiwanese supplier of bedposts to one based in the Caribbean, which resulted in a 50 percent reduction in price to Singer. From Singer's point of view, the primary advantages of entering into this arrangement were

> *Buying economies of scale.* IMX buys for several clients (including other furniture makers), which allows it to negotiate lower unit costs on larger orders. There are also economies of scale in shipping costs from overseas. IMX claims that it saves at least 20 percent for clients in this way.
>
> *Reduced management overhead.* Singer was able to eliminate its international purchasing unit and several related management functions.
>
> *Lower warehousing costs.* IMX bears much of the risk on several lines of product by absorbing local storage costs.
>
> *Above-board accounting.* The firms agreed on open procedures and disclosures to be sure that the quality programs are functioning and charges are in line with costs.

Channels of Distribution

Failure to establish solid channels of distribution can spell the end for many firms. The design of the distribution channel includes the number and the configuration of distribution centers; arrangements with third-party wholesalers; licensing and other agreements with retailers, including vendor-managed inventory programs; and establishment of the means to move product quickly through the channel. Direct selling to consumers has been an enormously successful strategy for some retailers, especially for products that become obsolete quickly. By eliminating intermediaries, manufacturers reduce the risk of product dying in the supply channel. This has been a successful strategy for computer maker Dell and for Amazon.com. Dell Computer's phenomenal success can be attributed partially to its outstanding supply chain design, highlighted in the Snapshot Application in this section.

Snapshot Application

DELL COMPUTER DESIGNS THE ULTIMATE SUPPLY CHAIN

Dell Computer was one of the biggest success stories of the 1990s. How successful? The stock price increased a whopping 27,000 percent during the decade. There is no question that a sleek, efficient supply chain design was a contributing factor to Dell's phenomenal success.

Michael Dell, the firm's founder, began by assembling and reselling IBM PCs from his dorm room at the University of Texas in the early 1980s. Later, in the mid-1980s, he formed PC's Limited, which offered one of the first of the mail order "clones." The computers were clones of the IBM XT, which was selling for several thousand dollars at the time. PC's Limited sold a basic box consisting of a motherboard with an Intel 8088 chip, a power supply, a floppy drive, and a controller for $795. The buyer had to add a graphics card, a monitor, and a hard drive to make the system functional, but the final product cost less than half as much as an equivalent IBM XT and ran faster. (This was, in fact, the first computer purchased by this writer.) From this modest beginning grew the multibillion-dollar Dell Computer Corporation which dominates the PC and laptop market today.

To understand Dell's success, one must understand the nature of the personal computer marketplace. The central processor is really the computer, and its power determines the power of the PC. In the PC marketplace, Intel has been the leader in designing every new generation of processor chip. A few companies, such as AMD and Texas Instruments, have had limited success in this market, but the relentless new-product introduction by Intel has resulted in competitors' processors becoming obsolete before they can garner significant market share. Each new generation of microprocessors renders old technology obsolete. For that reason, computers and computer components have a relatively short life span. As new chips are developed at an ever-increasing pace, the obsolescence problem becomes even more critical.

How does one avoid getting stuck with obsolete inventory? Dell's solution was simple and elegant. Don't keep *any* inventory! All PCs purchased from Dell are made to order. Dell does not build to stock. They do store components, however. Although Dell can't guarantee all components are used, their market strategy is designed to move as much of the component inventory as possible. Dell focuses only on the latest technology, and both systems and components are priced to sell quickly. Furthermore, because of their high volume, they can demand quantity discounts from suppliers. As the so-called clockspeed of the industry (a term coined by Fine, 1998) increases, Dell's advantage over manufacturers with more traditional supply chain designs also increases.

Dell's supply chain strategy is not designed to produce the least expensive computer. Less expensive brands, such as Asus and Acer, manufacture in low cost labor markets and in large production quantities. Dell's more agile supply chain allows them to quickly design and market products with the latest technology. However, it is true that personal computers have evolved into a much more commoditized market. For this reason, Dell has moved away from their configure-to-order strategy for many of its products. Also, this has prompted Dell and other U.S.-based manufacturers to expand into other areas, such as peripherals, servers, software, and services. Dell frequently contracts with large organizations (e.g., universities) to provide all of their computing needs. This is another example of servicization, which was discussed in Chapter 1.

6.9 MULTILEVEL DISTRIBUTION SYSTEMS

In many large commercial and military inventory systems, it is common for stock to be stored at multiple locations. For example, inventory may flow from manufacturer to regional warehouses, from regional warehouses to local warehouses, and from local warehouses to stores or other point-of-use locations. Determining the allocation of inventory among these multiple locations is an important strategic consideration, and can have a significant impact on the bottom line. A typical multilevel distribution system is pictured in Figure 6–11.

FIGURE 6–11
Typical multilevel distribution system

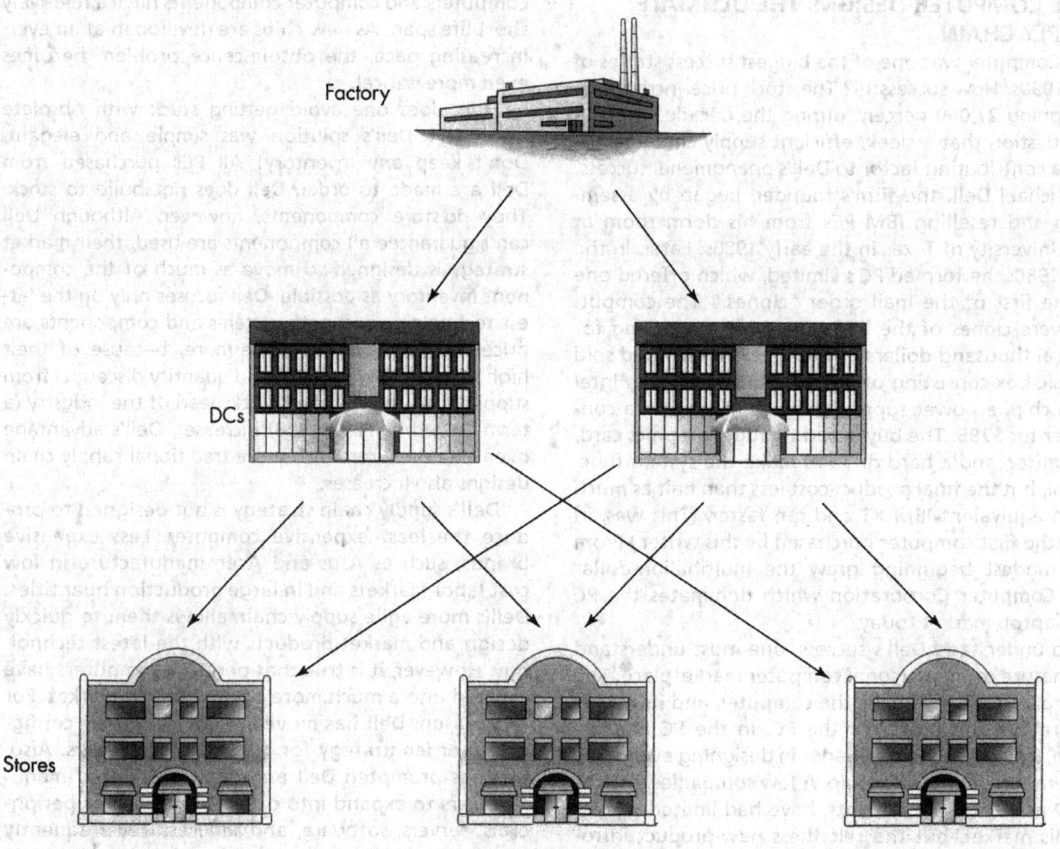

In the parlance of traditional inventory theory, such systems are referred to as multi-echelon inventory systems. The interest in this area was originally sparked by a seminal paper by Clark and Scarf (1960) that was part of a major initiative at the Rand Corporation to study logistics and inventory management problems arising in the military. This paper laid the theoretical framework for what later became a very large body of research in multi-echelon inventory theory. (There is a brief overview of multi-echelon inventory models in Chapter 5.)

Including intermediate storage locations in a large-scale distribution system has advantages and disadvantages. The advantages include

1. Risk pooling.
2. Distribution centers that can be designed to meet local needs.
3. Economies of scale in storage and movement of goods.
4. Faster response time.

Suppose a distribution center serves 50 retail outlets. As seen earlier, by holding the majority of the stock at the distribution center rather than at the stores, pooling implies that the same systemwide service level could be achieved with less total inventory.

In retailing, the mix of products sold depends on the location of the store. For example, one sells more short-sleeve shirts in Arizona than in Maine. Hence, *distribution centers* located in the Southwest would stock a different assortment of products than distribution centers located in the Northeast. Distribution centers could be designed to take these differences into account.

Distribution centers allow for *economies of scale* in the following way. If all product were shipped directly from the factory to the local outlet, shipment sizes would be relatively small. Large bulk shipments from factories located overseas could be made to distribution centers at a lower unit cost. In that way, the smaller shipments would be made over shorter distances from distribution centers to stores.

Finally, because distribution centers can be located closer to the customer than can factories, demands can be met more quickly. Retailers try to locate distribution centers in the United States within one day's drive away from any store. (This is why Ohio is a popular place for retail distribution centers, since this is the geographic center of the country.) In this way, store inventories can be replenished overnight if necessary.

Multilevel distribution systems could have several disadvantages as well. These include that they

1. May require more inventory than simpler distribution systems.
2. May increase total order lead times from the plant to the customer.
3. Could ultimately result in greater costs for storage and movement of goods.
4. Could contribute to the bullwhip effect.

Depending on the number of distinct locations used, it is likely that a multilevel system requires more overall total inventory than a single-level system, since safety stock is likely built in at each level. This means that more money is tied up in the pipeline.

When distribution centers experience stock-outs, the response time of the system from manufacturer to point of sale could actually be worse in a multilevel system. This is a consequence of the fact that in the multilevel case, the total lead time from plant to store is the sum of the lead times at each level. (However, in a well-managed system, stock-outs at the distribution center should be very rare occurrences.)

One must not ignore the cost of the distribution center itself. Building a modern, large-scale facility could cost upward of $500 million. In addition, there are recurring costs such as rent and labor. As a result, building and maintaining a multilocation distribution system is expensive.

The *bullwhip effect*, discussed earlier, is the propensity of the variance of orders to increase as one moves up the supply chain. Adding additional levels to a distribution system could cause a bullwhip effect.

Problems for Sections 6.7–6.9

22. Describe how inventory pooling works in a multiechelon inventory system. Under what circumstances does one derive the greatest benefit from pooling? The least benefit?

23. Cross training workers is one way to achieve capacity pooling in a manufacturing environment. What are the advantages and disadvantages to such cross-training?
24. Describe the concept of postponement in supply chains. If you were planning a trip to a distant place, what decisions would you want to postpone as long as possible?
25. Many automobiles can be ordered in one of two engine sizes (examples are the Lincoln LS, the Lexus Coupe, and the Jaguar S Type) but are virtually identical in every other way. How might these automakers use the concept of postponement in their production planning?
26. Discuss why having too many suppliers can be troublesome. Can having too few suppliers also be a problem?
27. Many large companies that have their own manufacturing facilities and logistics organizations outsource a portion of their production (such as IBM) or their supply chain operations (such as Saturn). Why do you suppose this is?
28. A 3PL provider may have only transport services or may also provide warehouse and inventory management services. What are the advantages and disadvantages to a firm in outsourcing its warehouse and inventory management operations along with transportation?
29. What types of companies are best suited to using 4PL providers?
30. Why might a retailer want to consider developing a three-level multilevel system? (The three levels might be labeled National Distribution Center, Regional Distribution Center, and Store.)
31. What are the characteristics of items from which one derives the greatest benefit from centralized storage? the least benefit?

6.10 INCENTIVES IN THE SUPPLY CHAIN

One of the key challenges in SCM is that a supply chain is rarely owned by any one firm. It generally involves different players, often with competing objectives. Consider the following example.

Example 6.5 Suppose that the retailer SnowInc buys ski jackets from the Chinese manufacturer JacketCo. Due to the short selling season and long delivery lead time for this fashion good, this is a one-time purchase decision. SnowInc estimates the season's demand for one type of jacket to be normally distributed with mean 500 and standard deviation 100. Retail price for the jacket is $100. If not sold at the end of the season they unload them for $10 per jacket. The wholesale price JacketCo charges is $30 per jacket and JacketCo's per unit manufacturing cost is $12. How many jackets should SnowInc order and what are the two firms' profits? If both firms were owned by the same company, how would these answers change?

Solution We first consider the decision from SnowInc's perspective. From the newsvendor model (see Section 5.3), they have an overage cost of $30 − $10 = $20 and an underage cost of $100 − $30 = $70. The critical ratio is therefore 70/(20 + 70) = 7/9 and it is best for SnowInc to order 576 jackets, as shown in the below spreadsheet.

	A	B
1	Price	$100
2	Cost	$30
3	Salvage Value	$10
4	Cost of inventory left (overage Cost)	$20
5	Cost of unsatisfied demand (underage Cost)	$70
6	Mean Demand	500
7	Standard Deviation of Demand	100
8		
9	Critical Fractile	0.7778
10	z	0.7647
11	Amount to Stock	576
12		
13	L(z) - loss function	0.1279
14	Expected lost sales	13
15	Expected sales	487
16	Expected left over inventory	89
17		
18	Expected cost	$ 2,680.21
19	Expected profit	$32,319.79

Cell Formulas

Cell	Formula
B4	=B2−B3
B5	=B1−B2
B9	=B5/(B4+B5)
B10	=NORMSINV(B9)
B11	=B6+B7*B10
B13	=NORM.S.DIST(B10,0)−B10*(1−NORM.S.DIST(B10,1))
B14	=B7*B13
B15	=B6−B14
B16	=B11−B15
B18	=(B4+B5)*B7*NORM.S.DIST(B10,0)
B19	=B5*B15−(B4*B16)

SnowInc has an expected profit of approximately $32,320 and JacketCo has a profit from this order of 576*($30 − $12) = $10,368 for a total channel profit of approximately $42,688. However, if SnowInc and JacketCo are owned by the same company, then by replacing the jacket cost of $30 with its true cost of $12 in the above spreadsheet it is seen that 701 jackets should be ordered for a total channel profit of approximately $43,524 ($30,906 to SnowInc and $12,618 to JacketCo), which is a 2 percent increase in total profit.

If 701 jackets are ordered then the supply chain creates more profit and availability improves. In fact, there is only a 2 percent chance that the retailer will stock out (one minus the critical ratio). The reason that so many jackets are ordered (relative to mean demand of 500 jackets) is because the margins are so high relative to the overstock costs.

Given that the supply chain makes more profit and customers are happier if the retailer orders 701 jackets in Example 6.5, why doesn't the retailer do this on their own initiative? The answer is clear from the number above. Ordering 576 jackets produces an expected profit of $32,320 for the retailer whereas ordering 701 jackets produces an expected profit of $30,906. There is no incentive for the retailer to make this change.

In general, the incentives in Example 6.5 can be written as follows. Suppose the manufacturer produces an item for c, sells it to the retailer for w, and the retailer sells it for p. Then the underage cost for the retailer is $p - w$, for the manufacturer is $w - c$, and for the supply-chain as a whole is $p - c$. Because $(p - w) > (p - c)$, the retailer will under stock from the standpoint of maximizing profit to the whole supply chain. In economics this is known as *double marginalization*. Because each firm naturally considers its own margin, the decisions are not what a centralized decision maker would do.

The issue of double marginalization arises because the firms are following a standard wholesale price contract agreement. With different contracts, it is often possible to align incentives of each party so that the optimal supply chain decision is reached; in this case, the supply chain is said to be *coordinated*. For example, many book publishers offer buy-back agreements to bookstores which allow the stores to return unsold copies for a full refund. In this way, the overage cost to retailers is reduced and they are encouraged to stock more. Pasternack (1985) showed how the right buy-back contract can coordinate the supply chain, resulting in system optimal profit; the question then becomes how to split the profits. Assuming that a win-win arrangement can be found, where both parties benefit, both parties will enter into such an agreement. However, buy-back contracts can be problematic in environments where the supplier really does not want to take the goods back or the goods may be damaged in transit.

Revenue sharing contracts are another type of contract that, with the right parameter choices, may coordinate the supply chain. In this case, the retailer pays much less for the goods up front but gives the supplier a portion of all revenue earned. Because there is less risk of overstock, the retailer is again incentivized to order more than they would with a simple wholesale price contract. Such contracts have proved particularly effective in the movie rental industry, where low upfront DVD (and previously video) costs incentivize the store to stock more, which both makes for happier customers and more rentals. The movie studios then take a cut from every movie rented.

Vendor-managed inventory is another way to mitigate double marginalization and coordinate the supply chain. Because the supplier is deciding inventory at the retailer's facility it need not consider the retailer's margins. Of course, restrictions such as shelf-space limitations need to be in place for such contracts to ensure the supplier doesn't overstock on the retailer's behalf.

There are many more kinds of contacts than those described here that, in the right situations, work to coordinate the supply chain. However, there has also been significant behavioral research to evaluate how such contacts perform in practice, when the parties may have considerations beyond expected profit, such as perceptions of fairness. Somewhat surprisingly, behavioral considerations often work against supply chain coordination, and in lab studies wholesale price contracts can do better than profit-maximizing theory would predict (e.g., Loch and Wu, 2008). This combined with their simplicity probably explains the continued widespread use of wholesale price contracts in practice.

Problems for Section 6.10

32. How is double marginalization affected by the profit margin of the retailer $(p - w)$ relative to the profit margin of the whole supply chain $(p - c)$? Is its effect greatest when most of the profit margin sits with the retailer or with the supplier?

33. Why might it not be practical for the supplier in Example 6.5 to simply tell the retailer to order 701 jackets and give the supplier a kick-back for the profit differential? Can you think of different supply chains where such an arrangement might be effective?

34. What types of industries, beyond book publishing, are likely to find buy-back agreements effective?

35. What types of industries, beyond movie rentals, are likely to find revenue sharing agreements effective? When are they least likely to be practical?

36. Why might the supplier be likely to overstock (relative to what is supply chain optimal) in a VMI arrangement if shelf-space restrictions or similar are not in place by the retailer?

6.11 GLOBAL SUPPLY CHAIN MANAGEMENT

Economic barriers between countries are coming down. China, a long time holdout, now participates in a free trade area with the Association of Southeast Asian Nations (ASEAN) and in 2008 signed a bilateral free trade agreement with New Zealand (its first such agreement). Today, few industries only produce in and serve their home market.

One example of a dramatic shift in the marketplace occurred in the automobile industry. Consider the experience from Womack et al. (1990). As a child in the 1950s, there was no question that the family car would be an American nameplate because almost *everybody* in the United States purchased American cars in those years. Foreign automakers began to make inroads into the American market during the late fifties and early sixties and, by 1970, the American firms had given up about 20 percent of the domestic market. During the 1970s, the market share of U.S.-based firms eroded more quickly. While the American firms clung to old designs and old ways of doing business, foreign manufacturers took advantage of changing tastes. The big winner was the Japanese who saw their share of the world auto market soar from almost zero in the mid-fifties to about 30 percent by 1990 (Womack et al., 1990). In 2007 Toyota surpassed American General Motors to take the world's top spot for quarterly sales (Chozick & Shirouzui, 2007).

In addition to the fact that U.S. consumers are buying more foreign cars, it is also true that U.S. firms are producing more cars in other countries, and foreign competitors are producing more cars in the United States. Mexico, and to a lesser extent Canada, have also become key manufacturing locations for U.S.-headquartered companies' automobile production. However, as of the time of this writing, China is the world's largest automobile producer with annual production that exceeds that of the United States and Japan combined. Nevertheless, China's labor costs have been rapidly rising in recent years (by 500 percent between 2000 and 2012) and are expected to continue to rise at a rate of 18 percent per year (Mayer, 2013). Another country may yet emerge as the world's largest automobile producer.

Automobile supply chains are simply one example of supply chains that have undergone major changes in the last few decades. In general, supply chains have become both more global and more complex. For example, between 1995 and 2007 the number of transnational companies more than doubled from 38,000 to 79,000, and foreign subsidiaries nearly tripled from 265,000 to 790,000, according to a supply chain survey by IBM (IBM, 2009). Further, managing global supply chains is made more challenging by the heterogeneity of government and local regulations and cultures across different countries.

A further complexity in managing global supply chains is managing volatile exchange rates. If revenue is reported in U.S. dollars but earned in a foreign currency then any changes in exchange rates can directly affect reported earnings. Similarly, if suppliers are paid in their local currency then exchange rate changes will affect the home country's reported costs. Companies often use *exchange rate hedging* to mitigate the risk from exchange rate movements. Currency options are purchased so that if the exchange rate moves in a favorable direction for the firm then there is no payout but if it moves in an unfavorable direction then the options pay out. The cost of the options depend in part on the *strike price* for the option, which is the point at which they begin to pay out. Southwest Airlines used fuel price options to successfully hedge against fuel price rises in the mid-2000s and is said to have, saved approximately $3.5 billion through fuel hedging between 1999 and 2008 (New York Times, 2008). Of course, when fuel prices dropped during the global financial crisis in 2009 these hedges were less successful, but such is the fundamental nature of options.

Fuel costs are a key issue in supply chain design. In particular, fuel prices have tripled between 2000 and 2012 (Mayer, 2013). One effect of rising fuel costs has been the decision by shipping companies to use *slow steaming*, where vessels designed to travel at 25 knots are deliberately slowed to between 18 and 20 knots to reduce the usage of bunker fuel. In fact, some companies are even using super slow steaming (12 to 14 knots) to reduce costs even further. Clearly, this has significant negative implications with respect to supply chain responsiveness and is particularly problematic for supply chains of perishable items.

One response to increasing labor costs in China and increasing shipping costs due to fuel is the rise of *on-shoring* or *re-shoring*, which is simply the returning of manufacturing operations that were offshored to back in-country (see also Chapter 1). This is most common in the United States where labor unions have become more flexible and automation has made routine tasks more cost effective (Booth, 2013). Another factor in this decision is to decrease risk, particularly in the face of increasing global tensions. In food supply chains, concerns over food miles, food safety, and sustainability have also led to changing supply chain configurations. Clearly, supply chain designs must be regularly evaluated and rethought as global trends change the key trade-offs that lead to one location being chosen over another.

Problems for Section 6.11

37. What do you see as the new emerging markets in the world in the next 20 years? For what reason has Africa been slow to develop as a new market and as a desirable location for manufacturing?
38. As noted earlier in this chapter, the share of U.S. sales accounted for by multinational firms is increasing. What events might reverse this trend?
39. What difficulties for supply chain management are created by the growth of globalization?
40. What industries do you think are particularly likely to have onshore manufacturing operations in the next few years?
41. What is the downside to using currency option hedging?

6.12 SUMMARY

With the rise of the information age has come the rise of interest in supply chain management. When firms can see data on supply chain costs they can work to reduce them, and there is anecdotal evidence to suggest that firms first worked to push costs out of manufacturing and then out of their supply chains (Henkoff, 1994). Because of this, supply chain software has become big business. Most of the biggest names in the information systems arena, including Oracle Corporation and German-based SAP, now offer supply chain modules as part of their total system solutions.

Both information systems and new technologies have allowed information to be gathered and shared in ways that were not previously possible. Supply chain partners can share data on market trends or even manage each other's inventory through vendor-managed inventory agreements. Point-of-sale entry systems based on barcoding are now ubiquitous and RFID technology solutions are becoming increasingly popular as well.

With information, or "big data" as it is often called these days, has come the rise of business analytics and mathematical modeling can play an important role in efficient supply chain management. The transportation and transshipment problems, discussed in this chapter, are examples of the kind of mathematical optimization models that can assist firms with determining efficient schedules for moving product from the factory to the market. There are also mathematically based techniques for efficient scheduling of delivery vehicles.

Delivering the product to the consumer was traditionally a secondary consideration for manufacturing firms. Today, however, supply chain considerations are taken into account even at the product design level. Products that are easily stacked can be shipped and stored more easily and less expensively. The strategy of postponement has turned out to be a fundamental design principle that has proven to be highly cost effective. By designing products whose final configuration can be postponed, firms can delay product differentiation. This allows them to gain valuable time in determining the realization of demand and also to pool intermediate inventory for a variety of end products.

An unusual phenomenon that was observed in the late 1980s is the bullwhip effect. The variance of orders seems to increase dramatically as one moves up the supply chain. While most agree that the bullwhip effect is the result of different agents acting to optimize their own positions, solutions for this problem are not trivial. Information sharing, reduced order batching, and decreased order lead times will help but they do not relieve the issue of each party operating under its own incentives.

Misaligned incentives in the supply chain are a major source of supply chain inefficiency. About the only way to mitigate these issues are through a change in approach to partnerships and contracts. When different parties in the supply chain consider themselves to be partners then they are more likely to work together to find win-win solutions, namely solutions that both increase the performance of the supply chain and also increase each party's individual profit. Moving beyond wholesale price contracts to agreements such as buy-back contracts, revenue sharing contracts, and vendor managed inventory agreements can all help to coordinate the supply chain if operated under appropriate parameter choices.

The problem of misaligned incentives becomes exacerbated in global supply chains because the parties are often located in different geographic areas, may come from different cultural backgrounds, and may have different local incentives provided by their governments. Variable exchange rates, rising fuel costs, and increased global tensions also form challenges for global supply chain management. Sustainability and risk management have also become of increasing importance to many global corporations.

Bibliography

Arntzen, B. C., G. G. Brown, T. P. Harrison, and L. L. Trafton. "Global Supply Chain Management at Digital Equipment Corporation." *Interfaces* 25 (1995), pp. 69–93.

Arrow, K. J. "Historical Background." Chapter 1 in *Studies in the Mathematical Theory of Inventory and Production*, ed. K. J. Arrow, S. Karlin, and H. Scarf. Stanford, CA: Stanford University Press, 1958.

Barrone, F. Private communication, 1996.

Bassamboo, A., R. S. Randhawa, and J. A. Van Mieghem. "A Little Flexibility Is All You Need: On the Asymptotic Value of Flexible Capacity in Parallel Queuing Systems." *Operations Research* 60 (2012), pp. 1423–1435.

Bassamboo, A., R. S. Randhawa, and J. A. Van Mieghem. "Optimal Flexibility Configurations in Newsvendor Networks: Going Beyond Chaining and Pairing." *Management Science* 56 (2010), pp. 1285–1303.

Bell, W. J. "Improving the Distribution of Industrial Gases with an Online Computerized Routing and Scheduling Optimizer." *Interfaces* 13, no. 6 (1983), pp. 4–23.

Booth, T. "Here, there and everywhere: After decades of sending work across the world, companies are rethinking their offshoring strategies." *The Economist*, Jan 19th 2013. Accessed from http://www.economist.com/news/special-report/21569572-after-decades-sending-work-across-world-companies-are-rethinking-their-offshoring

Bray, R. L., and H. Mendelson. "Information Transmission and the Bullwhip Effect: An Empirical Investigation." *Management Science* 58, no. 5 (2012), pp. 860–875.

Bustillo, M. "Wal-Mart Radio Tags to Track Clothing." *Wall Street Journal*, July 23, 2010.

Cachon, G. P., T. Randall, and G. M. Schmidt. "In Search of the Bullwhip Effect." *Manufacturing and Service Operations Management* 9, no. 4 (2007), pp. 457–479.

Cannon, E. EDI Guide. A Step by Step Approach. New York: Van Nostrand Reinhold, 1993.

Chozick, A. and Shirouzui, N. "GM Slips Into Toyota's Rearview Mirror. Japanese Firm Passes U.S. Rival for First Time in Quarterly Global Sales." *Wall Street Journal*, April 25, 2007. Accessed from http://online.wsj.com/article/SB117739853275580259.html

Clark, A. J., and H. E. Scarf. "Optimal Policies for a Multiechelon Inventory Problem." *Management Science* 6 (1960), pp. 475–90.

Clarke, G., and G. W. Wright. "Scheduling of Vehicles from a Central Depot to a Number of Delivery Points." *Operations Research* 12 (1964), pp. 568–81.

Cohen, M.; P. V. Kamesam; P. Kleindorfer; H. Lee; and A. Tekerian. "Optimizer: IBM's Multi-Echelon Inventory System for Managing Service Logistics." *Interfaces* 20, no. 1 (1990), pp. 65–82.

Cooke, J. A. "Software Takes Babel out of Vendor Managed Inventory." *Logistics Management & Distribution Report* 38, no. 2 (1999), p. 87.

Copacino, W. C. *Supply Chain Management: The Basics and Beyond*. Boca Raton, FL: St. Lucie Press, 1997.

Crawford, F. A. "ECR: A Mandate for Food Manufacturers?" *Food Processing*, February 1994.

Dauzere-Peres, S., et al. "Omya Hustadmarmor Optimizes Its Supply Chain for Delivering Calcium Carbonate Slurry to European Paper Manufacturers." *Interfaces* 37 (2007), pp. 39–51.

Degbotse, A., B. T. Denton, K. Fordyce, R. J. Milne, R. Orzell, C. T. Wang. "IBM Blends Heuristics and Optimization to Plan Its Semiconductor Supply Chain." *Interfaces* 43, no. 2 (2013), pp. 130–141.

Dinning, M., and E. W. Schuster. "Fighting Friction," *APICS—The Performance Advantage*, February 2003.

Dornier, P.-P.; R. Ernst; M. Fender; and P. Kouvelis. *Global Operations and Logistics, Text and Cases*. New York: John Wiley & Sons, 1998.

Dreifus, S. B., ed. *Business International's Global Desk Reference*. New York: McGraw-Hill, 1992.

Duff, C., and R. Ortega. "How Wal-Mart Outdid a Once-Touted Kmart in Discount Store Race." *The Wall Street Journal*, March 24, 1995.

Eilon, S.; C. D. T. Watson-Gandy; and N. Christofides. *Distribution Management: Mathematical Modeling and Practical Analysis*. London: Griffin, 1971.

Eppen, G. D. "Effects of Centralization on Expected Costs in a Multi-Location Newsboy Problem." *Management Science* 25 (1979), pp. 498–501.

Eppen, G. D., and L. Schrage. "Centralized Ordering Policies in a Multi-Warehouse System with Leadtimes and Random Demand." In *Multi-Level Production/Inventory Systems: Theory and Practice*, ed. L. B. Schwarz. New York: North Holland, 1981.

Erkip, N.; W. H. Hausman; and S. Nahmias. "Optimal Centralized Ordering Policies in Multi-Echelon Inventory Systems with Correlated Demands." *Management Science* 36 (1990), pp. 381–92.

Fine, C. H. Clockspeed. Reading, MA: Perseus Books, 1998.

Fisher, M. L. "What is the right supply chain for your product?" *Harvard Business Review* (1997), pp. 105–106.

Granneman, S. "RFID Chips Are Here," *The Register*, accessed June 27, 2003.

Hammond, Jan. Barilla SpA (A and B). Copyright © 1994 by the President and Fellows of Harvard Business School.

Handfield, R. B., and E. L. Nichols Jr. *Introduction to Supply Chain Management*. Upper Saddle River, NJ: Prentice Hall, 1999.

Henkoff, R. "Delivering the Goods." *Fortune*, November 25, 1994, pp. 64–78.

IBM. "The Smarter Supply Chain of the Future." *Global Chief Supply Chain Officer Study*. Accessed from http://www-07.ibm.com/events/my/industrialinsights/pdf/01_Randy_Sng_Smarter_SC_for_Mfg-10Dec-MY.pdf

Jacobson, G., and J. Hillkirk. *Xerox, American Samurai*. New York: Macmillan, 1986.

John, C. G. and M. Willis. "Supply chain re-engineering at Anheuser-Busch." *Supply Chain Management Review* 2 (1998), pp. 28–36.

Lee, H. L., C. Billington, and B. Carter. "Hewlett-Packard Gains Control of Inventory and Service through Design for Localization." *Interfaces* 23, no. 4 (1994), pp. 1–11.

Lee, H. L., P. Padmanabhan, and S. Whang. "The Bullwhip Effect in Supply Chains." *Sloan Management Review*, Spring 1997, pp. 93–102.

Loch, C. and Y. Wu. (2008). "Social Preferences and Supply Chain Performance: An Experimental Study." *Management Science* 54, no. 11 (2008), pp. 1835–1849.

Martin, A. J. *DRP: Distribution Resource Planning*. 2nd ed. Essex Junction, VT: Oliver Wight Limited Publications, 1990.

Mayer, L. "Why Onshoring High-tech Manufacturing Jobs Makes Economic Sense." *Huffington Post*, January 24, 2013. Accessed from http://www.huffingtonpost.com/linda-mayer/manufacturing-makes-economic-sense_b_2533593.html

Muckstadt, J. A., and L. J. Thomas. "Are Multi-Echelon Inventory Methods Worth Implementing in Systems with Low Demand Rate Items?" *Management Science* 26 (1980), pp. 483–94.

Nahmias, S., and S. A. Smith. "Mathematical Models of Retailer Inventory Systems: A Review." In *Perspectives in Operations Management*, ed. R. K. Sarin. Boston: Kluwer, 1993.

Nahmias, S., and S. A. Smith. "Optimizing Inventory Levels in a Two-Echelon Retailer System with Partial Lost Sales." *Management Science* 40 (1994), pp. 582–96.

New York Times. "Airlines try to hedge oil costs to stay in business." June 30, 2008. Accessed from http://www.nytimes.com/2008/06/30/business/worldbusiness/30iht-30hedge.14104427.html?_r=0

Palevich, R. F. "Supply Chain Management." *Hospital Materiel Management Quarterly* 20, no. 3 (1999), pp. 54–63.

Pasternack, B. "Optimal pricing and returns policies for perishable commodities." *Marketing Science* 4 (1985), pp. 166–176.

Pazour, J. A., and L. C. Neubert. "Routing and Scheduling of Cross-Town Drayage Operations at J.B. Hunt Transport." *Interfaces* 43, no. 2 (2013), pp. 117–129.

Ragsdale, C. T. *Spreadsheet Modeling and Decision Analysis*. 2nd ed. Cincinnati: South-Western, 1998.

Ross, David Frederick. *Competing through Supply Chain Management: Creating Market-Winning Strategies through Supply Chain Partnerships*. New York: Chapman & Hall, 1998.

Scheeres, J. "Tracking Junior with a Microchip," *Wired News*, October 10, 2003.

Schrage, L. "Formulation and Structure of More Complex/Realistic Routing and Scheduling Problems" *Networks* 11 (1981), pp. 229–32.

Schuster, E. W.; S. J. Allen; and D. L. Brock. *Global RFID: The Value of the EPCglobal Network for Supply Chain Management*. Berlin: Springer, 2007.

Schwarz, L. B., ed. *Multi-Level Production/Inventory Systems: Theory and Practice*. New York: North Holland, 1981.

Signorelli, S., and H. Heskett. "Benneton." Harvard Business School Case 9-685-014, 1984.

Simchi-Levi, D.; P. Kaminski; and E. Simchi-Levi. *Designing and Managing the Supply Chain: Concepts, Strategies, and Case Studies*. New York: McGraw-Hill/Irwin, 1999.

Sliwa, C. "Users Cling to EDI for Critical Transactions." *Computerworld* 33, no. 11 (1999), p. 48.

Sterman, R. "Modeling Managerial Behavior: Misperception of Feedback in a Dynamic Decision Making Experiment." *Management Science* 35, no. 3 (1989), pp. 321–39.

Supply Chain Forum. http://www.stanford.edu/group/scforum/, accessed August 1999.

Varchaver, N. "Scanning the Globe: The Humble Bar Code Began as an Object of Suspicion and Grew into a Cultural Icon. Today It's Deep in the Heart of the Fortune 500." *Fortune Magazine*, May 31, 2004. Accessed from http://money.cnn.com/magazines/fortune/fortune_archive/2004/05/31/370719/index.htm

Wilder, C., and M. K. McGee. "GE: The Net Pays Off." *Informationweek*, February 1997, pp. 14–16.

Womack, J. P., D. T. Jones, and D. Roos. *The Machine That Changed the World*. New York: Harper Perennial, 1990.

Yansouni, C. Private communication, 1999.

Chapter Eight

Push and Pull Production Control Systems: MRP and JIT

"The most dangerous kind of waste is the waste we do not recognize."
—Shigeo Shingo

Chapter Overview

Purpose

To understand the push and pull philosophies in production planning and compare MRP and JIT methods for scheduling the flow of goods in a factory.

Key Points

1. *Push versus pull.* There are two fundamental philosophies for moving material through the factory. A push system is one in which production planning is done for all levels in advance. Once production is completed, units are pushed to the next level. A pull system is one in which items are moved from one level to the next only when requested. *Materials requirements planning* (MRP) is the basic push system. Based on forecasts for end items over a specified planning horizon, the MRP planning system determines production quantities for each level of the system. It relies on the so-called explosion calculus, which requires knowledge of the gozinto factor (i.e., how many of part A are required for part B), and production lead times. The earliest of the pull systems is *kanban* developed by Toyota, which has exploded into the *just-in-time* (JIT) and lean production movements. Here the fundamental goal is to reduce work-in-process to a bare minimum. To do so, items are only moved when requested by the next higher level in the production process. Each of the methods has particular advantages and disadvantages.
2. *MRP basics.* The MRP explosion calculus is a set of rules for converting a *master production schedule* (MPS) to a build schedule for all the components comprising the end product. The MPS is a production plan for the end item or final product by period. It is derived from the forecasts of demand adjusted for returns, on-hand inventory, and the like. At each stage in the process, one computes the production amounts required at each level of the production process by doing two basic operations: (1) offsetting the time when production begins by the lead time required at the current level and (2) multiplying the higher-level requirement by the gozinto factor. The simplest production schedule at each level is lot-for-lot

(L4L), which means one produces the number of units required each period. However, if one knows the holding and setup cost for production, it is possible to construct a more cost efficient lot-sizing plan. Three heuristics we consider are (1) EOQ lot sizing, (2) the Silver–Meal heuristic, and (3) the least unit cost heuristic. Optimal lot sizing requires dynamic programming and is discussed in Appendix 8–A. We also consider lot sizing when capacity constraints are explicitly accounted for. This problem is difficult to solve optimally, but can be approximated efficiently.

MRP as a planning system has advantages and disadvantages over other planning systems. Some of the disadvantages include (1) forecast uncertainty is ignored; (2) capacity constraints are largely ignored; (3) the choice of the planning horizon can have a significant effect on the recommended lot sizes; (4) lead times are assumed fixed, but they should depend on the lot sizes; (5) MRP ignores the losses due to defectives or machine downtime; (6) data integrity can be a serious problem; and (7) in systems where components are used in multiple products, it is necessary to peg each order to a specific higher-level item.

3. *JIT basics.* The JIT philosophy grew out of the kanban system developed by Toyota. Kanban is the Japanese word for card or ticket. Kanban controls the flow of goods in the plant by using a variety of different kinds of cards. Each card is attached to a palette of goods. Production cannot commence until production ordering kanbans are available. This guarantees that production at one level will not begin unless there is demand at the next level. This prevents work-in-process inventories from building up between work centers when a problem arises anywhere in the system. Part of what made kanban so successful at Toyota was the development of single minute exchange of dies (SMED), which reduced changeover times for certain operations from several hours to several minutes. Kanban is not the only way to implement a JIT system. Information flows can be controlled more efficiently with a central information processor than with cards.

4. *Comparison of JIT and MRP.* JIT has several advantages and several disadvantages when compared with MRP as a production planning system. Some of the advantages of JIT include (1) reduce work-in-process inventories, thus decreasing inventory costs and waste, (2) easy to quickly identify quality problems before large inventories of defective parts build up, and (3) when coordinated with a JIT purchasing program, ensures the smooth flow of materials throughout the entire production process. Advantages of MRP include (1) the ability to react to changes in demand, since demand forecasts are an integral part of the system (as opposed to JIT which does no look-ahead planning); (2) allowance for lot sizing at the various levels of the system, thus affording the opportunity to reduce setups and setup costs; and (3) planning of production levels at all levels of the firm for several periods into the future, thus affording the firm the opportunity to look ahead to better schedule shifts and adjust workforce levels in the face of changing demand.

The supply chain is the set of all activities that convert raw materials to the final product. One of the key activities in the supply chain is the actual production process. How well things are managed in the factory plays a fundamental role in the reliability and quality of the final product. There are two fundamentally different philosophies for managing the flow of goods in the factory. As we will see in this chapter, the methods developed in Chapters 4 and 5 for managing inventories are not always appropriate in the factory context.

The two approaches we consider are *materials requirements planning (MRP)* and *just-in-time (JIT)*. These are often referred to respectively as "push" and "pull" control systems. To appreciate exactly what distinguishes push and pull systems will require an understanding of exactly how these methods work, which will be covered in detail in this chapter. The simplest definition that this writer has seen (due to Karmarkar, 1989) is that "a pull system initiates production as a reaction to present demand, while a push system initiates production in anticipation of future demand." Thus, MRP incorporates forecasts of future demand while JIT does not.

To better understand the difference between MRP and JIT, consider the following simple example. Garden spades are produced by a plant in Muncie, Indiana. Each spade consists of two parts: the metal digger and the wooden handle. The parts are connected by two screws. The plant produces spades at an average rate of 100 per week. The metal digger is produced in batches of 400 on the first two days of each month, and the handles are ordered from an outside supplier. The assembly of spades takes place during the first week of each month.

Consider now the demand pattern for the screws. Exactly 800 screws are needed during the first week of each month. Assuming four weeks per month, the weekly demand pattern for the screws is 800, 0, 0, 0, 800, 0, 0, 0, 800, 0, 0, 0, and so on. Using a weekly demand rate of 200 and appropriate holding and setup costs, suppose that the EOQ formula gives an order quantity of 1,400. A little reflection shows that ordering the screws in lots of 1,400 doesn't make much sense. If we schedule a delivery of 1,400 screws at the beginning of a month, 800 are used immediately and 600 are stored for later use. At the beginning of the next month another order for 1,400 has to be made, since the 600 screws stored are insufficient to meet the next month's requirement. It makes more sense to either order 800 screws at the beginning of each month or some multiple of 800 every several months.

The EOQ solution was clearly inappropriate here. Why? Recall that in deriving the EOQ formula, we assumed that demand was known and constant. The demand pattern in this example is known, but it is certainly not constant. In fact, it is very spiky. If we were to apply the methods of Chapter 5, we would assume that the demand was random. It is easy to show that over a one-year period the weekly demand has mean 200 and standard deviation 350. These values could be used to generate (Q, R) values assuming some form of a distribution for weekly demand. But this solution would not make any sense either. The demand pattern for the screws is not random; it is predictable, since it is a consequence of the production plan for the spades, which is known. The demand is *variable*, but it is not *random*.

We still have not solved the problem of how many screws to buy and when they should be delivered. One approach might be to just order once at the beginning of the year to meet the demand for an entire year. This would entail a one-time delivery of 10,400 screws at the start of each year (assuming 200 per week). What would be the advantage of this approach? Screws are very inexpensive items. By purchasing enough for an entire year's production, we would incur the fixed delivery costs only once.

There is a completely different way to approach this problem. One could simply decide to schedule deliveries of screws at the beginning of every month. This approach might be more expensive than the once-a-year delivery strategy, since fixed costs would be 12 times higher. However, it could have other advantages that more than compensate for the higher fixed costs. Monthly deliveries eliminate the need to store screws in the plant. If usage rates vary, delivery sizes could be adjusted to match need. Also, if a problem arose with the screws caused by either a defect in production or a design change in the spades, the company would not be stuck with a large inventory of useless items.

440 Chapter Eight *Push and Pull Production Control Systems: MRP and JIT*

These two policies illustrate the basic difference between MRP and JIT (although, as we will see, there is much more to these production control philosophies than this). In an MRP system, we determine lot sizes based on forecasts of future demands and possibly on cost considerations. In a JIT system, we try to reduce lot sizes to their minimum to eliminate waste and unnecessary buildups of inventory.

MRP may be considered to be a top-down planning system in that all production quantity decisions are derived from demand forecasts. Lot-sizing decisions are found for every level of the production system. Items are produced based on this plan and *pushed* to the next level. In JIT, requests for goods originate at a higher level of the system and are *pulled* through the various levels of production. This is the basic idea behind push and pull production control systems.

MRP Basics

In general, a production plan is a complete specification of the amounts of each end item or final product and subassembly produced, the exact timing of the production lot sizes, and the final schedule of completion. The production plan may be broken down into several component parts: (1) the **master production schedule (MPS)**, (2) the **materials requirements planning (MRP) system,** and (3) the detailed **job shop schedule.** Each of these parts can represent a large and complex subsystem of the entire plan.

At the heart of the production plan are the forecasts of demand for the end items produced over the planning horizon. An end item is the output of the productive system; that is, products shipped out the door. Components are items in intermediate stages of production, and raw materials are resources that enter the system. A schematic of the productive system appears in Figure 8–1. It is important to bear in mind that raw materials, components, and end items are defined in a relative and not an absolute sense. Hence, we may wish to isolate a portion of a company's operation as a productive system. End items associated with one portion of the company may be raw materials for another portion. A single productive system may be the entire manufacturing operation of the firm or only a small part of it.

The master production schedule (MPS) is a specification of the exact amounts and timing of production of each of the end items in a productive system. The MPS refers to *unaggregated* items. As such, the inputs for determining the MPS are forecasts for

FIGURE 8–1
Schematic of the productive system

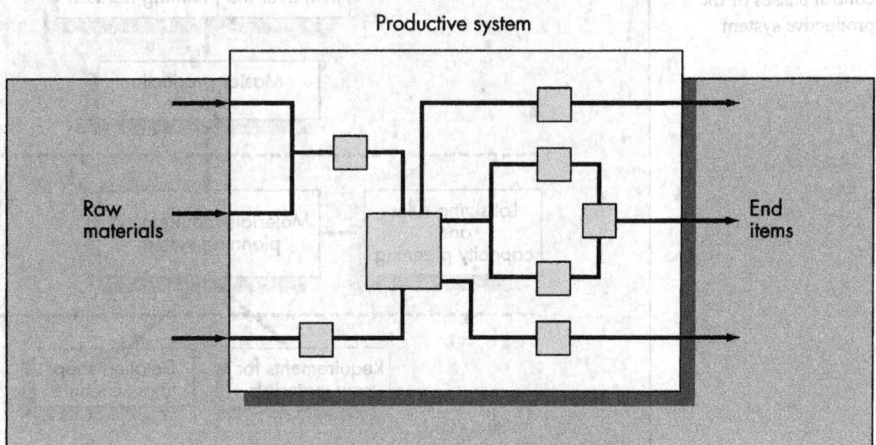

future demand by item rather than by aggregate items, as discussed in Chapter 3. The MPS is then broken down into a detailed schedule of production for each of the components that comprise an end item. The materials requirements planning (MRP) system is the means by which this is accomplished. Finally, the results of the MRP are translated into specific shop floor schedules (using methods such as those discussed in Chapter 9) and requirements for raw materials.

The data sources for determining the MPS include the following:

1. Firm customer orders.
2. Forecasts of future demand by item.
3. Safety stock requirements.
4. Seasonal plans.
5. Internal orders from other parts of the organization.

An important part of the success of MRP is the integrity and timeliness of the data. The information system that supports the MRP receives inputs from the production, marketing, and finance departments of the firm. A smooth flow of information among these three functional areas is a key ingredient to a successful production planning system.

We may consider the control of the production system to be composed of three major phases. Phase 1 is the gathering and coordinating of the information required to develop the master production schedule. Phase 2 is the determination of planned order releases using MRP, and phase 3 is the development of detailed shop floor schedules and resource requirements from the MRP planned order releases. Figure 8–2 is a schematic of these three control phases of the productive system.

This chapter is concerned with the way that the MPS is used as input to the MRP system. We will show in detail exactly how the MRP calculus works; that is, how product structures are converted to parent–child relationships between levels of the production system, how production lead times are used to obtain time-phased requirements, and how lot-sizing methods result in specific schedules. In the lot-sizing section we will

FIGURE 8–2
The three major control phases of the productive system

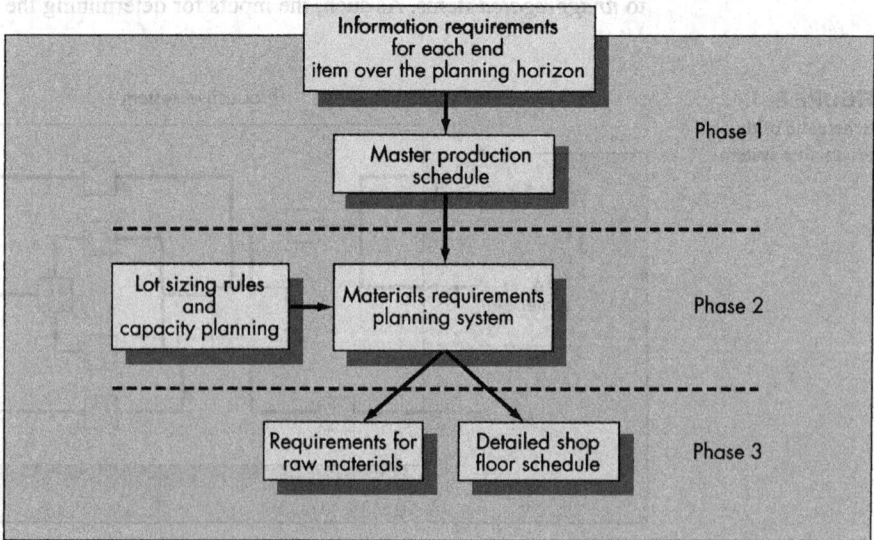

consider both optimal and heuristic lot-sizing techniques for uncapacitated systems and a straightforward heuristic technique for capacitated lot sizing.

JIT Basics

The just-in-time approach has its roots in the kanban system of material flow pioneered by Toyota. We will discuss the mechanics of kanban later in Section 8.6. The notion of JIT has grown significantly from its roots as a material flow technology. It has important strategic implications for firms, not just in manufacturing, but also in managing the supplier base and in distribution management.

The fundamental ideas behind JIT are

1. *Work-in-process (WIP) inventory is reduced to a bare minimum.* The amount of WIP inventory allowed is a measure of how tightly the JIT system is tuned. The less WIP designed in the system, the better balanced the various steps in the process need to be.
2. *JIT is a pull system.* Production at each stage is initiated only when requested. The flow of information in a JIT system proceeds sequentially from level to level.
3. *JIT extends beyond the plant boundaries.* Special relationships with suppliers must be in place to ensure that deliveries are made on an as-needed basis. Suppliers and manufacturers must be located in close proximity if the JIT design is to include the suppliers.
4. *The benefits of JIT extend beyond savings of inventory-related costs.* Plants can be run efficiently without the clutter of inventory of raw material and partially finished goods clogging the system. Quality problems can be identified before they build up to unmanageable proportions. Rework and inspection of finished goods are minimized.
5. *The JIT approach requires a serious commitment from top management and workers alike.* Workers need to maintain an awareness of their systems and products, and need to be empowered to stop the flow of production if they see something wrong. Management must allow these workers to have that flexibility.

Lately, the term "lean production" has been used to describe JIT. The term appears to have been coined by Womack et al. (1990) in their landmark study of the automobile industry, *The Machine That Changed the World*. In comparing the worst of American mass production and the best Japanese lean production, the authors show just how effective a properly implemented JIT philosophy can be. They described their experience at General Motors' Framingham, Massachusetts, plant in 1986:

> Next we looked at the line itself. Next to each work station were piles—in some cases weeks' worth—of inventory. Littered about were discarded boxes and other temporary wrapping material. On the line itself the work was unevenly distributed with some workers running madly to keep up and others finding time to smoke and even read a newspaper.... At the end of the line we found what is perhaps the best evidence of old-fashioned mass production: an enormous work area full of finished cars riddled with defects. All these cars needed further repair before shipment, a task that can prove enormously time-consuming and often fails to fix fully the problems now buried under layers of parts and upholstery.

Now contrast this with their experience at Toyota's Takaoka plant in Toyoda City:

> The differences between Takaoka and Framingham are striking to anyone who understands the logic of lean production. For a start hardly anyone was in the aisles. The armies of indirect workers so visible at GM were missing, and practically every worker in sight was actually

adding value to the car ... The final assembly line revealed further differences. Less than an hour's worth of inventory was next to each worker at Takaoka. The parts went on more smoothly and the work tasks were better balanced, so that every worker worked at about the same pace.... At the end of the line, the difference between lean and mass production was even more striking. At Takaoka we observed almost no rework area at all. Almost every car was driven directly from the line to the boat or the trucks taking cars to the buyer.

These differences are exciting and dramatic. We should note that GM has since closed Framingham and that the plants run by the "big three" (namely, GM, Ford, and Chrysler LLC) are far more efficient and better managed than Framingham. Still, we have a ways to go to duplicate the phenomenal success that the Japanese have had with lean production systems.

This chapter begins with a discussion of the basic explosion calculus of MRP and how lot-sizing strategies other than lot-for-lot are incorporated into a basic single-level MRP solution.

8.1 THE EXPLOSION CALCULUS

Explosion calculus is a term that refers to the set of rules by which gross requirements at one level of the product structure are translated into a production schedule at that level and requirements at lower levels. At the heart of any MRP system is the product structure. The product structure refers to the relationship between the components at adjacent levels of the system. The product structure diagram details the parent–child relationship of components and end items at each level, the number of periods required for production of each component, and the number of components required at the child level to produce one unit at the parent level.

A typical product structure appears in Figure 8–3. In order to produce one unit of the end item, two units of A and one unit of B are required. Assembly of A requires one week, and assembly of B requires two weeks. A and B are "children" of the end item. In order to produce A, one unit of C and two units of D are required. In order to produce B, two units of C and three units of E are required. The respective production lead times also appear on the product structure diagram. Product structure diagrams can be quite complex, with as many as 15 or more levels in some industries.

The explosion calculus (also known as the bill-of-materials explosion) follows a set of rules that translate the planned order releases for end items and components into production schedules for lower-level components. The method involves properly phasing requirements in time and accounting for the number of components required at the child level to produce a single parent item. The method is best illustrated by example.

FIGURE 8–3
Typical product structure diagram

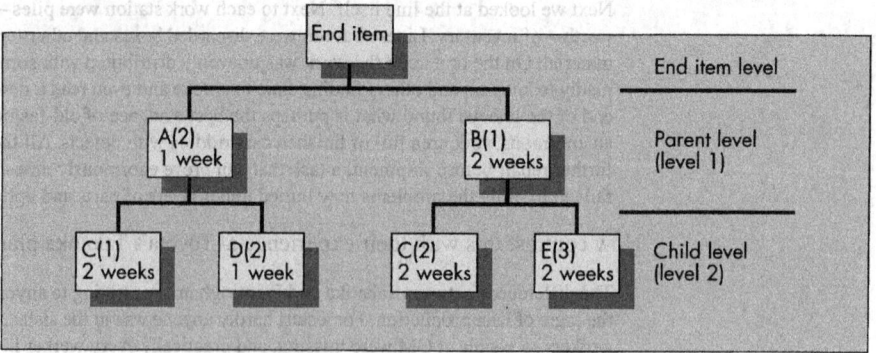

Example 8.1   The Harmon Music Company produces a variety of wind instruments at its plant in Joliet, Illinois. Because the company is relatively small, it would like to minimize the amount of money tied up in inventory. For that reason production levels are set to match predicted demand as closely as possible. In order to achieve this goal, the company has adopted an MRP system to determine production quantities.

One of the instruments produced is the model 85C trumpet. The trumpet retails for $800 and has been a reasonably, if not spectacularly, profitable item for the company. Based on orders from music stores around the country, the production manager receives predictions of future demand for about four months into the future.

Figure 8–4 shows the trumpet and its various subassemblies. Figure 8–5 gives the product structure diagram for the construction of the trumpet. The bell section and the lead pipe and valve sections are welded together in final assembly. Before the welding, three slide assemblies and three valves are produced and fitted to the valve casing assembly. The forming and shaping of the bell section requires two weeks, and the forming and shaping of the lead pipe and valve sections require four weeks. The valves require three weeks to produce, and the slide assemblies two weeks.

The trumpet assembly problem is a three-level MRP system. Level 0 corresponds to the final product or end item, which is the completed trumpet. Level 1, the child level relative to the trumpet, corresponds to the bell and valve casing assemblies. Level 2 corresponds to the slide

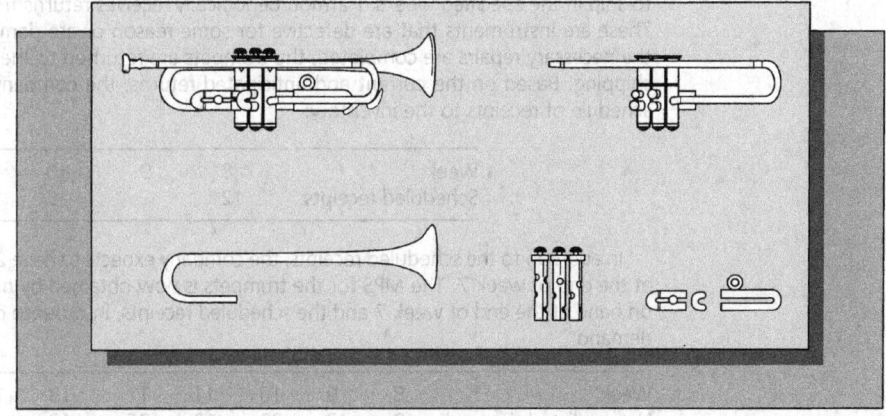

FIGURE 8–4
Trumpet and subassemblies

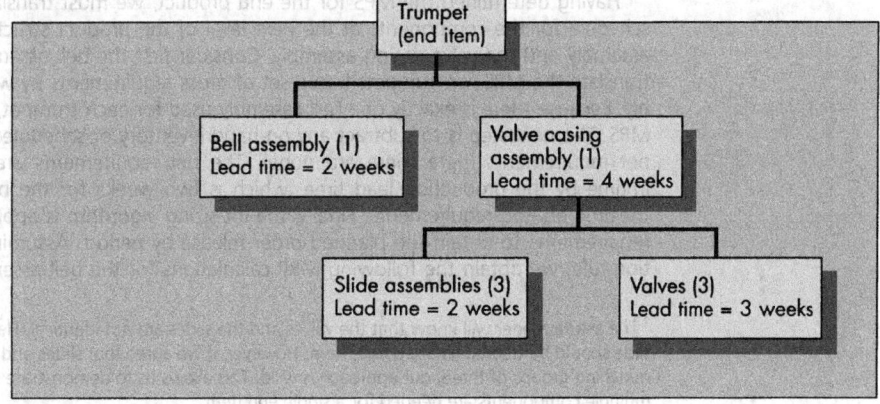

FIGURE 8–5
Product structure diagram for Harmon trumpet

and valve assemblies. The information in the product structure diagram is often represented as an indented bill of materials (BOM), which is a more convenient representation for preparation of computer input. The indented BOM for the trumpet is[1]

1 Trumpet
  1 Bell assembly
  1 Valve assembly
    3 Slide assemblies
    3 Valves

It takes seven weeks to produce a trumpet. Hence, the company must begin production now on trumpets to be shipped in seven weeks. For that reason we will consider only forecasts for demands that are at least seven weeks into the future. If we label the current week as week 1, then Harmon requires forecasts for the sales of trumpets for weeks 8 to 17. Suppose that the predicted demands for those weeks are

Week	8	9	10	11	12	13	14	15	16	17
Demand	77	42	38	21	26	112	45	14	76	38

These forecasts represent the numbers of trumpets that the firm would like to have ready to ship in the specified weeks. Harmon periodically receives returns from its various suppliers. These are instruments that are defective for some reason or are damaged in shipping. Once the necessary repairs are completed, the trumpets are returned to the pool of those ready for shipping. Based on the current and anticipated returns, the company expects the following schedule of receipts to the inventory:

Week	8	9	10	11
Scheduled receipts	12		6	9

In addition to the scheduled receipts, the company expects to have 23 trumpets in inventory at the end of week 7. The MPS for the trumpets is now obtained by netting out the inventory on hand at the end of week 7 and the scheduled receipts, in order to obtain the net predicted demand:

Week	8	9	10	11	12	13	14	15	16	17
Net predicted demand	42	42	32	12	26	112	45	14	76	38

Having determined the MPS for the end product, we must translate it into a production schedule for the components at the next level of the product structure. These are the bell assembly and the valve casing assembly. Consider first the bell assembly. The first step is to translate the MPS for trumpets into a set of gross requirements by week for the bell assembly. Because there is exactly one bell assembly used for each trumpet, this is the same as the MPS. The next step is to subtract any on-hand inventory or scheduled receipts to obtain the net requirements (here there are none). The net requirements are then translated back in time by the production lead time, which is two weeks for the bell assembly, to obtain the time-phased requirements. Finally, the lot-sizing algorithm is applied to the time-phased requirements to obtain the planned order release by period. Assuming a lot-for-lot production rule, we obtain the following MRP calculations for the bell assembly:

---

[1] The astute reader will know that the valves and the slides are not identical. Hence, each valve and each slide should be treated as a separate item. However, if we agree that slides and valves correspond to matching groups of three, our approach is valid. This allows us to demonstrate the multiplier effect when multiple components are needed for a single end item.

Week	6	7	8	9	10	11	12	13	14	15	16	17
Gross requirements			42	42	32	12	26	112	45	14	76	38
Net requirements			42	42	32	12	26	112	45	14	76	38
Time-phased net requirements	42	42	32	12	26	112	45	14	76	38		
Planned order release (lot for lot)	42	42	32	12	26	112	45	14	76	38		

Lot for lot means that the production quantity each week is just the time-phased net requirement. A lot-for-lot production rule means that no inventory is carried from one period to another. As we will see later, lot for lot is rarely an optimal production rule. Optimal and heuristic production scheduling rules will be examined in Section 8.2.

The calculation is essentially the same for the valve casing assembly, except that the production lead time is four weeks rather than two weeks. The calculations for the valve casing assembly are

Week	4	5	6	7	8	9	10	11	12	13	14	15	16	17
Gross requirements					42	42	32	12	26	112	45	14	76	38
Net requirements					42	42	32	12	26	112	45	14	76	38
Time-phased net requirements	42	42	32	12	26	112	45	14	76	38				
Planned order release (lot for lot)	42	42	32	12	26	112	45	14	76	38				

Now consider the MRP calculations for the valves. Let us assume that the company expects an on-hand inventory of 186 valves at the end of week 3 and a receipt from an outside supplier of 96 valves at the start of week 5. There are three valves required for each trumpet. (Note that the valves are not identical, and hence are not interchangeable. We could display three separate sets of MRP calculations, but this is unnecessary because each trumpet has exactly one valve of each type.) One obtains gross requirements for the valves by multiplying the production schedule for the valve casing assembly by 3. Net requirements are obtained by subtracting on-hand inventory and scheduled receipts. The MRP calculations for the valves are

Week	2	3	4	5	6	7	8	9	10	11	12	13
Gross requirements			126	126	96	36	78	336	135	42	228	114
Scheduled receipts				96								
On-hand inventory	186	60	30									
Net requirements			0	0	66	36	78	336	135	42	228	114
Time-phased net requirements	66	36	78	336	135	42	228	114				
Planned order release (lot for lot)	66	36	78	336	135	42	228	114				

Net requirements are obtained by subtracting on-hand inventory and scheduled receipts from gross requirements. Because the on-hand inventory of 186 in period 3 exceeds the gross requirement in period 4, the net requirements for period 4 are 0. The remaining 60 units (186 − 126) are carried into period 5. In period 5 the scheduled receipt of 96 is added to the starting inventory of 60 to give 156 units. The gross requirements for period 5 are 126, so the net requirements for period 5 are 0, and the additional 30 units are carried over to period 6. Hence, the resulting net requirements for period 6 are 96 − 30 = 66.

The net requirements are phased back three periods in order to obtain the time-phased net requirements and the production schedule. Note that the valves are produced internally. The scheduled receipt of 96 corresponds to defectives that were sent out for rework. A similar calculation is required for the slide assemblies.

Example 8.1 represents the essential elements of the explosion calculus. Note that we have assumed for the sake of the example that the production scheduling rule is lot for lot. That is, in each period the production quantity is equal to the net requirements for that period. However, such a policy may be suboptimal and even infeasible. For example, the schedule requires the delivery of 336 valves in week 9. However, suppose that the plant can produce only 200 valves in one week. If that is the case, a lot-for-lot scheduling rule is infeasible.

Problems for Section 8.1

1. The inventory control models discussed in Chapters 4 and 5 are often labeled *independent* demand models and MRP is often labeled a *dependent* demand system. What do the terms *independent* and *dependent* mean in this context?
2. What information is contained in a product structure diagram?
3. For the example of Harmon Music presented in this section, determine the planned order release for the slide assemblies. Assume lot-for-lot scheduling.
4. The Noname Computer Company builds a computer designated model ICU2. It imports the motherboard of the computer from Taiwan, but the company inserts the sockets for the chips and boards in its plant in Lubbock, Texas. Each computer requires a total of ninety 64K dynamic random access memory (DRAM) chips. Noname sells the computers with three add-in boards and two disk drives. The company purchases both the DRAM chips and the disk drives from an outside supplier. The product structure diagram for the ICU2 computer is given in Figure 8–6.

   Suppose that the forecasted demands for the computer for weeks 6 to 11 are 220, 165, 180, 120, 75, 300. The starting inventory of assembled computers in week 6 will be 75, and the production manager anticipates returns of 30 in week 8 and 10 in week 10.

   a. Determine the MPS for the computers.

   b. Determine the planned order release for the motherboards assuming a lot-for-lot scheduling rule.

   c. Determine the schedule of outside orders for the disk drives.

5. For Problem 4, suppose that Noname has 23,000 DRAM chips in inventory. It anticipates receiving a lot of 3,000 chips in week 3 from another firm that has gone out of

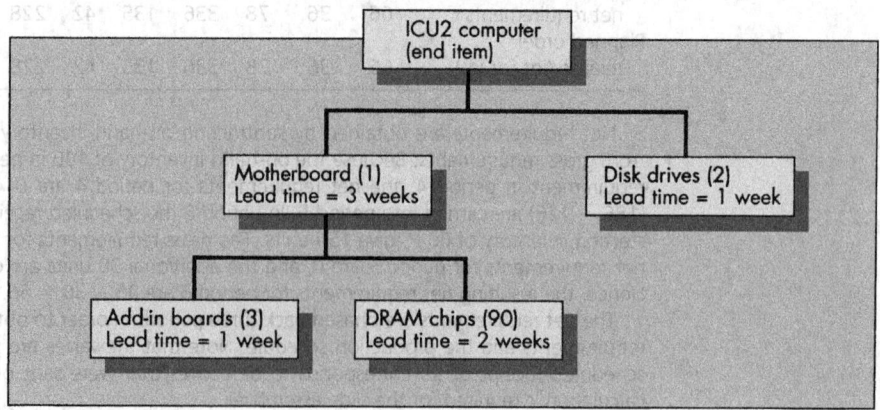

FIGURE 8–6
Product structure diagram for ICU2 computer (for Problem 4)

business. At the current time, Noname purchases the chips from two vendors, A and B. A sells the chips for less, but will not fill an order exceeding 10,000 chips per week.

    a. If Noname has established a policy of inventorying as few chips as possible, what order should it be placing with vendors A and B over the next six weeks?

    b. Noname has found that not all the DRAM chips purchased function properly. From past experience it estimates an 8 percent failure rate for the chips purchased from vendor A and a 4 percent failure rate for the chips purchased from vendor B. What modification in the order schedule would you recommend to compensate for this problem?

6. Consider the product structure diagram given in Figure 8–3. Assume that the MPS for the end item for weeks 10 through 17 is

Week	10	11	12	13	14	15	16	17
Net requirements	100	100	40	40	100	200	200	200

Assume that lot-for-lot scheduling is used throughout. Also assume that there is no entering inventory in period 10 and no scheduled receipts.

    a. Determine the planned order release for component A.

    b. Determine the planned order release for component B.

    c. Determine the planned order release for component C. (Hint: Note that C is required for both A and B.)

7. What alternatives are there to lot-for-lot scheduling at each level? Discuss the potential advantages and disadvantages of other lot-sizing techniques.

8. One of the inputs to the MRP system is the forecast of demand for the end item over the planning horizon. From the point of view of production, what advantages are there to a forecasting system that smooths the demand (that is, provides forecasts that are relatively constant) versus one that achieves greater accuracy but gives "spiky" forecasts that change significantly from one period to the next?

9. An end item has the product structure diagram given in Figure 8–7.

FIGURE 8–7
Product structure diagram (for Problem 9)

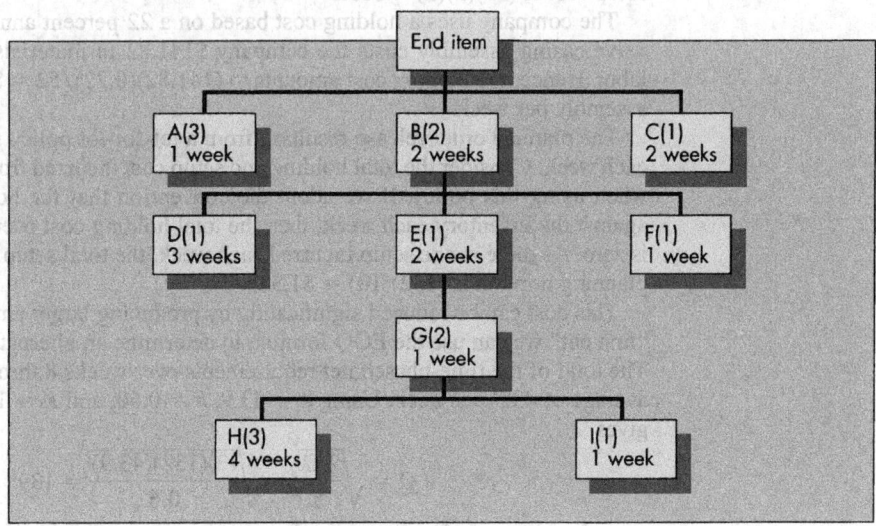

a. Write the product structure diagram as an indented bill-of-materials list.
b. Suppose that the MPS for the end item is

Week	30	31	32	33	34	35
MPS	165	180	300	220	200	240

If production is scheduled on a lot-for-lot basis, find the planned order release for component F.

c. Using the data in part (b), find the planned order release for component I.
d. Using the data in part (b), find the planned order release for component H.

8.2 ALTERNATIVE LOT-SIZING SCHEMES

In Example 8.1 we assumed that the production scheduling rule was lot for lot. That is, the number of units scheduled for production each period was the same as the net requirements for that period. In fact, this policy is assumed for convenience and ease of use only. It is, in general, not optimal. The problem of finding the best (or near best) production plan can be characterized as follows: we have a known set of time-varying demands and costs of setup and holding. What production quantities will minimize the total holding and setup costs over the planning horizon? Note that neither the methods of Chapter 4 (which assumes known but constant demands) nor those of Chapter 5 (which assumes random demands) are appropriate.

In this section we will discuss several popular heuristic (i.e., approximate) lot-sizing methods that easily can be incorporated into the MRP calculus.

EOQ Lot Sizing

To apply the EOQ formula, we need three inputs: the average demand rate, λ; the holding cost rate, h; and the setup cost, K. Consider the valve casing assembly in Example 8.1. Suppose that the setup operation for the machinery used in this assembly operation takes two workers about three hours. The workers average \$22 per hour. That translates to a setup cost of $(22)(2)(3) = \$132$.

The company uses a holding cost based on a 22 percent annual interest rate. Each valve casing assembly costs the company \$141.82 in materials and value added for labor. Hence, the holding cost amounts to $(141.82)(0.22)/52 = \$0.60$ per valve casing assembly per week.

The planned order release resulting from a lot-for-lot policy requires production in each week. Consider the total holding and setup cost incurred from weeks 6 through 15 when using this policy. If we adopt the convention that the holding cost is charged against the inventory each week, then the total holding cost over the 10-week horizon is zero. As there is one setup incurred each week, the total setup cost incurred over the planning horizon is $(132)(10) = \$1,320$.

This cost can be reduced significantly by producing larger amounts less often. As a "first cut" we can use the EOQ formula to determine an alternative production policy. The total of the time-phased net requirements over weeks 8 through 17 is 439, for an average of 43.9 per week. Using $\lambda = 43.9$, $h = 0.60$, and $K = 132$, the EOQ formula gives

$$Q = \sqrt{\frac{2K\lambda}{h}} = \sqrt{\frac{(2)(132)(43.9)}{0.6}} = 139.$$

If we schedule the production in lot sizes of 139 while guaranteeing that all net requirements are filled, the resulting MRP calculations for the valve casing assembly are

Week	4	5	6	7	8	9	10	11	12	13	14	15	16	17
Net requirements					42	42	32	12	26	112	45	14	76	38
Time-phased net requirements	42	42	32	12	26	112	45	14	76	38				
Planned order release (EOQ)	139	0	0	0	139	0	139	0	0	139				
Planned deliveries					139	0	0	0	139	0	139	0	0	139
Ending inventory					97	55	23	11	124	12	106	92	16	117

One finds the ending inventory each period from the formula

$$\text{Ending inventory} = \text{Beginning inventory} + \text{Planned deliveries} - \text{Net requirements}.$$

Consider the cost of using EOQ lot sizing rather than lot for lot. During periods 8 through 17 there are a total of four setups, resulting in a total setup cost of $(132)(4) = \$528$. The most direct way to compute the holding cost is to simply accumulate the ending inventories for the 10 periods and multiply by h. The cumulative ending inventory is $97 + 55 + 23 + \cdots + 117 = 653$. Hence, the total holding cost incurred over the 10 periods is $(0.6)(653) = \$391.80$. The total holding and setup cost when lot sizes are computed from the EOQ formula is $\$528 + \$391.80 = \$919.80$. This is a considerable improvement over the cost of $\$1,320$ obtained when using lot-for-lot production scheduling. (However, this savings does not consider the cost impact that lot sizing at this level may have upon lower levels in the product tree. It is possible, though unlikely, that in a global sense lot for lot could be more cost effective than EOQ. This point will be explored in more depth in Section 8.5.) Note that the use of the EOQ to set production quantities results in an entirely different pattern of gross requirements for the valve and slide assemblies one level down. In particular, the gross requirements for the valves are now

Week	4	5	6	7	8	9	10	11	12	13
Gross requirements	417	0	0	0	417	0	417	0	0	417

In the remainder of this section, we discuss three other popular lot-sizing schemes when demand is known and time is varying. It should be pointed out that the problem of determining lot sizes subject to time-varying demand occurs in contexts other than MRP. We have included it here to illustrate how these methods can be linked to the MRP explosion calculus.

The Silver–Meal Heuristic

The Silver–Meal heuristic (named for Harlan Meal and Edward Silver) is a forward method that requires determining the average cost per period as a function of the number of periods the current order is to span, and stopping the computation when this function first increases.

Define $C(T)$ as the average holding and setup cost per period if the current order spans the next T periods. As above, let $(r_1, \ldots, r_n)$ be the requirements over the n-period horizon. Consider period 1. If we produce just enough in period 1 to meet the demand in period 1, then we just incur the order cost K. Hence,

$$C(1) = K.$$

If we order enough in period 1 to satisfy the demand in both periods 1 and 2, then we must hold r_2 for one period. Hence,

$$C(2) = (K + hr_2)/2.$$

Similarly,

$$C(3) = (K + hr_2 + 2hr_3)/3$$

and, in general,

$$C(j) = (K + hr_2 + 2hr_3 + \cdots + (j-1)hr_j)/j.$$

Once $C(j) > C(j-1)$, we stop and set $y_1 = r_1 + r_2 + \cdots + r_{j-1}$, and begin the process again starting at period j.

Example 8.2 A machine shop uses the Silver–Meal heuristic to schedule production lot sizes for computer casings. Over the next five weeks the demands for the casings are r = (18, 30, 42, 5, 20). The holding cost is $2 per case per week, and the production setup cost is $80. Find the recommended lot sizing.

Solution Starting in period 1:

$C(1) = 80,$

$C(2) = [80 + (2)(30)]/2 = 70,$

$C(3) = [80 + (2)(30) + (2)(2)(42)]/3 = 102.67.$ Stop because $C(3) > C(2)$.

Set $y_1 = r_1 + r_2 = 18 + 30 = 48.$
Starting in period 3:

$C(1) = 80,$

$C(2) = [80 + (2)(5)]/2 = 45,$

$C(3) = [80 + (2)(5) + (2)(2)(20)]/3 = 56.67.$ Stop.

Set $y_3 = r_3 + r_4 = 42 + 5 = 47.$

Because period 5 is the final period in the horizon, we do not need to start the process again. We set $y_5 = r_5 = 20$. Hence, the Silver–Meal heuristic results in the policy **y** = (48, 0, 47, 0, 20). (Hint: You can streamline calculations by noting that $C(j+1) = [j/(j+1)][C(j) + hr_{j+1}]$.)

To show that the Silver–Meal heuristic will not always result in an optimal solution, consider the following counterexample.

Example 8.3 Let r = (10, 40, 30), K = 50, and h = 1. The Silver–Meal heuristic gives the solution **y** = (50, 0, 30), but the optimal solution is (10, 70, 0).

In closing this section, we note that Silver and Peterson (1985, p. 238) recommend conditions under which the Silver–Meal heuristic should be used instead of the EOQ. The condition is based on the variance of periodic demand: the higher the variance, the better the improvement the heuristic gives. However, our feeling is that given today's computing technology and the ease with which the heuristic solution can be found, the additional computational costs of using Silver–Meal (or one of the following two methods described) instead of EOQ are minimal and not an important consideration.

Least Unit Cost

The least unit cost (LUC) heuristic is similar to the Silver–Meal method except that instead of dividing the cost over j periods by the number of periods, j, we divide it by the total number of units demanded through period j, $r_1 + r_2 + \cdots + r_j$. We choose the order horizon that minimizes the cost per unit of demand rather than the cost per period.

Define $C(T)$ as the average holding and setup cost per unit for a T-period order horizon. Then,

$$C(1) = K/r_1,$$
$$C(2) = (K + hr_2)/(r_1 + r_2),$$
$$\vdots$$
$$C(j) = [K + hr_2 + 2hr_3 + \cdots + (j-1)hr_j]/(r_1 + r_2 + \cdots + r_j).$$

As with the Silver–Meal heuristic, this computation is stopped when $C(j) > C(j-1)$, and the production level is set equal to $r_1 + r_2 + \cdots + r_{j-1}$. The process is then repeated, starting at period j and continuing until the end of the planning horizon is reached.

Example 8.4 Assume the same requirements schedule and costs as given in Example 8.2.
Starting in period 1:

$$C(1) = 80/18 = 4.44,$$
$$C(2) = [80 + (2)(30)]/(18 + 30) = 2.92,$$
$$C(3) = [80 + (2)(30) + (2)(2)(42)]/(18 + 30 + 42) = 3.42.$$

Because $C(3) > C(2)$, we stop and set $y_1 = r_1 + r_2 = 48$.
Starting in period 3:

$$C(1) = 80/42 = 1.90,$$
$$C(2) = [80 + (2)(5)]/(42 + 5) = 1.92.$$

Because $C(2) > C(1)$, stop and set $y_3 = r_3 = 42$.
Starting in period 4:

$$C(1) = 80/5 = 16,$$
$$C(2) = [80 + (2)(20)]/(5 + 20) = 4.8.$$

As we have reached the end of the horizon, we set $y_4 = r_4 + r_5 = 5 + 20 = 25$. The solution obtained by the LUC heuristic is $y = (48, 0, 42, 25, 0)$. It is interesting to note that the policy obtained by this method is different from that for the Silver–Meal heuristic. It turns out that the Silver–Meal method gives the optimal policy, with cost $310, whereas the LUC gives a suboptimal policy, with cost $340.

Part Period Balancing

Another approximate method for solving this problem is part period balancing. Although the Silver–Meal technique seems to give better results in a greater number of cases, part period balancing seems to be more popular in practice.

The method is to set the order horizon equal to the number of periods that most closely matches the total holding cost with the setup cost over that period. The order horizon that exactly equates holding and setup costs will rarely be an integer number of periods (hence the origin of the name of the method).

Example 8.5 Again consider Example 8.2. Starting in period 1, we find

Order Horizon	Total Holding Cost
1	0
2	60
3	228

8.2 Alternative Lot-Sizing Schemes

Because 228 exceeds the setup cost of 80, we stop. As 80 is closer to 60 than to 228, the first order horizon is two periods. That is, $y_1 = r_1 + r_2 = 18 + 30 = 48$.

We start the process again in period 3.

Order Horizon	Total Holding Cost
1	0
2	10
3	90

We have exceeded the setup costs of 80, so we stop. Because 90 is closer to 80 than is 10, the order horizon is three periods. Hence $y_3 = r_3 + r_4 + r_5 = 67$. The complete part period balancing solution is $y = (48, 0, 67, 0, 0)$, which is different from both the Silver–Meal and LUC solutions. This solution is optimal, as it also has a total cost of $310.

All three of the methods discussed in this section are heuristic methods. That is, they are reasonable methods based on the structure of the problem but don't necessarily give the optimal solution. In Appendix 8–A, we discuss the Wagner–Whitin algorithm that guarantees an optimal solution to the problem of production planning with time-varying demands. While tedious to solve by hand, the Wagner–Whitin algorithm can be implemented easily on a computer and solved quickly and efficiently.

Problems for Section 8.2

10. Perform the MRP calculations for the valves in the example of this section, using the gross requirements schedule that results from EOQ lot sizing for the valve casing assemblies. Use $K = \$150$ and $h = 0.4$.

11. *a.* Determine the planned order release for the motherboards in Problem 4 assuming that one uses the EOQ formula to schedule production. Use $K = \$180$ and $h = 0.40$.

    b. Using the results from part (*a*), determine the gross requirements schedule for the DRAM chips, which are ordered from an outside supplier. The order cost is $25.00, and the holding cost is $0.01 per chip per week. What order schedule with the vendor results if the EOQ formula is used to determine the lot size?

    c. Repeat the calculation of part (*b*) for the add-in boards. Use the same value of the setup cost and a holding cost of 28 cents per board per week.

12. *a.* Discuss why the EOQ formula may give poor results for determining planned order releases.

    b. If the forecasted demand for the end item is the same each period, will the EOQ formula result in optimal lot sizing at each level of the product structure? Explain.

13. The problem of lot sizing for the valve casing assembly described for Harmon Music Company in Section 8.2 was solved using the EOQ formula. Determine the lot sizing for the 10 periods using the following methods instead:

    a. Silver–Meal.

    b. Least unit cost.

    c. Part period balancing.

    d. Which lot-sizing method resulted in the lowest cost for the 10 periods?

14. A single inventory item is ordered from an outside supplier. The anticipated demand for this item over the next 12 months is 6, 12, 4, 8, 15, 25, 20, 5, 10, 20, 5, 12. Current inventory of this item is 4, and ending inventory should be 8. Assume a holding cost of $1 per period and a setup cost of $40. Determine the order policy for this item based on

    a. Silver–Meal.
    b. Least unit cost.
    c. Part period balancing.
    d. Which lot-sizing method resulted in the lowest cost for the 12 periods?

15. For the counterexample (Example 6.3), which shows that the Silver–Meal heuristic may give a suboptimal solution, do either the least unit cost or the part period balancing heuristics give the optimal solution?

16. Discuss the advantages and disadvantages of the following lot-sizing methods in the context of an MRP scheduling system: lot for lot, EOQ, Silver–Meal, least unit cost, and part period balancing.

17. The time-phased net requirements for the base assembly in a table lamp over the next six weeks are

Week	1	2	3	4	5	6
Requirements	335	200	140	440	300	200

    The setup cost for the construction of the base assembly is $200, and the holding cost is $0.30 per assembly per week.

    a. What lot sizing do you obtain from the EOQ formula?
    b. Determine the lot sizes using the Silver–Meal heuristic.
    c. Determine the lot sizes using the least unit cost heuristic.
    d. Determine the lot sizes using part period balancing.
    e. Compare the holding and setup costs obtained over the six periods using the policies found in parts (a) through (d) with the cost of a lot-for-lot policy.

Problems 18–22 are based on the material appearing in Appendix 8–A.

18. Anticipated demands for a four-period planning horizon are 23, 86, 40, and 12. The setup cost is $300 and the holding cost is $h = \$3$ per unit per period.

    a. Enumerate all the exact requirements policies, compute the holding and setup costs for each, and find the optimal production plan.
    b. Solve the problem by backward dynamic programming.

19. Anticipated demands for a five-period planning horizon are 14, 3, 0, 26, 15. Current starting inventory is four units, and the inventory manager would like to have eight units on hand at the end of the planning horizon. Assume that $h = 1$ and $K = 30$. Find the optimal production schedule. (Hint: Modify the first and the last period's demands to account for starting and ending inventories.)

20. A small manufacturing firm that produces a line of office furniture requires casters at a fairly constant rate of 75 per week. The MRP system assumes a six-week planning horizon. Assume that it costs $266 to set up for production of the casters and the holding cost amounts to $1 per caster per week.

    a. Compute the EOQ and determine the number of periods of demand to which this corresponds by forming the ratio (EOQ)/(demand per period). Let T be this ratio rounded to the nearest integer. Determine the policy that produces casters once every T periods.

b. Using backward dynamic programming with $N = 6$ and $\mathbf{r} = (75, 75, \ldots, 75)$, find the optimal solution. (Refer to Appendix 8–A.) Does your answer agree with what you obtained in part (a)?

21. a. Based on the results of Problem 20, suggest an approximate lot-sizing technique. Under what circumstances would you expect this method to give good results?

 b. Use this method to solve Example 8A.2 (see Appendix 8–A). By what percentage does the resulting solution differ from the optimal?

22. Solve Problem 17 using the Wagner–Whitin algorithm. (Refer to Appendix 8–A.)

8.3 INCORPORATING LOT-SIZING ALGORITHMS INTO THE EXPLOSION CALCULUS

Example 8.6   Let us return to Example 8.1 concerning the Harmon Music Company and consider the impact of lot sizing on the explosion calculus. Consider first the valve casing assembly. The time-phased net requirements for the valve casing assembly are

Week	4	5	6	7	8	9	10	11	12	13
Time-phased net requirements	42	42	32	12	26	112	45	14	76	38

The setup cost for the valve casing assembly is $132, and the holding cost is $h = \$0.60$ per assembly per week. We will determine the lot sizing by the Silver–Meal heuristic.
Starting in week 4:

$$C(1) = 132,$$

$$C(2) = \frac{132 + 0.6(42)}{2} = 78.6,$$

$$C(3) = \frac{132 + 0.6[42 + (2)(32)]}{3} = 65.2,$$

$$C(4) = \frac{132 + 0.6[42 + (2)(32) + (3)(12)]}{4} = 54.3,$$

$$C(5) = \frac{132 + 0.6[42 + (2)(32) + (3)(12) + (4)(26)]}{5} = 55.92.$$

Since $C(5) > C(4)$, we terminate computations and set $y_4 = 42 + 42 + 32 + 12 = 128$.
Starting in week 8:

$$C(1) = 132,$$

$$C(2) = \frac{132 + 0.6(112)}{2} = 99.6,$$

$$C(3) = \frac{132 + 0.6[112 + (2)(45)]}{3} = 84.4,$$

$$C(4) = \frac{132 + 0.6[112 + (2)(45) + (3)(14)]}{4} = 69.6,$$

$$C(5) = \frac{132 + 0.6[112 + (2)(45) + (3)(14) + (4)(76)]}{5} = 92.16,$$

Hence, $y_8 = 26 + 112 + 45 + 14 = 197$.
Production occurs next in week 12. It is easy to show that $y_{12} = 76 + 38 = 114$.
A summary of the MRP calculations using the Silver–Meal (S–M) heuristic to determine lot sizes for the valve casing assembly is as follows:

Week	4	5	6	7	8	9	10	11	12	13	14	15	16	17
Net requirements						42	42	32	12		26	112	45	14	76	38
Time-phased net requirements	42	42	32	12		26	112	45	14		76	38			
Planned order release (S–M)	128	0	0	0	0	197	0	0	0	114	0			
Planned deliveries					128	0	0	0	197	0	0	0	114	0
Ending inventory					86	44	12	0	171	59	14	0	38	0

It is interesting to compare the holding and setup cost of the policy using the Silver–Meal heuristic with the previous solutions using lot for lot and the EOQ formula. There are exactly three setups in our solution, resulting in a total setup cost of $(132)(3) = \$396$. The sum of the ending inventories each week is $86 + 44 + \cdots + 38 + 0 = 424$. The total holding cost is $(0.6)(424) = \$254.40$. Hence, the total cost of the Silver–Meal solution for this assembly amounts to $\$650.40$. Compare this to the costs of $\$1,320$ using lot for lot and $\$919.80$ using the EOQ solution.

It is also interesting to note what would have been the result if we had employed the Wagner–Whitin algorithm to find the true optimal solution. The optimal solution for this problem turns out to be $y_4 = 154$, $y_9 = 171$, and $y_{12} = 114$, with a total cost of $\$610.20$, which is only a slight improvement over the Silver–Meal heuristic.

We will now consider how the planned order release for the valve casing assembly affects the scheduling for lower-level components. In particular, if we consider the MRP calculations for the valves and assume that the lot sizing for the valves is determined by the Silver–Meal heuristic as well, we obtain

Week	1	2	3	4	5	6	7	8	9	10	11	12	13
Gross requirements				384	0	0	0	591	0	0	0	342	0
Scheduled receipts					96								
On-hand inventory			186	0	96	96	96	0					
Net requirements				198	0	0	0	495	0	0	0	342	0
Time-phased net requirements	198	0	0	0	495	0	0	0	342	0			
Planned order release (S–M)	198	0	0	0	495	0	0	0	342	0			

Note in this calculation summary that the scheduled receipts in period 5 must be held until period 8 before they can be used to offset demand. This results from the zero gross requirements in periods 5 through 8.

The calculation of the planned order release is based on a setup cost of $\$80$ and a holding cost of $\$0.07$ per valve per week. It is interesting to note that the Silver–Meal heuristic resulted in a lot-for-lot production rule in this case. This results from the lumpy demand pattern caused by the lot sizing applied at a higher level of the product structure. Both Silver–Meal and Wagner–Whitin give the same results for this example.

Problems for Section 8.3

23. If we were to solve Example 8.6 using the Wagner–Whitin algorithm (described in Appendix 8–A), we would obtain (154, 0, 0, 0, 0, 171, 0, 0, 114, 0) as the planned order release for the valve casing assembly. What are the resulting planned order releases for the valves?

24. Consider the example of Noname Computer Company presented in Problem 4. Suppose that the setup cost for the production of the motherboards is $\$180$ and the

holding cost is $h = \$0.40$ per motherboard per week. Using part period balancing, determine the planned order release for the motherboards and the resulting gross requirements schedule for the DRAM chips. (Hint: Use the net demand for computers after accounting for starting inventory and returns.)

25. For the example presented in Problem 6, assume that the setup cost for both components A and B is $100 and that the holding costs are respectively $0.15 and $0.25 per component per week. Using the Silver–Meal algorithm, determine the planned order releases for both components A and B and the resulting gross requirements schedules for components C, D, and E.

8.4 LOT SIZING WITH CAPACITY CONSTRAINTS

We consider a variant of the problem treated in Section 8.3. Assume that in addition to known requirements $(r_1, \ldots, r_n)$ in each period, there are also production capacities $(c_1, \ldots, c_n)$. Hence, we now wish to find the optimal production quantities $(y_1, \ldots, y_n)$ subject to the constraints $y_i \leq c_i$, for $1 \leq i \leq n$.

The introduction of capacity constraints clearly makes the problem far more realistic. As lot-sizing algorithms can be incorporated into an MRP planning system, production capacities will be an important part of any realizable solution. However, they also make the problem more complex. The rather neat result that optimal policies always order exact requirements is no longer valid. Determining true optimal policies is difficult and time-consuming, and is probably not practical for most real problems.

Even finding a feasible solution may not be obvious. Consider our simple four-period example with vector $\mathbf{r} = (52, 87, 23, 56)$, but now suppose that the production capacity in each period is $\mathbf{c} = (60, 60, 60, 60)$. First we must determine if the problem is feasible; that is, whether at least one solution exists. On the surface the problem looks solvable, as the total requirement over the four periods is 218 and the total capacity is 240. But this problem is infeasible; the most that can be produced in the first two periods is 120, but the requirements for those periods sum to 139.

We have the following feasibility condition:

$$\sum_{i=1}^{j} c_i \geq \sum_{i=1}^{j} r_i \quad \text{for } j = 1, \ldots, n.$$

Even when the feasibility condition is satisfied, it is not obvious how to find a feasible solution. Consider the following example.

Example 8.7

$$\mathbf{r} = (20, 40, 100, 35, 80, 75, 25),$$
$$\mathbf{c} = (60, 60, 60, 60, 60, 60, 60).$$

Checking for feasibility, we have that:

$r_1 = 20$, $\quad c_1 = 60$;
$r_1 + r_2 = 60$, $\quad c_1 + c_2 = 120$;
$r_1 + r_2 + r_3 = 160$, $\quad c_1 + c_2 + c_3 = 180$;
$r_1 + r_2 + r_3 + r_4 = 195$, $\quad c_1 + c_2 + c_3 + c_4 = 240$;
$r_1 + r_2 + r_3 + r_4 + r_5 = 275$, $\quad c_1 + c_2 + c_3 + c_4 + c_5 = 300$;
$r_1 + r_2 + r_3 + r_4 + r_5 + r_6 = 350$, $\quad c_1 + c_2 + c_3 + c_4 + c_5 + c_6 = 360$;
$r_1 + r_2 + r_3 + r_4 + r_5 + r_6 + r_7 = 375$, $\quad c_1 + c_2 + c_3 + c_4 + c_5 + c_6 + c_7 = 420$.

458 Chapter Eight *Push and Pull Production Control Systems: MRP and JIT*

The feasibility test is satisfied, so we know at least that a feasible solution exists. However, it is far from obvious how we should go about finding one. Scheduling on a lot-for-lot basis is not going to work because of the capacity constraints in periods 3, 5, and 6.

We will present an approximate lot-shifting technique to obtain an initial feasible solution. The method is to back-shift demand from periods in which demand exceeds capacity to prior periods in which there is excess capacity. This process is repeated for each period in which demand exceeds capacity until we construct a new requirements schedule in which lot for lot is feasible. In the example, the first period in which demand exceeds capacity is period 3. We replace r_3 with c_3. The difference of 40 units must now be redistributed back to periods 1 and 2. We consider the first prior period, which is period 2. There are 20 units of excess capacity in period 2, which we absorb. We still have 20 units of demand from period 3 that are not yet accounted for; this is added to the requirement for period 1. Summarizing the results up until this point, we have

$$r' = (20, 40, 100, 35, 80, 75, 25),$$
$$c = (60, 60, 60, 60, 60, 60, 60).$$

The next period in which demand exceeds capacity is period 5. The excess demand of 20 units can be back-shifted to period 4. Finally, the 15 units of excess demand in period 6 can be back-shifted to periods 4 (5 units) and 1 (10 units). The feasibility condition guarantees that this process leads to a feasible solution.

This leads to

$$r' = (20, 40, 100, 35, 80, 75, 25),$$
$$c = (60, 60, 60, 60, 60, 60, 60).$$

Hence, the modified requirements schedule obtained is

$$r' = (50, 60, 60, 60, 60, 60, 25).$$

Setting **y** = **r**′ gives a feasible solution to the original problem.

The Improvement Step

We have that lot for lot for the modified requirements schedule **r**′ is feasible for the original problem. Next we would like to see if we can discover an improvement; that is, another feasible policy that has lower cost. There are a variety of reasonable improvement rules that one can use. We will employ the following one.

For each lot that is scheduled, starting from the last and working backward to the beginning, determine whether it is cheaper to produce the units composing that lot by shifting production to prior periods of excess capacity. By eliminating a lot, one reduces setup cost in that period to zero, but shifting production to prior periods increases the holding cost. The shift is made only if the additional holding cost is less than the setup cost. We illustrate the process with an example.

Example 8.8 Assume that $K = \$450$ and $h = \$2$.

$$r = (100, 79, 230, 105, 3, 10, 99, 126, 40),$$
$$c = (120, 200, 200, 400, 300, 50, 120, 50, 30).$$

Computing the cumulative sum of requirements and capacities for each period makes it easy to see the problem as feasible. However, because requirements exceed capacities in some periods, lot for lot is not feasible. We back-shift excess demand to prior periods in order to obtain the modified requirements schedule $r' = (100, 109, 200, 105, 28, 50, 120, 50, 30)$.

Lot for lot for the modified requirements schedule r' is feasible for the original problem. The initial feasible solution requires nine setups at a total setup cost of 9 × 450 = $4,050. The holding cost of the initial policy is 2(0 + 30 + 0 + 0 + 25 + 65 + 86 + 10) = $432. In order to do the improvement step, it is convenient to arrange the data in a table.

	1	2	3	4	5	6	7	8	9
r'	100	109	200	105	28	50	120	50	30
c	120	200	200	400	300	50	120	50	30
y	100	109	200	105	28	50	120	50	30
Excess capacity	20	91	0	295	272	0	0	0	0

Starting from the last period, consider the final lot of 30 units. There is enough excess capacity in prior periods to consider shifting this lot. The latest period that this lot can be scheduled for is period 5. The extra holding cost incurred by making the shift is 2 × 30 × 4 = $240. As this is cheaper than the setup cost of $450, we make the shift and increase y_5 from 28 to 58 and reduce the excess capacity in period 5 from 272 to 242.

Now consider the lot of 50 units scheduled in period 8. This lot can also be shifted to period 5 with a resulting additional holding cost of 2 × 50 × 3 = $300. Again this is cheaper than the setup cost, so we make the shift. At this point we have $y_5 = 108$, and the excess capacity in period 5 is reduced to 192.

The calculations are summarized on our table in the following way:

	1	2	3	4	5	6	7	8	9
r'	100	109	200	105	28	50	120	50	30
c	120	200	200	400	300 108 58	50	120	50	30
y	100	109	200	105	28 192 242	50	120	0 5̶0̶	0 3̶0̶
Excess capacity	20	91	0	295	2̶7̶2̶	0	0	0	0

Next consider the lot of 120 units scheduled in period 7. At this point, we still have 192 units of excess capacity in period 5. The additional holding cost of shifting the lot of 120 from period 7 to period 5 is 2 × 120 × 2 = $480. This exceeds the setup cost of $450, so we do not make the shift.

It is clearly advantageous to shift the lot of 50 units in period 6 to period 5, thus reducing the excess capacity in period 5 to 142 and increasing the lot size in period 5 from 108 to 158. Doing so results in the following:

	1	2	3	4	5	6	7	8	9
r'	100	109	200	105	28	50	120	50	30
c	120	200	200	400	300 158 108 58	50	120	50	30
y	100	109	200	105	28 142 192 242	0	120	0 5̶0̶	0 3̶0̶
Excess capacity	20	91	0	295	2̶7̶2̶	0	0	0	0

At this point it may seem that we are done. However, there is enough capacity in period 4 to shift the entire lot of 158 units from period 5 to period 4. The additional holding cost of this shift is 2 × 158 = $316. Because this is cheaper than the setup cost, we make the shift. Summarizing these calculations on the table gives

	1	2	3	4	5	6	7	8	9
r'	100	109	200	105	28	50	120	50	30
c	120	200	200	400	300	50	120	50	30
					0				
					158				
					108				
				263	58	0		0	0
y	100	109	200	105	28	50	120	50	30
					300				
					142				
					192				
				137	242	50		50	30
Excess capacity	20	91	0	295	272	0	0	0	0

At this point, no additional lot shifting is possible. The solution we have obtained is

$$y = (100, 109, 200, 263, 0, 0, 120, 0, 0)$$

for the original requirements schedule

$$r = (100, 79, 230, 105, 3, 10, 99, 126, 40).$$

We will compute the cost of this solution and compare it with that of our initial feasible solution. There are five setups at a total setup cost of 5 × 450 = $2,250. The holding cost is 2(0 + 30 + 0 + 158 + 155 + 145 + 166 + 40 + 0) = 2 × 694 = $1,388. The total cost of this policy is $3,638, compared with $4,482 for our initial feasible policy. For this example the improvement step resulted in a cost reduction of close to 20 percent.

Problems for Section 8.4

26. Consider the example presented in Section 8.2 of scheduling the production of the valve casing assembly.

    a. Suppose that the production capacity in any week is 100 valve casings. Using the algorithm presented in this section, determine the planned order release for the valve casings.
    b. What gross requirements schedule for the valves does the lot sizing you obtained in part (a) give?
    c. Suppose that the production capacity for the valves is 200 valves per week. Is the gross requirements schedule from part (b) feasible? If not, suggest a modification in the planned order release computed in part (a) that would result in a feasible gross requirements schedule for the valves.

27. Solve Problem 14 assuming a maximum order size of 20 per month.

28. a. Solve Problem 17 assuming the following production capacities:

Week	1	2	3	4	5	6
Capacity	600	600	600	400	200	200

b. On a percentage basis, how much larger are the total holding and setup costs in the capacitated case than in the solutions obtained from parts (*b*), (*c*), and (*d*) of Problem 17?

29. The method of rescheduling the production of a lot to one or more prior periods if the increase in the holding cost is less than the cost of a setup also can be used when no capacity constraints exist. This method is an alternative heuristic lot scheduling technique for the uncapacitated problem. For Problem 14, start with a lot-for-lot policy and consider shifting lots backward as we have done in this section, starting with the final period and ending with the first period. Compare the total cost of the policy that you obtain with the policies derived in Problem 14.

8.5 SHORTCOMINGS OF MRP

MRP is a closed production system with two major inputs: (1) the master production schedule for the end item and (2) the relationships between the various components, modules, and subassemblies composing the production process for that end item. The method is logical and seemingly sensible for scheduling production lot sizes. However, many of the assumptions made are unrealistic. In this section, we will discuss some of these assumptions, the problems that arise as a result of them, and the means for dealing with these problems.

Uncertainty

Underlying MRP is the assumption that all required information is known with certainty. However, uncertainties do exist. The two key sources of uncertainty are the forecasts for future sales of the end item and the estimation of the production lead times from one level to another. Forecast uncertainty usually means that the realization of demand is likely to be different from the forecast of that demand. In the production planning context, it also could mean that updated forecasts of future demands are different from earlier forecasts of those demands. Forecasts must be revised when new orders are accepted, prior orders are canceled, or new information about the marketplace becomes available. That has two implications in the MRP system. One is that *all* the lot-sizing decisions that were determined in the last run of the system could be incorrect, and, even more problematic, former decisions that are currently being implemented in the production process may be incorrect.

The analysis of stochastic inventory models in Chapter 5 showed that an optimal policy included safety stock to protect against the uncertainty of demand. That is, we would order to a level exceeding expected demand. The same logic can be applied to MRP systems. The manner in which uncertainty transmits itself through a complex multilevel production system is not well understood. For that reason, it is not recommended to include independent safety stock at all levels of the system. Rather, by using the methods in Chapter 5, suitable safety levels can be built into the forecasts for the end item. These will be transmitted automatically down through the system to the lower levels through the explosion calculus.

Example 8.9   Consider Example 8.1 on the Harmon Music Company. Suppose that the firm wishes to incorporate uncertainty into the demand forecasts for weeks 8 through 17. Based on historical records of trumpet sales maintained by the firm, an analyst finds that the ratio of the standard deviation of the forecast error to the mean demand each week is near 0.3.[2] Furthermore, weekly

[2] In symbols, this is written σ/μ and is known as the coefficient of variation.

demand is closely approximated by a normal distribution. Harmon has decided that it would like to produce enough trumpets to meet all the demand each week with probability .90. (In the terminology used in Chapter 5, this means that they are using a Type 1 service level of 90 percent for the trumpets.)

The safety stock is of the form σz where z is the appropriate cut-off point from the normal table. Here $z = 1.28$. Incorporating safety stock into the demand forecasts, we obtain

Week	8	9	10	11	12	13	14	15	16	17
Predicted demand (μ)	77	42	38	21	26	112	45	14	76	38
Standard deviation (σ)	23.1	12.6	11.4	6.3	7.8	33.6	13.5	4.2	22.8	11.4
Mean demand plus safety stock ($\mu + \sigma z$)	107	58	53	29	36	155	62	19	105	53

Of course, this is not the only way to compute safety stock. Alternatives are to employ a Type 2 service criterion or to use a stock-out cost model instead of a service level model. The next step is to net out the scheduled receipts and anticipated on-hand inventory to arrive at a revised MPS for the trumpets. The explosion calculus would now proceed as before, except that the safety stock that is included in the revised MPS would automatically be transmitted to the lower-level assemblies.

Safety lead times are used to compensate for the uncertainty of production lead times in MRP systems. Simply put, this means that the estimates for the time required to complete a production batch at one level and transport it to the next level would be multiplied by some safety factor. If a safety factor of 1.5 were used at Harmon Music Company, the lead times for the components would be revised as follows: bell assembly, 3 weeks; valve casing assembly, 6 weeks; slide assemblies, 3 weeks; valves, 4.5 weeks. Conceptually, safety lead times make sense if the essential uncertainty is in the production times from one level to the next, and safety stocks make sense if the essential uncertainty is in the forecast of the demand for the end item. In practice, both sources of uncertainty are generally present and some mixture of both safety stocks and safety lead times is used.

Capacity Planning

Another important issue that is not treated explicitly by MRP is the capacity of the production facility. The type of capacitated lot-sizing method we discussed earlier will deal with production capacities at one level of the system but will not solve the overall capacity problem. The problem is that even if lot sizes at some level do not exceed the production capacities, there is no guarantee that when these lot sizes are translated to gross requirements at a lower level, these requirements also can be satisfied with the existing capacity. That is, a feasible production schedule at one level may result in an infeasible requirements schedule at a lower level.

Capacity requirements planning (CRP) is the process by which the capacity requirements placed on a work center or group of work centers are computed by using the output of the MRP planned order releases. If the planned order releases result in an infeasible requirements schedule, there are several possible corrective actions. One is to schedule overtime at the bottleneck locations. Another is to revise the MPS so that the planned order releases at lower levels can be achieved with the current system capacity. This is clearly a cumbersome way to solve the problem, requiring an iterative trial-and-error process between the CRP and the MRP.

As an example of CRP, consider the manufacture of the trumpet discussed in Example 8.1 and throughout the rest of this chapter. Suppose that the valves are produced in three work centers: 100, 200, and 300. At work center 100, the molten brass is poured into the form used to shape the valve. At work center 200, the holes are drilled in the appropriate positions in the valves (there are three hole configurations, depending upon whether the valve is number 1, 2, or 3). Finally, at work center 300, the valve is polished and the surface appropriately graded to ensure that the valve does not stick in operation. A summary of the appropriate information for the work centers is given in the following table.

Work Center	Worker Time Required to Produce One Unit (hours/unit)	Machine Throughput (units/day)
100	0.1	120
200	0.25	100
300	0.15	160

According to this information, there would be a total of six minutes (0.1 hour) of worker time required to produce a single valve at work center 100, and the existing equipment can support a maximum throughput of 120 valves per day. Consider the planned order releases obtained for the valves resulting from the Silver–Meal lot scheduling rule given in Section 8.3:

Week	2	3	4	5	6	7	8	9	10	11
Planned order release (S–M)	198	0	0	0	495	0	0	0	342	0

This planned order release translates to the following capacity requirements at the three work centers:

Week	2	3	4	5	6	7	8	9	10	11
Labor time requirements (hours):										
Work center 100	19.8	0	0	0	49.5	0	0	0	34.2	0
Work center 200	49.5	0	0	0	123.75	0	0	0	85.5	0
Work center 300	29.7	0	0	0	72.25	0	0	0	51.3	0
Machine time requirements (days):										
Work center 100	1.65	0	0	0	4.125	0	0	0	2.85	0
Work center 200	1.98	0	0	0	4.95	0	0	0	3.42	0
Work center 300	1.24	0	0	0	3.09	0	0	0	2.14	0

The capacity requirements show whether the planned order release obtained from the MRP is feasible. For example, suppose that the requirement of 123.75 labor hours in week 6 at work center 200 exceeds the capacity of this work center. This means that the current lot sizing is infeasible and some corrective action is required. One possibility is to split the lot scheduled for week 6 by producing some part of it in a prior week. Another is to adjust the lot sizing for the valve casing assembly at the next higher level of the product structure to accommodate the capacity constraints at the current level. In either case, substantial changes in the initial production plan may be required.

This example suggests an interesting speculation. Would it not perhaps make more sense to determine where the bottlenecks occur *before* attempting to explode the MPS through the various levels of the system? In this way, a feasible production plan could be found that would meet capacity constraints. Additional refinements could then be considered.

Rolling Horizons and System Nervousness

Thus far, our view of MRP is that it is a static system. Given known requirements for the end items over a specified planning horizon, one determines both the timing and the sizes of the production lot sizes for all the lower-level components. In practice, however, the production planning environment is dynamic. The MRP system may have to be rerun each period and the production decisions reevaluated. Often it is the case that only the lot-sizing decisions for the current planning period need to be implemented. We use the term *rolling horizons* to refer to the situation in which only the first-period decision of an N-period problem is implemented. The full N-period problem is rerun each period to determine a new first-period decision.

When using rolling horizons, the planning horizon should be long enough to guarantee that the first-period decision does not change. Unfortunately, certain demand patterns are such that even for long planning horizons, the first-period decision does not remain constant. Consider the following simple example (from Carlson, Beckman, and Kropp, 1982).

Example 8.10 Suppose that the demand follows the cyclic pattern 190, 210, 190, 210, 190. . . . For a five-period planning horizon, the requirements schedule for periods 1 to 5 is

$$r = (190, 210, 190, 210, 190).$$

Furthermore, suppose that $h = 1$ and $K = 400$. The optimal solution for this problem obtained from the Wagner–Whitin algorithm is

$$y = (190, 400, 0, 400, 0).$$

However, suppose that the planning horizon is chosen to be six periods instead of five periods. The requirements schedule for a six-period planning horizon is

$$r = (190, 210, 190, 210, 190, 210).$$

The optimal solution in this case is

$$y = (400, 0, 400, 0, 400, 0).$$

That is, the first-period production quantity has changed from 190 to 400. If we go to a seven-period planning horizon, then y_1 will be 190. With an eight-period planning horizon, y_1 again becomes 400. One might think that this cycling of the value of y_1 would continue indefinitely. It turns out that this is *not* the case, however. For planning horizons of $n \geq 21$ periods, the value of y_1 remains fixed at 190.[3] However, even when there is eventual convergence of y_1, as in this example, the cycling for the first 20 periods could be troublesome when using rolling planning horizons.

Another common problem that results when using MRP is "nervousness." The term was coined by Steele (1973), who used it to refer to the changes that can occur in a schedule when the horizon is moved forward one period. Some of the causes of nervousness include unanticipated changes in the MPS because of updated forecasts, late deliveries of raw materials, failure of key equipment, absenteeism of key personnel, and unpredictable yields.

There has been some analytical work on the nervousness problem. Carlson, Jucker, and Kropp (1979 and 1983) use the term *nervousness* specifically to mean that a revised schedule requires a setup in a period in which the prior schedule did not. They have proposed an interesting technique to reduce this particular type of nervousness: Let $(\hat{y}_1, \hat{y}_2, \ldots, \hat{y}_N)$ be the existing production schedule and $(y_1, y_2, \ldots, y_N)$ be a revised schedule based on new demand information. Suppose that besides the usual costs of holding and setup, there is an additional cost of v if the new schedule y calls for a setup in a period that the old schedule $\hat{y}$ did not. This means that there is an additional

---

[3] I am grateful to Lawrence Robinson of Cornell University for pointing out that this anomaly does not continue for all values of n as was claimed in past editions and by Carlson, Beckman, and Kropp (1982).

setup cost associated with the new schedule in those periods in which no setup was called for in the old schedule. Their method is to increase the setup cost from K to $K + v$ if $\hat{y}_k = 0$ prior to determining the new schedule $\mathbf{y}$. Re-solving the problem with the modified setup costs using any of the lot-sizing algorithms previously discussed now will result in fewer setup revisions. The advantages of the various lot-sizing methods in this context are discussed in the two given references. The revision cost v reflects the relative importance of the cost of nervousness.

Additional Considerations

Although MRP would seem to be the most logical way to schedule production in batch-type operations, as we saw above the basic method has some very serious shortcomings. Other difficulties are considered.

Lead Times Dependent on Lot Sizes

The MRP calculus assumes that the production lead time from one level to the next is a fixed constant independent of the size of the lot. In many contexts this assumption is clearly unreasonable. One would expect the lead time to increase if the lot size increases. Including a dependence between the production lead time and the size of the production run into the explosion calculus seems to be extremely difficult.

MRP II: Manufacturing Resource Planning

As we have noted, MRP is a closed production planning system that converts an MPS into planned order releases. Manufacturing resource planning (MRP II) is a philosophy that attempts to incorporate the other relevant activities of the firm into the production planning process. In particular, the financial, accounting, and marketing functions of the firm are tied to the operations function. As an example of the difference between the perspectives offered by MRP and MRP II, consider the role of the master production schedule. In MRP, the MPS is treated as input information. In MRP II, the MPS would be considered a part of the system and, as such, would be considered a decision variable as well. Hence, the production control manager would work with the marketing manager to determine when the production schedule should be altered to incorporate revisions in the forecast and new order commitments. Ultimately, all divisions of the company would work together to find a production schedule consistent with the overall business plan and long-term financial strategy of the firm.

Another important aspect of MRP II is the incorporation of capacity resource planning (CRP). Capacity considerations are not explicitly accounted for in MRP. MRP II is a closed-loop cycle in which lot sizing and the associated shop floor schedules are compared to capacities and recalculated to meet capacity restrictions. However, capacity issues continue to be an important issue in both MRP and MRP II operating systems.

Obviously, such a global approach to the production scheduling problem is quite ambitious. Whether such a philosophy can be converted to a workable system in a particular operating environment remains to be seen.

Imperfect Production Processes

An implicit assumption made in MRP is that there are no defective items produced. Because requirements for components and subassemblies are computed to exactly satisfy end-item demand forecasts, losses due to defects can seriously upset the balance of the production plan. In some industries, such as semiconductors, yield rates can be as low as 10 to 20 percent for new products. As long as yields are stable, incorporating yield losses into the MRP calculus is not difficult. One computes net demands and lot

Snapshot Application

RAYMOND CORPORATION BUILDS WORLD-CLASS MANUFACTURING WITH MRP II

The Raymond Corporation is a major materials handling equipment manufacturer headquartered in Greene, New York. In order to achieve an estimated payback of 10 times in reduced inventories and organizational efficiencies, the organization underwent a process of implementation of MRP II that spanned over two years. The success of their effort was based on several basic principles. The first was that top management had to be committed to the process of change. For that reason, the first step was the education of the top management utilizing a "canned" educational package available from an outside consulting firm. The CEO facilitated on-site training for the vice presidents, who in turn were responsible for training the middle management implementation team. With top management on board, middle management could not simply ignore the issue and wait for it to go away. Training continued throughout the implementation phase of the project and ultimately included employees at every level of the company.

Once training was far enough along to begin thinking about implementation, a strategy for implementation was laid out. The first step was to take a hard look at the data that would be used as inputs to the system. As a result of this effort, stockroom reporting accuracy went from 66 percent to over 95 percent in about 16 months. Every inventory status report was measured for accuracy and corrected when necessary. Setting up standards and systems that give accurate information can be the lion's share of the benefit from an effort such as this. An early payoff was that reporting accuracy led to reduced need to closely monitor purchasing. Inventory status reports were used for ABC classification, and more time and energy were devoted to managing the "A" items.

In order to determine the effectiveness of new systems, the implementation team would meet weekly to review the progress of internal measures. An attempt was made to determine the cause of problems or lack of progress without pointing fingers and assigning blame. Performance measurements become an important part of the success of the implementation effort. Accurate and up-to-date performance measurements are the cornerstone of any systems change effort, but they must be put in place without threatening workers.

Finally, the author recommends that the *final* step should be the purchase of new software. If the underlying data and measurements systems in place are not sound, the software, no matter how sophisticated, won't help. Many firms believe that purchasing an expensive MRP software system is all that's necessary to achieve reduced inventory, lower materials costs, improved on-time delivery, and so on. However, without employees that are on-board, accurate data, and performance measurements, new software can be more of a hindrance than a help.

Aside from reaching class A status, what benefits did Raymond see from this process? Sheldon (1994) claimed elimination of overtime, elimination of shortages, improved on-time deliveries, reductions in setup times and costs, reductions in rework and scrap rates, and lower inventory and material handling costs. While it is hard to believe that the improvements were as dramatic as this, a carefully planned implementation of MRP II clearly paid off for the Raymond Corporation.

Source: This discription is based on Sheldon (1994).

---

sizes in the same way, and in the final step divides the planned order release figures by the average yield. For example, if a particular process has a yield rate of 78 percent, one would multiply the planned order releases by $1/0.78 = 1.28$. The problem is much more complex if yields are random and variances are too large to be ignored. Using mean yields would result in substantial stock-outs. One would have to develop a kind of newsboy model that balanced the cost of producing too many and too few and determine an appropriate safety factor. Because of the dependencies of successive levels, this would be a difficult problem to model mathematically. Monte Carlo computer simulation would be a good alternative. To this writer's knowledge, no one has attempted to develop a mathematical model of random yields in the context of MRP systems. (Random yields, however, are discussed by several researchers. For example, Nahmias and Moinzadeh, 1997, consider a mathematical model of random yields in a single-level lot-sizing problem.)

Data Integrity

An MRP system can function effectively only if the numbers representing inventory levels are accurate. It is easy for incorrect data to make their way into the scheduling system. This can occur if a shipment is not recorded or is recorded incorrectly at some level, items entering inventory for rework are not included, scrap rates are higher than anticipated, and so on. In order to ensure the integrity of the data used to determine the size and the timing of lot sizes, physical stock-taking may be required at regular intervals. An alternative to complex physical stock-taking is a technique known as *cycle counting*. Cycle counting simply means directly verifying the on-hand levels of the various inventories comprising the MRP system. For example, are the 45 units of part A557J indicated on the current record the actual count of this part number?

Efficient cycle counting can be achieved in a variety of ways. Stockrooms may have containers that only hold a fixed number or weight of items. Coded shelving systems could be used to more easily identify items with part numbers. Certain areas could be made accessible only to specific personnel. Cycle counting systems can be based on number or on weight. Furthermore, an error in the inventory level must be considered in relative terms. Based on the importance of the item, different percentage errors may be considered acceptable. Different error tolerances should be applied to weigh-counted items versus hand-counted items. If MRP is to have a positive impact on the overall production scheduling problem, the inventory records must be an accurate reflection of the actual state of the system.

Order Pegging

In some complex systems, a single component may be used in more than one item at the next higher level of the system. For example, a company producing many models of toy cars may use the same-sized axle in each of the cars. Gross requirements for axles would be the sum of the gross requirements generated by the MPS for each model of car. Hence, when one component is used in several items, the gross requirements schedule for this component comes from several sources. If a shortage of this component occurs, it is useful for the firm to be able to identify the particular items higher in the tree structure that would be affected. In order to do this, the gross requirements schedule is broken down by the items that generate it and each requirement is "pegged" with the part number of the source of the requirement. Pegging adds considerable complexity to the information storage requirements of the system and should only be considered when the additional information is important in the decision-making process.

Problems for Section 8.5

30. MRP systems have been used with varying degrees of success. Describe under what circumstances MRP might be successful and under what circumstances it would not be successful.

31. Discuss the advantages and disadvantages of including safety stock in MRP lot-sizing calculations. Do you think that a production control manager would be reluctant to build to safety stock if he or she is behind schedule?

32. For what reason is the capacitated lot-sizing method discussed in Section 8.5 not adequate for solving the overall capacity problem?

33. Planned order releases (POR) for three components, A, B, and C, are given below. Suppose that the yields for these components are respectively 84 percent, 92 percent,

and 70 percent. Assuming lot-for-lot scheduling, how should these planned order releases be adjusted to account for the fact that the yields are less than 100 percent?

Week	6	7	8	9	10	11	12	13	14	15	16	17
POR(A)				200	200	80	80	200	400	400	400	
POR(B)			100	100	40	40	100	200	200	200		
POR(C)	200	400	280	100	280	600	800	800	400			

34. Define the terms *rolling horizons* and *system nervousness* in the context of MRP systems.

8.6 JIT FUNDAMENTALS

Just-in-time, lean production, and zero inventories are all names for essentially the same thing: a system of moving material through a plant that requires a minimum of inventory. Some have speculated that the roots of the system go back to the situation in postwar Japan. Devastated by the war, the Japanese firms were cash poor and did not have the luxury of investing cash in excess inventories. Thus, lean production was born from necessity. However, as Japanese cars started gaining in popularity in the United States, it quickly became clear that they were far superior to American- and European-made cars in terms of quality, value, efficiency, and reliability. We know today that JIT and the quality initiatives of the 1950s played important roles in this success.

Two developments were key to the success of this new approach to mass production: the kanban system and SMED (which stands for single minute exchange of dies). Kanban is a Japanese word for *card* or *ticket*. It is a manual information system developed and used by Toyota for implementing just-in-time.

The Mechanics of Kanban

There are a variety of different types of kanban tickets, but two are the most prevalent. These are withdrawal kanbans and production ordering kanbans. A withdrawal kanban is a request for parts to a work center from the prior level of the system. A production ordering kanban is a signal for a work center to produce additional lots. The manner in which these two kanban tickets are used to control the flow of production is depicted in Figure 8–8.

The process is as follows: Parts are produced at work center 1, stored in an intermediate location (known as the store), and subsequently transported to work center 2. Parts are transported in small batches represented by the circles in the figure. Production flows from left to right in the diagram. The detailed steps in the process are as follows (the numbers below appear in the appropriate locations in Figure 8–8):

1. When the number of tickets on the withdrawal kanban reaches a predetermined level, a worker takes these tickets to the store location.
2. If there are enough canisters available at the store, the worker compares the part number on the production ordering kanbans at the store with the part number on the withdrawal kanbans.
3. If the part numbers match, the worker removes the production ordering kanbans from the containers, places them on the production ordering kanban post, and places the withdrawal kanbans in the containers.
4. When a specified number of production ordering kanbans have accumulated, work center 1 proceeds with production.

FIGURE 8–8
Kanban system for two production centers

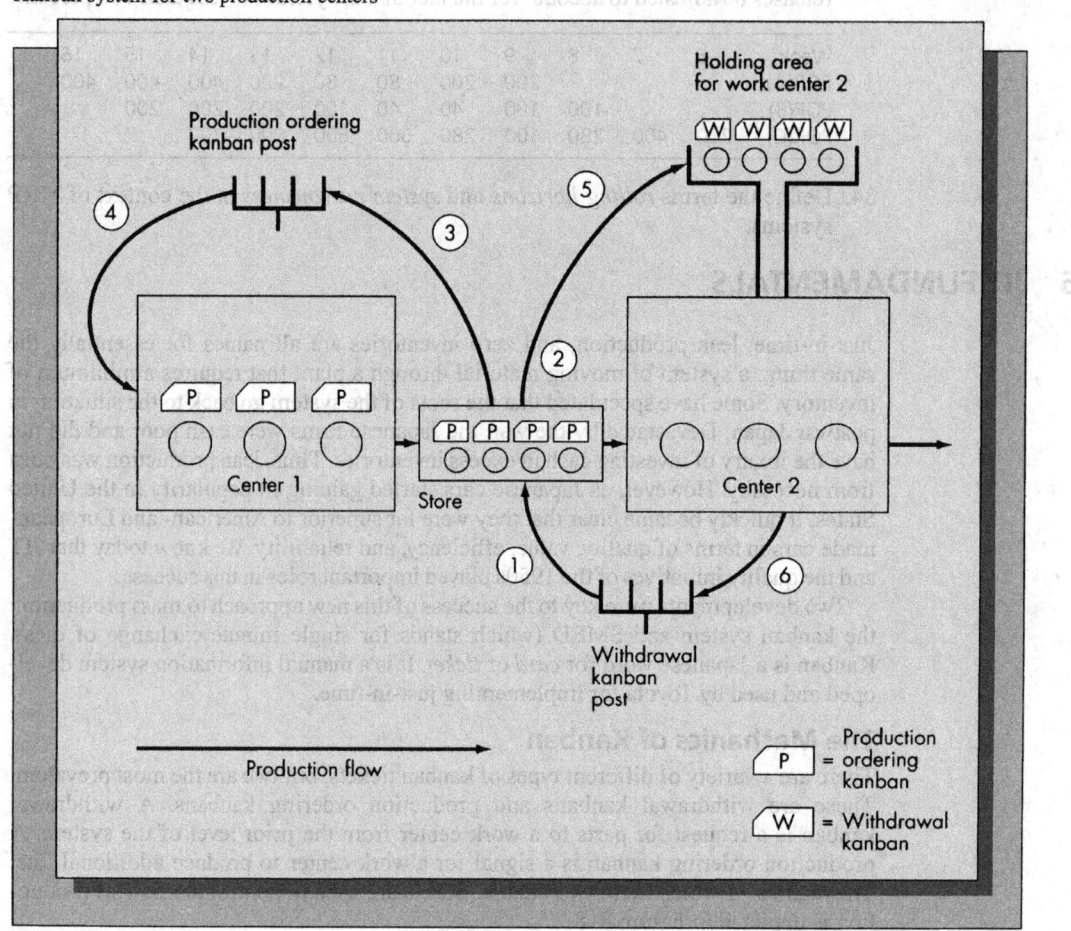

5. The worker transports parts picked up at the store to work center 2 and places them in a holding area until they are required for production.
6. When the parts enter production at work center 2, the worker removes the withdrawal kanbans and places them on the withdrawal kanban post. (Note that production ordering kanbans for work center 2 are then attached to the parts produced at that work center. These kanban tickets are not shown in Figure 8–8.)

One computes the number of kanban tickets in the system in advance. Toyota uses the following formula (Monden, 1981b):

$$y = \frac{\overline{D}L + w}{a},$$

where

y = Number of kanbans.
$\overline{D}$ = Expected demand per unit of time.

L = Lead time (processing time + waiting time between processes + conveyance time).

w = Policy variable specifying the level of buffer stock, generally around 10 percent of $\overline{D}L$.

a = Container capacity (usually no more than 10 percent of daily demand).

This formula implies that the maximum level of inventory is given by $ay = \overline{D}L + w$. The ideal value of w is zero. However, it is difficult to balance a system so perfectly that buffer stock is eliminated entirely.

As mentioned earlier, the kanban system is a manual information system for implementing just-in-time. JIT systems also can be implemented in other ways, which may be more efficient than the kanban method. More will be said about this later in the section.

Single Minute Exchange of Dies

One of the key components of the success of Toyota's production system was the concept of single minute exchange of dies (SMED), championed by Shigeo Shingo. Shingo is generally credited with developing and implementing SMED at Toyota in 1970, which has become an important part of the overall Toyota production system. The basic theory developed in Chapter 4 tells us that small lot sizes will be optimal only if fixed costs are small (as K decreases in the EOQ formula, so does the value of Q). The most significant component of the cost of setting up for a new operation in a plant is the time required to change over the machinery for that operation, since the production line must be frozen during the changeover operation. This requires changing some set of tools and/or dies required in the process, hence the origin of the term SMED. (A die is a tool used for shaping or impressing an object or material.)

Die-changing operations are required in automotive plants when switching over the production line from one car model to another. These operations typically required about four hours. The idea behind SMED is that a significant portion of the die-changing operation can be done off-line while the previous dies are still in place and the line continues to operate. According to Shingo (1981), this is accomplished by dividing the die-changing operation into two components: inside exchange of die (IED) and outside exchange of die (OID). The OID operation is to be performed while the line is running in advance of the actual exchange. The goal is to structure the die change so that there are as many steps as possible in the OID portion of the operation.

While this idea sounds simple, it has led to dramatic improvements in throughput rates in many circumstances, both within and outside the automotive industry. Shingo (1981) describes some of the successes:

- At Toyota, an operation that required eight hours for exchange of dies and tools for a bolt maker was reduced over a year's time to only 58 seconds.
- At Mitsubishi Heavy Industry, a tool-changing operation for a boring machine was reduced from 24 hours to only 2 minutes and 40 seconds.
- At H. Weidmann Company of Switzerland, changing the dies for a plastic molding machine was reduced from 2.5 hours to 6 minutes and 35 seconds.
- At Federal-Mogul Company of the United States, the time required to exchange the tools for a milling machine was reduced from 2 hours to 2 minutes.

Of course, SMED cannot be applied in all manufacturing contexts. Even in contexts where it can be applied, the benefits of the die-changing time reduction can be realized only if the process is integrated into a carefully designed and implemented overall manufacturing control system.

Advantages and Disadvantages of the Just-in-Time Philosophy

Champions of just-in-time would have one believe that all other production planning systems are now obsolete. The zeal with which they promote the method is reminiscent of the enthusiasm that heralded MRP in the early 1970s. At that time, some claimed that classical inventory analysis was no longer valid. However, each new production method should be viewed as an addition to, rather than a replacement for, what is already known. Just-in-time can be a useful tool in the right circumstances, but is far from a panacea for the problems facing industry today.

Just-in-time and EOQ are not mutually exclusive. Setup time and, consequently, setup cost reduction result in smaller lot sizes. Smaller lot sizes require increased efficiency and reliability of the production process, but considerably less investment in raw materials, work-in-process inventories, and finished-goods inventories.

Kanban is a manual information system used to support just-in-time inventory control. Just-in-time and kanban are not necessarily wedded. In future years, we expect to see just-in-time systems based on more current and sophisticated information transfer technology. A shortcoming of kanban is the time required to transmit new information through the system. Figure 8–9 considers a schematic of a serial production process with six levels. With the kanban system, the direction of the flow of information is opposite to the direction of the flow of the production. Consider the consequences of a sudden change in the requirements at level 6. This change is transmitted first to level 5, then to level 4, and so on. There could be a substantial time lag from the instant that the change occurs at level 6 until the information reaches level 1.

A centralized information processing system will help to alleviate this problem. If there are sudden changes in the requirements at one end of the system resulting from unplanned changes in demand or breakdowns of key equipment, these changes will be instantly transmitted to the entire system.

FIGURE 8–9
Kanban information system versus centralized information system

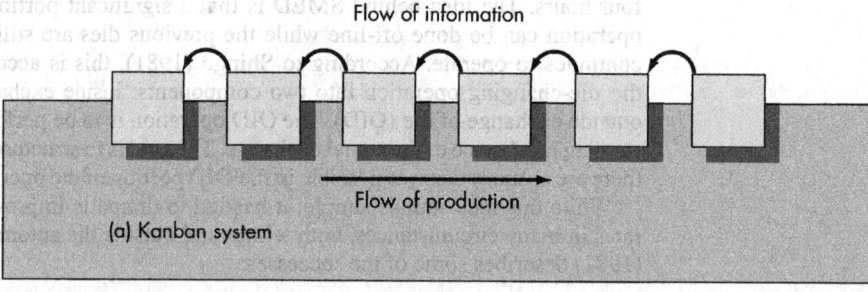

(a) Kanban system

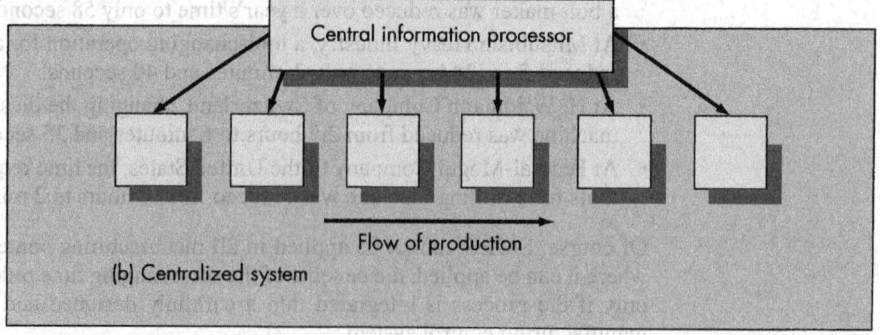

(b) Centralized system

MRP has an important advantage over kanban in this regard. One of the strengths of MRP is its ability to react to forecasted changes in the pattern of demand. The MRP system recomputes production quantities based on these changes and makes this information available to all levels simultaneously. MRP allows planning to take place at all levels in a way that just-in-time, and especially kanban, will not. As Meal (1984) points out:

> Just-in-time production works well when the overall production rate is constant, but it is unsatisfactory for communicating basic changes in production rate to earlier stages in the process. . . . On the other hand using the HPP [hierarchical production planning] approach, plant managers do not rely on their short term signals to establish their early stage production rates.

Just-in-time is most efficient when the pattern of demand is stable and predictable. Changes in the demand may result from predictable causes or random fluctuations or both. MRP makes use of forecasts of anticipated changes in demand and transmits this information to all parts of the productive system. However, neither MRP nor just-in-time is designed to protect against random fluctuations of demand. Both methods could be unstable in the face of high demand variance.

Another potential shortcoming of just-in-time is the idle time that may result when unscheduled breakdowns occur. Part of the Japanese philosophy is that workers should have a familiarity with more than one portion of the productive process. If a breakdown occurs, then workers' attention can be immediately focused on the problem. However, if workers are familiar with only their own operation, there will be significant worker idle time when a breakdown occurs. This is consistent with the trade-off curve presented in Figure 9–4 of Chapter 9 on shop floor control and sequence scheduling. Buffer inventories between successive operations provide a means of smoothing production processes. However, buffer inventories also have disadvantages. They can mask underlying problems. A popular analogy is to compare a production process with a river and the level of inventory with the water level in the river. When the water level is high, the water will cover the rocks. Likewise, when inventory levels are high, problems are masked. However, when the water level (inventory) is low, the rocks (problems) are evident (see Figure 8–10).

Because items are moved through the system in small batches, 100 percent inspection is feasible. Seen in this light, just-in-time can be incorporated easily into an overall quality control strategy. Total quality management (TQM), discussed in Chapter 12, and

FIGURE 8–10
River/inventory analogy illustrating the advantages of just-in-time

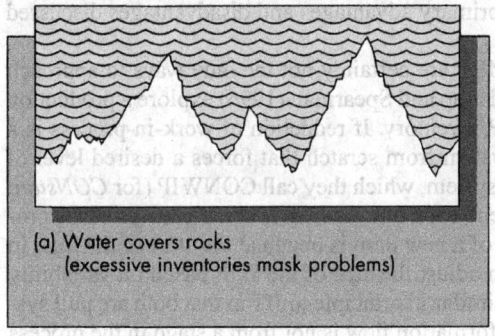

(a) Water covers rocks
(excessive inventories mask problems)

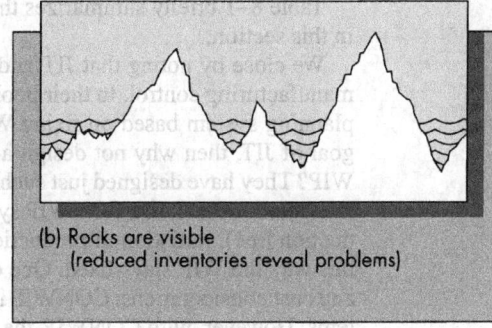

(b) Rocks are visible
(reduced inventories reveal problems)

TABLE 8–1
Summary of Advantages and Disadvantages of Just-in-Time and Kanban

Feature	Advantages	Disadvantages
Small work-in-process inventories	1. Decreases inventory costs. 2. Improves production efficiency. 3. Points out quality problems quickly.	1. May result in increased worker idle time. 2. May decrease the production rate.
Kanban information flow system	1. Provides for efficient lot tracking. 2. Inexpensive means of implementing just-in-time. 3. Allows for predetermined level of WIP inventory by presenting number of kanban tickets.	1. Slow to react to changes in demand. 2. Ignores known information about future demand patterns.
Coordinated inventory and purchasing	1. Inventory reduction. 2. Improved coordination of different systems. 3. Improved relationships with vendors.	1. Decreased opportunity for multiple sourcing. 2. Suppliers must react more quickly. 3. Improved reliability required of suppliers

JIT can work together not only to reduce inventory costs, but also to bring about significant improvements in product quality.

As users of just-in-time point out, it is not simply an inventory control system. For just-in-time to work properly, it must be coordinated with the purchasing system and with purchasing strategies. One complaint about just-in-time is that it merely pushes system uncertainty and higher inventories onto the supplier. There is no doubt that greater flexibility on the part of the suppliers is necessary; they must be able to react quickly and provide sufficiently reliable parts to relieve the manufacturer of the necessity to inspect all incoming lots. Furthermore, multiple sourcing becomes difficult under such a system. That is, the firm may be forced to deal with a single supplier in order to develop the close relationship that the system requires. Single sourcing presents risks for both suppliers and manufacturers. The manufacturer faces the risk that the supplier will be unable to supply parts when they are needed, and the supplier faces the risk that the manufacturer will suffer reverses and demand will drop.

Table 8–1 briefly summarizes the primary advantages and disadvantages discussed in this section.

We close by noting that JIT and MRP are certainly not the only ways to approach manufacturing control. In their book, Hopp and Spearman (1996) explore a production planning system based on fixing WIP inventory. If reduction of work-in-process is a goal of JIT, then why not design a system from scratch that forces a desired level of WIP? They have designed just such a system, which they call CONWIP (for *CONstant Work-In-Process*). In a CONWIP system, each time an item is completed (exits the production line), initiation of production of a new item is begun at the start of the line. In this way the WIP stays fixed. One can adjust the size of the WIP based on variability and cost considerations. CONWIP is similar in principle to JIT in that both are pull systems. However, with CONWIP, the information flow is not from a stage in the process to the previous stage, but from the end of the process to the beginning. The method sounds intriguing, but still needs to stand the test of implementation in the real world.

Implementation of JIT in the United States

A dramatic example of successful implementation of JIT in the United States is the Harley-Davidson Motorcycle Company. Until the early 1980s Harley-Davidson was owned by American Foundry Company (AMF). Harley, well known as a manufacturer of large-displacement motorcycles, faced severe competition from the Japanese. Honda, traditionally a manufacturer of small-displacement motorcycles, was beginning to make inroads into Harley's market. It appeared that motorcycles would become another consumer product produced only by foreign companies.

The first step in Harley's recovery was the purchase of the company from AMF by a group of employees. Shortly after the buyout, top management traveled to Japan to see how its competitors' factories were run. According to Willis (1986),

> The real "secret," the executives discovered, lay not in robotics or high-tech systems but in the intelligent, efficient organization of the company's employees and production systems.

As a result of these visits, Harley-Davidson was completely reorganized. Traditional management structure was replaced by a system in which each employee was given ownership of his or her area of the line. A large proportion of staff jobs were cut, resulting in a much shallower organization chart similar to that in Japanese companies. In this way, problems could not become buried in bureaucracy. The firm also instituted a quality circles program with active participation of the line personnel (see the discussion of quality circles in Chapter 12).

The firm invested in state-of-the-art computer-aided design/computer-aided manufacturing (CAD/CAM) and robotics equipment. The physical layout of the plant was restructured into work cells using a group technology layout (see Chapter 11). Motorcycles were no longer manufactured on a traditional assembly line.

A key change was the manner in which material was moved through the plant. Harley adopted the term MAN (materials as needed) to describe its system, but this was clearly just another name for JIT. To make JIT work, it instituted a program to reduce the number of setups each day. Prior to the restructuring, it produced 13 to 14 different models each day. Under the new system, improved forecasting allowed it to implement two-hour repeating cycles.

In order to make JIT work, Harley needed a commitment from its vendors as well as its own employees. To encourage its vendors to "buy in" to the program, Harley offered training sessions on the principles of JIT. These programs became so popular that Harley started to offer them to firms that were neither vendors nor clients. What is the result of this effort? Today Harley-Davidson's motorcycles are 99 percent defect-free, as compared to only 50 percent in 1982. In addition to achieving dramatic improvements in product quality, Harley developed new employee benefit programs and expanded its product line. All this was accomplished with a simultaneous reduction in costs.

Harley-Davidson is not the only example of successful implementation of JIT in the United States. Jacobson and Hillkirk (1986) describe the turnaround of Xerox, which was beleaguered by competition from Kodak and several Japanese firms (especially Canon) in the early 1980s. Xerox embarked on a self-examination program based on competitive benchmarking and undertook a complete restructuring of its business. Implementation of JIT systems played a major role in its turnaround. For example, it reduced the number of vendors supplying the company from 5,000 to only 400, which included a mix of sources overseas as low-cost suppliers and sources close by to provide timely deliveries when needed. Its systems allowed it to reduce copier parts inventories by $240 million.

The American auto industry has made significant moves toward embracing JIT, but there is still a long way to go. There are many examples of plants in the United States that have adopted the JIT philosophy. Two General Motors ventures are the NUMMI plant in northern California, a joint venture with Toyota, and the Saturn plant in Tennessee. Ironically, Ford, which pioneered the assembly line for mass production of automobiles, has been the most successful American firm at adopting Japanese manufacturing philosophies. Ford's assembly plant near Atlanta, Georgia, at which the Ford Taurus and the Mercury Sable are manufactured, is impressive on most productivity and quality measures, even when compared with the Japanese. When GM attempted to isolate the factors responsible for Ford's significantly better productivity in this plant as compared to GM's Fairfax, Kansas, plant, which makes the Pontiac Grand Prix, it found that 41 percent of the difference could be attributed to the manufacturability of the car's designs and 48 percent to factory practice (Womack et al., 1990, p. 96).

Although U.S. firms have certainly made significant progress toward adopting JIT principles, the conversion to "lean production" has not been as quick as one would have hoped. This is partly due to an environment that is less conducive to JIT. For example, in the U.S. auto industry, assembly plants and suppliers are often separated by large distances. Japanese firms can have daily and even hourly deliveries from suppliers, because those suppliers are located close to assembly plants. Also, JIT works best when product demand is relatively stable. Sales of automobiles in the United States have been far more cyclic than in Japan (Womack et al., 1990, p. 247), making a pure JIT system more difficult to implement here. Hence, the U.S. auto industry faces a more difficult environment for successful implementation of JIT. Even with these difficulties, both U.S. and European manufacturers will have to make the transition to lean production methods if they hope to remain competitive with the Japanese.

Problems for Section 8.6

35. Discuss the concepts of push versus pull and how they relate to just-in-time.
36. What is the difference between a just-in-time system and a kanban system? Can just-in-time be implemented without kanban?
37. A regional manufacturer of table lamps plans on using a manual kanban information system. On average the firm produces 1,200 lamps monthly. Production lead time is 18 days, and the firm plans to have 15 percent buffer stock. Assume 20 working days per month.

    a. If each container holds 15 lamps, what will be the total number of kanban tickets required? (Use the formula given in this section.)
    b. What is the maximum WIP inventory the company can expect to have using this system?
    c. Suppose that each lamp costs the firm $30 to produce. If carrying costs are based on a 20 percent annual interest rate, what annual carrying cost for WIP inventory is the company incurring? (You may wish to review the discussion of holding costs in Chapter 4.)

38. What is SMED? In what way can die-changing operations be reduced by orders of magnitude? Why is it an advantage to do so?
39. Explain how the dual-card kanban system operates.

40. Discuss the advantages and disadvantages of each of the following features of just-in-time:
    a. Small lot sizes.
    b. Integrated purchasing and inventory control.
    c. Kanban information system.

8.7 A COMPARISON OF MRP AND JIT

MRP and JIT are fundamentally different systems for manufacturing control. As we noted earlier, MRP is a push system and JIT is a pull system. JIT is a reactive system. If a problem develops and the line is shut down, JIT reacts immediately, since requests for new material are discontinued. In this way, one might say that JIT reacts to uncertainties and MRP does not. However, JIT is clearly not going to work well when it is known that demands will vary significantly over time. MRP builds this information into the planning structure while JIT does not.

For most manufacturing environments, implementing a pure JIT system is simply not feasible. Suppliers may not be located in close enough proximity to allow inputs to be delivered according to a rigid schedule. Demands for products may be highly variable, making it impractical to ignore this information in the planning process. It may be difficult to move products in small batches. Implementing SMED may not be possible in some environments. When setup costs are very high, it makes economic sense to produce in large lots and store items rather than change over production processes frequently. With that said, however, major reductions in WIP inventories can be achieved in the vast majority of traditional manufacturing plants. Plants that run lean run better.

Toyota's enormous success in reducing inventory-related costs while producing high-quality products with high throughput rates has formed the basis for much of the support for JIT-based systems. However, it is unclear if JIT is primarily responsible for Toyota's success. Toyota's way of doing business differs from that of American auto makers in many dimensions. Is its success a direct result of JIT methods, or can it be attributed to other factors that might be more difficult to emulate? In order to determine under what circumstances JIT would be most advantageous, Krajewski et al. (1987) developed a large-scale simulator to compare JIT, MRP, and ROP (reorder point) manufacturing environments. Their comparison included 36 distinct factors aggregated into eight major categories, with each factor varied from one to five levels. The eight categories considered and a brief summary of the factors in these categories are listed here:

1. *Customer influence.* Demand forecast error.
2. *Vendor influence.* Vendor reliability (order size received compared to order size requested, and time received compared to time requested).
3. *Buffer mechanisms.* Capacity buffer and safety stock and safety lead times.
4. *Product structure.* Considered pyramid (few end items) and inverted pyramid (many end items) structures.
5. *Facility design.* Routing patterns, shop emphasis, and length of routings.
6. *Process.* Scrap rates, equipment failures, worker flexibility, and capacity imbalances.
7. *Inventory.* Reporting accuracy, lot-sizing rules, and setup times.
8. *Other factors.* Number of items, number of workstations, and several other factors.

The results obtained were very interesting. JIT worked well only in favorable manufacturing environments. This means little or no demand variability, reliable vendors, and small setup times for production. JIT showed poor performance when one or more of these factors became unfavorable. In fact, in a favorable environment both ROP and MRP gave good results as well. This suggests that the primary benefit comes from creating a favorable manufacturing environment, as opposed to simply implementing a JIT system. Perhaps greater benefit would result from carefully evaluating and (where possible) rectifying the key problems affecting manufacturing than by blindly implementing a new production planning system. Alternatively, perhaps it is the *process* of implementing a JIT system from which the greatest benefit is obtained.

New approaches to manufacturing control are quickly tagged with three-letter acronyms and proselytized with the zealousness of a religion. JIT is no exception. At its best, JIT is a set of methods that should be implemented on a continuous improvement basis for reducing inventories at every level of the supply chain. At its worst, JIT is a romantic idea that when applied blindly can be very damaging to worker morale, relationships with suppliers, and ultimately the bottom line. Inventory savings can often be an illusion, as illustrated by Chhikara and Weiss (1995). They show in three case studies that if inventory reductions are not tied to accounting systems and cash flows, inventory reductions do not translate to reduced inventory costs. JIT for its own sake does not make sense. It must be carefully integrated into the entire supply and manufacturing chain in order to realize its benefits.

Zipkin (1991) offers a very thoughtful piece on the "JIT revolution." His main point is that JIT can have real benefits, but if the pragmatism is not distinguished from the romance, the consequence could be disaster. He cites an example of a manager of a computer assembly plant who was ordered to reduce his WIP inventory to zero in six months. This was the result, apparently, of the experiences of the CFO, who had attended a JIT seminar that inspired him to promote massive inventory reductions.

Finally, as noted by Karmarkar (1989), the issue is not to make a choice between MRP and JIT, but to make the best use of both techniques. JIT reacts very slowly to sudden changes in demand, while MRP incorporates demand forecasts into the plan. Does that mean that Toyota, famous for their JIT system, ignores demand forecasts in their manufacturing planning and control? Very unlikely. Understanding what different methodologies offer and their limitations leads to a manufacturing planning and control system that is well designed and efficient. Improvements should be incremental, not revolutionary.

8.8 JIT OR LEAN PRODUCTION?

In recent years the term *lean production* has become commonplace. Is lean production just another term for JIT? Yes and no. Lean production has come to encompass more than JIT, but the goal is the same, namely, to reduce work-in-process inventories to a bare minimum. The term lean production seems to be due to Womack et al. (1990) who used it to describe the Toyota Production System.

One might wonder why this chapter is about JIT and not lean production, considering that lean production (or lean manufacturing) seems to be the favored term these days. JIT is a set of principles for moving materiel through the factory that can be compared directly to MRP. Lean production encompasses all of the concepts of JIT elaborated on in this chapter, but has also been linked to six sigma quality programs (discussed in

Chapter 12), cellular manufacturing systems (discussed in Chapter 11), the focused factory (discussed in Chapter 1), and total productive maintenance (discussed in Chapter 12). Hence, lean production encompasses topics that are treated in depth throughout the book, in addition to JIT principles.

When one reads descriptions of lean production systems from practitioners [such as *The Portal to Lean Production* by Nicholas and Soni (2006)], one is struck by a few things. First, practitioners view lean production in a very broad sense as noted above. Second, there appear to be many success stories of lean production concepts implemented in the United States. We know that the EOQ and EPQ formulas developed in Chapter 4 can be used to determine appropriate run sizes in a factory. Are not these concepts fundamentally at odds with those of lean production? The answer is yes, they are. Run sizes recommended by these formulas could be large depending on costs and usage rates, which is verboten in a lean production system. Which is the better approach?

The answer is that it depends. If the objective is to set run sizes to balance holding and setup costs, the models of Chapter 4 (and Chapter 5 when uncertainty is included) are fine. However, there are many costs and benefits that these models ignore because they are difficult to quantify. How does one quantify the cost of having to rework a large batch of items because a setting on a machine was wrong? How does one quantify the chaos that results from having large stockpiles of work-in-process inventory all over the plant? Thus, many of the benefits of lean production and JIT are hard to incorporate into a model. Simple economic trade-offs tell only a small part of the story. This suggests that modeling the true benefits of lean production is an area of opportunity for researchers. When we have models that take into account all of the costs and benefits of these disparate approaches to running the factory, we can make more intelligent comparisons among different production planning philosophies.

8.9 HISTORICAL NOTES

The specific term *MRP* is relatively new, although the concept of materials planning based on predicted demand and product structures appears to have been around for quite a while. In fact, there is a reference to this approach by Alfred Sloan (1964), who refers to a purely technical calculation by analysts at General Motors in 1921 of the quantity of materials needed for production of a given number of cars. The term *BOM* (bill of materials) *explosion* was commonly used to describe what is now called MRP.

The books by Orlicky (1975) and New (1974) did a great deal to legitimize MRP as a valid and identifiable technique, although the term seems to have been around since the mid-1960s. In addition, the well-known practitioners George Plossl and Oliver Wight also must be given credit for popularizing the method (see, for example, Plossl and Wight, 1971). In Anderson, Schroeder, Tupy, and White (1982) the authors state that the first computerized MRP systems were implemented close to 1970. The number of installed systems has increased since that time at an exponential rate.

Interestingly, much of the work on optimal and suboptimal lot-sizing methods predates the formal recognition of MRP. The seminal paper in this area was by Wagner and Whitin (1958), who first recognized the optimality of an exact requirements policy for periodic-review inventory control systems with time-varying demand, and developed the dynamic programming algorithm described in this chapter. The

Silver–Meal heuristic when opportunities for replenishment are at the start of periods appeared in Silver and Meal (1973). DeMatteis (1968) is generally credited with the part period balancing approach. However, the paper by Gorham (1968) refers to both part period balancing (called the least total cost approach) and least unit cost methods, suggesting that these methods were well known at the time. It is likely that both methods were developed by practitioners before 1968 but were not reported in the literature.

The lot-shifting algorithm for the capacitated problem outlined in Section 8.4 is very similar to one developed by Karni (1981). Similar ideas were explored by Dixon and Silver (1981) as well. Lot sizing is not always used by practitioners in operational MRP systems because of the effect that small errors at a high level of the product structure are telescoped into large errors at a lower level. Furthermore, lot-sizing algorithms require estimation of the holding and setup costs and more calculations than the simple lot-for-lot policy.

The historical references to JIT are contained within the chapter. It is unclear who coined the term JIT, but the concept is clearly derived from Toyota's kanban system. SMED (single minute exchange of dies) has played an important role in the success of the Japanese lean production methods. Shigeo Shingo is generally credited with its development.

8.10 Summary

Materials requirements planning (MRP) is a set of procedures for converting forecast demand for a manufactured product into a requirements schedule for the components, subassemblies, and raw materials comprising that product. A closely related concept is that of the *master production schedule* (MPS), which is a specification of the projected needs of the end product by time period. The *explosion calculus* represents the set of rules and procedures for converting the MPS into the requirements at lower levels. The information required to do the explosion calculus is contained in the *product structure diagram* and the *indented bill-of-materials list*. The two key pieces of information contained in the product structure diagram are the production lead times needed to produce the specific component and the multiplier giving the number of units of the component required to produce one item at the next higher level of the product structure.

Many MRP systems are based on a *lot-for-lot* production schedule. That is, the number of units of a component produced in a period is the same as the requirements for that component in that period. However, if setup and holding costs can be estimated accurately, it is possible to find other lot-sizing rules that are more economical. The optimal lot-sizing procedure is the Wagner–Whitin algorithm. However, the method is rarely used in practice, largely because of the relative complexity of the calculations required (although such calculations take very little time on a computer). We explored three heuristic methods that require fewer calculations than the Wagner–Whitin algorithm, although none of these methods will necessarily give an optimal solution. They are the *Silver–Meal heuristic,* the *least unit cost heuristic,* and *part period balancing.*

We also treated the dynamic lot-sizing problem when capacity constraints exist. One of the limitations of MRP is that capacities are ignored. This is especially important if lot sizing is incorporated into the system. Finding optimal solutions to a capacity-constrained inventory system subject to time-varying demand is an extremely difficult problem. (For those of you familiar with the term, the problem is said to be NP complete, which is a reference to the level of difficulty.) A straightforward heuristic method for obtaining a solution to the capacitated lot-sizing problem was presented. However, incorporating such a method into the MRP system will, in and of itself, *not* solve the complete

480 Chapter Eight *Push and Pull Production Control Systems: MRP and JIT*

capacitated MRP problem, because even if a particular lot-sizing schedule is feasible at one level, there is no guarantee that it will result in a feasible requirements schedule at a lower level.

Truly optimal lot-sizing solutions for an MRP system would require formulating the problem as an integer program in order to determine the optimal decisions for all levels simultaneously. For real assembly systems, which can be as many as 10 to 15 levels deep, this would result in an enormous mathematical programming problem. In view of the host of other issues concerned with implementing MRP, the marginal benefit one might achieve from multilevel optimization would probably not justify the effort involved.

System nervousness is one problem that arises when implementing an MRP system. The term refers to the unanticipated changes in a schedule that result when the planning horizon is rolled forward by one period. Another difficulty is that in many circumstances, production lead times depend on the lot sizes: MRP assumes that production lead times are fixed. Still another problem is that the yields at various levels of the process may not be perfect. If the yield rates can be accurately estimated in advance, these rates can be factored into the calculations in a straightforward manner. However, in many industries the yield rates may be difficult to estimate in advance.

Manufacturing resource planning (MRP II) attempts to deal with some of the problems of implementing MRP by integrating the financial, accounting, and marketing functions into the production-planning function.

In this chapter we also discussed just-in-time. Just-in-time is an inventory control system whose goal is to reduce work-in-process to a bare minimum. The concepts are based on the production control systems used by Toyota in Japan in the 1970s. JIT is a pull system, whereas MRP is a push system. Parts are transferred from one level to the next only when requested. In addition to reduced inventories, this approach allows workers to quickly locate quality control problems. Because parts are moved through the system in small batches, defects can be identified quickly. By the nature of the system, stopping production at one location automatically stops production on the entire line so that the source of the problem can be identified and corrected before defective inventories build up.

An important aspect of JIT is reduction of production lot sizes. To make small lot sizes economical, it is necessary to reduce fixed costs of changeover. This is the goal of single minute exchange of dies (SMED). By dividing the die- or tool-changing operation into portions that can be done off-line and those that must be done on-line, enormous reductions in setup times can be achieved.

Kanban and JIT are closely related. Kanban is a manual information system for implementing JIT that relies on cards or tickets to signal the need for more product. While not very high-tech, the method has worked well in practice.

JIT has several disadvantages vis-à-vis MRP as well as several advantages. JIT will react more quickly if a problem develops. However, JIT systems are very slow to react to changes in the pattern of demand. MRP, on the other hand, builds forecasts directly into the explosion calculus.

Additional Problems for Chapter 8

41. CalcIt produces a line of inexpensive pocket calculators. One model, IT53, is a solar-powered scientific model with a liquid crystal display (LCD). The calculator is pictured in Figure 8–11.

    Each calculator requires four solar cells, 40 buttons, one LCD display, and one main processor. All parts are ordered from outside suppliers, but final assembly is done

FIGURE 8–11
CalcIt Model IT53
Scientific Calculator
(Problem 41)

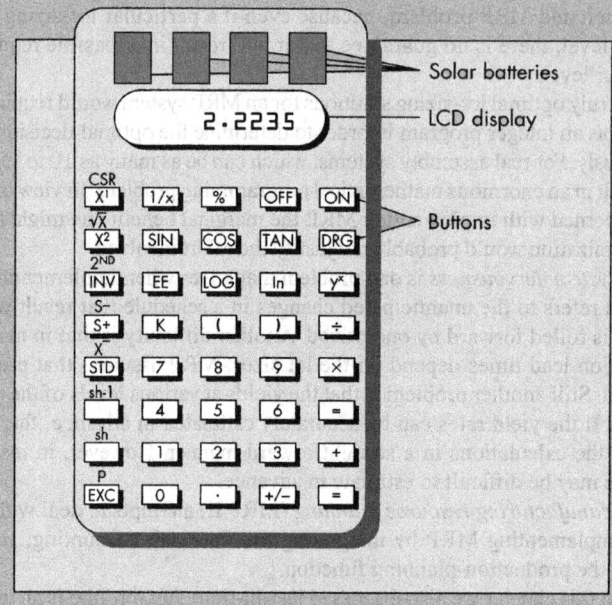

by CalcIt. The processors must be in stock three weeks before the anticipated completion date of a batch of calculators to allow enough time to set the processor in the casing, connect the appropriate wiring, and allow the setting paste to dry. The buttons must be in stock two weeks in advance and are set by hand into the calculators. The LCD displays and the solar cells are ordered from the same supplier and need to be in stock one week in advance.

Based on firm orders that CalcIt has obtained, the master production schedule for IT53 for a 10-week period starting at week 8 is given by

Week	8	9	10	11	12	13	14	15	16	17
MPS	1,200	1,200	800	1,000	1,000	300	2,200	1,400	1,800	600

Determine the gross requirements schedule for the solar cells, the buttons, the LCD display, and the main processor chips.

42. Consider the example of the CalcIt Company for Problem 41. Suppose that the buttons used in the calculators cost $0.02 each and the company estimates a fixed cost of $12 for placing and receiving orders of the buttons from an outside supplier. Assume that holding costs are based on a 24 percent annual interest rate and that there are 48 weeks to a year. Using the gross requirements schedule for the buttons determined in Problem 41, what order policy does the Silver–Meal heuristic recommend for the buttons? (Hint: Express h as a cost per 10,000 units and divide each demand by 10,000.)

43. Solve Problem 42 using part period balancing and least unit cost. Compare the costs of the resulting solutions to the cost of the solution obtained by using the Silver–Meal heuristic.

44. *Work-in-process* (WIP) *inventory* is a term that refers to the inventory of components and subassemblies in a manufacturing process. Assuming lot-for-lot scheduling at all

levels, theoretically the WIP inventory should be zero. Do you think that this is likely to be the case in a real manufacturing environment? Discuss the possible reasons for large WIP inventories occurring even when an MRP system is used.

45. Vivian Lowe is planning a surprise party for her husband's 50th birthday. She has decided to serve shish kabob. The recipe that she is using calls for two pineapple chunks for each shrimp. She plans to size the kabobs so that each has three shrimp. She estimates that a single pineapple will yield about 50 chunks, but from past experience, about 1 out of every 10 pineapples is bad and has to be thrown out. She has invited 200 people and expects that about half will show up. Each person generally eats about 2 kabobs.

    a. How many pineapples should she buy?
    b. Suppose that the number of guests is a random variable having the normal distribution with mean 100 and variance 1,680. If she wants to make enough kabobs to feed all the guests with probability 95 percent, how many pineapples should she buy?

46. In this chapter, we assumed that the "time bucket" was one week. This implies that forecasts are reevaluated and the MRP system rerun on a weekly basis.

    a. Discuss the potential advantages of using a shorter time bucket, such as a day.
    b. Discuss the potential advantages of using a longer time bucket, such as two weeks or a month.

47. Develop a spreadsheet that reproduces the calculations for Example 8.1. As in the example, the spreadsheet should include the net predicted demand for trumpets. The columns should correspond to weeks and should be labeled 1 to 18. Below the net predicted demand for trumpets should be the calculations for the valve casing assembly, and below that the calculations for the valves. For each component, include rows for the following information: (1) gross requirements, (2) scheduled receipts, (3) on-hand inventory, (4) time-phased net requirements, and (5) lot-for-lot planned order release. Your spreadsheet should automatically update all calculations if the net predicted demand for trumpets changes.

48. Two end products, EP1 and EP2, are produced in the Raleigh, North Carolina, plant of a large manufacturer of furniture products located in the Southeast. The product structure diagrams for these products appear in Figure 8–12.

FIGURE 8–12
Product structure diagrams (for Problem 48)

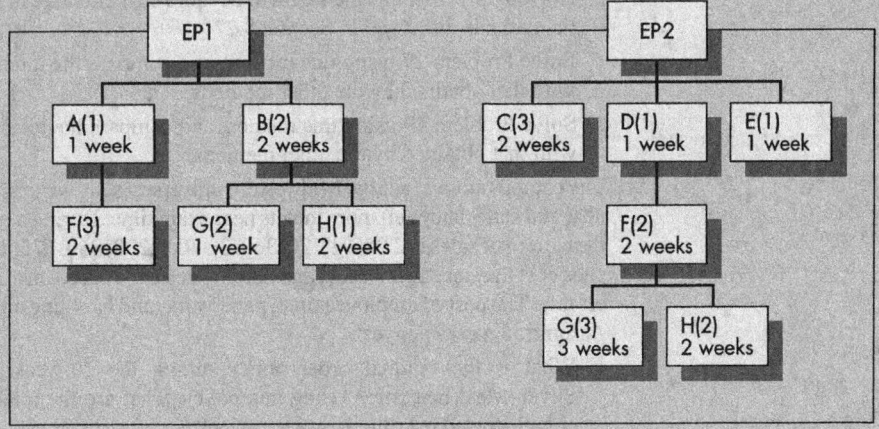

Suppose that the master production schedules for these two products are

Week	18	19	20	21	22	23	24
EP1	120	112	76	22	56	90	210
EP2	62	68	90	77	26	30	54

Assuming lot-for-lot production, determine the planned order releases for components F, G, and H.

49. A component used in a manufacturing facility is ordered from an outside supplier. Because the component is used in a variety of end products, the demand is high. Estimated demand (in thousands) over the next 10 weeks is

Week	1	2	3	4	5	6	7	8	9	10
Demand	22	34	32	12	8	44	54	16	76	30

The components cost 65 cents each and the interest rate used to compute the holding cost is 0.5 percent per week. The fixed order cost is estimated to be $200. (Hint: Express h as the holding cost per thousand units.)

a. What ordering policy is recommended by the Silver–Meal heuristic?

b. What ordering policy is recommended by the part period balancing heuristic?

c. What ordering policy is recommended by the least unit cost heuristic?

d. Which method resulted in the lowest-cost policy for this problem?

50. A popular heuristic lot-sizing method is known as period order quantity (POQ). The method requires determining the average number of periods spanned by the EOQ and choosing the lot size to equal this fixed period supply. Let λ be the total demand over an N-period planning horizon $[\lambda = (\Sigma\, r_i/n)]$ and assume that EOQ is computed as described in Section 8.2. Then $P = \text{EOQ}/\lambda$ rounded to the nearest integer. For the example in Section 8.2, $P = 139/43.9 = 3.17$, which is rounded to 3. The POQ would call for setting the lot size equal to three periods of demand. For the example in Section 8.2, the resulting planned order release would be 116, 0, 0, 150, 0, 0, 135, 0, 0, 38.

a. Compare the cost of the policy obtained by this method for the example in Section 8.2 to that obtained using the EOQ.

b. What are the advantages of this approach over EOQ?

c. Do you think that this method will be more cost effective in general than the heuristic methods discussed in Section 8.2?

d. Solve Problem 17 using this method, and compare the total holding and setup cost with that obtained by the other methods.

e. Solve Problem 49 using this method, and compare the total holding and setup cost with that obtained by the other methods.

51. The campus store at a large Midwestern university sells writing tablets to students, faculty, and staff. They sell more tablets near exam time. During a typical 10-week quarter, the pattern of sales is 2,280, 1,120, 360, 3,340, 1,230, 860, 675, 1,350, 4,600, 1,210. The pads cost the store $1.20 each, and holding costs are based on a 30 percent annual interest rate. The cost of employee time, paperwork, and handling amounts to $30 per order. Assume 50 weeks per year.

a. What is the optimal order policy during the 10-week quarter based on the Silver–Meal heuristic? Using this policy, what are the total holding and ordering costs incurred over the 10-week period?

484 Chapter Eight *Push and Pull Production Control Systems: MRP and JIT*

b. The bookstore manager has decided that it would be more economical if the demand were the same each week. In order to even out the demand he limits weekly sales (to the annoyance of his clientele). Hence, assume that the total demand for the 10-week quarter is still the same, but the sales are constant from week to week. Determine the optimal order policy in this case and compare the total holding and ordering cost over the 10 weeks to the answer you obtained in part (a). (You may assume continuous time for the purposes of your calculations, so that the optimal lot size is the EOQ.)

c. Based on the results of parts (a) and (b), do you think that it is more economical in general to face a smooth or a spiky demand pattern?

52. Develop a spreadsheet template for finding Silver–Meal solutions for general lot-sizing problems. Store the holding and setup cost parameters in separate cell locations so that they can be inputted and changed easily. Allow for 30 periods of demand to be inputted in column 2 of the spreadsheet. List the period numbers 1, 2, . . . , 30 in column 1. Work out the logic that gives $C(j)$ in column 3.

One would use such a spreadsheet in the following way: Input requirements period by period until an increase is observed in column 3. This identifies the first forecast horizon. Now replace entries in column 2 with zeros and input requirements starting at the current period. Continue until the next forecast horizon is identified. Repeat this process until the end of the planning horizon. Use this method to find the Silver–Meal solution for the following production planning problems:

a. Solve Problem 14 in this manner.

b. Weekly demands for 2-inch rivets at a division of an aircraft company are predicted to be (in gross)

Week	1	2	3	4	5	6	7	8	9	10	11	12
Demand	240	280	370	880	950	120	135	450	875	500	400	200
Week	13	14	15	16	17	18	19	20	21	22	23	24
Demand	600	650	1,250	250	800	700	750	200	100	900	400	700

Setup costs for ordering the rivets are estimated to be $200, and holding costs amount to 10 cents per gross per week. Find the lot sizing given by the Silver–Meal method.

53. Along the lines described in Problem 52, construct a spreadsheet for finding the least unit cost lot-sizing rule.

a. Solve both parts (a) and (b) of Problem 52.

b. Which method, least unit cost or Silver–Meal, gave the more cost-effective solution?

Appendix 8–A

Optimal Lot Sizing for Time-Varying Demand

The techniques considered in Section 8.3 are easy to use and give lot sizes with costs that are generally near the true optimal. This appendix considers how one would go about computing true optimal lot sizes. Optimal in this context means the policy that minimizes the total holding and setup cost over the planning horizon. This appendix shows how optimal policies can be determined by casting the problem as a shortest-path problem. It also shows how dynamic programming can be used to find the shortest path.

Assume that:

1. Forecasted demands over the next n periods are known and given by the vector $\mathbf{r} = (r_1, \ldots, r_n)$.
2. Costs are charged against holding at $\$h$ per unit per period and $\$K$ per setup. We will assume that the holding cost is charged against ending inventory each period.

In order to get some idea of the potential difficulty of this problem, consider the following simple example.

Example 8A.1

The forecast demand for an electronic assembly produced at Hi-Tech, a local semiconductor fabrication shop, over the next four weeks is 52, 87, 23, 56. There is only one setup each week for production of these assemblies, and there is no back-ordering of excess demand. Assume that the shop has the capacity to produce any number of the assemblies in a week.

Consider the total number of feasible production policies for Hi-Tech over the four-week period. Let $y_1, \ldots, y_4$ be the order quantities in each of the four weeks. Clearly $y_1 \geq 52$ in order to guarantee that we do not stock out in period 1. If we assume that ending inventory in period 4 is zero (which will be easy to show is optimal), then $y_1 \leq 218$, the sum of all the demands. Hence y_1 can take any one of 167 possible values. Consider y_2. The number of feasible values of y_2 depends upon the value of y_1. As no stock-out is permitted to occur in period 2, $y_1 + y_2 \geq 52 + 87 = 139$. If

$$y_1 \leq 139, \quad \text{then } 139 - y_1 \leq y_2 \leq 218 - y_1,$$

and if

$$y_1 > 139, \quad \text{then } 0 \leq y_2 \leq 218 - y_1.$$

With a little effort, one can show that this results in a total of 10,200 different values of just the pair (y_1, y_2). It is thus clear that for even moderately sized problems the number of feasible solutions is enormous.

Searching all the feasible policies is unreasonable. However, an important discovery by Wagner and Whitin reduces considerably the number of policies one must consider as candidates for optimality.

The Wagner–Whitin algorithm is based on the following observation:

Result. An optimal policy has the property that each value of $\mathbf{y}$ is exactly the sum of a set of future demands. (We will call this an exact requirements policy.) That is,

$$y_1 = r_1, \quad \text{or } y_1 = r_1 + r_2, \ldots, \quad \text{or } y_1 = r_1 + r_2 + \cdots + r_n.$$
$$y_2 = 0, \quad \text{or } y_2 = r_2, \quad \text{or } y_2 = r_2 + r_3, \ldots, \quad \text{or}$$
$$y_2 = r_2 + r_3 + \cdots + r_n$$
$$\vdots$$
$$y_n = 0 \quad \text{or } y_n = r_n.$$

An exact requirements policy is completely specified by designating the periods in which ordering is to take place. The number of exact requirements policies is much smaller than the total number of feasible policies.

Example 8A.1 (continued)

We continue with the four-period scheduling problem. Because y_1 must satisfy exact requirements, we see that it can assume values of 52, 139, 162, or 218 only; that is, only four distinct values. Ignoring the value of y_1, y_2 can assume values 0, 87, 110, 166. It is easy to see that every exact requirements policy is completely determined by specifying in what periods ordering should

FIGURE 8A–1
Network representation for lot scheduling (Example 8A.1)

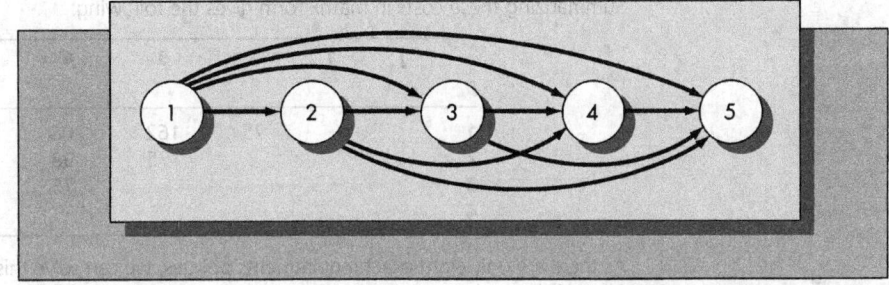

take place. That is, each such policy is the form $(i_1, \ldots, i_n)$, where the values of i_j are either 0 or 1. If $i_j = 1$, then production takes place in period j. Note that $i_1 = 1$ because we must produce in period 1 to avoid stocking out, whereas $i_2, \ldots, i_n$ will each be either 0 or 1. For example, the policy (1, 0, 1, 0) means that production occurs in periods 1 and 3 only. It follows that $\mathbf{y} = (139, 0, 79, 0)$. For this example, there are exactly $2^3 = 8$ distinct exact requirements policies.

A convenient way to look at the problem is as a one-way network with the number of nodes equal to exactly one more than the number of periods. Every path through the network corresponds to a specific exact requirements policy. The network for the four-period problem appears in Figure 8A–1.

For any pair (i, j) with $i < j$, if the arc (i, j) is on the path, it means that ordering takes place in period i and the order size is equal to the sum of the requirements in periods $i, i + 1, \ldots, j - 1$. Period j is the next period of ordering. Note that all paths end at period $n + 1$. The policy of ordering in periods 1 and 3 only would correspond to the path 1–3–5. The path 1–2–4–5 means that ordering is to take place in periods 1, 2, and 4.

The next step is to assign a value to each arc in the network. The value or "length" of the arc (i, j), called c_{ij}, is defined as the setup and holding cost of ordering in period i to meet requirements through period $j - 1$. For example, c_{15} = the cost of ordering in period 1 to satisfy the demands in periods 1 through 4.

Finally, we would like to determine the minimum-cost production schedule, or shortest path through the network. As we will see, *dynamic programming* is one method of solving this problem. However, for a small problem, the optimal policy can be found by simply enumerating the paths through the network and choosing one with minimum cost.

Example 8A.2 We will solve Example 8A.1 using path enumeration. Recall that $\mathbf{r} = (52, 87, 23, 56)$. In addition, assume that there is a cost of holding of $h = \$1$ per unit per period and a cost of $K = \$75$ per setup.

The first step is to compute c_{ij} for $1 \leq i \leq 4$ and $i + 1 \leq j \leq 5$.

$c_{12} = 75$ (setup cost only).
$c_{13} = 75 + 87 = 162$.
$c_{14} = 75 + (23 \times 2) + 87 = 208$.
$c_{15} = 75 + (56 \times 3) + (23 \times 2) + 87 = 376$.
$c_{23} = 75$.
$c_{24} = 75 + 23 = 98$.
$c_{25} = 75 + 23 + (56 \times 2) = 210$.
$c_{34} = 75$.
$c_{35} = 75 + 56 = 131$.
$c_{45} = 75$.

Summarizing these costs in matrix form gives the following:

i \ j	1	2	3	4	5
1		75	162	208	376
2			75	98	210
3				75	131
4					75

As there are only eight exact requirements policies, we can solve this problem by enumerating the policies and comparing the costs.

Path	Cost
1–2–3–4–5	$300
1–2–4–5	248
1–2–5	285
1–2–3–5	281
1–3–4–5	312
1–3–5	293
1–4–5	283
1–5	376

It follows that the optimal path is 1–2–4–5 at a cost of $248. This corresponds to ordering in periods 1, 2, and 4 only. The optimal ordering policy is $y_1 = 52$, $y_2 = 110$, $y_3 = 0$, $y_4 = 56$.

*SOLUTION BY DYNAMIC PROGRAMMING

The total number of exact requirements policies for a problem of n periods is 2^{n-1}. As n gets large, total enumeration is not efficient. Dynamic programming is a recursive solution technique that can significantly reduce the number of computations required, although it too can be quite cumbersome.

Dynamic programming is based on the *principle of optimality*. One version of this principle is that if a problem consists of exactly n stages and there are $r < n$ stages remaining, the optimal policy for the remaining stages is independent of policy adopted in the previous stages. Because dynamic programming is not used anywhere else in this text, we will not present a detailed discussion of it. The interested reader should refer to Hillier and Lieberman (1990) for a brief overview or Nemhauser (1966) for a more in-depth treatment at a mathematical level consistent with ours.

Define f_k as the minimum cost starting at node k, assuming that an order is placed in period k. The principle of optimality for this problem results in the following system of equations:

$$f_k = \min_{j>k}(c_{kj} + f_j) \quad \text{for } k = 1, \ldots, n.$$

The initial condition is $f_{n+1} = 0$.

Example 8A.3   We will solve Example 8A.1 by dynamic programming in order to illustrate the technique. One starts with the initial condition and works backward from period $n + 1$ to period 1.[4] In each period one determines the value of j that achieves the minimum.

[4] Actually, the original Wagner–Whitin (1958) algorithm is based on a forward dynamic programming formulation. Although the forward formulation has some advantages for planning horizon analysis, we feel that backward recursion is more natural and more intuitive.

$f_5 = 0$.

$$f_4 = \min_{j>4}(c_{4j} + f_j)$$
$$= 75 \quad \text{at } j = 5 \text{ (the only possible value of } j\text{)}.$$

$$f_3 = \min_{j>3}(c_{3j} + f_j) = \min\begin{Bmatrix} c_{34} + f_4 \\ c_{35} + f_5 \end{Bmatrix} = \min\begin{Bmatrix} 75 + 75 \\ 131 + 0 \end{Bmatrix} = \min\begin{Bmatrix} 150 \\ 131 \end{Bmatrix}$$
$$= 131 \quad \text{at } j = 5.$$

$$f_2 = \min_{j>2}(c_{2j} + f_j) = \min\begin{Bmatrix} c_{23} + f_3 \\ c_{24} + f_4 \\ c_{25} + f_5 \end{Bmatrix} = \min\begin{Bmatrix} 75 + 131 \\ 98 + 75 \\ 210 + 0 \end{Bmatrix} = \min\begin{Bmatrix} 206 \\ 173 \\ 210 \end{Bmatrix}$$
$$= 173 \quad \text{at } j = 4.$$

Finally,

$$f_1 = \min_{j>1}(c_{1j} + f_j) = \min\begin{Bmatrix} c_{12} + f_2 \\ c_{13} + f_3 \\ c_{14} + f_4 \\ c_{15} + f_5 \end{Bmatrix} = \min\begin{Bmatrix} 75 + 173 \\ 162 + 131 \\ 208 + 75 \\ 376 + 0 \end{Bmatrix} = \min\begin{Bmatrix} 248 \\ 293 \\ 283 \\ 376 \end{Bmatrix}$$
$$= 248 \quad \text{at } j = 2.$$

To determine the optimal order policy, we retrace the solution back from the beginning. In period 1 the optimal value of j is $j = 2$. This means that the production level in period 1 is equal to the demand in period 1, so that $y_1 = r_1 = 52$. The next order period is period 2. The optimal value of j in period 2 is $j = 4$, which implies that the production quantity in period 2 is equal to the sum of the demands in periods 2 and 3, or $y_2 = r_2 + r_3 = 110$. The next period of ordering is period 4. The optimal value of j in period 4 is $j = 5$. This gives $y_4 = r_4 = 56$. Hence, the optimal order policy is $\mathbf{y} = (52, 110, 0, 56)$.

Appendix 8–B

Glossary of Notation for Chapter 8

$C(T)$ = Average holding and setup cost per period (for Silver–Meal heuristic) or per unit (LUC heuristic) if the current order spans T periods.

c_i = Production capacity in period i.

c_{ij} = Cost associated with arc (i, j) in network representation of lot scheduling problem used for Wagner–Whitin algorithm.

f_j = Minimum cost from period i to the end of the horizon (refer to the dynamic programming algorithm for Wagner–Whitin).

h = Holding cost per unit per time period.

K = Setup cost for initiating an order.

r_i = Requirement for period i.

y_i = Production lot size in period i.

Bibliography

Anderson, J. C.; R. G. Schroeder; S. E. Tupy; and E. M. White. "Material Requirements Planning Systems: The State of the Art." *Production and Inventory Management* 23 (1982), pp. 51–66.

Carlson, R. C.; S. L. Beckman; and D. H. Kropp. "The Effectiveness of Extending the Horizon in Rolling Production Scheduling." *Decision Sciences* 13 (1982), pp. 129–46.

Carlson, R. C.; J. V. Jucker; and D. H. Kropp. "Less Nervous MRP Systems: A Dynamic Economic Lot-Sizing Approach." *Management Science* 25 (1979), pp. 754–61.

Carlson, R. C.; J. V. Jucker; and D. H. Kropp. "Heuristic Lot Sizing Approaches for Dealing with MRP System Nervousness." *Decision Sciences* 14 (1983), pp. 156–69.

Chhikara, J., and E. N. Weiss. "JIT Savings—Myth or Reality?" *Business Horizons* 38 (May–June 1995), pp. 73–78.

DeMatteis, J. J. "An Economic Lot Sizing Technique: The Part-Period Algorithm." *IBM Systems Journal* 7 (1968), pp. 30–38.

Dixon, P. S., and E. A. Silver. "A Heuristic Solution Procedure for the Multi-Item, Single-Level, Limited Capacity Lot Sizing Problem." *Journal of Operations Management* 2 (1981), pp. 23–39.

Gorham, T. "Dynamic Order Quantities." *Production and Inventory Management* 9 (1968), pp. 75–81.

Hillier, F. S., and G. J. Lieberman. *Introduction to Operations Research.* 5th ed. New York: McGraw-Hill, 1990.

Hopp, W., and M. Spearman. *Factory Physics.* Burr Ridge, IL: Richard D. Irwin, 1996.

Jacobson, G., and J. Hillkirk. *Xerox, American Samurai.* New York: MacMillan, 1986.

Karmarkar, U. "Getting Control of Just-In-Time." *Harvard Business Review* 67 (September–October 1989), pp. 122–31.

Karni, R. "Maximum Part Period Gain (MPG)—A Lot Sizing Procedure for Unconstrained and Constrained Requirements Planning Systems." *Production and Inventory Management* 22 (1981), pp. 91–98.

Krajewski, L. J.; B. E. King; L. P. Ritzman; and D. S. Wong. "Kanban, MRP, and Shaping the Manufacturing Environment." *Management Science* 33 (1987), pp. 39–57.

Love, Stephen. *Inventory Control.* New York: McGraw-Hill, 1979.

Meal, H. "Putting Production Decisions Where They Belong." *Harvard Business Review* 62 (1984), pp. 102–11.

Monden, Y. "What Makes the Toyota Production System Really Tick?" *Industrial Engineering* 13, no. 1 (1981a), pp. 36–46.

Monden, Y. "Adaptable Kanban System Helps Toyota Maintain Just-in-Time Production." *Industrial Engineering* 13, no. 5 (1981b), pp. 28–46.

Nahmias, S., and K. Moinzadeh. "Lot Sizing with Randomly Graded Yields." *Operations Research* 46, no. 6 (1997), pp. 974–86.

Nemhauser, G. L. *Introduction to Dynamic Programming.* New York: John Wiley & Sons, 1966.

New, C. *Requirements Planning.* Essex, England: Gower Press, 1974.

Nicholas, J., and A. Soni. *The Portal to Lean Production.* Boca Raton, Auerbach Publications, 2006.

Orlicky, J. *Materials Requirements Planning.* New York: McGraw-Hill, 1975.

Plossl, G., and O. Wight. *Materials Requirements Planning by Computer.* Washington, DC: American Production and Inventory Control Society, 1971.

Sheldon, D. "MRP II Implementation: A Case Study." *Hospital Materiel Management Quarterly* 15, no. 4 (1994), pp. 48–52.

Shingo, S. *Study of "Toyota" Production System from Industrial Engineering Viewpoint.* Tokyo: Japan Management Association, 1981.

Silver, E. A., and H. C. Meal. "A Heuristic for Selecting Lot Size Quantities for the Case of a Deterministic Time-Varying Demand Rate and Discrete Opportunities for Replenishment." *Production and Inventory Management* 14 (1973), pp. 64–74.

Silver, E. A., and R. Peterson. *Decision Systems for Inventory Management and Production Planning.* 2nd ed. New York: John Wiley & Sons, 1985.

Sloan, A. *My Years with General Motors.* Garden City, NY: Doubleday, 1964.

Steele, D. C. "The Nervous MRP System: How to Do Battle." *Production and Inventory Management* 16 (1973), pp. 83–89.

Vollman, T. E.; W. L. Berry; and D. C. Whybark. *Manufacturing and Control Systems.* 3rd ed. New York: McGraw-Hill/Irwin, 1992.

Wagner, H. M., and T. M. Whitin. "Dynamic Version of the Economic Lot Size Model." *Management Science* 5 (1958), pp. 89–96.

Willis, R. "Harley Davidson Comes Roaring Back." *Management Review* 75 (March 1986), pp. 20–27.

Womack, J. P.; D. T. Jones; and D. Roos. *The Machine That Changed the World: The Story of Lean Production.* New York: Harper Perennial, 1990.

Zipkin, P. "Does Manufacturing Need a JIT Revolution?" *Harvard Business Review* 69 (January–February 1991), pp. 40–50.

Chapter Nine

Operations Scheduling

"I have an unbelievable assistant who handles all of my scheduling! It's like a Tetris game."
—Neil Patrick Harris

Chapter Overview

Purpose

To gain an understanding of the key methods and results for sequence scheduling in a job shop environment.

Key Points

1. *The job shop scheduling problem.* A job shop is a set of machines and workers who use the machines. Jobs may arrive all at once or randomly throughout the day. For example, consider an automotive repair facility. On any day, one cannot predict in advance exactly what kinds of repairs will come to the shop. Different jobs require different equipment and possibly different personnel. A senior mechanic might be assigned to a complex job, such as a transmission replacement, while a junior mechanic would be assigned to routine maintenance. Suppose the customers bring their cars in first thing in the morning. The shop foreman must determine the sequence in which to schedule the jobs in the shop to make the most efficient use of the resources (both human and machine) available.

   The relevant characteristics of the sequencing problem include
   - The pattern of arrivals.
   - Number and variety of machines.
   - Number and types of workers.
   - Patterns of job flow in the shop.
   - Objectives for evaluating alternative sequencing rules.

2. *Sequencing rules.* The sequencing rules that we consider in this section include.
   - *First come first served (FCFS).* Schedule jobs in the order they arrive to the shop.
   - *Shortest processing time (SPT) first.* Schedule the next job with the shortest processing time.
   - *Earliest due date (EDD).* Schedule the jobs that have the earliest due date first.
   - *Critical ratio (CR) scheduling.* The critical ratio is (due date − current time)/processing time. Schedule the job with the smallest CR value next.

3. *Sequencing results.* A common criterion for evaluating the effectiveness of sequencing rules is the mean flow time. The flow time of any job is the amount of time that elapses from the point that the job arrives in the shop to the point

that the job is completed. The mean flow time is just the average of all the flow times for all the jobs. The main result of this section is that SPT scheduling minimizes the mean flow time. Another result of interest is that if the objective is to minimize the maximum lateness, then the jobs should be scheduled by EDD. This section also deals with several scheduling algorithms. Moore's algorithm minimizes the number of tardy jobs, and Lawler's algorithm is used when precedence constraints are present (that is, jobs must be done in a certain order).

All the preceding results apply to a single machine or single facility. When scheduling jobs on multiple machines, the problem is much more complex. In this case, there are a few known results. Consider the case of n jobs that must be scheduled on two machines. The main result discovered in this case is that the optimal solution is to sequence the jobs in the same order on both machines (this is known as a permutation schedule). This means that there are a possible $n!$ feasible solutions. This can, of course, be a very large number. However, a procedure discovered by Johnson (1954) efficiently computes the optimal sequence for n jobs on two machines. Essentially the same algorithm can be applied to three machines under very special circumstances. The problem of scheduling two jobs on m machines can be solved efficiently by a graphical procedure.

4. *Sequence scheduling in a stochastic environment.* The problems alluded to previously assume all information is known with certainty. Real problems are more complex in that there is generally some type of uncertainty present. One source of uncertainty could be the job times. In that case, the job times, say $t_1, t_2, \ldots, t_n$, are assumed to be independent random variables with a known distribution function. The optimal sequence for a single machine in this case is very much like scheduling the jobs in SPT order based on expected processing times.

When scheduling jobs with uncertain processing times on multiple machines, one must assume that the distribution of job times follows an exponential distribution. The exponential distribution is the only one possessing the so-called memoryless property, which turns out to be crucial in the analysis. When the objective is to minimize the expected makespan (that is, the total time to complete all jobs), it turns out that the longest expected processing time (LEPT) first rule is optimal.

Another source of uncertainty in a job shop is the order in which jobs arrive to the shop. In the automotive job shop example, we assumed that jobs arrived all at once at the beginning of the day. However, in a factory setting, jobs are likely to arrive at random times during the day. In this case, queueing theory can shed some light on how much time elapses from the point a job arrives until its completion. This section outlines several results under assumptions of FCFS, LCFS, and SPT sequencing.

5. *Line balancing.* Another problem that arises in the factory setting is that of balancing an assembly line. While line balancing is not a sequence scheduling problem found in a job shop environment, it is certainly a scheduling problem arising within the plant. Assume we have an item flowing down an assembly line and that a total of n tasks must be completed on the item. The problem is to determine which tasks should be placed where on the line. Typically, an assembly line is broken down into stations and some subset of tasks is assigned to each station. The goal is to balance the time required at each station while taking into account the precedence relationships existing among the individual tasks.

Optimal line balances are difficult to find. We consider one heuristic method, which gives reasonable results in most circumstances.

Scheduling is an important aspect of operations control in both manufacturing and service industries. With increased emphasis on time to market and time to volume as well as improved customer satisfaction, efficient scheduling will gain increasing emphasis in the operations function in the coming years.

In some sense, much of what has been discussed so far in this text can be considered a subset of production scheduling. Aggregate planning, treated in Chapter 3, is aimed at macroscheduling of workforce levels and overall production levels for the firm. Detailed inventory control, discussed in Chapters 4 and 5, concerns methods of scheduling production at the individual item level; Chapter 6 treated vehicle scheduling; and MRP, discussed in Chapter 8, provides production schedules for end items and subassemblies in the product structure.

There are many different types of scheduling problems faced by the firm. A partial list includes

1. *Job shop scheduling.* Job shop scheduling, known more commonly in practice as shop floor control, is the set of activities in the shop that transform inputs (a set of requirements) to outputs (products to meet those requirements). Much of this chapter will be concerned with sequencing issues on the shop floor, and more will be said about this problem in Section 9.1.

2. *Personnel scheduling.* Scheduling personnel is an important problem for both manufacturing and service industries. Although shift scheduling on the factory floor may be considered one of the functions of shop floor control, personnel scheduling is a much larger problem. Scheduling health professionals in hospitals and other health facilities is one example. Determining whether to meet peak demand with overtime shifts, night shifts, or subcontracting is another example of a personnel scheduling problem.

3. *Facilities scheduling.* This problem is particularly important when facilities become a bottleneck resource. Scheduling operating rooms at hospitals is one example. As the need for health care increases, some hospitals and health maintenance organizations (HMOs) find that facilities are strained. A similar problem occurs in colleges and universities in which enrollments have increased without commensurate increases in the size of the physical plant.

4. *Vehicle scheduling.* Manufacturing firms must distribute their products in a cost-efficient and timely manner. Some service operations, such as dial-a-ride systems, involve pick-ups and deliveries of goods and/or people. Vehicle routing is a problem that arises in many contexts. Problems such as scheduling snow removal equipment, postal and bank deliveries, and shipments to customers with varying requirements at different locations are some examples. Vehicle scheduling is discussed in Section 6.6.

5. *Vendor scheduling.* For firms with just-in-time (JIT) systems, scheduling deliveries from vendors is an important logistics issue. Purchasing must be coordinated with the entire product delivery system to ensure that JIT production systems function efficiently. Vollman et al. (1992, p. 191) discuss the application of vendor scheduling to the JIT system at Steelcase. (JIT is discussed in Chapters 1 and 8 of this book.)

6. *Project scheduling.* A project may be broken down into a set of interrelated tasks. Although some tasks can be done concurrently, many tasks cannot be started until others are completed. Complex projects may involve thousands of individual tasks that must be coordinated for the project to be completed on time and within budget. Project scheduling is an important component of the planning function, which we treat in detail in Chapter 10.

7. *Dynamic versus static scheduling.* Most scheduling theory that we review in this chapter views the scheduling problem as a static one. Numerous jobs arrive simultaneously to be processed on a set of machines. In practice, many scheduling problems are dynamic in the sense that jobs arrive continuously over time. One example is the problem faced by an air traffic controller who must schedule runways for arriving planes. The problem is a dynamic one in that planes arrive randomly and runways are freed up and committed randomly over time. Dynamic scheduling problems, treated in Section 9 of this chapter, are analyzed using the tools of queueing theory (discussed in detail in Supplement 2, which follows this chapter).

Scheduling is a complex but extremely important operations function. The purpose of this chapter is to give the reader the flavor of the kinds of results one can obtain using analytical models, and to show how these models can be used to solve certain classes of scheduling problems. Our focus is primarily on job shop scheduling, but we consider several other scheduling problems as well.

9.1 PRODUCTION SCHEDULING AND THE HIERARCHY OF PRODUCTION DECISIONS

Crucial to controlling production operations is the detailed scheduling of various aspects of the production function. We may view the production function in a company as a hierarchical process. First, the firm must forecast demand for aggregate sales over some predetermined planning horizon. These forecasts provide the input for determining the sales and operations planning function discussed in Chapter 3. The production plan then must be translated into the master production schedule (MPS). The MPS results in specific production goals by product and time period.

Materials requirements planning (MRP), treated in detail in Chapter 8, is one method for meeting specific production goals of finished-goods inventory generated by the MPS. The MRP system "explodes" the production levels one obtains from the MPS analysis back in time to obtain production targets at each level of assembly by time period. The result of the MRP analysis is specific planned order releases for final products, subassemblies, and components.

Finally, the planned order releases must be translated into a set of tasks and the due dates associated with those tasks. This level of detailed planning results in the shop floor schedule. Because the MRP or other lot scheduling system usually recommends revisions in the planned order releases, shop floor schedules change frequently. The hierarchy of production planning decisions is shown schematically in Figure 9–1.

Shop floor control means scheduling personnel and equipment in a work center to meet the due dates for a collection of jobs. Often, jobs must be processed through the machines in the work center in a unique order or sequence. Figure 9–2 shows the layout of a typical job shop.

FIGURE 9–1
Hierarchy of production decisions

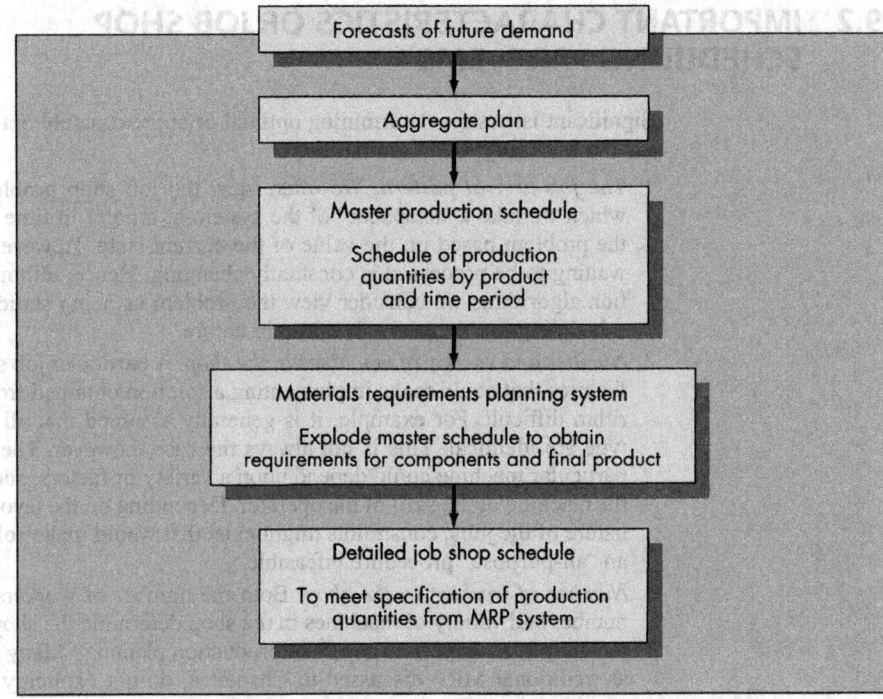

FIGURE 9–2
Typical job shop layout

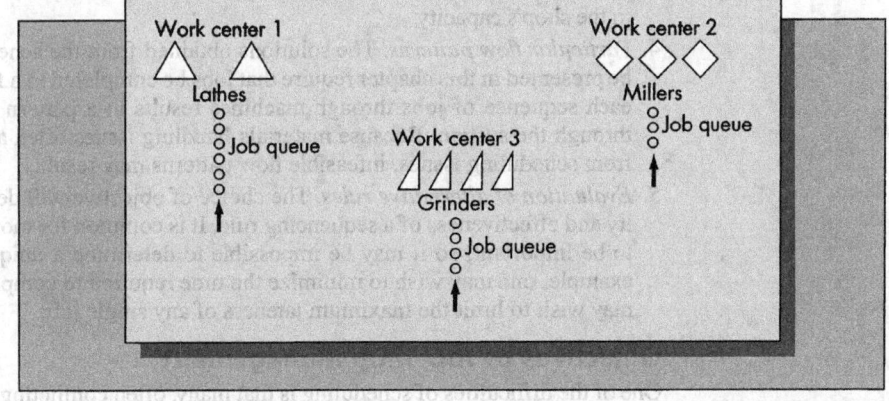

Both jobs and machines are treated as indivisible. Jobs must wait, or queue up, for processing when machines are busy. This is referred to as discrete processing. Production scheduling in continuous-process industries, such as sugar or oil refining, has a very different character.

Although there are many problems associated with operations scheduling, our concern in this chapter will be job sequencing. Given a collection of jobs remaining to be processed on a collection of machines, the problem is how to sequence these jobs to optimize some specified criterion. Properly choosing the sequencing rule can effect dramatic improvements in the throughput rate of the job shop.

9.2 IMPORTANT CHARACTERISTICS OF JOB SHOP SCHEDULING PROBLEMS

Significant issues for determining optimal or approximately optimal scheduling rules are the following:

1. *The job arrival pattern.* We often view the job shop problem as a static one in which we take a "snapshot" of the system at a point in time and proceed to solve the problem based on the value of the current state. However, the number of jobs waiting to be processed is constantly changing. Hence, although many of the solution algorithms we consider view the problem as being static, most practical shop scheduling problems are dynamic in nature.
2. *Number and variety of machines in the shop.* A particular job shop may have unique features that could make implementing a solution obtained from a scheduling algorithm difficult. For example, it is generally assumed that all machines of a given type are identical. This is not always the case, however. The throughput rate of a particular machine could depend upon a variety of factors, such as the condition of the machine or the skill of the operator. Depending on the layout of the shop and the nature of the jobs, constraints might exist that would make solutions obtained from an "all-purpose" procedure infeasible.
3. *Number of workers in the shop.* Both the number of workers in the shop and the number and variety of machines in the shop determine the shop's capacity. Capacity planning is an important aspect of production planning. Many control systems, such as traditional MRP discussed in Chapter 8, do not explicitly incorporate capacity considerations. Furthermore, capacity is dynamic. A breakdown of a single critical machine or the loss of a critical employee could result in a bottleneck and a reduction in the shop's capacity.
4. *Particular flow patterns.* The solutions obtained from the scheduling algorithms to be presented in this chapter require that jobs be completed in a fixed order. However, each sequence of jobs through machines results in a pattern of flow of materials through the system. Because materials-handling issues often are treated separately from scheduling issues, infeasible flow patterns may result.
5. *Evaluation of alternative rules.* The choice of objective will determine the suitability and effectiveness of a sequencing rule. It is common for more than one objective to be important, so it may be impossible to determine a unique optimal rule. For example, one may wish to minimize the time required to complete all jobs, but also may wish to limit the maximum lateness of any single job.

Objectives of Job Shop Management

One of the difficulties of scheduling is that many, often conflicting, objectives are present. The goals of different parts of the firm are not always the same. Some of the most common objectives are

1. Meet due dates.
2. Minimize work-in-process (WIP) inventory.
3. Minimize the average flow time through the system.
4. Provide for high machine/worker time utilization. (Minimize machine/worker idle time.)
5. Provide for accurate job status information.
6. Reduce setup times.
7. Minimize production and worker costs.

FIGURE 9–3
A process composed of two operations in series

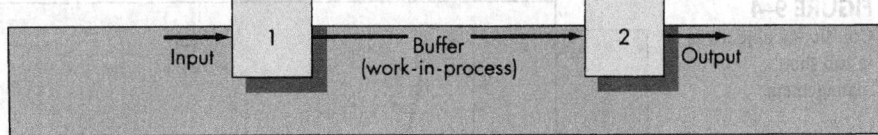

It is obviously impossible to optimize all seven objectives simultaneously. In particular, (1) and (3) are aimed primarily at providing a high level of customer service, and (2), (4), (6), and (7) are aimed primarily at providing a high level of plant efficiency. Determining the trade-off between cost and quality is one of the most important strategic issues facing a firm today.

Some of these objectives conflict. If the primary objective is to reduce work-in-process inventory (as, for example, with just-in-time inventory control systems, discussed in Chapter 8), it is likely that worker idle time will increase. As the system tightens up by reducing the inventory within and between manufacturing operations, differences in the throughput rate from one part of the system to another may force the faster operations to wait. Although not recommended by those espousing the just-in-time philosophy, buffer inventories between operations can significantly reduce idle time.

As an example, consider the simple system composed of two operations in series, pictured in Figure 9–3. If work-in-process inventory is zero, then the throughput of the system at any point in time is governed by the smaller of the throughputs of the two operations. If operation 1 is temporarily halted by a machine failure, then operation 2 also must remain idle. However, if there is a buffer inventory placed between the operations, then 2 can continue to operate while 1 is undergoing repair or recalibration.

Finding the proper mix between WIP inventory and worker idle time is equivalent to choosing a point on the trade-off curve of these conflicting objectives. (Trade-off, or exchange, curves were discussed in Chapter 5 in the context of multi-item inventory control.) Such a curve is pictured in Figure 9–4a. A movement from one point to another along such a curve does not necessarily imply that the system has improved, but rather that different weights are being applied to the two objectives. A true improvement in the overall system would mean that the entire trade-off curve undergoes a downward shift, such as that pictured in Figure 9–4b.

9.3 JOB SHOP SCHEDULING TERMINOLOGY

In general, a job shop scheduling problem is one in which n jobs must be processed through m machines. The complexity of the problem depends upon a variety of factors, such as what job sequences are permissible and what optimization criteria are chosen. In this section we define some of the terms that will be used throughout this chapter.

1. *Flow shop.* In a flow shop each of the n jobs must be processed through the m machines in the same order, and each job is processed exactly once on each machine. This is what we typically think of as an assembly line.

2. *Job shop.* A general job shop differs from a flow shop in that not all jobs are assumed to require exactly m operations, and some jobs may require multiple operations on a single machine. Furthermore, in a job shop each job may have a different required sequencing of operations. General job shop problems are extremely complex. All-purpose solution algorithms for solving general job shop problems do not exist.

FIGURE 9–4
Conflicting objectives in job shop management

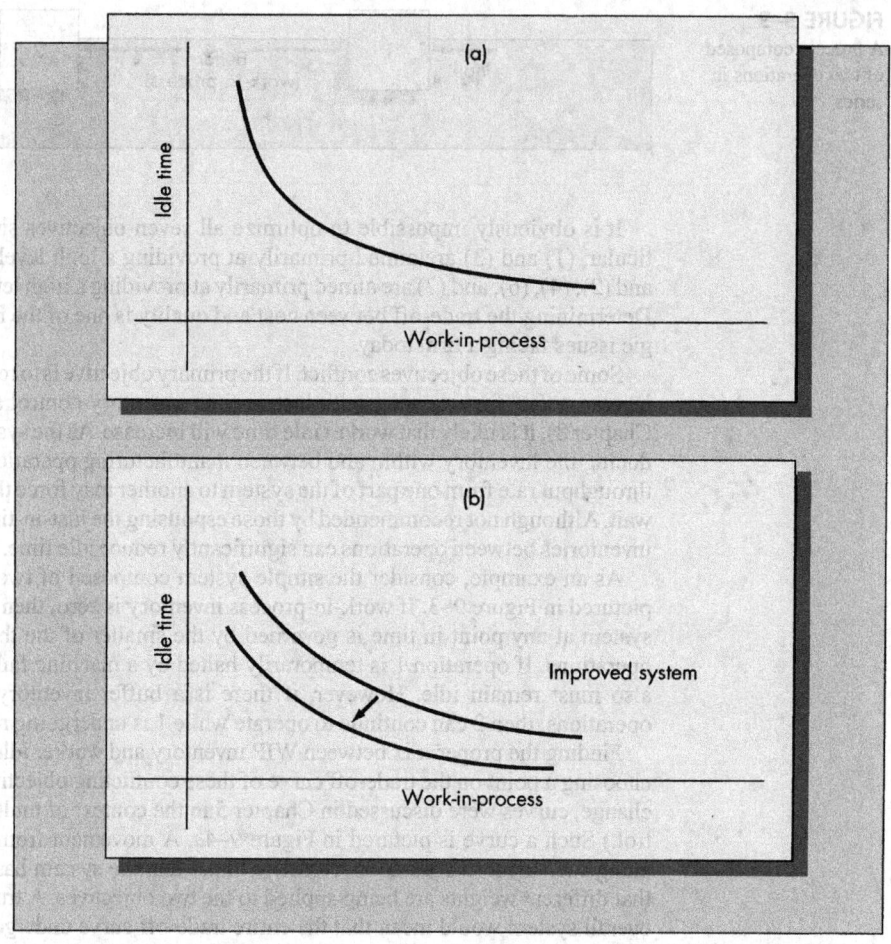

3. *Parallel processing versus sequential processing.* Most of the problems that we will consider involve sequential processing. This means that the m machines are distinguishable, and different operations are performed by different machines. In parallel processing we assume that the machines are identical, and any job can be processed on any machine. An example of parallel processing occurs in a phone switching center, in which calls are processed through the next available server. Parallel processing is discussed in the context of stochastic scheduling in Section 9.8.

4. *Flow time.* The flow time of job i is the time that elapses from the initiation of the first job on the first machine to the completion of job i. Equivalently, it is the amount of time that job i spends in the system. The *mean flow time,* which is a common measure of system performance, is the arithmetic average of the flow times for all n jobs.

5. *Makespan.* The makespan is the flow time of the job that is completed last. It is also the time required to complete all n jobs. Minimizing the makespan is a common objective in multiple-machine sequencing problems.

6. *Tardiness and lateness.* Tardiness is the positive difference between the completion time (flow time) and the due date of a job. A tardy job is one that is completed after

its due date. Lateness refers to the difference between the job completion time and its due date, and differs from tardiness in that lateness can be either positive or negative. Minimizing the average tardiness and the maximum tardiness is also a common scheduling objective.

9.4 A COMPARISON OF SPECIFIC SEQUENCING RULES

In the comparison and evaluation of sequencing rules, we consider the job shop at a fixed point in time. This section will focus on a single machine only. Assume that there is a collection of jobs that must be processed on the machine and that each job has associated with it a processing time and a due date. We compare the performance of four sequencing rules commonly used in practice. The purpose of this section is to illustrate how these sequencing rules affect various measures of system performance.

We compare the following four sequencing rules:

1. *First-come, first-served (FCFS).* Jobs are processed in the sequence in which they entered the shop.
2. *Shortest processing time (SPT).* Jobs are sequenced in increasing order of their processing times. The job with the shortest processing time is first, the job with the next shortest processing time is second, and so on.
3. *Earliest due date (EDD).* Jobs sequenced in increasing order of their due dates. The job with the earliest due date is first, the job with the next earliest due date is second, and so on.
4. *Critical ratio (CR).* Critical ratio scheduling requires forming the ratio of the processing time of the job, divided by the remaining time until the due date, and scheduling the job with the largest ratio next.

We compare the performance of these four rules for a specific case based on mean flow time, average tardiness, and number of tardy jobs. The purpose of the next example is to help the reader develop an intuition for the mechanics of scheduling before presenting formal results.

Example 9.1 A machining center in a job shop for a local fabrication company has five unprocessed jobs remaining at a particular point in time. The jobs are labeled 1, 2, 3, 4, and 5 in the order that they entered the shop. The respective processing times and due dates are given in the following table.

Job Number	Processing Time	Due Date
1	11	61
2	29	45
3	31	31
4	1	33
5	2	32

First-Come, First-Served

Because the jobs are assumed to have entered the shop in the sequence that they are numbered, FCFS scheduling means that the jobs are scheduled in the order 1, 2, 3, 4, 5.

9.4 A Comparison of Specific Sequencing Rules

This results in

Sequence	Completion Time	Due Date	Tardiness
1	11	61	0
2	40	45	0
3	71	31	40
4	72	33	39
5	74	32	42
Totals	268		121

Mean flow time = 268/5 = 53.6.
Average tardiness = 121/5 = 24.2.
Number of tardy jobs = 3.

The tardiness of a job is equal to zero if the job is completed prior to its due date and is equal to the number of days late if the job is completed after its due date.

Shortest Processing Time

Here jobs are sequenced in order of increasing processing time.

Job	Processing Time	Completion Time	Due Date	Tardiness
4	1	1	33	0
5	2	3	32	0
1	11	14	61	0
2	29	43	45	0
3	31	74	31	43
Totals		135		43

Mean flow time = 135/5 = 27.0.
Average tardiness = 43/5 = 8.6.
Number of tardy jobs = 1.

Earliest Due Date

Here jobs are completed in the order of their due dates.

Job	Processing Time	Completion Time	Due Date	Tardiness
3	31	31	31	0
5	2	33	32	1
4	1	34	33	1
2	29	63	45	18
1	11	74	61	13
Totals		235		33

Mean flow time = 235/5 = 47.0.
Average tardiness = 33/5 = 6.6.
Number of tardy jobs = 4.

Critical Ratio Scheduling

After each job has been processed, we compute

$$\frac{\text{Due date} - \text{Current time}}{\text{Processing time}},$$

which is known as the critical ratio, and schedule the next job in order to minimize the value of the critical ratio. The idea behind critical ratio scheduling is to provide a balance between SPT, which only considers processing time, and EDD, which only considers due dates. The ratio will grow smaller as the current time approaches the due date, and more priority will be given to those jobs with longer processing times. One disadvantage of the method is that the critical ratios need to be recalculated each time a job is scheduled.

It is possible that the numerator will be negative for some or all of the remaining jobs. When that occurs it means that the job is late, and we will assume that late jobs are automatically scheduled next. If there is more than one late job, then the late jobs are scheduled in SPT sequence.

First we compute the critical ratios starting at time $t = 0$.

Current time: $t = 0$

Job	Processing Time	Due Date	Critical Ratio
1	11	61	61/11 (5.545)
2	29	45	45/29 (1.552)
3	31	31	31/31 (1.000)
4	1	33	33/1 (33.00)
5	2	32	32/2 (16.00)

The minimum value corresponds to job 3, so job 3 is performed first. As job 3 requires 31 units of time to process, we must update all the critical ratios in order to determine the next job to process. We move the clock to time $t = 31$ and recompute the critical ratios.

Current time: $t = 31$

Job	Processing Time	Due Date − Current Time	Critical Ratio
1	11	30	30/11 (2.727)
2	29	14	14/29 (0.483)
4	1	2	2/1 (2.000)
5	2	1	1/2 (0.500)

The minimum is 0.483, which corresponds to job 2. Hence, job 2 is scheduled next. Since job 2 has a processing time of 29, we update the clock to time $t = 31 + 29 = 60$.

Current time: $t = 60$

Job	Processing Time	Due Date − Current Time	Critical Ratio
1	11	1	1/11 (.0909)
4	1	−27	−27/1 < 0
5	2	−28	−28/2 < 0

Jobs 4 and 5 are now late, so they are given priority and scheduled next. Since they are scheduled in SPT order, they are done in the sequence job 4, then job 5. Finally, job 1 is scheduled last.

Summary of the Results for Critical Ratio Scheduling

Job	Processing Time	Completion Time	Tardiness
3	31	31	0
2	29	60	15
4	1	61	28
5	2	63	31
1	11	74	13
Totals		289	87

Mean flow time = 289/5 = 57.8.
Average tardiness = 87/5 = 17.4.
Number of tardy jobs = 4.

We summarize the results of this section for all four scheduling rules:

Summary of the Results of Four Scheduling Rules

Rule	Mean Flow Time	Average Tardiness	Number of Tardy Jobs
FCFS	53.6	24.2	3
SPT	27.0	8.6	1
EDD	47.0	6.6	4
CR	57.8	17.4	4

9.5 OBJECTIVES IN JOB SHOP MANAGEMENT: AN EXAMPLE

Example 9.2 An air traffic controller is faced with the problem of scheduling the landing of five aircraft. Based on the position and runway requirements of each plane, she estimates the following landing times:

Plane:	1	2	3	4	5
Time (in minutes):	26	11	19	16	23

Only one plane may land at a time. The problem is essentially the same as that of scheduling five jobs on a single machine, with the planes corresponding to the jobs, the landing times to the processing times, and the runway to the machine.

1. With the given information, two reasonable objectives would be to minimize the total time required to land all planes (i.e., the makespan) or the average time required to land the planes (the mean flow time). The makespan for any sequence is clearly 95 minutes, the sum of the landing times. However, as we saw in Example 9.1, the mean flow time is not sequence independent and the shortest-processing-time rule minimizes the mean flow time. We will show in Section 9.6 that SPT is the optimal sequencing rule for minimizing mean flow time for a single machine in general.

2. An alternative objective might be to land as many people as quickly as possible. In this case we also would need to know the number of passengers on each plane. Suppose that

these numbers are as follows:

Plane	1	2	3	4	5
Landing time	26	11	19	16	23
Number of passengers	180	12	45	75	252

The appropriate objective in this case might be to minimize the *weighted* makespan or the weighted sum of the completion times, where the weights would correspond to the number of passengers in each plane. Notice that the objective function would now be in units of passenger-minutes.

3. An issue that we have not yet addressed is the time that each plane is scheduled to arrive. Assume the following data:

Plane	1	2	3	4	5
Landing time	26	11	19	16	23
Scheduled arrival time	5:30	5:45	5:15	6:00	5:40

Sequencing rules that ignore due dates could give very poor results in terms of meeting the arrival times. Some possible objectives related to due dates include minimizing the average tardiness and minimizing the maximum tardiness.

4. Thus far we have ignored special conditions that favor some planes over others. Suppose that plane number 4 has a critically low fuel level. This would probably result in plane 4 taking precedence. Priority constraints could arise in other ways as well: planes that are scheduled for continuing flights or planes carrying precious or perishable cargo also might be given priority.

The purpose of this section was to demonstrate the difficulties of choosing an objective function for job sequencing problems. The optimal sequence is highly sensitive to the choice of the objective, and the appropriate objective is not always obvious.

Problems for Sections 9.1–9.5

1. Discuss each of the following objectives listed and the relationship each has with job shop performance.
   a. Reduce WIP inventory.
   b. Provide a high level of customer service.
   c. Reduce worker idle time.
   d. Improve factory efficiency.
2. In Problem 1, why are (*a*) and (*c*) conflicting objectives, and why are (*b*) and (*d*) conflicting objectives?
3. Define the following terms:
   a. Flow shop.
   b. Job shop.
   c. Sequential versus parallel processing.
   d. Makespan.
   e. Tardiness.
4. Four trucks, 1, 2, 3, and 4, are waiting on a loading dock at XYZ Company that has only a single service bay. The trucks are labeled in the order that they arrived at the dock. Assume the current time is 1:00 P.M. The times required to unload each truck

and the times that the goods they contain are due in the plant are given in the following table.

Truck	Unloading Time (minutes)	Time Material Is Due
1	20	1:25 P.M.
2	14	1:45 P.M.
3	35	1:50 P.M.
4	10	1:30 P.M.

Determine the schedules that result for each of the rules FCFS, SPT, EDD, and CR. In each case compute the mean flow time, average tardiness, and number of tardy jobs.

5. Five jobs must be scheduled for batch processing on a mainframe computer system. The processing times and the promised times for each of the jobs are listed here.

Job	1	2	3	4	5
Processing time	40 min	2.5 hr	20 min	4 hr	1.5 hr
Promised time	11:00 A.M.	2:00 P.M.	2:00 P.M.	1:00 P.M.	4:00 P.M.

Assume that the current time is 10:00 A.M.

a. If the jobs are scheduled according to SPT, find the tardiness of each job and the mean tardiness of all jobs.

b. Repeat the calculation in part (a) for EDD scheduling.

9.6 AN INTRODUCTION TO SEQUENCING THEORY FOR A SINGLE MACHINE

Assume that n jobs are to be processed through one machine. For each job i, define the following quantities:

$t_i =$ Processing time for job i,
$d_i =$ Due date for job i,
$W_i =$ Waiting time for job i,
$F_i =$ Flow time for job i,
$L_i =$ Lateness of job i,
$T_i =$ Tardiness of job i,
$E_i =$ Earliness of job i.

The processing time and the due date are constants that are attached to the description of each job. The waiting time for a job is the amount of time that the job must wait before its processing can begin. For the cases that we consider, it is also the sum of the processing times for all the preceding jobs. The flow time is simply the waiting time plus the job processing time ($F_i = W_i + t_i$). The flow time of job i and the completion time of job i are the same. We will define the lateness of job i as $L_i = F_i - d_i$, and assume that lateness can be either a positive or a negative quantity. Tardiness is the positive part of lateness ($T_i = \max[L_i, 0]$), and earliness is the negative part of lateness ($E_i = \max[-L_i, 0]$).

Other related quantities are maximum tardiness T_{max}, given by the formula

$$T_{max} = \max\{T_1, T_2, \ldots, T_n\},$$

and the mean flow time F', given by the formula

$$F' = \frac{1}{n}\sum_{i=1}^{n} F_i.$$

As we are considering only a single machine, every schedule can be represented by a permutation (that is, ordering) of the integers $1, 2, \ldots, n$. There are exactly $n!$ different permutation schedules [$n! = n(n-1)\cdots(2)(1)$].

Shortest-Processing-Time Scheduling

We have the following result:

Theorem 9.1   **The scheduling rule that minimizes the mean flow time F' is SPT.**

Theorem 9.1 is easy to prove. Let $[1], [2], \ldots, [n]$ be any permutation of the integers $1, 2, 3, \ldots, n$. The flow time of the job that is scheduled in position k is given by

$$F_{[k]} = \sum_{i=1}^{k} t_{[i]}.$$

It follows that the mean flow time is given by

$$F' = \frac{1}{n}\sum_{k=1}^{n} F_{[k]} = \frac{1}{n}\sum_{k=1}^{n}\sum_{i=1}^{k} t_{[i]}.$$

The double summation term may be written in a different form. Expanding the double summation, we obtain

$$k = 1: t_{[1]}$$
$$k = 2: t_{[1]} + t_{[2]}$$
$$\vdots$$
$$k = n: t_{[1]} + t_{[2]} + \cdots + t_{[n]}.$$

By summing down the column rather than across the row, we may rewrite F' in the form

$$nt_{[1]} + (n-1)t_{[2]} + \cdots + t_{[n]},$$

which is clearly minimized by setting

$$t_{[1]} \leq t_{[2]} \leq \cdots \leq t_{[n]},$$

which is exactly the SPT sequencing rule.

We have the following corollary to Theorem 9.1.

Corollary 9.1   **The following measures are equivalent:**

1. **Mean flow time**
2. **Mean waiting time**
3. **Mean lateness**

Taken together, Corollary 9.1 and Theorem 9.1 establish that SPT minimizes mean flow time, mean waiting time, and mean lateness for single-machine sequencing.

Earliest-Due-Date Scheduling

If the objective is to minimize the maximum lateness, then the jobs should be sequenced according to their due dates. That is, $d_{[1]} \leq d_{[2]} \leq \cdots \leq d_{[n]}$. We will not present a proof of this result. The idea behind the proof is to choose some schedule that does not sequence the jobs in order of their due dates; that implies that there is some value of k such that $d_{[k]} > d_{[k+1]}$. One shows that by interchanging the positions of jobs k and $k+1$, the maximum lateness is reduced.

Minimizing the Number of Tardy Jobs

There are many instances in which the penalty for a late (tardy) job remains the same no matter how late it is. For example, any delay in the completion of all tasks required for preparation of a space launch would cause the launch to be aborted, independent of the length of the delay.

We will describe an algorithm from Moore (1968) that minimizes the number of tardy jobs for the single machine problem.

Step 1. Sequence the jobs according to the earliest due date to obtain the initial solution. That is $d_{[1]} \leq d_{[2]} \leq \cdots \leq d_{[n]}$.

Step 2. Find the first tardy job in the current sequence, say job $[i]$. If none exists, go to step 4.

Step 3. Consider jobs $[1], [2], \ldots, [i]$. Reject the job with the largest processing time. Return to step 2.

Step 4. Form an optimal sequence by taking the current sequence and appending to it the rejected jobs. The jobs appended to the current sequence may be scheduled in any order because they constitute the tardy jobs.

Example 9.3 A machine shop processes custom orders from a variety of clients. One of the machines, a grinder, has six jobs remaining to be processed. The processing times and promised due dates (both in hours) for the six jobs are given here.

Job	1	2	3	4	5	6
Due date	15	6	9	23	20	30
Processing time	10	3	4	8	10	6

The first step is to sequence the jobs according to the EDD rule.

Job	2	3	1	5	4	6
Due date	6	9	15	20	23	30
Processing time	3	4	10	10	8	6
Completion time	3	7	17	27	35	41

We see that the first tardy job is job 1, and there are a total of four tardy jobs. We now consider jobs 2, 3, and 1 and reject the job with the longest processing time. This is clearly job 1. At this point, the new current sequence is

Job	2	3	5	4	6
Due date	6	9	20	23	30
Processing time	3	4	10	8	6
Completion time	3	7	17	25	31

The first tardy job in the current sequence is now job 4. We consider the sequence 2, 3, 5, 4, and reject the job with the longest processing time, which is job 5. The current sequence is now

Job	2	3	4	6
Due date	6	9	23	30
Processing time	3	4	8	6
Completion time	3	7	15	21

Clearly there are no tardy jobs at this stage. The optimal sequence is 2, 3, 4, 6, 5, 1 or 2, 3, 4, 6, 1, 5. In either case the number of tardy jobs is exactly 2.

Precedence Constraints: Lawler's Algorithm

Lawler's algorithm (Lawler, 1973) is a powerful technique for solving a variety of constrained scheduling problems. The objective function is assumed to be of the form

$$\min \max_{1 \leq i \leq n} g_i(F_i)$$

where g_i is any nondecreasing function of the flow time F_i. Furthermore, the algorithm handles *any* precedence constraints. Precedence constraints occur when certain jobs must be completed before other jobs can begin; they are quite common in scheduling problems. Some examples of functions g_i that one might consider are $g_i(F_i) = F_i - d_i = L_i$, which corresponds to minimizing maximum lateness, or $g_i(F_i) = \max(F_i - d_i, 0)$, which corresponds to minimizing maximum tardiness.

The Algorithm

Lawler's algorithm first schedules the job to be completed last, then the job to be completed next to last, and so on. At each stage one determines the set of jobs not required to precede any other. Call this set V. Among the set V, choose the job k that satisfies

$$g_k(\tau) = \min_{i \in V} (g_i(\tau)),$$

where $\tau = \sum_{i=1}^{n} t_i$ and corresponds to the processing time of the current sequence.

Job k is now scheduled last. Consider the remaining jobs and again determine the set of jobs that are not required to precede any other remaining job. After scheduling job k, this set may have changed. The value of τ is reduced by t_k and the job scheduled next to last is now determined. The process is continued until all jobs are scheduled. Note that as jobs are scheduled, some of the precedence constraints may be relaxed, so the set V is likely to change at each iteration.

Example 9.4   Tony D'Amato runs a local body shop that does automotive painting and repairs. On a particular Monday morning he has six cars waiting for repair. Three (1, 2, and 3) are from a car rental company and he has agreed to finish these cars in the order of the dates that they were promised. Cars 4, 5, and 6 are from a retail dealer who has requested that car 4 be completed first because a customer is waiting for it. The resulting precedence constraints can be represented as two disconnected networks, as pictured in Figure 9–5.

The times required to repair each of the cars (in days) and the associated promised completion dates are

Job	1	2	3	4	5	6
Processing time	2	3	4	3	2	1
Due date	3	6	9	7	11	7

FIGURE 9–5
Precedence constraints for Example 9.4

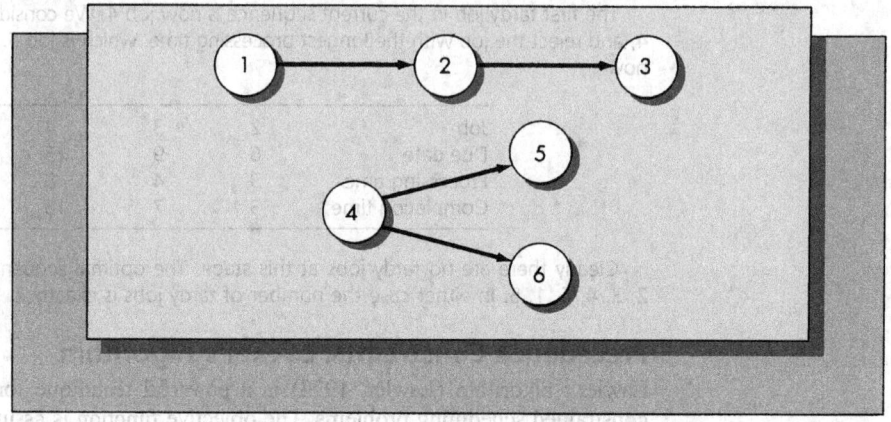

Determine how the repair of the cars should be scheduled through the shop in order to minimize the maximum tardiness.

Solution   1. First we find the job scheduled last (sixth). Among the candidates for the last position are those jobs that are not predecessors of other jobs. These are 3, 5, and 6. The total processing time of all jobs is $2 + 3 + 4 + 3 + 2 + 1 = 15$. (This is the current value of τ.) As the objective is to minimize the maximum tardiness, we compare the tardiness of these three jobs and pick the one with the smallest value. We obtain $\min\{15 - 9, 15 - 11, 15 - 7\} = \min\{6, 4, 8\} = 4$, corresponding to job 5. Hence job 5 is scheduled last (position 6).

2. Next we find the job scheduled fifth. The candidates are jobs 3 and 6 only. At this point the value of τ is $15 - 2 = 13$. Hence, we find $\min\{13 - 9, 13 - 7\} = \min\{4, 6\} = 4$, which corresponds to job 3. Hence, job 3 is scheduled in the fifth position.

3. Find the job scheduled fourth. Because job 3 is no longer on the list, job 2 now becomes a candidate. The current value of $\tau = 13 - 4 = 9$. Hence, we compare $\min\{9 - 6, 9 - 7\} = \min\{3, 2\} = 2$, which corresponds to job 6. Schedule job 6 in the fourth position.

4. Find the job scheduled third. Job 6 has been scheduled, so job 4 now becomes a candidate along with job 2, and $\tau = 9 - 1 = 8$. Hence, we look for $\min\{8 - 6, 8 - 7\} = \min\{2, 1\} = 1$, which occurs at job 4.

5. At this point we would find the job scheduled second. However, we are left with only jobs 1 and 2, which, because of the precedence constraints, must be scheduled in the order 1–2.

Summarizing the results, the optimal sequence to repair the cars is 1–2–4–6–3–5.

In order to determine the value of the objective function, the maximum tardiness, we compute the flow time for each job and compare it to the due date. We have

Job	Processing Time	Flow Time	Due Date	Tardiness
1	2	2	3	0
2	3	5	6	0
4	3	8	7	1
6	1	9	7	2
3	4	13	9	4
5	2	15	11	4

Hence, the maximum tardiness is four days. The reader should convince him- or herself that any other sequence results in a maximum tardiness of at least four days.

Snapshot Application

MILLIONS SAVED WITH SCHEDULING SYSTEM FOR FRACTIONAL AIRCRAFT OPERATORS

Celebrities, corporate executives, and sports professionals are a large part of the group that uses private planes for travel. For many of these people, it doesn't make economic sense to purchase planes. An attractive alternative is fractional ownership, especially for those that have only occasional need of a plane. Fractional ownership of private planes provides owners with the flexibility to fly to over 5,000 destinations (as opposed to about 500 for the commercial airlines). Other advantages include privacy, personalized service, fewer delays, and the ability to conduct business on the plane.

The concept of a fractional aircraft program is similar to that of a time-share condominium, except that the aircraft owners are guaranteed access at any time with as little as four hours notice. The fees are based on the number of flight hours the owner will require: one-eighth share owners are allotted 100 hours of annual flying time, one-quarter share owners 200 hours, and so forth. The entire system is coordinated by fractional management company (FMC). Clearly, the problem of scheduling the planes and crews can become quite complex.

When scheduling planes and crews, the FMC must determine schedules that (1) meet customer requests on time, (2) satisfy maintenance and crew restrictions, and (3) allow for specific aircraft trip assignments and requests. The profitability of the FMC will depend upon how efficiently they perform these tasks. A group of consultants attacked this problem and developed a scheduling system known as ScheduleMiser.[1] The inputs to this system are trip requests, aircraft availability, and aircraft restrictions over a specified planning horizon. Note that even though owners are guaranteed service with only four hours notice, the vast majority of trips are booked at least three days or more in advance. This gives the FMC a reliable profile of demand over a two- to three-day planning horizon. Note that aircraft schedules must be coordinated with crew schedules, as crew work rules cannot be violated.

ScheduleMiser is the underlying engine that drives the larger planning system known as Flight Ops. ScheduleMiser is based on a mixed-integer mathematical formulation of the problem. The objective function consists of five terms delineating the various costs in the system. Several sets of constraints are included to ensure that demands are filled, crews are properly scheduled, and planes are not overbooked. This system was adopted and implemented by Raytheon Travel Air in November of 2000 (now Flight Options) for scheduling their fleet of over 100 aircraft. Raytheon reported a savings of over $4.4 million in the first year of implementation of this system. This is only one example of many mathematical-based scheduling systems that have been implemented in the airline industry.

[1] Martin, C., D. Jones, and P. Keskinocak. "Optimizing On-Demand Aircraft Schedules for Fractional Aircraft Operators," *Interfaces*, 33, no. 5, September–October 2003, pp. 22–35.

Problems for Section 9.6

6. Consider the information given in Problem 4. Determine the sequence that the trucks should be unloaded in order to minimize

    a. Mean flow time.
    b. Maximum lateness.
    c. Number of tardy jobs.

7. On May 1, a lazy MBA student suddenly realizes that he has done nothing on seven different homework assignments and projects that are due in various courses. He estimates the time required to complete each project (in days) and also notes their due dates:

Project	1	2	3	4	5	6	7
Time (days)	4	8	10	4	3	7	14
Due date	4/20	5/17	5/28	5/28	5/12	5/7	5/15

Because projects 1, 3, and 5 are from the same class, he decides to do those in the sequence that they are due. Furthermore, project 7 requires results from projects 2 and 3, so 7 must be done after 2 and 3 are completed. Determine the sequence in which he should do the projects in order to minimize the maximum lateness.

8. Eight jobs are to be processed through a single machine. The processing times and due dates are given here.

Job	1	2	3	4	5	6	7	8
Processing time	2	3	2	1	4	3	2	2
Due date	5	4	13	6	12	10	15	19

Furthermore, assume that the following precedence relationships must be satisfied:

$$2 \to 6 \to 3.$$
$$1 \to 4 \to 7 \to 8.$$

Determine the sequence in which these jobs should be done in order to minimize the maximum lateness subject to the precedence restrictions.

9. Jane Reed bakes breads and cakes in her home for parties and other affairs on a contract basis. Jane has only one oven for baking. One particular Monday morning she finds that she has agreed to complete five jobs for that day. Her husband John will make the deliveries, which require about 15 minutes each. Suppose that she begins baking at 8:00 A.M.

Job	Time Required	Promised Time
1	1.2 hr	11:30 A.M
2	40 min	10:00 A.M.
3	2.2 hr	11:00 A.M.
4	30 min	1:00 P.M.
5	3.1 hr	12:00 NOON
6	25 min	2:00 P.M.

Determine the sequence in which she should perform the jobs in order to minimize

a. Mean flow time.
b. Number of tardy jobs.
c. Maximum lateness.

10. Seven jobs are to be processed through a single machine. The processing times and due dates are given here.

Job	1	2	3	4	5	6	7
Processing time	3	6	8	4	2	1	7
Due date	4	8	12	15	11	25	21

Determine the sequence of the jobs in order to minimize

a. Mean flow time.
b. Number of tardy jobs.
c. Maximum lateness.
d. What is the makespan for any sequence?

9.7 SEQUENCING ALGORITHMS FOR MULTIPLE MACHINES

We now extend the analysis of Section 9.6 to the case in which several jobs must be processed on more than one machine. Assume that n jobs are to be processed through m machines. The number of possible schedules is staggering, even for moderate values of both n and m. For each machine, there are $n!$ different orderings of the jobs. If the jobs may be processed on the machines in any order, it follows that there are a total of $(n!)^m$ possible schedules. For example, for $n = 5$, $m = 5$, there are $24,883 \times 10^{10}$, or about 25 billion, possible schedules. Even with the availability of inexpensive computing today, enumerating all feasible schedules for even moderate-sized problems is impossible or, at best, impractical.

In this section we will present some known results for scheduling jobs on more than one machine. A convenient way to represent a schedule is via a Gantt chart. As an example, suppose that two jobs, I and J, are to be scheduled on two machines, 1 and 2. The processing times are

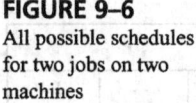

	Machine 1	Machine 2
Job I	4	1
Job J	1	4

Assume that both jobs must be processed first on machine 1 and then on machine 2. The possible schedules appear in four Gantt charts in Figure 9–6. The first two schedules are known as permutation schedules. That means that the jobs are processed in the same sequence on both machines. Clearly, for this example, the permutation schedules provide better system performance in terms of both total and average flow time.

FIGURE 9–6
All possible schedules for two jobs on two machines

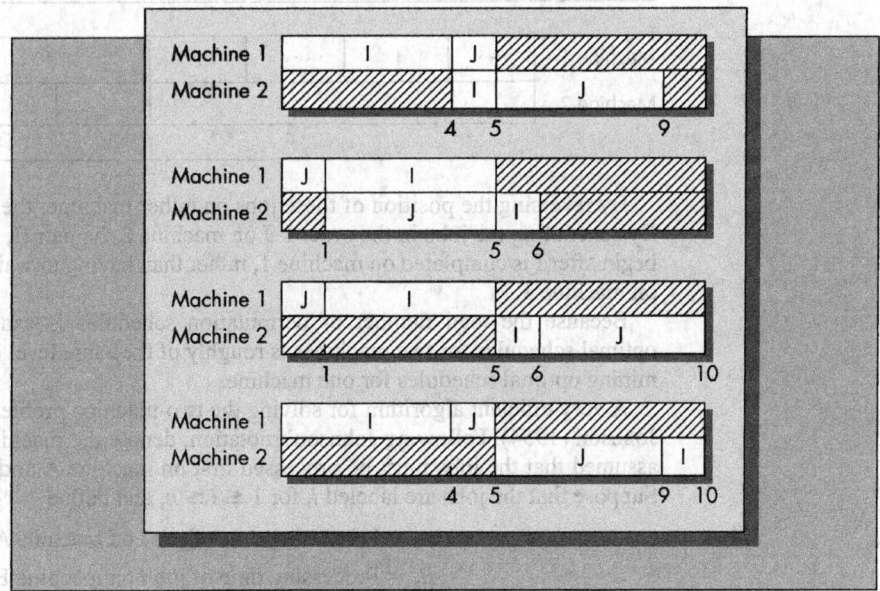

Recall that the total flow time (or makespan) is the total elapsed time from the initiation of the first job on the first machine until the completion of the last job on the last machine. For the given schedules, the makespans (total flow time) are respectively 9, 6, 10, and 10.

The mean flow time is also used as a measure of system performance. For the first schedule in the example, the mean flow time is $(5 + 9)/2 = 7$. For the second schedule, it is $(5 + 6)/2 = 5.5$, and so on.

A third possible objective is minimization of the mean idle time in the system. The mean idle time is the arithmetic average of the idle times for each machine. In schedule 1, we see that machine 1 is idle for 4 units of time (between times 5 and 9) and machine 2 is idle for 4 units of time as well (between times 0 and 4). Hence the mean idle time for schedule 1 is 4. In schedule 2, both machines 1 and 2 are idle for 1 unit of time, giving a mean idle time of 1. The mean idle times for schedules 3 and 4 are 5 units of time.

Scheduling n Jobs on Two Machines

Assume that n jobs must be processed through two machines and that each job must be processed in the order machine 1 then machine 2. Furthermore, assume that the optimization criterion is to minimize the makespan. The problem of scheduling on two machines turns out to have a relatively simple solution.

Theorem 9.2 **The optimal solution for scheduling n jobs on two machines is always a permutation schedule.**

Theorem 9.2 means that one can restrict attention to schedules in which the sequence of jobs is the same on both machines. This result can be demonstrated as follows. Consider a schedule for n jobs on two machines in which the sequencing of the jobs on the two machines is different. That is, the schedule looks as follows:

Machine 1	...	I	...	J			
Machine 2					...	J	...	I

By reversing the position of these jobs on either machine, the flow time decreases. By scheduling the jobs in the order I–J on machine 2 the pair (I, J) on machine 2 may begin after I is completed on machine 1, rather than having to wait until J is completed on machine 1.

Because the total number of permutation schedules is exactly $n!$, determining optimal schedules for two machines is roughly of the same level of difficulty as determining optimal schedules for one machine.

A very efficient algorithm for solving the two-machine problem was discovered by Johnson (1954). Following Johnson's notation, denote the machines by A and B. It is assumed that the jobs must be processed first on machine A and then on machine B. Suppose that the jobs are labeled i, for $1 \leq i \leq n$, and define

$$A_i = \text{Processing time of job } i \text{ on machine A}.$$
$$B_i = \text{Processing time of job } i \text{ on machine B}.$$

Johnson's result is that the following rule is optimal for determining an order in which to process the jobs on the two machines.

Rule: Job i precedes job $i+1$ if $\min(A_i, B_{i+1}) < \min(A_{i+1}, B_i)$.

An easy way to implement this rule is as follows:

1. List the values of A_i and B_i in two columns.
2. Find the smallest remaining element in the two columns. If it appears in column A, then schedule that job next. If it appears in column B, then schedule that job last.
3. Cross off the jobs as they are scheduled. Stop when all jobs have been scheduled.

Example 9.5 Five jobs are to be scheduled on two machines. The processing times are

Job	Machine A	Machine B
1	5	2
2	1	6
3	9	7
4	3	8
5	10	4

The first step is to identify the minimum job time. It is 1, for job 2 on machine A. Because it appears in column A, job 2 is scheduled first and row 2 is crossed out. The next smallest processing time is 2, for job 1 on machine B. This appears in the B column, so job 1 is scheduled last. The next smallest processing time is 3, corresponding to job 4 in column A, so that job 4 is scheduled next. Continuing in this fashion, we obtain the optimal sequence

$$2\text{--}4\text{--}3\text{--}5\text{--}1.$$

The Gantt chart for the optimal schedule is pictured in Figure 9–7. Note that there is no idle time between jobs on machine A. This is a feature of all optimal schedules.

Extension to Three Machines

The problem of scheduling jobs on three machines is considerably more complex. If we restrict attention to total flow time only, it is still true that a permutation schedule is optimal (this is not necessarily the case for average flow time). Label the machines A, B, and C. The three-machine problem can be reduced to (essentially) a two-machine problem if the following condition is satisfied:

$$\min A_i \geq \max B_i \quad \text{or} \quad \min C_i \geq \max B_i$$

FIGURE 9–7
Gantt chart for the optimal schedule for Example 9.5

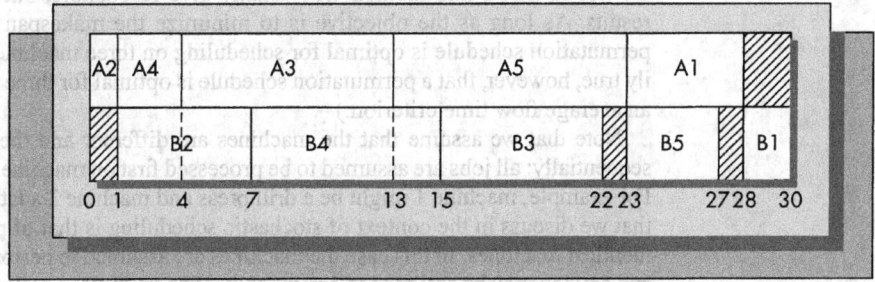

It is only necessary that *either one* of these conditions be satisfied. If that is the case, then the problem is reduced to a two-machine problem in the following way.

Define $A'_i = A_i + B_i$, and define $B'_i = B_i + C_i$. Now solve the problem using the rules described for two machines, treating A'_i and B'_i as the processing times. The resulting permutation schedule will be optimal for the three-machine problem.

Example 9.6   Consider the following job times for a three-machine problem. Assume that the jobs are processed in the sequence A–B–C.

Job	Machine A	Machine B	Machine C
1	4	5	8
2	9	6	10
3	8	2	6
4	6	3	7
5	5	4	11

Checking the conditions, we find

$$\min A_i = 4,$$
$$\max B_i = 6,$$
$$\min C_i = 6,$$

so that the required condition is satisfied. We now form the two columns A' and B'.

Job	Machine A'	Machine B'
1	9	13
2	15	16
3	10	8
4	9	10
5	9	15

The problem is now solved using the two-machine algorithm. The optimal solution is 1–4–5–2–3. Note that because of ties in column A, the optimal solution is not unique.

If the conditions for reducing a three-machine problem to a two-machine problem are not satisfied, this method will usually give reasonable, but possibly suboptimal, results. As long as the objective is to minimize the makespan or total flow time, a permutation schedule is optimal for scheduling on three machines. (It is not necessarily true, however, that a permutation schedule is optimal for three machines when using an average flow time criterion.)

Note that we assume that the machines are different and the processing proceeds sequentially: all jobs are assumed to be processed first on machine 1, then on machine 2. For example, machine 1 might be a drill press and machine 2 a lathe. A related problem that we discuss in the context of stochastic scheduling is that of parallel processing on identical machines. In this case the machines are assumed to perform the same function, and any job may be assigned to any machine. For example, a collection of 10 jobs might require processing on either one of two drill presses. The results for parallel processing suggest that SPT is an effective rule for minimizing mean flow time, but longest processing time first (LPT) is often more effective for minimizing total flow time or makespan. We will discuss parallel processing in the context of random job times in Section 9.8.

The Two-Job Flow Shop Problem

Assume that two jobs are to be processed through m machines. Each job must be processed by the machines in a particular order, but the sequences for the two jobs need not be the same. We present a graphical procedure for solving this problem developed by Akers (1956).

1. Draw a Cartesian coordinate system with the processing times corresponding to the first job on the horizontal axis and the processing times corresponding to the second job on the vertical axis. On each axis, mark off the operation times in the order in which the operations must be performed for that job.
2. Block out areas corresponding to each machine at the intersection of the intervals marked for that machine on the two axes.
3. Determine a path from the origin to the end of the final block that does not intersect any of the blocks and that minimizes the vertical movement. Movement is allowed only in three directions: horizontal, vertical, and 45-degree diagonal. The path with minimum vertical distance will indicate the optimal solution. Note that this will be the same as the path with minimum horizontal distance.

This procedure is best illustrated by an example.

Example 9.7

A regional manufacturing firm produces a variety of household products. One is a wooden desk lamp. Prior to packing, the lamps must be sanded, lacquered, and polished. Each operation requires a different machine. There are currently shipments of two models awaiting processing. The times required for the three operations for each of the two shipments are

Job 1		Job 2	
Operation	Time	Operation	Time
Sanding (A)	3	A	2
Lacquering (B)	4	B	5
Polishing (C)	5	C	3

The first step is to block out the job times on each of the axes. Refer to Figure 9–8 for this step. Every feasible schedule is represented by a line connecting the origin to the tip of block C, with the condition that the line not go through a block. Only three types of movement are allowed: horizontal, vertical, and 45-degree diagonal. Horizontal movement implies that only job 1 is being processed, vertical movement implies that only job 2 is being processed, and diagonal movement implies that both jobs are being processed. Minimizing the flow time is the same as maximizing the time that both jobs are being processed. This is equivalent to finding the path from the origin to the end of block C that maximizes the diagonal movement and therefore minimizes either the horizontal or the vertical movement.

Two feasible schedules for this problem are represented in Figure 9–8. The total time required by any feasible schedule can be obtained in two ways: it is either the total time represented on the horizontal axis (12 in this case) plus the total vertical movement (4 and 3 respectively), or the total time on the vertical axis (10 in this case) plus the total horizontal movement (6 and 5 respectively). Schedule 1 has total time 16, and schedule 2 has total time 15. Schedule 2 turns out to be optimal for this problem.

The Gantt chart for the optimal schedule appears in Figure 9–9.

FIGURE 9–8
Graphical solution of Example 9.7

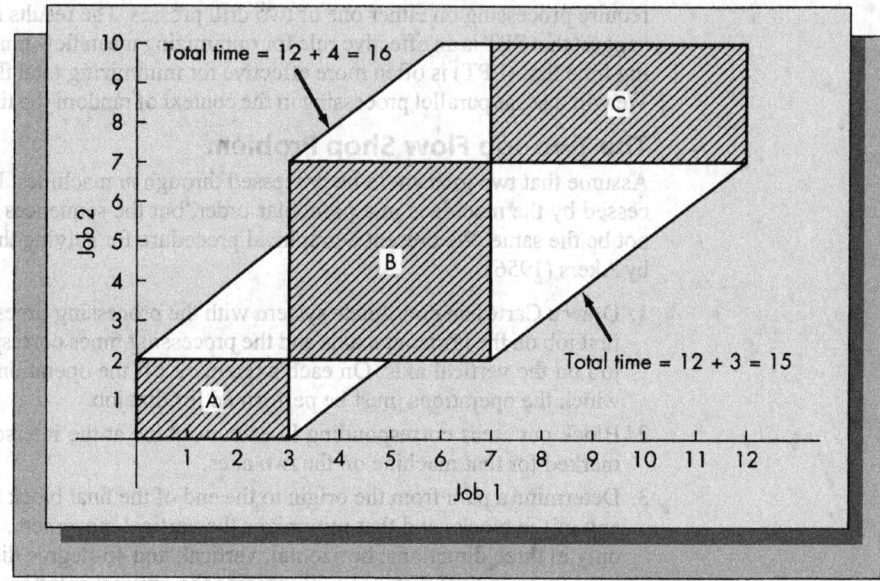

FIGURE 9–9
Gantt chart for optimal solution to Example 9.7

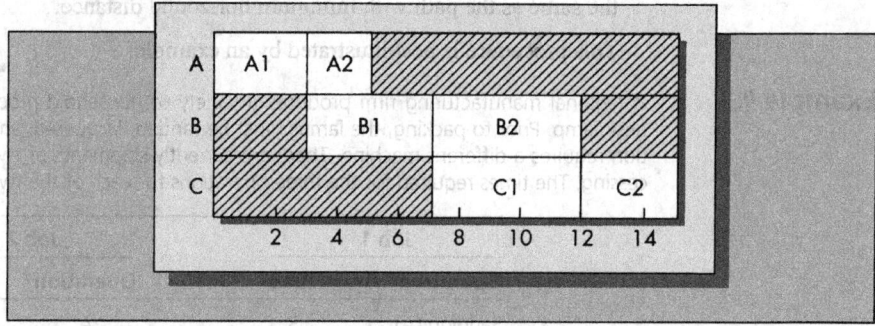

We should note that this method does *not* require the two jobs to be processed in the same sequence on the machines. We present another example to illustrate the case in which the sequence of the jobs is different.

Example 9.8 Reggie Sigal and Bob Robinson are roommates who enjoy spending Sunday mornings reading the Sunday newspaper. Reggie likes to read the main section first, followed by the sports section, then the comics, and finally the classifieds. Bob also starts with the main section, but then goes directly to the classifieds, followed by the sports section and finally the comics. The times required (in tenths of an hour) for each to read the various sections are

Reggie		Bob	
Required Sequence	Time	Required Sequence	Time
Main section (A)	6	Main section (A)	4
Sports (B)	1	Classifieds (D)	3
Comics (C)	5	Sports (B)	2
Classifieds (D)	4	Comics (C)	5

Solution

The goal is to determine the order of the sections read for each to minimize the total time required to complete reading the paper. In this problem we identify Reggie as job 1 and Bob as job 2. The sections of the paper correspond to the machines.

In order to obtain the optimal solution, we first block out the processing times for each of the jobs. Assume that job 1 (Reggie) is blocked out on the x axis and job 2 (Bob) on the y axis. The processing times are sequenced on each axis in the order stated. The graphical representation for this problem is given in Figure 9–10. In the figure, two different feasible schedules are represented as paths from the origin to the point (16, 14). The top path represents a schedule that calls for Bob to begin reading the main section first (job 2 is processed first on machine A), and the lower path calls for Reggie to begin first. The lower path turns out to be optimal for this problem with a processing time of 20.

The optimal processing time for this problem is 20. As the time units are in tenths of an hour, this is exactly two hours. One converts the lower path in Figure 9–10 to a Gantt chart in the following way: From time 0 to 6, Reggie reads A and Bob is idle. Between times 6 and 12, the 45-degree line indicates that both Bob and Reggie are reading. Reggie reads B for 1 time unit and C for 5 time units, and Bob reads A for 4 time units and D for 3 time units. Reggie is now idle for one time unit because the path is vertical at this point, and begins reading D at time 13. When Reggie completes D, he is done. Starting at time 15, Bob reads C and completes his reading at time 20. Figure 9–11 shows the Gantt chart indicating the optimal solution.

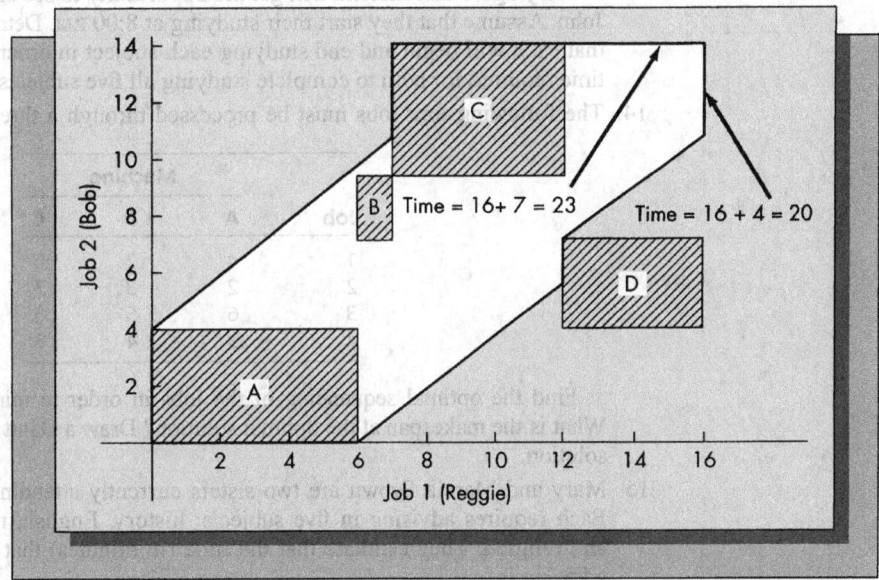

FIGURE 9–10
Graphical solution of Example 9.8

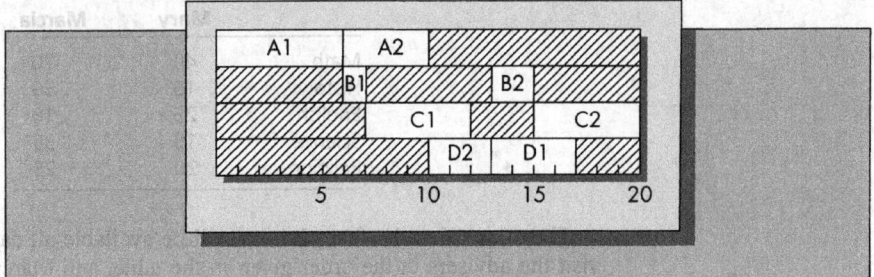

FIGURE 9–11
Gantt chart for optimal solution to Example 9.8

Problems for Section 9.7

11. Consider Example 9.6, illustrating the use of Johnson's algorithm for three machines. List all optimal solutions for this example.

12. Suppose that 12 jobs must be processed through six machines. If the jobs may be processed in any order, how many different possible schedules are there? If you were to run a computer program that could evaluate 100 schedules every second, how much time would the program require to evaluate all feasible schedules?

13. Two law students, John and Marsha, are planning an all-nighter to prepare for their law boards the following day. Between them they have one set of materials in the following five subjects: contracts, torts, civil law, corporate law, and patents. Based on their previous experience, they estimate that they will need the following amount of time (in hours) with each set of materials:

	Contracts	Torts	Civil	Corporate	Patents
John	1.2	2.2	0.7	0.5	1.5
Marsha	1.8	0.8	3.1	1.1	2.3

    They agree that Marsha will get the opportunity to see each set of notes before John. Assume that they start their studying at 8:00 P.M. Determine the exact times that each will begin and end studying each subject in order to minimize the total time required for both to complete studying all five subjects.

14. The following four jobs must be processed through a three-machine flow shop.

	Machine		
Job	A	B	C
1	4	2	6
2	2	3	7
3	6	5	6
4	3	4	8

    Find the optimal sequencing of the jobs in order to minimize the makespan. What is the makespan at the optimal solution? Draw a Gantt chart illustrating your solution.

15. Mary and Marcia Brown are two sisters currently attending university together. Each requires advising in five subjects: history, English, mathematics, science, and religion. They estimate that the time (in minutes) that each will require for advising is

	Mary	Marcia
Math	40	20
History	15	30
English	25	10
Science	15	35
Religion	20	25

    They think that the five advisers will be available all day. Mary would like to visit the advisers in the order given in the table, and Marcia would prefer to see them in the order math, religion, English, science, and history. At what times should each plan to see the advisers in order to minimize the total time for both to complete their advising?

16. Two jobs must be processed through four machines in the same order. The processing times in the required sequence are

Job 1		Job 2	
Machine	Time	Machine	Time
A	5	A	2
B	4	B	4
C	6	C	3
D	3	D	5

Determine how the two jobs should be scheduled in order to minimize the total makespan, and draw the Gantt chart indicating the optimal schedule.

17. Peter Minn is planning to go to the Department of Motor Vehicles to have his driver's license renewed. His friend, Patricia, who is accompanying him, is applying for a new license. In both cases there are five steps that are required: (A) having a picture taken, (B) signing a signature verification form, (C) passing a written test, (D) passing an eye test, and (E) passing a driving test.

For renewals the steps are performed in the order A, B, C, D, and E with average times required, respectively, of 0.2, 0.1, 0.3, 0.2, and 0.6 hour. In the case of new applications, the steps are performed in the sequence D, B, C, E, and A, with average times required of 0.3, 0.2, 0.7, 1.1, and 0.2 hour, respectively. Peter and Pat go on a day when the department is essentially empty. How should they plan their schedule in order to minimize the time required for both to complete all five steps?

9.8 STOCHASTIC SCHEDULING: STATIC ANALYSIS

Single Machine

An issue we have not yet addressed is uncertainty of the processing times. In practice it is possible and even likely that the exact completion time of one or more jobs may not be predictable. It is of interest to know whether or not there are some results concerning the optimal sequencing rules when processing times are uncertain. We assume that processing times are independent of one another.

In the case of processing on a single machine, most of the results are quite similar to those discussed earlier for the deterministic case. Suppose that n jobs are to be processed through a single machine. Assume that the job times, $t_1, t_2, \ldots, t_n$, are random variables with known distribution functions. The goal is to minimize the *expected* average weighted flow time; that is,

$$\text{Minimize } E\left(\frac{1}{n}\sum_{i=1}^{n} u_i F_i\right),$$

where u_i are the weights and F_i is the (random) flow time of job i.

Rothkopf (1966) has shown that the optimal solution is to sequence the jobs so that job i precedes job $i + 1$ if

$$\frac{E(t_i)}{u_i} < \frac{E(t_{i+1})}{u_{i+1}}.$$

Notice that if we set all the weights $u_i = 1$, then this rule is simply to order the jobs according to the minimum expected processing time; that is, it is essentially the same as SPT.

In the case of due date scheduling with random processing times, results are also similar to the deterministic case. Banerjee (1965) shows that if the objective is to minimize the maximum over all jobs of the probability that a job is late, then the optimal schedule is to order the jobs according to earliest due date (or according to earliest expected due date when due dates are themselves random).

Multiple Machines

Somewhat more interesting results exist for scheduling jobs with random job times on multiple machines. In fact, there are results available for this case that are *not* true for the deterministic problem.

An assumption that is usually made for the multiple-machine problem is that the distribution of job times is exponential. This assumption is needed because the exponential distribution is the only one having the *memoryless property*. (This property is discussed in detail in Chapter 13 on reliability and maintenance.) The requirement that job times be exponentially distributed is severe in the context of scheduling. In most job shops, if processing times cannot be predicted accurately in advance, it is unlikely that they would be exponentially distributed. Why? The memoryless property tells us that the probability that a job is completed in the next instant of time is independent of the length of time already elapsed in processing the job. Certain applications, such as telephone systems and shared computer applications, may be accurately modeled in this manner, but by and large the exponential law would not accurately describe processing times for most manufacturing job shops.

With these caveats in mind, we present several results for scheduling jobs on multiple machines with random job times. Consider the following problem: n jobs are to be processed through two identical parallel machines. Each job needs to be processed only once on either machine. The objective is to minimize the expected time that elapses from time zero until the last job has completed processing. This is known as the expected makespan. We assume that the n jobs have processing times $t_1, t_2, \ldots, t_n$, which are exponential random variables with rates $\mu_1, \mu_2, \ldots, \mu_n$. This means that the expected time required to complete job i, $E(t_i)$, is $1/\mu_i$.

Parallel processing is different from flow shop processing. In flow shop processing, the jobs are processed first on machine 1 and then on machine 2. In parallel processing, the jobs need to be processed on only one machine, and any job can be processed on either machine. Assume that at time $t = 0$ machine 1 is occupied with a prior job, job 0, and the remaining processing time of job 0 is t_0, which could be a random or deterministic variable. The remaining jobs are processed as follows: let $[1], [2], \ldots, [n]$ be a permutation of the n jobs. Job [1] is scheduled on the vacant machine. Job [2] follows either job 0 on machine 1 or job [1] on machine 2, depending on which is completed first. Each successive job is then scheduled on the next available machine.

Let $T_0 \leq T_1 \leq \cdots \leq T_n$ be the completion times of the successive jobs. The makespan is the time of completion of the last job, which is T_n. The expected value of the makespan is minimized by using the longest-expected-processing-time-first rule (LEPT).[1] Note that this is exactly the opposite of the SPT rule for a single machine. The optimality of scheduling the jobs in decreasing order of their expected size rather than in increasing order (as the SPT rule does) is more likely a result of parallel processing than of randomness of the job times.

---

[1] However, if we consider flow time, then SEPT (shortest expected processing time first) minimizes the expected flow time on two machines.

FIGURE 9–12
Realization of parallel processing on two machines with random job times

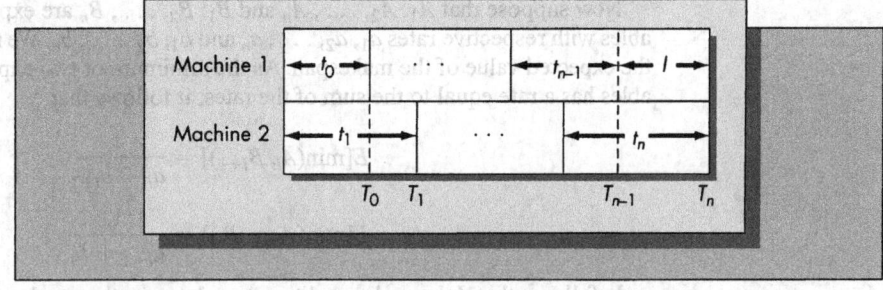

We intuitively show the optimality of LEPT for this problem as follows: Consider the schematic diagram in Figure 9–12, which gives a particular realization of the processing times for an arbitrary sequencing of the jobs. In Figure 9–12 the random variable I corresponds to the idle time of the machine that does not process the job completed last. Intuitively, we would like to make I as small as possible in order to minimize the expected makespan. This can be shown more rigorously as follows.

From the picture, it is clear that

$$T_n + T_{n-1} = \sum_{i=0}^{n} t_i$$

and

$$T_n = T_{n-1} - I.$$

Solving for T_{n-1} in the second equation and substituting into the first gives

$$T_n + T_n - I = \sum_{i=0}^{n} t_i$$

or

$$2T_n = \sum_{i=0}^{n} t_i + I.$$

As Σt_i is fixed independent of the processing sequence, it follows that minimizing $E(T_n)$ is equivalent to minimizing $E(I)$. Because I is minimized when the processing time of the last job is minimized, we schedule the jobs in order of decreasing expected processing time. Note that this result does *not* necessarily carry over to the case of parallel processing on two machines with deterministic processing times. However, in the deterministic case, scheduling the longest job first will generally give good results when minimizing total makespan. SPT is superior for minimizing mean flow time.

A class of problems we will not discuss, but for which there are several interesting results, are problems in which jobs are to be processed through m nonidentical processors and the processing time does not depend on the job. See Righter (1988) for the characterization of the optimal scheduling rule for this problem.

The Two-Machine Flow Shop Case

An interesting question is whether there is a stochastic analog to Johnson's algorithm for scheduling n jobs on two machines in a flow shop setting; that is, where each job must be processed through machine 1 first, then through machine 2. Johnson's algorithm tells us that job i precedes job $i + 1$ if

$$\min(A_i, B_{i+1}) < \min(A_{i+1}, B_i)$$

in order to minimize the makespan.

Now suppose that $A_1, A_2, \ldots, A_n$ and $B_1, B_2, \ldots, B_n$ are exponential random variables with respective rates $a_1, a_2, \ldots, a_n$ and $b_1, b_2, \ldots, b_n$. We now wish to minimize the expected value of the makespan. As the minimum of two exponential random variables has a rate equal to the sum of the rates, it follows that

$$E[\min(A_i, B_{i+1})] = \frac{1}{a_i + b_{i+1}}.$$

$$E[\min(A_{i+1}, B_i)] = \frac{1}{a_{i+1} + b_i}.$$

It follows that Johnson's condition translates in the stochastic case to the condition that

$$a_i - b_i \geq a_{i+1} - b_{i+1},$$

so that the jobs should be scheduled in the order of decreasing values of the difference in the rates.

Example 9.9

Consider Example 9.5, used to illustrate Johnson's algorithm, but let us assume that the job times are random variables having the exponential distribution with mean times given in the example. Hence, we have the following:

Job	Expected Times		Rates		Differences
	A	B	A	B	
1	5	2	0.20	0.500	−0.30
2	1	6	1.00	0.170	0.83
3	9	7	0.11	0.140	−0.03
4	3	8	0.33	0.125	0.21
5	10	4	0.10	0.250	−0.15

Ordering the jobs according to decreasing values of the differences in the final column results in the sequence

2–4–3–5–1.

which is exactly the same sequence we found in the deterministic case using Johnson's algorithm.

This section considered several solution procedures when job times are random variables. Even when job times are known with certainty, randomness resulting from other sources may still be present. For example, when considering scheduling as a dynamic problem, one must determine the pattern of arrivals to the system. It is common for jobs to arrive according to some random process and queue up for service. Queueing theory and simulation are useful tools for dealing with randomness of this type. Conway, Maxwell, and Miller (1967) discuss the application of both simulation and queueing to operations scheduling problems.

Problems for Section 9.8

18. Consider Example 9.2 in Section 9.5 on determining the optimal sequence to land the planes. Suppose that the landing times are random variables with standard deviation equal to one-third of the mean in each case.

a. In what sequence should the planes be landed in order to minimize the expected average weighted flow time, if the weights to be used are the reciprocals of the number of passengers on each plane?

b. For the sequence you found in part (a), what is the probability that all planes are landed within 100 minutes? Assume that the landing times are independent normally distributed random variables. Will your answer change if the planes are landed in a different sequence?

19. A computer center has two identical computers for batch processing. The computers are used as parallel processors. Job times are estimated by the user, but experience has shown that an exponential distribution gives an accurate description of the actual job times. Suppose that at a point in time there are eight jobs remaining to be processed with the following expected job times (expressed in minutes):

Job	1	2	3	4	5	6	7	8
Expected time	4	8	1	50	1	30	20	6

a. In what sequence should the jobs be processed in order to minimize the expected completion time of all eight jobs (i.e., the makespan)?

b. Assume that computer A is occupied with a job that has exactly two minutes of processing time remaining and computer B is idle. If job times are deterministic, show the start and end times of each job on each computer using the sequence derived in part (a).

20. Six ships are docked in a harbor awaiting unloading. The times required to unload the ships are random variables with respective means of 0.6, 1.2, 2.5, 3.5, 0.4, and 1.8 hours. The ships are given a priority weighting based on tonnage. The respective tonnages are 12, 18, 9, 14, 4, and 10. In what sequence should the ships be unloaded in order to minimize the expected weighted time?

21. Solve Problem 13 assuming that the times required by John and Marsha are exponentially distributed random variables with expected times given in Problem 13.

22. Five sorority sisters plan to attend a social function. Each requires hair styling and fitting for a gown. Assume that the times required are independent exponentially distributed random variables with the mean times for the fittings of 0.6, 1.2, 1.5, 0.8, and 1.1 hours, respectively, and mean times for the stylings of 0.8, 1.6, 1.0, 0.7, and 1.3 hours, respectively. Assume that the fittings are done before the stylings and that there is only a single hair stylist and a single seamstress available. In what sequence should they be scheduled in order to minimize the total expected time required for fittings and stylings?

9.9 STOCHASTIC SCHEDULING: DYNAMIC ANALYSIS

The scheduling algorithms discussed thus far in this chapter are based on the assumption that all jobs arrive for processing simultaneously. In practice, however, scheduling jobs on machines is a dynamic problem. We use the term *dynamic* here to mean that jobs are arriving randomly over time, and decisions must be made on an ongoing basis as to how to schedule those jobs.

Queueing theory provides a means of modeling some dynamic scheduling problems. Chapter 7 and Supplement 2, provide a review of basic queueing theory. In this section familiarity with the results presented in Supplement 2 is assumed.

Consider the following problem. Jobs arrive completely at random to a single machine. This means that the arrival process is a *Poisson* process. Assume that the mean arrival rate is λ. We initially will assume that processing times are exponentially distributed with mean $1/\mu$. This means that the average processing rate is μ and processing times are independent identically distributed exponential random variables. Finally, we assume that jobs are processed on a first-come, first-served (FCFS) basis. In queueing terminology, we are assuming an M/M/1/FCFS queue. Other processing sequences also will be considered.

Basic queueing theory answers several questions about the performance characteristics of this scheduling problem. First, the probability distribution of the number of jobs in the system (the number waiting to be processed plus the number being processed) in the steady state is known to be geometric with parameter $\rho = \lambda/\mu$. That is, if L is the number of jobs in the system in steady state, then

$$P\{L = i\} = \rho^i(1 - \rho) \quad \text{for } i = 0, 1, 2, 3, \ldots$$

The expected number of jobs in the system is $\rho/(1 - \rho)$. This implies that a solution exists only for $\rho < 1$. Intuitively this makes sense: the rate at which jobs arrive in the system must be less than the rate at which they are processed to guarantee that the queue does not grow without bound.[2]

Minimizing mean flow time is a common objective not only in static scheduling, but also in dynamic scheduling. The flow time of a job begins the instant the job joins the queue of unprocessed jobs and continues until its processing is completed. For the dynamic scheduling problem, the flow time of a job is a random variable; it depends on the realization of the processing times of preceding jobs as well as its own processing time. The queueing term for the flow time of a job is the waiting time in the system and is denoted by the symbol W. Supplement 2 shows that the distribution of the flow time for the M/M/1/FCFS queue is exponential with parameter $\mu - \lambda$. That is,

$$P\{W > t\} = e^{-(\mu-\lambda)t} \quad \text{for all } t > 0.$$

Also derived are the distribution for the waiting time in the queue and the expected number of jobs in the queue waiting to be processed. We can see the application of these formulas to the dynamic scheduling problem in the following example.

Example 9.10 A student computer laboratory has a single laser printer. Jobs queue up on the printer from the network server in the lab and are completed on a first-come, first-served basis. The average printing job requires four minutes, but the times vary considerably. Experience has shown that the distribution of times closely follows an exponential distribution. At peak times, about 12 students per hour require use of the printer, but the arrival of jobs to the printer can be assumed to occur completely at random.

Assuming a peak traffic period, determine the following:

a. The average number of jobs in the printer queue.
b. The average flow time of a job.

---

[2] What is not obvious, however, is what happens at the boundary when $\lambda = \mu$ or $\rho = 1$. It turns out that when the processing and the arrival rates are equal (and interarrival times and job processing times are random), the queue still grows without bound. The reason for this is certainly not obvious, but it appears to be a consequence of the randomness of the arrivals and processing times.

c. The probability that a job will wait more than 30 minutes before it begins processing.
d. The probability that there are more than six jobs in the system.

Solution

First we must determine the service and arrival rates. As each printing job requires an average of 4 minutes, it follows that the service *rate* is $\mu = 1/4$ per minute or 15 per hour. The arrival rate is given as $\lambda = 12$ per hour. The traffic intensity $\rho = 12/15 = .8$.

a. The average number of jobs in the queue is l_q which is given by (refer to Supplement 2)

$$l_q = \frac{\rho^2}{1 - \rho} = \frac{.64}{.2} = 3.2.$$

b. The average flow time of a job is the same as the waiting time in the system. From Chapter 7,

$$W = \frac{\rho}{\lambda(1 - \rho)} = \frac{.8}{(12)(.2)} = 0.3333 \text{ hour (20 minutes)}.$$

c. Here we are interested in $P\{W_q > 0.5\}$. The distribution of W_q is essentially exponential with parameter $\mu - \lambda$, but with positive mass at zero.

$$P\{W_q > t\} = \rho e^{-(\mu - \lambda)t} = .8 e^{-(3)(0.5)} = .1785.$$

d. Here we wish to determine $P\{L > 6\}$. From the solution of Example 7.5 in Chapter 7, we showed that

$$P\{L > k\} = \rho^{k+1} = .8^7 = .2097.$$

Selection Disciplines Independent of Job Processing Times

Although our sense of fair play says that the service discipline should be FCFS, there are many occasions when jobs are processed in other sequences. For example, consider a manufacturing process in which parts are stacked as they are completed. The next stage in the process may simply take the parts from the top of the stack, resulting in a last-come, first-served (LCFS) discipline. Similarly, one could envision a situation in which completed parts are thrown into a bin and taken out at random, resulting in service occurring in a random order.

Queueing theory tells us that as long as the selection discipline *does not depend on the processing times*, the mean flow times (and hence mean numbers in the system and mean queue lengths) are the same.[3] However, the **variance** of the flow times does depend on the selection discipline. The flow time variance is greatest with LCFS and least with FCFS among the three disciplines FCFS, LCFS, and random.[4] The second moments of the flow time are given by

$$E_{\text{LCFS}}(W^2) = \frac{1}{1 - \rho} E_{\text{FCFS}}(W^2),$$

$$E_{\text{RANDOM}}(W^2) = \frac{1}{1 - \rho/2} E_{\text{FCFS}}(W^2).$$

(The second equation has been proved for exponential processing times only, but it has been conjectured that it holds in general.) Recall that the variance of a random

---

[3] Many of the results quoted in this section are discussed more fully in Chapter 9 of Conway, Maxwell, and Miller (1967). In fact, even though this book is over 40 years old, it still provides the most comprehensive treatment of the application of queueing theory to scheduling problems.

[4] This is strictly true only if we eliminate the possibility of preemption. Preemption means that a newly arriving job is allowed to interrupt the service of a job already in progress. We will not treat preemptive disciplines here.

variable is the second moment minus the mean squared, so we can obtain the variance of W directly from these formulas.

Example 9.10 (continued) Determine the variance of the flow times for the laser printer during peak hours assuming (1) FCFS, (2) LCFS, and (3) random selection disciplines.

Solution Because under FCFS the flow time is exponentially distributed with parameter $\mu - \lambda$, it follows that the mean flow time is $1/(\mu - \lambda)$ and the variance of the flow time is $1/(\mu - \lambda)^2$.

$$E_{FCFS}(W) = \frac{1}{\mu - \lambda} = \frac{1}{15 - 12} = \frac{1}{3} \text{ hour.}$$

$$Var_{FCFS}(W) = \frac{1}{(3)^2} = \frac{1}{9}.$$

Because $Var(W) = E(W)^2 - (E(W))^2$, it follows that

$$E_{FCFS}(W)^2 = Var_{FCFS}(W) + (E_{FCFS}(W))^2 = \frac{1}{9} + \left(\frac{1}{3}\right)^2 = \frac{2}{9}.$$

From these results, we obtain

$$E_{LCFS}(W)^2 = \left(\frac{1}{1-.8}\right)\left(\frac{2}{9}\right) = \frac{10}{9}, \quad \text{giving}$$

$$Var_{LCFS}(W) = \frac{10}{9} - \left(\frac{1}{3}\right)^2 = 1.0.$$

Similarly,

$$E_{RANDOM}(W)^2 = \left(\frac{1}{1-.4}\right)\left(\frac{2}{9}\right) = 0.3704, \quad \text{giving}$$

$$Var_{RANDOM}(W) = 0.3704 - \left(\frac{1}{3}\right)^2 = 0.2593.$$

Hence, we see that if the jobs are processed on the printer on an LCFS basis, the variance of the flow time is 1.0, as compared to 2/9 for FCFS. Processing jobs in a random order also increases the variance of the flow time over FCFS, but by a much smaller degree. Intuitively, the variance is larger for LCFS than for FCFS, because when jobs are processed in the opposite order of their arrival, it is likely that a job that has been in the queue for a while will continue to be "bumped" by newly arriving jobs. The result will be a very long flow time. A similar phenomenon occurs in the random case, but the effect is not as severe.

Selection Disciplines Dependent on Job Processing Times

One of the goals of research into dynamic queueing models is to discover optimal selection disciplines. Previously we stated that the average measures of performance (w, w_q, l, and l_q) are independent of the selection discipline as long as the selection discipline does not depend on the job processing times. However, it was shown in Chapter 7 that selection based on shortest processing times can make a large difference to average waiting time. Furthermore, consider the case in which job processing times are realized at the instant the job joins the queue. This assumption is reasonable for most industrial scheduling applications. For machine processing problems, the work content is likely to be a multiple of the number of parts that have to be processed, so the processing time is known at the instant a job joins the queue. An example in which this does not hold

FIGURE 9–13

Relative flow times: SPT versus FCFS

Source: Adapted from tabled results in Conway, Maxwell, and Miller (1967), p. 184.

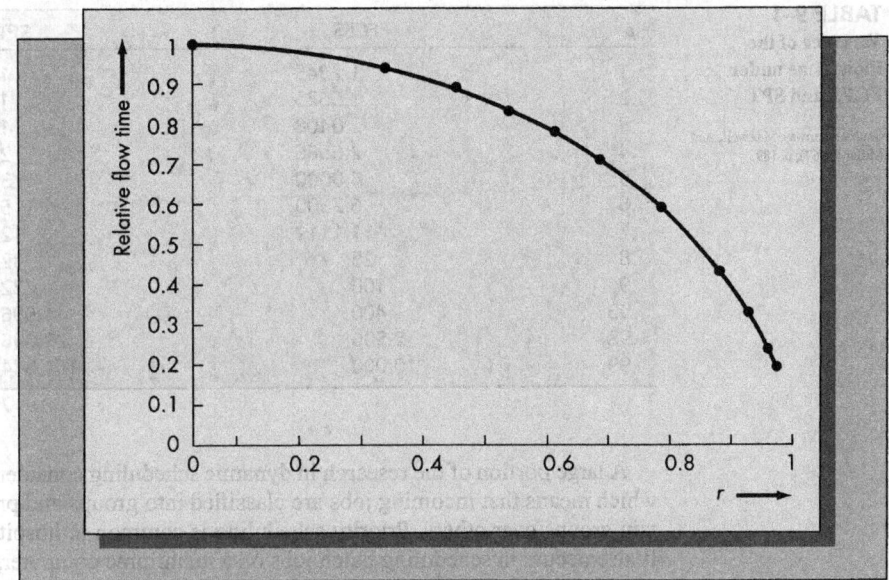

would be a bank. It is generally not possible to tell how long a customer will require for service until he or she enters service and reveals the nature of the transaction.

When job processing times are realized when a job joins the queue, it is possible to use a selection discipline that is dependent on job times. One such discipline, discussed at length earlier in this chapter, is the SPT rule: The next job processed is the one with the shortest processing time. It turns out that the SPT rule is effective for the dynamic problem as well as the static problem.

SPT scheduling can significantly reduce the size of the queue in the dynamic scheduling problem. In Figure 9–13 we show just how dramatic this effect can be. This figure assumes an M/M/1 queue. Define the relative flow time as the ratio

$$\frac{E_{SPT}(\text{Flow Time})}{E_{FCFS}(\text{Flow Time})}.$$

We see that as the traffic intensity increases, the advantage of SPT at reducing flow time (and hence the number in the system and the queue length) improves. The queue is reduced by "cleaning out" the shorter jobs. For values of ρ near 1, this ratio could be as low as 0.2. Because of Little's formula (see Chapter 7), the expected number in the system and the flow time are proportional, so this curve also represents the ratio of the expected numbers in the system for the respective selection disciplines.

An interesting question is what happens to the variance of the performance measures under each selection discipline. Again assuming exponential service times, Table 9–1 gives the variances of the flow times for SPT and FCFS as a function of the traffic intensity, ρ.

What we see from this table is that for low values of the traffic intensity (less than about .7), SPT has slightly lower variance than FCFS. However, as the traffic intensity approaches 1, the variance under SPT increases dramatically. For $\rho = .99$, the variance of the flow time under SPT is more than 16 times that for FCFS. Hence, the reduction in the mean flow time achieved by SPT comes at the cost of possibly increasing the variance.

TABLE 9–1
Variance of the Flow Time under FCFS and SPT

Source: Conway, Maxwell, and Miller (1967), p. 189.

ρ	FCFS	SPT
.1	1.2345	1.179
.2	1.5625	1.482
.3	2.0408	1.896
.4	2.6666	2.563
.5	4.0000	3.601
.6	6.2500	5.713
.7	11.1111	12.297
.8	25	32.316
.9	100	222.2
.95	400	1,596.5
.98	2,500	22,096
.99	10,000	161,874

A large portion of the research in dynamic scheduling considers priority disciplines, which means that incoming jobs are classified into groups and priority is given to certain groups over others. Priority scheduling is common in hospital emergency rooms. It also occurs in scheduling batch jobs on a mainframe computer, as certain users may be given priority over others. Priorities may be preemptive or nonpreemptive. Preemptive priority means that a newly arriving job with a higher priority than the job currently being processed is permitted to interrupt the service of the job in process. The interrupted job may continue where it left off at a later time, or it may have to start processing again from scratch. We will not pursue this complex area, but note that SPT is quite robust; it is optimal for a large class of priority scheduling problems.

The $c\mu$ Rule

Consider the following scheduling problem. Jobs arrive randomly to a single machine with exponential processing times. We allow the jobs in the queue to have different service rates μ_i. That is, at any moment, suppose that there are n jobs waiting to be processed. We index the jobs $1, 2, 3, \ldots, n$ and assume that the time required to complete job i has the exponential distribution with mean $1/\mu_i$. In addition, suppose that there is a return of c_i if job i is completed by some fixed time t. The issue is, what is the best choice for the next job to be processed if the objective is to maximize the total expected earnings?

Derman et al. (1978) showed that the optimal policy is to choose the job with the largest value of $c_i\mu_i$. Notice that if the weights are set equal to 1, the $c\mu$ rule is exactly the same as SPT in expectation. Hence, this can be considered to be a type of weighted SPT scheduling rule. It turns out that the $c\mu$ rule is optimal for several other versions of the stochastic scheduling problem. We refer the interested reader to Pinedo (1983) and the references listed there.

Problems for Section 9.9

23. A computer system queues up batch jobs and processes them on an FCFS basis. Between 2 and 5 P.M., jobs arrive at an average rate of 30 per hour and require an average of 1.2 minutes of computer time. Assume the arrival process is Poisson and the processing times are exponentially distributed.

    a. What is the expected number of jobs in the system and in the queue in the steady state?

b. What are the expected flow time and the time in the queue in the steady state?
c. What is the probability that the system is empty?
d. What is the probability that the queue is empty?
e. What is the probability that the flow time of a job exceeds 10 minutes?

24. Consider the computer system of Problem 23.
   a. Compute the variance of the flow times assuming FCFS, LCFS, and random selection disciplines.
   b. Using a normal approximation of the flow time distribution for the LCFS and random cases, estimate the probability that the flow time in the system exceeds 10 minutes in each case.

25. A critical resource in a manufacturing operation experiences a very high traffic intensity during the shop's busiest periods. During these periods the arrival rate is approximately 57 jobs per hour. Job processing times are approximately exponentially distributed with mean 1 minute.
   a. Compute the expected flow time in the system assuming an FCFS processing discipline, and the expected flow time under SPT using Figure 9–13.
   b. Compute the probability that a job waits more than 30 minutes for processing under FCFS.
   c. Using a normal approximation, estimate the probability that a job waits more than 30 minutes for processing under LCFS.

9.10 ASSEMBLY LINE BALANCING

The problem of balancing an assembly line is a classic industrial engineering problem. Even though much of the work in the area goes back to the mid-1950s and early 1960s, the basic structure of the problem is relevant to the design of production systems today, even in automated plants. The problem is characterized by a set of n distinct tasks that must be completed on each item. The time required to complete task i is a known constant t_i. The goal is to organize the tasks into groups, with each group of tasks being performed at a single workstation. In most cases, the amount of time allotted to each workstation is determined in advance, based on the desired rate of production of the assembly line. This is known as the cycle time and is denoted by C. A schematic of a typical assembly line is given in Figure 9–14. In the figure, circles represent tasks to be done at the corresponding stations.

FIGURE 9–14
Schematic of a typical assembly line

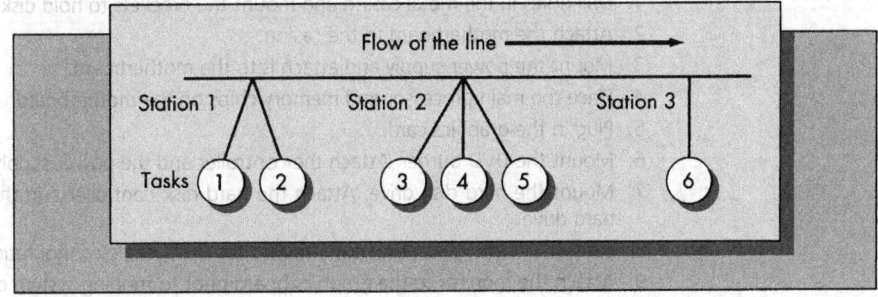

Assembly line balancing is traditionally thought of as a facilities design and layout problem, and one might argue that it would be more appropriately part of Chapter 11. Assigning tasks to workstations has traditionally been a one-shot decision made at the time the plant is constructed and the line is set up. However, the nature of the modern factory is changing. New plants are being designed with flexibility in mind, allowing new lines to be brought up and old ones restructured on a continuous basis. In such an environment, line balancing is more like a dynamic scheduling problem than a one-shot facilities layout problem.

There are a variety of factors that contribute to the difficulty of the problem. First, there are precedence constraints: some tasks may have to be completed in a particular sequence. Another problem is that some tasks cannot be performed at the same workstation. For example, it might not be possible to work on the front end and the back end of a large object such as an automobile at the same workstation. This is known as a *zoning restriction*. Still other complications might arise. For example, certain tasks may have to be completed at the same workstation, and other tasks may require more than one worker.

Finding the optimal balance of an assembly line is a difficult combinatorial problem even when the problems previously described are not present. Several relatively simple heuristics have been suggested for determining an approximate balance. Many of these methods require few calculations and make it possible to solve large problems by hand.

Let $t_1, t_2, \ldots, t_n$ be the time required to complete the respective tasks. The total work content associated with the production of an item, say T, is given by

$$T = \sum_{i=1}^{n} t_i.$$

For a cycle time of C, the minimum number of workstations possible is $[T/C]$, where the brackets indicate that the value of T/C is to be rounded to the next larger integer. Because of the discrete and indivisible nature of the tasks and the precedence constraints, it is often true that more stations are required than this ideal minimum value. If there is leeway in the choice of the cycle time, it is advisable to experiment with different values of C to see if a more efficient balance can be obtained.

We will present one heuristic method from Helgeson and Birnie (1961) known as the *ranked positional weight technique*. The method places a weight on each task based on the total time required by all the succeeding tasks. Tasks are assigned sequentially to stations based on these weights. We illustrate the method by example.

Example 9.11

The final assembly of Noname personal computers, a generic mail-order PC clone, requires a total of 12 tasks. The assembly is done at the Lubbock, Texas, plant using various components imported from the Far East. The tasks required for the assembly operations are

1. Drill holes in the metal casing and mount the brackets to hold disk drives.
2. Attach the motherboard to the casing.
3. Mount the power supply and attach it to the motherboard.
4. Place the main processor and memory chips on the motherboard.
5. Plug in the graphics card.
6. Mount the DVD burner. Attach the controller and the power supply.
7. Mount the hard disk drive. Attach the hard disk controller and the power supply to the hard drive.
8. Set switch settings on the motherboard for the specific configuration of the system.
9. Attach the monitor to the graphics board prior to running system diagnostics.
10. Run the system diagnostics.

FIGURE 9–15
Precedence constraints for Noname computer (Example 9.11)

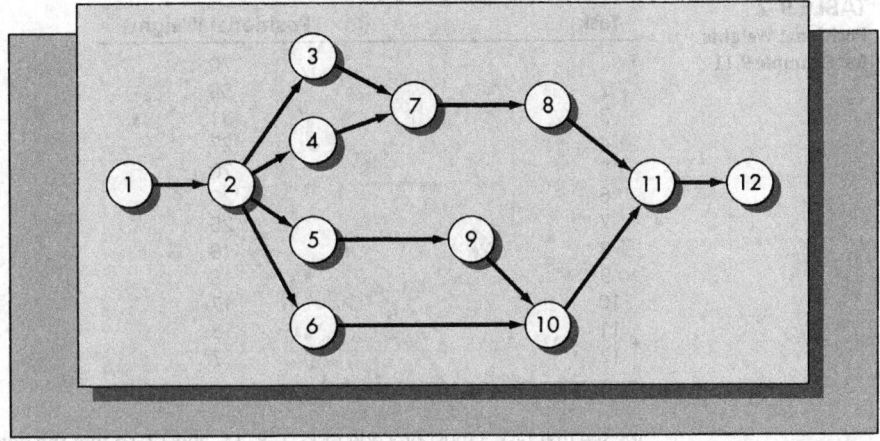

11. Seal the casing.
12. Attach the company logo and pack the system for shipping.

The holes must be drilled and the motherboard attached to the casing prior to any other operations. Once the motherboard has been mounted, the power supply, memory, processor chips, graphics card, and disk controllers can be installed. The floppy drives are placed in the unit prior to the hard drive and require that the power supply and controller be in place first. Based on the memory configuration and the choice of graphics adapter, the switch settings on the motherboard are determined and set. The monitor must be attached to the graphics board so that the results of the diagnostic tests can be read. Finally, after all other tasks are completed, the diagnostics are run and the system is packed for shipping. The job times and precedence relationships for this problem are summarized in the following table. The network representation of this particular problem is given in Figure 9–15.

Task	Immediate Predecessors	Time
1	—	12
2	1	6
3	2	6
4	2	2
5	2	2
6	2	12
7	3, 4	7
8	7	5
9	5	1
10	9, 6	4
11	8, 10	6
12	11	7

Suppose that the company is willing to hire enough workers to produce one assembled machine every 15 minutes. The sum of the task times is 70, which means that the minimum number of workstations is the ratio 70/15 = 4.67 rounded to the next larger integer, which is 5. This does not mean that a five-station balance necessarily exists.

The solution procedure requires determining the positional weight of each task. The positional weight of task *i* is defined as the time required to perform task *i* plus the times required to perform all tasks having task *i* as a predecessor. As task 1 must precede all other tasks, its positional weight is simply the sum of the task times, which is 70. Task 2 has positional weight 58. From Figure 9–15

9.10 Assembly Line Balancing

TABLE 9–2
Positional Weights for Example 9.11

Task	Positional Weight
1	70
2	58
3	31
4	27
5	20
6	29
7	25
8	18
9	18
10	17
11	13
12	7

we see that task 3 must precede tasks 7, 8, 11, and 12, so that the positional weight of task 3 is $t_3 + t_7 + t_8 + t_{11} + t_{12} = 31$. The other positional weights are computed similarly. The positional weights are listed in Table 9–2.

The next step is to rank the tasks in the order of decreasing positional weight. The ranking for this case is 1, 2, 3, 6, 4, 7, 5, 8, 9, 10, 11, 12. Finally, the tasks are assigned sequentially to stations in the order of the ranking, and assignments are made only as long as the precedence constraints are not violated.

Let us now consider the balance obtained using this technique assuming a cycle time of 15 minutes. Task 1 is assigned to station 1. That leaves a slack of three minutes at this station. However, because task 2 must be assigned next, in order not to violate the precedence constraints, and the sum $t_1 + t_2$ exceeds 15, we close station 1. Tasks 2, 3, and 4 are then assigned to station 2, resulting in an idle time of only one minute at this station. Continuing in this manner, we obtain the following balance for this problem:

Station	1	2	3	4	5	6
Tasks	1	2, 3, 4	5, 6, 9	7, 8	10, 11	12
Idle time	3	1	0	3	5	8

Notice that although the minimum possible number of stations for this problem is five, the ranked positional weight technique results in a six-station balance. As the method is only a heuristic, it is possible that there is a solution with five stations. In this case, however, the optimal balance requires six stations when $C = 15$ minutes.

The head of the firm assembling Noname computers is interested in determining the minimum cycle time that would result in a five-station balance. If we increase the cycle time from $C = 15$ to $C = 16$, then the balance obtained is

Station	1	2	3	4	5
Tasks	1	2, 3, 4, 5	6, 9	7, 8, 10	11, 12
Idle time	4	0	3	0	3

This is clearly a much more efficient balance: The total idle time has been cut from 20 minutes per unit to only 10 minutes per unit. The number of stations decreases by about 16 percent, while the cycle time increases by only about 7 percent. Assuming that a production day is seven hours, a value of $C = 15$ minutes would result in a daily production level of 28 units per assembly operation and a value of $C = 16$ minutes would result in a daily production level of 26.25 units per assembly operation. Management would have to determine whether the decline in the production rate of 1.75 units per day per operation is justified by the savings realized with five rather than six stations.

An alternative choice is to stay with the six stations, but see if a six-station balance can be obtained with a cycle time less than 15 minutes. It turns out that for values of the cycle time of both 14 minutes and 13 minutes, the ranked positional weight method will give six-station balances. The $C = 13$ solution is

Station	1	2	3	4	5	6
Tasks	1	2, 3	6	4, 5, 7, 9	8, 10	11, 12
Idle time	1	1	1	1	4	0

Thirteen minutes appear to be the minimum cycle time with six stations. The total idle time of eight minutes resulting from the balance above is two minutes less than that achieved with five stations when $C = 16$. The production rate with six stations and $C = 13$ would be 32.3 units per day per operation. Increasing the number of stations from five to six results in a substantial improvement in the throughput rate.

In this section we presented the ranked positional weight heuristic for solving the assembly line balancing problem. Other heuristic methods exist as well. One is COMSOAL, a computer-based heuristic developed by Arcus (1966). The method is efficient for large problems involving many tasks and workstations. Kilbridge and Wester (1961) suggest a method similar to the ranked positional weight technique.

There are optimal procedures for solving the line balancing problem, but the calculations are complex and time-consuming, requiring either dynamic programming (Held et al., 1963) or integer programming (Thangavelu and Shetty, 1971). More recent interest in the line balancing problem has focused on issues relating to uncertainty in the performance times for the individual tasks. (See Hillier and Boling, 1986, and the references contained there.)

Virtually all assembly line balancing procedures assume that the objective is to minimize the total idle time at all workstations. However, as we saw in this section, an optimal balance for a fixed cycle time may not be optimal in a global sense. Carlson and Rosenblatt (1985) suggest that most assembly line balancing procedures are based on an incorrect objective. The authors claim that maximizing profit (rather than minimizing idle time) would give a different solution to most assembly line balancing problems, and they present several models in which both numbers of stations and cycle time are decision variables.

Problems for Section 9.10

26. Consider the example of Noname computers presented in this section.

   a. What is the minimum cycle time that is possible? What is the minimum number of stations that would theoretically be required to achieve this cycle time?

   b. Based on the ranked positional weight technique, how many stations are actually required for the cycle time indicated in part (*a*)?

   c. Suppose that the owner of the company that sells Noname computers finds that he is receiving orders for approximately 100 computers per day. How many separate assembly lines are required assuming (*i*) the best five-station balance, (*ii*) the best six-station balance (both determined in the text), and (*iii*) the balance you obtained in part (*b*)? Discuss the trade-offs involved with each choice.

27. A production facility assembles inexpensive telephones on a production line. The assembly requires 15 tasks with precedence relationships and activity times as shown in Figure 9–16. The activity times appear next to the node numbers in the network.

FIGURE 9–16
(For Problem 27)

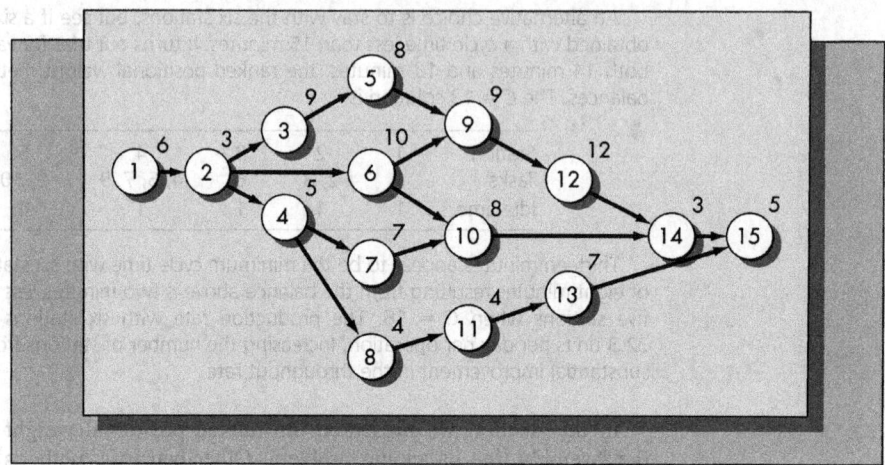

FIGURE 9–17
(For Problem 29)

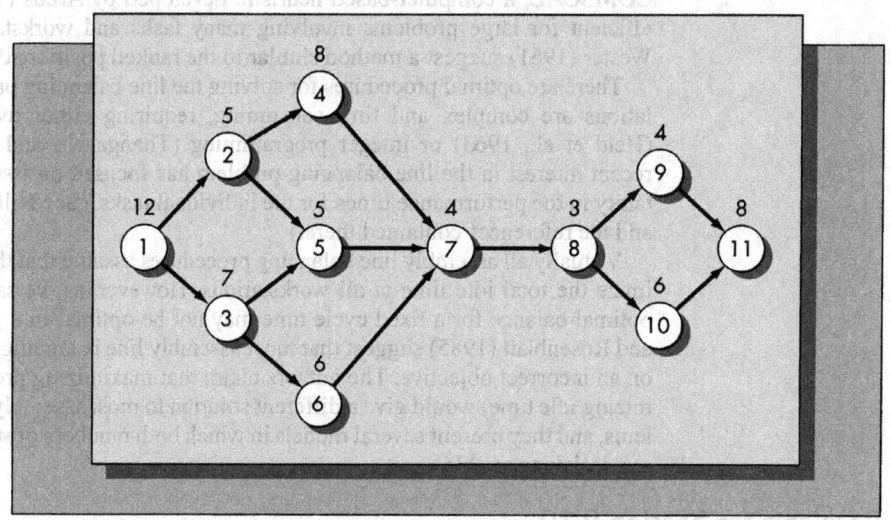

   a. Determine positional weights for each of the activities.
   b. For a cycle time of 30 units, what is the minimum number of stations that could be achieved? Find the $C = 30$ balance obtained using the ranked positional weight technique.
   c. Is there a solution with the same number of stations you found in part (b) but with a lower cycle time? In particular, what appears to be the minimum cycle time that gives a balance with the same number of stations you found in part (b)?

28. For the data given in Problem 27, determine by experimentation the minimum cycle time for a three-station balance.

29. Consider the assembly line balancing problem represented by the network in Figure 9–17. The performance times are shown above the nodes.
   a. Determine a balance for $C = 15$.
   b. Determine a balance for $C = 20$.

Snapshot Application

MANUFACTURING DIVISIONS REALIZE SAVINGS WITH SCHEDULING SOFTWARE

Motorola Goes for MOOPI

Motorola Corporation has adopted MOOPI from Berclain Group of Canada to schedule the remanufacture of 1,000 engine controllers each month in the Automotive and Industrial Electronics Group in its Seguin, Texas, plant. Utilization of used engine controllers has improved from 35 percent to over 70 percent and the time required for scheduling has reduced from 100 to only 8 hours per month as a consequence of implementing the software. The problem of scheduling cores remanufacture is a very complex one, requiring five or six employees when it was done manually. According to Eileen Svoboda, a process improvement manager:

> Remanufacturing in itself is a unique and complex process because the raw material—the core—arrives randomly through time, and the material required to remanufacture it is unknown until after the core is inspected. Right now in our business we have 7,000 Motorola core model numbers that can be remanufactured into approximately 800 different customer models. To keep all this straight in the old manual system we relied on paper trails, as well as the memory and expertise of a few key individuals in Texas, Michigan, and Illinois.

The software allows the group to schedule one month's worth of production in detail, as well as some additional planning functions for a 26-week time horizon. Motorola considered four different scheduling systems. MOOPI was chosen because it could both handle complex material assignment needs and easily run what-if simulations. Although the simulation feature played an important part in the decision, MOOPI is basically an optimization package, and, according to Berclain, Motorola's primary goal was optimization of materials utilization.

The system's database incorporates manufacturing data, including sequence of operations or routings, bills of materials, and setup sequencing information. It distinguishes raw materials, subassembly, and finished goods inventory levels. It can exchange data with other inventory control systems, and it details production orders for all work centers.

H.P. Implements FastMAN for Materials Scheduling

The Hewlett-Packard Corporation of Palo Alto, California, has experienced enormous growth in the highly competitive PC business. Part of this success is attributable to careful management of the materials in the PC product plants.

H.P.'s scheduling system is PC-based and is used in conjunction with its MRP II system. One post-MRP scheduler used by H.P. is FastMAN, produced by the company with the same name based in Chicago, Illinois. Today, H.P. has eight installations of FastMAN and three with APS, a workstation-based system recently made available on PCs. According to Dr. Lee Seaton, a senior industry analyst with H.P.:

> The materials content of a personal computer constitutes over 90 percent of its cost. Unfortunately, we frequently had too much of one thing and too little of something else. And we knew it was only going to get worse, since product life cycles continue to accelerate, recently down from 15 months to under one year. We had to reduce product write-offs and have a smoother cut-off for a given product set. Too often, we'd launch a successful product, but either not have enough to sell or at the end of the cycle have excessive material write-offs.

While material control is normally the domain of MRP II, H.P. was not having the desired level of success with MRP II. Dr. Seaton claims that 30 percent of the MRP runs were considered useless. Updates of inventory levels or bills of materials were not entered into the system in a timely fashion, making the results out of date. The new scheduling tools allowed H.P. employees to verify the validity of MRP runs with desktop systems. Also, the software provided the capability for determining the consequences of business decisions in a spreadsheet or graphical form. Engineering changes could more easily be incorporated into the materials plan, and excess material could be utilized more effectively by constructing "matched sets." The key to H.P.'s success was "getting information into the hands of the decision makers," says Seaton.

Source: These two applications are discussed in Parker (1995).

c. What appears to be the minimum cycle time that can be achieved using the number of stations you obtained in part (*a*)?

d. What appears to be the minimum cycle time that can be achieved using the number of stations you obtained in part (*b*)?

9.11 HISTORICAL NOTES

Interest in studying the effects of different sequencing strategies in the job shop is relatively recent. One of the earliest monographs in the open literature that considered sequencing issues is by Salveson (1952). The first significant published work to present analytical results for optimal sequencing strategies is Johnson (1954). Bellman's (1956) review article discusses sequence scheduling (among other topics) and presents an interesting proof of the optimality of Johnson's algorithm based on dynamic programming arguments. Bellman appears to be the first to have recognized the optimality of a permutation schedule for scheduling n jobs on three machines.

Johnson's work spawned considerable interest in scheduling. The excellent monograph by Conway, Maxwell, and Miller (1967), for example, lists over 200 publications up until 1967. It is likely that considerably more than 200 papers have been published since that time. Much of the recent research in sequence scheduling has focused on stochastic scheduling. Weiss (1982) provides an interesting synopsis of work in this area. That jobs should be scheduled in order of decreasing expected processing time when scheduling is on two parallel processors and the objective is to minimize the expected makespan appears to have been discovered at about the same time by Bruno and Downey (1977) and Pinedo and Weiss (1979). The elegant method of proof we present is from Pinedo and Weiss (1979).

Much of the work on dynamic scheduling under uncertainty appears in the Conway, Maxwell, and Miller (1967) monograph. The $c\mu$ rule, apparently discovered by Derman et al. (1978) in an entirely different context, led to several extensions. See, for example, Righter and Shanthikumar (1989).

9.12 Summary

Scheduling problems arise in many contexts in managing operations. One of the areas explored in this chapter was optimal sequencing rules for scheduling jobs on machines, a problem that arises in *shop floor control*. We also considered dynamic scheduling problems, which are more typical of the kinds of scheduling problems that one encounters in management of service systems.

Much of the emphasis of the chapter was on determining efficient *sequencing rules*. The form of the optimal sequencing rule depends on several factors, including the pattern of arrivals of jobs, the configuration of the job shop, constraints, and the optimization objectives. Typical objectives in job shop management include meeting due dates, minimizing work-in-process, minimizing the average flow time, and minimizing machine idle time.

We discussed four sequencing rules: FCFS (first-come, first-served), SPT (shortest processing time first), EDD (earliest due date), and CR (critical ratio). For sequencing jobs on a single machine, we showed that *SPT* optimized several objectives, including mean flow time. However, SPT sequencing could be problematic. Long jobs would be constantly pushed to the rear of the job queue and might never be processed. For that reason, pure SPT scheduling is rarely used in practice. *Critical ratio scheduling* attempts to balance the importance placed on processing time and the remaining time until the due date. However, there is little evidence to suggest that critical ratio scheduling performs well relative to the common optimization criteria such as mean flow time. As one would expect, *earliest-due-date* scheduling performs best when the goal is to minimize the maximum tardiness.

We considered a variety of algorithms for *single-machine sequencing,* including Moore's (1968) algorithm for minimizing the number of tardy jobs and Lawler's (1973) algorithm for minimizing any nondecreasing function of the flow subject to precedence constraints. An excellent summary of algorithms for sequence scheduling can be found in French (1982). Several techniques for *multiple-machine scheduling* also were presented in this chapter. Johnson's (1954) classic work on scheduling *n jobs through two machines* is discussed, as well as Akers's (1956) graphical method for *two jobs through m machines.*

Stochastic scheduling problems were treated in two contexts: static and dynamic. Static problems are stochastic counterparts to the problems treated earlier in the chapter, except that job completion times are random variables. Most of the simple results for static stochastic scheduling problems require the assumption that job times have the exponential distribution. Because of the memoryless property of the exponential distribution, this assumption is probably not satisfied in most manufacturing job shops. The dynamic case occurs when jobs arrive randomly over time. *Queueing theory,* discussed in detail in Chapter 7 and Supplement 2, is the means for analyzing such problems.

The *assembly line balancing problem* is one in which a collection of tasks must be performed on each item. Furthermore, the tasks must be performed in a specified sequence. The problem is to allot the tasks to workstations on an assembly line. The quality of the balance is measured by the idle time remaining at each station. Determining the best mix of cycle time (amount of time allotted to each station) and number of stations is an extremely difficult analytical problem. We discuss one very simple heuristic solution method from Helgeson and Birnie (1961), known as the ranked positional weight technique, which provides an efficient balance quickly.

While most of this chapter concerns analytical methods for developing schedules, it is important to keep in mind that many real scheduling problems are too complex to be modeled mathematically. In such cases, *simulation* can be a very valuable tool. A computer-based simulation is a model of a real process expressed as a computer program. By running simulations under different scenarios, consequences of alternative strategies can be evaluated easily. Simulations are particularly effective when significant randomness or variation exists.

Job shop *scheduling software* is a growing business. Programs designed to run on PCs and workstations are available from several vendors. Most of these programs provide convenient interfaces to existing enterprise and MRP systems. While the market for the post-MRP schedulers is much smaller than the market for full-blown integrated MRP II systems, it is growing and probably exceeds $100 million in the United States alone. These programs are designed to run in conjunction with an MRP system, and generally incorporate some combination of optimization and simulation. Many companies have been successful at implementing these programs on the factory floor.

There are a number of excellent texts on scheduling. For further reading in this area, we would suggest the books by Baker (1974), French (1982), and Conway, Maxwell, and Miller (1967). Pinedo (1995) provides comprehensive coverage.

Additional Problems on Scheduling

30. Mike's Auto Body Shop has five cars waiting to be repaired. The shop is quite small, so only one car can be repaired at a time. The number of days required to repair each car and the promised date for each are given in the following table.

Cars	Repair Time (days)	Promised Date
1	3	5
2	2	6
3	1	9
4	4	11
5	5	8

Mike has agreed to provide a rental car to each customer whose car is not repaired on time. Compare the performance of the four sequencing rules FCFS, SPT, EDD, and CR relative to minimizing average tardiness.

31. For each of the problems listed, indicate precisely what or who would correspond to jobs and who or what would correspond to machines. In each case discuss what objectives might be appropriate and special priorities that might exist.

    a. Treating patients in a hospital emergency room.
    b. Unloading cargo from ships at port.
    c. Serving users on a time-shared computer system.
    d. Transferring long-distance phone calls from one city to another.

32. Six patients are waiting in a hospital emergency room to receive care for various complaints, ranging from a sprained ankle to a gunshot wound. The patients are numbered in the sequence that they arrived and are given a priority weighting based on the severity of the problem. There is only one doctor available.

Patient	1	2	3	4	5	6
Time required	20 min	2 hr	30 min	10 min	40 min	1 hr
Priority	1	10	3	5	2	2

    a. Suppose that the patients are scheduled on an FCFS basis. Compute the mean flow time and the *weighted* mean flow time, where the weight is the priority number associated with each patient.
    b. Perform the calculations in part (a) for SPT sequencing.
    c. Determine a sequence different from those in parts (a) and (b) that achieves a lower value of the weighted mean flow time.

33. Consider Mike's Auto Body Shop mentioned in Problem 30. What sequencing of the jobs minimizes the

    a. Mean flow time?
    b. Maximum lateness?
    c. Number of tardy jobs?

34. Consider the situation of the emergency room mentioned in Problem 32. Determine the sequence in which patients should be treated in order to minimize the *weighted* value of the mean flow time.

35. Barbara and Jenny's Ice Cream Company produces four different flavors of ice cream: vanilla, chocolate, strawberry, and peanut fudge. Each batch of ice cream is produced in the same large vat, which must be cleaned prior to switching flavors. One day is required for the cleaning process.

    At the current time they have the following outstanding orders of ice cream:

Flavor	Order Size (gallons)	Due Date
Vanilla	385	3
Chocolate	440	8
Strawberry	200	6
Peanut fudge	180	12

It takes one day to produce the ice cream and a maximum of 100 gallons can be produced at one time. Cleaning is required only when flavors are switched. The production for one flavor will be completed prior to beginning production for another flavor. Cleaning is always started at the beginning of a day.

Treating each ice cream flavor as a different job, find the following:

a. The sequence in which the ice cream flavors should be produced in order to minimize the mean flow time for all of the flavors.

b. The optimal sequence to produce the flavors in order to minimize the number of flavors that are late.

36. Consider Barbara and Jenny's Ice Cream Company, mentioned in Problem 35. Suppose that if vanilla or strawberry is produced after chocolate or peanut fudge, an extra day of cleaning is required. For that reason they decide that the vanilla and strawberry will be produced before the chocolate and peanut fudge.

a. Find the optimal sequencing of the flavors to minimize the maximum lateness using Lawler's algorithm.

b. Enumerate all the feasible sequences and determine the sequence that minimizes the maximum lateness by evaluating and comparing the objective function value for each case.

37. Irving Bonner, an independent computer programming consultant, has contracted to complete eight computer programming jobs. Some jobs must be completed in a certain sequence because they involve program modules that will be linked.

Job	Time Required (days)	Due Date
1	4	June 8
2	10	June 15
3	2	June 10
4	1	June 12
5	8	July 1
6	3	July 6
7	2	June 25
8	6	June 29

Precedence restrictions:

$$1 \to 2 \to 5 \to 6.$$
$$4 \to 7 \to 8.$$

Assume that the current date is Monday, June 1, and that Bonner does not work on weekends. Using Lawler's algorithm, find the sequence in which he should be performing the jobs in order to minimize maximum lateness subject to the precedence constraints.

38. William Beebe owns a small shoe store. He has 10 pairs of shoes that require resoling and polishing. He has a machine that can resole one pair of shoes at a time, and the time required for the operation varies with the type and condition of the shoe and the type of sole that is used. Shoes are polished on a machine dedi-cated to this purpose as well, and polishing is always done after resoling. His assistant generally does the polishing while Mr. Beebe does the resoling. The resoling and polishing times (in minutes) are

Shoes	Resoling Time	Polishing Time
1	14	3
2	28	1
3	12	2
4	6	5
5	10	10
6	14	6
7	4	12
8	25	8
9	15	5
10	10	5

In what order should the shoes be repaired in order to minimize the total makespan for these 10 jobs?

39. A leatherworks factory has two punch presses for punching holes in the various leather goods produced in the factory prior to sewing. Suppose that 12 different jobs must be processed on one or the other punch press (i.e., parallel processing). The processing times (in minutes) for these 12 jobs are given in the following table.

Job	1	2	3	4	5	6	7	8	9	10	11	12
Time	26	12	8	42	35	30	29	21	25	15	4	75

Assume that both presses are initially idle. Compare the performance of SPT and LPT (longest processing time) rules for this example. (In parallel processing the next job is simply scheduled on the next available machine.)

40. An independent accountant is planning to prepare tax returns for six of her clients. Prior to her actually preparing each return, her secretary checks the client's file to be sure all the necessary documentation is there and obtains all the tax forms needed for the preparation of the return. Based on past experience with the clients, her secretary estimates that the following times (in hours) are required for preparation of the return and for the accountant to complete the necessary paperwork prior to filing each return:

Client	Secretary Time	Accountant Time
1	1.2	2.5
2	1.6	4.5
3	2.0	2.0
4	1.5	6.0
5	3.1	5.0
6	0.5	1.5

In what order should the work be completed in order to minimize the total time required for all six clients?

41. Five Hong Kong tailors—Simon, Pat, Choon, Paul, and Wu—must complete alterations on a suit for the duke and a dress for the duchess as quickly as possible. On the dress, Choon must first spend 45 minutes cutting the fabric, then Pat will spend 75 minutes sewing the bodice, Simon will need 30 minutes stitching the sleeves, Paul 2 hours lacing the hem, and finally Wu will need 80 minutes for finishing touches. As far as the suit is concerned, Pat begins with shortening the sleeves, which requires 100 minutes. He is followed by Paul, who sews in the lining in 1.75 hours; Wu, who spends 90 minutes sewing on the buttons and narrowing the lapels; and finally Choon, who presses and cleans the suit in 30 minutes.

Determine precisely when each tailor should be performing each task in order to minimize the total time required to complete the dress and the suit. Assume that the tailors start working at 9 A.M. and take no breaks. Draw the Gantt chart indicating your solution.

42. The assembly of a transistorized clock radio requires a total of 11 tasks. The task times and predecessor relationships are given in the following table.

Task	Time (seconds)	Immediate Predecessors
1	4	
2	38	
3	45	
4	12	1, 2
5	10	2
6	8	4
7	12	5
8	10	6
9	2	7
10	10	8, 9
11	34	3, 10

a. Develop a network for this assembly operation.

b. What is the minimum cycle time that could be considered for this operation? What is the minimum number of stations that could be used with this cycle time?

c. Using the ranked positional weight technique, determine the resulting balance using a cycle time of 45 seconds.

d. Determine by experimentation the minimum cycle time that results in a four-station balance.

e. What is the daily production rate for this product if the company adopts the balance you determined in part (c)? (Assume a six-hour day for your calculations.) What would have to be done if the company wanted a higher rate of production?

43. Suppose in Problem 42 that additional constraints arise from the fact that certain tasks cannot be performed at the same station. In particular suppose that the tasks are zoned in the following manner:

Zone 1	Tasks 2, 3, 1, 4, 6
Zone 2	Tasks 5, 8, 7, 9
Zone 3	Tasks 10, 11

Assuming that only tasks in the same zone category can be performed at the same station, determine the resulting line balance for Problem 42 based on a 45-second cycle time.

44. The Southeastern Sports Company produces golf clubs on an assembly line in its plant in Marietta, Georgia. The final assembly of the woods requires the eight operations given in the following table.

Task	Time Required (min.)	Immediate Predecessors
1. Polish shaft	12	
2. Grind the shaft end	14	
3. Polish club head	6	
4. Imprint number	4	3
5. Connect wood to shaft	6	1, 2, 4
6. Place and secure connecting pin	3	5
7. Place glue on other end of shaft	3	1
8. Set in grips and balance	12	6, 7

a. Draw a network to represent the assembly operation.
b. What is the minimum cycle time that can be considered? Determine the balance that results from the ranked positional weight technique for this cycle time.
c. By experimentation, determine the minimum cycle time that can be achieved with a three-station balance.

45. Develop a template that computes several measures of performance for first-come, first-served job sequencing. Allow for up to 20 jobs so that column 1 holds the numbers 1, 2, ..., 20. Column 2 should be the processing times to be inputted by the user, and column 3 the due dates also inputted by the user. Column 4 should be the tardiness and column 5 the flow time. Develop the logic to compute the mean flow time, the average tardiness, and the number of tardy jobs. (When computing the average of a column, be sure that your spreadsheet does not treat blanks as zeros.)

a. Use your template to find the mean flow time, average tardiness, and number of tardy jobs for Problem 7 (Section 8.6), assuming FCFS sequencing.
b. Find the mean flow time, average tardiness, and number of tardy jobs for Problem 8, assuming FCFS sequencing.
c. Find the mean flow time, average tardiness, and number of tardy jobs assuming FCFS sequencing for the following 20-job problem:

Job	Processing Time	Due Date	Job	Processing Time	Due Date
1	10	34	11	17	140
2	24	38	12	8	120
3	16	60	13	23	110
4	8	52	14	25	160
5	14	25	15	40	180
6	19	95	16	19	140
7	26	92	17	6	130
8	24	61	18	23	190
9	4	42	19	25	220
10	12	170	20	14	110

46. a. Solve Problem 45(a) assuming SPT sequencing. To do this you may use the spreadsheet developed in Problem 45 and simply sort the data in the first three columns, using column 2 (the processing time) as a sort key.
b. Solve Problem 45(b) assuming SPT sequencing.
c. Solve Problem 45(c) assuming SPT sequencing.

47. a. Solve Problem 45(a) assuming EDD sequencing. In this case one sorts on the due date column.
b. Solve Problem 45(b) assuming EDD sequencing.
c. Solve Problem 45(c) assuming EDD sequencing.

Bibliography

Akers, S. B. "A Graphical Approach to Production Scheduling Problems." *Operations Research* 4 (1956), pp. 244–45.

Arcus, A. L. "COMSOAL: A Computer Method for Sequencing Operations for Assembly Lines." *International Journal of Production Research* 4 (1966), pp. 259–77.

Baker, K. R. *Introduction to Sequencing and Scheduling.* New York: John Wiley & Sons, 1974.

Banerjee, B. P. "Single Facility Sequencing with Random Execution Times." *Operations Research* 13 (1965), pp. 358–64.

Bellman, R. E. "Mathematical Aspects of Scheduling Theory." *SIAM Journal of Applied Mathematics* 4 (1956), pp. 168–205.

Bruno, J., and P. Downey. "Sequencing Tasks with Exponential Service Times on Two Machines." Technical Report, Department of Electrical Engineering and Computer Science, University of California at Santa Barbara, 1977.

Carlson, R., and M. Rosenblatt. "Designing a Production Line to Maximize Profit." *IIE Transactions* 17 (1985), pp. 117–22.

Conway, R. W.; W. L. Maxwell; and L. W. Miller. *Theory of Scheduling.* Reading, MA: Addison Wesley, 1967.

Derman, C.; G. L. Lieberman; and S. M. Ross. "A Renewal Decision Problem." *Management Science* 24 (1978), pp. 554–61.

Fisher, M.; A. J. Greenfield; R. Jaikumar; and J. T. Lister III. "A Computerized Vehicle Routing Application." *Interfaces* 12 (1982), pp. 42–52.

Fishman, G. S. *Concepts and Methods in Discrete Event Digital Simulation.* New York: John Wiley & Sons, 1973.

French, S. *Sequencing and Scheduling: An Introduction to the Mathematics of the Job Shop.* Chichester, England: Ellis Horwood Limited, 1982.

Graves, S. C. "A Review of Production Scheduling." *Operations Research* 29 (1981), pp. 646–75.

Held, M.; R. M. Karp; and R. Shareshian. "Assembly Line Balancing—Dynamic Programming with Precedence Constraints." *Operations Research* 11 (1963), pp. 442–59.

Helgeson, W. P., and D. P. Birnie. "Assembly Line Balancing Using the Ranked Positional Weight Technique." *Journal of Industrial Engineering* 12 (1961), pp. 394–98.

Hillier, F. S., and R. W. Boling. "On the Optimal Allocation of Work in Symmetrically Unbalanced Production Line Systems with Variable Operation Times." *Management Science* 25 (1986), pp. 721–28.

Hutchison, J.; G. Leong; and P. T. Ward. "Improving Delivery Performance in Gear Manufacturing at Jeffrey Division of Dresser Industries." *Interfaces* 23, no. 2 (March–April 1993), pp. 69–83.

Johnson, S. M. "Optimal Two and Three Stage Production Schedules with Setup Times Included." *Naval Research Logistics Quarterly* 1 (1954), pp. 61–68.

Kilbridge, M. D., and L. Wester. "A Heuristic Method of Line Balancing." *Journal of Industrial Engineering* 12 (1961), pp. 292–98.

Lawler, E. L. "Optimal Sequencing of a Single Machine Subject to Precedence Constraints." *Management Science* 19 (1973), pp. 544–46.

Moore, J. M. "An n-job, One Machine Sequencing Algorithm for Minimizing the Number of Late Jobs." *Management Science* 15 (1968), pp. 102–109.

Nichols, J. C. "Planning for Real World Production." *Production* 106, no. 8 (August 1994), pp. 18–20.

Parker, K. "What New Tools Will Best Tame Time." *Manufacturing Systems* 12, no. 1 (January 1994), pp. 16–22.

Parker, K. "Dynamism and Decision Support." *Manufacturing Systems* 13, no. 4 (April 1995), pp. 12–24.

Pinedo, M. "Stochastic Scheduling with Release Dates and Due Dates." *Operations Research* 31 (1983), pp. 554–72.

Pinedo, M. *Scheduling, Theory, Algorithms and Systems.* Englewood Cliffs, NJ: Prentice Hall, 1995.

Pinedo, M., and G. Weiss. "Scheduling Stochastic Tasks on Two Parallel Processors." *Naval Research Logistics Quarterly* 26 (1979), pp. 527–36.

Randhawa, S. U., and R. Shroff. "Simulation-Based Design Evaluation of Unit Load Automated Storage/Retrieval Systems." *Computers and Industrial Engineering* 28, no. 1 (January 1995), pp. 71–79.

Righter, R. "Job Scheduling to Minimize Weighted Flowtime on Uniform Processors." *Systems and Control Letters* 10 (1988), pp. 211–16.

Righter, R., and J. G. Shanthikumar. "Scheduling Multiclass Single-Server Queuing Systems to Stochastically Maximize the Number of Successful Departures." *Probability in the Engineering and Informational Sciences* 3 (1989), pp. 323–33.

Rothkopf, M. S. "Scheduling with Random Service Times." *Management Science* 12 (1966), pp. 707–13.

Salveson, M. E. "Production Planning and Scheduling." *Econometrica* 20 (1952), pp. 554–90.

Swain, J. J. "Flexible Tools for Modeling." *OR/MS Today* 20, no. 6 (1993), pp. 62–78.

Thangavelu, S. R., and C. M. Shetty. "Assembly Line Balancing by Zero One Integer Programming." *AIIE Transactions* 3 (1971), pp. 61–68.

Vasilash, G. "Scheduling for the Shop Floor." *Production* 107, no. 6 (June 1995), pp. 46–47.

Vollman, T. E.; W. L. Berry; and D. C. Whybark. *Manufacturing Planning and Control Systems.* 3rd ed. Homewood, IL: Richard D. Irwin, 1992.

Chapter Eleven

Facilities Layout and Location

"When you come to a fork in the road, take it."
—Yogi Berra

Chapter Overview

Purpose

To understand the major issues faced by a firm when designing and locating new facilities, and to learn the quantitative techniques for assisting with the decision-making process.

Key Points

1. *Fundamentals.* Before deciding on the appropriate layout for a new facility, whether it be a factory, hospital, theme park, or anything else, one must first study the patterns of flow. The simplest flow pattern is straight-line flow, as might be encountered on an assembly line. Other patterns include U flow, L flow, serpentine flow, circular flow, and S flow. Another issue is desirability or undesirability of locating operations near each other. For example, in a hospital, the emergency room must be near the hospital entrance, and the maternity ward should be close to the area where premature babies are cared for. A graphical technique for representing the relative desirability of locating two facilities near each other is the activity relationship chart (or rel chart). From-to charts give the distances between activities, which can be used to compute costs associated with various layouts.

2. *Types of layouts.* In the factory setting, the appropriate type of layout depends on the manufacturing environment and the characteristics of the product. A *fixed position layout* is appropriate when building large items such as planes or ships that are difficult and costly to move. Workstations are located around the object, which remains stationary. More typical is the *product layout* where machines or workstations are organized around the sequence of operations required to produce the product. Product layouts are most typical for mass production. In the case of small- to medium-sized companies, a *process layout* makes more sense. Here one groups similar machines or similar processes together. Finally, *layouts based on group technology* might be appropriate. In this case, machines might be grouped into machine cells where each cell corresponds to a part family or group of part families.

3. *Computerized layout techniques.* For large complex factories or service facilities, determining the best layout manually is impractical. There are several computerized layout techniques available to assist with this function. They include CRAFT, COFAD, ALDEP, CORELAP, and PLANET. All of these methods are intended for the factory setting and share the objective of minimizing materials handling costs. Both CRAFT and COFAD are based on the principle of improvement. This means that the user must specify an initial layout. From there, one considers pairwise interchanges of departments and chooses the one with the largest improvement.

   Both ALDEP, CORELAP, and PLANET are construction routines rather than improvement routines. Layouts are determined from scratch, and there is no requirement that the user specify an initial layout. There is some controversy regarding whether human planners or computer programs produce better layouts. In one study where groups of 20 chosen from 74 people trained in layout techniques were compared with computerized layouts, the humans fared much better. Others criticized this study on the grounds that most layout departments are not that well staffed.

4. *Flexible manufacturing systems.* A flexible manufacturing system (FMS) is a collection of numerically controlled machines connected by a computer-controlled materials flow system. Typical flexible manufacturing systems are used for metal cutting and forming operations and certain assembly operations. Because the machines can be programmed, the same system can be used to produce a variety of different parts. Flexible manufacturing systems tend to be extremely expensive (some costing upwards of $10 million). As a result, the added flexibility may not be worth the cost. While the FMS can have many advantages (reducing work-in-process inventory, increased machine utilization, flexibility), these advantages are rarely justified by the high cost of these systems. An alternative that is more popular is flexible manufacturing cells. These are smaller than full-blown systems, but still provide more flexibility than single-function equipment.

5. *Locating new facilities.* Where to locate a new facility is a complex and strategically important problem. Hospitals need to be close to high-density population centers, and airports need to be near large cities, but not too near because of noise pollution. New factories are often located outside the United States to take advantage of the lower labor costs overseas. But these savings might come at a high price. Political instability, unfavorable exchange rates, infrastructure deficiencies, and long lead times are a few of the problems that arise from locating facilities abroad. Often such decisions are more strategic than tactical and require careful weighing of the advantages and disadvantages at the level of top management.

   However, in cases where the primary objective is to locate a facility to be closest to its customer base, quantitative methods can be very useful. In these cases, one must specify how distance is measured. Straight-line distance (also known as Euclidean distance) measures the shortest distance between two points. However, straight-line distance is not always the most appropriate measure. For example, when locating a firehouse, one must take into account the layout of streets. Using rectilinear distance (as measured by only horizontal and vertical movements) would make more sense in this context. Another consideration is that not all customers are of equal size. For example, a bakery would make larger deliveries to a supermarket or warehouse store than to a convenience store. Here one would use a weighted distance criterion. In the remainder of this chapter, we review several quantitative techniques for finding the best location of a single facility under various objectives.

Where to locate facilities and the efficient design of those facilities are important strategic issues for business as well as the military, nonprofit institutions, and government. During the 1980s, Northern California's Silicon Valley experienced tremendous growth in microelectronics and related industries. One can get some idea of how significant this growth was from the American Electronics Association Member Directory: more than 50 percent of the listings are in the Bay Area. Most of these firms were "start-ups," adapting a new technology to a specialized segment of the marketplace. With the surge in demand for microcomputers came support industries producing hard disk drives, floppy disks, semiconductor manufacturing equipment, local area networks, and a host of other related products. In many cases, large investments in capital equipment were required before the first unit could be sold. A typical example is the Read-Rite Corporation of Milpitas, California, the largest independent producer of thin film heads for reading from and writing to Winchester hard drives in the world. When the firm was founded in 1983, an initial capital investment of $40 million was required. The venture capital investors bore the risk that the firm would survive. Read-Rite is typical of hundreds of high-tech start-ups.

What equipment should be purchased, how facilities should be organized, and where the facilities should be located are fundamental strategy issues facing any manufacturing organization. Service industries also are faced with the problem of finding effective layouts. Achieving efficient patient flows in hospitals is one example. Another example is the obvious care used in laying out the many theme parks across the United States. Anyone who has visited the San Diego Zoo or Disney World in Orlando, Florida, can appreciate the importance of effective layout and efficient management of people in service industries.

Tompkins and White (1984) estimated that 8 percent of the U.S. gross national product has been spent on new facilities annually since 1955. This does not include the cost of modification of existing facilities. If the authors' estimates are correct, we are spending in excess of $500 billion annually on construction and modification of facilities. The authors go on to claim that from 20 to 50 percent of the total operating expenses in manufacturing are attributed to materials handling costs. Effective facilities planning could reduce these costs by 10 to 30 percent annually, the authors claim.

An important part of the enormous success of Japanese companies in achieving manufacturing dominance in several key industries is efficient production. Efficient production includes efficient design of the product, employee involvement, lean inventory material management systems, and intelligent layout and organization of facilities.

Chapter 1 touched on some of the qualitative issues that management must consider when deciding on the location of new facilities. This chapter treats in greater depth the issues associated with locating new facilities and the methods for determining the best layout of operations in those facilities. In addition to exploring the qualitative factors that should be taken into account, we will also consider how a manager can employ computers and quantitative techniques to assist with these complex decisions.

How a plant or workplace should be laid out is, in a sense, a special version of the location problem. Determining a suitable layout means finding the locations of departments within some specified boundary. When designing new facilities, the planner also must decide on the size and shape of the facility as well as the configuration of the departments within it.

Quantitative techniques are most useful when the goal is to minimize or maximize a single dimensional objective such as cost or profit. The objective function used in location problems generally involves either Euclidean or rectilinear distance (these terms will be defined later in Section 11.8). However, minimizing total distance traveled may not make sense in all cases. As an extreme example, consider the problem of locating a school. A location that requires 100 students to travel 10 miles each is clearly not equally desirable to one that requires 99 students to travel 1 mile and one student to travel 901 miles.

For layout problems, the most common objective used in mathematical models is to minimize the cost of materials handling. Furthermore, such models invariably assume that the number of materials handling trips from every work center to every other work center is known with certainty. In most real environments such assumptions are naive at best. Another deficiency of mathematical models is that they ignore such factors as plant safety, flexibility of the layout for future design changes, noise, and aesthetics.

This does not imply that mathematical and computer models are not useful for solving layout and location problems. What it does mean is that quantitative solutions must not be taken on blind faith. They must be carefully considered in the context of the problem. Used properly, the results of mathematical and computer models can reduce significantly the number of alternatives that the analyst must consider.

11.1 THE FACILITIES LAYOUT PROBLEM

Determining the best layout for a facility is a classical industrial engineering problem. Early industrial engineers often were known as efficiency experts and were interested in determining layouts to optimize some measure of production efficiency. For the most part, this view continues today, especially in plant layout. However, layout problems occur in many environments outside the plant. Some of these include

1. Hospitals
2. Warehouses
3. Schools
4. Offices
5. Workstations
6. Banks
7. Shopping centers
8. Airports
9. Industrial plants

Each of these layout problems has unique characteristics. Our focus in this chapter will be on techniques for finding layouts of industrial plants, although many of the methods can be applied to other facilities as well. The objectives in a plant layout study might include one or more of the following:

1. Minimize the investment required in new equipment.
2. Minimize the time required for production.
3. Utilize existing space most efficiently.
4. Provide for the convenience, safety, and comfort of the employees.
5. Maintain a flexible arrangement.
6. Minimize the materials handling cost.
7. Facilitate the manufacturing process.
8. Facilitate the organizational structure.

Vollmann and Buffa (1966) suggest nine steps as a guide for the analysis of layout problems:

1. Determine the compatibility of the materials handling layout models with the problem under study. Find all factors that can be modeled as materials flow.
2. Determine the basic subunits for analysis. Determine the appropriate definition of a department or subunit.
3. If a mathematical or computer model is to be used, determine the compatibility of the nature of costs in the problem and in the model. That is, if the model assumes that materials handling costs are linear and incremental (as most do), determine whether or not these assumptions are realistic.
4. How sensitive is the solution to the flow data assumptions? What is the impact of random changes in these data?
5. Recognize model idiosyncrasies and attempt to find improvements.
6. Examine the long-run issues associated with the problem and the long-run implications of the proposed solution.
7. Consider the layout problem as a systems problem.
8. Weigh the importance of qualitative factors.
9. Select the appropriate tools for analysis.

11.2 PATTERNS OF FLOW

As we noted in Section 11.1, the objective used most frequently for quantitative analysis of layout problems is to minimize the materials handling cost. When minimizing the materials handling cost is the primary objective, a flow analysis of the facility is necessary. Flow patterns can be classified as horizontal or vertical. A horizontal flow pattern is appropriate when all operations are located on the same floor, and a vertical pattern is appropriate when operations are in multistory structures. Francis and White (1974) give six horizontal flow patterns and six vertical flow patterns. The six horizontal patterns appear in Figure 11–1.

The simplest pattern is (a), which is straight-line flow. The main disadvantage of this pattern is that separate docks and personnel are required for receiving and shipping goods. The L shape is used to replace straight-line flow when the configuration of the building or the line requires it. The U shape has the advantage over the straight-line configuration of allowing shipping and receiving to be at the same location. The circular pattern is similar to the U shape. The remaining two patterns are used when the space required for production operations is too great to allow use of the other patterns.

Two charts that supply useful information regarding flows are (1) the activity relationship chart and (2) the from-to chart.

Activity Relationship Chart

An activity relationship chart (also called a rel chart for short) is a graphical means of representing the desirability of locating pairs of operations near each other. The following letter codes have been suggested for determining a "closeness" rating.

A   Absolutely necessary. Because two operations may use the same equipment or facilities, they must be located near each other.

E   Especially important. The facilities may require the same personnel or records, for example.

I   Important. The activities may be located in sequence in the normal work flow.

O   Ordinary importance. It would be convenient to have the facilities near each other, but it is not essential.

U   Unimportant. It does not matter whether the facilities are located near each other or not.

X   Undesirable. Locating a welding department near one that uses flammable liquids would be an example of this category.

FIGURE 11–1
Six horizontal flow patterns

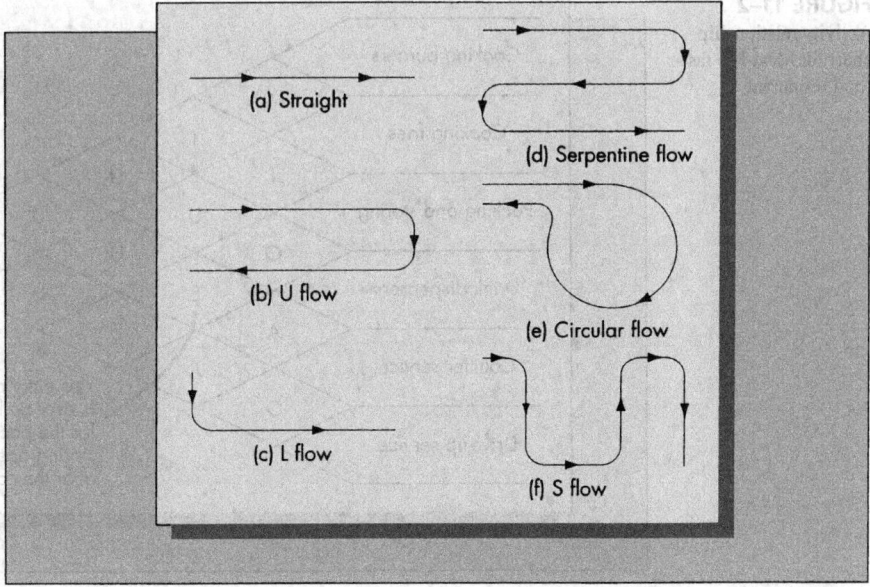

The closeness ratings are represented in an activity relationship chart that specifies the appropriate rating for each pair of departments. Consider the following example.

Example 11.1 Meat Me, Inc., is a franchised chain of fast-food hamburger restaurants. A new restaurant is being located in a growing suburban community near Reston, Virginia. Each restaurant has the following departments:

1. Cooking burgers.
2. Cooking fries.
3. Packing and storing burgers.
4. Drink dispensers.
5. Counter servers.
6. Drive-up server.

The burgers are cooked on a large grill, and the fries are deep fried in hot oil. For safety reasons the company requires that these cooking areas not be located near each other. All hamburgers are individually wrapped after cooking and stored near the counter. The service counter can accommodate six servers, and the site has an area reserved for a drive-up window.

An activity relationship chart for this facility appears in Figure 11–2. In the chart, each pair of activities is given one of the letter designations A, E, I, O, U, or X. Once a final layout is determined, the proximity of the various departments can be compared to the closeness ratings in the chart. Note that Figure 11–2 gives only the closeness rating for each pair of departments. In the original conception of the chart, a number giving the reason for each closeness rating is also included in every cell. These numbers do not appear in our example.

FIGURE 11–2
Activity relationship chart for Meat Me fast-food restaurant

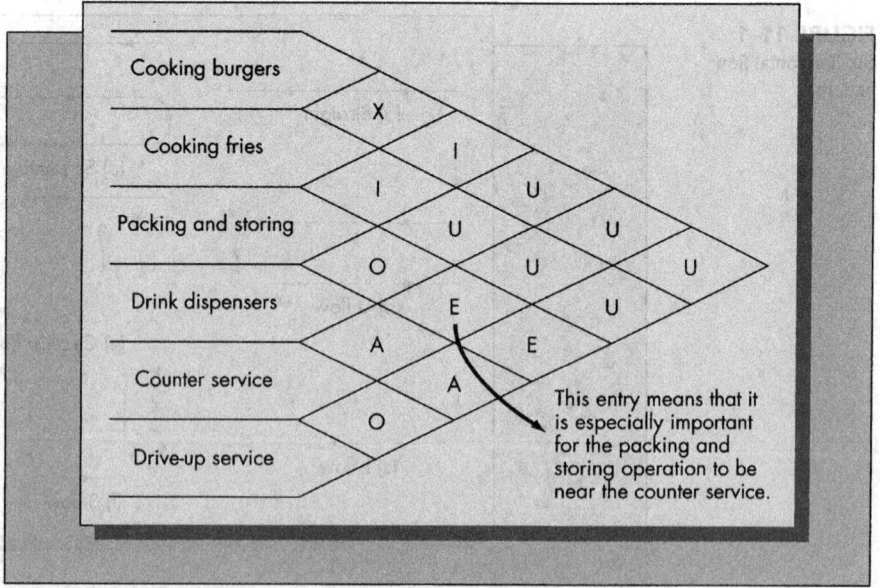

From-To Chart

A from-to chart is similar to the mileage chart that appears at the bottom of many road maps and gives the mileage between selected pairs of cities. From-to charts are used to analyze the flow of materials between departments. The two most common forms are charts that show the distances between departments and charts that show the number of materials handling trips per day between departments. A from-to chart differs from an activity relationship chart in that the from-to chart is based on a specific layout. It is a convenient means of summarizing the flow data corresponding to a given layout.

Example 11.2   A machine shop has six work centers. The work centers contain one or more of the following types of machines:

1. Saws
2. Milling machines
3. Punch presses
4. Drills
5. Lathes
6. Sanders

The from-to chart in Figure 11–3 shows the distance in feet between centers of the six departments. Note that the chart in the example is symmetric; that is, the travel distance between A and B is the same as the travel distance between B and A. This is not necessarily always the case, however. There may be one-way lanes, which allow material flow in one direction only, or an automated materials handling system that moves pallets in one direction only.

Figure 11–4 shows a from-to chart that gives the number of materials handling trips per day. These figures could be based on a specific product mix produced in the shop or simply be representative of an average day.

FIGURE 11–3
From-to chart showing distances between six department centers (measured in feet)

To \ From	Saws	Milling	Punch press	Drills	Lathes	Sanders
Saws		18	40	30	65	24
Milling	18		38	75	16	30
Punch press	40	38		22	38	12
Drills	30	75	22		50	46
Lathes	65	16	38	50		60
Sanders	24	30	12	46	60	

FIGURE 11–4
From-to chart showing number of materials handling trips per day

To / From	Saws	Milling	Punch press	Drills	Lathes	Sanders
Saws		43	26	14	40	
Milling			75	60		23
Punch press					45	16
Drills		22			28	
Lathes		45		30		60
Sanders		12				

Suppose that the firm's accounting department has estimated that the average cost of transporting material one foot in the machine shop is 20 cents. Using this fact, one can develop a third from-to chart that gives the average daily cost of materials handling from every department to every other department. For example, the distance separating saws and milling in the current layout is 18 feet (from Figure 11–3) and there are an average of 43 materials handling trips between these two departments (from Figure 11–4). This translates to a total of (43)(18) = 774 feet traveled in a day or a total cost of (774)(0.2) = $154.80 per day for materials handling between saws and milling. The materials handling costs for the other pairs of departments appear in Figure 11–5.

FIGURE 11–5
From-to chart showing materials handling cost per day (in $)

To / From	Saws	Milling	Punch press	Drills	Lathes	Sanders
Saws		154.8	208	84	520	
Milling			570	900		138
Punch press					342	38.4
Drills		330			280	
Lathes		144		300		720
Sanders		72				

From-to charts are not a means of determining layouts, but simply a convenient way to express important flow characteristics of an existing layout. They can be useful in comparing the materials handling costs of a small number of alternatives. Because criteria other than the materials handling cost are relevant, the from-to chart should be supplemented with additional information, such as that contained in an activity relationship chart.

11.3 TYPES OF LAYOUTS

Different philosophies of layout design are appropriate in different manufacturing environments. Chapter 1 discussed the problem of matching the product life cycle with the process life cycle represented by the product–process matrix (see Figure 1–5 in particular). The upper left-hand corner of the product–process matrix corresponds to low-volume production and little product standardization. Such a product structure is usually characterized by a job-shop-type environment. In a job shop there are a wide variety of jobs with different flow patterns associated with each job. A commercial printer is a typical example of a jumbled flow shop such as this. As volume increases, the number of products declines and flow patterns become more standardized. For discrete parts manufacture, an auto assembly plant is a good example of this case. A different approach for designing production facilities would be appropriate in such a setting.

Fixed Position Layouts

Some products are too big to be moved, so the product remains fixed and the layout is based on the product size and shape. Examples of products requiring *fixed position* layouts are large airplanes, ships, and rockets. For such projects, once the basic frame is built, the various required functions would be located in fixed positions around the product. A project layout is similar in concept to the fixed position layout. This would be appropriate for large construction jobs such as commercial buildings or bridges. The required equipment is moved to the site and removed when the project is completed. A typical fixed position layout is shown in Figure 11–6.

Product Layouts

In a *product layout* (or product flow layout) machines are organized to conform to the sequence of operations required to produce the product. The product layout is typical

FIGURE 11–6
Fixed position layout

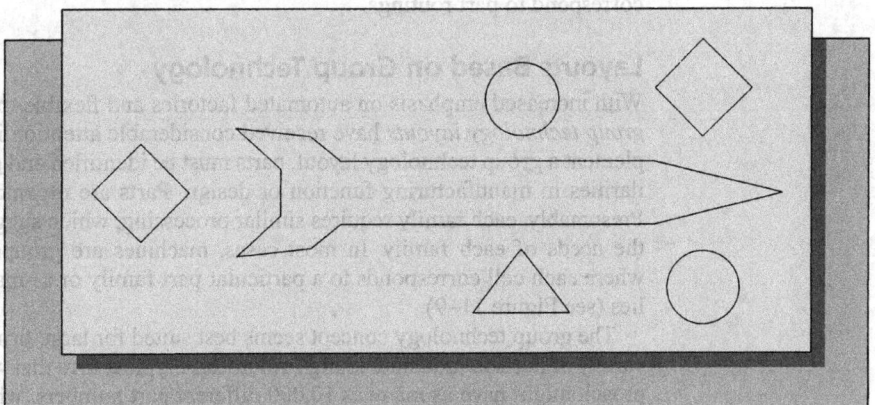

FIGURE 11-7
Product layout

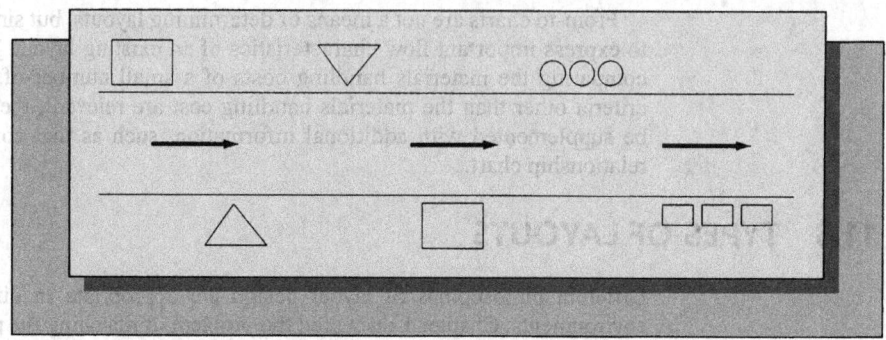

of high-volume standardized production (the lower right-hand corner in Figure 1–5 in Chapter 1). An assembly line (or transfer line) is a product layout, because assembly facilities are organized according to the sequence of steps required to produce the item. Product layouts are desirable for flow-type mass production and provide the fastest cycle times in this environment. Transfer lines are expensive and inflexible, however, and become cumbersome when changes in the product flow are required. Furthermore, a transfer line can experience significant idle time. If one part of the line stops, the entire line may have to remain idle until the problem is corrected. Figure 11–7 shows a typical product layout.

Process Layouts

Process layouts are the most common for small- to medium-volume manufacturers. A *process layout* groups similar machines having similar functions. A typical process layout would group lathes in one area, drills in one area, and so on. Process layouts are most effective when there is a wide variation in the product mix. Each product has a different routing sequence associated with it. In such an environment it would be difficult to organize the machines to conform with the production flow because flow patterns are highly variable. Process layouts have the advantage of minimizing machine idle time. Parts from multiple products or jobs queue up at each work center to facilitate high utilization of critical resources. Also, when design changes are common, parts routings will change frequently. In such an environment, a process layout affords minimal disruption. Figure 11–8 shows a typical process layout. The arrows correspond to part routings.

Layouts Based on Group Technology

With increased emphasis on automated factories and flexible manufacturing systems, *group technology layouts* have received considerable attention in recent years. To implement a group technology layout, parts must be identified and grouped based on similarities in manufacturing function or design. Parts are organized into part families. Presumably, each family requires similar processing, which suggests a layout based on the needs of each family. In most cases, machines are grouped into machine cells where each cell corresponds to a particular part family or a small group of part families (see Figure 11–9).

The group technology concept seems best suited for large firms that produce a wide variety of parts in moderate to high volumes. A typical firm that would consider this approach might have as many as 10,000 different part numbers, which might be grouped

604 Chapter Eleven *Facilities Layout and Location*

FIGURE 11–8
Process layout

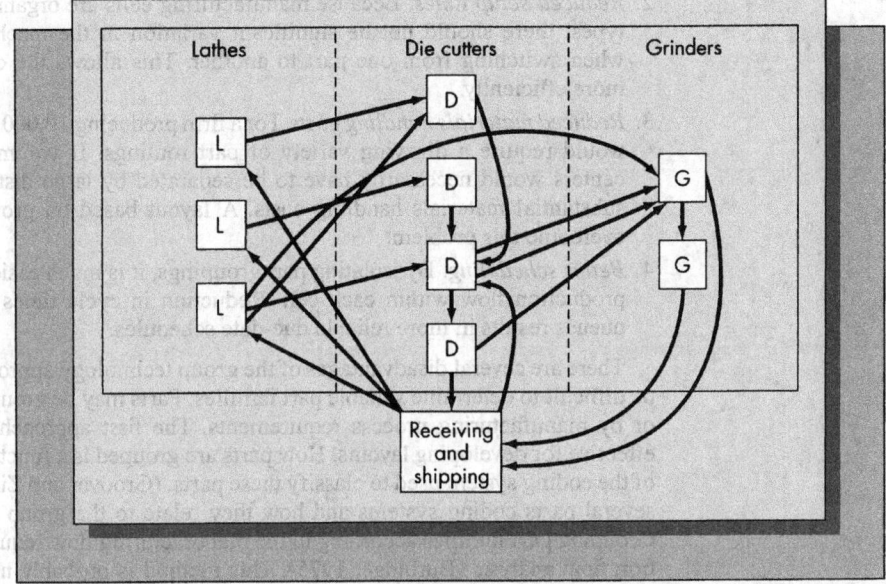

FIGURE 11–9
Group technology layout

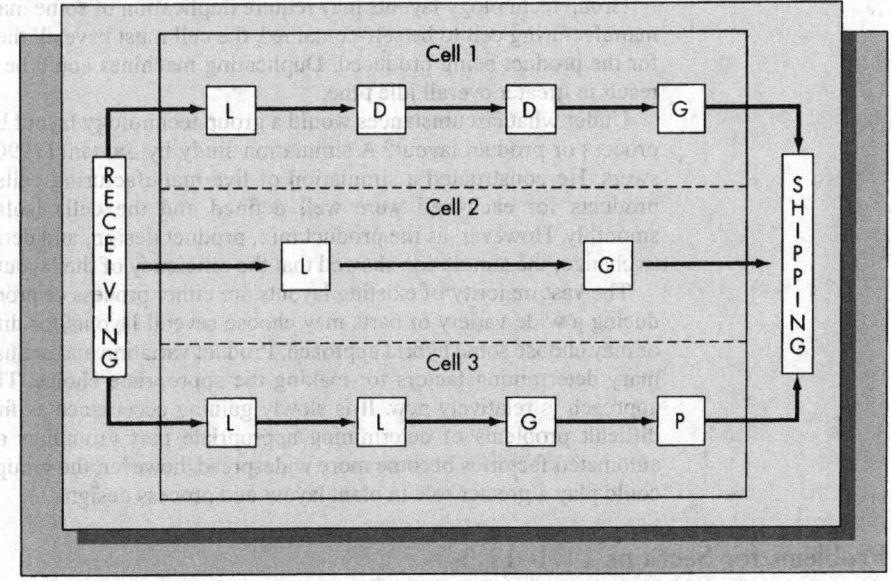

into 50 or so part families. Some of the advantages of using the group technology concept are

1. *Reduced work-in-process inventories.* Each manufacturing cell operates as an independent unit, allowing much tighter controls on the flow of production. Large work-in-process inventories are not needed to maintain low cycle times. A side benefit of this is reduced queues of parts and the confusion that results.

2. *Reduced setup times.* Because manufacturing cells are organized according to part types, there should not be significant variation in the machine settings required when switching from one part to another. This allows the cells to operate much more efficiently.
3. *Reduced materials handling costs.* For a firm producing 10,000 parts, a process layout would require a dizzying variety of part routings. If volumes are large, process centers would necessarily have to be separated by large distances, thus requiring substantial materials handling costs. A layout based on group technology would overcome this problem.
4. *Better scheduling.* By isolating part groupings, it is much easier to keep track of the production flow within each cell. Reduction in cycle times and work-in-process queues results in more reliable due-date schedules.

There are several disadvantages of the group technology approach. One is that it can be difficult to determine suitable part families. Parts may be grouped by size and shape or by manufacturing process requirements. The first approach is easier but not as effective for developing layouts. How parts are grouped is a function, to a large degree, of the coding system used to classify these parts. (Groover and Zimmers, 1984, discuss several parts coding systems and how they relate to the group technology concept.) Grouping part families according to the manufacturing flow requires a careful production flow analysis (Burbidge, 1975). This method is probably not feasible for a firm with a large number of parts, however.

Group technology layouts may require duplication of some machines. In order for a manufacturing cell to be self-contained, the cell must have all the machines necessary for the product being produced. Duplicating machines could be expensive and could result in greater overall idle time.

Under what circumstances would a group technology layout be preferred to a pure process or product layout? A simulation study by Sassani (1990) provides some answers. He constructed a simulation of five manufacturing cells. Initially, when the products for each cell were well defined and the cells isolated, the system ran smoothly. However, as the product mix, product design, and demand patterns started to change, the simulation showed that the efficiency of the layout deteriorated.

The vast majority of existing layouts are either process or product type. Firms producing a wide variety of parts may choose several layouts for different product lines, or may choose some hybrid approach. Product variation and annual volume are the primary determining factors for making the appropriate choice. The group technology approach is relatively new. It is slowly gaining acceptance as firms wrestle with the difficult problems of determining appropriate part groupings and cell designs. As automated factories become more widespread, however, the group technology concept could play a greater role in plant layout and process design.

Problems for Sections 11.1–11.3

1. For each of the eight objectives of a layout study listed in Section 11.1, give examples of situations in which that objective would be important and examples in which it would be unimportant.
2. A manufacturing facility consists of five departments: A, B, C, D, and E. At the current time, the facility is laid out as in Figure 11–10. Develop a from-to distance chart for this layout. Estimate the distance separating departments based on the flow pattern of the materials handling system in the figure. Assume that all departments are located at their centers as marked in Figure 11–10.

FIGURE 11–10
Layout of manufacturing facility (for Problem 2)

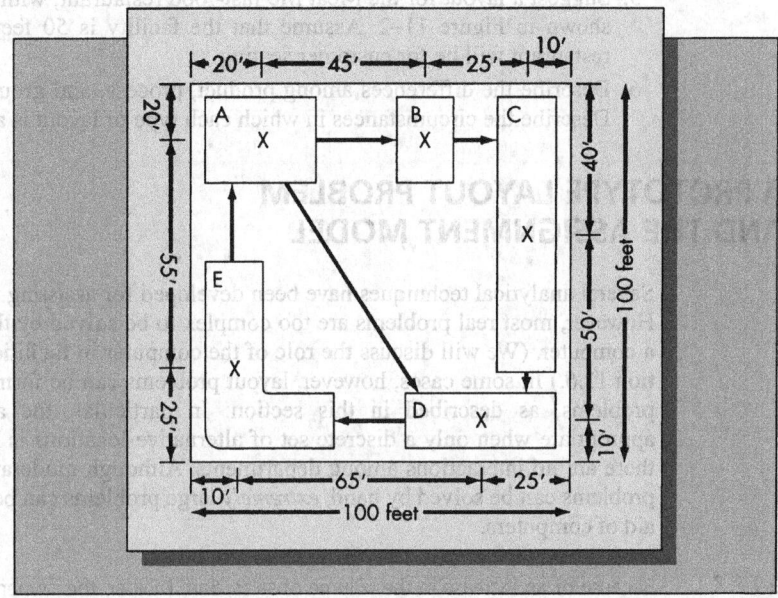

3. Four products are produced in the facility described in Problem 2. The routing for these products and their forecasted production rates are

Product	Routing	Forecasted Production (units/week)
1	A–B–C–D–E	200
2	A–D–E	900
3	A–B–C–E	400
4	A–C–D–E	650

Suppose that all four products are produced in batches of size 50.

 a. Convert this information into a from-to chart similar to Figure 11–4 but giving the number of materials handling trips per week between departments.

 b. Suppose that the cost of transporting goods 1 foot is estimated to be $2. Using the from-to chart you determined in part (a), obtain a from-to chart giving materials handling cost per week between departments.

 c. Develop an activity relationship chart for this facility based on the materials handling cost from-to chart you obtained in part (b). Use only the rankings A, E, I, O, U, with A being assigned to the highest cost and U the least.

 d. Based on the results of parts (b) and (c), would you recommend a different layout for this facility?

4. Consider the example of the machine shop with the from-to charts given in Figures 11–3 through 11–5. Based on the results of Figure 11–5, in what ways might the current layout be improved?

5. Suggest a layout for the Meat Me fast-food restaurant, with the relationship chart shown in Figure 11–2. Assume that the facility is 50 feet square and half the restaurant will be for customer seating.
6. Describe the differences among product, process, and group technology layouts. Describe the circumstances in which each type of layout is appropriate.

11.4 A PROTOTYPE LAYOUT PROBLEM AND THE ASSIGNMENT MODEL

Several analytical techniques have been developed for assisting with layout problems. However, most real problems are too complex to be solved by these methods without a computer. (We will discuss the role of the computer in facilities layout later in Section 11.6.) In some cases, however, layout problems can be formulated as *assignment* problems, as described in this section. In particular, the assignment model is appropriate when only a discrete set of alternative locations is being considered and there are no interactions among departments. Although moderately sized assignment problems can be solved by hand, *extremely* large problems can be solved only with the aid of computers.

Example 11.3

Because of an increase in the volume of sales, Sam Melder, the owner of Melder, Inc., a small manufacturing firm located in Muncie, Indiana, has decided to expand production capacity. A new wing has been added to the plant that will house four machines: (1) a punch press, (2) a grinder, (3) a lathe, and (4) a welding machine. There are only four possible locations for these machines, say A, B, C, and D. However, the welding machine, which is the largest machine, will not fit in location B.

The plant foreman has made estimates of the impact in terms of materials handling costs of locating each of the machines in each of the possible locations. These costs, expressed in terms of dollars per hour, are represented in the following table.

		Location			
		A	B	C	D
Machines	1	94	13	62	71
	2	62	19	84	96
	3	75	88	18	80
	4	11	M	81	21

The entry M stands for a very large cost. It is used to indicate that machine 4 is not permitted in location B. As the objective is to assign the four machines to locations in order to minimize the total materials handling cost, an optimal solution will never assign machine 4 to location B.

Minimum cost assignments can rarely be found by inspection. For example, one reasonable approach might be to assign the machines to the lowest cost locations in sequence. The lowest cost in the matrix is 11, so machine 4 would be located in location A. Eliminating the last row and the first column, we see that the next remaining lowest cost is 13, so machine 1 would be assigned to location B. Now also eliminating the first row and the second column, the smallest remaining cost is 18, so machine 3 would be assigned to location C. Finally, machine 2 must be assigned to location D. The total cost of this solution is 11 + 13 + 18 + 96 = $138. As we will see, this solution is suboptimal. (The optimal cost is $114. Can you find the optimal solution?)

The Assignment Algorithm

A simple approach such as this will rarely result in an optimal solution. A solution algorithm will be presented from which one can obtain an optimal solution to the assignment problem by hand for moderately sized problems.

The Assignment Algorithm

The solution algorithm presented in this section is based on the following observation:

Result: If a constant is added to, or subtracted from, all entries in a row or column of an assignment cost matrix, the optimal assignment is unchanged.

In applying this result, the objective is to continue subtracting constants from rows and columns in the cost matrix until a zero cost assignment can be made. The zero cost assignment for the modified matrix is optimal for the original problem. This leads to the following algorithm for solving assignment problems:

Solution Procedure for Assignment Problems

1. Locate the smallest number in row 1 and subtract it from all the entries in row 1. Repeat for all rows in the cost matrix.
2. Locate the smallest number in column 1 and subtract it from all the entries in column 1. Repeat for all columns in the cost matrix.
3. At this point each row and each column will have at least one zero. If it is possible to make a zero cost assignment, then do it. That will be the optimal solution. If not, go to step 4.
4. Determine the maximum number of zero cost assignments. This will equal the smallest number of lines required to cover all zeros. The lines are found by inspection and are not necessarily unique. The important point is that the number of lines drawn not exceed the maximum number of zero cost assignments.
5. Choose the smallest uncovered number and do the following:
    a. Subtract it from all other uncovered numbers.
    b. Add it to the numbers where the lines cross.
    c. Return to step 3.

The process is continued until one can make a zero cost assignment. Notice that step 5 is merely an application of the result in the following way: If the smallest uncovered number is subtracted from every element in the matrix and then added to every covered element, it will be subtracted once and added twice where lines cross.

Example 11.3 (continued) Let us return to Example 11.3. The original cost matrix is

		Location			
		A	B	C	D
	1	94	13	62	71
Machine	2	62	19	84	96
	3	75	88	18	80
	4	11	M	81	21

11.4 A Prototype Layout Problem and the Assignment Model

Step 1. Subtracting the smallest number from each row gives

81	0	49	58
43	0	65	77
57	70	0	62
0	M	70	10

Because M is very large relative to the other costs, subtracting 11 from M still leaves a very large number, which we again denote as M for convenience. At this point at least one zero appears in each row, and in each column except the last.

Step 2. Subtracting 10 from every number in the final column gives

81	0	49	48
43	0	65	67
57	70	0	52
0	M	70	0

At this point we have at least one zero in every row and every column (step 3). However, that does not necessarily mean that a zero cost assignment is possible. In fact, it is possible to make at most three zero cost assignments at this stage, as shown in step 4.

Step 4.

81	[0]	49	48
43	0	65	67
57	70	[0]	52
[0]	M	70	0

The three assignments shown in step 4 are 1–B, 3–C, and 4–A. There are other ways of assigning three locations at zero cost as well. It does not matter which we choose at this stage, only that we know three are possible. The next step is to find three lines that cover all the zeros. These are shown here.

81	0̸	49	48
43	0̸	65	67
~~57~~	~~7̸0~~	~~0~~	~~52~~
~~0~~	~~M~~	~~70~~	~~0~~

Again, the choice of lines is not unique. However, it is important that no more than three lines be used. Finding three lines to cover all zeros is done by trial and error.

Step 5. The smallest uncovered number, 43, is subtracted from all other uncovered numbers and added to the numbers where the lines cross. The resulting matrix is

		Location			
		A	B	C	D
Machine	1	38	[0]	6	5
	2	[0]	0	22	24
	3	57	113	[0]	52
	4	0	M	70	[0]

It is now possible to make a zero cost assignment, as shown in the matrix. The optimal assignment is machine 1, the punch press, to location B; machine 2, the grinder, to location A;

machine 3, the lathe, to location C; machine 4, the welder, to location D. The total materials handling cost per hour of the optimal solution is obtained by referring to the original assignment cost matrix. It is 13 + 62 + 18 + 21 = $114 per hour.

The assignment algorithm also can be used when the number of sites is larger than the number of machines. For example, suppose that there were six potential sites for locating the four machines and the original cost matrix was

		Location					
		A	B	C	D	E	F
Machine	1	94	13	62	71	82	25
	2	62	19	84	96	24	29
	3	75	88	18	80	16	78
	4	11	M	81	21	45	14

The procedure is to add two dummy machines, 5 and 6, with zero costs. The problem is then solved using the assignment algorithm as if there were six machines and six locations. The locations to which the dummy machines are assigned are the ones that are not used.

Problems for Section 11.4

7. Solve the following assignment problem:

	A	B	C	D
1	21	24	26	23
2	29	27	30	29
3	24	25	34	27
4	28	26	28	25

8. Each of four machines is to be assigned to one of five possible locations. The objective is to assign the machines to locations that will minimize the materials handling cost. The machine–location costs are given in the following matrix. Find the optimal assignment.

	A	B	C	D	E
1	26	20	22	21	25
2	35	31	33	40	26
3	15	18	23	16	25
4	31	34	33	30	M

9. University of the Atlantic is moving its business school into a new building, which has been designed to house six academic departments. The average time required for a student to get to and from classes in the building depends upon the location of the department in which he or she is taking the class. Based on the distribution of

class loads, the dean has estimated the following mean student trip times in minutes, given the departmental locations.

		Location					
		A	B	C	D	E	F
Department	1	13	18	12	20	13	13
	2	18	17	12	19	17	16
	3	16	14	12	17	15	19
	4	18	14	12	13	15	12
	5	19	20	16	19	20	19
	6	22	23	17	24	28	25

Find the optimal assignment of departments to locations to minimize mean student trip time in and out of the building.

*11.5 MORE ADVANCED MATHEMATICAL PROGRAMMING FORMULATIONS

The assignment model described in Section 11.4 can be useful for determining optimal layouts for a limited number of real problems. The primary limitation of the simple assignment model is that, in most cases, the number of materials handling trips and the associated materials handling cost are assumed to be independent of the location of the other facilities. In Example 11.3, the cost of assigning the punch press to location A was assumed to be $94 per hour. However, in most cases this cost would depend upon the location of the other machines as well.

A formulation of the problem that takes this feature into account is considerably more complex. In order to avoid confusion, we will assume that the problem is to assign machines to locations. The problem could be to assign other types of subfacilities to locations, of course, but we will retain this terminology for convenience. Define the following quantities:

n = Number of machines;

c_{ij} = Cost per time period of assigning machine i to location j. This cost could be a one-time relocation cost that is converted to an annual equivalent;

d_{jr} = Cost of making a single materials handling trip from location j to location r;

f_{ik} = Mean number of trips per time period from machine i to machine k;

S_i = The set of locations to which machine i could feasibly be assigned;

$$a_{ijkr} = \begin{cases} f_{ik}d_{jr} & \text{if } i \neq k \text{ or } j \neq r, \\ c_{ij} & \text{if } i = k \text{ and } j = r; \end{cases}$$

$$x_{ij} = \begin{cases} 1 & \text{if machine } i \text{ is assigned to location } j, \\ 0 & \text{otherwise.} \end{cases}$$

Interpret a_{ijkr} as the materials handling cost per unit time when machine i is assigned to location j and machine k is assigned to location r. This cost is incurred only if both x_{ij} and x_{kr} are equal to 1. Hence, it follows that the total cost of assigning machines to locations is given by

$$\frac{1}{2}\sum_{i=1}^{n}\sum_{j=1}^{n}\sum_{k=1}^{n}\sum_{r=1}^{n} a_{ijkr} x_{ij} x_{kr}. \tag{1}$$

As all indices are summed from 1 to n, each assignment will be counted twice; hence the need to multiply by $\frac{1}{2}$. Constraints are included to ensure that each machine gets assigned to exactly one location and each location is assigned exactly one machine. These are

$$\sum_{i=1}^{n} x_{ij} = 1, \quad j = 1, \ldots, n; \tag{2}$$

$$\sum_{j=1}^{n} x_{ij} = 1, \quad i = 1, \ldots, n; \tag{3}$$

$$x_{ij} = 0 \text{ or } 1, \quad i = 1, \ldots, n \text{ and } j = 1, \ldots, n; \tag{4}$$

$$x_{ij} = 0, \quad i = 1, \ldots, n \text{ and } j \notin S(i). \tag{5}$$

The mathematical programming formulation is to minimize the total materials handling cost of the assignment, (1), subject to the constraints (2), (3), (4), and (5). This formulation is known as the quadratic assignment problem. In general, such problems are extremely difficult to solve. One should consider using such a method only for moderately sized problems.

Problem for Section 11.5

10. Consider the following problem with two locations and three machines. Suppose that the costs of transporting a unit load from location j to location r are given in the following table:

		To location	
		A	B
From location	A		6
	B	9	

The average numbers of trips required from machine i to machine k per hour are

		To machine		
		1	2	3
From machine	1	0	3	1
	2	0	0	3
	3	0	4	0

Relocation costs are ignored. Write out the complete quadratic assignment formulation for this location problem.

11.6 COMPUTERIZED LAYOUT TECHNIQUES

The quadratic assignment formulation given in Section 11.5 has several shortcomings. First, one must specify the costs of all materials handling trips and the expected number of trips from every department to every other department. When many departments are involved, this information could be difficult to obtain. Furthermore, an efficient solution technique for solving large quadratic assignment problems has yet to be discovered.

For these reasons there has been considerable interest in computer-aided methods. These methods are heuristics; they do not guarantee an optimal solution but generally yield efficient solutions. They can be used for solving problems that are too large to be solved analytically. The methods that we discuss in this section are CRAFT, COFAD, ALDEP, CORELAP, and PLANET.

For each of these methods the objective is to minimize the cost of materials handling. However, the solutions generated by these computer programs must be considered in the context of the problem. Issues such as plant safety, noise, and aesthetics are ignored. The layout obtained from a computer program may have to be modified in order to take these factors into account.

Computer programs for determining layouts generally fall into two classes: (1) improvement routines and (2) construction routines. An improvement routine takes an existing layout and considers the effect of interchanging the location of two or more facilities. A construction routine constructs the layout from scratch from flow data and the information in the activity relationship chart. CRAFT and COFAD are both improvement routines, and PLANET, CORELAP, and ALDEP are construction routines. The improvement routines have the disadvantage of requiring specification of an initial layout. However, improvement routines generally result in more usable layouts. Construction routines often give layouts with oddly shaped departments.

CRAFT

CRAFT (*computerized relative allocation of facilities technique*) was one of the first computer-aided layout routines developed. As noted earlier, CRAFT is an improvement routine and requires the user to specify an initial layout. The objective used in CRAFT is to minimize the total transportation cost of a layout, where transportation cost is defined as the product of the cost to move a unit load from department i to department j and the distance between departments i and j. To be more specific, define

$n =$ Number of departments,

$v_{ij} =$ Number of loads moved from department i to department j in a given time,

$u_{ij} =$ Cost to move a unit load a unit distance from department i to department j,

$d_{ij} =$ Distance separating departments i and j.

It follows that $y_{ij} = u_{ij}v_{ij}$ is the cost to move total product flow during the specified time interval a unit distance from i to j, and that $y_{ij}d_{ij}$ is the cost of the product flow from i to j. The total cost of the product flow between all pairs of departments is

$$\frac{1}{2}\sum_{i=1}^{n}\sum_{j=1}^{n} y_{ij}d_{ij}.$$

Note that the input information v_{ij} and u_{ij} may be represented as from-to charts, as shown in Figures 11–3 and 11–4.

Two implicit assumptions made in CRAFT are

1. Move costs are independent of the equipment utilization.
2. Move costs are a linear function of the length of the move.

When these assumptions cannot be justified, CRAFT may be used to minimize the product of flows and distances only by assigning the unit cost u_{ij} a value of 1. The entries d_{ij} are computed by the program from a specification of an initial layout. Based on an initial layout, CRAFT considers exchanging the position of adjacent departments and computes the materials handling cost of the resulting exchange. The program chooses the pairwise interchange that results in the greatest cost reduction.

Departments are assumed to be either rectangularly shaped or composed of rectangular pieces. Furthermore, departments are assumed to be located at their *centroids*. The centroid is another term for the coordinates of the center of gravity or balance point. A discussion of centroids and how they are computed for objects in the plane appears in Appendix 11–A. The accuracy of assuming that a department is located at its centroid depends upon the shape of the department. The assumption is most accurate when the shape of the department is square or rectangular, but is less accurate for oddly shaped departments.

To better understand how CRAFT determines layouts, consider the following example.

Example 11.4   A local manufacturing firm has recently completed construction of a new wing of an existing building to house four departments: A, B, C, and D. The wing is 100 feet by 50 feet. The plant manager has chosen an initial layout of the four departments. This layout appears in Figure 11–11. We have marked the centroid locations of the departments with a dot. From the figure we see that department A requires 1,800 square feet, B requires 1,200 square feet, C requires 800 square feet, and D requires 1,200 square feet.

One of the inputs required by CRAFT is the flow data, that is, the number of materials handling trips per unit time from every department to every other department. These data are given in the from-to chart appearing in Figure 11–12a. The distance between departments is assumed to be the rectilinear distance between centroid locations. From Figure 11–11, we see that the centroid locations of the initial layout are

$$(x_A, y_A) = (30, 35), \quad (x_C, y_C) = (20, 10),$$
$$(x_B, y_B) = (80, 35), \quad (x_D, y_D) = (70, 10).$$

The rectilinear distance between A and B, for example, is given by the formula

$$|x_A - x_B| + |y_A - y_B| = |30 - 80| + |35 - 35| = 50.$$

One computes distances between other pairs of departments in a similar way. The calculations are summarized in the from-to chart in Figure 11–12b. Notice that we have assumed that the distance from department i to department j is the same as the distance from department j to department i. As we noted earlier, this may not necessarily be true if material is transported in one direction only.

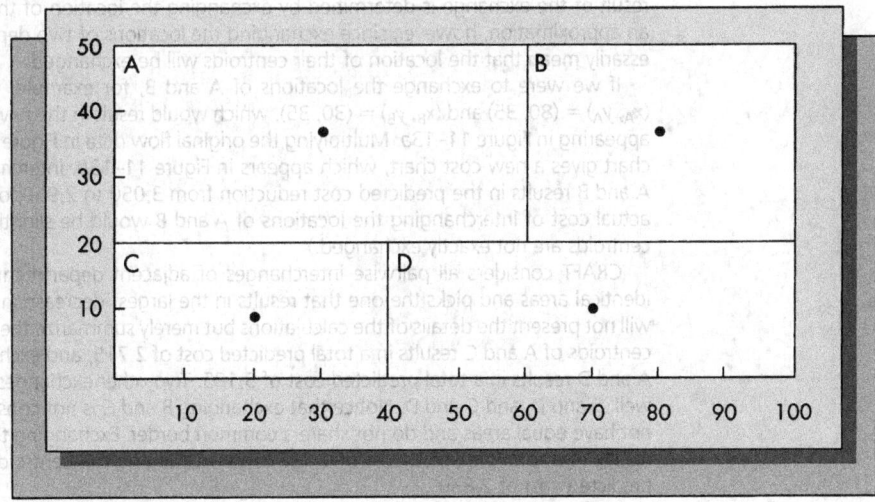

FIGURE 11–11
Initial layout for CRAFT example (Example 11.4)

FIGURE 11–12
From-to charts for initial layout

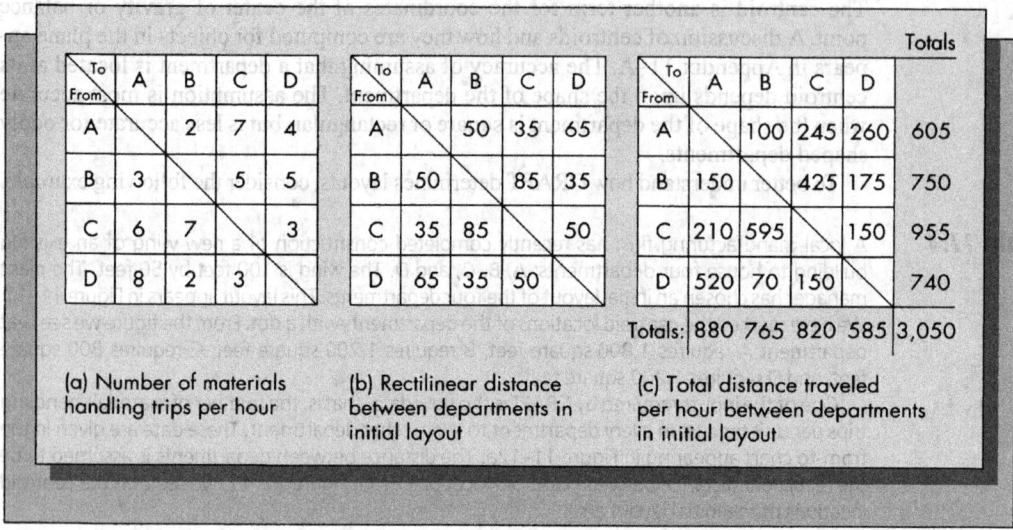

(a) Number of materials handling trips per hour

(b) Rectilinear distance between departments in initial layout

(c) Total distance traveled per hour between departments in initial layout

Normally, a third from-to chart also would be required. This would give the cost of transporting a unit load a unit distance from department i to department j. As noted, CRAFT may be used to minimize the product of flows and distances by assigning a value of 1 to these transport costs. We will assume this to be the case in our example. Hence, one obtains the hourly cost of transporting materials to and from each of the departments by simply multiplying the entries in the from-to chart of Figure 11–12a by the entries in the from-to chart of Figure 11–12b. These calculations are summarized in Figure 11–12c. The total distance traveled per hour for the initial layout is 3,050 feet.

CRAFT now considers the effect of pairwise interchanges of two departments that either have adjacent borders or have the same area. (CRAFT can also consider the effect of exchanging the locations of three departments. We will not consider this option in our example.) The result of the exchange is determined by exchanging the location of the centroids. This is only an approximation, however, since exchanging the locations of two departments does *not* necessarily mean that the location of their centroids will be exchanged.

If we were to exchange the locations of A and B, for example, we would assume that $(x_A, y_A) = (80, 35)$ and $(x_B, y_B) = (30, 35)$, which would result in the new from-to distance chart appearing in Figure 11–13a. Multiplying the original flow data in Figure 11–12a by this distance chart gives a new cost chart, which appears in Figure 11–13b. Interchanging the centroids of A and B results in the predicted cost reduction from 3,050 to 2,950, or about 3 percent. (The actual cost of interchanging the locations of A and B would be slightly different because the centroids are not exactly exchanged.)

CRAFT considers all pairwise interchanges of adjacent departments or departments with identical areas and picks the one that results in the largest decrease in the predicted cost. We will not present the details of the calculations but merely summarize the results. Exchanging the centroids of A and C results in a total predicted cost of 2,715, and exchanging the centroids of A and D results in a total predicted cost of 3,185. Two other exchanges must be considered as well: B and D, and C and D. Notice that exchanging B and C is not considered because they do not have equal areas and do not share a common border. Exchanging the centroids of B and D results in a total predicted cost of 2,735, and exchanging the centroids of C and D in a total predicted cost of 2,830.

FIGURE 11–13
New distance and cost from-to charts after exchanging centroids for A and B

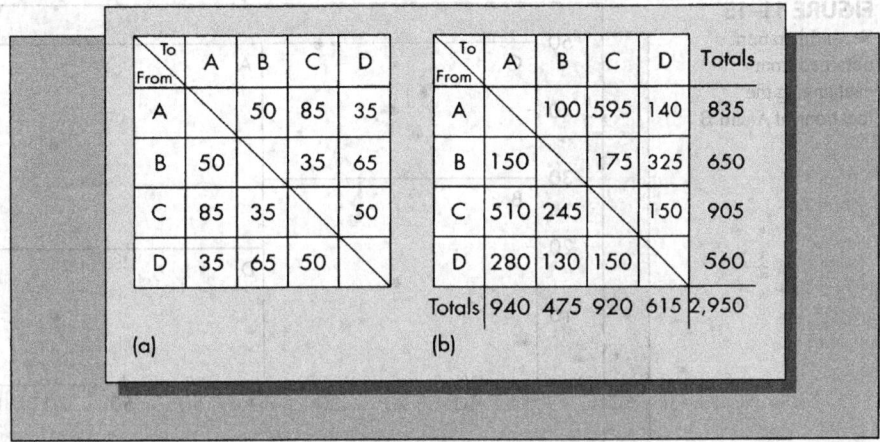

(a)   (b)

The maximum predicted cost reduction is achieved by exchanging A and C. The new layout with A and C exchanged appears in Figure 11–14. Because C has the smaller area, it is placed in the upper left-hand corner of the space formerly occupied by A, so that the remaining space allows A to be contiguous. Notice that A is no longer rectangular. The actual cost of the new layout is not necessarily equal to the predicted value of 2,715. The centroid of A is computed using the method outlined in Appendix 11–A. It is determined by first finding the moments M_x and M_y given by

$$M_x = (40^2 - 0)(30 - 0)/2 + (60^2 - 40^2)(50 - 20)/2 = 54,000,$$
$$M_y = (30^2 - 0)(40 - 0)/2 + (50^2 - 20^2)(60 - 40)/2 = 39,000,$$

and dividing by the area of A to obtain

$$x_A = 54,000/1,800 = 30,$$
$$y_A = 39,000/1,800 = 21.66667.$$

FIGURE 11–14
New layout with A and C interchanged

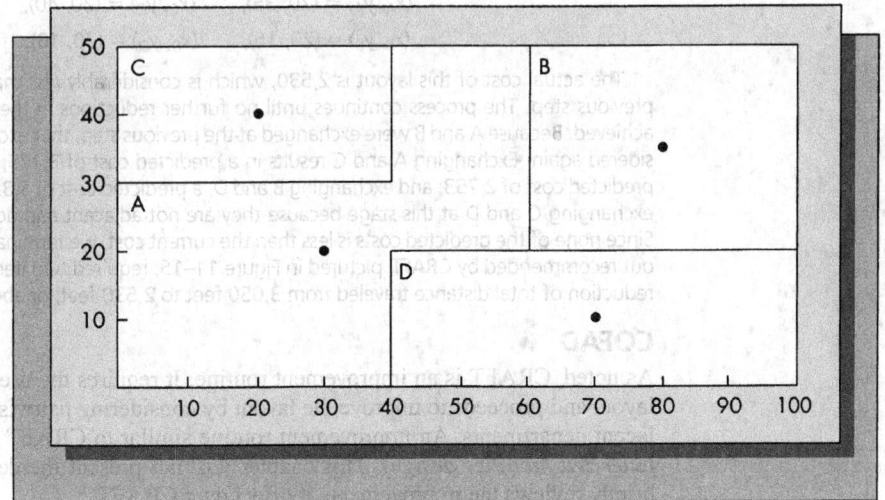

FIGURE 11–15
Second iteration, obtained from exchanging the locations of A and B

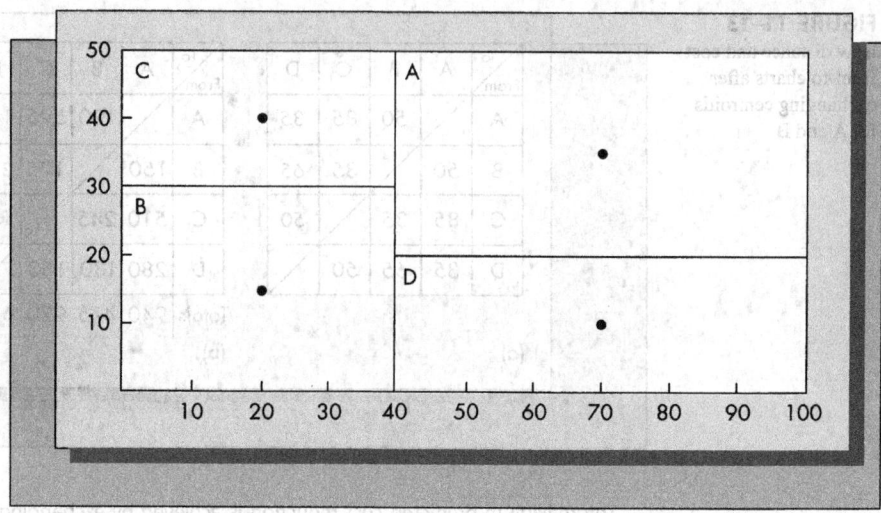

The centroid of C is located at the center of symmetry, which is

$$(x_C, y_C) = (20, 40).$$

The centroids for B and D are unchanged. The cost of the new layout is actually 2,810, which is somewhat more than the 2,715 predicted at the last step, but is still less than the original cost. The process is continued until predicted cost reductions are no longer possible. At this point only three exchanges need to be considered: A and B, A and D, and B and D. Obviously, we need not consider exchanging A and C, and C and D may not be exchanged because they do not share a common border. The predicted cost resulting from exchanging the centroids of A and B is 2,763.33; of A and D, 3,641.33; and of B and D, 2,982. Clearly, the greatest predicted reduction is now achieved by exchanging the locations of A and B.

The new layout is pictured in Figure 11–15. The centroids for the respective departments are now

$$(x_A, y_A) = (70, 35), \quad (x_C, y_C) = (20, 40),$$
$$(x_B, y_B) = (20, 15), \quad (x_D, y_D) = (70, 10).$$

The actual cost of this layout is 2,530, which is considerably *less* than that predicted in the previous step. The process continues until no further reductions in the predicted costs can be achieved. Because A and B were exchanged at the previous step, that exchange need not be considered again. Exchanging A and C results in a predicted cost of 3,175; exchanging A and D, a predicted cost of 2,753; and exchanging B and D, a predicted cost of 3,325. (We do not consider exchanging C and D at this stage because they are not adjacent and do not have equal areas.) Since none of the predicted costs is less than the current cost, we terminate calculations. The layout recommended by CRAFT, pictured in Figure 11–15, required two iterations and resulted in a reduction of total distance traveled from 3,050 feet to 2,530 feet, or about 17 percent.

COFAD

As noted, CRAFT is an improvement routine. It requires the user to specify an initial layout and proceeds to improve the layout by considering pairwise interchanges of adjacent departments. An improvement routine similar to CRAFT is COFAD (for *computerized facilities design*). This chapter will not present the details of COFAD, but briefly reviews the improvements it offers over CRAFT.

618 Chapter Eleven *Facilities Layout and Location*

COFAD is a modification of CRAFT that incorporates the choice of a materials handling system as part of the decision process. For a given layout, COFAD calculates the total move cost of the layout for a variety of materials handling alternatives and chooses the one with the minimum cost. Improvements are made by considering the equipment utilization of alternatives and exchanging assignments of poorly utilized equipment with equipment with better utilization. Once the best choice of equipment for a given layout is determined, the program considers improving the layout in much the same way as CRAFT. The program terminates when no additional improvements are possible. Once the program claims to have reached a steady state, the problem may be re-solved using from-to charts obtained from perturbing the original data from 10 to 50 percent. The purpose of re-solving the problem with the new data is to provide further assurance that the optimal solution has been reached, and to test the sensitivity of the solution to the flow data.

ALDEP

Both CRAFT and COFAD are improvement routines. That is, they start out with an initial layout and consider improvements by interchanging locations of departments. The other class of computerized layout techniques includes programs that develop the layouts essentially from scratch; they do not require an initial layout. Experience has shown that construction programs often tend to result in oddly shaped layouts, and for that reason they have not received as much attention in the literature as CRAFT.

ALDEP (for *automated layout design program*), is a construction routine rather than an improvement routine. That means that layouts are determined from scratch and the program does not require the user to specify an initial layout. ALDEP makes use of the closeness ratings that appear in the activity relationship chart. Figure 11–2 is an example of a rel chart. ALDEP first selects a department at random and places it in the upper left-hand corner of the layout. The next step is to scan the rel chart and place a department with a high closeness rating (A or E) in the layout adjacent to the first department. Successive departments are placed in the existing area in a top-down fashion, following a "sweep" pattern. The process is continued until all departments have been placed. At that point, a score for the layout is computed. The score is based on a numerical scale attached to the closeness ratings. ALDEP uses the following closeness rating values:

$$A = 4^3 = 64,$$
$$E = 4^2 = 16,$$
$$I = 4^1 = 4,$$
$$O = 4^0 = 1,$$
$$U = 0,$$
$$X = -4^5 = -1,024.$$

The entire process is repeated several times, and the layout with the largest score chosen. Because ALDEP tries to achieve a high closeness rating score, it often recommends layouts that have departments with very unusual shapes. The use of the sweep pattern helps to avoid this problem, but means that the resulting layout always appears as a set of adjacent strips. This type of layout may not be appropriate or desirable for some applications. The user specifies the sweep width to be used; the choice of the sweep width can have a significant effect upon the configuration of the final layout. For example, suppose that department A is 14 squares, B is 8 squares, the sweep width is 2 squares, and the

FIGURE 11–16
Method of placing departments used by ALDEP

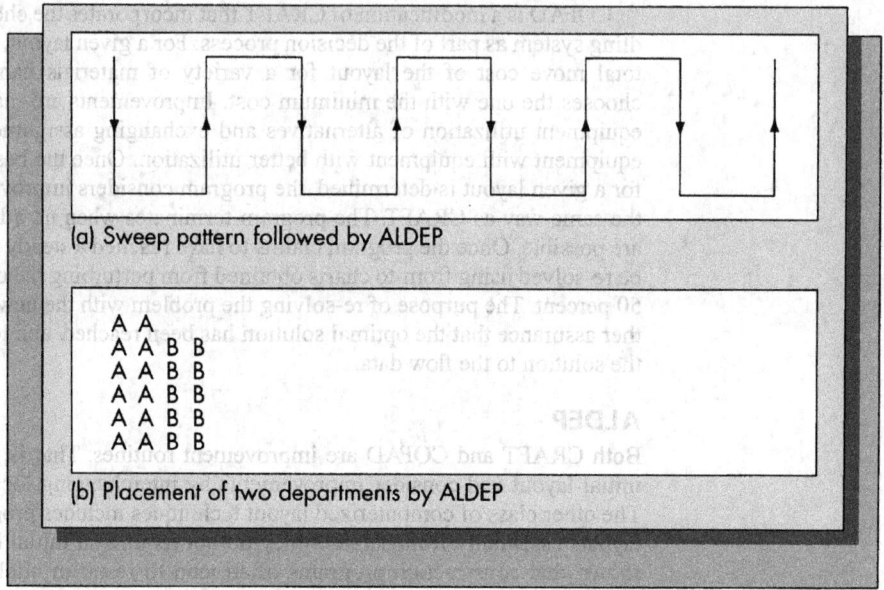

facility width is 6 squares. The layout of these two departments given by ALDEP is shown in Figure 11–16b, assuming that the departments are placed in the order A, B.

CORELAP

Like ALDEP, CORELAP (for *computerized relationship layout planning*) is a construction routine that places departments within the layout using closeness rating codes. The major difference between CORELAP and ALDEP is that CORELAP does not randomly select the first department to be placed. Rather, a total closeness rating (TCR) is computed for each department. The TCR is based on the numerical values $A = 6, E = 5, I = 4, O = 3, U = 2, X = 1$. Each department is compared to every other department to obtain a TCR.

For example, consider the Meat Me fast-food restaurant described in Example 11.1, with the rel chart shown in Figure 11–2. The closeness rating codes for the cooking-burgers department are X, I, U, U, and U, giving a TCR for this department of 11. The remaining values of the TCR are

Cooking fries: X, I, U, U, U—11,
Packing and storing: I, I, O, E, E—21,
Drink dispensers: U, U, O, A, A—19,
Counter service: U, U, E, A, A—21,
Drive-up service: O, A, E, U, U—18.

CORELAP now selects the department with the highest TCR and places that department in the center of the existing facility. When there is a tie (as in this case between the packing and storing department and the counter service department), the department with the largest area is placed first. Once the initial department is selected, the rel chart is scanned to see what departments have the highest closeness rating compared with the department just placed. Suppose that counter service is placed first. Then, scanning Figure 11–2, we see that only the drink dispensers department has a closeness rating code of A relative to the counter service department. Hence, drink dispensers would be placed in the layout next. Each time that a department is chosen to be placed in the layout, alternative placements are considered and placing ratings based on user-specified numerical values for the rel codes are computed. The new department is placed to maximize the placing rating. (Detailed examples of this procedure can be found in Francis and White, 1974, and Tompkins and White, 1984.)

PLANET

PLANET (for *plant layout analysis and evaluation technique*) has essentially the same required inputs as COFAD, and unlike both CORELAP and ALDEP does not use information contained in the rel chart to generate a layout. However, unlike CRAFT, PLANET is not an improvement routine. PLANET converts input data into a flow-between chart that gives the cost of sending a unit of flow between each pair of departments. In addition to the flow-between chart entries, the program also requires the user to input a priority rating for each department. The priority rating is a number from 1 to 9, with 1 representing the highest priority. The program selects departments to enter the layout in a sequential fashion, based first on the priority rating and second on the entries in the flow-between chart. Because PLANET does not restrict the final layout to conform to the shape of the building or allow fixing the location of certain departments, it suffers from the problems of other construction routines. Layouts obtained from PLANET, like those from ALDEP and CORELAP, may result in departments having unrealistic shapes. For that reason, such methods are better for providing the planner with some alternative ideas and initial layouts than for giving a final solution.

Computerized Methods versus Human Planners

An interesting debate concerning the effectiveness of computerized layout techniques versus expert human judgment appeared in the management science literature. The debate was sparked by a paper by Scriabin and Vergin (1975). In their study, the authors compared the layouts produced by three computerized layout routines, including CRAFT, and the layouts obtained without the use of these specific programs by 74 human subjects who were trained in manual layout techniques. The authors showed that the best solution obtained by groups of 20 of the 74 human subjects was better than the best solution obtained by the three computer routines. The largest difference in total cost occurred when the number of departments was the largest (20). Percentage differences ranged from 0 to 6.7. The authors concluded that humans will generally outperform computer layout routines because "in problems of a larger size the ability of man to recognize and visualize complex patterns gives him an edge over the essentially mechanical procedures followed by the computer programs."

Scriabin and Vergin's conclusions came under fire by a number of researchers. Buffa (1976) noted that the issue of flow dominance was not treated properly. Flow dominance refers to the tendency of materials to flow in the same sequence in the layout. Complete dominance occurs when a factory manufactures only a single product in an identical manner each time. In such a case, the final layout can easily be obtained by visual inspection. The other extreme occurs when products flow randomly through the factory. In that case all layouts are equivalent. (Block, 1977, gives a formal definition of flow dominance.) Buffa claimed that for problems in which flow dominance is over 200 percent, human subjects could be expected to obtain good solutions easily. The average flow dominance in the problems used by Scriabin and Vergin was apparently over 200 percent.

Another problem with their conclusions, as pointed out by Coleman (1977), was that in a typical industrial setting one does not have 20 professionals solving a layout problem. When comparing the layouts produced by the computer programs with those produced by individual human subjects, Coleman showed that the computer-generated layouts were superior. Finally, Block (1977) performed a separate experiment to test Buffa's contention that when flow dominance was under 200 percent, the computer will outperform the human. Block compared layouts produced by CRAFT with those produced by eight humans (four engineers and four laypeople) for a set of layout problems generated by Nugent, Vollmann, and Ruml (1968), in which the average flow dominance was 115 percent. He found that COFAD obtained better results in every case. The largest differences were observed when the number of departments was larger than 10.

What can we learn from these studies? It would appear that Scriabin and Vergin's conclusions are not justified. Later results showed that the computer-aided methods are, in fact, extremely useful and can result in significantly better layouts than can be obtained by simple visual or graphical methods when the number of departments is large and when material flow patterns are highly variable.

Dynamic Plant Layouts

Thus far, this chapter has considered only static layout problems. That is, we assumed that the costs appearing in the from-to charts are fixed. In some circumstances, this assumption may not be accurate, however. Nicol and Hollier (1983) note that: "Radical layout changes occur frequently and that management should therefore take this into account in their forward planning." A dynamic plant layout is based on the recognition that demands on the system, and hence costs of any given configuration, may change over time. When information on how the environment will change is available, one can incorporate this information into a model by allowing the costs in the from-to charts to change each planning period. This is precisely the scenario considered by Rosenblatt (1986). He showed how dynamic from-to charts would form the basis of a multiperiod planning model and developed a dynamic programming scheme to solve the resulting system of equations. With an example he shows how dynamic layouts can result in cost savings over fixed layouts in a changing environment. Models of this type will gain an even greater importance as firms continue to move toward structures based on agile manufacturing and increased flexibility.

Other Computer Methods

A variety of other analytical methods have been developed in addition to those already discussed. A method called bias sampling, suggested by Nugent, Vollmann, and Ruml (1968), is a straightforward modification of CRAFT that involves a randomization procedure for selecting departments to exchange. The method is considerably slower computationally but often results in better layouts. Considering the enormous strides that have been made in computing technology, the computational issues are less serious today than they were in 1968. SPACECRAFT (see Johnson, 1982) is an extension of CRAFT designed to produce layouts for multistory structures. The two primary modifications required were that (1) constraints had to be incorporated into the computational procedures that allowed certain departments to be located on specific floors and (2) the nonlinearity of the time required to go between floors required more complex cost calculations.

Not all layout problems are easily amenable to the methods reviewed here. There are applications in which assuming rectangular-shaped departments is not appropriate. Examples include the layouts of office buildings, an airplane's dashboard, a city or a neighborhood, or an integrated circuit. Drezner (1980) introduced a method called DISCON (for *dispersion and concentration*) that considers facilities as disks. The disks are first dispersed in the plane mathematically, using a system of differential equations simulating a system of springs connecting the disks. The dispersion phase provides an initial solution, which is later improved upon in the concentration phase. Drezner's approach works better than CRAFT when departments are not rectangular and when the number of facilities is large. Techniques based on graph theoretic methods (Foulds, 1983) and statistical cluster analysis (Scriabin and Vergin, 1985) also have been considered.

The "classic" software reviewed in this section illustrate the basic concepts used in most software products for facilities layout and design. Special products have been designed for distinct market segments. Office design, process piping, and industrial facilities planning are inherently very different layout problems and require specially tailored software products.

The problem of designing office facilities requires blocking out space for well-defined activities. These problems are the concern of interior designers and architects. Drafting tools with extensive libraries of symbols are the most popular for these applications. The most popular is AutoCAD, which allows for both two- and three-dimensional layouts. Process piping and layout design are typically used in conjunction with chemical plants and are almost always displayed as three-dimensional layouts. Industrial facilities layout and design usually involve some variant of the software tools discussed in this chapter, or the use of a specially tailored graphical-based simulation package, such as Pro-Model.

Intelligent design and layout of industrial facilities is a problem that is continuing to grow in importance. For example, the cost of a new fab (fabrication facility) in the semiconductor industry typically exceeds $1 billion. Similar investments are required for new automotive assembly plants. Firms cannot afford to make mistakes when planning the organization of these enormously expensive facilities.

Problems for Section 11.6

11. Briefly describe each of the following computerized layout techniques. In each case, indicate whether the method is a construction or improvement method.

    a. CRAFT
    b. COFAD
    c. ALDEP
    d. CORELAP
    e. PLANET

12. a. Discuss the advantages and disadvantages of using computer programs to develop layouts.

    b. Do the results of the studies discussed in Section 11.6 suggest that human planners or computer programs produce superior layouts? For what reasons are these studies not conclusive?

13. For Example 11.4, which illustrated CRAFT, verify the values of the predicted costs (2,715, 3,185, 2,735, and 2,830) obtained in the first iteration.

14. Consider the initial layout for Example 11.4, which appears in Figure 11–11. Draw a figure showing the layout obtained from exchanging the locations of A and D, and find the centroids of A and D in the new layout.

15. Determine the centroids for the six departments in the layout pictured in Figure 11–17 using the methods outlined in Appendix 11–A.

FIGURE 11–17
Layout (for Problem 15)

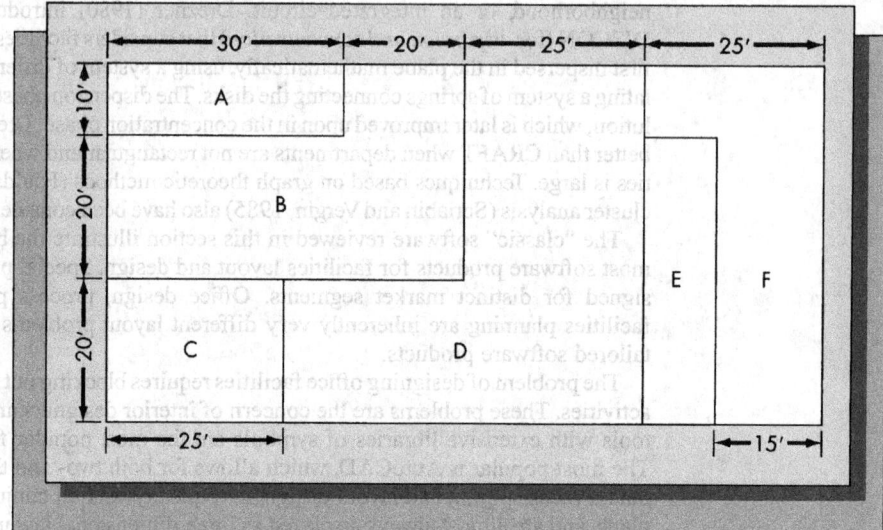

FIGURE 11–18
Layout and from-to chart (for Problem 16)

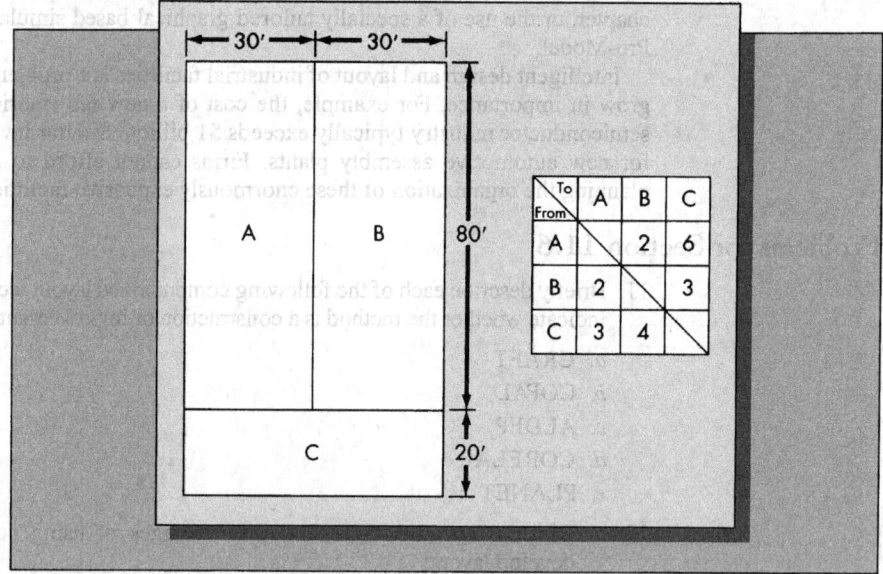

16. Consider the initial layout and from-to chart appearing in Figure 11–18. Assuming the goal is to minimize the total distance traveled, determine the final layout recommended by CRAFT using the pairwise exchange method described in this section. Compare the predicted and the actual figures for total distance traveled in the final layout.

17. Consider the initial layout pictured in Figure 11–19 and the two from-to charts giving the flow and cost data. Use the CRAFT approach to obtain a final layout. Compare the total cost of each layout predicted by CRAFT to the actual cost of each layout.

18. A facility consisting of eight departments has the activity relationship chart pictured in Figure 11–20. Compute the TCR for each department that would be used by CORELAP.

FIGURE 11–19
Layout and from-to charts
(for Problem 17)

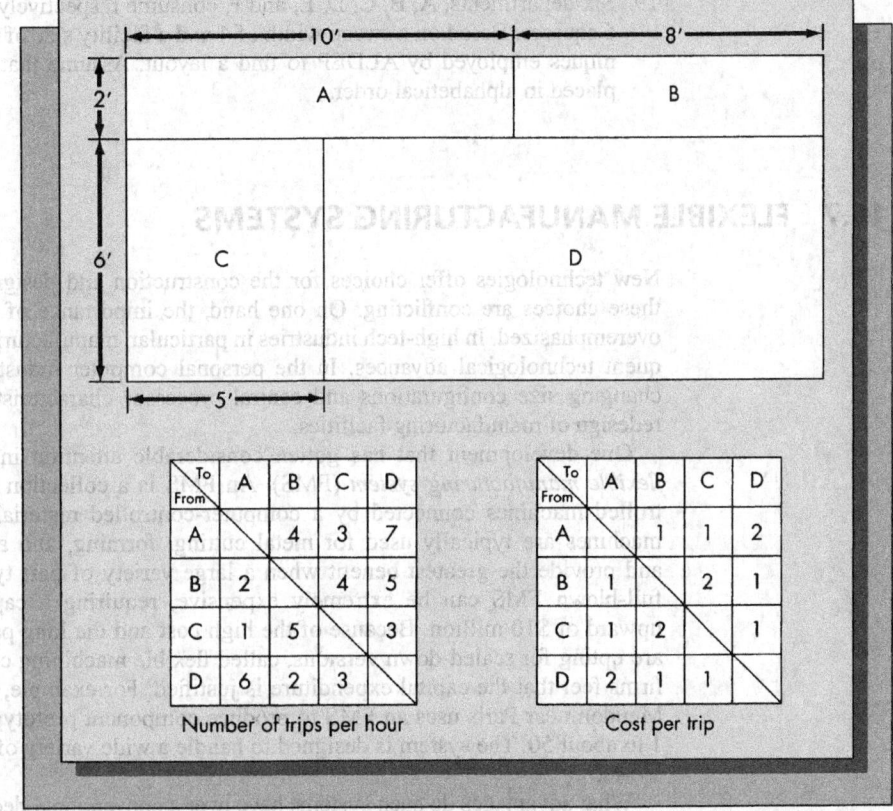

FIGURE 11–20
Rel chart
(for Problem 18)

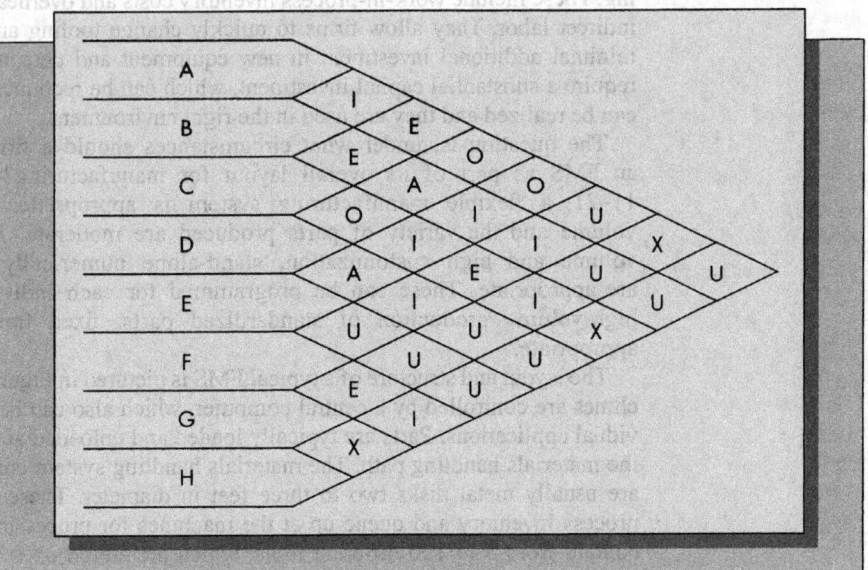

19. Six departments, A, B, C, D, E, and F, consume respectively 12, 6, 9, 18, 22, and 6 squares. Based on a sweep width of 4 and a facility size of 5 by 16, use the techniques employed by ALDEP to find a layout. Assume that the departments are placed in alphabetical order.

11.7 FLEXIBLE MANUFACTURING SYSTEMS

New technologies offer choices for the construction and design of facilities. Often these choices are conflicting. On one hand, the importance of flexibility cannot be overemphasized. In high-tech industries in particular, manufacturing must adapt to frequent technological advances. In the personal computer industry, for example, the changing size configurations and central processor characteristics require constant redesign of manufacturing facilities.

One development that has gotten considerable attention in recent years is the *flexible manufacturing system* (FMS). An FMS is a collection of numerically controlled machines connected by a computer-controlled materials flow system. The machines are typically used for metal cutting, forming, and assembly operations, and provide the greatest benefit when a large variety of part types are required. A full-blown FMS can be extremely expensive, requiring a capital expenditure of upward of $10 million. Because of the high cost and the long payback period, firms are opting for scaled-down versions, called flexible machining cells. However, many firms feel that the capital expenditure is justified. For example, the Citroen plant in Meudon near Paris uses an FMS to produce component prototypes in batch sizes of 1 to about 50. The system is designed to handle a wide variety of part types (Hartley, 1984).

What advantages do such systems have over a conventional dedicated machine layout? They provide the opportunity to drastically slash the hidden costs of manufacturing. These include work-in-process inventory costs and overhead costs associated with indirect labor. They allow firms to quickly change tooling and product design with minimal additional investment in new equipment and personnel. However, they do require a substantial capital investment, which can be recouped only if their potential can be realized and they are used in the right environment.

The question is, under what circumstances should a firm consider employing an FMS as part of its overall layout for manufacturing? As shown in Figure 11–21, a flexible manufacturing system is appropriate when the production volume and the variety of parts produced are moderate. For systems with low volume and high customization, stand-alone numerically controlled machines are appropriate. These can be programmed for each individual application. For high-volume production of standardized parts, fixed transfer lines are more appropriate.

The layout and structure of a typical FMS is pictured in Figure 11–22. Often the machines are controlled by a central computer, which also can be programmed for individual applications. Parts are typically loaded and unloaded at a single location along the materials handling path. The materials handling system consists of pallets, which are usually metal disks two to three feet in diameter. These pallets carry work-in-process inventory and queue up at the machines for processing. Each machine may contain from 5 to 100 different tools, which are stored on a carousel. Tools can be

FIGURE 11–21
The position of FMS in the manufacturing hierarchy

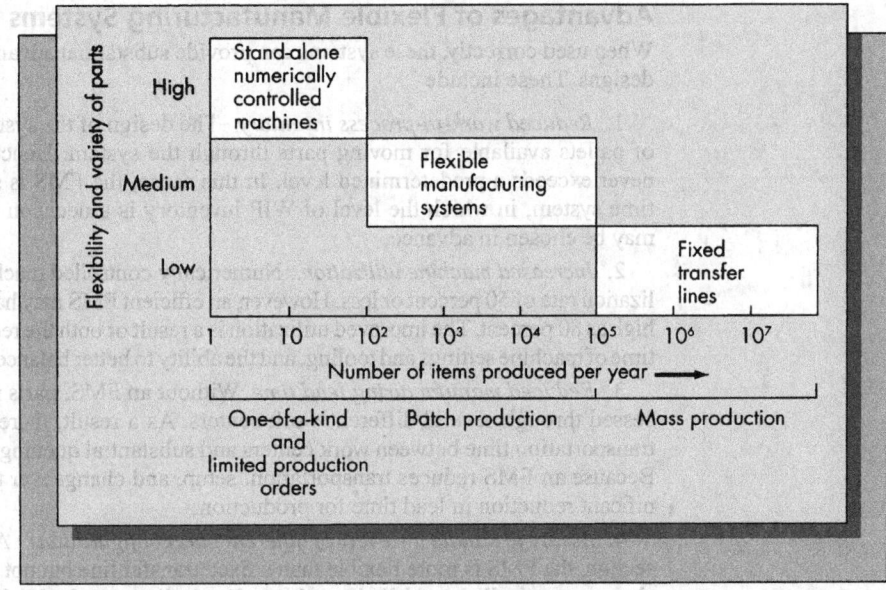

FIGURE 11–22
A typical flexible manufacturing system

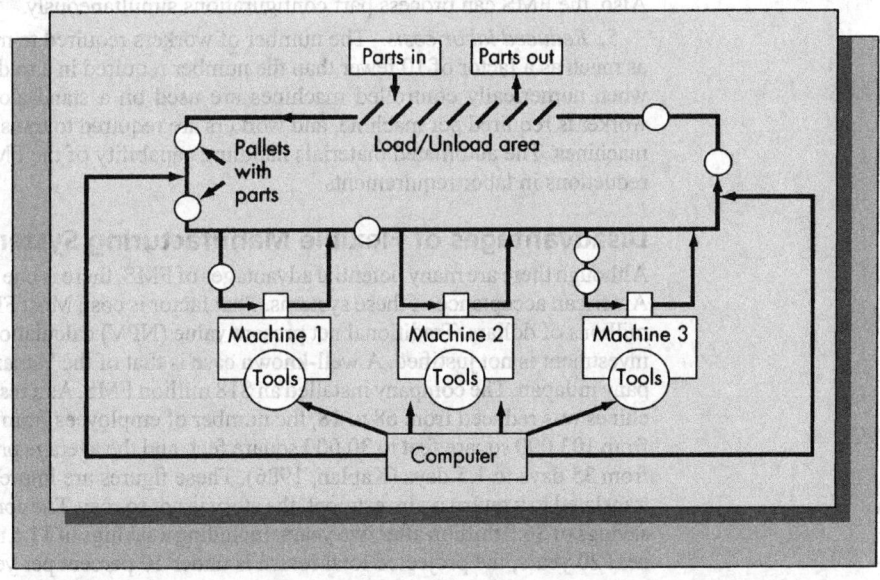

exchanged in a matter of seconds. Note that the routing of parts must also be programmed into the system, as not all products require the same sequencing of machine operations. Although Figure 11–22 shows a centralized computer, some systems use individually programmed machines.

Advantages of Flexible Manufacturing Systems

When used correctly, these systems can provide substantial advantages over more rigid designs. These include

1. *Reduced work-in-process inventory.* The design of the system limits the number of pallets available for moving parts through the system. Hence, the WIP inventory never exceeds a predetermined level. In this sense, the FMS is similar to the just-in-time system, in which the level of WIP inventory is a decision variable whose value may be chosen in advance.

2. *Increased machine utilization.* Numerically controlled machines often have a utilization rate of 50 percent or less. However, an efficient FMS may have a utilization rate as high as 80 percent. The improved utilization is a result of both the reduction of changeover time of machine settings and tooling, and the ability to better balance the system workload.

3. *Reduced manufacturing lead time.* Without an FMS, parts might have to be processed through several different work centers. As a result, there could be substantial transportation time between work centers and substantial queuing time at work centers. Because an FMS reduces transportation, setup, and changeover time, it results in significant reduction in lead time for production.

4. *Ability to handle a variety of different part configurations.* As noted earlier in this section, the FMS is more flexible than a fixed transfer line but not as flexible as a stand-alone numerically controlled machine. Depending on the tooling available for the machines, parts may be launched into the system with little or no setup time required. Also, the FMS can process part configurations simultaneously.

5. *Reduced labor costs.* The number of workers required to manage an FMS can be as much as a factor of 10 fewer than the number required in a traditional job shop. Even when numerically controlled machines are used on a stand-alone basis, at least one worker is required per machine, and workers are required to transport the parts between machines. The automated materials handling capability of the FMS leads to significant reductions in labor requirements.

Disadvantages of Flexible Manufacturing Systems

Although there are many potential advantages of FMS, there is one factor that has delayed American acceptance of these systems. That factor is cost. Most FMSs cost in the tens of millions of dollars. Traditional net present value (NPV) calculations often show that the investment is not justified. A well-known case is that of the Yamazaki Machinery Company in Japan. The company installed an $18 million FMS. As a result, the number of machines was reduced from 68 to 18, the number of employees from 215 to 12, floor space from 103,000 square feet to 30,000 square feet, and the average processing time of parts from 35 days to 1.5 days (Kaplan, 1986). These figures are impressive. However, when translated to a return on investment, the story is not so rosy. The company reported a total savings of $6.9 million after two years. Including a savings of $1.5 million per year for the next 20 years, the projected total return is under 10 percent per year. In most American companies, the "hurdle rate" is generally 15 percent or higher, thus making this particular FMS operation a poor investment by NPV considerations alone. (The hurdle rate is the minimum acceptable rate of return on new projects.)

In addition to the direct costs of the equipment and the space, several indirect costs also are incurred. In order to manage the flow of materials, a sophisticated software system is required. Effective software can be extremely expensive, may require customization, often has bugs, and generally requires worker training. The cost of equipment such as feeders, conveyors, and transfer devices may not be part of the initial purchase cost. Other indirect costs include site preparation, spare parts to support the machinery, and disruptions that might result during the installation period. Furthermore, any company that purchases an FMS must anticipate a decline in productivity that accompanies the introduction of new technology.

It is no wonder that so many American companies have trouble justifying the investment in FMS. However, Kaplan (1986) argues that traditional cost accounting methods may ignore some important considerations. One is that evaluation of alternative investments based on discounted cash flow assumes a status quo. That is, NPV analysis assumes that factors such as market share, price, labor costs, and the company's competitive position in the marketplace will remain constant. However, the values of some of these variables will change, and are more likely to degenerate if the company retains outmoded production methods.

Furthermore, most firms prefer to invest in a variety of small projects rather than make a major capital outlay for a single project. Such a philosophy is safer in the short run, but could be suboptimal in the long run. An example of an industry that failed to invest in new technology is the railroad industry. Because of outmoded equipment and facilities, many firms in this industry have been unable to stay competitive and profitable.

Cost is not the only problem. The FMS may experience downtime for a variety of reasons. Planned downtime could be the result of scheduled maintenance and scheduled tool changeovers. Unplanned downtime could result from mechanical failures of the machines or electrical failures. If a single machine goes down, the system can continue to function, but if either the materials handling system or the central computer fails, the entire FMS is crippled.

Decision Making and Modeling of the FMS

Mathematical modeling can help with the decisions required to design and manage an FMS. Flexible manufacturing systems, like all job shops, must be managed on a continual basis. Some decisions, such as whether to purchase a system at all, have very far-reaching consequences. Other decisions, such as what action should be taken when a machine breaks down or a tool is damaged, may only affect the flow of materials for the next few hours. This suggests that a natural way to categorize these decisions is by the time horizon associated with their consequences. Table 11–1 summarizes the various levels of FMS decision making broken down in this manner.

TABLE 11–1 Levels of Decision Making in Flexible Manufacturing Systems

Time Horizon	Major Issues	Modeling Methods
Long term (months–years)	Design of the system Parts mix changes System modification and/or expansion	Queuing networks Simulation Optimization
Medium term (days–weeks)	Production batching Maximizing of machine utilization Planning for fluctuations in demand and/or availability of resources	Balancing methods Network simulation
Short term (minutes–hours)	Work order scheduling and dispatching Tool management Reaction to system failures	Tool operation and allocation program Work order dispatching algorithm Simulation

FIGURE 11–23
A single-server queue

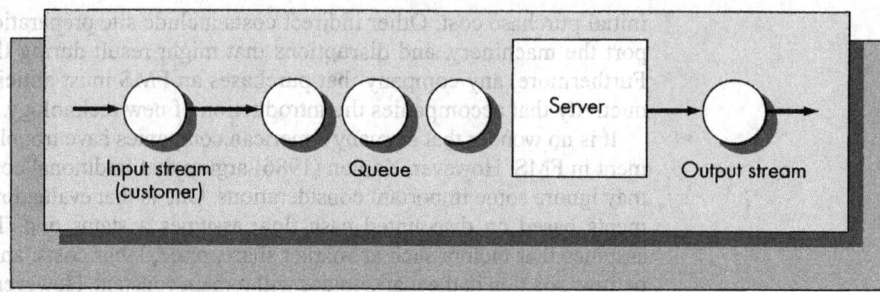

FIGURE 11–24
A network of queues

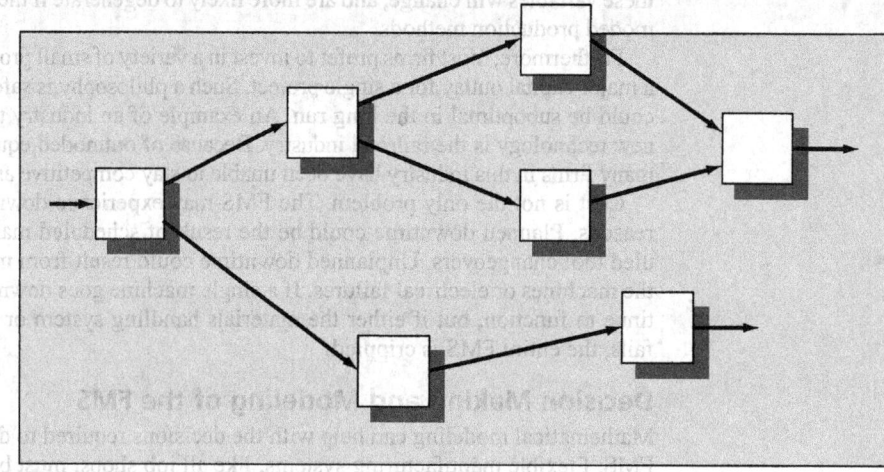

Queuing-Based Models

Queuing theory is the basis for many models that can assist with long-term decisions. A queue is simply a waiting line. A single-server queuing system is characterized by an input stream (known as customers), a service discipline specifying the order or sequence that customers are served, and a service mechanism. Most queuing models assume that both the arrival stream of customers and the service times are random variables. It is the random nature of arrivals and services and their interactions that makes queuing problems interesting.[1] Figure 11–23 shows a simple schematic of a single-server queuing system.

In an FMS, each machine corresponds to a separate queue. The jobs correspond to the customers, and the queue is the stack of jobs waiting for processing at a machine. Because an FMS is a collection of machines connected by a materials handling system, the entering stream of customers for one machine is the result of the accumulation of departing streams from other machines. Hence, an FMS is a special kind of queuing network. A typical queuing network appears in Figure 11–24.

Queuing models are most useful in aiding with system design. They can be used to compute a variety of measures relating to machine utilization and system performance. An important issue that arises during the initial design phase is system capacity. The system capacity is the maximum production rate that the FMS can sustain. It depends

---

[1] A summary of basic queuing theory appears in Supplement 2, which follows Chapter 8.

on both the configuration of the FMS and the assumptions one makes about the nature of the arrival stream of jobs. Schweitzer's (1977) analysis shows that the output rate of a flexible manufacturing system is simply the capacity of the slowest machine in the system.

To be more precise, suppose that machine i can process jobs at a rate μ_i. If the probabilities that an entering job visits machines in a given order are known, one can find e_i, the expected number of visits of a newly arriving job to machine i, using queuing theory methods. It follows that $1/e_i$ is the rate that jobs arrive to machine i, so μ_i/e_i is the output rate of machine i. The "slowest" machine, where slow is used in a relative sense, is that machine whose output rate is least. Hence, the output rate of the system is $\min_{1 \leq i \leq n} (\mu_i/e_i)$.

Such results can be very valuable when considering the design of the system and its potential utility to the firm. However, in some circumstances queuing models are only of limited value. In particular, in order to obtain explicit results for complex queuing networks, one often must assume that the arrival and the service processes are purely random. That is, both the time between the arrival of successive jobs and the time required for a machine to complete its task are exponential random variables.[2] It is unlikely that both interarrival times and job performance times in flexible manufacturing systems are accurately described by exponential distributions. There are circumstances under which exponential queuing formulas do give reasonable approximations to more complex cases, but simulation should be used to validate analytical formulas. Approximate analytical results are available for nonexponential cases as well (see Suri and Hildebrant, 1984, for example). Also, the exponential assumption is not required for some simple network configurations. A review of the analytical results for network queuing models of flexible manufacturing systems can be found in Buzacott and Yao (1986).

Even with these limitations, queuing models provide a powerful means for analyzing the performance characteristics and capacity limitations of flexible manufacturing systems. Eventually, network queuing models will accurately reflect the nature of FMSs and provide an effective means for assisting with system design and management.

Mathematical Programming Models

Stecke (1983) considers the use of mathematical programming for solving several decision problems arising in FMS management. These problems include the following:

1. *Part type selection problem.* From a given set of part types that have associated known requirements, determine a subset for immediate and simultaneous processing.
2. *Machine grouping problem.* Partition the machines into groups so that each machine in a group can perform the same set of operations.
3. *Production ratio problem.* Determine the relative ratios to produce the part types selected in step 1.
4. *Resource allocation problem.* Allocate the limited number of pallets and fixtures among the selected part types.
5. *Loading problem.* Allocate the operations and required tools of the selected part types among the machine groups subject to technological capacity constraints of the FMS.

---

[2] The properties of the exponential distribution are discussed in detail in Chapter 2 and in Supplement 2 on queuing.

We will not present the details of the mixed integer programming formulations. Our purpose is simply to note that mathematical programming is another means of helping with long-range and medium-range decisions affecting the FMS. Stecke (1983) shows how one would apply these models using actual data from an existing FMS.

The Future of FMS

There is substantial potential for the application of FMS both in the United States and abroad. It is estimated that about half of the annual expenditures on manufacturing is in the metal-working industry, and two-thirds of metal working is metal cutting (Stecke, 1983). Furthermore, about three-fourths of the dollar volume of metal-worked parts is manufactured in batches of fewer than 50 parts (Cook, 1975). Evidently, there is a huge market for FMSs in the United States. Similar potential exists in other industrialized countries as well. In fact, the rate of growth of installed FMSs is higher in Japan than in any other country in the world (Jaikumar, 1984).

The rate of growth of FMSs in the United States has been healthy if not spectacular. In 1981 there were about 18 systems operational in the United States (Jaikumar, 1984), and by late 1986 this number had grown to about 50. Krouse (1986) estimated that there should have been 284 systems in place in the United States by 1990. As we noted earlier, the primary concern among companies considering purchasing an FMS is cost. The average cost of such systems was estimated to be $12.5 million in 1986 and is probably higher today. Also, installation generally requires from 18 to 24 months.

Both hardware and changeover costs discourage many potential users of FMSs. Furthermore, many factories in this country have yet to invest in numerically controlled machine tools, let alone a full-blown FMS. As a response to this, vendors are offering scaled-down versions of the FMS known as flexible manufacturing cells. Flexible manufacturing cells are small FMSs offering fewer machines, a less extensive materials handling system, and fewer tools per machine. Vendors anticipate healthy sales of these cells, which should result in an expanded customer base and a larger market for scaled-up systems.

Cost is not the only factor retarding acceptance. The performance of many existing FMSs has been disappointing. Zygmont (1986) reported that some installed systems did not meet the expectations of the companies that purchased them. In one case, three years were required to debug a system purchased by Electro-Optical and Data Systems of Hughes Aircraft and in the end the system was still less flexible than originally expected. One of the problems encountered was that the level of precision required was higher than the system was capable of delivering. Similarly, Deere and Co. was disappointed with its $20 million system, and was especially disappointed with the lack of flexibility afforded by the software for handling complex and varying part sequences.

Jaikumar (1986) makes a case that the problem with FMSs in the United States is not the systems themselves but the way they are used. In a comparison of FMSs in the United States and Japan, he found some striking differences. These differences are listed in Table 11–2.

Most telling is the fact that there are almost 10 times more part types produced on each Japanese system than on each American system. That, coupled with the enormous difference in annual volume per part, indicates that American firms are using FMSs improperly. That is, they are used as if they were simply another set of machines for high-volume standardized production rather than for producing the varied part mix for which they were designed. Another important difference is that many Japanese systems are run both day and night and often unattended. Jaikumar (1986) claims that this is a consequence of the improved design and reliability of the Japanese systems.

TABLE 11–2
A Comparison of FMSs in the United States and Japan

	United States	Japan
System development times (years)	25 to 3	1 to 1.25
Types of parts produced per system	10	93
Annual volume per part	1.727	258
Number of new parts introduced per year	1	22
Number of systems with unattended operations	0	18
Average metal-cutting time per day	83	202

As firms install additional FMSs, vendors will gain a better understanding of their power and their limitations. Advances in both hardware and software should make future systems more capable of dealing with the problems discussed. As both the systems and the understanding of the circumstances under which they can be most effective improve, we should see many more companies installing FMSs in the next decade.

Problems for Section 11.7

20. In each case listed, state whether the factor listed is an advantage or a disadvantage of FMS. Discuss the reasons for your choice.

    a. Cost.
    b. Ability to handle different parts requirements.
    c. Advances in manufacturing technology.
    d. Reliability.

21. For each of the case situations described, state which of the three types of manufacturing systems would be most appropriate: (1) stand-alone numerically controlled machines, (2) FMS, (3) fixed transfer line, or (4) another system. Explain your choice in each case.

    a. A local machine shop that accepts custom orders from a variety of clients in the electronics industry.
    b. An international supplier of standard-sized metal containers.
    c. The metal-working division of a large aircraft manufacturer, which must serve the needs of a variety of divisions in the firm.

22. For what reason might a traditional NPV (net present value) analysis not be an appropriate means for evaluating the desirability of purchasing an FMS?

23. With which decisions related to FMS design or control can the following methods assist? Also, briefly describe how each method would be used.

    a. Queuing theory
    b. Simulation
    c. Mathematical programming

11.8 LOCATING NEW FACILITIES

Chapter 1 discussed several qualitative considerations when deciding on the best location for a new plant or other facility. The remainder of this chapter will consider quantitative techniques that can help with location decisions. There are many circumstances in which the objective can be quantified easily, and it is in these cases that analytical solution methods are most useful.

Snapshot Application

KRAFT FOODS USES OPTIMIZATION AND SIMULATION TO DETERMINE BEST LAYOUT

In the mid-1990s Kraft decided to renovate one of its major manufacturing facilities located in the Midwest. New higher-capacity production lines were to replace the old lines. The new lines would have increased throughput and more mixing capabilities and would be able to operate at a variety of speeds. One of the concerns in designing the new facility was determining the optimum number of new lines to install to maintain current capacity levels while also allowing for future growth. Management needed to decide the line configuration quickly because the lines required a six-month delivery lead time.

Kraft management asked the firm's operations research group to develop a detailed mathematical model of the system. A "seat of the pants" approach was simply unacceptable: a wrong decision would be costly. Too many lines would result in wasted space and money, and too few in a capacity bottleneck. A further difficulty was that none of Kraft's plants had used these lines before, so there was no prior experience from which to draw.

Staff members from the firm's operations research group were asked to consider both the problem of optimizing the number of new lines and the flow of material within the plant. To address the optimization problem, the group developed an integer programming formulation of the problem. The objective was to ensure that the makespan of any schedule Kraft was likely to encounter did not exceed one eight-hour shift. (Refer to Chapter 8 for a discussion of makespan.) They determined that six lines would easily take care of existing capacity requirements and include a substantial margin for future growth. The model was solved using the AMPL optimization package on a personal computer.

Once the optimal number of new lines was determined, the next step was to develop a detailed simulation of the factory floor to show graphically how the new design would work in practice. For this task, the group decided to use F&H Simulation's Taylor II software package, a graphical-based simulation package especially well-suited for considering the effects of different work schedules on a given layout. The simulation model consisted of 139 elements including lines, machines, work-in-process buffers, loading areas for raw materials, and shipping areas. By simulating the process with the heaviest schedules, the group demonstrated that the new layout would easily have enough capacity to handle the most severe demands the plant is likely to see. Furthermore, the simulation afforded factory personnel a means to see how the flow of materials would change prior to the time that the plant was renovated and the new layout implemented.

Source: Based on Sengupta and Combes (1995).

In some sense, the plant layout problem is a special case of the location problem. However, the problems considered in the remainder of this chapter differ from layout problems in the following way: we will assume that there are one or more existing facilities already in place and we wish to find the optimal location of a new facility. We will concentrate on the problem of locating a single new facility, although there are versions of the problem in which one must determine the locations of multiple facilities.

Examples of the type of one-facility location problems that can be solved by the methods discussed in this chapter include

1. Location of a new storage warehouse for a company with an existing network of production and distribution centers.
2. Determining the best location for a new machine in a job shop.
3. Locating the computer center in a university.
4. Finding the best location for a new hospital in a metropolitan area.
5. Finding the most suitable location for a power generating plant designed to serve a geographic region.
6. Determining the placement of an ATM in a neighborhood.
7. Locating a new police station in a community.

Undoubtedly, the reader can think of many other examples of location problems. Analytical methods assume that the objective is to locate the new facility to minimize some function of the distance of the new location from existing locations. For example, when locating a new warehouse, an appropriate objective would be to minimize the total distance traveled to the warehouse from production facilities and from the warehouse to retail outlets. A hospital would be located to be most easily accessible to the largest proportion of the population in the area it serves. A machine would be placed to minimize the weighted sum of materials handling trips to and from the machine. Clearly, choosing the location of a facility to minimize some function of the distance separating the new facility from existing facilities is appropriate for many real location problems.

Measures of Distance

Two measures of distance are most common: *Euclidean distance* and *rectilinear distance*. Euclidean distance is also known as straight-line distance. The Euclidean distance separating two points is simply the length of the straight line connecting the points. Suppose that an existing facility is located at the point (a, b) and let (x, y) be the location of the new facility. Then the Euclidean distance between (a, b) and (x, y) is

$$\sqrt{(x-a)^2 + (y-b)^2}.$$

The rectilinear distance (also known as metropolitan distance, recognizing the fact that streets usually run in a crisscross pattern) is given by the formula

$$|x - a| + |y - b|.$$

Figure 11–25 illustrates the difference between these two distance measures.

Rectilinear distance is appropriate for many location problems. Distances in metropolitan areas tend to be more closely approximated by rectilinear distances than by Euclidean distances even when the street pattern is not a perfect grid. In many manufacturing environments, material is transported across aisles arranged in regular patterns. It is a fortunate coincidence that rectilinear distance is more common than Euclidean distance, because the rectilinear distance problem is easier to solve.

FIGURE 11–25
Euclidean and rectilinear distances

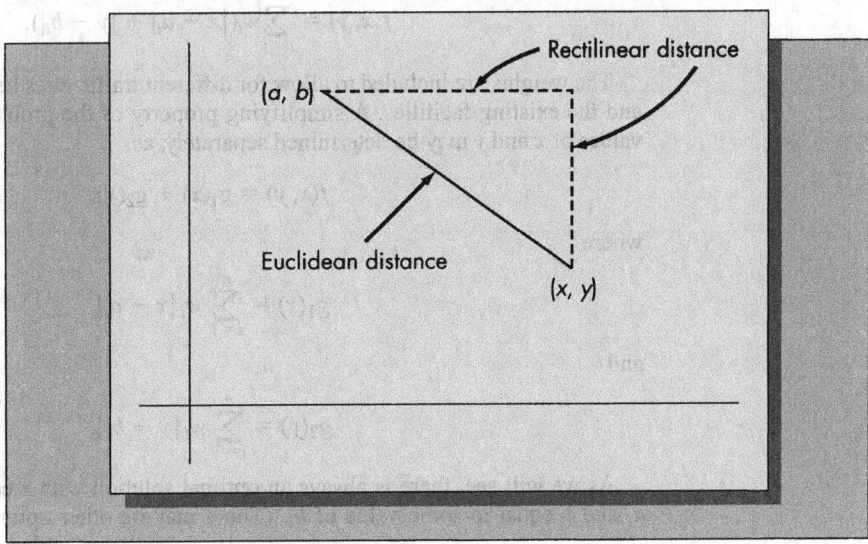

Problems for Section 11.8

24. Consider the problem of locating a new hospital in a metropolitan area. List the factors that can be quantified and those that cannot. Comment on the usefulness of quantitative methods in the decision-making process.

25. A coordinate system is superimposed on a map. Three existing facilities are located at (5, 15), (10, 20), and (6, 9). Compute both the rectilinear and the Euclidean distances separating each facility from a new facility located at $(x, y) =$ (8, 8).

26. For the situation described in Problem 25, suppose that there are only three feasible locations for the new facility: (8, 16), (6, 15), and (4, 18).

    a. What is the optimal location if the objective is to minimize the total rectilinear distance to the three existing facilities?
    b. What is the optimal location if the objective is to minimize the total Euclidean distance to the three existing facilities?

27. For each of the seven examples of location problems listed in this section, indicate which distance measure, Euclidean or rectilinear, would be more appropriate. (Discuss how, in some cases, one or the other objective could be appropriate for the same problem, depending upon the optimization criterion used.)

11.9 THE SINGLE-FACILITY RECTILINEAR DISTANCE LOCATION PROBLEM

In this section we will present a solution to the general problem of locating a new facility among n existing facilities. The objective is to locate the new facility to minimize a weighted sum of the rectilinear distances from the new facility to existing facilities. Assume that the existing facilities are located at points $(a_1, b_1), (a_2, b_2), \ldots, (a_n, b_n)$. Then the goal is to find values of x and y to minimize

$$f(x, y) = \sum_{i=1}^{n} w_i(|x - a_i| + |y - b_i|).$$

The weights are included to allow for different traffic rates between the new facility and the existing facilities. A simplifying property of the problem is that the optimal values of x and y may be determined separately, as

$$f(x, y) = g_1(x) + g_2(y),$$

where

$$g_1(x) = \sum_{i=1}^{n} w_i |x - a_i|$$

and

$$g_2(y) = \sum_{i=1}^{n} w_i |y - b_i|.$$

As we will see, there is always an optimal solution with x equal to some value of a_i and y equal to some value of b_i. (There may be other optimal solutions as well.)

FIGURE 11–26
Optimal locations of the new facility for a rectilinear distance measure

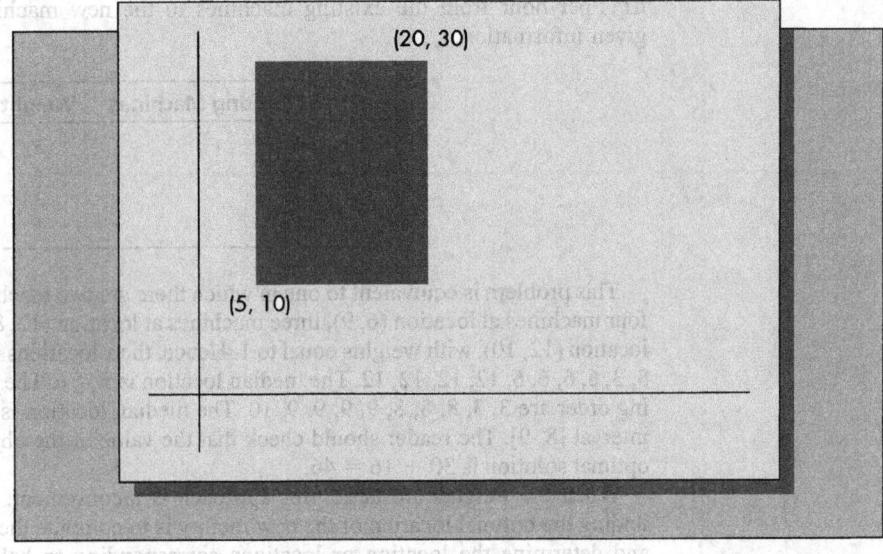

However, before presenting the general solution algorithm for finding the optimal location of the new facility, we consider a few simple examples in order to provide the reader with some intuition. Consider first the case in which there are exactly two existing facilities, located at (5, 10) and (20, 30) as pictured in Figure 11–26. Assume that the weight applied to each of these facilities is 1. If x assumes any value between 5 and 20, the value of $g_1(x)$ is equal to 15. (For example, if $x = 13$, then $g_1(x) = |5 - 13| + |13 - 20| = 8 + 7 = 15$.) Similarly, if y assumes any value between 10 and 30, then $g_2(y) = 20$. Any value of x outside the closed interval [5, 20] and any value of y outside the closed interval [10, 30] results in larger values of $g_1(x)$ and $g_2(y)$. Hence, the optimal solution is (x, y) with $5 \leq x \leq 20$ and $10 \leq y \leq 30$. All locations in the shaded region pictured in Figure 11–26 are optimal.

As in the example, there always will be an optimal location of the new facility with coordinates coming from the set of coordinates of the existing facilities. Suppose that the existing facilities have locations (3, 3), (6, 9), (12, 8), and (12, 10). Again assume that the weight applied to these locations is 1. Ranking the x locations in increasing order gives 3, 6, 12, 12. A *median* value is such that half of the x values lie above it and half of the x values lie below it. Any value of x between 6 and 12 is a median location and is optimal for this problem. The optimal value of $g_1(x)$ is 15. (The reader should experiment with a number of different values of x between 6 and 12 to satisfy himself or herself that this is the case.) Ranking the y values in increasing order gives 3, 8, 9, 10. The median value of y is between 8 and 9, and the optimal value of $g_2(y) = 8$.

The optimal solution is to locate (x, y) at the median of the existing facilities. This result carries over to the case in which there are weights different from 1. Suppose in Example 11.4 that we were given the locations of four machines in a job shop. The goal is to find the location of a fifth machine to minimize the total distance traveled to transport material between the new machine and the existing ones. Assume that on average there are respectively 2, 4, 3, and 1 materials handling trips per hour from the existing machines to the new machine. Summarizing the given information,

Location of Existing Machines	Weight
(3, 3)	2
(6, 9)	4
(12, 8)	3
(12, 10)	1

This problem is equivalent to one in which there are two machines at location (3, 3), four machines at location (6, 9), three machines at location (12, 8), and one machine at location (12, 10), with weights equal to 1. Hence, the x locations in increasing order are 3, 3, 6, 6, 6, 6, 12, 12, 12, 12. The median location is $x = 6$. The y locations in increasing order are 3, 3, 8, 8, 8, 9, 9, 9, 9, 10. The median location is any value of y on the interval [8, 9]. The reader should check that the value of the objective function at the optimal solution is $30 + 16 = 46$.

When the weights are large, this approach is inconvenient. A quicker method of finding the optimal location of the new facility is to compute the accumulated weights and determine the location or locations corresponding to half of the accumulated weight. The procedure is best illustrated by example.

Example *11.5* University of the Far West has purchased equipment that permits faculty to prepare videotapes of lectures. The equipment will be used by faculty from six schools on campus: business, education, engineering, humanities, law, and science. The locations of the buildings on the campus are pictured in Figure 11-27. The coordinates of the locations and the numbers of faculty

FIGURE 11–27
Location of six campus buildings (refer to Example 11.5)

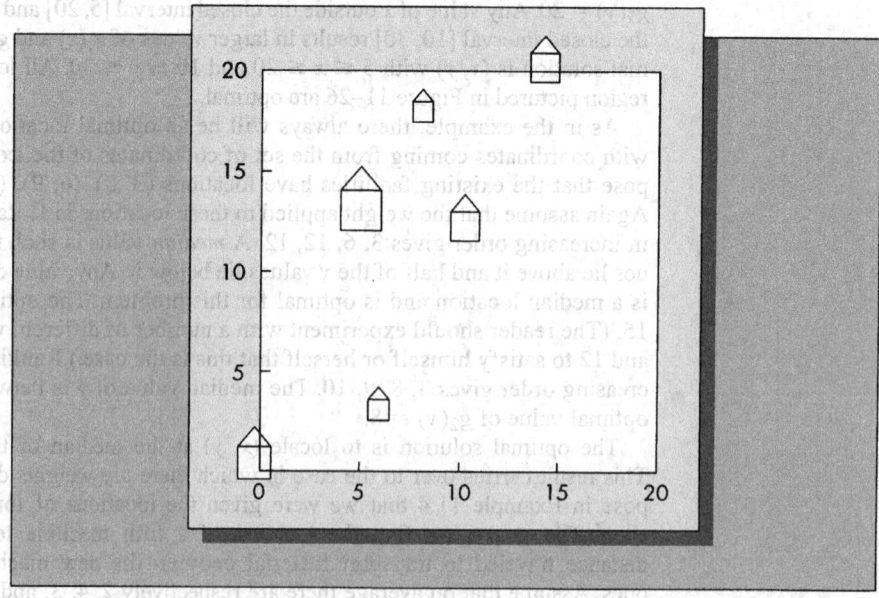

that are anticipated to use the equipment are as follows:

School	Campus Location	Number of Faculty
Business	(5, 13)	31
Education	(8, 18)	28
Engineering	(0, 0)	19
Humanities	(6, 3)	53
Law	(14, 20)	32
Science	(10, 12)	41

The campus is laid out with large grassy areas separating the buildings, and walkways are mainly east–west or north–south, so that distances between buildings are rectilinear. The university planner would like to locate the new facility so as to minimize the total travel time of all faculty planning to use it.

We will find the optimal values of the x and y coordinates separately. Consider the optimal x coordinate value. We first rank x coordinates in increasing value and accumulate the weights.

School	x Coordinate	Weight	Cumulative Weight
Engineering	0	19	19
Business	5	31	50
Humanities	6	53	103
Education	8	28	131
Science	10	41	172
Law	14	32	204

The optimal value of the x coordinate is found by dividing the total cumulative weight by 2 and identifying the first location at which the cumulative weight exceeds this value. In the example this is the first time that the cumulative weight exceeds $204/2 = 102$. This occurs at $x = 6$, when the cumulative weight is 103. Hence, the optimal $x = 6$.

We use the same procedure to find the optimal value of the y coordinate. The rankings are given here.

School	y Coordinate	Weight	Cumulative Weight
Engineering	0	19	19
Humanities	3	53	72
Science	12	41	113
Business	13	31	144
Education	18	28	172
Law	20	32	204

In this case the cumulative weight first exceeds 102 when $y = 12$. Hence, $y = 12$ is optimal. The optimal location of the new facility is (6, 12). This solution is unique. Multiple optima will occur when a value of the cumulative weight exactly equals half of the total cumulative weight. For example, suppose that the weight for science were 19 instead of 41. Then the cumulative weight for science would be 91, exactly half of the total weight of 182, and all values of y on the closed interval [12, 13] would be optimal.

Contour Lines

Example 11.5 suggests an interesting question. Suppose that the location (6, 12) is infeasible. How can the university gauge the cost penalty when locating the new facility elsewhere? Contour lines, or isocost lines, can assist with determining the penalty of nonoptimal solutions. A contour line is a line of constant cost: locating a new facility anywhere along a contour line results in exactly the same cost.

FIGURE 11-28
Contour lines for the two-facility problem pictured in Figure 11-26

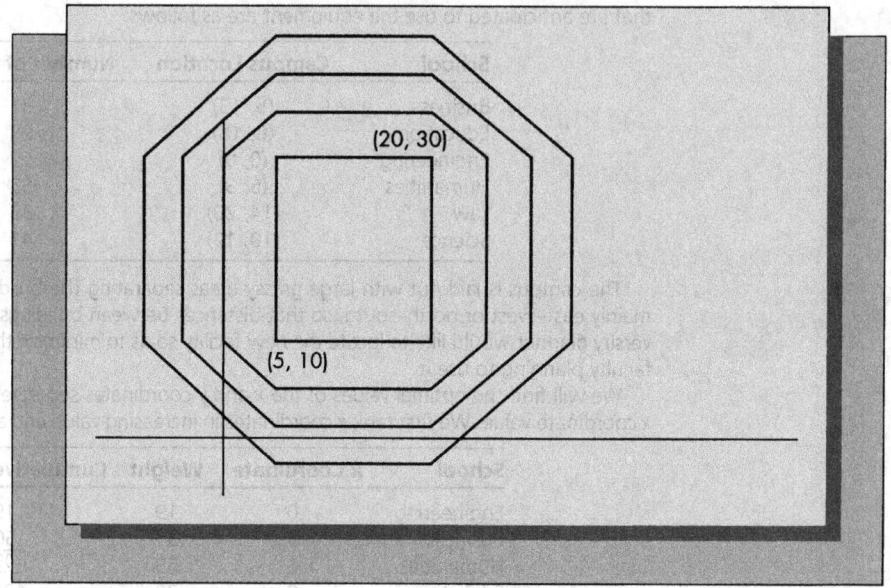

We have pictured the contour lines for the simple example of Figure 11–26, in which there are only two existing facilities and the weights are equal, in Figure 11–28. The reader should convince himself or herself that the total rectilinear distance from any point along a contour line to the two points (5, 10) and (20, 30) is the same. Determining contour lines involves computing the appropriate slope for each of the regions obtained by drawing vertical and horizontal lines through each of the points (a_i, b_i). The procedure for determining contour lines is outlined in Appendix 11–B at the end of this chapter.

In Figure 11–29 we have pictured contour lines for the Example 11.5 problem in which the university must locate an audiovisual center. If the optimal location (6, 12) is infeasible, the university administration could use this map to see the penalties associated with alternative sites.

Minimax Problems

We have assumed thus far that the new facility should be placed so as to minimize the sum of the weighted distances to all existing facilities. There are circumstances in which this objective is inappropriate, however. Consider the following example. The city is considering locations for a paramedic facility. The paramedics should be able to respond to emergency calls anywhere in the city. Certain conditions, such as a severe heart attack, must be treated quickly if the patient is to have any chance of surviving. Hence, the facility should be located so that *all* locations in the city can be reached in a given time.

In such a case the objective would be to determine the location of the new facility to minimize the maximum distance to the existing facilities rather than the total distance. Let $f(x, y)$ be the maximum distance from the new facility to the existing facilities. Then

$$f(x, y) = \max_{1 \leq i \leq n} (|x - a_i| + |y - b_i|).$$

The objective is to find (x^*, y^*) that satisfies

$$f(x^*, y^*) = \min_{x,y} f(x, y).$$

FIGURE 11–29
Contour lines for the university location in Example 11.5

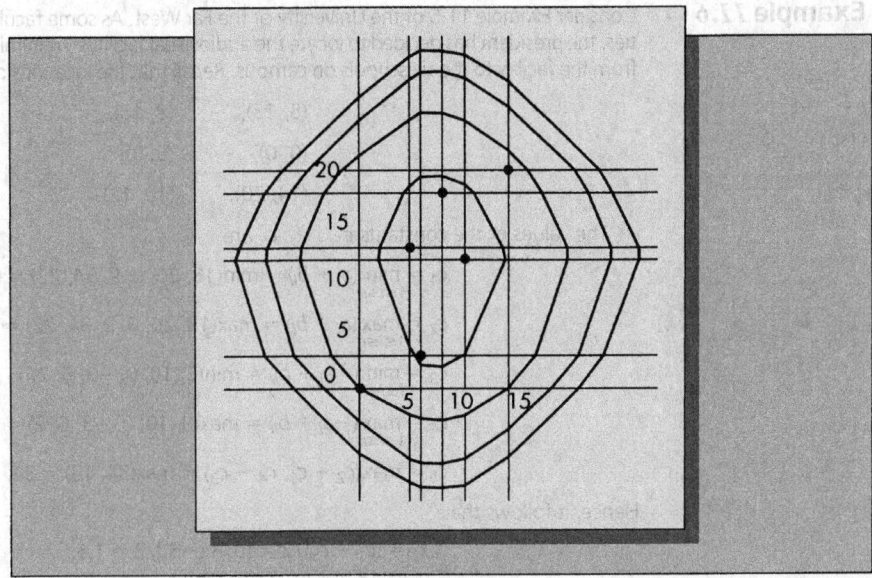

The procedure for finding the optimal minimax location is straightforward. Linear programming can be used to show that the procedure we will outline is optimal. (We will not present the details here. The interested reader should refer to Francis and White, 1974.) Define the numbers c_1, c_2, c_3, c_4, and c_5:

$$c_1 = \min_{1 \leq i \leq n} (a_i + b_i),$$
$$c_2 = \max_{1 \leq i \leq n} (a_i + b_i),$$
$$c_3 = \min_{1 \leq i \leq n} (-a_i + b_i),$$
$$c_4 = \max_{1 \leq i \leq n} (-a_i + b_i),$$
$$c_5 = \max(c_2 - c_1, c_4 - c_3).$$

Let
$$x_1 = (c_1 - c_3)/2,$$
$$y_1 = (c_1 + c_3 + c_5)/2,$$

and
$$x_2 = (c_2 - c_4)/2,$$
$$y_2 = (c_2 + c_4 - c_5)/2.$$

Then all points that lie along the line connecting (x_1, y_1) and (x_2, y_2) are optimal. That is, every optimal solution to the minimax problem, (x^*, y^*), can be expressed in the form

$$x^* = \lambda x_1 + (1 - \lambda)x_2,$$
$$y^* = \lambda y_1 + (1 - \lambda)y_2,$$

where λ is a constant satisfying $0 \leq \lambda \leq 1$. The optimal value of the objective function is $c_5/2$.

11.9 The Single-Facility Rectilinear Distance Location Problem

Example 11.6 Consider Example 11.5 of the University of the Far West. As some faculty members have disabilities, the president has decided to locate the audiovisual facility to minimize the maximum distance from the facility to the six schools on campus. Recall that the locations of the schools are

$$(5, 13), \quad (8, 18),$$
$$(0, 0), \quad (6, 3),$$
$$(14, 20), \quad (10, 12).$$

The values of the constants $c_1, \ldots, c_5$ are

$$c_1 = \min_{1 \leq i \leq n} (a_i + b_i) = \min(18, 26, 0, 9, 34, 22) = 0,$$

$$c_2 = \max_{1 \leq i \leq n} (a_i + b_i) = \max(18, 26, 0, 9, 34, 22) = 34,$$

$$c_3 = \min_{1 \leq i \leq n} (-a_i + b_i) = \min(8, 10, 0, -3, 6, 2) = -3,$$

$$c_4 = \max_{1 \leq i \leq n} (-a_i + b_i) = \max(8, 10, 0, -3, 6, 2) = 10,$$

$$c_5 = \max(c_2 - c_1, c_4 - c_3) = \max(34, 13) = 34.$$

Hence, it follows that

$$x_1 = (c_1 - c_3)/2 = [0 - (-3)]/2 = 1.5,$$
$$y_1 = (c_1 + c_3 + c_5)/2 = (0 - 3 + 34)/2 = 15.5,$$

and

$$x_2 = (c_2 - c_4)/2 = (34 - 10)/2 = 12,$$
$$y_2 = (c_2 + c_4 - c_5)/2 = (34 + 10 - 34)/2 = 5.$$

All points on the line connecting (x_1, y_1) and (x_2, y_2) are optimal. The value of the objective function at the optimal solution(s) is $34/2 = 17$. The optimal locations for the minimax problem are pictured in Figure 11–30. Recall that the optimal solution when we used a weighted objective was (6, 12). It is interesting to note that one optimal solution to this problem, (6, 11), is quite close to that solution.

FIGURE 11–30
Optimal solutions for minimax location objective

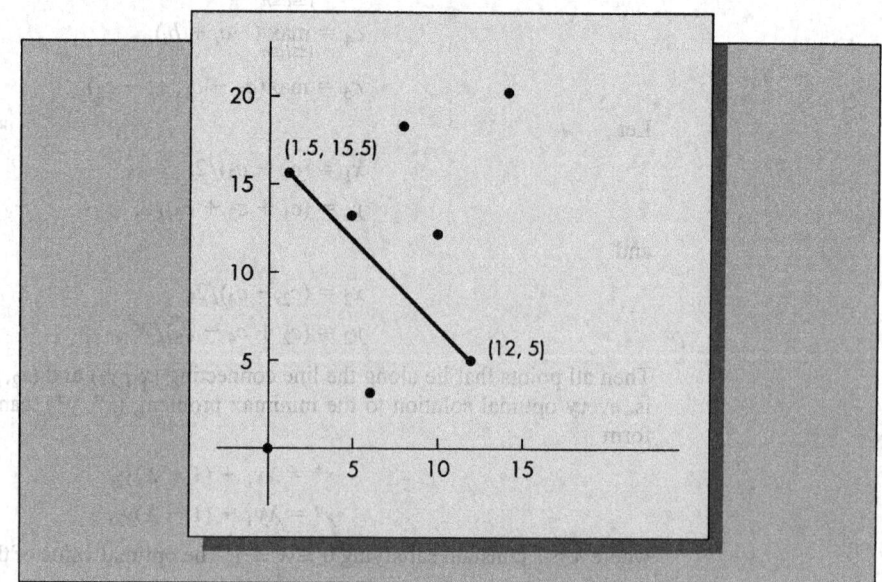

Problems for Section 11.9

28. A machine shop has five machines, located at (3, 3), (3, 7), (8, 4), (12, 3), and (14, 6), respectively. A new machine is to be located in the shop with the following expected numbers of loads per hour transported to the existing machines: $\frac{1}{8}, \frac{1}{8}, \frac{1}{4}, 1$, and $\frac{1}{6}$. Material is transported along parallel aisles, so a rectilinear distance measure is appropriate. Find the coordinates of the optimal location of the new machine to minimize the weighted sum of the rectilinear distances from the new machine to the existing machines.

29. Solve the problem of locating the new audiovisual center at the University of the Far West described in Example 11.5, assuming that the weights are respectively 80, 12, 56, 104, 42, and 17 for the schools of business, education, engineering, humanities, law, and science.

30. Armand Bender plans to visit six customers in Manhattan. Three are located in a building at 34th Street and 7th Avenue. The remaining customers are at 48th and 8th, 38th and 3rd, and 42nd and 5th. Streets are separated by 200 feet and avenues by 400 feet. He plans to park once and walk to all of the customers. Assume that he must return to his car after each visit to pick up different samples. At what location should he park in order to minimize the total distance traveled to the clients? (Hint: In designing your grid, be sure that you account for the fact that avenues are twice as far apart as streets.)

31. In Problem 30, suppose that Mr. Bender can park only in lots located at (1) 40th Street and 8th Avenue, (2) 46th Street and 6th Avenue, and (3) 33rd Street and 5th Avenue. Where should he plan to park?

32. An industrial park consists of 16 buildings. The corporations in the park are sharing the cost of construction and maintenance for a new first-aid center. Because of the park's layout, distances between buildings are most closely approximated by a rectilinear distance measure. Weights for the buildings are determined based on the frequency of accidents. Find the optimal location of the first-aid center to minimize the weighted sum of the rectilinear distances to the 16 buildings.

Building	a_i	b_i	w_i	Building	a_i	b_i	w_i
1	0	0	9	9	14	6	11
2	10	3	7	10	19	0	17
3	8	8	4	11	20	4	14
4	12	20	3	12	14	25	6
5	4	9	2	13	3	14	5
6	18	16	12	14	6	6	8
7	4	1	4	15	9	21	15
8	5	3	5	16	10	10	4

33. Draw contour lines for the problem of locating a machine shop described in Problem 28. (Refer to Appendix 11-B.)

34. Draw contour lines for the location problem described in Problem 30. (Refer to Appendix 11-B.)

35. Two facilities, located at (0, 0) and (0, 10), have respective weights 2 and 1. Draw contour lines for this problem. (Refer to Appendix 11-B.)

36. Solve Problem 28 assuming a minimax rectilinear objective.

37. Solve Problem 30 assuming a minimax rectilinear objective.

38. Solve Problem 32 assuming a minimax rectilinear objective.

11.10 EUCLIDEAN DISTANCE PROBLEMS

Although the rectilinear distance measure is appropriate for many real problems, there are applications in which the appropriate measure of distance is the straight-line measure. An example is locating power-generating facilities in order to minimize the total amount of electrical cable that must be laid to connect the plant to the customers. This section will consider the Euclidean problem and a variant of it known as the gravity problem, which has a far simpler solution.

The Gravity Problem

The gravity problem corresponds to the case of an objective equal to the square of the Euclidean distance. Hence, the objective is to find values of (x, y) to minimize

$$f(x, y) = \sum_{i=1}^{n} w_i[(x - a_i)^2 + (y - b_i)^2].$$

This objective is appropriate when the cost of locating new facilities increases as a function of the square of the distance of the new facility to the existing facilities. Although such an objective is not common, the solution to this problem is straightforward and often has been used as an approximation to the more common straight-line distance problem.

The optimal values of (x, y) are easily determined by differentiation. The partial derivatives of the objective function with respect to x and y are

$$\frac{\partial f(x, y)}{\partial x} = 2 \sum_{i=1}^{n} w_i(x - a_i),$$

$$\frac{\partial f(x, y)}{\partial y} = 2 \sum_{i=1}^{n} w_i(y - b_i).$$

Setting these partial derivatives equal to zero and solving for x and y gives the optimal solution

$$x^* = \frac{\sum_{i=1}^{n} w_i a_i}{\sum_{i=1}^{n} w_i}$$

$$y^* = \frac{\sum_{i=1}^{n} w_i b_i}{\sum_{i=1}^{n} w_i}$$

The term *gravity problem* arises for the following reason. Suppose that one places a map of the area in which the facility is to be located on a heavy piece of cardboard. Weights proportional to the numbers w_i are placed at the locations of the existing facilities. Then the gravity solution is the point on the map at which the entire thing would balance. (This particular description is by Keefer, 1934.) Although one could certainly solve the gravity problem this way, it is so easy to find (x^*, y^*) using the given formulas that there seems little reason to employ the physical model.

Example 11.7 We will find the solution to the problem of locating the audiovisual center for the University of the Far West assuming a squared Euclidean distance location measure. Substituting the values of the weights and the building locations into the given formulas, we obtain

$$x^* = 1{,}555/204 = 7.6,$$
$$y^* = 2{,}198/204 = 10.8,$$

which is somewhat different from the rectilinear solution (6, 12).

The Straight-Line Distance Problem

The straight-line distance measure arises much more frequently than does the squared-distance measure discussed in Section 11.9. The objective in this case is to find (x, y) to minimize

$$f(x, y) = \sum_{i=1}^{n} w_i \sqrt{(x - a_i)^2 + (y - b_i)^2}.$$

Unfortunately, it is not as easy to find the optimal solution mathematically when using a Euclidean distance measure as it is when using squared Euclidean distance. As with the gravity problem, there is also a physical model that one could construct to find the optimal solution. In this case one places a map of the area on a table top. Holes are punched in the table top at the locations of existing facilities, and weights are suspended on strings through the holes. The size of the weights should be proportional to the relative weights of the locations. The strings are attached to a ring. If there is no friction, the ring will come to rest at the location of the optimal solution (see Figure 11–31). Although this method can be used to find a solution, it does have drawbacks. In particular, the friction between the string and the table must be negligible to be sure that the ring comes to rest in the correct position.

Determining the optimal solution mathematically is more difficult for Euclidean distance than for either rectilinear or squared Euclidean distance. There are no known

FIGURE 11–31
Solution of the Euclidean distance problem using a physical model

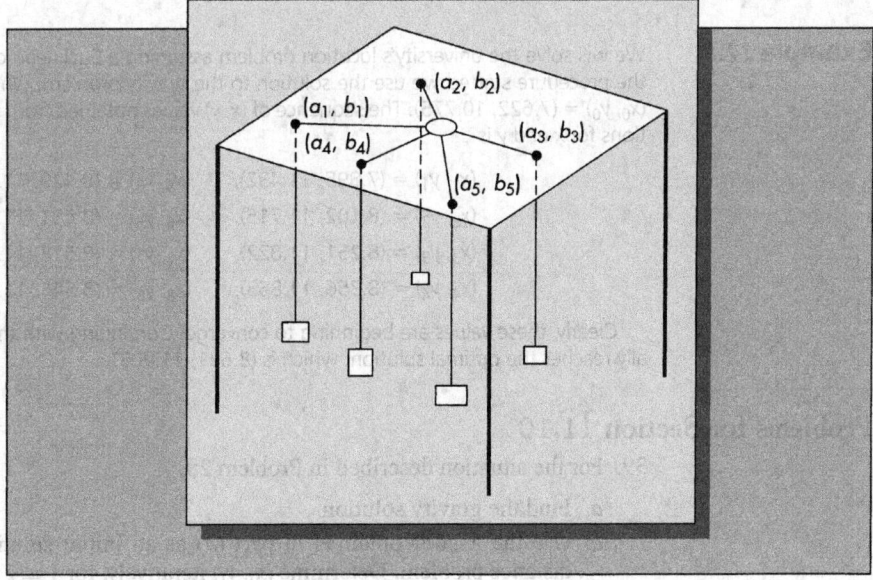

simple algebraic solutions; all existing methods require an iterative procedure. We will describe a procedure that appears in Francis and White (1974) that will yield an optimal solution as long as the location of the new facility does not overlap with the location of an existing facility.

Define

$$g_i(x, y) = \frac{w_i}{\sqrt{(x - a_i)^2 + (y - b_i)^2}}.$$

Let

$$x = \frac{\sum_{i=1}^{n} a_i g_i(x, y)}{\sum_{i=1}^{n} g_i(x, y)},$$

$$y = \frac{\sum_{i=1}^{n} b_i g_i(x, y)}{\sum_{i=1}^{n} g_i(x, y)}.$$

The procedure is as follows: Begin the process with an initial solution (x_0, y_0). The gravity solution is generally recommended to get the method started. Compute the values of $g_i(x, y)$ at this solution and determine new values of x and y from the given formulas. Then, recompute $g_i(x, y)$ using the new values of x and y, giving rise to yet another pair of (x, y) values. Continue to iterate in this fashion until the values of the coordinates converge. This procedure will give an optimal solution as long as the values of (x, y) at each iteration do not correspond to some existing location. The problem is that if we substitute $x = a_i$ and $y = b_i$, $g_i(x, y)$ is undefined, because the denominator is zero. It is unlikely that this will happen, but if it does, a modification of this method is required (see Francis and White, 1974).

Example 11.8 We will solve the university's location problem assuming a Euclidean distance measure. To get the procedure started we use the solution to the gravity problem, which, to three decimals, is $(x_0, y_0) = (7.622, 10.775)$. The sequence of (x, y) values obtained from iterating the given equations for x and y is

$(x_1, y_1) = (7.895, 11.432)$, $(x_5, y_5) = (8.429, 11.880)$,
$(x_2, y_2) = (8.102, 11.715)$, $(x_6, y_6) = (8.481, 11.889)$,
$(x_3, y_3) = (8.251, 11.822)$, $(x_7, y_7) = (8.518, 11.894)$,
$(x_4, y_4) = (8.356, 11.863)$, $(x_8, y_8) = (8.545, 11.899)$.

Clearly, these values are beginning to converge. Continuing with the iterations one eventually reaches the optimal solution, which is $(8.621, 11.907)$.

Problems for Section 11.10

39. For the situation described in Problem 28,
    a. Find the gravity solution.
    b. Use the answer obtained in part (a) as an initial solution for the Euclidean distance problem. Determine (x_i, y_i) iteratively, for $1 \leq i \leq 5$ if you are solving

the problem by hand, or for $1 \leq i \leq 20$ if you are solving with the aid of a computer. Based on your results, estimate the final solution.

40. Three existing facilities are located at (0, 0), (5, 5), and (10, 10). The weights applied to these facilities are 1, 2, and 3, respectively. Find the location of a new facility that minimizes the weighted Euclidean distance to the existing facilities.

41. A telecommunications system is going to be installed at a company site. The switching center that governs the system must be located in one of the five buildings to be served. The goal is to minimize the amount of underground cabling required. In which building should the switching center be located? Assume a straight-line distance measure.

Building	Location
1	(10, 10)
2	(0, 4)
3	(6, 15)
4	(8, 20)
5	(15, 0)

11.11 OTHER LOCATION MODELS

The particular models discussed in Sections 11.9 and 11.10 have been referred to as "planar location models" by Francis, McGinnis, and White (1983). As they noted, there are seven assumptions associated with these models of location problems:

1. A plane is an adequate approximation of a sphere.
2. Any point on the plane is a valid location for a facility.
3. Facilities may be idealized as points.
4. Distances between facilities are adequately represented by planar distance.
5. Travel costs are proportional to distance.
6. Fixed costs are ignored.
7. Issues of distribution can be ignored.

Unless distances separating facilities are extremely large, assumption (1) should be a reasonable approximation of reality. Assumption (2) can be very restrictive. In some circumstances, only a small number of feasible locations exist, in which case the simplest approach is to evaluate the cost of locating the new facility at each of these locations and choose the one with the lowest cost. When the number of feasible alternatives is large, one could construct contour lines and consider only those locations along a given contour line with an acceptably low cost.

Depending upon the nature of the problem, assumption (3) may or may not be problematic. For example, if one uses location models to solve factory layout problems, then the size of the facilities becomes an issue. However, for a problem such as locating warehouses nationwide, idealizing facilities as points is reasonable. Assumption (4) requires that one use a particular measure of distance to compare various configurations. However, one distance measure may not be sufficient to explain all facility interactions. For example, rectilinear distances are typically used in problems in which facilities are to be located in cities. However, closed roads, rivers, or unusual street patterns could make this assumption inaccurate.

The final three assumptions deal with issues that typically arise in distribution problems. Transportation costs depend on the terrain: It is more expensive to transport goods over mountains than on flat interstate highways, for example. Fixed costs of transporting goods can be substantial depending on the mode of transportation. The fixed cost of transporting goods by air, for example, is very high.

More complex location models exist that deal with several of these shortcomings. We briefly review these in the following.

Locating Multiple Facilities

Section 11.10 treated the problem of locating a single facility among n existing facilities. However, applications exist in which the goal is to locate multiple facilities among n existing facilities. For example, a nationwide consumer products producer might be considering where to locate five new regional warehouses.

In some circumstances, multifacility location problems can be solved as a sequence of single location problems. That is, the optimal locations of the new facilities can be determined one at a time. However, when there is any interaction among the new facilities, this approach will not work.

This section will show how linear programming can be used to solve the multiple-facility rectilinear distance location problem. Assume that existing facilities have locations at points $(a_1, b_1), \ldots, (a_n, b_n)$ as in Section 11.10. Suppose that m new facilities are to be located at $(x_1, y_1), \ldots, (x_m, y_m)$. Then the objective function to be minimized may be written in the form

$$\text{Minimize } f_1(\mathbf{x}) + f_2(\mathbf{y})$$

where

$$f_1(\mathbf{x}) = \sum_{1 \le j < k \le m} v_{jk} |x_j - x_k| + \sum_{j=1}^{m} \sum_{i=1}^{n} w_{ij} |x_j - a_i|$$

and

$$f_2(\mathbf{y}) = \sum_{1 \le j < k \le m} v_{jk} |y_j - y_k| + \sum_{j=1}^{m} \sum_{i=1}^{n} w_{ij} |y_j - b_i|.$$

The v_{jk} measure the interaction of new facilities j and k. It is the presence of these terms that prevents us from solving the multifacility problem as a sequence of one-facility problems. However, as with the single-facility problem, the optimal x and y locations may be determined independently. We present the linear programming formulation for finding the optimal x coordinates. The optimal y coordinates may be found in the same way.

The trick in transforming the problem of finding $\mathbf{x}$ to minimize $f_1(\mathbf{x})$ is to eliminate the absolute value function from the objective, as this is not a strictly linear function. The means for doing so is a standard trick in linear programming. (A similar technique was applied in the linear programming formulation of the aggregate planning problem in Section 3.5.)

For any constants a and b write $|a - b| = c + d$, but require that $cd = 0$ (either c or d or both must be zero). If $a > b$, then $|a - b| = c$, and if $a < b$, then $|a - b| = d$. Hence, we may think of c as the positive part of $a - b$ and d as the negative part of $a - b$. Substituting $|x_j - x_k| = c_{jk} + d_{jk}$ and $|x_j - a_i| = e_{ij} + f_{ij}$, we obtain the linear programming formulation of the problem of determining $\mathbf{x}$:

$$\text{Minimize } \sum_{1 \le j < k \le m} v_{jk}(c_{jk} + d_{jk}) + \sum_{j=1}^{m} \sum_{i=1}^{n} w_{ij}(e_{ij} + f_{ij})$$

subject to

$$x_j - x_k - c_{jk} + d_{jk} = 0, \quad 1 \leq j < k \leq n;$$
$$x_j - a_i - e_{ij} + f_{ij} = 0, \quad 1 \leq i \leq n, \quad 1 \leq j \leq n;$$
$$c_{jk} \geq 0, \quad d_{jk} \geq 0, \quad 1 \leq j < k \leq n;$$
$$e_{ij} \geq 0, \quad f_{ij} \geq 0, \quad 1 \leq i \leq n, \quad 1 \leq j \leq n;$$

x_j unrestricted in sign.

We do not need to explicitly include the constraints $c_{jk}d_{jk} = 0$ and $e_{ij}f_{ij} = 0$. One can show that at the minimum cost solution these relationships always hold (which is certainly fortunate as these are not linear relationships). One additional substitution is necessary prior to solving the problem. Since linear programming codes require that all variables be nonnegative, we must substitute $x_j = x_j^+ - x_j^-$, where $x_j^+ \geq 0$ and $x_j^- \geq 0$. Commercial linear programming codes are based on the Simplex Method, which is extremely efficient. One can solve realistically sized problems easily even on a personal computer.

Multifacility gravity problems require the solution of a system of linear equations, so that gravity problems involving large numbers of facilities are easily solved as well. Multifacility Euclidean problems are solved by utilizing a multidimensional version of the iterative solution method described in Section 11.10. We will not review these methods here. The interested reader should refer to Francis and White (1974).

Further Extensions

Facilities Having Positive Areas

All previous models assumed that facilities are approximated by points in the plane. When the area of the facilities is small compared to the area covered by the available locations, this assumption is reasonable. However, in certain applications the areas of the facilities cannot be ignored. For example, when finding locations for machines in a job shop, the machines must be far enough apart for them to be able to operate efficiently. Tompkins and White (1984) present an approach that requires the assumptions that the facilities are rectangular in shape and that the weights are uniformly distributed over the areas. The method is based on developing an analogy between the location problem and the problem of locating forces on a beam and is similar to the procedure for constructing contour lines discussed in Appendix 11–B.

Location–Allocation Problems

Often the decision of where to locate new facilities must be accompanied by the decision of which of the existing locations will be served by each new facility. For example, a firm may be considering where to locate several regional warehouses. In addition to determining the location and the number of these new warehouses, the firm also must decide which of the retail outlets will be serviced by which warehouses.

Location–allocation problems are difficult to solve owing to the large number of decision variables. The mathematical programming formulation of the problem, assuming that a rectangular distance measure is used, is

$$\text{Minimize} \sum_{j=1}^{m} \sum_{i=1}^{n} z_{ij} w_{ij} [|x_j - a_i| + |y_j - b_i|] + g(m)$$

subject to

$$\sum_{j=1}^{m} z_{ij} = 1 \quad \text{for } 1 \leq i \leq n,$$

where

w_{ij} = Cost per unit time per unit distance if the existing facility i is serviced by new facility j;

$$z_{ij} = \begin{cases} 1 & \text{if existing facility } i \text{ is serviced by new facility } j, \\ 0 & \text{otherwise;} \end{cases}$$

m = Total number of new facilities, $1 \le m \le n$;

(x_j, y_j) = Coordinates of new facility j, $1 \le j \le m$;

(a_i, b_i) = Coordinates of existing facility i, $1 \le i \le n$;

$g(m)$ = Cost per unit time of providing m new facilities.

This problem formulation has decision variables m, the number of new facilities; z_{ij}, the specification of which of the existing locations i will be serviced by facility j; and (x_j, y_j), the location of the new facilities. The optimization is difficult due to the presence of the zero-one variables z_{ij} and the inclusion of m as a decision variable. The problem is typically solved by considering successive values of $m = 1, 2, \ldots$, and enumerating all combinations of z_{ij} for each value of m. Given a fixed m and set of z_{ij} values, the solution can be obtained using the methods for locating multiple facilities discussed earlier in this section. However, the number of different z_{ij} values grows quickly as a function of m, so only moderately sized problems can be solved in this fashion.

Discrete Location Problems

The models considered in this chapter for location of new facilities assumed that the new facilities could be located anywhere in the plane. This is not the case for most applications. Contour lines assist with evaluating alternative locations but cannot be constructed for problems in which one must locate multiple facilities. An alternative approach is to restrict a priori the possible locations to some discrete set of possibilities. When there is only a single facility and the number of possible locations is small, the easiest approach is to evaluate the cost of each location and pick the smallest.

When there are multiple facilities, the assignment model discussed in Section 11.4 can be used to determine the optimal locations of the new facilities. In certain types of warehouse-layout problems, new facilities can take up more than one potential site. For example, suppose that we must determine in which locations in a warehouse to store k items. Suppose that the appropriate storage area in the warehouse is composed of n grid squares and each item stored takes up more than a single square. Each square would be numbered and the storage location of an item specified by the numbers of the grid squares covered by the item. The resulting model, discussed in Francis and White (1974), is a generalization of the simple assignment model appearing in Section 11.4. We will not present the details of the model here.

Network Location Models

Planar location models assume that the goal is to locate one or more new facilities in order to minimize some function of the distance separating the new and the existing facilities. A rectilinear, Euclidean, or other distance measure is generally assumed. In certain applications, the distances should be measured over an existing network and are not accurately approximated by standard measures. Overland transport must follow road networks, water transport must follow shipping lanes and sea routes, and air transport is confined to predetermined air corridors. In other applications the network may correspond to a network of power cables or telephone wires. In many of these applications the new facility or facilities must be placed on or very near to a location on the network, and distances can be measured only in terms of the network. Network location models are beyond the scope of our coverage. The interested reader should refer to the review articles of Francis, McGinnis, and White (1983) and Tansel, Francis, and Lowe (1983).

International Issues

The problem of locating facilities is a part of the larger issue of global supply chain management. It is truer and truer that businesses are evolving into global corporations. This is no longer just the case for the industry giants. Globalization now plays a greater role than ever before, and its importance will continue to grow. Arntzen et al. (1995) discuss the supply chain configuration for Digital Equipment Corporation. In one case, they show how various parts of computers are shipped from the United States to Europe, from Europe to Brazil, and from Brazil to Europe and back to the United States. Fabrication may be done in two or three different countries, and distribution networks may be equally complex.

Lower wage rates were traditionally the primary reason for firms based in developed countries to locate plants in less developed countries. This is certainly true today. General Motors does much of its auto assembly in Mexico. Virtually all the large semiconductor manufacturers have fabrication facilities overseas, typically in places like Malaysia and the Philippines.

Cohen and Lee (1989) provide a good overview of some of the issues that one must take into account when locating facilities in other countries. They include

1. Duties and tariffs are based on material flows. Their impact must be incorporated into international shipping schedules of materials, intermediate product, and finished product.
2. Currency exchange rates fluctuate unpredictably and affect profit levels in each country.
3. Corporate tax rates vary considerably from country to country.
4. Global sourcing must take into account lead times, costs, new technologies, and dependence on particular countries.
5. Local content rules and quotas constrain material flow between countries.
6. Product designs may vary by national market.
7. Transfer price mechanisms must be put in place to take the place of centralized control.
8. Differences in language, cultural norms, education, and skills must be incorporated into location decisions.

Only recently have we begun to understand the complexity of the problem of locating new facilities and their effect on global supply chain operations. Well-constructed and well-thought-out mathematical models will continue to assist us in managing these increasingly complex networks. However, many of the issues alluded to in this section are difficult to quantify, thus making good judgment crucial.

Problems for Section 11.11

42. For each of the location problems described, discuss which of the seven assumptions listed in this section are likely to be violated:

    a. Locating three new machines in a machine shop.
    b. Locating an international network of telecommunications facilities.
    c. Locating a hospital in a sparsely populated area.
    d. Locating spare parts depots to support a field repair organization.

43. Consider Problem 28 of this chapter. Suppose that two new machines, A and B, are to be located in the shop. Machine A has $\frac{1}{8}, \frac{1}{8}, \frac{1}{4}, 1$, and $\frac{1}{6}$ as the expected numbers of loads transported to the existing five machines, respectively, and machine B has $\frac{1}{4}, \frac{1}{6}, 3, \frac{1}{5}$, and $\frac{1}{2}$ as the expected numbers of loads transported, respectively. Furthermore, suppose that there are two loads per hour on average transported between the new machines. Assume a rectilinear distance measure.

   a. Formulate the problem of determining the optimal locations of the new machines as a linear program.

   b. If you have access to a computerized linear programming code, solve the problem formulated in part (a).

44. Consider the University of the Far West described in Example 11.5. Suppose that the university administration has decided that two audiovisual centers are needed. Each center would have different facilities. The anticipated numbers of faculty members using each center are

School	Faculty Members Using Center A	Faculty Members Using Center B
Business	13	18
Education	40	23
Engineering	24	17
Humanities	20	23
Law	30	9
Science	16	21

   Furthermore, there will be a total of 16 staff persons at centers A and B. They will need to interact frequently.

   a. Formulate the problem of determining the optimal locations of the two audiovisual centers as a linear program. Assume that rectilinear distances are used throughout.

   b. If you have access to a computerized linear programming code, solve the problem formulated in part (a).

45. Describe the following location problems and how they differ from those previously treated in this chapter:

   a. Location–allocation problems
   b. Discrete location problems
   c. Network location problems

11.12 HISTORICAL NOTES

The problems discussed in this chapter have a long history. Determining suitable layouts for production facilities is a problem that dates back to the start of the industrial revolution, although it appears that the development of analytical techniques for finding layouts is recent. Little seems to have been published concerning analytical layout methods prior to 1950. Apple (1977) lists a number of texts dealing with the plant layout problem published in the early 1950s. The computerized layout techniques discussed in this chapter were developed in the 1960s and 1970s. CRAFT, one of the first computerized methods and most popular even today, is from Buffa, Armour, and Vollmann (1964). ALDEP is from Seehof and Evans (1967), CORELAP from Lee and Moore (1967), COFAD from Tompkins and Reed (1976), and PLANET from Deisenroth and Apple (1972). Both ALDEP and CRAFT are available from the IBM Corporation as part of its SHARE library.

Some of the location problems discussed in this chapter go back hundreds of years. The problem of finding the location of a single new facility to minimize the sum of the Euclidean distances to the existing facilities has been referred to as the Steiner–Weber problem or the general Fermat problem. Francis and White (1974) state that the problem with exactly three facilities was posed by Fermat and solved by the mathematician Torricelli prior to 1640. The work on the rectilinear distance problem is relatively recent and was sparked by a paper by Hakimi (1964). Research continues today on discovering efficient solution techniques for locating multiple facilities using various distance measures.

11.13 Summary

This chapter dealt with two important logistics problems: the most efficient layout of facilities and the best location of new facilities relative to the existing ones. In a sense, the layout problem is a special type of location problem, because the goal is to find the best location of facilities within a specified boundary.

The analytical methods for layout discussed in this chapter assume that the objective is to minimize some function of the distance separating facilities. This viewpoint is probably most appropriate for plant layout problems and less so for other problems in which qualitative factors play a greater role. Two charts are important for layout analysis: the *activity relationship chart* (or rel chart for short) and the *from-to chart*. In order to construct a rel chart, each pair of facilities is given a letter code *A* (absolutely necessary), *E* (especially important), *I* (important), *O* (ordinary importance), *U* (unimportant), or *X* (undesirable), representing the desirability of locating facilities near each other. A from-to chart may specify the distance between pairs of facilities, numbers of materials handling trips per unit time between facilities, or the cost of materials handling trips between facilities. Both rel charts and from-to charts are useful for evaluating the quality of a layout.

Section 11.3 discussed types of layouts. The two most common types are *product layouts* and *process layouts*. The product layout is usually a fixed transfer line arranged in the sequence of the manufacturing steps required. A process layout groups machines with similar functions. Part routings vary from product to product. The product layout is appropriate for high-volume production of a small number of products. The process layout is appropriate for a low-volume job-shop environment. *Fixed position layouts* are used for products that are too large to move. Recently, there has been considerable interest in layouts based on *group technology*. Parts are grouped into families, and machine cells are developed consistent with this grouping. Group technology layouts are appropriate for automated factories.

The *assignment model* can be used for solving relatively simple layout and location problems. In order to use the assignment algorithm, we assume that for each placement of a machine (say) in a location, we can evaluate the cost of that assignment. This assumes that there is no interaction between the machines. When interaction does occur, a *quadratic assignment* formulation exists, but quadratic assignment models are far more difficult to solve than simple assignment models.

We discussed five *computerized layout* techniques: CRAFT, COFAD, ALDEP, PLANET, and CORELAP. Both CRAFT and COFAD are improvement routines. That means that both require that the user specify an initial layout. The program proceeds to consider interchanging adjacent pairs of facilities in order to achieve an improvement. On the other hand, ALDEP, PLANET, and CORELAP are construction routines, which build the layout from scratch. Because construction routines often result in departments with odd shapes, improvement routines are generally preferred. We also noted that there are a host of new software products now available for the personal computer and for UNIX workstations. Many of these products are based on drafting programs with large libraries of graphical icons. These products use methods conceptually similar to the earlier programs previously mentioned, but are far more user friendly.

The chapter included a discussion of *flexible manufacturing systems* (FMSs). An FMS is a collection of machines linked by an automated materials handling system and is generally controlled by a central computer. FMSs are used primarily in the metal-working industries and are an appropriate choice when there is medium to large volume and a moderate variety of part types required. The downside to these systems is cost, which can run as high as $10 million or more. Flexible manufacturing cells are a scaled-down lower-cost alternative.

The second part of the chapter was concerned with methods for locating new facilities. *Location models* are appropriate when locating one or more new facilities within a specified area already containing a finite number of existing facilities. The objective is to locate new facilities to minimize some function of the distance separating new and existing facilities. Three distance measures were considered: rectilinear, Euclidean, and squared Euclidean. The first two are the most common for describing real problems and depend on whether movement occurs according to a crisscross street pattern (rectilinear) or is measured by straight-line distances (Euclidean).

The optimal solution to the weighted rectilinear distance problem is to locate the (x, y) coordinates at the *median* of the existing coordinates. When using a squared Euclidean distance measure, the optimal location of the new facility is at the center of gravity of the existing coordinates. No simple algebraic solution for the Euclidean distance problem is known, but iterative solution techniques exist. The chapter also included a brief discussion of several more complex location problems, including location of multiple facilities, location of facilities having nonzero areas, location–allocation problems, discrete location problems, and network location models. Finally, the chapter concluded with a discussion of issues of concern when locating new facilities in other countries. As globalization of manufacturing and supply chain networks increases, these issues will play an even greater role in location planning.

Additional Problems on Layout and Location

46. A real estate firm wishes to open four new offices in the Boston area. There are six potential sites available. Based on the number of employees in each office and the location of the properties that each employee will manage, the firm estimated the total travel time in hours per day for each office and each location. Find the optimal assignment of offices to sites to minimize employee travel time.

		Offices			
		A	B	C	D
Sites	1	10	3	3	8
	2	13	5	2	6
	3	12	9	9	4
	4	14	2	7	7
	5	17	7	4	3
	6	12	8	5	5

47. A large supermarket chain in the Southeast requires five additional warehouses in the Atlanta area. It has identified five sites for these warehouses. The annual transportation costs (in $000) for each warehouse at each site are given in the following table. Find the assignment of warehouses to sites to minimize the total annual transportation costs.

		Warehouses				
		A	B	C	D	E
Sites	1	41	47	38	46	50
	2	39	37	42	36	45
	3	43	46	45	42	46
	4	51	54	47	58	56
	5	44	40	42	41	45

48. A machine shop located on the outskirts of Los Angeles accepts custom orders from a number of high-tech firms in southern California. The machine shop consists of four departments: A (lathes), B (drills), C (grinders), and D (sanders). The from-to chart showing distances in feet between department centers is given here.

		To department			
		A	B	C	D
From department	A		45	63	32
	B	29		27	46
	C	63	75		68
	D	40	30	68	

The shop has accepted orders for production of four products: P1, P2, P3, and P4. The routing for production of these products and the weekly production rates are

Product	Routing	Weekly Production
P1	A–B–C–D	200
P2	A–C–D	600
P3	B–D	400
P4	B–C–D	500

Assume that products are produced in batches of size 25.

a. Convert this information into a from-to chart giving numbers of materials handling trips per week between departments.
b. If the cost to transport one batch 1 foot is estimated to be $1.50, convert the from-to chart you found in part (a) to one giving the materials handling cost per week between departments.
c. Develop an activity relationship chart for these four departments based on the results of part (b). Assume that A is assigned to the highest cost and O to the least, with the rankings E and I assigned to the costs falling in between the extremes.
d. Suppose that the machine shop is located in a building that is 60 feet by 80 feet. Furthermore, suppose that departments are rectangularly shaped with the

FIGURE 11–32
Shape of facility
(for Problem 49)

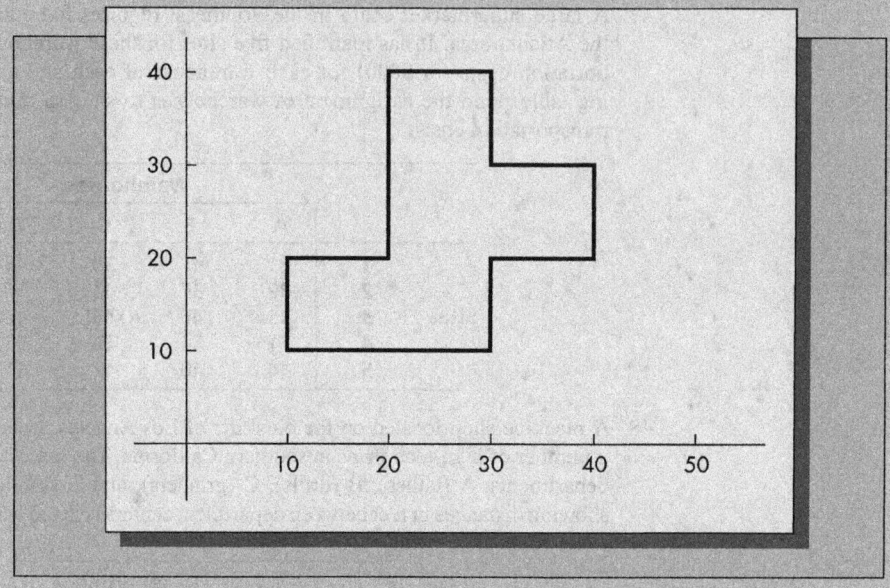

following dimensions:

Department	Dimensions
A	20 × 30
B	40 × 20
C	45 × 55
D	37 × 25

Sketch a layout consistent with the rel chart you obtained in part (c).

49. A facility has the shape shown in Figure 11–32. Using the methods described in Appendix 11–A, find the location of the centroid of this facility.

50. An initial layout for four departments and from-to charts giving distances separating departments and unit transportation costs appear in Figure 11–33. Using the CRAFT pairwise exchange technique, find the layout recommended by CRAFT to minimize total materials handling costs.

51. An initial layout for five departments and a from-to flow data chart are given in Figure 11–34. Assuming that departments A and D are in fixed locations and cannot be moved, find the layout recommended by CRAFT for departments B, C, and E. Assume that the objective is to minimize the total distance traveled.

52. Consider the rel chart for the Meat Me fast-food restaurant, given in Figure 11–2. Assume that the areas required for each department are

Department	Area Required (square feet)
Cooking burgers	200
Cooking fries	200
Packing and storing	100
Drink dispensers	100
Counter servers	400
Drive-up server	100

FIGURE 11–33
Layout and from-to charts (for Problem 50)

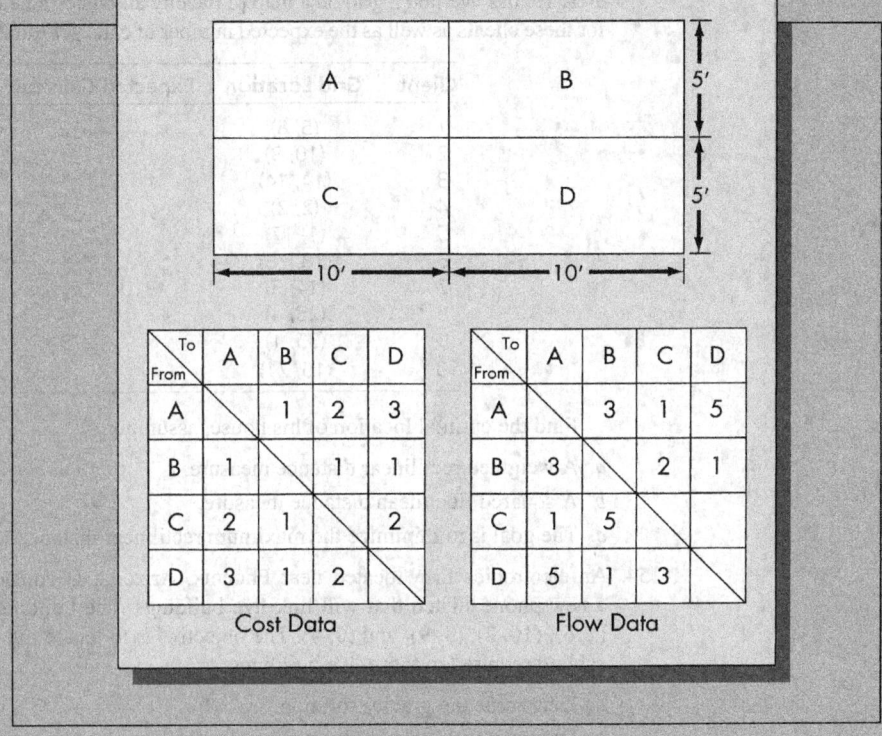

FIGURE 11–34
Layout and from-to chart (for Problem 51)

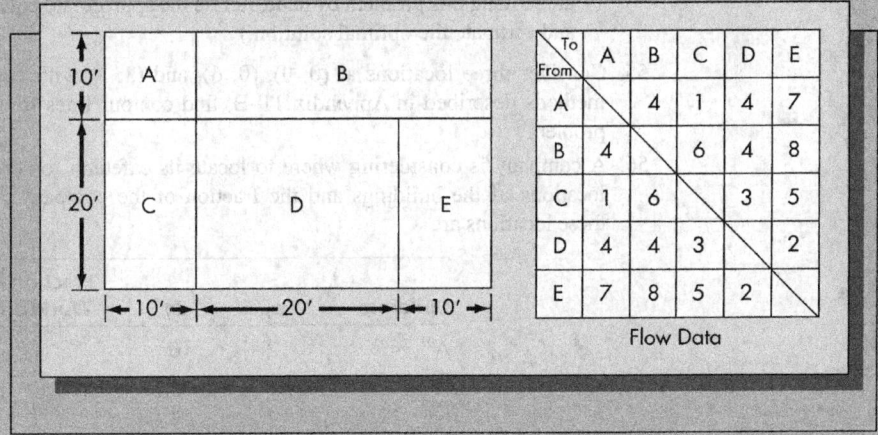

Assume a sweep width of 2 squares and facility dimensions of 5 by 9 squares, where each square is 5 feet on a side. As a result, for example, the cooking-burgers department requires 8 squares. Use the ALDEP approach to develop a layout for the restaurant. Comment on the practicality of your results.

53. Frank Green, an independent TV repairman, is considering purchasing a home in Ames, Iowa, that he will use as a base of operations for his repair business. Frank's primary sources of business are 10 industrial accounts located throughout the Ames

area. He has overlaid a grid on a map of the city and determined the following locations for these clients as well as the expected number of calls per month he receives:

Client	Grid Location	Expected Calls per Month
1	(5, 8)	2
2	(10, 3)	1
3	(14, 14)	1
4	(2, 2)	3
5	(1, 17)	1
6	(18, 25)	$\frac{1}{2}$
7	(14, 3)	$\frac{1}{4}$
8	(25, 4)	4
9	(35, 1)	3
10	(16, 21)	$\frac{1}{6}$

Find the optimal location of his house, assuming

a. A weighted rectilinear distance measure.

b. A squared Euclidean distance measure.

c. The goal is to minimize the maximum rectilinear distance to any client.

54. An electronics firm located near Phoenix, Arizona, is considering where to locate a new phone switch that will link five buildings. The buildings are located at (0, 0), (2, 6), (10, 2), (3, 9), and (0, 4). The objective is to locate the switch to minimize the cabling required to those five buildings.

a. Determine the gravity solution.

b. Determine the optimal location assuming a straight-line distance measure. (If you are solving this problem by hand, iterate the appropriate equations at least five times and estimate the optimal solution.)

55. Consider three locations at (0, 0), (0, 6), and (3, 3) with equal weights. Using the methods described in Appendix 11-B, find contour lines for the rectilinear location problem.

56. A company is considering where to locate its cafeteria to service six buildings. The locations of the buildings and the fraction of the company's employees working at these locations are

Building	a_i	b_i	Fraction of Workforce
A	2	6	$\frac{1}{12}$
B	1	0	$\frac{1}{12}$
C	3	3	$\frac{1}{6}$
D	5	9	$\frac{1}{4}$
E	4	2	$\frac{1}{4}$
F	10	7	$\frac{1}{6}$

a. Find the optimal location of the cafeteria to minimize the weighted rectilinear distance to all the buildings.

b. Find the optimal location of the cafeteria to minimize the maximum rectilinear distance to all the buildings.

658 Chapter Eleven *Facilities Layout and Location*

       c. Find the gravity solution.

       d. Suppose that the cafeteria must be located in one of the buildings. In which building should it be located if the goal is to minimize weighted rectilinear distance?

       e. Solve part (*d*) assuming weighted Euclidean distance.

Spreadsheet Problems for Chapter 11

57. Design a spreadsheet to compute the total rectilinear distance from a set of up to 10 existing locations to any other location. Assume that existing locations are placed in Columns A and B and the new location in cells D1 and E1. Initialize column A with the value of cell D1 and column B with the value of cell E1, so that the total distance will be computed correctly when there are fewer than 10 locations.

       a. Suppose that existing facilities are located at (0, 0), (5, 15), (110, 120), (35, 25), (80, 10), (75, 20), (8, 38), (50, 65), (22, 95), and (44, 70), and the new facility is to be located at (50, 50). Determine the total rectilinear distance of the new facility to the existing facilities.

       b. Suppose the new facility in part (*a*) can be located only at $x = 0, 5, 10, \ldots, 100$ and $y = 0, 10, 20, \ldots, 100$. By systematically varying the x and y coordinates, find the optimal location of the new facility.

58. Solve Problem 57, assuming a Euclidean distance measure.

59. Solve Problem 32 using an electronic spreadsheet. To do so, enter the building numbers in column A, the x coordinates in column B, and the associated weights in column C. Sort columns A, B, and C in ascending order by using column B as the primary sort key. Now accumulate the weights (column C) in column D using the sum function. Divide the total accumulated weight by 2 and visually identify the optimal x coordinate value. It will be where the cumulative weight first exceeds half the total cumulative weight. Repeat the process for the y coordinates.

60. Design an electronic spreadsheet to compute the optimal solution to the gravity problem. Allow for up to 20 locations. Let column A be the location number, column B the x coordinates ($a_1, \ldots, a_n$) of existing locations, and column C the y coordinates ($b_1, \ldots, b_n$) of existing locations. Store the optimal solution in cell D1. Find the gravity solution to Problem 32 using your spreadsheet.

61. Extend the results of Problem 60 to find the optimal location of a new facility among a set of existing facilities assuming a straight-line Euclidean distance measure. Let column E correspond to $g_i(x, y)$, where the initial (x, y) values appear in F1 and F2. In locations G1 and G2, store

$$x = \frac{\sum_{i=1}^{n} a_i g_i(x, y)}{\sum_{i=1}^{n} g_i(x, y)}.$$

$$y = \frac{\sum_{i=1}^{n} b_i g_i(x, y)}{\sum_{i=1}^{n} g_i(x, y)}.$$

Start with the gravity solution in cells F1 and F2. After calculation, replace the values in cells F1 and F2 with the values in cells G1 and G2. Continue in this manner until the solution converges. Using your spreadsheet,

a. Solve Problem 32.
b. Solve Problem 41.
c. Solve Problem 53 assuming a Euclidean distance measure.
d. Solve Problem 56 assuming a Euclidean distance measure.

Appendix 11-A

Finding Centroids

The centroid of any object is another term for the physical coordinates of the center of gravity. For a plate of uniform density, it would be the point at which the plate would balance exactly. Let R be any region in the plane. The centroid for R is defined by two points $\bar{x}, \bar{y}$. In order to find these two points, we first must obtain the moments of R, M_x, and M_y, which are given by the formulas

$$M_x = \int\int_R x \, dx \, dy,$$

$$M_y = \int\int_R y \, dx \, dy.$$

Let $A(R)$ be the area of R. Then the centroid of R is given by

$$\bar{x} = \frac{M_x}{A(R)}, \quad \bar{y} = \frac{M_y}{A(R)}.$$

We now obtain explicit expressions for the moments when R is a finite sum of rectangles. Suppose that R is a simple rectangle as pictured in Figure 11–35. Then

$$M_x = \int_{y_1}^{y_2} dy \int_{x_1}^{x_2} x \, dx = \int_{y_1}^{y_2} dy \left.\frac{x^2}{2}\right|_{x_1}^{x_2}$$

$$= \int_{y_1}^{y_2} \frac{dy(x_2^2 - x_1^2)}{2} = \frac{x_2^2 - x_1^2}{2}(y_2 - y_1),$$

$$M_y = \int_{x_1}^{x_2} dx \int_{y_1}^{y_2} y \, dy = \int_{x_1}^{x_2} dx \left.\frac{y^2}{2}\right|_{y_1}^{y_2}$$

$$= \int_{x_1}^{x_2} \frac{dx(y_2^2 - y_1^2)}{2} = \frac{y_2^2 - y_1^2}{2}(x_2 - x_1).$$

Note that because the area of the rectangle is $(x_2 - x_1)(y_2 - y_1)$, and $x_2^2 - x_1^2 = (x_2 - x_1)(x_1 + x_2)$ (and similarly for $y_1^2 - y_2^2$), we obtain

$$\bar{x} = \frac{x_1 + x_2}{2}, \quad \bar{y} = \frac{y_1 + y_2}{2}.$$

The formulas for the moments of a rectangle may be used to find the centroid when R consists of a collection of rectangles as well. Suppose that R can be subdivided into

FIGURE 11–35
The centroid of a rectangle

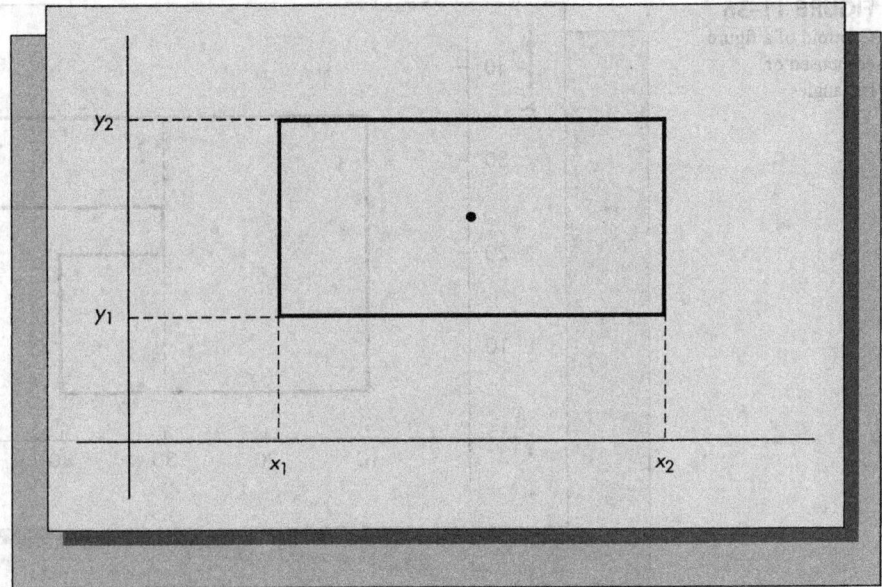

k rectangles labeled $R_1, R_2, \ldots, R_k$ with respective boundaries defined by $[(x_{1i}, x_{2i}), (y_{1i}, y_{2i})]$ for $1 \leq i \leq k$. Since

$$M_x = \int_R \int x\, dx\, dy = \sum_{i=1}^{k} \int_{R_i} \int x\, dx\, dy,$$

it follows that

$$M_x = \sum_{i=1}^{k} \frac{x_{2i}^2 - x_{1i}^2}{2}(y_{2i} - y_{1i}).$$

Similarly,

$$M_y = \sum_{i=1}^{k} \frac{y_{2i}^2 - y_{1i}^2}{2}(x_{2i} - x_{1i}).$$

Example 11A.1 Consider the region R pictured in Figure 11–36. We will determine the centroid of the region using the given formulas. The region can be broken down into three rectangles in a number of different ways. For the one pictured in Figure 11–36, we have

$$x_{11} = 10, \quad x_{21} = 30,$$
$$y_{11} = 5, \quad y_{21} = 35,$$
$$x_{12} = 30, \quad x_{22} = 40,$$
$$y_{12} = 5, \quad y_{22} = 20,$$
$$x_{13} = 30, \quad x_{23} = 50,$$
$$y_{13} = 25, \quad y_{23} = 35.$$

FIGURE 11-36
Centroid of a figure composed of rectangles

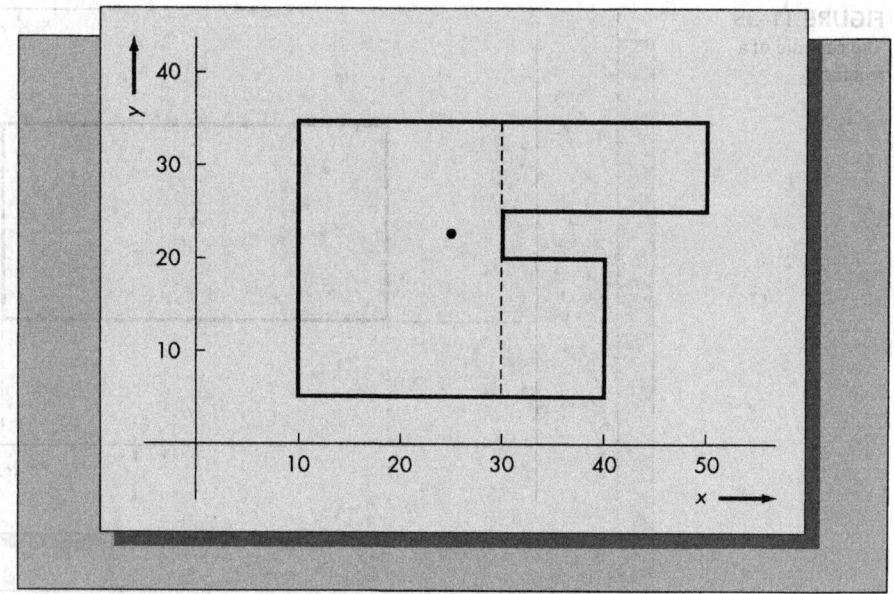

Substituting into the given formulas, we obtain

$$M_x = \frac{30^2 - 10^2}{2}(35 - 5) + \frac{40^2 - 30^2}{2}(20 - 5) + \frac{50^2 - 30^2}{2}(35 - 25)$$
$$= (400)(30) + (350)(15) + (800)(10) = 25{,}250,$$

$$M_y = \frac{35^2 - 5^2}{2}(30 - 10) + \frac{20^2 - 5^2}{2}(40 - 30) + \frac{35^2 - 25^2}{2}(50 - 30)$$
$$= (600)(20) + (187.5)(10) + (300)(20) = 19{,}875.$$

The total area of R is

$$A(R) = (20)(30) + (10)(15) + (20)(10) = 950.$$

It follows that the centroid is

$$\bar{x} = \frac{25{,}250}{950} = 26.579,$$

$$\bar{y} = \frac{19{,}875}{950} = 20.921.$$

The centroid is marked with a dot on Figure 11-36.

Appendix 11-B

Computing Contour Lines

This appendix outlines the procedure for computing contour lines, or isocost lines, such as those pictured in Figures 11-28 and 11-29. The theoretical justification for this procedure appears in Francis and White (1974).

1. Plot the points $(a_1, b_1), (a_2, b_2), \ldots, (a_n, b_n)$ on graph paper. Draw a horizontal line (parallel to the x axis) and a vertical line (parallel to the y axis) through each point.

2. Number the horizontal and vertical lines in sequence from left to right and from top to bottom. (If none of the original points is collinear, there will be exactly n horizontal and n vertical lines.)

3. Let C_i be the sum of the weights associated with the points along vertical line j, and D_i the sum of the weights associated with the points along horizontal line i.

4. Compute the following numbers:

$$M_0 = -\sum_{i=1}^{n} w_i, \quad N_0 = M_0 = -\sum_{i=1}^{n} w_i,$$

$$M_1 = M_0 + 2C_1, \quad N_1 = N_0 + 2D_1,$$

$$M_2 = M_1 + 2C_2, \quad N_2 = N_1 + 2D_2,$$

and so on.

(The final values of M_i and N_j will both be $+\sum_{i=1}^{n} w_i$.)

5. Define the region (i, j) as the region bounded by the ith and $(i + 1)$th vertical lines and the jth and $(j + 1)$th horizontal lines. The regions to the left of the first vertical line are labeled $(0, j)$, and those below the first horizontal line are labeled $(i, 0)$. The slope of any contour line passing through region (i, j) is given by

$$S_{i,j} = -M_i/N_j.$$

Once the slopes are determined, a contour line is constructed by starting at any point and moving through each region at the angle determined by the slope computed in step 5. We will present a simple example to illustrate the method.

Example 11B.1 Assume $(a_1, b_1) = (1, 1)$, $(a_2, b_2) = (5, 3)$, and $(a_3, b_3) = (3, 8)$, and $w_1 = 2$, $w_2 = 3$, and $w_3 = 6$. The first step is to plot these points on a grid as we have done in Figure 11–37. Drawing vertical and horizontal lines through each of the three points yields three vertical lines labeled 1, 2,

FIGURE 11–37
Regions for Example 11B.1

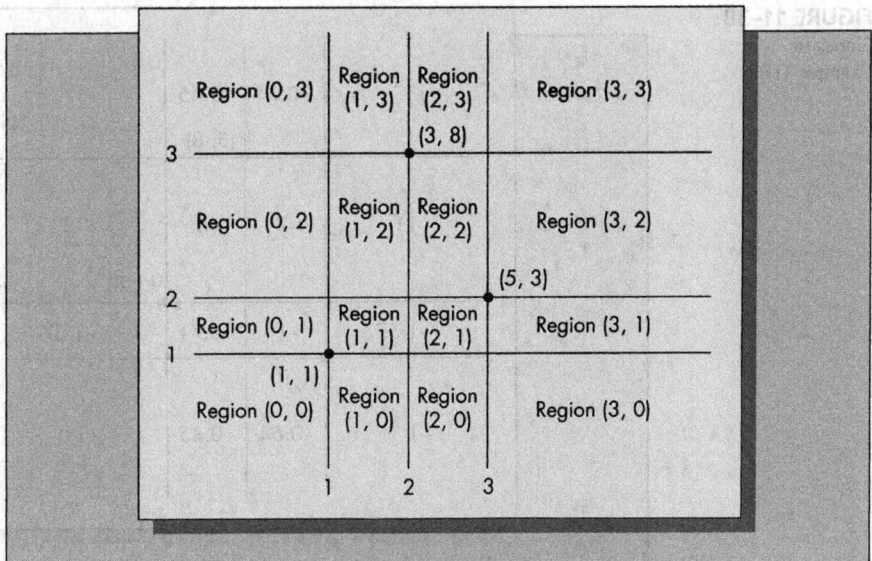

and 3 and three horizontal lines labeled 1, 2, 3 as well. Regions are labeled from (0, 0) to (3, 3) as in the figure.

Next we compute $M_0, \ldots, M_3$ and $N_0, \ldots, N_3$.

$$M_0 = -(2 + 3 + 6) = -11 = N_0,$$
$$M_1 = -11 + (2)(2) = -7, \quad N_1 = -11 + 2(2) = -7,$$
$$M_2 = -7 + (2)(6) = +5, \quad N_2 = -7 + (2)(3) = -1,$$
$$M_3 = +5 + (2)(3) = +11, \quad N_3 = -1 + (2)(6) = +11.$$

Next the ratios are computed to find the slope for each region.

$$S_{0,0} = -(-11)/(-11) = -1, \quad S_{0,2} = -(-11)/(-1) = -11,$$
$$S_{1,0} = -(-7)/(-11) = -0.64, \quad S_{1,2} = -(-7)/(-1) = -7,$$
$$S_{2,0} = -(5)/(-11) = +0.45, \quad S_{2,2} = -(5)/(-1) = 5,$$
$$S_{3,0} = -(11)/(-11) = +1, \quad S_{3,2} = -(11)/(-1) = 11,$$
$$S_{0,1} = -(-11)/(-7) = -1.57, \quad S_{0,3} = -(-11)/(11) = 1,$$
$$S_{1,1} = -(-7)/(-7) = -1, \quad S_{1,3} = -(-7)/(11) = 0.64,$$
$$S_{2,1} = -(5)/(-7) = +0.71, \quad S_{2,3} = -(5)/(11) = -0.45,$$
$$S_{3,1} = -(11)/(-7) = +1.57, \quad S_{3,3} = -(11)/(11) = -1.$$

Before constructing the contour lines, it is convenient to place the slopes in the appropriate regions, as shown in Figure 11–38. A contour line may be started at any point on a region boundary. From the initial point, one draws a line with the appropriate slope for that region to the boundary of the next region. At that point the slope changes to the value associated with the next region. One continues until the line segments return to the originating point. (If the slopes are correct and the drawing accurate, one will always return to the point of origination.) Two typical contour lines for the example problem are shown in Figure 11–39.

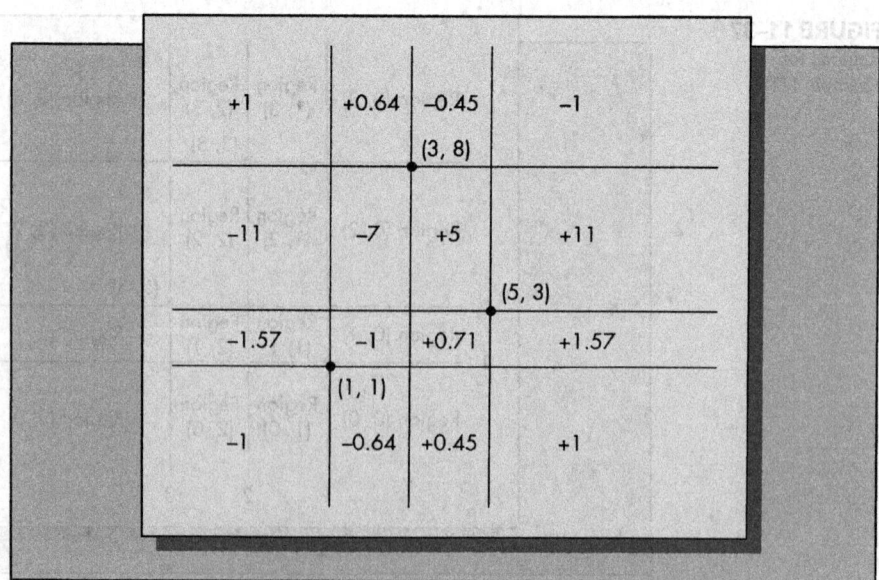

FIGURE 11–38
Slopes for Example 11B.1

514

FIGURE 11-39
Sample contour lines for Example 11B.1

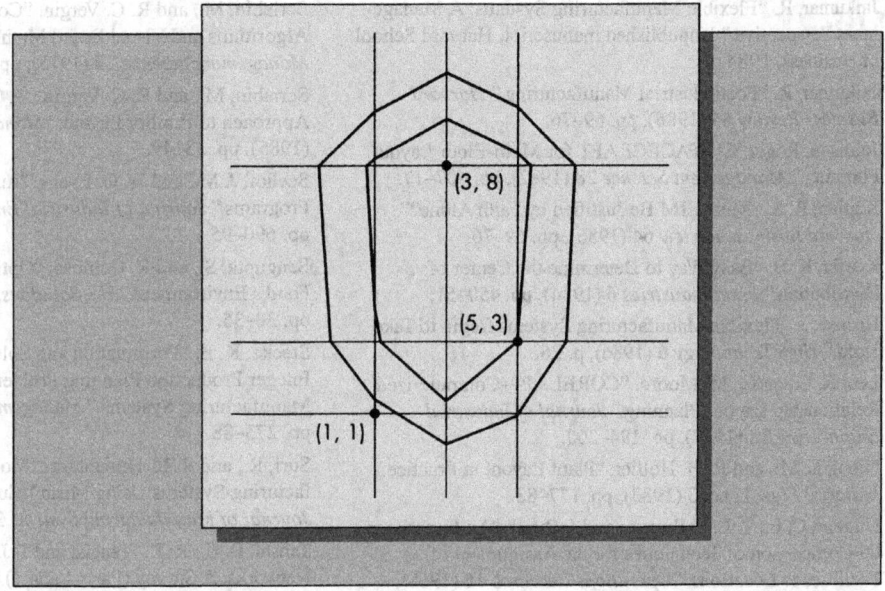

Bibliography

Apple, J. M. *Plant Layout and Material Handling*. 3rd ed. New York: John Wiley & Sons, 1977.

Arntzen, B. C.; G. G. Brown; T. P. Harrison; and L. L. Trafton. "Global Supply Chain Management at Digital Equipment Corporation." *Interfaces* 25, no. 1 (1995), pp. 69–93.

Block, T. E. "A Note on 'Comparison of Computer Algorithms and Visual Based Methods for Plant Layout' by M. Scriabin and R. C. Vergin." *Management Science* 24 (1977), pp. 235–37.

Bruno, G., and P. Biglia. "Performance Evaluation and Validation of Tool Handling in Flexible Manufacturing Systems Using Petri Nets." In *Proceedings of the International Workshop on Timed Petri Nets*, pp. 64–71. Torino, Italy, 1985.

Buffa, E. S. "On a Paper by Scriabin and Vergin." *Management Science* 23 (1976), p. 104.

Buffa, E. S.; G. C. Armour; and T. E. Vollmann. "Allocating Facilities with CRAFT." *Harvard Business Review* 42 (1964), pp. 136–58.

Burbidge, J. L. *The Introduction of Group Technology*. London: Heinemann, 1975.

Buzacott, J. A., and D. D. Yao. "On Queuing Network Models of Flexible Manufacturing Systems." *Queuing Systems* 1 (1986), pp. 5–27.

Cohen, M., and H. L. Lee. "Resource Deployment Analysis of Global Manufacturing and Distribution Networks." *Journal of Manufacturing and Operations Management* 2 (1989), pp. 81–104.

Coleman, D. R. "Plant Layout: Computers versus Humans." *Management Science* 24 (1977), pp. 107–12.

Conway, R. W.; W. L. Maxwell; J. O. McClain; and S. L. Worona. *Users Guide to XCELL+Factory Modeling System*. Redwood City, CA: Scientific Press, 1987.

Cook, N. H. "Computer Managed Parts Manufacture." *Scientific American* 232 (1975), pp. 23–29.

Deisenroth, M. P., and J. M. Apple. "A Computerized Plant Layout Analysis and Evaluation Technique (PLANET)." In *Technical Papers 1962*. Norcross, GA: American Institute of Industrial Engineers, 1972.

Drezner, Z. "DISCON: A New Method for the Layout Problem." *Operations Research* 28 (1980), pp. 1375–84.

Foulds, L. R. "Techniques for Facilities Layout." *Management Science* 29 (1983), pp. 1414–26.

Francis, R. L.; L. F. McGinnis; and J. A. White. "Locational Analysis." *European Journal of Operational Research* 12 (1983), pp. 220–52.

Francis, R. L., and J. A. White. *Facility Layout and Location: An Analytical Approach*. Englewood Cliffs, NJ: Prentice Hall, 1974.

Groover, M. P., and E. W. Zimmers. *CAD/CAM: Computer Aided Design and Manufacturing*. Englewood Cliffs, NJ: Prentice Hall, 1984.

Hakimi, S. L. "Optimum Location of Switching Centers and the Absolute Centers and Medians of a Graph." *Operations Research* 12 (1964), pp. 450–59.

Jaikumar, R. "Flexible Manufacturing Systems: A Management Perspective." Unpublished manuscript, Harvard School of Business, 1984.

Jaikumar, R. "Postindustrial Manufacturing." *Harvard Business Review* 64 (1986), pp. 69–76.

Johnson, Roger V. "SPACECRAFT for Multi-Floor Layout Planning." *Management Science* 28 (1982), pp. 407–17.

Kaplan, R. S. "Must CIM Be Justified by Faith Alone?" *Harvard Business Review* 64 (1986), pp. 69–76.

Keefer, K. B. "Easy Way to Determine the Center of Distribution." *Food Industries* 6 (1934), pp. 450–51.

Krouse, J. "Flexible Manufacturing Systems Begin to Take Hold." *High Technology* 6 (1986), p. 26.

Lee, R. C., and J. M. Moore. "CORELAP—Computerized Relationship Layout Planning." *Journal of Industrial Engineering* 18 (1967), pp. 194–200.

Nicol, L. M., and R. H. Hollier. "Plant Layout in Practice." *Material Flow* 1, no. 3 (1983), pp. 177–88.

Nugent, C. E.; T. E. Vollmann; and J. Ruml. "An Experimental Comparison of Techniques for the Assignment of Facilities to Locations." *Operations Research* 16 (1968), pp. 150–73.

Pritsker, A. A. B. *Introduction to Simulation and SLAM II.* 3rd ed. New York: John Wiley & Sons, 1986.

Rosenblatt, M. J. "The Dynamics of Plant Layout." *Management Science* 32, no. 1 (1986), pp. 76–86.

Sassani, F. "A Simulation Study on Performance Improvement of Group Technology Cells." *International Journal of Production Research* 28 (1990), pp. 293–300.

Schweitzer, P. J. "Maximum Throughput in Finite Capacity Open Queuing Networks with Product-Form Solutions." *Management Science* 24 (1977), pp. 217–23.

Scriabin, M., and R. C. Vergin. "Comparison of Computer Algorithms and Visual Based Methods for Plant Layout." *Management Science* 22 (1975), pp. 172–81.

Scriabin, M., and R. C. Vergin. "A Cluster Analytic Approach to Facility Layout." *Management Science* 31 (1985), pp. 33–49.

Seehof, J. M., and W. O. Evans. "Automated Layout Design Programs." *Journal of Industrial Engineering* 18 (1967), pp. 690–95.

Sengupta, S., and R. Combes. "Optimizing and General Food's Environment." *IIE Solutions,* August 1995, pp. 30–35.

Stecke, K. E. "Formulation and Solution of Nonlinear Integer Production Planning Problems for Flexible Manufacturing Systems." *Management Science* 29 (1983), pp. 273–88.

Suri, R., and R. R. Hildebrant. "Modeling Flexible Manufacturing Systems Using Mean Value Analysis." *SME Journal of Manufacturing Systems* 3 (1984), pp. 27–38.

Tansel, B. C.; R. L. Francis; and T. J. Lowe. "Location on Networks: A Survey (Parts 1 and 2)." *Management Science* 29 (1983), pp. 482–511.

Tompkins, J. A., and R. Reed Jr. "An Applied Model for the Facilities Design Problem." *International Journal of Production Research* 14 (1976), pp. 583–95.

Tompkins, J. A., and J. A. White. *Facilities Planning.* New York: John Wiley & Sons, 1984.

Vollman, T. E., and E. S. Buffa. "The Facilities Layout Problem in Perspective." *Management Science* 12 (1966), pp. 450–68.

Zygmont, J. "Flexible Manufacturing Systems: Curing the Cure-all." *High Technology* 6 (1986), pp. 22–27.

Appendix

Tables

TABLE A-1 Areas under the Normal Curve

Z	.00	.01	.02	.03	.04	.05	.06	.07	.08	.09
.00	.0000	.0040	.0080	.0120	.0160	.0199	.0239	.0279	.0319	.0359
.10	.0398	.0438	.0478	.0517	.0557	.0596	.0636	.0675	.0714	.0753
.20	.0793	.0832	.0871	.0910	.0948	.0987	.1026	.1064	.1103	.1141
.30	.1179	.1217	.1255	.1293	.1331	.1368	.1406	.1443	.1480	.1517
.40	.1554	.1591	.1628	.1664	.1700	.1736	.1772	.1808	.1844	.1879
.50	.1915	.1950	.1985	.2019	.2054	.2088	.2123	.2157	.2190	.2224
.60	.2257	.2291	.2324	.2357	.2389	.2422	.2454	.2486	.2517	.2549
.70	.2580	.2611	.2642	.2673	.2703	.2734	.2764	.2793	.2823	.2852
.80	.2881	.2910	.2939	.2967	.2995	.3023	.3051	.3078	.3106	.3133
.90	.3159	.3186	.3212	.3238	.3264	.3289	.3315	.3340	.3365	.3389
1.00	.3413	.3438	.3461	.3485	.3508	.3531	.3554	.3577	.3599	.3621
1.10	.3643	.3665	.3686	.3708	.3729	.3749	.3770	.3790	.3810	.3830
1.20	.3849	.3869	.3888	.3907	.3925	.3944	.3962	.3980	.3997	.4015
1.30	.4032	.4049	.4066	.4082	.4099	.4115	.4131	.4147	.4162	.4177
1.40	.4192	.4207	.4222	.4236	.4251	.4265	.4279	.4292	.4306	.4319
1.50	.4332	.4345	.4357	.4370	.4382	.4394	.4406	.4418	.4429	.4441
1.60	.4452	.4463	.4474	.4484	.4495	.4505	.4515	.4525	.4535	.4545
1.70	.4554	.4564	.4573	.4582	.4591	.4599	.4608	.4616	.4625	.4633
1.80	.4641	.4649	.4656	.4664	.4671	.4678	.4686	.4693	.4699	.4706
1.90	.4713	.4719	.4726	.4732	.4738	.4744	.4750	.4756	.4761	.4767
2.00	.4772	.4778	.4783	.4788	.4793	.4798	.4803	.4808	.4812	.4817
2.10	.4821	.4826	.4830	.4834	.4838	.4842	.4846	.4850	.4854	.4857
2.20	.4861	.4864	.4868	.4871	.4875	.4878	.4881	.4884	.4887	.4890
2.30	.4893	.4896	.4898	.4901	.4904	.4906	.4909	.4911	.4913	.4916
2.40	.4918	.4920	.4922	.4925	.4927	.4929	.4931	.4932	.4934	.4936
2.50	.4938	.4940	.4941	.4943	.4945	.4946	.4948	.4949	.4951	.4952
2.60	.4953	.4955	.4956	.4957	.4959	.4960	.4961	.4962	.4963	.4964
2.70	.4965	.4966	.4967	.4968	.4969	.4970	.4971	.4972	.4973	.4974
2.80	.4974	.4975	.4976	.4977	.4977	.4978	.4979	.4979	.4980	.4981
2.90	.4981	.4982	.4982	.4983	.4984	.4984	.4985	.4985	.4986	.4986
3.00	.4987	.4987	.4987	.4988	.4988	.4989	.4989	.4989	.4990	.4990
3.10	.4990	.4991	.4991	.4991	.4992	.4992	.4992	.4992	.4993	.4993
3.20	.4993	.4993	.4994	.4994	.4994	.4994	.4994	.4995	.4995	.4995
3.30	.4995	.4995	.4995	.4996	.4996	.4996	.4996	.4996	.4996	.4997
3.40	.4997	.4997	.4997	.4997	.4997	.4997	.4997	.4997	.4997	.4998
3.50	.4998	.4998	.4998	.4998	.4998	.4998	.4998	.4998	.4998	.4998
3.60	.4998	.4998	.4999	.4999	.4999	.4999	.4999	.4999	.4999	.4999
3.70	.4999	.4999	.4999	.4999	.4999	.4999	.4999	.4999	.4999	.4999
3.80	.4999	.4999	.4999	.4999	.4999	.4999	.4999	.4999	.4999	.4999

The values in the body of the table are the areas between the mean and the value of Z. Example: If we want to find the area under the standard normal curve between $Z = 0$ and $Z = 1.96$, we find the $Z = 1.90$ row and .06 column (for $Z = 1.90 + .06 = 1.96$) and read .4750 at the intersection. For convenience, this information also appears in Table A-4.

Source: P. Billingsley, D. J. Croft, D. V. Huntsberger, and C. J. Watson, *Statistical Inference for Management and Economics* (Boston: Allyn & Bacon, 1986). Reprinted with permission.

TABLE A–2 Cumulative Binomial Probabilities

$$P(X \leq r) = \sum_{k=0}^{r} \binom{n}{k} p^k (1-p)^{n-k}$$

where X is the number of successes in n trials

$n = 5$

r	.01	.05	.10	.20	.30	.40	p .50	.60	.70	.80	.90	.95	.99	r
0	0.9510	0.7738	0.5905	0.3277	0.1681	0.0778	0.0313	0.0102	0.0024	0.0003	0.0000	0.0000	0.0000	0
1	0.9990	0.9774	0.9185	0.7373	0.5282	0.3370	0.1875	0.0870	0.0308	0.0067	0.0005	0.0000	0.0000	1
2	1.0000	0.9988	0.9914	0.9421	0.8369	0.6826	0.5000	0.3174	0.1631	0.0579	0.0086	0.0012	0.0000	2
3	1.0000	1.0000	0.9995	0.9933	0.9692	0.9130	0.8125	0.6630	0.4718	0.2627	0.0815	0.0226	0.0010	3
4	1.0000	1.0000	1.0000	0.9997	0.9976	0.9898	0.9688	0.9222	0.8319	0.6723	0.4095	0.2262	0.0490	4

$n = 10$

r	.01	.05	.10	.20	.30	.40	p .50	.60	.70	.80	.90	.95	.99	r
0	0.9044	0.5987	0.3487	0.1074	0.0282	0.0060	0.0010	0.0001	0.0000	0.0000	0.0000	0.0000	0.0000	0
1	0.9957	0.9139	0.7361	0.3758	0.1493	0.0464	0.0107	0.0017	0.0001	0.0000	0.0000	0.0000	0.0000	1
2	0.9999	0.9885	0.9298	0.6778	0.3828	0.1673	0.0547	0.0123	0.0016	0.0001	0.0000	0.0000	0.0000	2
3	1.0000	0.9990	0.9872	0.8791	0.6496	0.3823	0.1719	0.0548	0.0106	0.0009	0.0000	0.0000	0.0000	3
4	1.0000	0.9999	0.9984	0.9672	0.8497	0.6331	0.3770	0.1662	0.0473	0.0064	0.0001	0.0000	0.0000	4
5	1.0000	1.0000	0.9999	0.9936	0.9527	0.8338	0.6230	0.3669	0.1503	0.0328	0.0016	0.0001	0.0000	5
6	1.0000	1.0000	1.0000	0.9991	0.9894	0.9452	0.8281	0.6177	0.3504	0.1209	0.0128	0.0010	0.0000	6
7	1.0000	1.0000	1.0000	0.9999	0.9984	0.9877	0.9453	0.8327	0.6172	0.3222	0.0702	0.0115	0.0001	7
8	1.0000	1.0000	1.0000	1.0000	0.9999	0.9983	0.9893	0.9536	0.8507	0.6242	0.2639	0.0861	0.0043	8
9	1.0000	1.0000	1.0000	1.0000	1.0000	0.9999	0.9990	0.9940	0.9718	0.8926	0.6513	0.4013	0.0956	9

$n = 15$

r	.01	.05	.10	.20	.30	.40	p .50	.60	.70	.80	.90	.95	.99	r
0	0.8601	0.4633	0.2059	0.0352	0.0047	0.0005	0.0000	0.0000	0.0000	0.0000	0.0000	0.0000	0.0000	0
1	0.9904	0.8290	0.5490	0.1671	0.0353	0.0052	0.0005	0.0000	0.0000	0.0000	0.0000	0.0000	0.0000	1
2	0.9996	0.9638	0.8159	0.3980	0.1268	0.0271	0.0037	0.0003	0.0000	0.0000	0.0000	0.0000	0.0000	2
3	1.0000	0.9945	0.9444	0.6482	0.2969	0.0905	0.0176	0.0019	0.0001	0.0000	0.0000	0.0000	0.0000	3
4	1.0000	0.9994	0.9873	0.8358	0.5155	0.2173	0.0592	0.0093	0.0007	0.0000	0.0000	0.0000	0.0000	4
5	1.0000	0.9999	0.9978	0.9389	0.7216	0.4032	0.1509	0.0338	0.0037	0.0001	0.0000	0.0000	0.0000	5
6	1.0000	1.0000	0.9997	0.9819	0.8689	0.6098	0.3036	0.0950	0.0152	0.0008	0.0000	0.0000	0.0000	6
7	1.0000	1.0000	1.0000	0.9958	0.9500	0.7869	0.5000	0.2131	0.0500	0.0042	0.0000	0.0000	0.0000	7
8	1.0000	1.0000	1.0000	0.9992	0.9848	0.9050	0.6964	0.3902	0.1311	0.0181	0.0003	0.0000	0.0000	8
9	1.0000	1.0000	1.0000	0.9999	0.9963	0.9662	0.8491	0.5968	0.2784	0.0611	0.0022	0.0001	0.0000	9
10	1.0000	1.0000	1.0000	1.0000	0.9993	0.9907	0.9408	0.7827	0.4845	0.1642	0.0127	0.0006	0.0000	10
11	1.0000	1.0000	1.0000	1.0000	0.9999	0.9981	0.9824	0.9095	0.7031	0.3518	0.0556	0.0055	0.0000	11
12	1.0000	1.0000	1.0000	1.0000	1.0000	0.9997	0.9963	0.9729	0.8732	0.6020	0.1841	0.0362	0.0004	12
13	1.0000	1.0000	1.0000	1.0000	1.0000	1.0000	0.9995	0.9948	0.9647	0.8329	0.4510	0.1710	0.0096	13
14	1.0000	1.0000	1.0000	1.0000	1.0000	1.0000	1.0000	0.9995	0.9953	0.9648	0.7941	0.5367	0.1399	14

TABLE A–2 (continued)

n = 20

r	.01	.05	.10	.20	.30	.40	p .50	.60	.70	.80	.90	.95	.99	r
0	0.8179	0.3585	0.1216	0.0115	0.0008	0.0000	0.0000	0.0000	0.0000	0.0000	0.0000	0.0000	0.0000	0
1	0.9831	0.7358	0.3917	0.0692	0.0076	0.0005	0.0000	0.0000	0.0000	0.0000	0.0000	0.0000	0.0000	1
2	0.9990	0.9245	0.6769	0.2061	0.0355	0.0036	0.0002	0.0000	0.0000	0.0000	0.0000	0.0000	0.0000	2
3	1.0000	0.9841	0.8670	0.4114	0.1071	0.0160	0.0013	0.0000	0.0000	0.0000	0.0000	0.0000	0.0000	3
4	1.0000	0.9974	0.9568	0.6296	0.2375	0.0510	0.0059	0.0003	0.0000	0.0000	0.0000	0.0000	0.0000	4
5	1.0000	0.9997	0.9887	0.8042	0.4164	0.1256	0.0207	0.0016	0.0000	0.0000	0.0000	0.0000	0.0000	5
6	1.0000	1.0000	0.9976	0.9133	0.6080	0.2500	0.0577	0.0065	0.0003	0.0000	0.0000	0.0000	0.0000	6
7	1.0000	1.0000	0.9996	0.9679	0.7723	0.4159	0.1316	0.0210	0.0013	0.0000	0.0000	0.0000	0.0000	7
8	1.0000	1.0000	0.9999	0.9900	0.8867	0.5956	0.2517	0.0565	0.0051	0.0001	0.0000	0.0000	0.0000	8
9	1.0000	1.0000	1.0000	0.9974	0.9520	0.7553	0.4119	0.1275	0.0171	0.0006	0.0000	0.0000	0.0000	9
10	1.0000	1.0000	1.0000	0.9994	0.9829	0.8725	0.5881	0.2447	0.0480	0.0026	0.0000	0.0000	0.0000	10
11	1.0000	1.0000	1.0000	0.9999	0.9949	0.9435	0.7483	0.4044	0.1133	0.0100	0.0001	0.0000	0.0000	11
12	1.0000	1.0000	1.0000	1.0000	0.9987	0.9790	0.8684	0.5841	0.2277	0.0321	0.0004	0.0000	0.0000	12
13	1.0000	1.0000	1.0000	1.0000	0.9997	0.9935	0.9423	0.7500	0.3920	0.0867	0.0024	0.0000	0.0000	13
14	1.0000	1.0000	1.0000	1.0000	1.0000	0.9984	0.9793	0.8744	0.5836	0.1958	0.0113	0.0003	0.0000	14
15	1.0000	1.0000	1.0000	1.0000	1.0000	0.9997	0.9941	0.9490	0.7625	0.3704	0.0432	0.0026	0.0000	15
16	1.0000	1.0000	1.0000	1.0000	1.0000	1.0000	0.9987	0.9840	0.8929	0.5886	0.1330	0.0159	0.0000	16
17	1.0000	1.0000	1.0000	1.0000	1.0000	1.0000	0.9998	0.9964	0.9645	0.7939	0.3231	0.0755	0.0010	17
18	1.0000	1.0000	1.0000	1.0000	1.0000	1.0000	1.0000	0.9995	0.9924	0.9308	0.6083	0.2642	0.0169	18
19	1.0000	1.0000	1.0000	1.0000	1.0000	1.0000	1.0000	1.0000	0.9992	0.9885	0.8784	0.6415	0.1821	19

n = 25

r	.01	.05	.10	.20	.30	.40	p .50	.60	.70	.80	.90	.95	.99	r
0	0.7778	0.2774	0.0718	0.0038	0.0001	0.0000	0.0000	0.0000	0.0000	0.0000	0.0000	0.0000	0.0000	0
1	0.9742	0.6424	0.2712	0.0274	0.0016	0.0001	0.0000	0.0000	0.0000	0.0000	0.0000	0.0000	0.0000	1
2	0.9980	0.8729	0.5371	0.0982	0.0090	0.0004	0.0000	0.0000	0.0000	0.0000	0.0000	0.0000	0.0000	2
3	0.9999	0.9659	0.7636	0.2340	0.0332	0.0024	0.0001	0.0000	0.0000	0.0000	0.0000	0.0000	0.0000	3
4	1.0000	0.9928	0.9020	0.4207	0.0905	0.0095	0.0005	0.0000	0.0000	0.0000	0.0000	0.0000	0.0000	4
5	1.0000	0.9988	0.9666	0.6167	0.1935	0.0294	0.0020	0.0001	0.0000	0.0000	0.0000	0.0000	0.0000	5
6	1.0000	0.9998	0.9905	0.7800	0.3407	0.0736	0.0073	0.0003	0.0000	0.0000	0.0000	0.0000	0.0000	6
7	1.0000	1.0000	0.9977	0.8909	0.5118	0.1536	0.0216	0.0012	0.0000	0.0000	0.0000	0.0000	0.0000	7
8	1.0000	1.0000	0.9995	0.9532	0.6769	0.2735	0.0539	0.0043	0.0001	0.0000	0.0000	0.0000	0.0000	8
9	1.0000	1.0000	0.9999	0.9827	0.8106	0.4246	0.1148	0.0132	0.0005	0.0000	0.0000	0.0000	0.0000	9
10	1.0000	1.0000	1.0000	0.9944	0.9022	0.5858	0.2122	0.0344	0.0018	0.0000	0.0000	0.0000	0.0000	10
11	1.0000	1.0000	1.0000	0.9985	0.9558	0.7323	0.3450	0.0778	0.0060	0.0001	0.0000	0.0000	0.0000	11
12	1.0000	1.0000	1.0000	0.9996	0.9825	0.8462	0.5000	0.1538	0.0175	0.0004	0.0000	0.0000	0.0000	12
13	1.0000	1.0000	1.0000	0.9999	0.9940	0.9222	0.6550	0.2677	0.0442	0.0015	0.0000	0.0000	0.0000	13
14	1.0000	1.0000	1.0000	1.0000	0.9982	0.9656	0.7878	0.4142	0.0978	0.0056	0.0000	0.0000	0.0000	14
15	1.0000	1.0000	1.0000	1.0000	0.9995	0.9868	0.8852	0.5754	0.1894	0.0173	0.0001	0.0000	0.0000	15
16	1.0000	1.0000	1.0000	1.0000	0.9999	0.9957	0.9461	0.7265	0.3231	0.0468	0.0005	0.0000	0.0000	16
17	1.0000	1.0000	1.0000	1.0000	1.0000	0.9988	0.9784	0.8464	0.4882	0.1091	0.0023	0.0000	0.0000	17
18	1.0000	1.0000	1.0000	1.0000	1.0000	0.9997	0.9927	0.9264	0.6593	0.2200	0.0095	0.0002	0.0000	18
19	1.0000	1.0000	1.0000	1.0000	1.0000	0.9999	0.9980	0.9706	0.8065	0.3833	0.0334	0.0012	0.0000	19
20	1.0000	1.0000	1.0000	1.0000	1.0000	1.0000	0.9995	0.9905	0.9095	0.5793	0.0980	0.0072	0.0000	20
21	1.0000	1.0000	1.0000	1.0000	1.0000	1.0000	0.9999	0.9976	0.9668	0.7660	0.2364	0.0341	0.0001	21
22	1.0000	1.0000	1.0000	1.0000	1.0000	1.0000	1.0000	0.9996	0.9910	0.9018	0.4629	0.1271	0.0020	22
23	1.0000	1.0000	1.0000	1.0000	1.0000	1.0000	1.0000	0.9999	0.9984	0.9726	0.7288	0.3576	0.0258	23
24	1.0000	1.0000	1.0000	1.0000	1.0000	1.0000	1.0000	1.0000	0.9999	0.9962	0.9282	0.7226	0.2222	24

Source: P. Billingsley, D. J. Croft, D. V. Huntsberger, and C. J. Watson, *Statistical Inference for Management and Economics* (Boston: Allyn & Bacon, 1986). Reprinted with permission.

TABLE A–3 Cumulative Poisson Probabilities

$$\sum_{x=x'}^{\infty} \frac{e^{-m}m^x}{x!}$$

x'	0.1	0.2	0.3	0.4	m 0.5	0.6	0.7	0.8	0.9	1.0
0	1.0000	1.0000	1.0000	1.0000	1.0000	1.0000	1.0000	1.0000	1.0000	1.0000
1	.0952	.1813	.2592	.3297	.3935	.4512	.5034	.5507	.5934	.6321
2	.0047	.0175	.0369	.0616	.0902	.1219	.1558	.1912	.2275	.2642
3	.0002	.0011	.0036	.0079	.0144	.0231	.0341	.0474	.0629	.0803
4	.0000	.0001	.0003	.0008	.0018	.0034	.0058	.0091	.0135	.0190
5	.0000	.0000	.0000	.0001	.0002	.0004	.0008	.0014	.0023	.0037
6	.0000	.0000	.0000	.0000	.0000	.0000	.0001	.0002	.0003	.0006
7	.0000	.0000	.0000	.0000	.0000	.0000	.0000	.0000	.0000	.0001

x'	1.1	1.2	1.3	1.4	m 1.5	1.6	1.7	1.8	1.9	2.0
0	1.0000	1.0000	1.0000	1.0000	1.0000	1.0000	1.0000	1.0000	1.0000	1.0000
1	.6671	.6988	.7275	.7534	.7769	.7981	.8173	.8347	.8504	.8647
2	.3010	.3374	.3732	.4082	.4422	.4751	.5068	.5372	.5663	.5940
3	.0996	.1205	.1429	.1665	.1912	.2166	.2428	.2694	.2963	.3233
4	.0257	.0338	.0431	.0537	.0656	.0788	.0932	.1087	.1253	.1429
5	.0054	.0077	.0107	.0143	.0186	.0237	.0296	.0364	.0441	.0527
6	.0010	.0015	.0022	.0032	.0045	.0060	.0080	.0104	.0132	.0166
7	.0001	.0003	.0004	.0006	.0009	.0013	.0019	.0026	.0034	.0045
8	.0000	.0000	.0001	.0001	.0002	.0003	.0004	.0006	.0008	.0011
9	.0000	.0000	.0000	.0000	.0000	.0000	.0001	.0001	.0002	.0002

x'	2.1	2.2	2.3	2.4	m 2.5	2.6	2.7	2.8	2.9	3.0
0	1.0000	1.0000	1.0000	1.0000	1.0000	1.0000	1.0000	1.0000	1.0000	1.0000
1	.8775	.8892	.8997	.9093	.9179	.9257	.9328	.9392	.9450	.9502
2	.6204	.6454	.6691	.6916	.7127	.7326	.7513	.7689	.7854	.8009
3	.3504	.3773	.4040	.4303	.4562	.4816	.5064	.5305	.5540	.5768
4	.1614	.1806	.2007	.2213	.2424	.2640	.2859	.3081	.3304	.3528
5	.0621	.0725	.0838	.0959	.1088	.1226	.1371	.1523	.1682	.1847
6	.0204	.0249	.0300	.0357	.0420	.0490	.0567	.0651	.0742	.0839
7	.0059	.0075	.0094	.0116	.0142	.0172	.0206	.0244	.0287	.0335
8	.0015	.0020	.0026	.0033	.0042	.0053	.0066	.0081	.0099	.0119
9	.0003	.0005	.0006	.0009	.0011	.0015	.0019	.0024	.0031	.0038
10	.0001	.0001	.0001	.0002	.0003	.0004	.0005	.0007	.0009	.0011
11	.0000	.0000	.0000	.0000	.0001	.0001	.0001	.0002	.0002	.0003
12	.0000	.0000	.0000	.0000	.0000	.0000	.0000	.0000	.0001	.0001

TABLE A-3 (*continued*)

					m					
x'	3.1	3.2	3.3	3.4	3.5	3.6	3.7	3.8	3.9	4.0
0	1.0000	1.0000	1.0000	1.0000	1.0000	1.0000	1.0000	1.0000	1.0000	1.0000
1	.9550	.9592	.9631	.9666	.9698	.9727	.9753	.9776	.9798	.9817
2	.8153	.8288	.8414	.8532	.8641	.8743	.8838	.8926	.9008	.9084
3	.5988	.6201	.6406	.6603	.6792	.6973	.7146	.7311	.7469	.7619
4	.3752	.3975	.4197	.4416	.4634	.4848	.5058	.5265	.5468	.5665
5	.2018	.2194	.2374	.2558	.2746	.2936	.3128	.3322	.3516	.3712
6	.0943	.1054	.1171	.1295	.1424	.1559	.1699	.1844	.1994	.2149
7	.0388	.0446	.0510	.0579	.0653	.0733	.0818	.0909	.1005	.1107
8	.0142	.0168	.0198	.0231	.0267	.0308	.0352	.0401	.0454	.0511
9	.0047	.0057	.0069	.0083	.0099	.0117	.0137	.0160	.0185	.0214
10	.0014	.0018	.0022	.0027	.0033	.0040	.0048	.0058	.0069	.0081
11	.0004	.0005	.0006	.0008	.0010	.0013	.0016	.0019	.0023	.0028
12	.0001	.0001	.0002	.0002	.0003	.0004	.0005	.0006	.0007	.0009
13	.0000	.0000	.0000	.0001	.0001	.0001	.0001	.0002	.0002	.0003
14	.0000	.0000	.0000	.0000	.0000	.0000	.0000	.0000	.0001	.0001

					m					
x'	4.1	4.2	4.3	4.4	4.5	4.6	4.7	4.8	4.9	5.0
0	1.0000	1.0000	1.0000	1.0000	1.0000	1.0000	1.0000	1.0000	1.0000	1.0000
1	.9834	.9850	.9864	.9877	.9889	.9899	.9909	.9918	.9926	.9933
2	.9155	.9220	.9281	.9337	.9389	.9437	.9482	.9523	.9561	.9596
3	.7762	.7898	.8026	.8149	.8264	.8374	.8477	.8575	.8667	.8753
4	.5858	.6046	.6228	.6406	.6577	.6743	.6903	.7058	.7207	.7350
5	.3907	.4102	.4296	.4488	.4679	.4868	.5054	.5237	.5418	.5595
6	.2307	.2469	.2633	.2801	.2971	.3142	.3316	.3490	.3665	.3840
7	.1214	.1325	.1442	.1564	.1689	.1820	.1954	.2092	.2233	.2378
8	.0573	.0639	.0710	.0786	.0866	.0951	.1040	.1133	.1231	.1334
9	.0245	.0279	.0317	.0358	.0403	.0451	.0503	.0558	.0618	.0681
10	.0095	.0111	.0129	.0149	.0171	.0195	.0222	.0251	.0283	.0318
11	.0034	.0041	.0048	.0057	.0067	.0078	.0090	.0104	.0120	.0137
12	.0011	.0014	.0017	.0020	.0024	.0029	.0034	.0040	.0047	.0055
13	.0003	.0004	.0005	.0007	.0008	.0010	.0012	.0014	.0017	.0020
14	.0001	.0001	.0002	.0002	.0003	.0003	.0004	.0005	.0006	.0007
15	.0000	.0000	.0000	.0001	.0001	.0001	.0001	.0001	.0002	.0002
16	.0000	.0000	.0000	.0000	.0000	.0000	.0000	.0000	.0001	.0001

					m					
x'	5.1	5.2	5.3	5.4	5.5	5.6	5.7	5.8	5.9	6.0
0	1.0000	1.0000	1.0000	1.0000	1.0000	1.0000	1.0000	1.0000	1.0000	1.0000
1	.9939	.9945	.9950	.9955	.9959	.9963	.9967	.9970	.9973	.9975
2	.9628	.9658	.9686	.9711	.9734	.9756	.9776	.9794	.9811	.9826
3	.8835	.8912	.8984	.9052	.9116	.9176	.9232	.9285	.9334	.9380
4	.7487	.7619	.7746	.7867	.7983	.8094	.8200	.8300	.8396	.8488
5	.5769	.5939	.6105	.6267	.6425	.6579	.6728	.6873	.7013	.7149
6	.4016	.4191	.4365	.4539	.4711	.4881	.5050	.5217	.5381	.5543
7	.2526	.2676	.2829	.2983	.3140	.3297	.3456	.3616	.3776	.3937
8	.1440	.1551	.1665	.1783	.1905	.2030	.2159	.2290	.2424	.2560
9	.0748	.0819	.0894	.0974	.1056	.1143	.1234	.1328	.1426	.1528

(*continued*)

TABLE A-3 (continued)

x'	m									
	5.1	5.2	5.3	5.4	5.5	5.6	5.7	5.8	5.9	6.0
10	.0356	.0397	.0441	.0488	.0538	.0591	.0648	.0708	.0772	.0839
11	.0156	.0177	.0200	.0225	.0253	.0282	.0314	.0349	.0386	.0426
12	.0063	.0073	.0084	.0096	.0110	.0125	.0141	.0160	.0179	.0201
13	.0024	.0028	.0033	.0038	.0045	.0051	.0059	.0068	.0078	.0088
14	.0008	.0010	.0012	.0014	.0017	.0020	.0023	.0027	.0031	.0036
15	.0003	.0003	.0004	.0005	.0006	.0007	.0009	.0010	.0012	.0014
16	.0001	.0001	.0001	.0002	.0002	.0002	.0003	.0004	.0004	.0005
17	.0000	.0000	.0000	.0001	.0001	.0001	.0001	.0001	.0001	.0002
18	.0000	.0000	.0000	.0000	.0000	.0000	.0000	.0000	.0000	.0001

x'	m									
	6.1	6.2	6.3	6.4	6.5	6.6	6.7	6.8	6.9	7.0
0	1.0000	1.0000	1.0000	1.0000	1.0000	1.0000	1.0000	1.0000	1.0000	1.0000
1	.9978	.9980	.9982	.9983	.9985	.9986	.9988	.9989	.9990	.9991
2	.9841	.9854	.9866	.9877	.9887	.9897	.9905	.9913	.9920	.9927
3	.9423	.9464	.9502	.9537	.9570	.9600	.9629	.9656	.9680	.9704
4	.8575	.8658	.8736	.8811	.8882	.8948	.9012	.9072	.9129	.9182
5	.7281	.7408	.7531	.7649	.7763	.7873	.7978	.8080	.8177	.8270
6	.5702	.5859	.6012	.6163	.6310	.6453	.6594	.6730	.6863	.6993
7	.4098	.4258	.4418	.4577	.4735	.4892	.5047	.5201	.5353	.5503
8	.2699	.2840	.2983	.3127	.3272	.3419	.3567	.3715	.3864	.4013
9	.1633	.1741	.1852	.1967	.2084	.2204	.2327	.2452	.2580	.2709
10	.0910	.0984	.1061	.1142	.1226	.1314	.1404	.1498	.1505	.1695
11	.0469	.0514	.0563	.0614	.0668	.0726	.0786	.0849	.0916	.0985
12	.0224	.0250	.0277	.0307	.0339	.0373	.0409	.0448	.0490	.0534
13	.0100	.0113	.0127	.0143	.0160	.0179	.0199	.0221	.0245	.0270
14	.0042	.0048	.0055	.0063	.0071	.0080	.0091	.0102	.0115	.0128
15	.0016	.0019	.0022	.0026	.0030	.0034	.0039	.0044	.0050	.0057
16	.0006	.0007	.0008	.0010	.0012	.0014	.0016	.0018	.0021	.0024
17	.0002	.0003	.0003	.0004	.0004	.0005	.0006	.0007	.0008	.0010
18	.0001	.0001	.0001	.0001	.0002	.0002	.0002	.0003	.0003	.0004
19	.0000	.0000	.0000	.0000	.0001	.0001	.0001	.0001	.0001	.0001

x'	m									
	7.1	7.2	7.3	7.4	7.5	7.6	7.7	7.8	7.9	8.0
0	1.0000	1.0000	1.0000	1.0000	1.0000	1.0000	1.0000	1.0000	1.0000	1.0000
1	.9992	.9993	.9993	.9994	.9994	.9995	.9995	.9996	.9996	.9997
2	.9933	.9939	.9944	.9949	.9953	.9957	.9961	.9964	.9967	.9970
3	.9725	.9745	.9764	.0781	.9797	.9812	.9826	.9839	.9851	.9862
4	.9233	.9281	.9326	.9368	.9409	.9446	.9482	.9515	.9547	.9576
5	.8359	.8445	.8527	.8605	.8679	.8751	.8819	.8883	.8945	.9004
6	.7119	.7241	.7360	.7474	.7586	.7693	.7797	.7897	.7994	.8088
7	.5651	.5796	.5940	.6080	.6218	.6354	.6486	.6616	.6743	.6866
8	.4162	.4311	.4459	.4607	.4754	.4900	.5044	.5188	.5330	.5470
9	.2840	.2973	.3108	.3243	.3380	.3518	.3657	.3796	.3935	.4075

TABLE A-3 (continued)

					m					
x'	7.1	7.2	7.3	7.4	7.5	7.6	7.7	7.8	7.9	8.0
10	.1798	.1904	.2012	.2123	.2236	.2351	.2469	.2589	.2710	.2834
11	.1058	.1133	.1212	.1293	.1378	.1465	.1555	.1648	.1743	.1841
12	.0580	.0629	.0681	.0735	.0792	.0852	.0915	.0980	.1048	.1119
13	.0297	.0327	.0358	.0391	.0427	.0464	.0504	.0546	.0591	.0638
14	.0143	.0159	.0176	.0195	.0216	.0238	.0261	.0286	.0313	.0342
15	.0065	.0073	.0082	.0092	.0103	.0114	.0127	.0141	.0156	.0173
16	.0028	.0031	.0036	.0041	.0046	.0052	.0059	.0066	.0074	.0082
17	.0011	.0013	.0015	.0017	.0020	.0022	.0026	.0029	.0033	.0037
18	.0004	.0005	.0006	.0007	.0008	.0009	.0011	.0012	.0014	.0016
19	.0002	.0002	.0002	.0003	.0003	.0004	.0004	.0005	.0006	.0006
20	.0001	.0001	.0001	.0001	.0001	.0001	.0002	.0002	.0002	.0003
21	.0000	.0000	.0000	.0000	.0000	.0000	.0001	.0001	.0001	.0001

					m					
x'	8.1	8.2	8.3	8.4	8.5	8.6	8.7	8.8	8.9	9.0
0	1.0000	1.0000	1.0000	1.0000	1.0000	1.0000	1.0000	1.0000	1.0000	1.0000
1	.9997	.9997	.9998	.9998	.9998	.9998	.9998	.9998	.9999	.9999
2	.9972	.9975	.9977	.9979	.9981	.9982	.9984	.9985	.9987	.9988
3	.9873	.9882	.9891	.9900	.9907	.9914	.9921	.9927	.9932	.9938
4	.9604	.9630	.9654	.9677	.9699	.9719	.9738	.9756	.9772	.9788
5	.9060	.9113	.9163	.9211	.9256	.9299	.9340	.9379	.9416	.9450
6	.8178	.8264	.8347	.8427	.8504	.8578	.8648	.8716	.8781	.8843
7	.6987	.7104	.7219	.7330	.7438	.7543	.7645	.7744	.7840	.7932
8	.5609	.5746	.5881	.6013	.6144	.6272	.6398	.6522	.6643	.6761
9	.4214	.4353	.4493	.4631	.4769	.4906	.5042	.5177	.5311	.5443
10	.2959	.3085	.3212	.3341	.3470	.3600	.3731	.3863	.3994	.4126
11	.1942	.2045	.2150	.2257	.2366	.2478	.2591	.2706	.2822	.2940
12	.1193	.1269	.1348	.1429	.1513	.1600	.1689	.1780	.1874	.1970
13	.0687	.0739	.0793	.0850	.0909	.0971	.1035	.1102	.1171	.1242
14	.0372	.0405	.0439	.0476	.0514	.0555	.0597	.0642	.0689	.0739
15	.0190	.0209	.0229	.0251	.0274	.0299	.0325	.0353	.0383	.0415
16	.0092	.0102	.0113	.0125	.0138	.0152	.0168	.0184	.0202	.0220
17	.0042	.0047	.0053	.0059	.0066	.0074	.0082	.0091	.0101	.0111
18	.0018	.0021	.0023	.0027	.0030	.0034	.0038	.0043	.0048	.0053
19	.0008	.0009	.0010	.0011	.0013	.0015	.0017	.0019	.0022	.0024
20	.0003	.0003	.0004	.0005	.0005	.0006	.0007	.0008	.0009	.0011
21	.0001	.0001	.0002	.0002	.0002	.0002	.0003	.0003	.0004	.0004
22	.0000	.0000	.0001	.0001	.0001	.0001	.0001	.0001	.0002	.0002
23	.0000	.0000	.0000	.0000	.0000	.0000	.0000	.0000	.0001	.0001

					m					
x'	9.1	9.2	9.3	9.4	9.5	9.6	9.7	9.8	9.9	10
0	1.0000	1.0000	1.0000	1.0000	1.0000	1.0000	1.0000	1.0000	1.0000	1.0000
1	.9999	.9999	.9999	.9999	.9999	.9999	.9999	.9999	1.0000	1.0000
2	.9989	.9990	.9991	.9991	.9992	.9993	.9993	.9994	.9995	.9995
3	.9942	.9947	.9951	.9955	.9958	.9962	.9965	.9967	.9970	.9972
4	.9802	.9816	.9828	.9840	.9851	.9862	.9871	.9880	.9889	.9897

(continued)

TABLE A-3 (continued)

					m					
x'	9.1	9.2	9.3	9.4	9.5	9.6	9.7	9.8	9.9	10
5	.9483	.9514	.9544	.9571	.9597	.9622	.9645	.9667	.9688	.9707
6	.8902	.8959	.9014	.9065	.9115	.9162	.9207	.9250	.9290	.9329
7	.8022	.8108	.8192	.8273	.8351	.8426	.8498	.8567	.8634	.8699
8	.6877	.6990	.7101	.7208	.7313	.7416	.7515	.7612	.7706	.7798
9	.5574	.5704	.5832	.5958	.6082	.6204	.6324	.6442	.6558	.6672
10	.4258	.4389	.4521	.4651	.4782	.4911	.5040	.5168	.5295	.5421
11	.3059	.3180	.3301	.3424	.3547	.3671	.3795	.3920	.4045	.4170
12	.2068	.2168	.2270	.2374	.2480	.2588	.2697	.2807	.2919	.3032
13	.1316	.1393	.1471	.1552	.1636	.1721	.1809	.1899	.1991	.2084
14	.0790	.0844	.0900	.0958	.1019	.1081	.1147	.1214	.1284	.1355
15	.0448	.0483	.0520	.0559	.0600	.0643	.0688	.0735	.0784	.0835
16	.0240	.0262	.0285	.0309	.0335	.0362	.0391	.0421	.0454	.0487
17	.0122	.0135	.0148	.0162	.0177	.0194	.0211	.0230	.0249	.0270
18	.0059	.0066	.0073	.0081	.0089	.0098	.0108	.0119	.0130	.0143
19	.0027	.0031	.0034	.0038	.0043	.0048	.0053	.0059	.0065	.0072
20	.0012	.0014	.0015	.0017	.0020	.0022	.0025	.0028	.0031	.0035
21	.0005	.0006	.0007	.0008	.0009	.0010	.0011	.0013	.0014	.0016
22	.0002	.0002	.0003	.0003	.0004	.0004	.0005	.0005	.0006	.0007
23	.0001	.0001	.0001	.0001	.0001	.0002	.0002	.0002	.0003	.0003
24	.0000	.0000	.0000	.0000	.0001	.0001	.0001	.0001	.0001	.0001

					m					
x'	11	12	13	14	15	16	17	18	19	20
0	1.0000	1.0000	1.0000	1.0000	1.0000	1.0000	1.0000	1.0000	1.0000	1.0000
1	1.0000	1.0000	1.0000	1.0000	1.0000	1.0000	1.0000	1.0000	1.0000	1.0000
2	.9998	.9999	1.0000	1.0000	1.0000	1.0000	1.0000	1.0000	1.0000	1.0000
3	.9988	.9995	.9998	.9999	1.0000	1.0000	1.0000	1.0000	1.0000	1.0000
4	.9951	.9977	.9990	.9995	.9998	.9999	1.0000	1.0000	1.0000	1.0000
5	.9849	.9924	.9963	.9982	.9991	.9996	.9998	.9999	1.0000	1.0000
6	.9625	.9797	.9893	.9945	.9972	.9986	.9993	.9997	.9998	.9999
7	.9214	.9542	.9741	.9858	.9924	.9960	.9979	.9990	.9995	.9997
8	.8568	.9105	.9460	.9684	.9820	.9900	.9946	.9971	.9985	.9992
9	.7680	.8450	.9002	.9379	.9626	.9780	.9874	.9929	.9961	.9979
10	.6595	.7576	.8342	.8906	.9301	.9567	.9739	.9846	.9911	.9950
11	.5401	.6528	.7483	.8243	.8815	.9226	.9509	.9696	.9817	.9892
12	.4207	.5384	.6468	.7400	.8152	.8730	.9153	.9451	.9653	.9786
13	.3113	.4240	.5369	.6415	.7324	.8069	.8650	.9083	.9394	.9610
14	.2187	.3185	.4270	.5356	.6368	.7255	.7991	.8574	.9016	.9339
15	.1460	.2280	.3249	.4296	.5343	.6325	.7192	.7919	.8503	.8951
16	.0926	.1556	.2364	.3306	.4319	.5333	.6285	.7133	.7852	.8435
17	.0559	.1013	.1645	.2441	.3359	.4340	.5323	.6250	.7080	.7789
18	.0322	.0630	.1095	.1728	.2511	.3407	.4360	.5314	.6216	.7030
19	.0177	.0374	.0698	.1174	.1805	.2577	.3450	.4378	.5305	.6186

TABLE A–3 (*concluded*)

x'	m									
	11	12	13	14	15	16	17	18	19	20
20	.0093	.0213	.0427	.0765	.1248	.1878	.2637	.3491	.4394	.5297
21	.0047	.0116	.0250	.0479	.0830	.1318	.1945	.2693	.3528	.4409
22	.0023	.0061	.0141	.0288	.0531	.0892	.1385	.2009	.2745	.3563
23	.0010	.0030	.0076	.0167	.0327	.0582	.0953	.1449	.2069	.2794
24	.0005	.0015	.0040	.0093	.0195	.0367	.0633	.1011	.1510	.2125
25	.0002	.0007	.0020	.0050	.0112	.0223	.0406	.0683	.1067	.1568
26	.0001	.0003	.0010	.0026	.0062	.0131	.0252	.0446	.0731	.1122
27	.0000	.0001	.0005	.0013	.0033	.0075	.0152	.0282	.0486	.0779
28	.0000	.0001	.0002	.0006	.0017	.0041	.0088	.0173	.0313	.0525
29	.0000	.0000	.0001	.0003	.0009	.0022	.0050	.0103	.0195	.0343
30	.0000	.0000	.0000	.0001	.0004	.0011	.0027	.0059	.0118	.0218
31	.0000	.0000	.0000	.0001	.0002	.0006	.0014	.0033	.0070	.0135
32	.0000	.0000	.0000	.0000	.0001	.0003	.0007	.0018	.0040	.0081
33	.0000	.0000	.0000	.0000	.0000	.0001	.0004	.0010	.0022	.0047
34	.0000	.0000	.0000	.0000	.0000	.0001	.0002	.0005	.0012	.0027
35	.0000	.0000	.0000	.0000	.0000	.0000	.0001	.0002	.0006	.0015
36	.0000	.0000	.0000	.0000	.0000	.0000	.0000	.0001	.0003	.0008
37	.0000	.0000	.0000	.0000	.0000	.0000	.0000	.0001	.0002	.0004
38	.0000	.0000	.0000	.0000	.0000	.0000	.0000	.0000	.0001	.0002
39	.0000	.0000	.0000	.0000	.0000	.0000	.0000	.0000	.0000	.0001
40	.0000	.0000	.0000	.0000	.0000	.0000	.0000	.0000	.0000	.0001

Source: *CRC Standard Mathematical Tables*, 16th ed., The Chemical Rubber Company, 1968.

TABLE A–4
Normal Probability Distribution and Partial Expectations

Standardized Variate z	Probabilities		Partial Expectations	
	F(z)	1 − F(z)	L(z)	L(−z)
.00	.5000	.5000	.3989	.3989
.01	.5040	.4960	.3940	.4040
.02	.5080	.4920	.3890	.4090
.03	.5120	.4880	.3841	.4141
.04	.5160	.4840	.3793	.4193
.05	.5200	.4800	.3744	.4244
.06	.5239	.4761	.3697	.4297
.07	.5279	.4721	.3649	.4349
.08	.5319	.4681	.3602	.4402
.09	.5359	.4641	.3556	.4456
.10	.5398	.4602	.3509	.4509
.11	.5438	.4562	.3464	.4564
.12	.5478	.4522	.3418	.4618
.13	.5517	.4483	.3373	.4673
.14	.5557	.4443	.3328	.4728
.15	.5596	.4404	.3284	.4784
.16	.5636	.4364	.3240	.4840
.17	.5685	.4325	.3197	.4897
.18	.5714	.4286	.3154	.4954
.19	.5753	.4247	.3111	.5011
.20	.5793	.4207	.3069	.5069
.21	.5832	.4168	.3027	.5127
.22	.5871	.4129	.3027	.5186
.23	.5910	.4090	.2944	.5244
.24	.5948	.4052	.2904	.5304
.25	.5987	.4013	.2863	.5363
.26	.6026	.3974	.2824	.5424
.27	.6064	.3936	.2784	.5484
.28	.6103	.3897	.2745	.5545
.29	.6141	.3859	.2706	.5606
.30	.6179	.3821	.2668	.5668
.31	.6217	.3783	.2630	.5730
.32	.6255	.3745	.2592	.5792
.33	.6293	.3707	.2555	.5855
.34	.6331	.3669	.2518	.5918
.35	.6368	.3632	.2481	.5981
.36	.6406	.3594	.2445	.6045
.37	.6443	.3557	.2409	.6109
.38	.6480	.3520	.2374	.6174
.39	.6517	.3483	.2339	.6239
.40	.6554	.3446	.2304	.6304
.41	.6591	.3409	.2270	.6370
.42	.6628	.3372	.2236	.6436
.43	.6664	.3336	.2203	.6503
.44	.6700	.3300	.2169	.6569
.45	.6736	.3264	.2137	.6637
.46	.6772	.3228	.2104	.6704
.47	.6808	.3192	.2072	.6772
.48	.6844	.3156	.2040	.6840
.49	.6879	.3121	.2009	.6909
.50	.6915	.3085	.1978	.6978

TABLE A-4 (continued)

Standardized Variate z	Probabilities		Partial Expectations	
	F(z)	1 − F(z)	L(z)	L(−z)
.51	.6950	.3050	.1947	.7047
.52	.6985	.3015	.1917	.7117
.53	.7019	.2981	.1887	.7187
.54	.7054	.2946	.1857	.7257
.55	.7088	.2912	.1828	.7328
.56	.7123	.2877	.1799	.7399
.57	.7157	.2843	.1771	.7471
.58	.7190	.2810	.1742	.7542
.59	.7224	.2776	.1714	.7614
.60	.7257	.2743	.1687	.7687
.61	.7291	.2709	.1659	.7759
.62	.7324	.2676	.1633	.7833
.63	.7357	.2643	.1606	.7906
.64	.7389	.2611	.1580	.7980
.65	.7422	.2578	.1554	.8054
.66	.7454	.2546	.1528	.8128
.67	.7486	.2514	.1503	.8203
.68	.7517	.2483	.1478	.8278
.69	.7549	.2451	.1453	.8353
.70	.7580	.2420	.1429	.8429
.71	.7611	.2389	.1405	.8505
.72	.7642	.2358	.1381	.8581
.73	.7673	.2327	.1358	.8658
.74	.7703	.2297	.1334	.8734
.75	.7733	.2267	.1312	.8812
.76	.7764	.2236	.1289	.8889
.77	.7793	.2207	.1267	.8967
.78	.7823	.2177	.1245	.9045
.79	.7852	.2148	.1223	.9123
.80	.7881	.2119	.1202	.9202
.81	.7910	.2090	.1181	.9281
.82	.7939	.2061	.1160	.9360
.83	.7967	.2033	.1140	.9440
.84	.7996	.2004	.1120	.9520
.85	.8023	.1977	.1100	.9600
.86	.8051	.1949	.1080	.9680
.87	.8067	.1922	.1061	.9761
.88	.8106	.1894	.1042	.9842
.89	.8133	.1867	.1023	.9923
.90	.8159	.1841	.1004	1.0004
.91	.8186	.1814	.0986	1.0086
.92	.8212	.1788	.0968	1.0168
.93	.8238	.1762	.0955	1.0250
.94	.8264	.1736	.0953	1.0330
.95	.8289	.1711	.0916	1.0416
.96	.8315	.1685	.0899	1.0499
.97	.8340	.1660	.0882	1.0582
.98	.8365	.1635	.0865	1.0665
.99	.8389	.1611	.0849	1.0749
1.00	.8413	.1587	.0833	1.0833
1.01	.8438	.1562	.0817	1.0917
1.02	.8461	.1539	.0802	1.1002
1.03	.8485	.1515	.0787	1.1087
1.04	.8508	.1492	.0772	1.1172
1.05	.8531	.1469	.0757	1.1257

(continued)

TABLE A–4 (continued)

Standardized Variate z	Probabilities		Partial Expectations	
	F(z)	1 − F(z)	L(z)	L(−z)
1.06	.8554	.1446	.0742	1.1342
1.07	.8577	.1423	.0728	1.1428
1.08	.8599	.1401	.0714	1.1514
1.09	.8621	.1379	.0700	1.1600
1.10	.8643	.1357	.0686	1.1686
1.11	.8665	.1335	.0673	1.1773
1.12	.8686	.1314	.0659	1.1859
1.13	.8708	.1292	.0646	1.1946
1.14	.8729	.1271	.0634	1.2034
1.15	.8749	.1251	.0621	1.2121
1.16	.8770	.1230	.0609	1.2209
1.17	.8790	.1210	.0596	1.2296
1.18	.8810	.1190	.0584	1.2384
1.19	.8830	.1170	.0573	1.2473
1.20	.8849	.1151	.0561	1.2561
1.21	.8869	.1131	.0550	1.2650
1.22	.8888	.1112	.0538	1.2738
1.23	.8907	.1093	.0527	1.2827
1.24	.8925	.1075	.0517	1.2917
1.25	.8943	.1057	.0506	1.3006
1.26	.8962	.1038	.0495	1.3095
1.27	.8980	.1020	.0485	1.3185
1.28	.8997	.1003	.0475	1.3275
1.29	.9015	.0985	.0465	1.3365
1.30	.9032	.0968	.0455	1.3455
1.31	.9049	.0951	.0446	1.3446
1.32	.9066	.0934	.0436	1.3636
1.33	.9082	.0918	.0427	1.3727
1.34	.9099	.0901	.0418	1.3818
1.35	.9115	.0885	.0409	1.3909
1.36	.9131	.0869	.0400	1.4000
1.37	.9147	.0853	.0392	1.4092
1.38	.9162	.0838	.0383	1.4183
1.39	.9177	.0823	.0375	1.4275
1.40	.9192	.0808	.0367	1.4367
1.41	.9207	.0793	.0359	1.4459
1.42	.9222	.0778	.0351	1.4551
1.43	.9236	.0764	.0343	1.4643
1.44	.9251	.0749	.0336	1.4736
1.45	.9265	.0735	.0328	1.4828
1.46	.9279	.0721	.0321	1.4921
1.47	.9292	.0708	.0314	1.5014
1.48	.9306	.0694	.0307	1.5107
1.49	.9319	.0681	.0300	1.5200
1.50	.9332	.0668	.0293	1.5293
1.51	.9345	.0655	.0286	1.5386
1.52	.9357	.0643	.0280	1.5480
1.53	.9370	.0630	.0274	1.5574
1.54	.9382	.0618	.0267	1.5667
1.55	.9394	.0606	.0261	1.5761
1.56	.9406	.0594	.0255	1.5855
1.57	.9418	.0582	.0249	1.5949
1.58	.9429	.0571	.0244	1.6044
1.59	.9441	.0559	.0238	1.6138

TABLE A-4 (continued)

Standardized Variate z	Probabilities		Partial Expectations	
	F(z)	1 − F(z)	L(z)	L(−z)
1.60	.9460	.0540	.0232	1.6232
1.61	.9463	.0537	.0227	1.6327
1.62	.9474	.0526	.0222	1.6422
1.63	.9484	.0516	.0216	1.6516
1.64	.9495	.0505	.0211	1.6611
1.65	.9505	.0495	.0206	1.6706
1.66	.9515	.0485	.0201	1.6801
1.67	.9525	.0475	.0197	1.6897
1.68	.9535	.0465	.0192	1.6992
1.69	.9545	.0455	.0187	1.7087
1.70	.9554	.0446	.0183	1.7183
1.71	.9564	.0436	.0178	1.7278
1.72	.9573	.0427	.0174	1.7374
1.73	.9582	.0418	.0170	1.7470
1.74	.9591	.0409	.0166	1.7566
1.75	.9599	.0401	.0162	1.7662
1.76	.9608	.0392	.0158	1.7558
1.77	.9616	.0384	.0154	1.7854
1.78	.9625	.0375	.0150	1.7950
1.79	.9633	.0367	.0146	1.8046
1.80	.9641	.0359	.0143	1.8143
1.81	.9649	.0351	.0139	1.8239
1.82	.9656	.0344	.0136	1.8436
1.83	.9664	.0336	.0132	1.8432
1.84	.9671	.0329	.0129	1.8529
1.85	.9678	.0322	.0126	1.8626
1.86	.9685	.0314	.0123	1.8723
1.87	.9693	.0307	.0119	1.8819
1.88	.9699	.0301	.0116	1.8916
1.89	.9706	.0294	.0113	1.9013
1.90	.9713	.0287	.0111	1.9111
1.91	.9719	.0281	.0108	1.9208
1.92	.9726	.0274	.0105	1.9305
1.93	.9732	.0268	.0102	1.9402
1.94	.9738	.0262	.0100	1.9500
1.95	.9744	.0256	.0097	1.9597
1.96	.9750	.0250	.0094	1.9694
1.97	.9756	.0244	.0092	1.9792
1.98	.9761	.0239	.0090	1.9890
1.99	.9767	.0233	.0087	1.9987
2.00	.9772	.0228	.0085	2.0085
2.01	.9778	.0222	.0083	2.0183
2.02	.9783	.0217	.0080	2.0280
2.03	.9788	.0212	.0078	2.0378
2.04	.9793	.0207	.0076	2.0476
2.05	.9798	.0202	.0074	2.0574
2.06	.9803	.0197	.0072	2.0672
2.07	.9808	.0192	.0072	2.0770
2.08	.9812	.0188	.0068	2.0868
2.09	.9817	.0183	.0066	2.0966
2.10	.9821	.0179	.0065	2.1065
2.11	.9826	.0174	.0063	2.1163
2.12	.9830	.0170	.0061	2.1261
2.13	.9834	.0166	.0060	2.1360
2.14	.9838	.0162	.0058	2.1458

(continued)

TABLE A-4 (continued)

Standardized Variate z	Probabilities		Partial Expectations	
	F(z)	1 − F(z)	L(z)	L(−z)
2.15	.9842	.0158	.0056	2.1556
2.16	.9846	.0154	.0055	2.1655
2.17	.9850	.0150	.0053	2.1753
2.18	.9854	.0146	.0052	2.1852
2.19	.9857	.0143	.0050	2.1950
2.20	.9861	.0139	.0049	2.2049
2.21	.9864	.0136	.0048	2.2148
2.22	.9868	.0132	.0046	2.2246
2.23	.9871	.0129	.0045	2.2345
2.24	.9875	.0125	.0044	2.2444
2.25	.9878	.0122	.0042	2.2542
2.26	.9881	.0119	.0041	2.2641
2.27	.9884	.0116	.0040	2.2740
2.28	.9887	.0113	.0039	2.2839
2.29	.9890	.0110	.0038	2.2938
2.30	.9893	.0107	.0037	2.3037
2.31	.9896	.0104	.0036	2.3136
2.32	.9898	.0102	.0035	2.3235
2.33	.9901	.0099	.0034	2.3334
2.34	.9904	.0096	.0033	2.3433
2.35	.9906	.0094	.0032	2.3532
2.36	.9909	.0091	.0031	2.3631
2.37	.9911	.0089	.0030	2.3730
2.38	.9913	.0087	.0029	2.3829
2.39	.9916	.0084	.0028	2.3928
2.40	.9918	.0082	.0027	2.4027
2.41	.9920	.0080	.0026	2.4126
2.42	.9922	.0078	.0026	2.4226
2.43	.9925	.0075	.0025	2.4325
2.44	.9927	.0073	.0024	2.4424
2.45	.9929	.0071	.0023	2.4523
2.46	.9931	.0069	.0023	2.4623
2.47	.9932	.0068	.0022	2.4722
2.48	.9934	.0066	.0021	2.4821
2.49	.9936	.0064	.0021	2.4921
2.50	.9938	.0062	.0020	2.5020
2.51	.9940	.0060	.0019	2.5119
2.52	.9941	.0059	.0019	2.5219
2.53	.9943	.0057	.0018	2.5318
2.54	.9945	.0055	.0018	2.5418
2.55	.9946	.0054	.0017	2.5517
2.56	.9948	.0052	.0017	2.5617
2.57	.9949	.0051	.0016	2.5716
2.58	.9951	.0049	.0016	2.5816
2.59	.9952	.0048	.0015	2.5915
2.60	.9953	.0047	.0015	2.6015
2.61	.9955	.0045	.0014	2.6114
2.62	.9956	.0044	.0014	2.6214
2.63	.9957	.0043	.0013	2.6313
2.64	.9959	.0041	.0013	2.6413
2.65	.9960	.0040	.0012	2.6512
2.66	.9961	.0039	.0012	2.6612
2.67	.9962	.0038	.0012	2.6712
2.68	.9963	.0037	.0011	2.6811
2.69	.9964	.0036	.0011	2.6911
2.70	.9965	.0035	.0011	2.7011

TABLE A–4 (concluded)

Standardized Variate z	Probabilities		Partial Expectations	
	F(z)	1 − F(z)	L(z)	L(−z)
2.71	.9966	.0034	.0010	2.7110
2.72	.9967	.0033	.0010	2.7210
2.73	.9968	.0032	.0010	2.7310
2.74	.9969	.0031	.0009	2.7409
2.75	.9970	.0030	.0009	2.7509
2.76	.9971	.0029	.0009	2.7609
2.77	.9972	.0028	.0008	2.7708
2.78	.9973	.0027	.0008	2.7808
2.79	.9974	.0026	.0008	2.7908
2.80	.9974	.0026	.0008	2.8008
2.81	.9975	.0025	.0007	2.8107
2.82	.9976	.0024	.0007	2.8207
2.83	.9977	.0023	.0007	2.8307
2.84	.9977	.0023	.0007	2.8407
2.85	.9978	.0022	.0006	2.8506
2.86	.9979	.0021	.0006	2.8606
2.87	.9979	.0021	.0006	2.8706
2.88	.9980	.0020	.0006	2.8806
2.89	.9981	.0019	.0006	2.8906
2.90	.9981	.0019	.0005	2.9005
2.91	.9982	.0018	.0005	2.9105
2.92	.9982	.0018	.0005	2.9205
2.93	.9983	.0017	.0005	2.9305
2.94	.9984	.0016	.0005	2.9405
2.95	.9984	.0016	.0005	2.9505
2.96	.9985	.0015	.0004	2.9604
2.97	.9985	.0015	.0004	2.9704
2.98	.9986	.0014	.0004	2.9804
2.99	.9986	.0014	.0004	2.9904
3.00	.9986	.0014	.0004	3.0004

Source: R. G. Brown, *Decision Rules for Inventory Management* (Hinsdale, IL.: Dryden, 1967). Adapted from Table VI, pp. 95–103.

TABLE A–5
Factors d_2 for R Charts

Number of Observations in Subgroup, n	Factor d_2, $d_2 = \dfrac{\bar{R}}{\sigma}$
2	1.128
3	1.693
4	2.059
5	2.326
6	2.534
7	2.704
8	2.847
9	2.970
10	3.078
11	3.173
12	3.258
13	3.336
14	3.407
15	3.472
16	3.532
17	3.588
18	3.640
19	3.689
20	3.735
21	3.778
22	3.819
23	3.858
24	3.895
25	3.931
30	4.086
35	4.213
40	4.322
45	4.415
50	4.498
55	4.572
60	4.639
65	4.699
70	4.755
75	4.806
80	4.854
85	4.898
90	4.939
95	4.978
100	5.015

Note: These factors assume sampling from a normal population.
Source: E. L. Grant and R. S. Leavenworth, *Statistical Quality Control*, 6th ed. (New York: McGraw-Hill, 1988).

TABLE A–6
Factors d_3 and d_4 for R Charts

Number of Observations in Subgroup, n	Factors for R Chart	
	Lower Control Limit d_3	Upper Control Limit d_4
2	0	3.27
3	0	2.57
4	0	2.28
5	0	2.11
6	0	2.00
7	.08	1.92
8	.14	1.86
9	.18	1.82
10	.22	1.78
11	.26	1.74
12	.28	1.72
13	.31	1.69
14	.33	1.67
15	.35	1.65
16	.36	1.64
17	.38	1.62
18	.39	1.61
19	.40	1.60
20	.41	1.59

Note: These factors assume sampling from a normal population. They give the upper and the lower control limits for an R chart as follows:

$$LCL = d_3 R$$
$$UCL = d_4 R$$

Source: E. L. Grant and R. S. Leavenworth, *Statistical Quality Control*, 6th ed. (New York: McGraw-Hill, 1988).

Index

A

Abernathy, W. J., 28, 36
Acceptance sampling, 670, 699–701
Ackoff, E. L., 240
Ackoff, R. L., 240
Activity relationship chart, 598–599
Advanced Forecasting, Inc. (AFI), 60
Aerospace products and parts, 7
Age replacement strategies, 768–773
Aggregate planning methodology, 130, 138–154
   chase strategy, 143
   cost parameters, 145
   costs in, 139–141
   disaggregating aggregate plans, 157–159
   extensions, 148–154
   HP Enterprise Services, case of, 144
   level strategy, 143
   linear programming formulation, 147–149
   mixed strategies, 143
   problem constraints, 146–147
   problem variables, 146
   rounding of variables, 147–148
   techniques for solving, 141–143
Agrarian economy, 5–6
Akers (1956), 514
ALDEP (for automated layout design program), 618–619
Alyeska Pipeline Service Company, 545
American auto industry, 475
American management style, 4
Apple Corporation, 2–3, 55
Arcus, A. L., 532
ARIMA models, 97–101
   predicting performance of the U.S. economy, 105
Arrow, K. A., 240, 295
Arthur Andersen, 5
The Art of War (Sun Tzu), 2
Assembly line balancing, 528–532
Autocorrelation coefficient, 91
Autocovariance, 91
Autoregressive model, 94–95
Average outgoing quality (AOQ), 714–715
Average outgoing quality limit (AOQL), 715

B

Balance Principle, 420
Baldrige Award, 722–724
Baumgartner, P., 23
Becker, Gary S., 6
Bellman, R. E., 535
Benchmarking quality, 721–722
Benetton Group, 351
Bessler, S. A., 295
Best practices benchmarking, 722
Binomial approximation, 737–738
Birnie, D. P., 529

Birth and death analysis, 418
Blackburn, J. D., 19
"Black swan" events, 137
BMW, 8, 13
Boards of directors, 4
BOM (bill of materials) explosion, 478
Boodman, D. M., 241
Bowman (1956), 162
Bowman, E. H., 241
Box-Jenkins models, 88–101
   criticism of, 105
   monthly international airline passenger totals, predicting, 101–104
Boyd, E. A., 408
Brown, R. G., 112, 116, 295
Bruno, J., 535
Buffa, E. S., 162
Buffering, 133
Bullwhip effect, 322–326, 358
Business process reengineering (BPR), 14–16
   downsizing and, 16
Business strategy, 2
   Apple story, 3
   defined, 3
Business to business (B2B), 327
Business to consumer (B2C), 327

C

Call or contact center. *see also* Queueing systems
   basics, 405–406
   call routing, 407
   metrics, 406–407
Capacity growth planning, 38–46
Capacity resource planning (CRP), 462–463, 465
Caterpillar Inc., 326
Causal models, 58–59
C charts, 688–689
Central limit theorem, 568
Centroids, 659–660
Champy, J., 14–15
Chaos, 137
Charnes, A., 584
Chase strategy, 143
Chemical industry, 7–8
Chinese economy, 23
Churchman, C. W., 240
Clark, A., 295
Clark, A. J., 357
Clarke, G., 342
COFAD (for computerized facilities design), 617–618
Cohen, M. A., 295
Cohen, S. S., 6
Coleman, D. R., 621
Coleman, Debbi, 4
Company mission statement, 2
Compaq Computer, 54, 109
Competing on quality, 20–22

Competitive advantage, 12
Compton, Ronald, 16
Computer and electronic products, 8, 54
Construction of a new plant, issues related to, 38
Contingency planning, 133
Continuous review, 204, 253
Contour lines, 638–639, 661–662
Control charts, 670
   for attributes, 683–686
   c charts, 688–689
   classical statistical hypothesis testing, 678–680
   classical statistical methods and, 691
   notations, 702
   p charts, 685–686
   R charts, 680–681
   statistical basis of, 671–673
   for variables, 675–680
   X chart, 678
Convex piecewise-linear functions, 149–150
   cost of hiring, 150
Conway, R. W., 521, 535
CONWIP (CONstant Work-In-Process), 473
Cooper, W. W., 584
CORELAP (for computerized relationship layout planning), 619–620
Correlation coefficient, 91
Costco, 8
Costs
   in aggregate capacity planning, 139–141
   control, 202
   holding, 139–140, 204–206, 269
   idle time, 140–141
   order, 206–207
   overtime and subcontracting, 140
   penalty, 207, 270
   setup, 269–270
   shortage, 140
   smoothing, 139, 202
   underage, 259
CRAFT (computerized relative allocation of facilities technique), 613–617
Critical chain project management (CCPM), 576
Critical path analysis, 545–546, 548–554
   finding critical path, 551–553
Critical path method (CPM), 545
Critical ratio scheduling, 498, 500–501
$C\mu$ *rule*, 527
Cumulative distribution function, 422
Customer surveys, 57

D

Dalleck, W. C., 241
Davis, D., 20
Davis, E. W., 584
Delivery reliability, 9
Delivery speed, 9
Dell Computer, 356
Delphi method, 58

DeMatteis, J. J., 479
De Meyer et al. (2002), 137
Deming, W. Edwards, 722
Deming Prize, 722–724
Deseasonalized series methods, 83–84
Design for logistics (DFL), 354
Design for manufacturability (DFM), 353
Design for manufacturability (DFM) movement, 728
Deuermeyer, B. L., 295
Dhalla, N. K., 28
Dingell, John D., 5
Disaggregation of aggregate plans, 157–159
DISCON(for dispersion and concentration), 622
Disney theme park, 4
Distribution centers (DCs), 351
Dixon, P. S., 479
Double exponential smoothing method, 79
Double marginalization, 361
Double sampling for attributes, 707
Douglas Aircraft, 36
Downey, P., 535
Dreifus, S. B., 355
Dynamic capacity expansion policy, 40–44
Dynamic programming, 486–487
Dynamic random access memory (DRAM) industry, 19–20
Dynamic vs static scheduling, 493

E

Earliest due date (EDD), 498–499
Economic order quantity (EOQ) model, 203, 439
  basic, 210–212
  example, 212–213
  finite production rate, 218–219
  inclusion of order lead time, 213–214
  JIT and, 215–216
  lot sizing, 449–450
  mathematical derivations for multiproduct constrained, 246–247
  for production planning, 231–233
  sensitivity, 214–215
Economies of scale, 38–39, 355, 376
  inventories and, 202
Economies of scope, 38–39
Edmondson, Harold E., 352
Efficiency-driven regime, 385
Ehrhardt, R., 295
Electronic commerce, 326–327
Enron, 5
Entity-based logic, 414–415
Eppen, G., 295, 350
Erkip, N., 350
Erlang, A. K., 411
Erlang distribution, 758
ET Water Systems, 7
Euclidean distance, 634
  gravity problem, 643
  straight-line distance measure problem, 644–645
Excel spreadsheet program
  linear programming, solving, 181–187
  service levels in (Q, R) systems, calculation of, 279

Expected value of demand, $E(D)$, 304
Experience curves, 34–36
  manufacturing strategy and, 36
Explosion calculus, 443–447
  lot-sizing algorithms in, 455–456
Exponential failure law, 749–750
Exponential interarrival times, 382–383
Exponential smoothing method, 69–73, 255
  differences between moving averages and, 74
  forecast errors, calculation of, 124
  single or simple, 66

F

Facilities planning. see also Layout design
  activity relationship chart, 598–599
  contour lines, 638–639
  discrete location problems, 649
  facilities having positive areas, 648
  for flexible manufacturing systems, 625–632
  flow patterns, 597–602
  from-to chart, 600
  historical notes, 651–652
  international issues, 650
  layout design, 602–607
  layout problem analysis, 596–597
  locating new facilities, 632–635
  location–allocation problems, 648–649
  measures of distance, 634
  minimax problems, 639–640
  multiple location models, 647–648
  network location models, 649–650
  single-facility rectilinear distance location problem, 635–641
Facilities scheduling, 492
Failure rate function, 748–749
  of complex equipment, 762–766
  expected values, 763–764
  increasing and decreasing, 754–755
  series systems subject to purely random failures, 760–761
Feasible region, graphing, 176–177
Federgruen, A., 295
Feigenbaum, A. V., 722
Fetter, R. B., 241
Firm's performance evaluation, 4
First-come, first-served (FCFS), 498–499, 523
Fitzsimmons, J. A., 411
Fitzsimmons, M. J., 411
Flexibility, 10, 28
Flexible manufacturing systems, 625–632
  advantages, 627
  decision making and modeling of, 628–629
  disadvantages, 627–628
  future of, 631–632
  mathematical programming models, 630–631
  queuing-based models, 629–630
Florida Power and Light (FPL), 586
Flow systems, 377–380
  capacity of, 378
  flow rates and utilization, 378–379
  process flow diagrams, 377
Food manufacturing, 8
Ford, Henry, 2, 9
Ford Motors, 36, 409

Forecast errors, 122–124
Forecasting
  aggregate forecasts, 57
  American presidential elections, 85
  ARIMA models, 97–101
  autocorrelation function, 91
  autoregressive model, 94–95
  Box-Jenkins models, 88–101
  causal models, 58–59
  characteristics of, 56–57
  customer surveys, 57
  cyclic variation in, 59
  Delphi method, 58
  demand in presence of lost sales, 109–110
  differences between exponential smoothing and moving averages, 74
  double exponential smoothing method, 79
  evaluation of, 62–64
  exponential smoothing method, 69–73
  Facebook, predicting growth of, 112–116
  good forecast requirements, 56
  historical notes for, 116–117
  Holt's method, 79
  inventory management and, 111–112
  jury of executive opinion, 57
  model identification and monitoring, 106–107
  moving averages and, 66–68
  moving averages model, 95–96
  multiple-step-ahead forecasts, 69–71, 73–74
  notation conventions, 62
  objective methods of, 58–60
  one-step-ahead forecast, 70–71
  Pfizer's drug sales, example, 65
  random series method, 60
  regression analysis, 77–78
  sales force composites, 57
  seasonal pattern, 59
  seasonal series methods, 81–84
  simple vs. complex time series methods, 107–108
  simulation as tool for, 108–109
  Sport Obermeyer, case of, 76
  stationary series, methods for, 66
  subjective methods of, 57–58
  τ-step-ahead forecast, 79
  time horizon in, 55–56
  time series methods, 59–60
  trend-based methods, 59, 77–80
  Winters's method, 85–88
Foreseen uncertainty, 137
Freeland, J. R., 18, 295
Free replacement warranty, 782–784
From-to chart, 600
Functional benchmarking, 722

G

Gantt chart, 546
Gates, Bill, 2
General Electric Corporation, 2
General Motors (GM), 8, 409, 442
Gilford, D. M., 241
Global supply chain management (SCM), 362–363
Goldhar, J. P., 39

816 Index

Goldratt, Elihu, 576
Graves, S. C., 295
Gray stock, 351
Green leasing, 26
Gross, D., 411

H

Hakseven, C., 411
Halfin-Whitt scaling, 431
Hammer, M. S., 14–15
Hansmann, F., 162, 241
Harley-Davidson, 474–475
Harris, C. M., 411
Harris, Ford, 240
Hartung, P., 295
Hausman, W. H., 295, 350
Hayes, R. H., 4, 29, 35–36
Heineken International, 132
    planning and control framework for, 134
Helgeson, W. P., 529
Hess, S. W., 162
Hewlett-Packard (HP), 351–352, 534
Hill, Terry, 9
Hillkirk, J., 354, 474
Histogram, 256
Holding costs, 139–140, 204–206, 269
Hollerith, Herman, 24
Holt, C. C., 161
Holt's method, 79
Honda, 13
Hyundai, 23

I

IBM Credit Corporation, 14–16
Iglehart, D. L., 295
IMX Corporation, 355
Incremental quantity discounts, 223–225
Industrial revolution, 5
Inspection paradox, 383, 418
International competitiveness, 10–12
International Organization for Standardization (ISO) 9000, 724–725
Inventory system. *see also* Economic order quantity (EOQ) model; Multiproduct inventory systems
    Caterpillar Corporation inventory control system, case of, 227
    characteristics of, 203–204
    determining optimal policy, 221–223
    excess demand and, 204
    finished goods, 202
    historical notes, 240–241, 295
    incremental quantity discounts, 223–225
    in-transit or pipeline, 202
    inventory management software for small business, 273
    motivation for holding, 202–203
    notational conventions, 303–304
    notation glossary, 248
    power-of-two policies, 236–240
    probability distributions for, 308–312
    quantity discount models, 220–226
    raw materials, 201
    resource-constrained multiple product systems, 227–228
    review time of, 204
    Tropicana, inventory management of, 285
    work-in-process (WIP), 201

J

Jackson network, 432
Jacobson, G., 354, 474
Japanese auto industry, 4
J.B. Hunt Transport Services, Inc., 346
Jelinek, M., 39
Jobs, Steve, 3
Job shop scheduling, 440, 492, 495–498
    example, 501–502
    flow shop, 496
    flow time of job, 497
    makespan, 497
    objectives, 495–496
    optimal scheduling rules, 495
    parallel processing *vs* sequential processing, 497
    tardiness, 497–498
    terminology, 496–498
Johnson, S. M., 535
Jones, D. T., 4
Jones, P., 2
Juran, Joseph M., 722
Just-in-time systems (JIT), 17–18, 215–216, 439–440
    advantages, 471–474
    basics, 442–443
    centralized information processing system, 471
    comparison with MRP, 476–477
    disadvantages, 471–474
    inside exchange of die (IED), 470
    mechanics of kanban, 468–470
    outside exchange of die (OID), 470
    single minute exchange of dies (SMED), 470
    in United States, 474–475

K

Kahaner, L., 2
Kalman, Rudolph, 116
Kalman filter, 116
Kamien, M. I., 162
Kanban system, 17
Kaplan, R., 295
Karlin, S., 240, 295
Karni, R., 479
Kettering, Charles F., 54
Key performance indicators (KPIs), 129–130, 135–136
    challenges in choosing, 136
    effectiveness related, 135
    efficiency related, 135
    evaluation criteria for merits of, 135–136
Kilbridge, M. D., 532
Kleinrock, L., 411
Known unknowns, 130

Kodak, 474
K out of N system, 764–766
Kraft Foods, 633
Krugman, Paul, 12
Krywko, Mark, 23

L

Lagrange multiplier, 230
Laplace distribution, 310–311
Lariviere, M., 382
Last-come, first-served (LCFS) discipline, 524
Lawler's algorithm, 506
Layout design, 602–607. *see also* Facilities planning
    algorithm for assignment model, 608–610
    assignment model, 607–610
    based on group technology, 603–607
    computerized, 612–622
    determining optimal, 61–612
    dynamic layouts, 621
    fixed position layout, 602
    planar location models, 646–647
    process layout, 603
    product layout, 602–603
Leach, A. G., 116
Lead time, 204
Lead time demand distributions, 311–312
Lead time pricing, 409–410
Lean production, 442, 477–478
Learning curve, 32–34
    criticism of, 36
    manufacturing strategy and, 36
Leasing
    green, 26
    vs buying, 25–26
Least unit cost (LUC) heuristic, 451–452
Lee, H. L., 325
LEED, 26
Leibniz's rule, 304
Level strategy, 143
Li, L., 162
Lieberman, M., 44
Linear inequalities, graphing, 174–176
Linear programming, 147–149
    application of, 195–196
    constraints in, 172
    continuity in, 173–174
    critical path problems with, 561–564
    degeneracy, 194
    extreme points, 172
    feasible region of, 172
    feasible solution, 172
    for finding optimal solution, 150–151
    formulation of cost–time problem, 564
    graphical problems, solving, 174–180
    linearity in, 173
    multiple optimal solutions, 194
    objective function, 172
    optimal solution, 172, 177–180
    prototype problem, 169–171
    recognizing several problems, 191–195
    redundant constraints, 194–195
    right-hand side in, 172
    set of constraints in, 151–154

Index

Simplex Method, 180–181
  solving with Excel, 181–187
  statement of general problem, 171–174
  unbounded solutions, 191
Little's law, 388–389, 423, 428
Logistics, 202
Longest-expected-processing-time-first rule (LEPT), 519
Lost sales, 140
Lot size-reorder point systems, 267–273
  cost function, 270–272
  decision variables, 268
  derivation of expected cost functions, 268–270
  describing demand, 268
  holding cost, 269
  inventory level *vs.* position, 272–273
  penalty cost, 270
  proportional ordering cost component, 270
  setup cost, 269–270
Lot-sizing schemes, 449–453
  with capacity constraints, 457–458
  EOQ lot sizing, 449–450
  lot-sizing algorithms, 455–456
  for time-varying demand, 484–485
Love, S. F., 295

M

Machinery manufacturing, 8
Magee, J. F., 241
Maintenance of complex equipment, 766
Make-or-buy decision, 39–40
Malcolm Baldrige National Quality Award, 722–724
Manne, A. S., 40
Manufacturers and manufacturing, 5–8
  business process reengineering and, 14–16
  competing on quality, 20–22
  global manufacturing strategies in the automobile industry, 13
  global marketplace, competing, 10–13
  just-in-time systems, 17–18
  operations strategy, 8–9
  servicization, 23–26
  time-based competition, 19–20
Manufacturing jobs
  international trend, 5
  outlook, 7–8
Manufacturing productivity growth, 5
Manufacturing resource planning (MRP II), 465
Master production schedule (MPS), 440
Materials as needed (MAN), 474
Materials requirements planning (MRP), 17, 439–440, 472
  basics, 440–442
  capacity resource planning (CRP), 462–463, 465
  comparison with JIT, 476–477
  control phases of productive system, 441
  data integrity, 467
  EOQ lot sizing, 449–450
  explosion calculus, 443–447
  historical notes, 478–479
  imperfect production processes, 465–466

least unit cost (LUC) heuristic, 451–452
lot-sizing schemes, 449–453
lot-sizing schemes with capacity constraints, 457–458
notation glossary, 488
order pegging, 467
part period balancing, 452–453
Raymond Corporation, case example, 466
rolling horizons and system nervousness, 463–464
shortcomings of, 461–467
Silver–Meal heuristic, 450–451
uncertainties and, 461
Materials requirements planning (MRP) system, 440
Maxwell, W. L., 535
Meal, H. C., 450, 472, 479
Mean absolute deviation (MAD), 62, 112
Mean absolute percentage error (MAPE), 62
Mean squared error (MSE), 62
Memoryless property, 519
Mercedes Benz, 13
Metters, R. D., 411
Microsoft® Project, 585
Military strategy, 2
Miller, D. W., 241
Miller, L. W., 535
Mission statements, 2
M/M/1 queue, 389–390, 418–428
  Balance Principle, 420, 422
  with a finite capacity, 427–429
  process $L(t)$, 418–419
  single-server queue, 424–425
  state changes for, 419
  state-dependent model, 424–425
  waiting time distribution, 421–422
M/M/s queue, 384
Moder, J. J., 584
Modigliani, F., 161
Modularization, 28
Monte Carlo simulation, 400, 414
MOOPI, 534
Mortgage crisis of 2008, 26
Motorola Corporation, 534, 701, 716
Motor vehicles and parts, 8
Moving averages, 66–68, 95–97
  average age of data for, 73
  differences between exponential smoothing and, 74
  forecast errors, calculation of, 123
Muckstadt, J. A., 350
Muckstadt, J. M., 295
Multi-echelon systems, 291–293
  Intel Corporation, case example, 294
Multilevel distribution systems, 356–358. *see also* Supply chain management (SCM)
  advantages, 357
  disadvantages, 358
  distribution centers, 358
Multiperiod stochastic inventory models, 253
Multiple-step-ahead forecasts, 73–74
Multiproduct inventory systems
  ABC analysis, 286–287
  exchange curves, 288–290
Murray, G. R., 295
Muth, J. F., 161

N

Nahmias, S., 109, 295, 350
Navistar International, 701
New, C., 478
Newsvendor model
  development of cost function, 259
  discrete demand and optimal policy, 262
  expected cost function, 260
  inclusion of starting inventory, 262–263
  for infinite horizon assuming lost sales, 307
  for infinite sequence of demands, 306–307
  interpretation of overage and underage costs for single period problem, 304–305
  multiple planning periods, 264–265
  for normal demand, 305–306
  notation, 258–259
  optimal policy, 260–262
  of Syngenta Seeds, case example, 263
Normal approximation, 738
Normal density function, 255
Normal distribution, 255
Notations, 126
N-period average, 67–68
NP hard, 341
Nugent, C. E., 621

O

Occupational Outlook Handbook (OOH), 7
Offshoring, 7
Operating characteristic (OC) curve measures, 702–704
Operations strategy, 3
  for manufacturing firms, 3
  of service firms, 4
  strategic dimensions, 9–10
Optimization criterion, 256–257
Order batching, 324
Order costs, 206–207
Orlicky, J., 478
Overtime and subcontracting costs, 140

P

Padmanabhan, P., 325
Panzer, J. C., 38
Part period balancing, 452–453
PASTA—Poisson Arrivals. *See* Time Averages, 384
P charts, 685–686
PC market, 21
Pekelman, D., 295
Penalty costs, 207, 270
Performance based contracting (PBC), 25
Periodic review, 204, 253
  fixed order size model, 284
  (s, S) policies, 282–283
  service levels in (Q, R) systems, 282–284
Perishable inventory problems, 293–294
Personnel scheduling, 492
Peterson, R., 295
Pfizer, 65
Pharmaceuticals and medicine, 8
Phillips, C. R., 584

Pinedo, M., 535
Pisano, G.P., 6
Plan, Do, Check, Act (PDCA) method, 723
PLANET (for plant layout analysis and evaluation technique), 620
Planned replacement under uncertainty, 774–780
Plant location
  environmental issues, 45
  interactions with other plants, 45
  international considerations, 45
  labor costs and, 45
  labor force requirements, 45
  process technologies, 45
  product lines, 45
  proximity of markets, 45
  proximity to other facilities, 46
  proximity to suppliers and resources, 45
  quality of life, 46
  size of plant decisions, 44
  tax treatment, 45
  transportation needs, 45
  unionization and, 45
  utilities requirements, 45
Point-of-sale (POS) data, 325
Poisson approximation, 738
Poisson distribution, 309
Poisson process, 380–382
Pollaczek-Khintchine (P-K) formula, 393
Pooling, 133
Pooling in services, 384
Porter, M. E., 7–8, 10–12
Porteus, E. L., 295
The Prince (Machiavelli), 2
Principle of optimality, 487
Printing industry, 8
Probability approximations, 737–738
Probability of delay, 384–385
Process life cycle, 28–29
  curve, 29
  first phase of, 28
  last phase of, 29
  middle phase of, 28–29
Process optimization, 16
Product benchmarking, 722
Production and operations strategy
  business process reengineering and, 14–16
  capacity growth planning, 38–46
  competing on quality, 20–22
  economies of scale, 38–39
  economies of scope, 38–39
  global marketplace, competing, 10–13
  just-in-time systems, 17–18
  make-or-buy decision, 39–40
  process life cycle, 28–29
  product life cycle, 27–28
  product–process matrix, 29–31
  servicization, 23–26
  time-based competition, 19–20
Production planning, 130
Production scheduling
  comparison and evaluation of sequencing rules, 498
  critical ratio, 498, 500–501
  earliest due date (EDD), 498–499
  earliest-due-date scheduling, 505
  first-come, first-served (FCFS), 498–499

hierarchy of production decisions, 493–494
historical notes, 535
job shop scheduling, 492, 495–498
minimizing the number of tardy jobs, 505
sequencing theory for single machine, 503–507
shortest processing time (SPT), 498–499
shortest-processing-time scheduling, 504
Productivity growth, 11
Product life cycle (PLC), 27–28
  life-cycle curve, 27
  major segments, 27
  maturation phase, 28
  product–process matrix, 29–31
  rapid growth phase, 28
  stabilization or decline phase, 28
  start-up phase, 27
Project evaluation and review technique (PERT), 545, 566–572
  beta-distributed activity times, 566–567
  central limit theorem, 568
  path independence, 571–572
  uniform distribution, 567
Project network, 546–548
Project scheduling, 493
Project scheduling and management, 544–545
  critical path analysis, 548–554
  critical path problems with linear programming, 561–564
  of Florida Power and Light (FPL), 586
  historical notes, 584–585
  minimum project completion time, 562
  notation glossary, 591–592
  organizational issues in, 583–584
  project evaluation and review technique (PERT), 566–572
  resource constraints for multiproject scheduling, 578–579
  resource constraints for single-project scheduling, 576–578
  resource loading profiles, 579–581
  software for, 585
  of Thomas Brothers Maps, Inc., 586
  time costing methods, 556–557
  of United Airlines, 586
Pro rata warranty, 784–785
Pull system, 17
Push system, 17

Q

Quality, 9
  acceptance sampling, 670
  benchmarking, 721–722
  control, 20–21
  designing of product and, 726–728
  double sampling for attributes, 707
  historical notes, 730–731
  measures, 20–22
  notations, 739–740
  operating characteristic (OC) curve measures, 702–704
  organizing for, 720–721
  single sampling for attributes, 702–704
Quality-and-efficiency (QED) driven regime, 385, 431
Quantity discount models, 220–226

Queueing network analyzer (QNA), 433
Queueing networks, 432–433
Queueing systems, 386–390, 392–401. *see also* Call or contact center
  in emergency departments (EDs), 402
  expected time in system for a single server system, 393
  exponential distribution, 417–418
  improving a service process, 400–401
  infinite server limits, 431–432
  Little's law, 388–389
  M/G/∞ queue, 430
  M/M/1 queue, 389–390, 418–422
  modeling framework, 434–435
  multiple parallel servers, 395–396
  notation for, 387–388
  optimization of, 433–435
  Poisson arrival processes, 417–418
  priorities, 397–399
  psychology of, 402–403
  queueing networks and polling models, 399
  simulation, 399–400
  structural elements, 387
  systems with abandonment, 396–397

R

Radio frequency identification (RFID) tags, 327–329
Rand Corporation, 357
Randomness, 254–256
Random numbers, generating, 414–415
Ranked positional weight technique, 529
Raymond Corporation, 466
R charts, 680–681
Rectilinear distance, 634
Regression analysis, 77–78
  derivation of equations for slope and intercept for, 124–126
Relative frequency histogram, 255
Reliability, 744
  distribution and density functions, 747–748
  historical notes, 789
  Poisson process in modeling of, 757–759
  risks of poor, 745
  of single component, 746
  software, 787–789
  Three Mile Island nuclear facility, maintenance of, 788
Research and development (R&D), 6
Reshoring, 7
Resource-constrained multiple product systems, 227–228
Retailer-warehouse systems, 295
Return on investment (ROI), 4
Revenue management of service operations, 407–410
  in airline industry, 407–408
  basics, 408–409
  lead time pricing, 409–410
  nontraditional applications for, 410
Review time, 204
Risk pooling, 57, 347–353
Rivkin, J. W., 7
Roos, D., 4
Rosenblatt, M. J., 241
Ruml, J., 621

S

Safety capacity, 352
Sakasegawa approximation, 385
Sales, inventory, and operations planning (SIOP). *see* Sales and operations planning (S&OP) process
Sales and operations planning (S&OP) process, 129–130, 137
    elements, 131
    on a global scale, 160–161
    historical notes, 161–162
    key inputs required for, 131
    overview, 132
    standard agenda for, 132–133
    strategies for dealing with uncertainty, 133
    uncertainty or risk, management of, 137–138
Sales force composites, 57
Salveson, M. E., 535
Sample autocorrelation function, 107
Scarf, H., 240–241, 295, 357
Scheduling system for fractional aircraft operators, 508
Schmenner (1982), 45
Schrage, L., 295, 350
Schwarz, L.B., 295
Seasonal factors, 81–82
Seasonal series methods, 81–84
Sensitivity report
    decision variables and constraints, 188–189
    objective function coefficients and right-hand sides, 188
    shadow prices, 187–188
    use of, 189–190
Sequencing algorithms for multiple machines, 510–516
    Gantt chart for optimal schedule, 514–516
    longest processing time first (LPT), 514
    n jobs on two machines, 511–512
    on three machines, 512–514
    two-job flow shop problem, 514–515
Sequencing theory for single machine, 503–507
Sequential sampling plans, 709–713
Service dominant logic (SDL), 369
Service economy, 5–6
Service levels in (Q, R) systems
    estimating sigma, inventory control and forecasting linked, 278
    Excel calculations, 279
    imputed shortage cost, 277
    lead time variability, 278
    negative safety stock, 280
    optimal (Q, R) policy, 308
    periodic review, 282–284
    scaling of lead time demand, 277
    Type 1 service, 274
    Type 2 constraint, 275–276
    Type 2 service, 274–275
Service operations management, 369
    call or contact center, 405–407
    of competition in service environments, 375–376
    controlling quality for services, 372
    exit barriers, 376
    exponential interarrival times, 382–383
    flow systems, 377–380
    general arrival processes, 383

guidelines for service guarantees and refunds, 404
historical notes, 411
human element in, 401–404
managing variability, 374–375
measure quality for services, 372
minimal opportunities for economies of scale, 376
modeling unscheduled arrivals, 380–385
paying for quality, 372–373
Poisson process, 380–382
pooling in services, 384
probability of delay, 384–385
product substitution, 376
queueing systems, 386–390, 392–401
revenue management, 407–410
role of technology in services, 403–404
service business, decisions of, 373
service system design problems, 433
of Southwest Airlines, 374
strategy, 370–376
Service quality, 371–372
Services sector economy, 370–371
Servicization, 23–26
    downstream, 23–24
    green leasing, 26
    IBM story, 24–25
    leasing vs buying, 25–26
    performance based contracting (PBC), 25
Setup costs, 269–270
Shelly, M. W., 241
Shen, Y., 25
Sherbrooke, C. C., 295
Shih, W.C., 6
Shortage costs, 140
Shortage gaming, 324
Shortest processing time (SPT), 498–499, 504
Silver, E. A., 295, 450, 479
Silver–Meal heuristic, 450–451
Simon, H. A., 161
Simplex Method, 180–181
Simulation, 108–109
Single-minute exchange of dies (SMED), 17–18
Single sampling for attributes, 702–704
Six-sigma, 22, 701, 716
Six-tenths rule, 42
Sleek Audio, 23
Sloan, Alfred, 478
Smith, Adam
    The Wealth of Nations, 31
Smith, S. A., 350
Smoothing costs, 139
    inventories and, 202
Southwest Airlines, 374
SPACECRAFT, 621
Speculation and inventories, 202
Squared coefficient of variation, 392
Star, M. K., 241
Stasey and McNair (1990), 18
Statistical control charts, 64
Steel industry, 8
Stochastic demand models, 203
Stochastic process, 380
Stochastic scheduling
    $c\mu$ rule, 527
    dynamic analysis, 522–527

minimizing mean flow time in, 523
multiple machine, 519–520
optimal selection disciplines, 525–527
selection disciplines independent of job processing times, 524–525
single machine, 518–519
static analysis, 518–521
two-machine flow shop case, 520–521
Strategic benchmarking, 722
Strategy, defined, 2
Supply chain management (SCM), 317–318. *see also* Multilevel distribution systems
    of Anheuser-Busch, 322
    bullwhip effect, 322–326
    capacity pooling, 352–353
    channel alignment, 325
    channels of distribution, 355
    configuration of the supplier base, 354
    of Dell Computer, 356
    designing products for supply chain efficiency, 353–355
    determining delivery routes in, 341–346
    electronic commerce, 326–327
    global, 362–363
    IBM's success, 325
    incentives in, 359–361
    information sharing, 325
    inventory/location pooling, 348–350
    issue of double marginalization, 361
    just-in-time distribution (JITD), 321–322
    order batching, 324
    outsource warehousing, 355
    practical issues in vehicle scheduling, 345–346
    pricing promotions, 325
    product pooling and postponement, 351–352
    radio frequency identification (RFID) tags, 327–329
    revenue sharing contracts, 361
    risk pooling, 347–353
    role of information in, 321–329
    shortage gaming, 324
    as a strategic weapon, 318–319
    strategy, 319–312
    transportation logistics of J.B. Hunt Transport Services, Inc., 346
    transportation problem, 329–338
    vendor-managed inventory, 361
    of Wal-Mart, 320
Svoboda, Eileen, 534

T

Talluri, K., 411
Taubert, W. H., 162
Textiles and apparels, 8
Thomas, L. J., 295, 350
Thomas Brothers Maps, Inc., 586
Three-dimensional concurrent engineering (3-DCE), 354
Three Mile Island nuclear facility, maintenance of, 788
Throughput, defined, 136
Time-based competition, 19–20
Time series methods, 59–60

Time value of money
  present value of a cost, 50
Tompkins, J. A., 595
Total quality management (TQM)
  competition based on quality, 719–720
  customer wants and, 717–719
  definition, 717
Townsend, P. L., 28
Toyota, 10, 13, 442
Tracking signal, 107
Transportation problem, 329–338
  general network formulations, 335–338
  generalizations of, 333–338
  infeasible routes, 334
  linear programming constraints, 332
  unbalanced problems, 334–335
Trigg, D. W., 116

U

Uncertainty
  demand, 252
  management of, 251–252
  in materials requirements planning (MRP), 461
  notation glossary, 312
  randomness and, 254–256
Uncertainty, in sales and operations planning, 137–138
  inventories and, 202
Unforeseen uncertainty, 137–138
United Airlines, 586
Universal Studios Theme Parks, 54
Unknown unknowns, 130
U.S. Bureau of Labor Statistics, 7

V

Van Mieghem, J. A., 382
Van Ryzin, G., 411
Vandermerwe and Rada (1988), 23
Variability
  arrival, 369
  capability, 369
  effort, 369
  request, 369
  subjective preference, 369
Variation, 137
Vehicle scheduling, 492
Veinott, A. F., 295
Vendor scheduling, 492
Vollmann, T. E., 621

W

Wagner, H. M., 241, 295, 478
Wagner–Whitin algorithm, 485
Waiting time distribution, 421–422
Waiting time paradox, 418
Wal-Mart, 8
Warner Robins Air Logistics Center, 576
Warranties, 782–786
Wayne, K., 36
Weiss, G., 535
Welch, Jack, 2
Wester, L., 532
Whang, S., 325
Wheelwright, S., 4, 29, 35–36
White, J. A., 595
Whitin, T. M., 295, 478
Whitt, W., 431
Wiener, Norbert, 116
Willing, R. O., 38
Wills, Faye, 21
Wilson, R. H., 240
Winters's method for seasonal problems, 85–88
Wise, R., 23
Womack, J. P., 4
Womack et al. (1990), 442
Work-in-process (WIP) inventories, 17
Wozniak, Steve, 3
Wright, G. W., 342

X

X chart, 678
  economic design of, 692–696
Xerox Corporation, 354, 474

Y

Yule-Walker equations, 94
Yuspeh, S., 28

Z

Zero defects, 670
Zero inventory plan, 143
Zipkin, P., 295
Zoning restriction, 529
Zysman, J., 6